W9-CRG-034

BEGINNING JAPANESE

PART I

by Eleanor Harz Jorden
with the assistance of Hamako Ito Chaplin

CHARLES E. TUTTLE COMPANY
Suido 1-chome, 2-6, Bunkyo-ku, Tokyo

Published by the Charles E. Tuttle Company, Inc.
of Rutland, Vermont and Tokyo, Japan
with editorial offices at
Suido 1-chome, 2-6, Bunkyo-ku, Tokyo, Japan
by special arrangement with
Yale University Press, New Haven, Connecticut

First Tuttle edition, 1974
Eighth.printing, 1983

PRINTED IN JAPAN

For

W. J. J.

Acknowledgments

I am indebted to many people—in Japan and the United States—for their assistance in the preparation of this book:

to Hajime Aikawa, Shiro Sugata, Hiroshi Sakamoto, Mayako Matsuda, Kazuhiko Mitsumoto, and Akira Kobayashi, who participated in the preparation of a short course, the expansion and revision of which was the basis for this text. I deeply appreciate their tireless efforts.

to Sayoko Kawamoto, Hiroshi Takano, Masayuki Minami, Yasukazu Tsukagoshi, and Reiko Hummel—and to Gabriel Cordova, supervisor of recording—for assistance in the preparation of the tape recordings that accompany the text. Mrs. Kawamoto was particularly helpful in performing many of the tiresome chores that preceded and followed actual recording, as well as in assisting in the final revision of the text.

to Mrs. Tomoko Tanaka Campen for her excellent illustrations, drawn with such meticulous care.

to the Language Development Section of the Department of Health, Education, and Welfare, for a grant which expedited the completion of the book and made possible the preparation of the accompanying tapes.

to the Center for Applied Linguistics of the Modern Language Association, for a grant which expedited the publishing of the book.

to Samuel E. Martin, of Yale University, for discussions which suggested several useful revisions.

to Kyoko Edayoshi, for her careful typing of the manuscript and for several valuable suggestions pertaining to the text.

To my teacher, Bernard Bloch of Yale University, who directed my formal study of linguistics and introduced me to the Japanese language, I continue to owe an immeasurable debt.

To Hamako Ito Chaplin, of Yale University, who has been directly involved in the preparation of this text—and previous versions of it—during the past six years, I wish to express my deepest appreciation for her capable assistance and enthusiastic cooperation. Mrs. Chaplin has willingly and cheerfully performed innumerable tasks of writing, rewriting, checking, editing, and recording, always giving evidence of her outstanding ability and uncompromising standards of excellence. It is impossible to express adequately my gratitude to her.

To my husband, William J. Jorden, I wish to express my thanks for his encouragement, his advice, and his patience.

E. H. J.

Washington, D.C.
January 1962

Contents

Contents

Introduction

Beginning Japanese (Parts I and II) contains thirty-five lessons, all of which have the same basic pattern and involve the same procedures. Each lesson requires many hours of class work supplemented by outside study and, if possible, laboratory work.

The method underlying this text is guided imitation; the aim is automaticity. Ideally, there are two teachers: under the supervision of a scientific linguist, who talks ABOUT Japanese, the student learns to speak the language in direct imitation of a tutor who is a native speaker of Japanese. The tutor drills on the Japanese in the text, providing an authentic model for the student to imitate. Statements on how the language is manipulated are included in the explanatory notes in the text, which may be supplemented, if necessary, by further discussions on the part of the linguist.

Language learning is overlearning. Through memorization of whole utterances, and substitution within and manipulation of these utterances, a student achieves the fluency and automaticity that are necessary for control of a language. Language learning involves acquiring a new set of habits, and habits must be automatic. Just as the experienced driver performs the mechanics of driving—turning on the engine, shifting gears, applying the brakes, etc.—unconsciously, and concentrates on where he is going, so the fluent speaker of a language is concerned with what he is saying rather than the mechanics of how he is saying it.

This textbook is concerned only with spoken Japanese. Reading and writing involve a different set of habits and are best begun after acquiring some basic control of the spoken language. It is suggested that students interested in studying written Japanese begin using an introductory reading text only after completing at least ten or fifteen lessons of this volume. [1]

The student should note the following general suggestions and warnings:

ALWAYS USE NORMAL SPEED. Do not permit yourself to speak more slowly than your tutor, and do not ask him to speak more slowly than is natural for him. The ability to understand slow, deliberate speech never heard outside of a classroom is of little practical value. The aim of the student should be to learn Japanese as it is spoken by the Japanese—not an artificial classroom dialect.

DRILL HOURS WITH A NATIVE TUTOR SHOULD BE CONDUCTED ENTIRELY IN JAPANESE FROM THE FIRST DAY. A class which fluctuates between Japanese and English, where valuable repetition and drill aimed at developing fluency are constantly interrupted by English questions and comments, never achieves the desired results. It is recommended that a specific time be designated as discussion period and that interruption of drill at

---

[1] For students who have completed Parts I and II, the forthcoming publication A Manual of Japanese Writing, by Chaplin and Martin, is suggested.

other times be avoided. A tutor who has not had technical linguistic training
should not attempt technical explanations <u>about</u> Japanese. These are provided
by the explanatory notes in the book and/or the scientific linguist.

REVIEW CONSTANTLY. DO NOT GO AHEAD TOO RAPIDLY. Remember
that e a c h new lesson presupposes thorough mastery of what has gone before.

Do not assume that the patterns of Japanese will resemble those of English,
or that distinctions made in English will be present in Japanese. EXPECT
DIFFERENCES AND BE SURPRISED AT SIMILARITIES.

Remember that USAGE—NOT LOGIC—DETERMINES WHAT IS ACCEPTED
IN A LANGUAGE. A native speaker is the final judge of whether or not an utterance is acceptable in his dialect. Differences of dialect, of course, cause
frequent disagreement among native speakers. Not all dialect differences are
geographical; many are social and educational.

PROCEDURES

1. Basic Dialogues

Each of the thirty-five lessons begins with a group of <u>Basic Dialogues</u> which
form the core of the lesson. A student controls a lesson to the extent to which
he has learned the dialogues by heart. Thorough memorization of the dialogues means thorough mastery of the text. Memorization is achieved by
direct imitation of the native tutor in class, and by repeated use of tapes in the
laboratory or at home.

Basic Dialogues are presented with their English equivalents. Numbered
utterances in the dialogues are <u>Basic Sentences</u>. New words or phrases occurring in a Basic Sentence for the first time are listed separately, immediately before the s e n t e n c e, as <u>breakdowns</u>. They a r e indented and not
numbered.

Some lessons contain <u>Additional Vocabulary</u>, at the end of the Basic Dialogues. The words in these sections are always to be drilled within an appropriate pattern sentence, never in isolation.

Following the Basic Dialogues are <u>Notes on the Basic Dialogues</u>, containing
assorted information on specific sentences. The numbering of the notes
corresponds to that of the sentences.

2. Grammatical Notes

Discussions of new patterns introduced in the Basic Dialogues are found in
the <u>Grammatical Notes</u>. These are to be read outside of class after the Basic
Dialogues have been introduced, but before proceeding to the drills.

In the Grammatical Notes, the procedure has been to introduce only material which will be of immediate practical use to a beginning student. No
attempt is made to present the full scientific analysis of Japanese on which the
text is based; rather, explanations are provided which will be useful within the
framework of the Japanese material being studied.

3. Drills

There are five basic kinds of drill in <u>Beginning Japanese</u>, each having a special purpose. However, the aim of all drills is the over-all aim of the course: to develop fluency and automaticity. Drills are to be performed in class with a tutor, and in the laboratory or at home with tapes. TEXTBOOKS SHOULD BE CLOSED DURING DRILL PRACTICE IN CLASS.

a. Substitution Drills

The tutor gives a pattern sentence which the student repeats. Immediately the tutor gives a word or phrase (called a cue) which the student substitutes appropriately in the original sentence. The tutor follows immediately with a new cue.

Example (English substitution drill):

Tutor:	Where did you put my book?
Student:	Where did you put my book?
Tutor:	pen
Student:	Where did you put my pen?
Tutor:	dictionary
Student:	Where did you put my dictionary?
	etc.

In more complicated substitution drills, there may be several substitution items (a compound cue) for each new sentence; or the successive cues may have to be substituted in different parts of the sentence; or the cue may require changes in the pattern sentence; or the cue may be given in its citation form (i.e. the basic form that regularly occurs in a dictionary) and have to be changed in order to occur within the pattern sentence.

Substitution drills whose cues occur in the same form in the pattern sentence are printed in two columns, with English equivalents on the left and drill sentences with cues underlined on the right. A drill that looks like this—

1.	Please give me a cigarette.	Ta⌐bako o kudasa⌐i.
2.	Please give me a match.	Ma⌐tti o kudasai.
3.	Please give me a book.	Ho⌐ñ o kudasai.
	etc.	

is to be drilled:

Tutor:	Ta⌐bako o kudasa⌐i.
Student:	Ta⌐bako o kudasa⌐i.
Tutor:	ma⌐tti
Student:	Ma⌐tti o kudasai.
Tutor:	ho⌐ñ
Student:	Ho⌐ñ o kudasai.
	etc.

When cues occur in their citation forms and must be changed by the student, they are given between virgules (//) immediately after the English equivalents on the left. A drill that looks like this—

1.	Please wait here.	Ko⌐ko de ma⌐tte kudasai.
2.	Please study here. /beñkyoo-suru/	Ko⌐ko de beñkyoo-site kudasa⌐i.

3. Please read here.   Ko꜀ko de yo꜒nde kudasai.
/yo꜒mu/
etc.

is to be drilled:

Tutor: Ko꜀ko de ma꜒tte kudasai.
Student: Ko꜀ko de ma꜒tte kudasai.
Tutor: beñkyoo-suru
Student: Ko꜀ko de beñkyoo-site kudasa꜒i.
Tutor: yo꜒mu
Student: Ko꜀ko de yo꜒nde kudasai.

b. Grammar Drills

Here, on the basis of a model provided at the beginning of the drill, the
student is required to perform parallel manipulation on a series of utterances
by the tutor. For example, he may be required to change each of the tutor's
utterances to the corresponding negative, or the past tense, etc.

Grammar Drills are printed in two columns, with the tutor's utterances on
the left and the student's responses on the right.

c. Response Drill

On the basis of the model or directions occurring at the beginning of the
drill, the student provides a parallel response to a series of questions or re-
marks by the tutor.

Like Grammar Drills, Response Drills are printed in two columns, with the
tutor's utterances on the left and the student's responses on the right. In
cases requiring a response clue from the tutor, this is given between virgules
immediately following the tutor's utterance.

Example (English response drill):

Tutor	Student
What did you buy? /a book/	I bought a book.
What did you borrow? /a pencil/	I borrowed a pencil.
etc.	

d. Level Drill

Here, the student is asked to change the tutor's utterances to a different
level of speech—to a more formal level, to the informal level, etc.

Again, this kind of drill is printed in two columns, with the tutor's utterance
on the left and the student's equivalent on the right.

e. Expansion Drills

The usual kind of expansion drill in this text is a repetition drill which
involves the buildup from short to long sentences. The tutor begins with a

short sentence and gradually adds words and phrases to form a long, complex sentence. At each stage, the student repeats what the tutor has just said. These drills are printed in two columns, with the successively longer Japanese sentences on the right and English equivalents on the left.

In another kind of expansion drill, the student expands a pattern sentence with the cue provided by the tutor. A model is provided at the beginning of the drill. For such drills, the tutor's pattern sentence and cue (marked off with virgules) are in the left column, and the student's responses in the right column.

Drills are not meant to be grammatical puzzles for tricking the student; they are intended to develop fluency. The pace of all drills should be rapid. A student has mastered a drill only when he can provide the required oral responses promptly, fluently, and without reference to his textbook.

4. Supplementary Material

The supplementary material following the drills occurs in various forms: conversations of varying length (with English equivalents), narrative passages, and question drills.

When read aloud by the tutor, this material is a good test of comprehension—but it must be read at normal speed, and the students' books must be closed. It also provides a stimulus to conversation. The class can ask and answer questions pertaining to the material and make up similar material; and with conversations for which English equivalents are given, they may reconstruct the original conversations by referring only to the English.

5. Exercises

The final section of each lesson contains suggestions for additional practice appropriate to each lesson. These exercises should be performed orally. Only the student who is able to do them fluently and accurately is ready to proceed to the next lesson.

TAPES

The tape series which accompanies Beginning Japanese includes all Basic Dialogues, Drills, and Supplementary Material.

1. Basic Dialogues

Each dialogue is recorded four times:

(a) For listening

The dialogue (in its most contracted form) is spoken at normal speed just as you might overhear it.

LISTEN WITH YOUR BOOK CLOSED.

(b) For memorization

This phase includes breakdowns and Basic Sentences, followed by pauses[1] for students' repetition. Breakdowns are said once and Basic Sentences twice. When a contracted alternant occurs, it is said once, following the second repetition of the uncontracted equivalent.

REPEAT EVERYTHING ALOUD AND FOLLOW IN YOUR BOOK.

(c) For fluency

Each complete Basic Sentence is said once, with pause for repetition. For sentences which have a contracted equivalent, only the uncontract-alternant is included in this phase.

REPEAT ALOUD WITH YOUR BOOK CLOSED.

(d) For comprehension

This is a repetition of (a) above (the Dialogue for listening), but this time the student is expected to understand everything he hears.

LISTEN WITH YOUR BOOK CLOSED.

2. Drills

Students are expected to participate in the drills when working with tapes exactly as they do in the classroom, except that they may follow in their books as necessary.

For drills which require repetition — that is, most expansion drills — there are pauses on the tapes following each utterance to be repeated. For drills which require answering by the student — substitution, grammar, response, level, and some expansion drills — there is a pause on the tape permitting him to give his answer orally. This pause is followed by the correct response, which serves to reinforce — or correct — the student's response.

REPEAT OR ANSWER. FOLLOW IN YOUR BOOK AS NECESSARY.

3. Supplementary Material

During question drills, turn off the tape recorder after each question and take whatever time is necessary to answer. All other supplementary material is presented for comprehension practice.

LISTEN WITH YOUR BOOK CLOSED.

---

[1] All pauses on the tapes are timed to require the student to speak at a normal rate of speed. The student who cannot repeat within the allotted time is talking too slowly and needs more practice.

PRONUNCIATION

The so-called 'standard' dialect of Japanese (spoken by educated natives of Tokyo) can be described in terms of 113 distinct syllables, of the following kinds:

    5   single vowel
   67   consonant + vowel
   36   consonant + y + vowel
    5   single consonant

The student's first task is to learn (1) how the sounds of Japanese are pronounced and (2) how the Japanese sounds—which are different from the sounds of English—are represented in this text with the letters of our own alphabet. For (1), the student needs as a model a native speaker of Japanese and/or a recording made by a native speaker. For (2), he must study the chart and notes below, always bearing in mind that the letters are no more than arbitrary symbols which are meant to remind him of the actually occurring Japanese sounds. Although the symbols may seem unnecessarily arbitrary at the beginning, while the structure of Japanese is still unknown, the student becomes accustomed to them very quickly as he becomes familiar with the language.

Syllables of Japanese

1	2	3	4	5	6	7	8	9	10	11	12	13	14	15	16	17
a	ka	ga	ḡa	sa	za	ta	da	na	ha	pa	ba	ma	ya	ra	wa	k
i	ki	gi	ḡi	si	zi	ti	--	ni	hi	pi	bi	mi	--	ri	--	s
u	ku	gu	ḡu	su	zu	tu	--	nu	hu	pu	bu	mu	yu	ru	--	t
e	ke	ge	ḡe	se	ze	te	de	ne	he	pe	be	me	--	re	--	p
o	ko	go	ḡo	so	zo	to	do	no	ho	po	bo	mo	yo	ro	--	ñ
	kya	gya	ḡya	sya	zya	tya	--	nya	hya	pya	bya	mya	--	rya	--	
	kyu	gyu	ḡyu	syu	zyu	tyu	--	nyu	hyu	pyu	byu	myu	--	ryu	--	
	kyo	gyo	ḡyo	syo	zyo	tyo	--	nyo	hyo	pyo	byo	myo	--	ryo	--	

(In the following discussion, row numbers correspond to the numbers of the vertical rows in the chart above. IN THIS SECTION ONLY, syllables within a word are separated by hyphens to show syllable division, and capital letters represent a pitch level higher than that represented by lower-case letters.)

Row 1	The symbol:	stands for a sound approximately like:	but the Japanese sound:
a	'a' in 'father'	is short and clipped	
i	'i' in 'machine'	is short and clipped	
u	'u' in 'put'	is short, clipped, and without lip-rounding	
e	'e' in 'bet'	is short and clipped	
o	'o' in 'horse'	is short and clipped	

When two or more Japanese vowels follow each other directly, each one retains its original quality and length, but the sequence is regularly pronounced as a continuum. The occurrence of the same vowel symbol twice indicates a long vowel: e.g. aa represents a + a pronounced without a break.

A word in Japanese has at least as many syllables as it has vowels.

Practice 1 [1]

a 'oh!'	A-o 'blue'	u-E 'top'	e 'picture'
A-a 'oh!'	I-i 'is good'	o-I 'nephew'	E-e 'yes'
A-i 'love'	i-E 'house'	o-O-i 'are many'	o-U 'owe'
A-u 'meet'	i-I-E 'no'	a-O-i 'is blue'	o-O-u 'conceal'

Row 2	The symbol:	stands for a sound approximately like:	but the Japanese sound:
k before a, u, e, o	'c' in 'coot'	has less aspiration [2]	
ky, and k before i	'c' in 'cute'	has less aspiration [2]	

The values of the vowel symbols remain the same as in Row 1 above.

Practice 2

ka-U 'buy'	a-KA-I 'is red'	ka-I-KE-E 'account'
ka-O 'face'	o-O-KI-i 'is big'	KYA-a 'eek!'
i-KE 'pond'	KE-e-ko 'practice'	KYO-o 'today'
ko-KO 'here'	ku-U-KO-O 'airport'	KYU-u 'grade'

[1] All the practice drills that follow are for pronunciation practice only.

[2] The corresponding English sound is followed by a strong puff of breath.

Row 3	The symbol:	stands for a sound approximately like:	but the Japanese sound:
	g before a, u, e, o	'g' in 'begone'	in initial position is more fully voiced than the corresponding English initial [1]
	gy, and g before i	'g' in 'regular'	in initial position is more fully voiced than the corresponding English initial [1]

Practice 3

GA-i 'injury'	gi-KO-O 'art'	GU-ke-e 'my elder brother'
GE-e 'craft'	GI-ka-i 'the Diet'	GYA-ku-i 'traitorous mind'
GO-i 'vocabulary'	go-KA-I 'misunderstanding'	gyo-O-KO-O 'good fortune'
gi-KE-E 'brother-in-law'	gu-U-I 'a moral'	GYU-u 'beef'

Row 4

The symbol ḡ represents a sound like the 'ng' of 'singer' [2] — that is, it is a sound made with the tongue in position for a g but with the air escaping through the nasal passages. In Japanese, this sound never occurs at the beginning of an utterance.

Like gy and g before i, ḡy and ḡ before i are pronounced with the tongue raised in a 'y' position, somewhat like the 'ngy' of 'bring you.'

The occurrence of ḡ is a matter of dialect. While it is usually considered a feature of Tokyo Japanese, there are many Tokyo speakers who

---

[1] A voiced sound is one accompanied by vibration of the vocal cords. In English, a voiced consonant at the beginning of a word begins without voice (vibration); in Japanese, an initial voiced consonant is voiced throughout its articulation.

[2] This is a valid comparison only for those speakers of English who distinguish between the medial sounds of 'singer' and 'finger,' with the latter containing the medial sound of 'singer' + 'g.'

regularly use g̲ instead, and there are still others who alternate freely be-
between the two. The situation, as far as this text is concerned, is
as follows:

> Where g is written, g̃ is NOT to be substituted.
> Where g̃ is written, g can ALWAYS be substituted.

Example:

> GA̲-i: G occurs in the speech of all speakers of Tokyo Japanese.

> KA-g̃u: Some speakers say KA-g̃u (with the nasal g̃) consistently,
> others say KA-gu consistently, and still others alternate
> freely between the two pronunciations.

Whichever pronunciation a student uses, he must be able to understand both.[1] However, it s h o u l d be pointed out that the dialect which
includes g̃ is considered the "prestige" dialect of Tokyo.

Practice 4

E-e-g̃a	KA-g̃e	ka-I-ḠI
'movie'	'shade'	'conference'
i-KA-g̃a	GO-g̃o	ka-I-ḠYA-KU[2]
'how?'	'afternoon'	'a jest'
KA-g̃u	ko-O-ḠO	ka-I-ḠYU-U
'furniture'	'spoken language'	'sea-cow'
a-O-g̃u	ku-ḠI	KO-o-g̃yo-o
'look up'	'nail'	'industry'

Row 5	The symbol:	stands for a sound approximately like:	but the Japanese sound:
	s̲ before a̲, u̲, e̲, o̲ sy̲, and s̲ be- fore i̲	's' in 'see' 'sh' in 'she'	is pronounced further forward in the mouth

---

[1] Accordingly, examples of g substitution for g̃ have been included on the
tapes that accompany this text.

[2] See the section on Whispered Syllables below.

Practice 5

A-sa 'morning'	o-SA-KE 'rice wine'	SYA-ka-i 'society'
a-SU 'tomorrow'	SU-ğu 'right away'	HA-i-sya 'dentist'
A-se 'perspiration'	ko-O-SU-I 'perfume'	KYU-u-syu-u 'Kyushu'
a-SI 'leg'	o-I-SI-I 'is delicious'	sya-SYO-O 'conductor'
a-SO-KO 'there'	o-KA-SI-i 'is funny'	syu-U-SYO-O 'grief'

Row 6	The symbol:	stands for a sound approximately like:	but the Japanese sound:
	z before a, u, [1] e, o	'z' in 'bazaar'	is pronounced further forward in the mouth and is regularly fully voiced [2]
	zy, and z before i	'j' in 'reject'	

Practice 6

za-I-KA 'inventory'	GO-zi 'five o'clock'	ZYU-u 'ten'
KA-zu 'number'	KA-zi 'a fire'	KA-zyu 'fruit tree'
ki-ZU 'a cut'	zi-E-E 'self-defense'	zyo-O 'feeling'
ZE-e 'a tax'	ZYA-a 'well then'	zyo-SE-E 'womanhood'
ZO-o 'elephant'	zya-KO-O 'musk'	ko-O-ZYO-o 'factory'

Row 7	The symbol:	stands for a sound approximately like:	but the Japanese sound:
	t before a, e, o	't' in 'tip'	is pronounced with the tongue touching the teeth and with little aspiration
	ty, and t before i	'ch' in 'cheap'	is pronounced further forward in the mouth
	t before u	'ts' in 'tsetse fly'	is pronounced further forward in the mouth

---

[1] An alternate pronunciation of z before u is 'dz.'

[2] See footnote 1 on page xxiii.

Practice 7

ka-TA 'person'	TI-zu 'map'	o-SI-ḠO-TO-TYU-U 'in the middle of work'
ta-KA-i 'is high'	ti-I-SA-i 'is small'	ko-O-TYO-O 'director'
ki-I-TE 'listening'	o-TYA 'tea'	TYO-o-me-e 'long life'
to-O-KA 'ten days'	ko-O-TYA 'black tea'	TU-i-te 'concerning'
si-ḠO-TO 'work'	TYU-u-i 'warning'	tu-ZU-KI 'continuation'

Row 8	The symbol:	stands for a sound approximately like:	but the Japanese sound:
	<u>d</u>	'd' in 'redeem'	is pronounced with the tongue touching the teeth and is regularly fully voiced [1]

Practice 8

e-DA 'branch'	DE-te 'leaving'	KA-do 'street corner'
o-KA-DA (family name)	i-SO-i-de 'hurrying'	DO-ko 'where?'
ku-DA-SA-i 'give me'	de-KI-ḠO-to 'occurrence'	do-O-ḠU 'tool'

Row 9	The symbol:	stands for a sound approximately like:	but the Japanese sound:
	<u>n</u> before <u>a</u>, <u>u</u>, <u>e</u>, <u>o</u>	'n' in 'deny'	is pronounced with the tongue touching the teeth and is regularly fully voiced [1]
	<u>ny</u>, and <u>n</u> before <u>i</u>	'n' in 'menu,' 'avenue,'[2] etc.	

---

[1] See footnote 1 on page xxiii.

[2] Applicable only for those speakers who use a ' —nyu' pronunciation.

Practice 9

NA-ka 'inside'	o-KA-NE 'money'	NYA-o 'meow'
KI-nu 'silk'	so-NO 'that'	gyu-U-NYU-U 'milk'
te-NU-ḠU-I 'towel'	NA-ni 'what?'	nyu-U-ZYO-O 'entrance'
NE-ko 'cat'	ni-KA-I 'second floor'	NYO-o-ḡo 'court lady'

Row 10	The symbol:	stands for a sound approximately like:	but the Japanese sound:
	h before a, e, o	'h' in 'hot'	
	hy, and h before i	'h' in 'humid'	has more friction
	H before u is made by bringing the upper and lower lips together and then puffing air out between them. Unlike English 'f,' which is the closest English sound, Japanese h before u does not involve the lower teeth in its production.		

Practice 10

HA-i 'yes'	hi-ḠE 'beard'	HYO-o 'hail'
HA-ha 'mother'	ko-O-HI-i 'coffee'	HU-u 'manner'
he-E 'wall'	HYU-u-zu 'fuse'	HU-ne 'boat'
HO-o 'direction'	hya-KU-DO '100 times'	HU-zi 'Fuji'

Row 11	The symbol:	stands for a sound approximately like:	but the Japanese sound:
	p before a, u, e, o	'p' in 'poor'	
	py, and p before i	'p' in 'pure'	has less aspiration

Practice 11

PA-a-zi 'purge'	PU-u-pu-u (noise of a horn)	PO-o-zu 'a pause'
a-PA-a-to 'apartment'	pe-E-ZI 'page'	PYU-u-pyu-u (noise of a whistle)
de-PA-a-to 'department store'	PO-ka-po-ka 'repeatedly'	pi-A-NO 'piano'

Row 12	The symbol:	stands for a sound approximately like:	but the Japanese sound:
	b before a, u, e, o	'b' in 'rebel'	is regularly fully voiced [1]
	by, and b before i	'b' in 'rebuke'	

Practice 12

BA-ta 'butter'	ka-BE 'wall'	sa-BI-SI-i 'is lonely'
ta-BA-KO 'cigarette'	bo-O 'stick'	BYA-ku-e 'white robe'
a-SO-BU 'play'	o-BO-e-te 'remembering'	BYU-u-byu-u (noise of a whistle)
a-BU-NA-I 'is dangerous'	e-BI 'shrimp'	byo-O-BU 'screen'

Row 13	The symbol:	stands for a sound approximately like:	but the Japanese sound:
	m before a, u, e, o	'm' in 'remind'	is regularly fully voiced [1]
	my, and m before i	'm' in 'amuse'	

Practice 13

MA-e 'front'	mu-SU-ME 'daughter'	kyo-O-MI 'interest'
ma-TA 'again'	ME-e-zi 'Meiji'	mya-KU-DO-O 'pulse'
NO-mu 'drink'	I-tu mo 'always'	MYU-u-zu 'muse'
mu-KO-O 'over there'	MI-se-te 'showing'	ko-O-MYO-O 'great deed'

_____

[1] See footnote 1 on page xxiii.

Row 14	The symbol:	stands for a sound approximately like:	but the Japanese sound:
y	'y' in 'year'	is regularly fully voiced [1]

Practice 14

ya-O-YA 'vegetable store'	o-YU 'hot water'	yo-SI-DA (family name)
NA-ḡo-ya 'Nagoya'	yu-KI-yo 'snowy night'	sa-YO-O 'that way'
o-YA-SU-MI-NA-SA-i 'good night'	yu-U-ME-E 'famous'	o-HA-YO-O 'good morning'

Row 15

The Japanese r is a flap-r, made by flicking the tip of the tongue against the alveolar ridge (area behind the upper teeth). This sound closely resembles the 'r' in the British English pronunciation of 'very.' To speakers of American English, it often sounds like a d, but there are two main differences: (1) the Japanese r is shorter than d; and (2) in the production of r, the tip of the tongue makes contact with the alveolar ridge, whereas in the production of d, it is the area of the tongue immediately behind the tip that makes contact against the upper teeth. When r is immediately followed by i or y, the r articulation just described is accompanied by palatalization — that is, the back part of the tongue is in position to make a y sound, while the tip makes the flap-r.

Practice 15

ra-KU 'comfortable'	o-HU-ro 'bath'	rya-KU-ZI 'simplified character'
sa-YO-NA-RA 'goodbye'	o-MO-SI-RO-i 'is interesting'	ka-I-RYU-U 'ocean current'
BI-ru 'building'	ri-KO-O 'clever'	ryu-U-KO-O 'fashion'
RU-u-ru 'rule'	ko-O-RI 'ice'	RYO-o-zi 'consul'
KI-re-e 'pretty'	a-RI-ḡa-to-o 'thank you'	ryo-O-RI-ya 'restaurant'

---

[1] See footnote 1 on page xxiii.

Row 16	The symbol: <u> </u>	stands for a sound approximately like:	but the Japanese sound:
	<u>w</u>	'w' in 'want'	is regularly fully voiced [1]

Practice 16

wa-KA-i   wa-KA-ru   wa-RE-WA-RE
'is young'   'understand'   'we'
he-E-WA   yu-BI-WA   wa-SU-RE-RU
'peace'   'ring'   'forget'

Row 17

    <u>K</u> occurs as a syllable by itself immediately preceding a syllable having initial <u>k</u> (i.e. a syllable of Row 2). The back of the tongue is raised as in the production of a single (that is, short) <u>k</u> and is held in that position for a full syllable beat before being released (compare the somewhat similar long 'k' in English 'bookkeeper'). The following syllable, which has initial <u>k</u>, is pronounced without aspiration—that is, without a puff of breath after the <u>k</u>.

    <u>S</u> occurs as a syllable by itself immediately preceding a syllable having initial <u>s</u> (i.e. a syllable of Row 5). Its articulation lasts for a full syllable beat and has the same quality as the <u>s</u> that follows (compare the somewhat similar long 's' in English 'less sleep' and the long 'sh' in 'horse-show').

    <u>T</u> occurs as a syllable by itself immediately preceding a syllable having initial <u>t</u> (i.e. a syllable of Row 7). The front of the tongue is pushed against the back of the upper teeth as in the production of a single (that is, short) <u>t</u> and is held in that position for a full syllable beat before being released (compare the somewhat similar long 't' in English 'hot tip'). The following syllable, which has initial <u>t</u>, is pronounced without aspiration.

    <u>P</u> occurs as a syllable by itself immediately preceding a syllable having initial <u>p</u> (i.e. a syllable of Row 11). The lips are brought together as in the production of a single (that is, short) <u>p</u> and are held in that position for a full syllable beat before being released (compare the somewhat similar long 'p' in English 'top part'). The following syllable, which has initial <u>p</u>, is pronounced without aspiration.

---

[1] See footnote 1 on page xxiii.

All double (that is, long) consonants in Japanese are characterized by tenseness.

Practice 17 a

mi-K-KA 'three days'	a-S-SA-ri 'briefly'
yu-K-KU-ri 'slowly'	ma-S-SU-ḡu 'straight'
NI-k-ko-o 'Nikko'	i-S-SO-O 'more'
ha-K-KI-ri 'clearly'	za-S-SI 'magazine'
se-K-KYO-o 'sermon'	ma-S-SI-RO 'all white'
ha-K-KYU-U 'small salary'	i-S-SYU-U 'one round'
ka-T-TA 'bought'	i-P-PA-I 'full'
i-T-TE 'going'	i-P-PU-U 'odd'
TYO-t-to 'a bit'	ri-P-PO-O 'legislation'
ma-T-TI-ba-ko 'matchbox'	ha-P-PI 'workman's coat'
ko-MA-t-tya-t-ta '[I]'m upset'	ha-P-PYA-KU-ME '800 momme'
yo-T-TU-ME 'fourth thing'	ha-P-PYO-O 'announcement'

Row 17 (continued)

N̲ represents a syllabic nasal: it is a sound which always has a full syllable beat of its own—that is, it constitutes a syllable—and is always pronounced with the nasal passage open; but its pronunciation varies depending on the sound that immediately follows in the same word or a following word.

1. Before a syllable beginning with p̲, b̲, or m̲ (that is, a syllable of Row 11, 12, or 13), ñ represents a syllabic m̲. [1]

2. Before a syllable beginning with z̲, t̲, d̲, n̲, or r̲ (that is, a syllable of Row 6, 7, 8, 9, or 15), ñ represents a syllabic n̲. [1]

3. Before a syllable beginning with k̲, g̲, or ḡ̲ (that is, a syllable of Row 2, 3, or 4), ñ represents a syllabic ḡ̲. [1]

4. Elsewhere—that is, before a vowel (i.e. a syllable of Row 1) or a syllable beginning with s̲, h̲, y̲, or w̲ (i.e. a syllable of Row 5, 10, 14, or 16) or at the end of an utterance—ñ represents syllabic nasalization, articulated by raising the tongue toward the roof of the mouth but not making contact anywhere, and at the same time releasing the flow of air through the nasal passage and vibrating the vocal cords. When ñ is followed by o̲, the o̲ is anticipated and the combination sounds like ñ + w̲ + o̲. Similarly, ñ followed by e̲ sounds like ñ + y̲ + e̲.

---

[1] It constitutes a full syllable and is longer than the related sound which occurs as the initial part of a syllable.

Practice 17b

(1) sa-N̄-PO   (2) be-N̄-ZYO   (3) be-N̄-KYO-O
     'a walk'   'toilet'   'study'
     SA-ñ-ba-i   ke-N̄-TO-o   ni-HO-N̄-GI-ñ-ko-o
     'three cupfuls'   'a guess'   'Bank of Japan'
     a-N̄-MA-RI   KO-ñ-do   ni-HO-N̄-GO
     'too much'   'this time'   'Japanese language'
                                  da-N̄-NA-SA-ma
                                  'master'
                                  BE-ñ-ri
                                  'convenient'

                          (4) te-N̄-I-N̄ 'store clerk'
                               ni-HO-ñ o 'Japan (as direct object)'
                               ni-HO-ñ e 'to Japan'
                               sa-N̄-SE-E 'approval'
                               HA-ñ-ha-ñ 'half and half'
                               HO-ñ-ya 'bookstore'
                               de-N̄-WA 'telephone'
                               a-RI-MA-SE-ñ 'there isn't any'

Whispered Syllables

   The Tokyo dialect of Japanese is characterized by the frequent occurrence
of whispered (that is, voiceless[1]) syllables. Whenever an i or u vowel[2] occurs
between any two voiceless consonants (k, s, t, p, or h), the vowel automatically becomes voiceless or, in some cases, is lost. This happens whether the
two consonants come in the same word or in consecutive words.

---

[1] A voiceless sound is one which is not accompanied by vibration of the
vocal cords.

[2] Other vowels are only occasionally affected.

Practice 18

In the following practice drills, whispered (i.e. voiceless or lost) vowels are crossed by a virgule (/).

ki̸-SYA	si̸-SU-MU	hi̸-SYO
'train'	'advance'	'secretary'
ki̸-TE	si̸-TE-RU	hi̸-TO
'coming'	'throw away'	'person'
ki̸-T-TE	na-SU̸-t-te	hi̸-P-PA-ru
'stamp'	'doing'	'pull'
ku̸-SYA-mi	ti̸-KA-i	hu̸-KA-i
'sneeze'	'is close'	'is deep'
NA-ku̸-te	ti̸-T-TO-mo	hu̸-SI-GĪ
'not being any'	'[not] a bit'	'strange'
si̸-TE	tu̸-KI-MA-si̸-ta	hu̸-TO-i
'doing'	'[I] arrived'	'is big around'
si̸-T-TE	tu̸-TO-me-te	hu̸-T-TO-BO-o-ru
'knowing'	'being employed'	'football'
su̸-KI-i	hi̸-KI-MA-si̸-ta	hi̸-HA-N̄
'skiing'	'[I] pulled'	'criticism'

In the phrases in the left-hand column below, the final vowel of the first word is preceded AND followed by a voiceless consonant and accordingly is itself voiceless. In the phrases in the right-hand column, the final vowel of the first word is preceded but not followed by a voiceless consonant and accordingly has its full, voiced value—that is, it is accompanied by vibration of the vocal cords.

Practice 19

DO-t-ti̸ ka 'either one'   DO-t-ti ḡa 'which one (as subject)?'

DE-su̸ kara 'therefore'   DE-su ḡa 'however'

I-tu̸ kara 'since when?'   I-tu ma-de 'until when?'

hi̸-KO-o-ki̸ to 'airplane and'   hi̸-KO-o-ki no 'of an airplane'

When an i or u vowel preceded by a voiceless consonant comes at the end of an utterance, the vowel either has its full voiced value or is whispered. There is variation depending on the speaker, the occasion, and the word in question. Alternants like the following occur commonly:

Practice 20

hi̸-TO-tu̸ or hi̸-TO-tu 'one unit'

SO-o de-su̸ or SO-o de-su 'that's right'

o-HA-YO-O GO-ZA-I-MA-su̸ or o-HA-YO-O GO-ZA-I-MA-su
  'good morning'

Accent

The rhythm of Japanese, unlike that of English, is regular and even: each syllable is given moderate, approximately equal stress, and has approximately equal length. However, some syllables seem more prominent than others. This prominence — or accent — is primarily a matter of pitch in Japanese, and only secondarily a matter of stress.

Any continuous Japanese sequence of one or more words is said to be accented if it contains at least one example of a single high-pitched syllable, or an uninterrupted series of high-pitched syllables, followed by an abrupt drop to a low-pitched syllable; and the accent is said to occur on the last (or only) high-pitched syllable, which is slightly stressed. Thus, an utterance that sounds like this:

$$\text{a}^{\text{merikaryoozi}}\text{kañ} \quad \text{'American Consulate'}$$

is an accented utterance, and the accent occurs on the syllable zi, which is slightly stressed (i.e. louder).

For the purposes of this text, we recognize four significant pitch levels: two accented levels (high and medium-high) and two unaccented levels (neutral and low). These are not absolute pitch levels but are relative to each other within a given utterance.

Some Japanese utterances are accented and some are unaccented. The first syllable of an unaccented sequence of more than one syllable is automatically pronounced with low pitch, and the following syllables all have neutral pitch. An unaccented sequence which follows pause (that is, which occurs at the beginning of a sentence, or within a sentence after a pause) appears in this text without any special accent marks.

koko is pronounced ko^{ko} 'here'

asoko is pronounced a^{soko} 'there'

ano sakana is pronounced a$^{\text{no sakana}}$ 'that fish'

soko e iku is pronounced so$^{\text{ko e iku}}$ 'I'll go there'

moo iti-do itte is pronounced mo$^{\text{o iti-do itte}}$ 'saying it again'

However, when an unaccented word or phrase having the above pitch contour occurs in the middle of a sequence, the superscript symbol ⌐ appears over the single syllable which has low pitch: ⌐ indicates a rise in pitch from low level to neutral level. Thus:

kore wa zăssi da   is pronounced   ko$^{\text{re wa}}$za$^{\text{ssi da}}$

'this is a magazine'

An accented sequence contains one or more of the following superscript symbols:[1]

Symbol	Meaning
⌐	Rise from neutral to high pitch
¬	Drop from high to neutral or low pitch
˻	Rise from neutral to medium-high pitch
˺	Drop from medium-high to neutral or low pitch

Thus:

do⌐ozo is pronounced do^{o}zo 'please'

a˻na¬ta is pronounced a^{na}ta 'you'

a⌐o¬i is pronounced a^{o}i 'is blue'

wa˻karimase¬ñ is pronounced wa^{karimase}ñ 'it isn't clear'

da˻izyo¬obu is pronounced da^{izyo}obu 'safe'

mo˻o iti-do itte kudasa¬i is pronounced mo^{o} iti-do itte kudasa$_{i}$
   'please say it again'

ki¬ree na o˻zyo¬osañ is pronounced ki$^{}$ree na o^{zyo}osañ
   'a pretty girl'

na¬gaku ka˻karima˺su kara is pronounced na$^{}$gaku ka^{karima}su kara
   'because it takes long'

o⌐oki¬i i˻e˺ desu is pronounced o^{oki}i i^{e} desu 'it's a big house'

Note the following rules and conventions:

(1) Only a word which contains ¬ or ˺ is said to be accented, and the accent is said to occur on the syllable at whose end ¬ or ˺ occurs.[2]

(2) Any word containing ⌐ or ˻, or the first word after a pause, or any word beginning with low plus neutral pitch, marks the start of a new accent phrase.

(3) Except in special circumstances, the first or only accented sequence of syllables of an utterance is said to be within the pitch

---

[1] A single accented word never has more than one high-pitched sequence and therefore cannot contain more than two of the accent superscripts— one rising and one falling.

[2] Actually the rise in pitch symbolized by ⌐ or ˻ is automatic, given the

range designated as "high." Subsequent accented sequences in the same sentence which have the same[1] or higher pitch are also said to be within the high range; those which have significantly lower pitch (i.e. lower than high but higher than neutral) are said to be "medium-high."

Whispered syllables in Japanese cannot be distinguished by pitch. Their position within the pitch coutour is determined by other linguistic criteria.

Since accent in Japanese is a matter of high pitch relative to a following low pitch, it is impossible to hear accent without a following low syllable. The occurrence of ˥ at the end of a single word in this text means that the word ordinarily has that accent when a following low syllable occurs. For example, hasi 'edge' and ha˥si˥ 'bridge' sound alike in isolation—in both, the first syllable is lower pitched than the second syllable—but when they are followed by a neutral or low syllable, they contrast with each other:

hasi wa (ha $^{si\ wa}$) 'as for the edge,' but

ha˥si˥ wa (ha ^{si} wa) 'as for the bridge';

hasi da (ha $^{si\ da}$) 'it's the edge,' but

ha˥si˥ da (ha ^{si} da) 'it's the bridge'; etc.

Similarly, ki 'spirit' and ki˥ 'tree' are alike in isolation, but compare:

ki wa (ki ^{wa}) 'as for the spirit' and

ki˥ wa (^{ki} wa) 'as for the tree.'

Accordingly we do speak of Japanese words that are accented on the final syllable, although we recognize that the accent can be heard in only some occurrences.

When a word is accented on its next-to-last syllable and the final syllable has a whispered alternant, the accent is regularly marked. For example, i˥kima˥su means either i——kima——su[2] or i——kima——su.

---

boundaries of the accent phrase. It always occurs on the second syllable of the accent phrase, unless the accent itself falls on the first syllable, in which case only the first syllable is high-pitched. Symbols for the rise are included here to simplify the reading of the transcription for the beginning student. It is possible to represent Japanese accent by using a traditional accent mark on the last high syllable (where this text has ˥ or ˦), with no symbol to indicate the automatic rise—provided the boundaries of the accent phrase are identified. Thus: ho˥n might be written hón, a˥na˥ta as anáta, i˥kima˥sita as ikimásita, mo˥o iti-do itte kudasa˥i as moo iti-do itte kudasái, and so on.

[1] 'Same' here refers to linguistic sameness, i. e. variation is within the bounds permitted by the native speaker for identification as the same. Usually, each successive occurrence of a given pitch level within a pause group represents a slightly lower alternant of that pitch.

[2] This is the more common alternant in Tokyo speech.

In animated or emphatic speech, the interval between pitch levels increases. In some cases, the interval between low and neutral pitch within one emphatic unaccented phrase may be as great as or greater than that between neutral and high pitch in a following unemphatic accented phrase. The symbol | (appearing only in Part II) marks the end of such an emphatic phrase. Thus:

oyoso kyo⌐omi na⌐i is pronounced o$^{yoso\ kyo^{omi\ na}}$i

'on the whole I have no interest'

but:

oyoso | kyo⌐omi na⌐i is pronounced o^{yoso} kyo$^{omi\ na}$i

'ON THE WHOLE I have no interest'

Accent presents difficulty for a foreign student of Japanese largely because of accent variation.[1] This variation is of three kinds:

(1) Variation in basic word accent

Many words have alternate accents within the Tokyo dialect. Thus, the accepted pronunciation of the word for 'policeman' is zyuñsa or zyu⌐ñsa; for 'streetcar,' deñsya or de⌐ñsya; for 'I,' boku or bo⌐ku.

(2) Gain and loss of accent in particular environments

Many basically unaccented words sometimes acquire an accent, and many accented words sometimes lose their accent. For example, accented ku⌐dasa⌐i loses its accent following an accented -te word:

i⌐tte kudasa⌐i 'please say [it]'
ha⌐na⌐site kudasai 'please talk'

An unaccented -te word acquires an accent before mo and kara:

itte 'saying [it]'

but:

i⌐tte⌐ mo 'even if [I] say [it]'

and:

i⌐tte⌐ kara 'after saying [it]'

(3) Variation in phrase accent

Many pairs of utterances, otherwise identical, are distinguished only by a difference in their phrase accent. Compare:

---

[1] The accents and intonations marked in this text follow those of the tapes that were recorded to accompany it, for all the material that was recorded.

(a) Kyo⌐oto e i├kima⌐sita ka 'did you go to Kyoto (or did you go somewhere else)?'

(b) Kyo⌐oto e i⌐kima⌐sita ka 'did you (or didn't you) go to Kyoto?'

(a) are wa ⌐na⌐ñ desu ka 'what is that?'

(b) a⌐re wa na⌐ñ desu ka 'what is THAT (in comparison with the other things)?'

(a) zu⌐ibuñ ya⌐su⌐i desu ⌐ne⌐e 'it's very CHEAP, isn't it'

(b) zu⌐ibuñ ya├su⌐i desu ⌐ne⌐e 'it's VERY cheap, isn't it'

(a) mo⌐tto úsiro 'further BACK'

(b) mo⌐tto usiro 'FURTHER back'

In general, it can be said that the occurrence of ⌐ or ⌐ on a word is a sign of primary interest in that word. Conversely, ├ is never a sign of interest or emphasis.

Superimposed on these kinds of variation is dialectal variation. The accent of Tokyo Japanese is different from that of other parts of Japan. A student working with a tutor who is not a native of Tokyo will find that the pitch contours marked in this text often do not match those used by his tutor.

Doesn't this mean, then, that the student of Japanese might just as well ignore accent? Not at all! The fact that two different accents are sometimes acceptable does not mean that any accent at all is permitted. (Some native speakers of English say 'dry cléaning' and others say 'drý cleaning,' but no speaker says 'dry cleaning.') Further indication of the importance of accent is the fact that many pairs of utterances with different meanings are distinguished only by their accent.

Intonation

The following intonation symbols are used in this text:

1. Period .

A period ending a sentence indicates that the final syllable and all immediately preceding unaccented syllables are pronounced with low pitch level, with the final syllable — if it is not whispered — lowest of all. In the event that the sentence, or its final accent phrase, contains no accent — that is, if the final or only pitch contour of the sentence is low + neutral — a final period indicates only the onset of silence.

Period intonation occurs most commonly at the end of statements, suggestions, rhetorical questions, and questions asked indirectly. At the end of direct questions, it often indicates abruptness, stiffness, aloofness, etc.

Examples:

Wa⌈karimase⌉n̄ desita. 'I didn't understand.' <u>is pronounced</u>

wa^{karimase} n̄ desi_{ta}

Asuko e iku. 'I'm going to go there.' <u>is pronounced</u>

_asuko e iku

2. Question mark _?_

A question mark ending a sentence indicates a rise in pitch on the final syllable, [1] usually with lengthening of that syllable. Question-mark intonation regularly changes a statement into a question, and is typical of familiar style.

Examples:

Wa⌈ka⌉ru? 'Is it clear?' <u>is pronounced</u> wa^{ka}ru^u

Kore? 'This one?' <u>is pronounced</u> ko^{re}^e

3. Rising hook _⌣_

A rising hook ending a sentence indicates a slight rise in pitch on the final syllable only, usually without lengthening of that syllable. The final syllable may start on a high or a low pitch. [2] This intonation occurs with certain sentence particles and implies friendliness and interest in the reaction of the person addressed. Wherever a rising hook occurs, it is possible to substitute a period as an alternate intonation without changing the meaning beyond m a k i n g the sentence more abrupt. Examples:

Wa⌈karima⌉sita ka⌣ 'Did you understand?' <u>is pronounced</u>

wa^{karima}sita ka⌣ <u>or</u> wa^{karima}sita ^{ka⌣}

I⌈i desu yo⌣ 'It's all right!' <u>is pronounced</u>

ⁱi desu yo⌣ <u>or</u> ⁱi desu ^{yo⌣}

---

[1] With this intonation, the final syllable is never whispered.

[2] A high-pitched start is more common in women's speech.

4. Low bar $\_$

A low bar ending a sentence indicates that the final syllable has neutral pitch. It usually is lengthened and there is a gradual fading into silence. This intonation denotes incompleteness.

Examples:

Ka⌐mawana⌐kereba_ 'If it doesn't matter . . .'   is pronounced

$$ka^{mawana}kerebaa\_$$

So⌐o desu ḡa_ 'That's so but . . .'   is pronounced

$$so^{so}o\ desu\ \bar{g}aa\_$$

5. Exclamation point $\underline{!}$

An exclamation point ending a sentence indicates that the final syllable starts high and has slightly falling pitch. Articulation ends abruptly and there is no significant lengthening of the final syllable.

Example:

Ano ne! 'Say there!'   is pronounced $a^{no^{ne}}$

6. Asterisk $\underline{*}$

An asterisk at the beginning of a sequence indicates a special exclamatory intonation in which all pitch levels of the sequence become successively higher with each occurrence.

Examples:

* Yo⌐ku wa⌐karima⌐su ⌐ne⌐e. 'How well you understand!'

is pronounced $yo^{o}ku\ wa^{karima}su^{ne}e$

* I⌐i o⌐te⌐ñki desu ⌐ne⌐e. 'What nice weather!'   is pronounced

$$i_{i}\ o^{te}\bar{n}ki\ de^{su\ ne}e$$

7. Comma $\underline{,}$ and Semicolon $\underline{;}$

A comma within a sentence indicates a break within the utterance: $\underline{X}, \underline{Y}$ means that there is a slight slowing down of articulation, with or without accompanying pause, at the end of $\underline{X}$; that neutral syllables at the end of $\underline{X}$ have a low alternant of neutral pitch; and that $\underline{Y}$ starts a new accent phrase. [1]

---

[1] This means that if the first two syllables of $\underline{Y}$ have unaccented pitch, the first is low and the second neutral.

A semicolon marks the same general kind of division as a comma, but in sentences containing more than one such division, the semicolon is used to indicate a division of major rank.

Examples:

Su⌐peiñḡo o yamema⌐sita ḡa, ni⌐hoñḡo wa ma⌐da be⌐ñkyoo-site ima⌐su.
'I gave up Spanish, but Japanese I'm still studying.'

is pronounced

peiñḡo o yamema   hoñḡo wa ma

su   sita ḡa ni   da beñkyoo-site ima
                                                            su.

Zi⌐kañ ḡa na⌐i kara, su⌐peiñḡo o yamema⌐sita ḡa; ni⌐hoñḡo wa ma⌐da
be⌐ñkyoo-site ima⌐su.
'I gave up Spanish because I have no time, but Japanese I'm still studying.'   is pronounced

kañ ḡa na   peiñḡo o yamema   hoñḡo wa ma

zi   i kara su   sita ḡa ni   da be ñkyoo-

    site ima

        su.

8. Dash —

A dash occurs within inverted sentences (cf. Lesson 11, Grammatical Note 5), indicating that what follows is to be pronounced without pause as if it were part of the preceding phrase. An accented sequence following the dash is medium-high.

Examples:

I⌐i desu ⌐ne⌐e — sore wa.   'Isn't it nice — that.'   is pronounced

i i desu ne e sore wa

I⌐kima⌐sita yo ⌐ — Kyo⌐oto e.   'I went — to Kyoto.'   is pronounced

i kima sita yo kyo oto e

---

[1] An intonation symbol which ordinarily occurs at the end of a sentence may occur in the middle of an inverted sentence.

Supplementary Pronunciation Drills

1. Vowel Combinations

aˈraimaˈsu 'wash   hiatari 'exposure   huañ
   (formal)'   to the sun'   'uneasiness'
arau 'wash   iu (yuu) [1]   huite
   (informal)'   'say'   'wiping'
aˈraeˈ   suˈmiˈe 'ink   suehiro
   'wash!'   drawing'   'folding fan'
aˈraoˈo   kiˈkioˈku 'hear (and   huoñ
   'let's wash'   keep in mind)'   'unrest'

deasi 'start'   doˈa 'door'
deiri 'going in and out' hiˈroˈi 'is wide'
neuti 'value'   oˈmoˈu 'think'
neoki 'lying down and getting   koˈe 'voice'
   up'

2. Short and Long Vowels

obasañ 'aunt'   haˈ 'tooth'
oˈbaˈasañ 'grandmother' haˈa 'yes'

ozisañ 'uncle'   kiˈteˈ 'coming'
oˈziˈisañ 'grandfather' kiite 'listening'

kuˈroo 'trouble'   husetu 'construction'
kuˈuro 'air route'   huusetu 'rumor'

kiˈreˈ 'cloth'   seḡyoo 'management'
kiˈree 'pretty'   seˈeḡyo 'control'

toˈtte 'taking'   muˈko 'bridegroom'
toˈotte 'going through' mukoo 'beyond'

tori 'bird'   oki 'open sea'
toˈoriˈ 'avenue'   oˈokiˈi 'is big'

---

[1] I + u is regularly pronounced yuu.

3. Short and Long Consonants

maki 'firewood'   ite 'being'
ma˥kki 'the last years'   itte 'going'

Masao (proper name)   ko˥na˥ 'flour'
ma˥ssa˥o 'deep blue'   koñna 'this kind'

nisi 'west'   kono boosi 'this hat'
ni˥ssi 'Japan and China'   ko˥ñ no boosi 'navy blue hat'

ma˥ti˥ 'town'   Su˥pe˥iñ 'Spain'
ma˥tti 'match'   su˥ppa˥i 'is sour'

4. su ~ tu Contrast

masu 'increase'   su˥ri 'pickpocket'   su˥ki˥ 'liking'
ma˥tu 'wait'   turi 'fishing'   tu˥ki˥ 'moon'

su˥mi 'corner'   su˥gi˥ 'past'   susumu 'advance'
tu˥mi 'crime'   tu˥gi˥ 'next'   tu˥tu˥mu 'wrap'

5. d ~ r Contrast

do˥o 'how?'   hodo 'extent'   muda 'useless'
ro˥o 'prison'   ho˥ro 'hood'   mura 'village'

dañboo 'heating'   ma˥de 'until'   sode 'sleeve'
rañboo 'rough'   ma˥re˥ 'rare'   sore 'that thing'

6. n ~ g̃ ~ ñ ~ ñg̃ Contrast

kani 'crab'   kaneñ 'a combustible'   sa˥ ni 'in what follows'
ka˥g̃i˥ 'key'   kag̃eñ 'moderation'   sa˥g̃i 'fraud'
ka˥ñi severe cold'   ka˥ñeñ 'hepatitis'   sañi 'approval'
ka˥ñg̃i 'Korean   kañg̃eñ 'restoration'   sa˥ñg̃i 'participation in
   singing girl'   government'

7. Even Rhythm Practice

a 'oh!'
are 'that one'
asoko 'there'
to˥kidoki˥ 'sometimes'
ano sakana 'that fish'
ano tomodati 'that friend'
ano tomodati da 'it's that friend'
asoko no tomodati 'a friend from that place'
Amerika no tomodati 'an American friend'
Amerika no tomodati da 'it's an American friend'

8. Accent Contrasts

I⌐ma desu.   'It's now.'
I⌐ma¬ desu.   'It's a living room.'

Ma¬initi desu.   'It's every day.'
Ma⌐initi de¬su.   'It's the Mainichi (a newspaper).'

Yo¬ñde kudasai.   'Please read [it].'
Yo⌐ñde kudasa¬i.   'Please call [him].'

Tu⌐yu de¬su.   'It's the rainy season.'
Tu¬yu desu.   'It's broth.'

A¬tuku simasu.   'I'll make it hot.'
A⌐tuku sima¬su.   'I'll make it thick.'

So⌐re o ki¬ru kara_   'Since I'm going to cut it. . .'
So⌐re o kiru¬ kara_   'Since I'm going to wear it. . .'

Ha¬si desu.   'They're chopsticks.'
Ha⌐si de¬su.   'It's the edge.'
Ha⌐si¬ desu.   'It's a bridge.'

9. Intonation Contrasts

De⌐ki¬ru.   'It's possible.'
De⌐ki¬ru?   'Is it possible?'

So¬o desyoo.   'That's probably so.'
So¬o desyoo?   'That's so, isn't it?'

Sore.   'That one.'
Sore?   'That one?'

I⌐soḡasi¬i.   'I'm busy.'
I⌐soḡasi¬i?   'Are you busy?'

So¬o desu ka.   'Oh.'
So¬o desu ka⌐   'Oh?'

Ti⌐ḡaima¬su yo.   'They're different.'
Ti⌐ḡaima¬su yo⌐   'They're different.' [1]

---

[1] Differences in the English equivalents are also differences of intonation.

Oʳwarimaꜙsita yo.   'I've finished.'
Oʳwarimaꜙsita yo⌐   'I've finished.' [1]

Iʳkimaꜙsu ka⌐   'Are you going?'
Iʳkimaꜙsu ḡa_   'I'm going but . . .'

Oʳnazi deꜙsu yo.   'They're the same.'
Oʳnazi deꜙsu ḡa_   'They're the same but . . .'

Zyoʳozuꜙ ni naʳrimaꜙsita ꜛneꜙe.   'How proficient you've become!'
* Zyoʳozuꜙ ni naʳrimaꜙsita ꜛneꜙe.   'How proficient you've become!' [1]

Aꜛnmari dekimaseꜙn ꜛneꜙe.   'He can't do very much, can he!'
* Aꜛnmari dekimaseꜙn ꜛneꜙe.   'He can't do very much, can he!' [1]

SPECIAL SYMBOLS AND CONVENTIONS

1. ( ), [ ], [ ]

In a Japanese sequence, material enclosed in parentheses ( ) may be omitted. In every case, the shorter utterance is less formal and/or less polite. Thus, a(b) means that ab and a both occur with the same meaning except that a is less formal and/or less polite than ab.

Italicized brackets [ ], on the other hand, enclose material that is optional without a difference of formality and/or politeness level: a[b] means that both ab and a occur in the given context without significant distinction.

Square brackets [ ] in the English equivalent of a Japanese sequence enclose material which is needed for natural English but does not correspond to anything in the Japanese sequence. Conversely, parentheses in the English equivalent enclose explanatory material or something literally translated from the Japanese which is not needed in the English. Compare:

Iʳkimaꜙsita ka⌐ 'Did [you] go?'

Eꜛe, iʳkimaꜙsita. 'Yes, [I] did (go).'

---

[1] Differences in the English equivalents are also differences of intonation.

'You' and 'I' are needed for natural English but do not correspond to anything in the Japanese. 'Go' in the second sentence corresponds to something in the Japanese that is usually omitted in the English equivalent.

Square brackets and parentheses are used more frequently in the earlier lessons, as an aid to the beginning student.

2. ↑, ↓, +

A raised arrow pointing upward ↑ following a Japanese word or phrase indicates that the word or phrase is polite-honorific—that is, it exalts the person to whom it refers. Such a word is used only in reference to persons other than the speaker.

A raised arrow pointing downward ↓ following a Japanese word or phrase indicates that the word or phrase is polite-humble—that is, it humbles the person to whom it refers in deference to the person addressed. Such a word is used only in reference to the speaker, members of his family, or persons closely connected with him.

A raised plus sign + following a Japanese word or phrase indicates that the word or phrase is polite-neutral—that is, it is polite but does not exalt or humble the person to whom it refers or the person to whom it is addressed. Such a word is a neutral indication of politeness.

3. Miscellaneous

A radical √ enclosing the citation form of an inflected word indicates the given word in any or all of its derived inflected forms. Thus, √go (in English) is an abbreviation for go, goes, went, gone, etc.

Lit. is used throughout the text as an abbreviation for 'literally.'

In the Japanese material, only the first word in a sentence and names of persons and places are capitalized.

ROMANIZATION

Various systems of romanization—representation of the Japanese language by letters of the Roman alphabet—are in use in Japan today. The system used in this book is an adaptation of the Shin-kunrei-shiki 'New Official System' and will be designated as BJ Romanization.[1] Other common romanizations are

---

[1] However, Japanese words appearing throughout the book as non-quoted parts of English sentences (as in this explanatory paragraph) are spelled in Hepburn romanization.

Hepburn (also called Hyōjun-shiki 'Standard System') and Nippon-shiki 'Japanese System.' The differences among them are slight and can be learned with little difficulty. For example, the word for 'romanization' is variously represented as follows:

BJ :	roomazi
Shin-kunrei-shiki :	rômazi [1]
Hepburn :	rōmaji [1]
Nippon-shiki :	rōmadi [1]

Hepburn romanization is the system most familiar to Westerners; but there are three cogent reasons for not using it in a Japanese language textbook.

1. BJ, Shin-kunrei-shiki, and Nippon-shiki bear a direct relation to Japanese structure, whereas Hepburn has no such connection. Thus, in describing Japanese inflection, many statements become unnecessarily complicated and parallelism is obscured if Hepburn romanization is used. For example, compare the following:

In a text using BJ, Shin-kunrei-shiki, or Nippon-shiki:

To form the stem of -u-class verbals, change final -u to -i.

Corresponding statement in a text using Hepburn romanization:

To form the stem of -u-class verbals, change final -u to -i, but change final -tsu to -chi and final -su to -shi.

The complexity of the latter statement results not from "special cases" in Japanese verbal structure, but only from the fact that Hepburn romanization is based on languages of the West (its vowels have values roughly as in the Romance languages, its consonants as in English) rather than on the Japanese language.

2. For the student who plans to learn the native Japanese writing system, the transition from Hepburn is more difficult than from the other systems.

3. The Japanese themselves do not adhere consistently to any single system; in fact, they sometimes use a mixture of several within the same word! It therefore becomes necessary for the foreign student to familiarize himself with the symbols used in all the systems. BJ, Shin-kunrei-shiki, and Nippon-shiki romanizations take a little longer for the English-speaking student to master (though only in the initial stages); but once he has learned any one of them, he can switch to Hepburn with no trouble. The student who has used only Hepburn, however, finds the conversion to other systems a difficult one.

The minor differences between BJ on the one hand and Shin-kunrei-shiki and Nippon-shiki on the other result from an attempt to avoid certain inconsistencies and ambiguity in the latter systems. For example, in BJ, ee and ei consistently represent different and distinct sequences of sounds of Tokyo Japanese. The spelling of these sequences in all the other romanizations (including Hepburn) is inconsistent, so that it is often impossible for a student to be certain which value a given occurrence of ei represents.

---

[1] The long mark over the o is sometimes omitted.

CONVERSION TABLE OF ROMANIZATION[1]

Symbol in another romanization	Corresponding symbol in BJ
ā [2]	aa
ū [2]	uu
ē [2]	ee
ei	ee (or ei)
ye [2]	e
ō [2]	oo
wo	o
-g-	-ḡ- (or -g-)
shi	si
sha	sya
shu	syu
sho	syo
ji	zi
ja	zya
ju	zyu
jo	zyo
di	zi
dz	z
chi	ti
cha	tya
chu	tyu
cho	tyo
tsu	tu
fu	hu
-n'-	-ñ-
-n (final)	-ñ
-n + consonant other than y-	-ñ-
-mp-	-ñp-
-mb-	-ñb-
-mm-	-ñm-

---

[1] The left-hand column includes symbols and combinations which either do not occur in BJ Romanization, or else they correspond to more than one BJ symbol so that their interpretation is ambiguous.

[2] A circumflex (ˆ) over a vowel has the same meaning as a macron (ˉ).

Classroom Instructions

1. Please listen.

   Ki⌐ite kudasa⌐i. or
   Ki⌐ite (i)te kudasa̅i. [2]

2. Please say [it].

   I⌐tte kudasa⌐i.

3. Please say [it] again.

   Mo⌐o iti-do itte kudasa⌐i.

4. Please answer.

   Ko⌐ta⌐ete kudasai.

5. Please speak in Japanese.

   Ni⌐hoñgo de hana⌐site kudasai.

6. Please don't use English.

   Eego (wa) tu⌐kawana⌐i de kudasai.

7. Please open [your] book.

   Hóñ (o) a⌐kete kudasa⌐i.

8. Please look at [your] book.

   Hóñ (o) ⌐mi⌐te kudasai.

9. Please don't look at [your] book.

   Hóñ (wa) ⌐mi⌐nai de kudasai.

10. Please close [your] book.

    Hóñ (o) ⌐to⌐zite kudasai.

11. Please say [it] in chorus.

    Mi⌐ñna⌐ de i⌐tte kudasa⌐i.

12. Please say [it] one (person) at a time.

    Hi⌐tori-zu⌐tu i⌐tte kudasa⌐i.

13. Please speak more quickly.

    Mótto ⌐ha⌐yaku ha⌐na⌐site kudasai.

14. Please speak more clearly.

    Mótto ha⌐kki⌐ri ha⌐na⌐site kudasai.

15. Please speak in a louder voice.

    Mótto ⌐o⌐oki na ⌐ko⌐e de ha⌐na⌐site kudasai.

16. Please ask Mr. (or Mrs. or Miss) Tanaka.

    Ta⌐naka-sañ ni kiite kudasa⌐i.

---

[1] These sentences are primarily for use by a Japanese instructor in giving classroom directions. It is suggested that introductory drill on them be conducted for the purpose of aural recognition.

[2] Accent of contracted alternant: Ki⌐ite⌐ te kudasai.

1

Introductory Lesson: Greetings and Useful Phrases

BASIC SENTENCES: FOR MEMORIZATION[1]

1. Oh, Mr. (or Mrs. or Miss) Tanaka!   A˺a, Tanaka-sañ.
2. Good morning.   O˺hayoo (gozaima˺su).
3. Good afternoon.   Koñniti wa.
4. Good evening.   Koñbañ wa.
5. How are you? or Are you well? (Lit. Is it health?)   O˺ge˺ñki desu ka⌐
6. Yes.   Ha˺i. or E˺e.
7. [I'm fine,] thank you. And you? (Lit. As for you?)   Okağesama de. A˺na˺ta wa?
8. Goodnight.   O˺yasumi-nasa˺i.
9. Goodbye.   Sayo(o)nara.[2]
10. Excuse me (on leaving).   Si˺tu˺ree(-simasu).
11. Excuse me (for what I did).   Si˺tu˺ree-(simasita).
12. No. or Not at all.   Iie.
13. Don't mention it. or You're welcome.   Do˺o itasimasite.
14. I'm sorry. or Thank you for your trouble.   Su˺(m)imase˺ñ.
15. I'm sorry (for what I did). or Thank you (for the trouble you took).   Su˺(m)imase˺ñ desita.
16. [Thanks] very much.   Do˺o mo.
17. Thank you.   A˺ri˺ğatoo (gozaimasu).
18. Thank you very much.   Do˺o mo a˺ri˺ğatoo (gozaimasu).
19. Thank you (for what you did).   A˺ri˺ğatoo (gozaimasita).
20. Please (speaker requesting something).   O˺neğai-sima˺su.
21. Please (speaker offering something).   Do˺ozo.

NOTES ON THE BASIC SENTENCES[3]

1. -Sañ is added to a family name (as in Tanaka-sañ), a given name (as in Ta˺roo-sañ), or a family name plus a given name (as in Tanaka ˹Ta˺roo-sañ), but it is NOT added to one's own name or to that of members of one's

---

[1] Be sure to read the Introduction before beginning.

[2] Alternate accent: Sa˺yo(o)na˺ra.

[3] Numbers in this section correspond to Basic Sentence numbers.

own family or household when speaking to outsiders. Thus, Mr. Yamamoto calls Mr. Tanaka <u>Tanaka-sañ</u>, but Mr. Tanaka identifies himself simply as <u>Tanaka</u>.

2. <u>Ohayoo</u> is used when addressing a friend or colleague or inferior informally. O⌐hayoo gozaima⌐su is a formal greeting used in addressing a superior, or in any situation requiring formality.

5. O⌐ge⌐ñki is the honorific (†) equivalent of <u>ge⌐ñki</u>. Only the latter may be used in reference to oneself. In referring to others, <u>ge⌐ñki</u> is plain and o⌐ge⌐ñki is polite. (O)⌐ge⌐ñki desu ka꜄ may occur as the equivalent of 'How are you?' 'How is he?' 'How is she?' or 'How are they?,' provided the context makes the meaning clear.

6. In general, <u>ha⌐i</u> is a rather stiff word, whereas e⌐e is conversational. However, <u>ha⌐i</u> is the regular response to a knock at the door or the calling of one's name.

7. <u>Okagesama de</u> indicates the speaker's appreciation for interest in his personal affairs ('thanks for asking') and/or appreciation for assistance ('thanks to you'). It always accompanies, or itself implies, favorable or pleasant information.

9. <u>Sayonara</u> is the contracted, less formal equivalent of <u>sayoonara</u>.

10. Si⌐tu⌐ree-simasu means literally 'I [am about to] commit a rudeness.' It is a polite way of excusing oneself from someone's presence, sometimes in the sense 'Excuse me for a moment' and sometimes as 'Excuse me—goodbye.' Other uses will be introduced later.

11. Si⌐tu⌐ree-simasita is the past equivalent of the preceding and means literally 'I committed a rudeness.' It is an apology for something that has already been done.

12. <u>Iie</u> is used in negative replies to questions, in contradictions and denials, and as an informal reply to apologies, expressions of thanks, and compliments.

13. Do⌐o itasimasite is used alone, or with <u>iie</u>, as a formal reply to apologies, expressions of thanks, and compliments.

14. Su⌐imase⌐ñ is the contracted, less formal equivalent of su⌐mimase⌐ñ.

15. Su⌐(m)imase⌐ñ desita is the past equivalent of su⌐(m)imase⌐ñ and refers to an action already completed. It is commonly used to apologize or say thank you, by someone who is on the point of leaving. However, the non-past form is used in expressing thanks immediately upon receiving something.

16. Do⌐o mo, used alone as an expression of thanks, is informal. It means literally 'in every way.'

17, 18, 19. The forms with <u>gozaimasu</u> (or <u>gozaimasita</u>) are formal, and those without are informal. Compare 2, above.

19. A⌐ri⌐gatoo gozaimasita is the past equivalent of a⌐ri⌐gatoo gozaimasu and refers to an action already completed. See 15, above.

20. Among the more common English equivalents of o⌐negai-sima⌐su are such expressions as: 'Would you please do it?'; 'Please take care of things';

'Please do'; 'May I have it?'; 'I'd like to have it'; etc. The equivalent differs depending upon the context, but the basic meaning is always the same—'I make a request'—and the word is humble (✝).

21. Do⌐ozo, which occurs by itself as an expression of offering or invitation ('Please have some'; 'Go ahead'; 'Here you are'; etc.), also occurs within sentences of request, making the request softer and less abrupt. Thus, do⌐ozo o⌐negai-sima⌐su is a softer equivalent of o⌐negai-sima⌐su alone.

DRILLS

A. Response Drill

1.	Tanaka-sañ⌐	Ha⌐i.
2.	Ohayoo.	Ohayoo.
3.	O⌐hayoo gozaima⌐su.	O⌐hayoo gozaima⌐su.
4.	O⌐hayoo gozaima⌐su.	Ohayoo.
5.	Koñniti wa.	Koñniti wa.
6.	Koñbañ wa.	Koñbañ wa.
7.	O⌐ge⌐ñki desu ka⌐	Okaḡesama de.
8.	O⌐ge⌐ñki desu ka⌐	E⌐e, okaḡesama de. A⌐na⌐ta wa?
9.	O⌐ge⌐ñki desu ka⌐	E⌐e, a⌐ri⌐ḡatoo gozaimasu.
10.	O⌐yasumi-nasa⌐i.	O⌐yasumi-nasa⌐i.
11.	O⌐yasumi-nasa⌐i.	Sayonara.
12.	Sa⌐yoona⌐ra.	Sayoonara.
13.	Sayonara.	Sayonara.
14.	Sa⌐yoona⌐ra.	Sayonara.
15.	Sayonara.	O⌐yasumi-nasa⌐i.
16.	Si⌐tu⌐ree.	Do⌐ozo.
17.	Si⌐tu⌐ree-simasu.	Do⌐ozo.
18.	Si⌐tu⌐ree.	Sayonara.
19.	Si⌐tu⌐ree-simasu.	Sayoonara.
20.	Si⌐tu⌐ree.	Iie.
21.	Si⌐tu⌐ree-simasita.	Do⌐o itasimasite.
22.	Si⌐tu⌐ree-simasita.	Iie, do⌐o itasimasite.
23.	Su⌐mimase⌐ñ.	Iie.
24.	Su⌐mimase⌐ñ.	Iie, do⌐o itasimasite.
25.	Su⌐mimase⌐ñ desita.	Iie.
26.	Su⌐mimase⌐ñ desita.	Do⌐o itasimasite.
27.	A⌐ri⌐ḡatoo.	Iie.
28.	A⌐ri⌐ḡatoo gozaimasu.	Do⌐o itasimasite.
29.	A⌐ri⌐ḡatoo gozaimasita.	Iie, do⌐o itasimasite.
30.	Do⌐o mo a⌐ri⌐ḡatoo gozaimasita.	Iie, do⌐o itasimasite.
31.	Do⌐o mo.	Iie.
32.	Do⌐ozo.	Su⌐mimase⌐ñ.
33.	Do⌐ozo.	A⌐ri⌐ḡatoo gozaimasu.
34.	Do⌐ozo.	Do⌐o mo.
35.	O⌐negai-sima⌐su.	Do⌐ozo.
36.	O⌐negai-sima⌐su.	Ha⌐i ⌐do⌐ozo.
37.	Do⌐ozo o⌐negai-sima⌐su.	Do⌐ozo.

B. Level Drill[1]

1. Ohayoo.   O‌ʰhayoo -gozaima‌ꞌsu.
2. Sayonara.   Sa‌ꞌyoona‌ꞌra.
3. Si‌ꞌtu‌ꞌree.   Si‌ꞌtu‌ꞌree-simasu.   or
                                     Si‌ꞌtu‌ꞌree-simasita.
4. Ge‌ꞌñki desu ka‿   O‌ꞌge‌ꞌñki desu ka‿
5. Su‌ꞌimase‌ꞌñ.   Su‌ꞌmimase‌ꞌñ.
6. Su‌ꞌimase‌ꞌñ desita.   Su‌ꞌmimase‌ꞌñ desita.
7. A‌ꞌri‌ꞌḡatoo.   A‌ꞌri‌ꞌḡatoo gozaimasu.   or
                                     A‌ꞌri‌ꞌḡatoo gozaimasita.
8. Do‌ꞌo mo.   Do‌ꞌo mo a‌ꞌri‌ꞌḡatoo gozaimasu.   or
                                     Do‌ꞌo mo a‌ꞌri‌ꞌḡatoo gozaimasita.
9. Do‌ꞌo mo a‌ꞌri‌ꞌḡatoo.   Do‌ꞌo mo a‌ꞌri‌ꞌḡatoo gozaimasu.   or
                                     Do‌ꞌo mo a‌ꞌri‌ꞌḡatoo gozaimasita.

EXERCISES

1. What would you say to Mr. Tanaka under the following circumstances?

    a. You have just met him in the morning.
    b. You have just met him in the afternoon.
    c. You have just met him in the evening.
    d. You offer him a cigarette.
    e. He has just given you something.
    f. He has just thanked you for something.
    g. You have just bumped into him.
    h. You are leaving.

2. Give Mr. Tanaka's reply to the preceding, wherever possible.

---

[1] The utterances in the right-hand column are more formal or polite equivalents of the utterances in the left-hand column.

Lesson 1. Getting Around

BASIC DIALOGUES: FOR MEMORIZATION

(a)

Smith

a bit or a little	tyo˥tto
please wait	ma˥tte kudasai

1. Just a minute!   Tyo˥tto ˥ma˞tte kudasai.

2. I don't understand.   Wa˩karimase˥ñ.

Tanaka

3. You don't understand?   Wa˩karimase˥ñ ka˩

Smith

one time	iti-do
one time more	moo iti-do
please say	i˞tte kudasa˥i

4. No (i.e. that's right). Please say [it] once more.   E˥e. Mo˞o iti-do itte kudasa˥i.

(b)

Smith

5. Do you understand?   Wa˩karima˥su ka˩

Yamamoto

6. Yes, I do (understand).   E˥e, wa˩karima˥su.

Smith

7. How about Mr. Tanaka? (Lit. As for Mr. Tanaka?)   Tanaka-sañ wa?

Yamamoto

8. Mr. Tanaka doesn't understand.   Ta˩naka-sañ wa wakarimase˥ñ.

(c)

Tanaka

9. Did you understand?   Wa˩karima˥sita ka˩

Smith

10. Yes, I did (understand).   E˥e wa˩karima˞sita.

Tanaka

well or a good deal or often	yo˥ku

11.	You understand [very] well, don't you.	Yo⌉ku wakarimasu ⌈ne⌉e.

Smith

12.	Oh, no!	Do⌉o itasimasite.

(d)

Smith

13.	Did you do [it]?	Si⌈ma⌉sita ka⌴

Tanaka

	all <u>or</u> the whole thing	ze⌉ñbu
14.	Yes, I did [it] all.	E⌉e, ze⌉ñbu si⊢ma⊣sita.

Smith

15.	Thanks for your trouble.	Go⌈ku⌉roosama (desita).

Tanaka

16.	Don't mention it.	Do⌉o itasimasite.

(e)

Smith

17.	Did you go?	I⌈kima⌉sita ka⌴

Tanaka

18.	No, I didn't (go).	Iie, i⌈kimase⌉ñ desita.

Smith (to Yamamoto)

19.	How about you?	A⌈na⌉ta wa?

Yamamoto

	yesterday	ki⌈no⌉o
20.	I went yesterday.	Ki⌈noo ikima⌉sita.

(f)

Smith

	tomorrow	a⌈sita⌉
21.	Are you going to go tomorrow?	A⌈sita ikima⌉su ka⌴

Yamamoto

	today	kyo⌉o
22.	No, I'm going to go today.	Iie, kyo⌉o ikimasu.

Smith

23.	How about Mr. Tanaka?	Tanaka-sañ wa?

Yamamoto

24.	He isn't going to go.	I⌈kimase⌉ñ.

NOTES ON THE BASIC DIALOGUES[1]

7. When addressing Mr. Tanaka, <u>Tanaka-sañ wa</u>? is equivalent to 'How about you, Mr. Tanaka?' It is less direct and more polite in Japanese to refer to the person by his name than by a⌐na⌐ta 'you.'

12. <u>Do⌐o itasimasite</u>, in addition to its use as a reply to expressions of thanks and apology, occurs as a polite reply to compliments.

15. Go⌐ku⌐roosama desita — lit. 'it has been toil on your part' — is used especially commonly in addressing a subordinate. The alternant without <u>desita</u> is informal.

GRAMMATICAL NOTES

1. V e r b a l s

wa⌐karima⌐su[2]   'understanding takes place'   <u>or</u>
                     'understanding will take place'

wa⌐karima⌐sita   'understanding took place'   <u>or</u>
                     'understanding has taken place'

wa⌐karimase⌐ñ   'understanding does not take place'   <u>or</u>
                     'understanding will not take place'   <u>or</u>
                     'understanding has not taken place'

wa⌐karimase⌐ñ desita   'understanding did not take place'

In Japanese there are words which are constant (i.e. have only one form) and those which are inflected (i.e. take particular sets of endings; compare English 'listen, listened, listening, listens'). Among the inflected words is a large group having forms similar to the four listed above (in addition to other forms). All such words are hereafter called VERBALS. [3]

The four forms listed above are named as follows:

(a) Form ending in -<u>ma</u>⌐su: Formal non-past affirmative
     Meaning: 'something happens (or exists)'   <u>or</u>
     'something is going to or will happen (or exist)'

---

[1] Numbers in this section correspond to those of the sentences in the Basic Dialogues.

[2] For the accent, see Introduction, page xxxvi.

[3] Note that the term 'verbal' is being defined with particular respect to Japanese. It names the word-class to which all words inflected like wa⌐karima⌐su belong—namely, words having other forms ending in -<u>ma</u>⌐sita, -<u>mase</u>⌐ñ, etc.

(b) Form ending in -ma⌐sita: Formal past affirmative
     Meaning: 'something has happened (or existed)' or
              'something happened (or existed)'

(c) Form ending in -mase⌐n̄: Formal non-past negative
     Meaning: 'something does not happen (or exist)' or
              'something is not going to or will not happen (or exist)'   or
              'something has not happened (or existed) up to the present
              time'

(d) Form ending in -mase⌐n̄ desita: Formal past negative
     Meaning: 'something did not happen (or exist)'

The particular meaning of a given form is determined by context.

Verbals are impersonal and can occur by themselves as complete standard
sentences. They can indicate the occurrence of an action or the existence of a
state without grammatical reference to a subject.   Contrast English 'I understand,' 'he understands,' 'they understand,' etc., with Japanese wa⌐karima⌐su
'understanding takes place,' 'there is understanding.' Most commonly, a verbal occurring alone refers to the speaker in a statement and to the person addressed in a question. For example:

     I⌐kima⌐sita ka⌐ 'Did you go?' (Lit. 'Did going take place?')
     E⌐e i⌐kima⌐sita. 'Yes, I went.' (Lit. 'Yes, going took place.')

Different topics are indicated sometimes by the context, sometimes by the specific mention of a topic (which in some circumstances is followed by the particle wa 'as for,' about which more will be said later). For example, continuing
the immediately preceding conversation:

     Tanaka-sañ wa? 'How about Mr. Tanaka?' (Lit. 'As for Mr. Tana-
     ka?')
     I⌐kimase⌐n̄ desita. 'He didn't go.' (Lit. 'Going didn't take place.')
     or
     Tanaka-sañ wa i⌐kimase⌐n̄ desita. 'Mr. Tanaka didn't go.' (Lit. 'As
     for Mr. Tanaka, going didn't take place.')

In the lessons that follow, new verbals will be introduced first alone in their
-ma⌐su form, with the dictionary form of the closest English equivalent, and
then in a sentence (in the -ma⌐su form or another form) with an appropriate
contextual equivalent. For example:

     write   ka⌐kima⌐su
     Are you going to write?   Ka⌐kima⌐su ka⌐

WARNING: Note that the -ma⌐su form of a verbal regularly refers to repeated action or future action, but not present action. Thus si⌐ma⌐su means '[I] do'
or '[I] will do,' but never '[I] am doing.'

2.   Question Particle ka

A Japanese sentence ending with the question particle[1] ka is a question. Any

---

[1] More will be said about particles in general later on.

statement can be made into a question by adding ka, provided the meaning makes sense. Compare:

(a) Wa⌐karimase⌐ñ. '[I] don't understand.' (Lit. 'There isn't understanding.')

(b) Wa⌐karimase⌐ñ ka⌐ '[You] don't understand?' or 'Don't [you] understand?' (Lit. 'There isn't understanding?')

Questions with ka end in rising intonation (represented in this text by the symbol ⌐) or in low intonation (represented by a period).

All sentences ending with the question particle ka are questions; but not all questions end with ka. For example, the phrase a⌐na⌐ta wa 'as for you' becomes a question when pronounced with question intonation (represented by a question mark).

3. Answers to Yes-or-No Questions

Ha⌐i[1] usually means 'what you just said is right.' In answer to affirmative questions, it corresponds to English 'yes,' but in answer to negative questions that anticipate a negative answer, it usually confirms the negative and corresponds to English 'no.' Iie, the opposite of ha⌐i, means 'what you just said is wrong' and behaves in a parallel way: in answer to affirmative questions it corresponds to English 'no,' but in answer to negative questions that anticipate a negative answer, it usually contradicts the negative and corresponds to English 'yes.'

	Literal English Equivalent	Normal English Equivalent
I⌐kima⌐sita ka⌐	'Going took place?'	'Did you go?'
Ha⌐i. [I⌐kima⌐sita.] [2]	'That's right. [Going took place.]'	'Yes. [I did (go).]'
Iie. [I⌐kimase⌐ñ desita.]	'That's wrong. [Going didn't take place.]'	'No. [I didn't (go).]'
I⌐kimase⌐ñ desita ka⌐	'Going didn't take place?'	'Didn't you go?'
Ha⌐i. [I⌐kimase⌐ñ desita.]	'That's right. [Going didn't take place.]'	'No. [I didn't (go).]'
Iie. [I⌐kima⌐sita.]	'That's wrong. [Going took place.]'	'Yes. [I did (go).]'

WARNING: English usage is as unexpected for a Japanese studying English as Japanese usage is for an American studying Japanese. Be wary of single-word answers given by a Japanese who is not yet fluent in English. In answer to 'Don't you have any bananas?' a 'Yes' from many Japanese means 'Yes. We have no bananas.'

---

[1] Throughout this note, whatever is said about ha⌐i applies equally to e⌐e.

[2] Diagonal brackets ([---]) enclose optional portions of the answer.

To sum up: The meaning of ha⌐i and iie occurring in answer to a yes-or-no question usually depends on the inflected form of the preceding question: Ha⌐i means that the affirmative or negative of the question applies and iie means that it does not apply.

4. ne⌐e

Ne⌐e 'isn't it true!' at the end of a sentence indicates an exclamation. It sometimes indicates reflection or consideration, and it often implies agreement—actual or assumed—between speaker and person addressed, but it is not a question-word in its occurrences with statement intonation. Compare:

Tanaka-san wa ⌐yo⌐ku wakarimasu.   'Mr. Tanaka understands [very] well.'

Tanaka-san wa ⌐yo⌐ku wa⌐karima⁻su   'Does Mr. Tanaka understand well?'
ka.⌡

Tanaka-san wa ⌐yo⌐ku wakarimasu   'Doesn't Mr. Tanaka understand well!'
⌐ne⌐e.   'How well Mr. Tanaka understands!'
                                            'Mr. Tanaka understands [very] well,
                                            doesn't he!' 'Come to think of it, Mr.
                                            Tanaka does understand well!' etc.

As always, unless the subject is explicitly stated, it is inferred from context. Thus, Wa⌐karimase⌐n ⌐ne⌐e. may mean 'You don't understand, do you!' or 'He doesn't understand, does he!' or 'They don't understand, do they!' or 'Come to think of it, I don't understand!' etc.

DRILLS

A. Substitution Drill

1. I did [it] all.   Ze⌐nbu si⌐ma⁻sita.
2. I did a little.   Tyo⌐tto si⌐ma⁻sita.
3. I did [it] once.   I⌐ti-do sima⌐sita.
4. I did [it] yesterday.   Ki⌐noo sima⌐sita.
5. I did [it] today.   Kyo⌐o si⌐ma⁻sita.
6. I did [it] once more.   Mo⌐o iti-do sima⌐sita.

B. Substitution Drill

1. I went yesterday.   Ki⌐noo ikima⌐sita.
2. I went today.   Kyo⌐o i⌐kima⁻sita.
3. I did [it] today.   Kyo⌐o si⌐ma⁻sita.
4. I did [it] all.   Ze⌐nbu si⌐ma⁻sita.
5. I understood [it] all.   Ze⌐nbu wa⌐karima⁻sita.
6. I understood a little.   Tyo⌐tto wa⌐karima⁻sita.
7. I'll do a little.   Tyo⌐tto simasu.
8. I'll do [it] tomorrow.   A⌐sita sima⌐su.

C. Grammar Drill (based on Grammatical Note 1)

        Tutor: Iᴿkimaᴸsu. (non-past verbal)
        Student: Iᴿkimaᴸsita. (past verbal)

   1. Yoᴸku wakarimasu.   Yoᴸku waᴿkarima⁴sita.
   2. Aᴿriᴸḡatoo gozaimasu.   Aᴿriᴸḡatoo gozaimasita.
   3. Zeᴸñbu simasu.   Zeᴸñbu siᴿma⁴sita.
   4. Waᴿkarimaseᴸñ ka⌐   Waᴿkarimaseᴸñ desita ka⌐
   5. Kyoᴸo ikimasu.   Kyoᴸo iᴿkima⁴sita.
   6. Suᴹmimaseᴸñ.   Suᴹmimaseᴸñ desita.
   7. Kyoᴸo siᴿma⁴su ka⌐   Kyoᴸo siᴿma⁴sita ka⌐
   8. Iᴿkimaᴸsu ka⌐   Iᴿkimaᴸsita ka⌐
   9. Yoᴸku waᴿkarimase⁴ñ.   Yoᴸku waᴿkarimaseᴸñ desita.
  10. Tanaka-sañ wa iᴿki-   Tanaka-sañ wa iᴿkimaseᴸñ desita.
       maseᴸñ.

D. Response Drill (based on Grammatical Note 3)

   (What does the <u>Ha</u>ᴸi. or <u>Iie</u>. answer to each of the following questions
   mean?)

   1. Iᴿkimaᴸsu ka⌐ /Haᴸi./   Haᴸi, iᴿkimaᴸsu.
   2. Siᴹmaseᴸñ ka⌐ /Iie./   Iie, siᴹmaᴸsu.
   3. Waᴿkarimaᴸsita ka⌐   Haᴸi, waᴿkarimaᴸsita.
       /Haᴸi./
   4. Iᴿkimaᴸsita ka⌐ /Iie./   Iie, iᴿkimaseᴸñ desita.
   5. Siᴹmaᴸsita ka⌐ /Haᴸi./   Haᴸi, siᴹmaᴸsita.
   6. Waᴿkarimaᴸsu ka⌐ /Iie./   Iie, waᴿkarimaseᴸñ.
   7. Iᴿkimaseᴸñ ka⌐ /Haᴸi./   Haᴸi, iᴿkimaseᴸñ.
   8. Siᴹmaᴸsu ka⌐ /Iie./   Iie, siᴹmaseᴸñ.
   9. Waᴿkarimaseᴸñ ka⌐   Haᴸi, waᴿkarimaseᴸñ.
       /Haᴸi./
  10. Iᴿkimaseᴸñ desita ka⌐   Iie, iᴿkimaᴸsita.
       /Iie./
  11. Siᴹmaseᴸñ desita ka⌐   Haᴸi, siᴹmaseᴸñ desita.
       /Haᴸi./
  12. Waᴿkarimaseᴸñ desita   Iie, waᴿkarimaᴸsita.
       ka⌐ /Iie./

E. Expansion Drill

   1. Please say [it].   Iᴿtte kudasa⁴i.
       Please say [it] all.   Zeᴸñbu iᴿtte kudasa⁴i.
       Please say [it] all once.   Iti-do ᴿzeᴸñbu iᴿtte kudasa⁴i.
       Please say [it] all once   Moo iti-do ᴿzeᴸñbu iᴿtte kudasa⁴i.
           more.
   2. [He] understands. [1]   Waᴿkarimaᴸsu.

----

[1] Remember that the English equivalents given are not the only equivalents.
Depending on context, there are various possibilities.

[He] understands, doesn't he!	Wa⌐karima⌐su ⌐ne⌐e.
How well [he] understands!	Yo⌐ku wakarimasu ⌐ne⌐e.
How well Mr. Tanaka understands!	Tanaka-sañ wa ⌐yo⌐ku wakarimasu ⌐ne⌐e.
3. [He]'s going to go.	I⌐kima⌐su.
Is [he] going to go?	I⌐kima⌐su ka⌐
Is [he] going to go tomorrow?	A⌐sita ikima⌐su ka⌐
Is Mr. Tanaka going to go tomorrow?	Tanaka-sañ wa a⌐sita ikima⌐su ka⌐
4. [He]'s not going to do [it].	Si⌐mase⌐ñ.
[He] didn't do [it].	Si⌐mase⌐ñ desita.
Didn't [he] do [it]?	Si⌐mase⌐ñ desita ka⌐
Didn't Mr. Tanaka do [it]?	Tanaka-sañ wa si⌐mase⌐ñ desita ka⌐

EXERCISES

1. Tell Tanaka-sañ:

   a. to wait a minute.
   b. to repeat.
   c. that you didn't understand.
   d. that you are going tomorrow.
   e. that you'll do the whole thing.
   f. that you appreciate his trouble.

2. Ask Tanaka-sañ:

   a. if he understood.
   b. if he is going today.
   c. if he did [it] yesterday.
   d. if he understood the whole thing.
   e. if he is well.

3. Exclaim (using ne⌐e) to Tanaka-sañ:

   a. how well Yamamoto-sañ understands.
   b. how well Yamamoto-sañ understood.
   c. how well Yamamoto-sañ is.
   d. that Yamamoto-sañ doesn't understand.

Lesson 2. Getting Around (cont.)

BASIC DIALOGUES: FOR MEMORIZATION

(a)

Tanaka (looking at a new kind of ball-point pen)

that thing	sore
as for that thing	sore wa
what?	na⌐ñ or
	na⌐ni
what is it?	na⌐ñ desu ka

1. What is that? (Lit. As for that thing, what is it?) — Sore wa ⌐na⌐ñ desu ka⌐

Smith

which thing (of 3 or more)	do⌐re

2. Which one is it? or Which one do you mean? — Do⌐re desu ka⌐

Tanaka (pointing)

3. It's that one. or I mean that one. — So⌐re de⌐su.

Smith

oh	a⌐a
pen	pe⌐ñ

4. Oh, that's a pen. — A⌐a, sore wa ⌐pe⌐ñ desu.

Tanaka

pencil	eñpitu
[it] isn't a pencil	e⌐ñpitu zya arimase⌐ñ

5. Isn't it a pencil? — E⌐ñpitu zya arimase⌐ñ ka⌐

Smith

is new	a⌐tarasi⌐i
new pen	a⌐tarasi⌐i ⌐pe⌐ñ

6. No (i.e. that's right). It's a new pen. — E⌐e. A⌐tarasi⌐i ⌐pe⌐ñ desu yo⌐

Tanaka

that way or thus or so	so⌐o

7. Oh, is that so? or Oh, really? or Oh? — A⌐a, so⌐o desu ka.

14

(b)

Smith

that thing over there	are
as for that thing over there	are wa
dictionary	ziˢbikiˀ or
	ziˀsyo

8. Is that (over there) a dictionary?   Are wa ziˢbikiˀ desu ka⤸

Tanaka

9. Yes, that's right (lit. it's that   Eˀe, soˀo desu.
    way).

Smith

is small	tiˢisaˀi

10. Isn't it small!   Tiˢisaˀi desu ˥ne˧e.

Tanaka

11. It is, isn't it!   Soˀo desu ˢneˀe.

Smith

is good or fine or all right	iˀi
good dictionary	iˀi zibiki

12. Is it a good dictionary?   Iˀi ziˢbikiˢ desu ka⤸

Tanaka

isn't good	yoˀku aˢrimaseˀñ

13. No, it isn't (good)!   Iie, yoˀku aˢrimaseˀñ yo⤸

Smith

14. Oh, really?   Aˀa, soˀo desu ka.

(c)

Smith (looking for something to read)

this thing	kore
as for this thing	kore wa
is interesting or unusual or fun	oˢmosiroˀi
book	hoˀñ
interesting book	oˢmosiroˀi ˥ho˧ñ

15. Is this an interesting book?   Kore wa oˢmosiroˀi ˥ho˧ñ desu ka⤸

Tanaka

16. No, it isn't (interesting).   Iie, oˢmosiˀroku aˢrimaseˀñ.

Smith

then or well then or in that case	zyaˀa

17. Well then, [how about] that?   Zyaˀa, sore wa?

Tanaka

magazine   zassi
18. Do you mean the magazine?   Zaˢssi de˥su kaↄ

19. That's [very] good!   Soˢre wa i˥i desu yoↄ

20. Here!   Do˥ozo.

(d)

Smith (looking at some Japanese paperbacks)

21. Is that a magazine?   Sore wa zaˢssi de˥su kaↄ

Tanaka

22. No, it isn't.   Iie, so˥o zya aˡrimaseˤn̄.

23. It's a book.   Hoˤn̄ desu yoↄ

Smith

24. How about this one?   Kore wa?

Tanaka

be different or be wrong   tiˢḡaima˥su
25. Oh, that's different.   A˥a, soˢre wa tiḡaima˥su.

26. That's a magazine.   Soˢre wa zassi de˥su.

(e)

Tanaka (to Smith, who is about to buy a newspaper)

newspaper   siñbuñ
good newspaper   i˥i siñbuñ
27. That's not a [very] good news-   Sore wa ˢi˥i siñbuñ zya aˡrimaseˤn̄
    paper, you know.   yoↄ

Smith

28. Oh?   So˥o desu ka.

how?   do˥o
29. How is this one?   Koˢre wa do˥o desu kaↄ

Tanaka

same   onazi
30. It's the same.   Oˢnazi de˥su.

no good   daˢme˥
31. It's no good!   Daˢme˥ desu yo.

ADDITIONAL VOCABULARY: OPPOSITES

Aˢtarasi˥i desu. 'It's new or   Huˢru˥i desu. 'It's old (i.e. not new)
    fresh.'   or stale.'
Oˢmosiro˥i desu. 'It's interesting   Tuˢmara˥nai desu. 'It's dull or bor-
    or fun or unusual.'   ing or trifling.'

Ti⌐isa˥i desu. 'It's small.' O⌐oki˥i desu. 'It's big.'
I˥i desu. 'It's good.' {Wa⌐ru˥i desu. 'It's bad.'
 {Da⌐me˥ desu. 'It's no good.'

NOTES ON THE BASIC DIALOGUES

1. Na˥n̄ occurs before d-, both na˥n̄ and na˥ni before t- and n-, and na˥ni else-where.

7, 9, 11, 14. So˥o desu. 'That's right.' occurs in answer to questions. So˥o desu ⌐ne˥e. 'That's right, isn't it.' follows statements (especially excla-mations ending in ne˥e.) containing known or recognized information, and indicates agreement. So˥o desu ka. 'Is that so?' follows statements con-taining information previously unknown or unrecognized, and indicates attention and interest. Thus:

O⌐mosiro˥i ⌐ho˥n̄ desu ka⏌ 'Is it an interesting book?'
So˥o desu. 'That's right.'

O⌐mosiro˥i ⌐ho˥n̄ desu ⌐ne˥e. 'It's an interesting book, isn't it.'
So˥o desu ⌐ne˥e. 'It is, isn't it.' (i.e. I knew that, and I agree.)

O⌐mosiro˥i ⌐ho˥n̄ desu. 'It's an interesting book.'
So˥o desu ka. 'Is that so?' (i.e. I didn't know until you told me.)

12. Note these additional equivalents of i˥i desu: 'it's fine,' 'it's nice,' 'it's all set,' 'it's all right,' 'it's all right as it is,' 'never mind,' 'don't both-er.'

20. In this context, do˥ozo means 'take it,' or 'read it,' or 'look at it,' etc. — i.e. Tanaka is offering it to Smith.

25. Ti⌐gaima˥su is a verbal (cf. Lesson 1, Grammatical Note 1). However, the non-past negative ti⌐gaimase˥n̄ is comparatively rare and should be avoided by the beginning student.

31. Da⌐me˥ desu may also refer to something that is broken or out of order or spoiled.

GRAMMATICAL NOTES

1. Adjectivals

o⌐mosiro˥i desu 'it's interesting'
o⌐mosi˥roku a⌐rimase˥n̄ 'it isn't interesting'

The words o⌐mosiro˥i 'it's interesting,' tu⌐mara˥nai 'it's dull,' a⌐tarasi˥i 'it's new,' hu⌐ru˥i 'it's old,' ti⌐isa˥i 'it's small,' o⌐oki˥i 'it's big,' i˥i 'it's good,' and wa⌐ru˥i 'it's bad' are all members of a class of inflected Japanese words having the following characteristics: they have a form ending in -ai, -oi, -ui, or -ii, and a form ending in -ku (in addition to others). All such words will hereafter be called ADJECTIVALS. The form ending in -i will be called the INFORMAL NON-PAST (it refers to present or future time) or the CITATION

FORM; it is the form under which an adjectival is regularly listed in a dictionary and the form by which it is cited. The form ending in -ku will be called the
ADVERBIAL. The adverbial is regularly made from the -i form (i.e. the informal non-past) by dropping the -i and adding -ku.[1] Thus:

Informal Non-Past (Citation Form)	Adverbial
o˹mosiro˺i	o˹mosi˺roku
tu˹mara˺nai	tu˹mara˺naku
a˹tarasi˺i	a˹tara˺siku
hu˹ru˺i	hu˹ruku
ti˹isa˺i	ti˹isaku
o˹oki˺i	o˹okiku
wa˹ru˺i	wa˹ruku

The only exception is i˹i : yo˺ku. I˹i is a newer form of yo˹i (which still occurs in present-day Japanese, alternating with i˹i), but the -ku form of the
word is always based on the older root.

Adjectivals, like verbals, are impersonal and may refer to any subject.
Context or a stated topic (sometimes followed by particle wa 'as for') makes
clear what is described.

An adjectival may occur in its -i form alone as a sentence in informal
speech; with a following desu,[2] it becomes formal. In other words, the only
difference between an -i form alone and an -i form plus desu is degree of formality. Thus:

	Informal	Formal
'It's interesting.'	O˹mosiro˺i.	O˹mosiro˺i desu.
'It's dull.'	Tu˹mara˺nai.	Tu˹mara˺nai desu.
'It's new.'	A˹tarasi˺i.	A˹tarasi˺i desu.
'It's old.'	Hu˹ru˺i.	Hu˹ru˺i desu.
'It's small.'	Ti˹isa˺i.	Ti˹isa˺i desu.
'It's big.'	O˹oki˺i.	O˹oki˺i desu.
'It's good.'	I˹i.	I˹i desu.
'It's bad.'	Wa˹ru˺i.	Wa˹ru˺i desu.

An adjectival which describes a verbal or any other inflected expression
occurs in its adverbial (-ku) form (cf. Yo˹ku wakarimasu ˺ne˹e. 'You understand [very] well, don't you!'). When adjectivals occur before the negative
a˹rimase˺n 'there isn't any,' we find:

---

[1] If the dictionary form is accented, the -ku form is also accented, but the
high-pitched sequence usually ends on an earlier syllable in the -ku form. However, many -ku forms occur with alternate accents.

[2] In this position, the adjectival is always accented, and the high-pitched
sequence normally ends on the next-to-last syllable. De˹su after an accented
word loses its accent.

O͡mosi͞roku a͞rimase͞ñ.	'It isn't interesting.'
Tu͡mara͞naku a͞rimase͞ñ.	'It isn't dull.'
A͡tara͞siku a͞rimase͞ñ.	'It isn't new.'
Hu͞ruku a͞rimase͞ñ.	'It isn't old.'
Ti͞isaku a͞rimase͞ñ.	'It isn't small.'
O͞okiku a͞rimase͞ñ.	'It isn't big.'
Yo͞ku a͞rimase͞ñ.	'It isn't good.'
Wa͞ruku a͞rimase͞ñ.	'It isn't bad.'

Since -mase͞ñ forms are formal, non-past, and negative, the above combinations are also formal, non-past, and negative. They are further identified as the negative equivalents of adjectivals in their -i form plus desu. The formal adjectival pattern is outlined as follows:

Formal Non-Past Adjectival

Affirmative		Negative	
-ai		-aku	
-oi	+ desu.	-oku	+ a͞rimase͞ñ.
-ui		-uku	
-ii		-iku	

Note that in the negative combination, it is the a͞rimase͞ñ that is negative—not the -ku form. Ti͞isaku a͞rimase͞ñ, for example, means literally something like 'being small, there isn't.'

WARNING: All adjectivals end in -ai, -oi, -ui, or -ii (in their informal non-past form); but not every word ending in one of these combinations is an adjectival. The word must also have a -ku form in order to be classified as an adjectival.

Hereafter, all new adjectivals will be introduced first in their citation form followed immediately by /-ku/ and defined without a subject, and then in a sentence with an appropriate contextual equivalent. For example:

| is hot | a͞tu͞i /-ku/ |
| Isn't it hot? | A͞tuku a͞rimase͞ñ ka⌐ |

2. Nominals

The major word class of Japanese is a class of constants (i.e. uninflected words; those having only one form) which will hereafter be called NOMINALS. Any constant which in some of its uses occurs with de͞su (meaning 'it is ——' or 'it will be ——') as a complete utterance is classed as a nominal.[1] The negative equivalent of nominal + de͞su is nominal + zya + a͞rimase͞ñ 'it's not ——' or 'it won't be ——.' For example, so͞o is a constant which may occur with desu as a complete utterance: So͞o desu. 'It's that way' or 'That's right.'

---

[1] Not all words classed as nominals occur in this pattern. Other identifying characteristics of nominals will be introduced later.

So⌐o is therefore classed as a nominal. The negative of So⌐o desu. is So⌐o zya a⌐rimase⌐n. 'It's not that way' or 'That's n o t right.'   Other examples are:

ho⌐ñ 'book': Ho⌐ñ desu. 'It's a book.'
           Ho⌐ñ zya a⌐rimase⌐ñ. 'It's not a book.'

Tanaka-sañ 'Mr. Tanaka': Ta⌐naka-sañ de⌐su. 'It's Mr. Tanaka.'
                       Ta⌐naka-sañ zya arimase⌐ñ. 'It's not Mr. Tana-
                       ka.'

a⌐na⌐ta 'you': A⌐na⌐ta desu. 'It's you.'
            A⌐na⌐ta zya a⌐rimase⌐ñ. 'It's not you.'

kore 'this thing': Ko⌐re de⌐su. 'It's this (thing).'
                Ko⌐re zya arimase⌐ñ. 'It's not this (thing).'

The class of nominals includes—but is by no means limited to—all Japanese words which stand for tangible objects: chair, man, milk, book, etc.

De⌐su regularly loses its accent when it follows an accented nominal. Compare:

        Pe⌐ñ desu. 'It's a pen.'
        E⌐ñpitu de⌐su. 'It's a pencil.'

For the accent of zya + a⌐rimase⌐ñ following accented and unaccented nominals, note the examples above.

Nominals do not distinguish between singular and plural number. For example, ho⌐ñ may refer to one book or more than one; kore to this thing or these things; etc.

Nominal + de⌐su sequences, like verbals and adjectivals, are impersonal and may refer to any topic, stated explicitly or indicated only by the context. Thus, depending on context, Ta⌐naka de⌐su m a y be equivalent to 'I'm Tanaka,' 'he's Tanaka,' 'it's Tanaka,' etc.   Kore wa ⌐ho⌐ñ desu, with the topic indicated by kore wa, means either 'this is a book' or 'these are books,' since nominals do not distinguish between singular and plural.

An adjectival in its c i t a t i o n form may precede a nominal directly as a descriptive word:

        o⌐mosiro⌐i ⌐ho⌐ñ 'an interesting book'
        o⌐oki⌐i zibiki 'a big dictionary'

This form may also precede an adjectival + nominal sequence:

        ti⌐isa⌐i o⌐mosiro⌐i ⌐ho⌐ñ 'a small interesting book'
        a⌐tarasi⌐i o⌐oki⌐i zibiki 'a new big dictionary'

Compare now these three constantly recurring, basic patterns of Japanese:

	Formal Non-Past	
	Affirmative	Negative
Verbal Pattern	Verbal ending in -ma⌐su (wa⌐karima⌐su)	Verbal ending in -mase⌐ñ (wa⌐karimase⌐ñ)
Adjectival Pattern	Adjectival ending in -i + desu (o⌐oki⌐i desu)	Adjectival ending in -ku + a⌐rimase⌐ñ (o⌐okiku a⌐rimase⌐ñ)
Nominal Pattern	Nominal + de⌐su (ho⌐ñ desu)	Nominal + zya + a⌐rimase⌐ñ (ho⌐ñ zya a⌐rimase⌐ñ)

So⌐o desu 'that's right' and so⌐o zya a⌐rimase⌐n̄ 'that's not right' are frequently used in answer to a question that ends with a nominal + de⌐su ka, but less commonly in answer to verbal or adjectival questions. Thus:

I⌐kima⌐su ka˩	E⌐e, i⌐kima⌐su.
	Iie, i⌐kimase⌐n̄.
O⌐oki⌐i desu ka˩	E⌐e, o⌐oki⌐i desu.
	Iie, o⌐okiku a⌐rimase⌐n̄.
Pe⌐n̄ desu ka˩	E⌐e, pe⌐n̄ desu. or E⌐e, so⌐o desu.
	Iie, pe⌐n̄ zya a⌐rimase⌐n̄. or Iie, so⌐o zya a⌐rimase⌐n̄.

In changing a sentence that ends with an adjectival + desu to its precise negative equivalent, the adjectival pattern is used; but a sentence that ends with a nominal + de⌐su follows the nominal pattern in forming its exactly corresponding negative. Compare:

Ho⌐n̄ wa o⌐mosiro⌐i desu.	Ho⌐n̄ wa o⌐mosi⌐roku a⌐rimase⌐n̄.
'The book is interesting.'	'The book isn't interesting.'
O⌐mosiro⌐i ⌐ho⌐n̄ desu.	O⌐mosiro⌐i ⌐ho⌐n̄ zya a⌐rimase⌐n̄.
'It's an interesting book.'	'It's not an interesting book.'

In conversation, however, a reply to a question does not always follow the question pattern exactly. Thus, in answer to:

Sore wa a⌐tarasi⌐i ⌐pe⌐n̄ desu ka˩ 'Is that a new pen?' (nominal pattern)

a common reply would be:

Iie, a⌐tara⌐siku a⌐rimase⌐n̄. 'No, it isn't new.' (adjectival pattern)

However, the exact negative equivalent would be:

Sore wa a⌐tarasi⌐i ⌐pe⌐n̄ zya a⌐rimase⌐n̄. 'That is not a new pen.'

Most new nominals can be recognized in the lessons that follow by a process of elimination: if a word is not a verbal (identified by a -ma⌐su ending) or an adjectival (identified by /-ku/) and is first introduced singly rather than in a phrase, it is a nominal. Other nominals, more difficult to recognize, can be identified on the basis of other criteria to be introduced later.

3. **kore, sore, are, do⌐re**

These four words are all nominals.

Kore refers to a thing or things[1] close to the speaker—i. e. 'near me.'

Sore refers to a thing or things (a) removed from the speaker but close to the person addressed—i. e. 'near you'; (b) within sight but slightly removed —

---

[1] These words are also used in reference to certain people: those who are inferiors, members of one's own family, etc.

i.e. neither 'here' nor 'over yonder'—from both speaker and person addressed; or (c) already identified in what has gone before—i.e. 'that thing (or those things) already under discussion.' In meaning (c), the English equivalent is often 'it.'

Are refers to a thing or things 'over there' or 'over yonder,' removed from both speaker and person addressed, either within sight or out of sight. Like sore, it too may refer to something already identified in what has gone before, but it always refers to something removed and usually indicates some particular concrete object(s) being pointed out and defined in terms of a particular location. For example, 'medicine being manufactured today' would, after its first mention, usually be referred to as sore, whereas Mount Fuji would most often be referred to as are.

In a sequence containing both sore and are, are usually implies greater distance. But when sore—with meaning (b)—and are occur singly, it is impossible to define the distance from the speaker at which sore ceases to be used and are begins; the most that can be said is that sore means 'that-rather-near' and are means 'that-over-there.'

Do⌐re is an interrogative nominal meaning 'which one (of a specified group, usually containing at least three things)?'

4. Particle yo

Like question particle ka, yo occurs at the end of sentences. It is a particle of emphasis: it means that the sentence is being stated with assurance. It is often used in warnings, in contradictions, and in informative exclamations. Sometimes it corresponds to conversational English 'you know,' 'I tell you,' 'say!' 'I'm sure,' etc.; but many times it corresponds to English exclamatory intonation and therefore is difficult to indicate in a written equivalent. Like sentences ending in ka, those ending in yo occur with rising or low intonation.

Compare:

Da⌐me⌐ desu. 'It's no good.'
Da⌐me⌐ desu ka.⌐ 'Isn't it any good?'
Da⌐me⌐ desu ⌐ne⌐e. 'It's no good, is it!'   or 'Isn't it awful!' (i.e. I assume you know)
Da⌐me⌐ desu yo. 'It's no good!'   or 'It's no good, you know!'   or 'Contrary to what you think, it's no good'   or 'I'm telling you it's no good,' etc.

DRILLS

A. Substitution Drill

1. What is that?   Sore wa ⌐na⌐n̄ desu ka.⌐
2. Is that a book?   Sore wa ⌐ho⌐n̄ desu ka.⌐
3. Is that a magazine?   Sore wa za⌐ssi de⌐su ka.⌐
4. Is that a newspaper?   Sore wa si⌐n̄buñ de⌐su ka.⌐
5. Is that a dictionary?   Sore wa ⌐zi⌐syo desu ka.⌐

6. Is that the same?   Sore wa o⌐nazi deˀsu ka⌐
7. Is that out of order?   Sore wa da⌐meˀ desu ka⌐
8. Is that today?   Sore wa ⌐kyoˀo desu ka⌐
9. Is that tomorrow?   Sore wa a⌐sitaˀ desu ka⌐
10. How is that?   Sore wa ⌐doˀo desu ka⌐

B. Substitution Drill

1. This is an interesting   Kore wa o⌐mosiroˀi ⌐hoⁿ desu ⌐neˀe.
   book, isn't it.
2. That is an interesting   Sore wa o⌐mosiroˀi ⌐hoⁿ desu ⌐neˀe.
   book, isn't it.
3. That is a good book,   Sore wa ⌐iˀi ⌐hoⁿ desu ⌐neˀe.
   isn't it.
4. That is a good diction-   Sore wa ⌐iˀi zi⌐bikiˀ desu ⌐neˀe.
   ary, isn't it.
5. That (over there) is a   Are wa ⌐iˀi zi⌐bikiˀ desu ⌐neˀe.
   good dictionary, isn't it.
6. That (over there) is a   Are wa o⌐okiˀi zi⌐bikiˀ desu ⌐neˀe.
   big dictionary, isn't it.
7. That (over there) is a   Are wa o⌐okiˀi zaˀssi deˀsu ⌐neˀe.
   big magazine, isn't it.
8. That (over there) is a   Are wa tu⌐maraˀnai zaˀssi deˀsu
   dull magazine, isn't it.   ⌐neˀe.
9. That (over there) is a   Are wa tu⌐maraˀnai siⁿbuñ deˀsu
   dull newspaper, isn't it.   ⌐neˀe.

C. Response Drill (based on Grammatical Note 2)

(What does the Eˀe. or Iie. answer to each of the following questions
mean?)

1. Peˀñ desu ka⌐ /Eˀe./   Eˀe, peˀñ desu.
2. Eⁿpitu deˀsu ka⌐ /Iie./   Iie, eⁿpitu zya arimaseˀñ.
3. Soˀo desu ka⌐ /Eˀe./   Eˀe, soˀo desu.
4. Kyoˀo desu ka⌐ /Iie./   Iie, kyoˀo zya a⌐rimaseⁿñ.
5. Siⁿbuñ deˀsu ka⌐ /Eˀe./   Eˀe, siⁿbuñ deˀsu.
6. O⌐nazi deˀsu ka⌐ /Iie./   Iie, o⌐nazi zya arimaseˀñ.
7. Zaˀssi deˀsu ka⌐ /Eˀe./   Eˀe, zaˀssi deˀsu.
8. A⌐sitaˀ desu ka⌐ /Iie./   Iie, a⌐sitaˀ zya a⌐rimaseⁿñ.
9. Da⌐meˀ desu ka⌐ /Eˀe./   Eˀe, da⌐meˀ desu.
10. Ta⌐naka-sañ deˀsu ka⌐   Iie, Ta⌐naka-sañ zya arimaseˀñ.
    /Iie./

D. Response Drill (based on Grammatical Note 1)

(What does the Eˀe. or Iie. answer to each of the following questions
mean?)

1. O⌐okiˀi desu ka⌐ /Eˀe./   Eˀe, o⌐okiˀi desu.
2. A⌐tarasiˀi desu ka⌐ /Iie./   Iie, a⌐taraˀsiku a⌐rimaseˀñ.
3. Hu⌐ruˀi desu ka⌐ /Eˀe./   Eˀe, hu⌐ruˀi desu.
4. Iˀi desu ka⌐ /Iie./   Iie, yoˀku a⌐rimaseⁿñ.

5. Oˈmosiroˈi desu kaˌ /Eˈe./   Eˈe, oˈmosiroˈi desu.
6. Tiˈisaˈi desu kaˌ /Iie./   Iie, tiˈisaku aˈrimaseˈñ.
7. Waˈruˈi desu kaˌ /Eˈe./   Eˈe, waˈruˈi desu.
8. Tuˈmaraˈnai desu kaˌ /Iie./   Iie, tuˈmaraˈnaku aˈrimaseˈñ.
9. Iˈi desu kaˌ /Eˈe./   Eˈe, iˈi desu.
10. Oˈokiˈi desu kaˌ /Iie./   Iie, oˈokiku aˈrimaseˈñ.

E. Response Drill

(What does the Iie. answer to each of the following questions mean?)

1. Iˈkimaˈsu kaˌ /Iie./   Iie, iˈkimaseˈñ.
2. Huˈruˈi desu kaˌ /Iie./   Iie, huˈruku aˈrimaseˈñ.
3. Oˈnazi deˈsu kaˌ /Iie./   Iie, oˈnazi zya arimaseˈñ.
4. Waˈkarimaseˈñ desita kaˌ   Iie, waˈkarimaˈsita.
    /Iie./
5. Siˈñbuñ zya arimaseˈñ kaˌ   Iie, siˈñbuñ deˈsu.
    /Iie./
6. Oˈmosiˈroku aˈrimaseˈñ   Iie, oˈmosiroˈi desu.
    kaˌ /Iie./
7. Siˈmaˈsu kaˌ /Iie./   Iie, siˈmaseˈñ.
8. Ziˈsyo zya aˈrimaseˈñ kaˌ   Iie, ziˈsyo desu.
    /Iie./
9. Aˈtarasiˈi desu kaˌ /Iie./   Iie, aˈtaraˈsiku aˈrimaseˈñ.
10. Koˈre deˈsu kaˌ /Iie./   Iie, koˈre zya arimaseˈñ.

F. Response Drill

Answer with soˈo desu, soˈo desu ˈneˈe, or soˈo desu ka, whichever is appropriate. Assume that each statement not ending with ˈneˈe contains new information.

1. Waˈkarimaseˈñ desita.   Soˈo desu ka.
2. Oˈmosiroˈi desu ˈneˈe.   Soˈo desu ˈneˈe.
3. Zeˈñbu waˈkarimaˈsita.   Soˈo desu ka.
4. Peˈñ desu kaˌ   Soˈo desu.
5. Daˈmeˈ desu yoˌ   Soˈo desu ka.
6. Ziˈsyo desu kaˌ   Soˈo desu.
7. Iˈi desu ˈneˈe.   Soˈo desu ˈneˈe.
8. Tiˈgaimaˈsu yoˌ   Soˈo desu ka.

G. Expansion Drill

1. [It] isn't a pen.   Peˈñ zya aˈrimaseˈñ.
    [It] isn't a new pen.   Aˈtarasiˈi ˈpeˈñ zya aˈrimaseˈñ.
    That isn't a new pen.   Sore wa aˈtarasiˈi ˈpeˈñ zya aˈri-
                                   maseˈñ.
    Isn't that a new pen?   Sore wa aˈtarasiˈi ˈpeˈñ zya aˈri-
                                   maseˈñ kaˌ
2. [It]'s a book.   Hoˈñ desu.
    [It]'s an interesting book.   Oˈmosiroˈi ˈhoˈñ desu.
    This is an interesting book.   Kore wa oˈmosiroˈi ˈhoˈñ desu.
    Isn't this an interesting   Kore wa oˈmosiroˈi ˈhoˈñ desu ˈneˈe.
    book!

3. [It]'s dull.   Tu⌐mara⌐nai desu.
    That's dull.   Sore wa tu⌐mara⌐nai desu.
    You know, that's dull.   Sore wa tu⌐mara⌐nai desu yo⌐
    You know, Mr. Tanaka, that's   Tanaka-sañ, sore wa tu⌐mara⌐nai
    dull.   desu yo⌐
4. [It] isn't [any] good.   Yo⌐ku a⌐rimase⌐ñ.
    The dictionary isn't [any]   Zi⌐biki⌐ wa ⌐yo⌐ku a⌐rimase⌐ñ.
    good.
    The small dictionary isn't   Ti⌐isa⌐i zi⌐biki⌐ wa ⌐yo⌐ku a⌐rimase⌐ñ.
    [any] good.
    The small dictionary isn't   Ti⌐isa⌐i zi⌐biki⌐ wa ⌐yo⌐ku a⌐rimase⌐ñ
    [any] good, is it!   ⌐ne⌐e.

EXERCISES

1. Tanaka-sañ asks you what it is. You answer that:

    a. it's a book.
    b. it's a newspaper.
    c. it's a pencil.
    d. it's an old magazine.
    e. it's a new pen.

2. Tanaka-sañ asks: Your answer:

    a. if it's interesting.   Yes, it is (interesting).
    b. if it's small.   No, it's big.
    c. if it's new.   No, it isn't (new).
    d. if it's the same.   No, it's different.
    e. if it's an interesting book.   No, it isn't interesting.
    f. if it's a new magazine.   No, it's old.
    g. what it is.   Which one do you mean?

3. Following the Basic Dialogues of this lesson, make up new conversations by replacing the nominals and adjectivals with other words of the same word-class, wherever possible. Practice the new conversations using appropriate props. For example, using a newspaper and a magazine, you might practice Basic Dialogue (c) as follows:

    Smith: Kore wa a⌐tarasi⌐i za⌐ssi de⌐su ka⌐
    Tanaka: Iie, a⌐tara⌐siku a⌐rimase⌐ñ.
    Smith: Zya⌐a, sore wa?
    Tanaka: Si⌐ñbuñ de⌐su ka⌐
        So⌐re wa atarasi⌐i desu yo⌐ Do⌐ozo.

Lesson 3. Shopping

NUMERALS

1 i⌐ti¬	10 zyu¬u	20 ni¬zyuu	30 sa¬ñzyuu
2 ni¬	11 zyu⌐uiti¬	21 ni¬zyuu iti	31 sa¬ñzyuu iti
3 sañ	12 zyu⌐uni¬	22 ni¬zyuu ni	32 sa¬ñzyuu ni
4 si¬ or yo¬n	13 zyu¬usañ	23 ni¬zyuu sañ	33 sa¬ñzyuu sañ
5 go¬	14 zyu⌐usi¬	24 ni¬zyuu si	34 sa¬ñzyuu si
6 ro⌐ku¬	15 zyu¬ugo	25 ni¬zyuu go	35 sa¬ñzyuu go
7 si⌐ti¬ or na¬na	16 zyu⌐uroku¬	26 ni¬zyuu roku	36 sa¬ñzyuu roku
8 ha⌐ti¬	17 zyu⌐usiti¬	27 ni¬zyuu siti	37 sa¬ñzyuu siti
9 ku¬ or kyu¬u	18 zyu⌐uhati¬	28 ni¬zyuu hati	38 sa¬ñzyuu hati
	19 zyu¬uku	29 ni¬zyuu ku	39 sa¬ñzyuu ku

40 yo¬ñzyuu	50 go⌐zyu¬u	60 ro⌐kuzyu¬u	70 na⌐na¬zyuu
41 yo¬ñzyuu iti	51 go⌐zyuu iti¬	61 ro⌐kuzyuu iti¬	71 na⌐na¬zyuu iti
42 yo¬ñzyuu ni	52 go⌐zyuu ni¬	62 ro⌐kuzyuu ni¬	72 na⌐na¬zyuu ni
43 yo¬ñzyuu sañ	53 gozyuu sañ	63 rokuzyuu sañ	73 na⌐na¬zyuu sañ
44 yo¬ñzyuu si	54 go⌐zyuu si¬	64 ro⌐kuzyuu si¬	74 na⌐na¬zyuu si
45 yo¬ñzyuu go	55 go⌐zyuu go¬	65 ro⌐kuzyuu go¬	75 na⌐na¬zyuu go
46 yo¬ñzyuu roku	56 go⌐zyuu roku¬	66 ro⌐kuzyuu roku¬	76 na⌐na¬zyuu roku
47 yo¬ñzyuu siti	57 go⌐zyuu siti¬	67 ro⌐kuzyuu siti¬	77 na⌐na¬zyuu siti
48 yo¬ñzyuu hati	58 go⌐zyuu hati¬	68 ro⌐kuzyuu hati¬	78 na⌐na¬zyuu hati
49 yo¬ñzyuu ku	59 go⌐zyuu ku¬	69 ro⌐kuzyuu ku¬	79 na⌐na¬zyuu ku

80 ha⌐tizyu¬u	90 kyu¬uzyuu
81 ha⌐tizyuu iti¬	91 kyu¬uzyuu iti
82 ha⌐tizyuu ni¬	92 kyu¬uzyuu ni
83 hatizyuu sañ	93 kyu¬uzyuu sañ
84 ha⌐tizyuu si¬	94 kyu¬uzyuu si
85 ha⌐tizyuu go¬	95 kyu¬uzyuu go
86 ha⌐tizyuu roku¬	96 kyu¬uzyuu roku
87 ha⌐tizyuu siti¬	97 kyu¬uzyuu siti
88 ha⌐tizyuu hati¬	98 kyu¬uzyuu hati
89 ha⌐tizyuu ku¬	99 kyu¬uzyuu kyuu

100 hya⌐ku¬	1000 se¬ñ or i⌐sse¬ñ	10,000 i⌐tima¬ñ
200 ni⌐hyaku¬	2000 ni⌐se¬ñ	20,000 ni⌐ma¬ñ
300 sa¬ñbyaku	3000 sa¬ñze¬ñ	30,000 sa¬ñma¬ñ
400 yo¬ñhyaku	4000 yo⌐ñse¬ñ	40,000 yo⌐ñma¬ñ
500 go⌐hyaku¬	5000 go⌐se¬ñ	50,000 go⌐ma¬ñ
600 ro⌐ppyaku¬	6000 ro⌐kuse¬ñ	60,000 ro⌐kuma¬ñ
700 na⌐na¬hyaku	7000 na⌐nase¬ñ	70,000 na⌐nama¬ñ
800 ha⌐ppyaku¬	8000 ha⌐sse¬ñ	80,000 ha⌐tima¬ñ
900 kyu¬uhyaku	9000 kyu⌐use¬ñ	90,000 kyu⌐uma¬ñ

BASIC DIALOGUES: FOR MEMORIZATION

(a)

Smith

cigarette(s) or tobacco	tabako
that cigarette or those cigarettes	sono tabako
how much?	i⌐kura¬ or oikura[+]
1. How much are those cigarettes?	Sono tabako wa ⌐i¬kura desu ka⌟

Clerk

which cigarette(s)?	do¬no tabako
2. Which cigarettes are they? or Which cigarettes do you mean?	Do¬no tabako desu ka⌟

Smith (picking up cigarettes)

this cigarette or these cigarettes	kono tabako
3. They're these cigarettes. or I mean these cigarettes.	Ko⌐no tabako de¬su.

Clerk

1 yen	iti-eñ
2 yen	ni-eñ
3 yen	sañ-eñ
4 yen	yo¬-eñ
4. They're ¥40.	Yo⌐ñzyu¬u-eñ desu.

Smith

match(es)	ma¬tti
this match or these matches	ko⌐no ma¬tti
5. How about these matches?	Ko⌐no ma¬tti wa?

Clerk

6. They're ¥2.	Ni-⌐eñ de¬su.

Smith

here you are	ha¬i
7. Here you are. ¥42.	Ha¬i. Yo⌐ñzyuu ⌐ni¬-eñ.

Clerk

8. Thank you.	A⌐ri¬ḡatoo gozaimasu.

(b)

Tanaka (examining Smith's purchases on the counter)

ashtray(s)	ha⌐iza¬ra
that little ashtray	sono ti⌐isa¬i ha⌐iza⌐ra
pretty or clean	ki¬ree
9. Isn't that little ashtray pretty!	Sono ti⌐isa¬i ha⌐iza⌐ra wa ⌐ki¬ree desu ⌐ne¬e.

10. Was it ¥400?   Yo⌐nhyaku⌐-eñ desita ka↲

                          Smith

11. No, it wasn't (that way).   Iie. So⌐o zya a⌐rimase⌐n desita.

12. It was ¥200.   Ni⌐hyaku⌐-eñ desita yo↲

                          Tanaka

13. (It was) ¥200?   Ni⌐hyaku⌐-eñ desita ka↲

      is cheap or inexpensive   ya⌐su⌐i /-ku/
14. How cheap! (Lit. It's cheap,   Ya⌐su⌐i desu ⌐ne⌐e.
      isn't it.)

                          (c)

                          Smith

      that big dictionary over   ano o⌐oki⌐i zibiki
        there
15. How much was that big diction-   Ano o⌐oki⌐i zi⌐biki⌐ wa ⌐i⌐kura desita
      ary over there?   ka↲

                          Tanaka

16. It was ¥1200.   Se⌐n nihyaku⌐-eñ desita.

                          Smith

      truth or true   hoñtoo
17. Is that true? or Really?   Ho⌐ñtoo de⌐su ka↲
      or Do you really mean it?

      extremely or to a con-   zu⌐ibuñ
        siderable degree
18. How (very) cheap! (Lit. It's   Zu⌐ibuñ ya⌐su⌐i desu ⌐ne⌐e.
      very cheap, isn't it.)

                          (d)

                          Smith

19. How much was that?   Sore wa ⌐i⌐kura desita ka↲

                          Tanaka

      this book   ko⌐no ho⌐ñ
20. Is it this book? or Do you   Ko⌐no ho⌐ñ desu ka↲
      mean this book?

21. It was ¥250.   Ni⌐hyaku gozyu⌐u-eñ desita.

                          Smith

      not very much or not so   añmari + negative
        much or not too much
      is expensive   ta⌐ka⌐i /-ku/
22. It wasn't very expensive, was   A⌐ñmari ta⌐kaku a⌐rimase⌐n desita
      it.   ⌐ne⌐e.

NOTES ON THE BASIC DIALOGUES

1. When 'cigarette' is being distinguished from other things to smoke—cigars, pipes, etc.—ma⌐kita⌐bako is used.

    Oikura, the polite (+) equivalent of i⌐kura, is used more commonly—but not exclusively—by women.

7. Ha⌐i is frequently used when handing something over to someone.

17. Ho⌐ñtoo de⌐su ka‿ 'Is that true?' indicates livelier interest and greater surprise than So⌐o desu ka‿ 'Is that so?' or 'Oh?'

GRAMMATICAL NOTES

1. Numerals of Series I and Counter -eñ

The numerals listed on page 26 are Japanese numerals of Chinese origin; they will hereafter be designated as SERIES I NUMERALS. A second series, of native Japanese origin, will be introduced later.

Three numerals have alternate forms: '4' is yo⌐ñ or si⌐;[1] '7' is na⌐na or si⌐ti⌐; '9' is kyu⌐u or ku⌐. Depending on what follows, either the alternants are used interchangeably, or one alternant occurs much more commonly, or only one alternant occurs. Unfortunately, no general rules apply which will assist the student in choosing the correct alternant(s); he must learn each combination as it occurs.

Si⌐zyu⌐u occurs as a less common alternant of yo⌐ñzyuu, and si⌐tizyu⌐u as a less common alternant of na⌐na⌐zyuu.

Numerals from 1 to 100 are listed at the beginning of this lesson. Three-digit numerals are read in terms of the number of hundreds, the number of tens, and the single units. If a zero occurs within a written number, it is usually omitted in the spoken number. Thus:

236: ni⌐hyaku sa⌐ñzyuu ro⌐ku⌐ (lit. '2 hundreds, 3 tens, 6')
632: ro⌐ppyaku sa⌐ñzyuu ⌐ni⌐ (lit. '6 hundreds, 3 tens, 2')
801: ha⌐ppyaku iti⌐ (lit. '8 hundreds, 1')

Four-digit numerals are read in terms of the number of thousands, the number of hundreds, the number of tens, and the single units. Thus:

4578: yo⌐ñse⌐ñ gohyaku na⌐na⌐zyuu ha⌐ti⌐ (lit. '4 thousands, 5 hundreds, 7 tens, 8')
8754: ha⌐sse⌐ñ na⌐na⌐hyaku go⌐zyuu si⌐ (lit. '8 thousands, 7 hundreds, 5 tens, 4')
9023: kyu⌐use⌐ñ ⌐ni⌐zyuu sañ (lit. '9 thousands, 2 tens, 3')

---

[1] A third, less common alternant which occurs only in certain compounds is yo-.

Higher numerals often cause difficulties for English speakers and therefore require special attention. In reading numerals containing from five to eight digits,[1] the numeral is read in terms of how many ten-thousands (up to thousands of ten-thousands), how many thousands, how many hundreds, how many tens, and how many single units it contains. This can be simplified in the case of a written number by inserting a comma between the fourth and fifth digit counting from the right,[2] and reading what precedes the comma as an independent numeral + -ma⌐ñ 'ten-thousands.' Study the following examples:

12,345 (rewritten 1,2345) is read: i⌐tima⌐ñ ni⌐se⌐ñ ⌐sa⌐ñbyaku ⌐yo⌐ñzyuu ⌐go⌐ (lit. '1 ten-thousand, 2 thousands, 3 hundreds, 4 tens, 5')

123,456 (rewritten 12,3456) is read: zyu⌐unima⌐ñ sa⌐ñze⌐ñ ⌐yo⌐ñhyaku go-⌐zyuu roku⌐ (lit. '12 ten-thousands, 3 thousands, 4 hundreds, 5 tens, 6')

1,234,567 (rewritten 123,4567) is read: hya⌐ku ni⌐zyuu sa⌐ñma⌐ñ yo⌐ñse⌐ñ gohyaku ro⌐kuzyuu siti⌐ (lit. '123 ten-thousands, 4 thousands, 5 hundreds, 6 tens, 7')

12,345,678 (rewritten 1234,5678) is read: se⌐ñ nihyaku ⌐sa⌐ñzyuu yo⌐ñma⌐ñ go⌐se⌐ñ roppyaku na⌐na⌐zyuu hati (lit. '1234 ten-thousands, 5 thousands, 6 hundreds, 7 tens, 8')

Note that the Japanese equivalent of a million is hya⌐kuma⌐ñ (lit. '100 ten-thousands,' i. e. 100,0000).

The occurrence of -ma⌐ñ in a numeral is always a signal of four digits to come. The digits may be zero. Thus:

go⌐ma⌐ñ   '50,000'
go⌐ma⌐ñ i⌐sse⌐ñ   '51,000'
go⌐ma⌐ñ hya⌐ku⌐   '50,100'
go⌐ma⌐ñ ⌐zyu⌐u   '50,010'
go⌐ma⌐ñ i⌐ti⌐   '50,001'

The numerals of Series I regularly occur independently in mathematics, in counting cadence, and in serial counting.

The monetary unit of Japan is the yen. To count yen, -eñ is added to the numerals of Series I. Note, however, that before -eñ, '4' is yo⌐- instead of the more usual yo⌐ñ or si⌐. The forms from 1 to 10[3] are:

iti-eñ	'1 yen'	roku-eñ	'6 yen'
ni-eñ	'2 yen'	na⌐na⌐-eñ or siti-eñ	'7 yen'
sañ-eñ	'3 yen'	hati-eñ	'8 yen'
yo⌐-eñ	'4 yen'	kyu⌐u-eñ	'9 yen'
go⌐-eñ	'5 yen'	zyuu-eñ	'10 yen'

The corresponding question word is na⌐ñ-eñ 'how many yen?'

---

[1] Numerals larger than this are not treated in this text.

[2] In English, numerals are divided into groups of threes; in Japanese, into groups of fours.

[3] In all such lists in this text, only commonly occurring alternants are included.

Forms like -eñ, which do not occur as independent words but are joined with numerals in compounds, will hereafter be called COUNTERS; and compounds that consist of numeral + counter will be called NUMBERS. All numerals and numbers are nominals.

2. Demonstratives: kono, sono, ano, do⌐no

Kono 'this —,' sono 'that —,' ano 'that — over there,' and do⌐no 'which — [of three or more]?' belong to a small class of Japanese constants (words having only one form) which occur only as a modifier of a following nominal.[1] Words of this class will be called DEMONSTRATIVES. Examples:

> ko⌐no pe⌐ñ 'this pen' (or, of course, 'these pens')
> sono eñpitu 'that pencil'
> a⌐no ho⌐ñ 'that book over there'
> kono o⌐mosiro⌐i ⌐ho⌐ñ 'this interesting book'
> do⌐no tabako 'which cigarettes?'
> do⌐no Tanaka-sañ 'which Mr. Tanaka?'

These four words must not be confused with kore, sore, are, and do⌐re, which are nominals. Compare:

> Ko⌐re de⌐su. 'It's this.'
> Kore wa ⌐ho⌐ñ desu. 'This is a book.'
> Ko⌐no ho⌐ñ desu. 'It's this book.'
> So⌐re zya arimase⌐ñ. 'It's not that.'
> Sore wa ⌐pe⌐ñ zya a⌐rimase⌐ñ. 'That is not a pen.'
> So⌐no pe⌐ñ zya a⌐rimase⌐ñ. 'It's not that pen.'

The spatial and referential relationships of kore, sore, and are described above (pages 21–22) apply equally to the corresponding demonstratives kono, sono, and ano.

3. Copula

De⌐su is a member of a certain set of inflected forms[2] which is neither a verbal (there are no forms ending in -ma⌐su, -ma⌐sita, etc.) nor an adjectival (there are no forms ending in -i or -ku). Actually, it is a unique set of forms; there are no other Japanese words with the same shapes or usage. Hereafter, de⌐su and its derived forms — symbolized as √de⌐su —[3] will be called the COPULA. The de⌐su form itself is the formal non-past of the copula, corresponding to the -ma⌐su form of a verbal.

---

[1] The nominal may have other modifiers as well. Note the fourth example.

[2] I.e. is one shape of a word having several shapes.

[3] The symbol √ indicates the enclosed word and its other forms. Thus √wa-⌐karima⌐su is a short-cut way of writing wa⌐karima⌐su, wa⌐karima⌐sita, etc.

It has already been pointed out that:

(a) de⌐su may follow an adjectival in its citation (-i) form, making the expression formal. The -i form alone is non-past informal; the -i form + de⌐su is non-past formal.

  o⌐oki⌐i desu 'it's big' (negative: o⌐okiku a⌐rimase⌐ñ 'it's not big')

(b) de⌐su may follow a nominal, meaning 'it is ——' or 'it will be ——' (non-past formal).

  ho⌐ñtoo de⌐su 'it's true' (negative: ho⌐ñtoo zya arimase⌐ñ 'it's not true')

In this lesson, the following new information is introduced:

(c) The past of de⌐su is de⌐sita[1] (also formal). It regularly occurs after a nominal, meaning 'it was ——.'

  kyo⌐o desu 'it's today'; kyo⌐o desita 'it was today.'

It sometimes follows an adjectival in its -i form, as the past equivalent of adjectival + de⌐su. However, this is only one of several formal past adjectival patterns,[2] and is not the most common pattern. An -i + desita pattern should not be used by a student without first checking with a native speaker of Japanese. If he hears it, however, he will have no trouble understanding it.

  (ya⌐su⌐i desu 'it's cheap'; ya⌐su⌐i desita 'it was cheap')

(d) Desita added to a formal non-past negative (ending in -mase⌐ñ) produces a formal past negative.

Formal Negatives

	Non-Past	Past
Verbal Pattern	wa⌐kariMASE⌐N̄ 'it isn't clear'	wa⌐kariMASE⌐N̄ DESITA 'it wasn't clear'
Adjectival Pattern	o⌐okiKU A⌐RIMASE⌐N̄ 'it isn't big'	o⌐okiKU A⌐RIMASE⌐N̄ DESITA 'it wasn't big'
Nominal Pattern	ho⌐ñtoo ZYA ARIMASE⌐N̄ 'it isn't true'	ho⌐ñtoo ZYA ARIMASE⌐N̄ DESITA 'it wasn't true'

---

[1] De⌐sita regularly loses its accent after an accented word.

[2] The others will be introduced later.

DRILLS

A. Substitution Drill

1. Do you mean this dictionary?   Ko⌐no zibiki⌐ desu ka◡
2. Do you mean those cigarettes?   So⌐no tabako de⌐su ka◡
3. Do you mean those matches over   A⌐no ma⌐tti desu ka◡
   there?
4. Which book do you mean?   Do⌐no ⌐ho⌐ñ desu ka◡
5. Do you mean this magazine?   Ko⌐no zassi de⌐su ka◡
6. Do you mean that newspaper?   So⌐no siñbuñ de⌐su ka◡
7. Do you mean that ashtray over   A⌐no haiza⌐ra desu ka◡
   there?
8. Which Mr. Tanaka do you mean?   Do⌐no Ta⌐naka-sañ de⌐su ka◡

B. Substitution Drill

1. How much were those cigarettes?   Sono tabako wa ⌐i⌐kura desita ka◡
2. How much was that ashtray?   So⌐no haiza⌐ra wa ⌐i⌐kura desita
                                       ka◡
3. How much were those matches?   So⌐no ma⌐tti wa ⌐i⌐kura desita ka◡
4. How much was that newspaper?   Sono siñbuñ wa ⌐i⌐kura desita ka◡
5. How much was that magazine?   Sono zassi wa ⌐i⌐kura desita ka◡
6. How much was that book?   So⌐no ho⌐ñ wa ⌐i⌐kura desita ka◡
7. How much was that dictionary?   So⌐no zibiki⌐ wa ⌐i⌐kura desita ka◡
8. How much was that pencil?   Sono eñpitu wa ⌐i⌐kura desita ka◡
9. How much was that pen?   So⌐no pe⌐ñ wa ⌐i⌐kura desita ka◡

C. Substitution Drill

1. That big dictionary wasn't very   Sono o⌐oki⌐i zi⌐biki⌐ wa a⌐ñmari
   expensive, was it!   ta⌐kaku a⌐rimase⌐ñ desita ⌐ne⌐e.
2. That new dictionary wasn't very   Sono a⌐tarasi⌐i zi⌐biki⌐ wa a⌐ñma-
   expensive, was it!   ri ta⌐kaku a⌐rimase⌐ñ desita
                                       ⌐ne⌐e.
3. That new dictionary wasn't very   Sono a⌐tarasi⌐i zi⌐biki⌐ wa a⌐ñ-
   big, was it!   mari o⌐okiku a⌐rimase⌐ñ desita
                                       ⌐ne⌐e.
4. That expensive dictionary wasn't   Sono ta⌐ka⌐i zi⌐biki⌐ wa a⌐ñmari
   very big, was it!   o⌐okiku a⌐rimase⌐ñ desita ⌐ne⌐e.
5. That expensive dictionary wasn't   Sono ta⌐ka⌐i zi⌐biki⌐ wa a⌐ñmari
   very good, was it!   yo⌐ku a⌐rimase⌐ñ desita ⌐ne⌐e.
6. That small dictionary wasn't   Sono ti⌐isa⌐i zi⌐biki⌐ wa a⌐ñmari
   very good, was it!   yo⌐ku a⌐rimase⌐ñ desita ⌐ne⌐e.
7. That small dictionary wasn't   Sono ti⌐isa⌐i zi⌐biki⌐ wa a⌐ñmari
   too bad, was it!   wa⌐ruku a⌐rimase⌐ñ desita ⌐ne⌐e.
8. That cheap dictionary wasn't   Sono ya⌐su⌐i zi⌐biki⌐ wa a⌐ñmari
   too bad, was it!   wa⌐ruku a⌐rimase⌐ñ desita ⌐ne⌐e.

D. Response Drill (based on Grammatical Note 3)

(Give the iie answer for each of the following.)

1.	A⌐no tabako de⌐sita ka⌐	Iie, a⌐no tabako zya arimase⌐ñ desita.
2.	Zi⌐syo desita ka⌐	Iie, zi⌐syo zya a⌐rimase⌐ñ desita.
3.	Ki⌐ree desita ka⌐	Iie, ki⌐ree zya a⌐rimase⌐ñ desita.
4.	Ho⌐ñtoo de⌐sita ka⌐	Iie, ho⌐ñtoo zya arimase⌐ñ desita.
5.	Ta⌐naka-sañ de⌐sita ka⌐	Iie, Ta⌐naka-sañ zya arimase⌐ñ desita.
6.	Hya⌐ku-eñ de⌐sita ka⌐	Iie, hya⌐ku-eñ zya arimase⌐ñ desita.
7.	Ki⌐no⌐o desita ka⌐	Iie, ki⌐no⌐o zya a⌐rimase⌐ñ desita.
8.	O⌐nazi de⌐sita ka⌐	Iie, o⌐nazi zya arimase⌐ñ desita.

E. Response Drill (based on Grammatical Note 3)

(Give the iie answer for each of the following, using the adjectival pattern.)

1.	O⌐mosiro⌐i za⌐ssi de⌐sita ka⌐	Iie, o⌐mosi⌐roku a⌐rimase⌐ñ desita.
2.	Ya⌐su⌐i ha⌐iza⌐ra desita ka⌐	Iie, ya⌐suku a⌐rimase⌐ñ desita.
3.	O⌐oki⌐i zi⌐biki⌐ desita ka⌐	Iie, o⌐okiku a⌐rimase⌐ñ desita.
4.	I⌐i ⌐ho⌐ñ desita ka⌐	Iie, yo⌐ku a⌐rimase⌐ñ desita.
5.	Tu⌐mara⌐nai za⌐ssi de⌐sita ka⌐	Iie, tu⌐mara⌐naku a⌐rimase⌐ñ desita.
6.	Ta⌐ka⌐i ta⌐bako de⌐sita ka⌐	Iie, ta⌐kaku a⌐rimase⌐ñ desita.
7.	A⌐tarasi⌐i si⌐ñbuñ de⌐sita ka⌐	Iie, a⌐tara⌐siku a⌐rimase⌐ñ desita.
8.	Ti⌐isa⌐i zi⌐biki⌐ desita ka⌐	Iie, ti⌐isaku a⌐rimase⌐ñ desita.
9.	Wa⌐ru⌐i ⌐ho⌐ñ desita ka⌐	Iie, wa⌐ruku a⌐rimase⌐ñ desita.
10.	Hu⌐ru⌐i si⌐ñbuñ de⌐sita ka⌐	Iie, hu⌐ruku a⌐rimase⌐ñ desita.

F. Grammar Drill (based on Grammatical Note 2)

Tutor: Ko⌐no ho⌐ñ wa ta⌐ka⌐i desu ⌐ne⌐e. 'Isn't this book expensive!'
Student: Kore wa ta⌐ka⌐i desu ⌐ne⌐e. 'Isn't this expensive!'

1.	Ko⌐no pe⌐ñ wa ya⌐su⌐i desu ⌐ne⌐e.	Kore wa ya⌐su⌐i desu ⌐ne⌐e.
2.	So⌐no zibiki⌐ wa ta⌐ka⌐i desu yo⌐	Sore wa ta⌐ka⌐i desu yo⌐
3.	A⌐no haiza⌐ra wa ⌐i⌐kura desita ka⌐	Are wa ⌐i⌐kura desita ka⌐
4.	Do⌐no za⌐ssi de⌐su ka⌐	Do⌐re desu ka⌐
5.	Sono eñpitu wa da⌐me⌐ desu ka⌐	Sore wa da⌐me⌐ desu ka⌐
6.	Ano siñbuñ wa hu⌐ru⌐i desu yo⌐	Are wa hu⌐ru⌐i desu yo⌐
7.	Ko⌐no ho⌐ñ wa o⌐mosiro⌐i desu ⌐ne⌐e.	Kore wa o⌐mosiro⌐i desu ⌐ne⌐e.

G. Expansion Drill

1. It's pretty.	Ki⌐ree desu.
Isn't it pretty!	Ki⌐ree desu ⌐ne⌐e.
Isn't the ashtray pretty!	Ha⌐iza⌐ra wa ⌐ki⌐ree desu ⌐ne⌐e.
Isn't that ashtray pretty!	So⌐no haiza⌐ra wa ⌐ki⌐ree desu ⌐ne⌐e.

2. How much was it?   I⌐kura desita ka⌐
    How much was the dictionary?   Zi⌐biki⌐ wa ⌐i⌐kura desita ka⌐
    How much was the big dic-   O⌐oki⌐i zi⌐biki⌐ wa ⌐i⌐kura desita ka⌐
    tionary?
    How much was this big dic-   Kono o⌐oki⌐i zi⌐biki⌐ wa ⌐i⌐kura de-
    tionary?   sita ka⌐

3. It isn't expensive.   Ta⌐kaku a⌐rimase⌐ñ.
    It wasn't expensive.   Ta⌐kaku a⌐rimase⌐ñ desita.
    It wasn't very expensive.   A⌐ñmari ta⌐kaku a⌐rimase⌐ñ desita.
    This book wasn't very expen-   Ko⌐no ho⌐ñ wa a⌐ñmari ta⌐kaku a⌐ri-
    sive.   mase⌐ñ desita.

4. It isn't true.   Ho⌐ñtoo zya arimase⌐ñ.
    It wasn't true.   Ho⌐ñtoo zya arimase⌐ñ desita.
    That wasn't true.   Sore wa ho⌐ñtoo zya arimase⌐ñ desita.
    You know, that wasn't true!   Sore wa ho⌐ñtoo zya arimase⌐ñ desita
                                                yo⌐

SUPPLEMENTARY CONVERSATION

Smith: (Pointing) O⌐neḡai-sima⌐su.
Clerk: Ko⌐re de⌐su ka⌐
Smith: E⌐e.
Clerk: Do⌐ozo.
Smith: I⌐kura desu ka⌐
Clerk: Ni⌐señ-eñ de⌐su.
Smith: Tyo⌐tto ta⌐ka⌐i desu ⌐ne⌐e.
Clerk: (Showing another one) Ko⌐re wa yasu⌐i desu. (Checking price tag) Se⌐ñ
        nihyaku⌐-eñ desu.
Smith: A⌐a, ko⌐re wa i⌐i desu ⌐ne⌐e. O⌐neḡai-sima⌐su. (Handing over money)
        Se⌐ñ nihyaku⌐-eñ. Ha⌐i.
Clerk: A⌐ri⌐ḡatoo gozaimasu.

English Equivalent

Smith: May I see that, please? (Lit. I make a request.)
Clerk: (Do you mean) this one?
Smith: Yes.
Clerk: Here you are.
Smith: How much is it?
Clerk: (It's) ¥2000.
Smith: It's a little expensive, isn't it.
Clerk: This one is cheap. . . . It's ¥1200.
Smith: Oh, this one is fine! I'll take it. Here you are. ¥1200.
Clerk: Thank you.

EXERCISES

1. Read the following in Japanese:

    a. 27   c. 604
    b. 64   d. 358

e.	891	m.	3,456,789
f.	3,487	n.	7,250,000
g.	8,926	o.	10,500,000
h.	6,044	p.	¥360
i.	10,000	q.	¥1,800
j.	23,487	r.	¥36,000
k.	46,020	s.	¥650,000
l.	321,321	t.	¥1,000,000

2. The customer asks the price of the following objects and the clerk answers
    with the price indicated:

a.	those cigarettes.	(¥40)
b.	this ashtray.	(¥350)
c.	these matches.	(¥2)
d.	that pen over there.	(¥1000)
e.	that small dictionary.	(¥400)
f.	that big book.	(¥1800)

3. You ask: Tanaka-san answers:
    a. if this book is interest-   No, it isn't very interesting.
        ing.
    b. if that book was ¥350.   No, it was ¥450.
    c. if these cigarettes are   Which cigarettes do you mean?
        ¥40.
    d. if that thing over there   No, it's a pencil.
        is a pen.
    e. if these books are the   No, they're different.
        same.
    f. if this pen was ¥2500.   Yes, that's right.
    g. if that pencil is ¥10.   No, it's ¥15.
    h. if these pens are dif-   Yes, they are.
        ferent.
    i. if that is a good pen.   No, it's not very good.
    j. if it was an expensive   No, it wasn't very expensive.
        dictionary.

4. Practice the Basic Dialogues with variations and appropriate props.

Lesson 4. Shopping (cont.)

BASIC DIALOGUES: FOR MEMORIZATION

(a)

Clerk

1. Welcome!	I⌐rassya⌐i. <u>or</u>
	I⌐rassyaima⌐se.

Smith

furoshiki (cloth square for wrapping)	hurosiki
furoshiki (as direct object)	hurosiki o
show <u>or</u> let [someone] see	mi⌐sema⌐su
please show <u>or</u> please let [someone] see	mi⌐sete kudasai
2. Please show [me] that furoshiki over there.	A⌐no hurosiki (o) mi⌐sete kudasai.

Clerk

is red	akai /-ku/[1]
red one(s)	a⌐ka⌐i no
3. Do you mean the red one? Here you are.	A⌐ka⌐i no desu ka⌐ Do⌐ozo.

Smith

is blue <u>or</u> green	a⌐o⌐i /-ku/
blue one(s)	a⌐o⌐i no
blue one(s) too	a⌐o⌐i no mo
4. Please show me that blue one too.	Sono a⌐o⌐i no mo ⌐mi⌐sete kudasai.

(. . . looking them over)

a little <u>or</u> a few	su⌐ko⌐si
a little more <u>or</u> a few more	mo⌐o suko⌐si
big one(s)	o⌐oki⌐i no
little bigger ones (as emphatic subject)	mo⌐o suko⌐si o⌐oki⌐i no ḡa
be necessary <u>or</u> need <u>or</u> want	i⌐rima⌐su
[I] need but	i⌐rima⌐su ḡa
5. I need a little bigger one but . . .	Mo⌐o suko⌐si o⌐oki⌐i no ḡa i⌐rima⌐su ḡa⌐

---

[1] This is the first example of an unaccented adjectival: <u>akai</u>, <u>akaku</u>, <u>akai hurosiki</u>, but a⌐ka⌐i <u>desu</u>, a⌐ka⌐i <u>no</u>.

Clerk (showing a third one)

	is yellow	kiiroi /-ku/
	yellow one(s)	ki⌐iro⌐i no
	as for a yellow one	ki⌐iro⌐i no wa
	how?	i⌐ka⌐ḡa+
6.	How about this yellow one? or How is this yellow one?	Kono ki⌐iro⌐i no(wa) i⌐ka⌐ḡa desu ka⌐

Smith

7.	Let me see. . . . or Hmmm. . . .	So⌐o desu ⌐ne⌐e.
	it's pretty but	ki⌐ree desu ḡa
8.	It's pretty but I'm afraid it won't do. . . (Lit. It's pretty but a bit. . .)	Ki⌐ree desu ḡa, tyo⌐tto⌐
	oh well or I guess	ma⌐a
	this one (as direct object)	kore o
	please give me	ku⌐dasa⌐i
9.	Oh well, I'll take (lit. give me) this one.	Ma⌐a, ko⌐re (o) kudasa⌐i.
	after that or and then or and	sore kara
	red one(s) too	a⌐ka⌐i no mo
10.	And give me this red one too.	Sore kara, kono a⌐ka⌐i no mo kudasai.

Clerk

	in addition	hoka ni
	something or anything	na⌐ni ka
11.	Anything else?	Ho⌐ka ni na⌐ni ka?

Smith

	just that	so⌐re dake⌐
12.	That's all.	So⌐re dake⌐ desu.
13.	Here you are — ¥1000.	Ha⌐i señ-eñ.

Clerk

	a little	syo⌐osyoo+
	please wait	o⌐mati-kudasa⌐i or o⌐mati-kudasaima⌐se
14.	Just a moment, please.	Syo⌐osyoo o⌐mati-kudasa⌐i. or Syo⌐osyoo o⌐mati-kudasaima⌐se.

(. . . returning with the wrapped package)

15.	I'm sorry to have kept you waiting.	O⌐matase-itasima⌐sita. ↓
	every time	maido
16.	Thank you (again and again).	Ma⌐ido ari⌐ḡatoo gozaimasu.

	again	mata
17.	Please [come] again.	Maˤta doˀozo.

(b)

Smith

18.	Say there!	Tyoˀtto—
	ashtray (as emphatic subject)	ˋhaˤizaˀra ḡa
	be in a place (of inanimate objects) or have	aˤrimaˀsu or goˤzaimaˀsu +
19.	Are there any ashtrays? or Do you have any ashtrays?	Haˤizaˀra (ḡa) aˤrimaˀsu ka⌐

Clerk

	yes	haˀa+
20.	Yes, there are. or Yes, I have. Here you are.	Haˀa, goˤzaimaˀsu. Doˀozo.

Smith

	is black	kuˤroˀi /-ku/
	black one(s)	kuˤroˀi no
	black one(s) (as direct object)	kuˤroˀi no o
21.	Please show me that black one.	Sono kuˤroˀi no (o) ˋmi┤sete kudasai.
	is white	siˤroˀi /-ku/
	white one(s) too	siˤroˀi no mo
22.	And please show me that white one, too.	Sore kara, sono siˤroˀi no mo ˋmi┤sete kudasai.

. . .

23.	I'll take this black one.	Kono kuˤroˀi no (o) kudasai.

Clerk

	as for the white one	siˤroˀi no wa
24.	How about the white one?	Siˤroˀi no wa i┐kaˀḡa desu ka⌐

Smith

	as for that one	sore wa
25.	That one I don't want.	Soˤre wa irimaseˀn̄.

Clerk

26.	Certainly. (I.e. I have understood your request and will do as you ask.)	Kaˤsikomarimaˀsita. +

(c)

Smith

	what (as direct object)?	naˀni o
	buy	kaˤimaˀsu

27. What did you buy?   Na⌐ni (o) ka⌐ima⌐sita ka⌐

                          Tanaka

        book and magazine   ho⌐ñ to zāssi
        book and magazine (as   ho⌐ñ to zāssi o
          direct object)
28. I bought a book and a magazine.   Ho⌐ñ to za⌐ssi (o) kaima⌐sita.

                          Smith

29. What about a newspaper?   Siñbuñ wa?

                          Tanaka

        oh!   a
        forget   wa⌐surema⌐su
30. Oh, I forgot. I'm sorry.   A. Wa⌐surema⌐sita. Su⌐mimase⌐ñ.

        as for a newspaper   siñbuñ wa
31. I didn't buy a newspaper.   Siñbuñ wa ka⌐imase⌐ñ desita.

                          Smith

        later   a⌐to de
32. Well then, would you [get it]   Zya⌐a, a⌐to de onegai-simasu.
    later?

        match (as emphatic sub-   ma⌐tti ga
          ject)
33. Say, have you got a match?   Tyo⌐tto, ma⌐tti (ga) a⌐rima⌐su ka⌐

                          Tanaka

        as for a match   ma⌐tti wa
        there isn't but or I don't   a⌐rimase⌐ñ ga
          have but
        lighter   ra⌐itaa
        lighter (as emphatic sub-   ra⌐itaa ga
          ject)
34. A match I don't have but I have   Ma⌐tti wa a⌐rimase⌐ñ ga, ra⌐itaa ga
    a lighter. Here you are.   arimasu. Do⌐ozo.

NOTES ON THE BASIC DIALOGUES

1. I⌐rassya⌐i and i⌐rassyaima⌐se, imperatives of the honorific verbal i⌐ras-
   syaima⌐su 'come,' are regularly used for greeting a customer entering a
   store, restaurant, inn, etc., and also for welcoming a guest to one's home.
   The form with -ma⌐se, which is formal, is used by women and by male employees of shops, restaurants, hotels, etc.

2. A furoshiki is a square of silk or cotton—or, more recently, plastic—used
   for wrapping packages which are to be hand-carried.

4. A⌐o⌐i covers that portion of the spectrum which includes both the 'blue' and
   'green' of English. Additional Japanese color words of more limited meaning will be introduced later.

5. With the meaning 'a little' or 'a few,' su⌐ko¬si and tyo¬tto are interchangeable, except that tyo¬tto is less formal; but only tyo¬tto is used as a means
of attracting attention (sentence 18) and as a polite refusal (sentence 8).

The affirmative forms of i⌐rima¬su more often mean 'need' and the negative forms 'not want' (sentence 25).

6. I⌐ka¬ḡa is a more polite equivalent of do¬o which occurs in a more limited
number of constructions.   Both are used in suggestions and in inquiring

how something or someone is.   Thus, X (wa) $\begin{Bmatrix} \text{do}^\neg\text{o} \\ \text{i}^\ulcorner\text{ka}^\neg\bar{\text{g}}\text{a} \end{Bmatrix}$ desu ka 'how about

X?' or 'how is X?'

7. Context, intonation, and/or rhythm make it possible to distinguish between
so¬o desu ⌐ne¬e 'that's right, isn't it,' 'isn't that true!' and so¬o desu ⌐ne¬e
'hmmm . . .'   The latter is often pronounced so¬oo desu ⌐ne⌐ee.

8. Tyo¬tto. is an indirect, hesitant—and polite—refusal of a suggestion, request, or invitation.

9. Ma¬a indicates that what follows is said after some hesitation or with some
reluctance.

14. Syo¬osyoo is a more polite equivalent of su⌐ko¬si which occurs commonly
in this sentence.   O⌐mati-kudasa¬i is a more polite equivalent of ma¬tte
kudasai.   The formal -ma¬se alternant is used most often by women.
(Compare the two alternants of sentence 1.)

15. O⌐matase-itasima¬sita is a humble (ǂ) word meaning literally 'I have caused
you to wait.'

16. Ma⌐ido ari¬ḡatoo gozaimasu is commonly used only by shopkeepers, clerks,
restaurant employees, etc.

18. Tyo¬tto is an informal word used to attract attention.

20. Ha¬a is a polite equivalent of ha¬i which occurs in the same kinds of patterns.

26. Ka⌐sikomarima¬sita means 'certainly—I have understood what you want me
to do' (never 'certainly—that's right').   It is addressed to a superior: for
example, an employer or a customer.

GRAMMATICAL NOTES

1. Particles: ḡa, o, wa, mo, to

There is a class of uninflected (i.e. non-changing) Japanese words which
occur within or at the end of a sentence, but never at the beginning.   They are
never preceded by pause but rather they are regularly pronounced as though
they were part of the word before them.   Within sentences, they relate what
precedes to what follows.   At the end of sentences, they color the meaning of
the sentence as a whole, making it into a question, an exclamation, an emphatic
statement, etc.   All such words are PARTICLES.   Those that regularly occur
at the end of sentences—like question particle ka and emphatic particle yo—are
SENTENCE PARTICLES.

Japanese particles often correspond to English prepositions. Many times, however, they are reflected instead in a particular word order or stress-intonation pattern in English; and sometimes there is nothing that specifically corresponds to them in a natural English equivalent.

(a) g̲a̲

(1) When preceded by a non-past or past inflected word (i.e. verbal, or adjectival, or copula), g̲a̲ marks a major division within a sentence: often it connects two sequences which are in contrast (corresponding to English 'but'); many times it separates a statement of fact from a related question or request (in which case, the most natural English equivalent is two independent sentences instead of two clauses with a connective).

Examples:

Ta⌐naka-sañ wa ikima⌐sita g̲a, Ya⌐mamoto-sañ wa ikimase⌐ñ desita.
'Mr.Tanaka went but Mr. Yamamoto didn't go.'
Ya⌐su⌐i desu g̲a, ki⌐ree desu. 'It's cheap but it's pretty.'
Ko⌐re wa ki⌐ree desu g̲a, so⌐re wa ki⌐ree zya a⌐rimase⌐ñ. 'This is pretty but that isn't (pretty).'
O⌐mosiro⌐i ⌐ho⌐ñ g̲a a⌐rima⌐su g̲a, i⌐ka⌐g̲a desu ka⌐ 'I have an interesting book. How about [reading] it?'

(2) G̲a̲ preceded by a nominal singles out the nominal as the subject[1] of a following inflected expression. Observe the location of the emphasis in the English equivalents.

Examples:

Ta⌐naka-sañ g̲a sima⌐sita. ' MR. TANAKA did [it].' (tells who did it)
Ko⌐re g̲a atarasi⌐i desu. ' THIS is new.' (tells which one is new)
So⌐re g̲a dame⌐ desu. ' THAT's out of order.' (tells which one is out of order)

(b) o̲

The particle o̲ singles out the preceding nominal as the direct object[1] of a following inflected expression. Note the location of the emphasis in the English equivalents.

Examples:

So⌐re o kudasa⌐i. 'Give me THAT.' (tells which one I want)
Ra⌐itaa o ⌐mi⌐sete kudasai. 'Please show me some LIGHTERS.' (tells what I want to see)
Ta⌐bako o oneg̲ai-sima⌐su. 'I'd like a CIGARETTE.' (tells what I want to have)
Hu⌐rosiki o kaima⌐sita. 'I bought a FUROSHIKI.' (tells what I bought)

----

[1] The subject tells who or what does or is something, and the direct object tells who or what is directly acted upon. Thus, in 'Bill called John,' 'Bill' is the subject and 'John' the direct object; in 'John called Bill,' 'John' is the subject and 'Bill' the direct object.

(c) <u>wa</u>

The particle <u>wa</u> 'as for,' 'in reference to' following a nominal occurs in two kinds of constructions:

(1) It follows the general topic (often one already under discussion) about which something new or significant is about to be stated or asked:[1] X wa 'I am talking about X—listen to what I am about to say'; 'as for X, the following is significant.'

Examples:

Tabako wa a⌐rimase⌐n. 'There AREN'T any cigarettes.' (in answer to the question 'Are there any cigarettes?'; i.e. 'I'm talking about cigarettes: what I want to say is that there AREN'T any.')

Sore wa ta⌐ka⌐i desu yo⌐ 'That one is EXPENSIVE, you know.' (i.e. 'I'm talking about that: what I want to say is that it's EXPENSIVE.')

Kore wa ⌐ra⌐itaa desu. 'This is a LIGHTER.' (i.e. 'I'm talking about this: what I want to say is that it's a LIGHTER.')

(2) <u>Wa</u> also occurs as the particle of comparison following a topic which is being compared:[2] X wa 'X in comparison with others' or 'insofar as we're talking about X.'

Examples:

Ta⌐bako wa arimase⌐n. 'Cigarettes I don't have.'

So⌐re wa taka⌐i desu yo⌐ 'That one (in comparison with others) is expensive, you know.'

Ko⌐re wa ra⌐itaa desu. 'This (in comparison with others) is a lighter.'

Note: Wa NEVER follows an interrogative word (i.e. a word that asks a question: 'what?' 'who?' 'when?' 'where?' etc.) and it NEVER follows the word or phrase that answers an interrogative word in a preceding question.

Now compare the following pairs:

Ma⌐tti ḡa a⌐rimase⌐n. 'There aren't any MATCHES.' (tells what is lacking)

Ma⌐tti wa a⌐rimase⌐n. 'There AREN'T any matches.' (answers the question 'Are there any matches?')

Ko⌐re ḡa aka⌐i desu. 'THIS is red.' (tells which one is red)

Kore wa a⌐ka⌐i desu. 'This is RED.' (tells what color this is)

_____

[1] In this construction, the word after w a regularly begins a new accent phrase. (See Introduction, page xxxv.)

[2] In this construction, the word after <u>wa</u> often does not begin a new accent phrase. (See Introduction, page xxxv.)

Ta⌐bako o kaima⌐sita.   'I bought CIGARETTES.'   (tells what I bought)
Ta⌐bako wa kaima⌐sita.   'Cigarettes I bought.'   (tells what happened to
cigarettes in comparison with other things)

Si⌐ñbuñ o wasurema⌐sita.   'I forgot the NEWSPAPER.'   (tells what I forgot)
Si⌐ñbuñ wa wasurema⌐sita.   'The newspaper I forgot.'   (tells what happened
to the newspaper in comparison with other things)

A phrase ending with <u>wa</u> usually occurs at, or near, the beginning of the
sentence. A phrase ending with subject particle <u>g̃a</u> usually precedes one ending
with <u>o</u>. However, a departure from the usual order changes only the emphasis.

Now study and compare the following examples.

Tanaka-sañ wa ⌐ho⌐ñ o ka⌐ima⌐sita.   'Mr. Tanaka bought a BOOK.'   (tells
what Mr. Tanaka bought)
Tanaka-sañ g̃a ⌐ho⌐ñ o ka⌐ima⌐sita.   'MR. TANAKA bought a BOOK.'
(tells who bought what)
Ho⌐ñ wa Ta⌐naka-sañ g̃a kaima⌐sita.   'MR. TANAKA bought the book.'
(tells who bought the book being talked about)

There are some verbals which may occur with both a <u>wa</u> and a <u>g̃a</u> phrase but
never with an <u>o</u> phrase.   Three such verbals have already been introduced:
wa⌐karima⌐su 'understand' or 'be clear'; a⌐rima⌐su 'be in a place' or 'have';
i⌐rima⌐su 'need' or 'be necessary.' With all such verbals, both the person who
understands (has, needs, etc.) and the thing or person affected are followed by
<u>wa</u> or <u>g̃a</u>, depending on emphasis.   Note the following examples of some of the
possible combinations:

Ta⌐naka-sañ g̃a irima⌐su.   'MR. TANAKA needs [it].'
Pe⌐ñ g̃a irimasu.   'I need a PEN.'
Tanaka-sañ wa ⌐pe⌐ñ g̃a irimasu.   'Mr. Tanaka needs a PEN.'
Pe⌐ñ wa Ta⌐naka-sañ g̃a irima⌐su.   'The pen, MR. TANAKA needs.'
Ko⌐re g̃a wakarimase⌐ñ.   'I don't understand THIS.'
Ko⌐re wa Tanaka-sañ wa wakarima⌐su.   'This (in comparison with others)
Mr. Tanaka (in comparison with others) UNDERSTANDS.'
Tanaka-sañ wa zi⌐biki⌐ g̃a a⌐rimase⌐ñ.   'Mr. Tanaka doesn't have a DIC-
TIONARY.'

G̃a, wa, and o are frequently o m i t t e d, [1] p a r t i c u l a r l y in s h o r t
sentences; the result is a slightly less formal alternant. (Watch the parentheses
in the Basic Dialogues and note where these particles are optional.)

(d) <u>mo</u>

The particle <u>mo</u> following a nominal means 'also,' 'too,' or—with a negative —'/not/ either.' A phrase ending in <u>mo</u> occurs as the subject or object or
topic of a following inflected expression, without particles <u>ga</u>, <u>o</u>, <u>wa</u>.

---

[1] But the <u>wa</u> of comparison is rarely omitted.

Examples:

Ta⌐naka-sañ mo ikima⌐sita.   'Mr. Tanaka went too.'
Ta⌐naka-sañ mo wasurema⌐sita.   'Mr. Tanaka forgot too.' or 'I forgot
Mr. Tanaka, too.'
Ko⌐re mo i⌐i desu.   'This is good, too.'
So⌐re mo so⌐o desu.   'That's right, too.'
Ko⌐re mo wakarimase⌐ñ.   'I don't understand this either.'

(e) <u>to</u>

The particle <u>to</u> 'and' joins nominals (which may be preceded by descriptive
phrases. It does not regularly join verbals or adjectivals.

Examples:

ta⌐bako to ma⌐tti 'cigarettes and matches'
kore to sore 'this and that'
a⌐na⌐ta to Tánaka-sañ 'you and Mr. Tanaka'
ho⌐ñ to zássi to siñbuñ 'a book and a magazine and a newspaper'
o⌐oki⌐i zi⌐biki to ti⌐isa⌐i ⌐ho⌐ñ 'a big dictionary and a small book'

A series of two or more nominals joined by <u>to</u> occurs in the same kinds of
constructions as a nominal alone. Thus:

Ta⌐bako to ma⌐tti o ku⌐dasa⌐i.   'Please give me a cigarette and match.'
Tanaka-sañ to Ya⌐mamoto-sañ de⌐su.   'It's Mr. Tanaka and Mr. Yamamoto.'
Ho⌐ñ to zássi to siñbuñ ḡa arima⌐su.   'There's a book and a magazine
and a newspaper.'

2. <u>a⌐rima⌐su</u> ~ <u>go⌐zaima⌐su</u>

A⌐rima⌐su and go⌐zaima⌐su, meaning 'some THING is located in a place' or
'have,' are verbals of identical lexical meaning, but a⌐rima⌐su is plain and
go⌐zaima⌐su is polite-neutral.[1]

An utterance containing √a⌐rima⌐su may be made more polite by substituting
√go⌐zaima⌐su in its corresponding form. The reverse, however, is not always
true: some utterances containing √go⌐zaima⌐su do not occur with a corresponding form of √a⌐rima⌐su (for example, o⌐hayoo gozaima⌐su).

In general, persons of equal status in the Japanese social structure use the
same politeness and formality level in conversing. Which level they use is determined by the formality of the situation and of the individuals involved as
well as by the closeness of their friendship. In conversations between persons
occupying different positions in the social scale (for example, employer and
employee, customer and salesgirl, etc.), the person of lower position usually

---

[1] Both are formal because of their -<u>ma⌐su</u> endings.

uses a more polite and/or formal level of speech.[1] In general, women use
polite speech more commonly than men; √go⌐zaima˺su, for example, is much
more typical of women's speech than of men's.

It is important to distinguish carefully between the use of nominal + √a⌐ri-
ma˺su and nominal + √de˺su. Note the following contrasts:

Affirmative	Negative
Zi⌐biki˺ (g̃a) arimasu.	Zi⌐biki˺ (g̃a) aʳrimase⁻ñ.
'There's a DICTIONARY.'	'There isn't a DICTIONARY.'
or 'I have a DICTIONARY.'	or 'I don't have a DICTIONARY.'
Zi⌐biki˺ wa arimasu.	Zi⌐biki˺ wa aʳrimase⁻ñ.
'There is a dictionary (in	'There isn't a dictionary (in com-
comparison with other things).'	parison with other things).' or
or 'A dictionary I have.'	'A dictionary I don't have.'
Zi⌐biki˺ desu.	Zi⌐biki˺ zya aʳrimase⁻ñ.
'It's a dictionary.'	'It isn't a dictionary.'

In each column the first two examples express existence or location in a place,
or possession; the last example expresses equivalence or definition.

3. ku⌐dasa˺i and Verbal Gerunds

Ku⌐dasa˺i is the imperative of the verbal ku⌐dasaima˺suᵗ '[someone] gives
me.' Since it is a polite word, the imperative is often translated as 'please give
me' and the -ma˺su form as '[someone] is kind enough to give me.'

In addition to the four inflected forms described in Lesson 1, verbals have
a form ending in -te (or -de). This form will be called the GERUND or, more
simply, the -TE FORM.

	Formal Non-Past	Gerund
'be (inanimate)' or 'have'	a⌐rima˺su	a˺tte
'say'	i⌐ima˺su	itte
'go'	i⌐kima˺su	itte
'need'	i⌐rima˺su	itte
'buy'	ka⌐ima˺su	katte
'wait'	ma⌐tima˺su	ma˺tte
'show'	mi⌐sema˺su	mi˺sete
'do'	si⌐ma˺su	site
'be different'	ti⌐g̃aima˺su	tig̃atte
'understand'	wa⌐karima˺su	waʳka˺tte
'forget'	wa⌐surema˺su	wasurete

---

[1] This, of course, is not necessarily reflected in every part of the conversation but refers to the over-all level.

A verbal in its gerund form + ku⌐dasa⌐i is a polite imperative expression. Ku⌐dasa⌐i regularly loses its accent when the preceding word or phrase is accented. Examples:

mi⌐sema⌐su '[I] show'	mi⌐sete kudasai 'please show'
	[lit. 'please give me showing']
ka⌐ima⌐su '[I] buy'	ka⌐tte kudasa⌐i 'please buy'
ma⌐tima⌐su '[I] wait'	ma⌐tte kudasai 'please wait'
i⌐ima⌐su '[I] say'	i⌐tte kudasa⌐i 'please say'
i⌐kima⌐su '[I] go'	i⌐tte kudasa⌐i 'please go' [1]
si⌐ma⌐su '[I] do'	si⌐te kudasa⌐i 'please do'

The -te form has other uses which will be introduced later.

Ku⌐dasa⌐i may also be preceded by a nominal (+ o): [2] E⌐npitu (o) kudasa⌐i. 'Please give me a pencil.'

O⌐mati-kudasa⌐i, in Basic Sentence 14, is an example of another ku⌐dasa⌐i pattern which will be discussed in a later lesson. It is equivalent to ma⌐tte kudasai except that it is more polite. Ku⌐dasaima⌐se is a formal equivalent of ku⌐dasa⌐i and is used most commonly by women.

4. no 'one(s)'

The no introduced in this lesson [3] is a nominal meaning 'one' or 'ones.' Like its English equivalents, it is used to refer to something or someone whose specific identity is known from the context. Thus, Japanese ya⌐su⌐i no (o) ka⌐ima⌐sita and its English equivalents 'I bought a cheap one' or 'I bought cheap ones' are used when the objects referred to are known.

Unlike the nominals which have occurred previously, no is always preceded by a modifier. An adjectival preceding no is always accented, as it is before √de⌐su: an unaccented adjectival acquires an accent on its pre-final syllable (cf. akai, but a⌐ka⌐i no and a⌐ka⌐i desu).

5.   Fragments

All Japanese sentences which consist of, or end with, a past or non-past or imperative[4] inflected form, with or without one or more sentence particles

---

[1] I⌐tte kudasa⌐i 'please say' and i⌐tte kudasa⌐i 'please go' are distinguished in the spoken language only by context.

[2] See Grammatical Note 1 above.

[3] See Basic Sentences 3, 4, 5, 6, 10, 21, 22, 23, 24.

[4] Or tentative (to be introduced later).

immediately following, are MAJOR SENTENCES.   All other sentences are
MINOR SENTENCES or FRAGMENTS.   Some of the fragments that have ap-
peared are: <u>Koñbañ wa. Tyo⌐tto. Ha⌐i.</u>

In conversational Japanese, a sentence may end in the middle of what would
be a major sentence if a portion of the preceding context were repeated and the
complete meaning is clear to the hearer; such utterances are also fragments.
Examples:

Na⌐ni (o) ka├ima⌐sita ka⌐   'What did you buy?'
Siñbuñ (o). 'A newspaper.' (i. e. S⌐iñbuñ (o) kaima⌐sita. 'I bought a
newspaper.')

Ta├ka⌐i desu ⌐ne⌐e. 'It's expensive, isn't it.'
E⌐e, zu⌐ibuñ. 'Yes, very.' (i. e. E⌐e, zu⌐ibuñ ta├ka⌐i desu. 'Yes, it's
very expensive.')

Ta├naka-sañ wa wakarima⌐sita. A⌐na⌐ta wa? (i.e. A⌐na⌐ta wa wa├karima⌐sita
ka⌐) 'Mr. Takana understood.   How about you?   (i.e. As for you, was
there understanding?)'

Particularly common are fragments ending with <u>g̱a</u> 'but.'   In some cases,
the <u>g̱a</u> implies a specific contrast to be supplied by the listener, as:

Si├nbuñ to zassi o kaima⌐sita ka⌐   'Did you buy a newspaper and a magazine?'
Si├nbuñ wa kaima⌐sita g̱a_   'A newspaper I bought but [I didn't buy a maga-
zine].'

Many times, however, <u>X</u> <u>g̱a</u> is simply a softer, more hesitant, less positive
way of saying <u>X</u>—indicating for example 'so-and-so is the case but. . . is that
all right? <u>or</u> should I do anything about it? <u>or</u> do you want to say something
different? <u>or</u> why do you ask? etc. In contrast with sentence-final <u>yo</u>, which
indicates finality and assurance on the part of the speaker, final <u>g̱a</u> is indirect
and polite. Often, the closest English equivalent of this <u>g̱a</u> is an intonation expressing hesitation.

Examples:

Ma⌐tti o kudasai. 'Please give me a match.'
A⌐rimase⌐ñ g̱a_ 'I haven't any but [do you want me to get some?]'
Ko├re wa irimase⌐ñ. So⌐re o kudasa⌐i. 'I don't want this one. Give me that
one.'
O├nazi de⌐su g̱a_ 'It's the same but [I'll give it to you if you want it].'

Ta├naka-sañ de⌐su ka⌐ 'Are you Mr. Tanaka?'
E⌐e, Ta├naka de⌐su g̱a_ 'Yes, I'm Tanaka but [what would you like? <u>or</u>
why do you ask?]'

DRILLS

A. Substitution Drill

1. Do you have a furoshiki?	Hu⌐rosiki (g̃a) arima⌐su ka⌐
2. Do you have a lighter?	Ra⌐itaa (g̃a) a⌐rima⌐su ka⌐
3. Do you have a match?	Ma⌐tti (g̃a) a⌐rima⌐su ka⌐
4. Do you have a cigarette?	Ta⌐bako (g̃a) arima⌐su ka⌐
5. Do you have an ashtray?	Ha⌐iza⌐ra (g̃a) a⌐rima⌐su ka⌐
6. Do you have a pencil?	E⌐ñpitu (g̃a) arima⌐su ka⌐
7. Do you have a pen?	Pe⌐ñ (g̃a) a⌐rima⌐su ka⌐
8. Do you have a dictionary?	Zi⌐syo (g̃a) a⌐rima⌐su ka⌐

B. Substitution Drill

1. Please give me that furoshiki over there.	A⌐no hurosiki (o) kudasa⌐i.
2. Please give me that lighter.	So⌐no ra⌐itaa (o) kudasai.
3. Please give me those matches over there.	A⌐no ma⌐tti (o) kudasai.
4. Please give me those cigarettes.	So⌐no tabako (o) kudasa⌐i.
5. Please give me that ashtray over there.	A⌐no haiza⌐ra (o) kudasai.
6. Please give me that pencil.	So⌐no eñpitu (o) kudasa⌐i.
7. Please give me that pen over there.	A⌐no pe⌐ñ (o) kudasai.
8. Please give me that dictionary.	So⌐no zi⌐syo (o) kudasai.
9. Please give me that book over there.	A⌐no ho⌐ñ (o) kudasai.
10. Please give me that newspaper.	So⌐no siñbuñ (o) kudasa⌐i.

C. Substitution Drill

1. Please let me see that blue furoshiki.	Sono a⌐o⌐i hurosiki (o) ⌐mi⌐sete kudasai.
2. Please let me see that small dictionary over there.	Ano ti⌐isa⌐i zi⌐biki⌐ (o) ⌐mi⌐sete kudasai.
3. Please let me see that big book.	Sono o⌐oki⌐i ⌐ho⌐ñ (o) ⌐mi⌐sete kudasai.
4. Please let me see that white ashtray over there.	Ano si⌐ro⌐i ha⌐iza⌐ra (o) ⌐mi⌐sete kudasai.
5. Please let me see that new magazine.	Sono a⌐tarasi⌐i zassi (o) ⌐mi⌐sete kudasai.
6. Please let me see that black pen over there.	Ano ku⌐ro⌐i ⌐pe⌐ñ (o) ⌐mi⌐sete kudasai.

7. Please let me see that red   Sono a⌐kai eñpitu (o) mi⌐sete kudasai.
    pencil.
8. Please let me see that old   Ano hu⌐ru⌐i siñbuñ (o) ⌐mi⌐sete kuda-
    newspaper over there.   sai.

D. Substitution Drill

(Make whatever particle changes are necessary.)

1. What did you buy?   Na⌐ni (o) ka⌐ima⌐sita ka⌐
2. What did you do?   Na⌐ni (o) si⌐ma⌐sita ka⌐
3. What did you forget?   Na⌐ni (o) wa⌐surema⌐sita ka⌐
4. What do you need?   Na⌐ni (ḡa) i⌐rima⌐su ka⌐
5. What do you have? or   Na⌐ni (ḡa) a⌐rima⌐su ka⌐
    What is there?
6. What don't you understand?   Na⌐ni (ḡa) wa⌐karimase⌐ñ ka⌐
7. Which one don't you under-   Do⌐re (ḡa) wa⌐karimase⌐ñ ka⌐
    stand?
8. Which one is the same?   Do⌐re (ḡa) o⌐nazi de⌐su ka⌐
9. Which one is no good?   Do⌐re (ḡa) da⌐me⌐ desu ka⌐
10. Which one is a dictionary?   Do⌐re (ḡa) zi⌐biki⌐ desu ka⌐

E. Grammar Drill (based on Grammatical Notes 1 and 4)

    Tutor: Sono a⌐kai ho⌐ñ (o) kudasai.   / a⌐o⌐i/ 'Please give me that red
            book.'
    Student: Sono a⌐o⌐i no mo kudasai.   'Please give me that blue one,
              too.'

1. O⌐oki⌐i zi⌐biki⌐ (o) ka⌐ima⌐sita.   Ti⌐isa⌐i no mo ka⌐ima⌐sita.
    /ti⌐isa⌐i/
2. A⌐kai eñpitu (o) oneḡai-sima⌐su.   Ku⌐ro⌐i no mo oneḡai-simasu.
    /ku⌐ro⌐i/
3. Kono hu⌐ru⌐i ⌐ma⌐tti (wa) da⌐me⌐   Kono a⌐tarasi⌐i no mo da⌐me⌐
    desu. /a⌐tarasi⌐i/   desu.
4. Ya⌐su⌐i hurosiki (o) ka⌐ima⌐sita.   Ta⌐ka⌐i no mo ka⌐ima⌐sita.
    / ta⌐ka⌐i /
5. Sono ku⌐ro⌐i ⌐ho⌐ñ (o) ⌐mi⌐sete   Sono a⌐ka⌐i no mo ⌐mi⌐sete kuda-
    kudasai. /akai/   sai.
6. Kono si⌐ro⌐i hurosiki (wa) ta⌐ka⌐i   Kono ku⌐ro⌐i no mo ta⌐ka⌐i desu.
    desu. /ku⌐ro⌐i /
7. Sono ki⌐iroi haiza⌐ra (o) kudasai.   Sono a⌐o⌐i no mo kudasai.
    / a⌐o⌐i/
8. Tu⌐mara⌐nai ⌐ho⌐ñ (o) ka⌐i-   O⌐mosiro⌐i no mo ka⌐ima⌐sita.
    ma⌐sita. / o⌐mosiro⌐i/

F. Response Drill (based on Grammatical Note 1)[1]

1. Are wa ⌐na⌐n̄ desu ka⌐   /Are wa/ hu⌐rosiki de⌐su.
    /hurosiki/
2. Na⌐ni ḡa i⌐rima⌐su ka⌐   E⌐n̄pitu ḡa irima⌐su.
    /en̄pitu/
3. Na⌐ni o ka⌐ima⌐sita ka⌐   Ha⌐iza⌐ra o ka⌐ima⌐sita.
    /ha⌐iza⌐ra/
4. A⌐tarasi⌐i zassi wa ⌐do⌐re   /A⌐tarasi⌐i zassi wa/ a⌐re de⌐su.
    desu ka⌐   /are/
5. Do⌐re ḡa da⌐me⌐ desu ka⌐   Ko⌐re ḡa dame⌐ desu.
    /kore/
6. Kore wa i⌐ka⌐ḡa desu ka⌐   /Kore wa/ da⌐me⌐ desu.
    /da⌐me⌐/
7. Do⌐re o ka⌐ima⌐sita ka⌐   A⌐o⌐i no o ka⌐ima⌐sita.
    /a⌐o⌐i no/
8. Do⌐no ⌐pe⌐n̄ ḡa da⌐me⌐   A⌐no pe⌐n̄ ḡa da⌐me⌐ desu.
    desu ka⌐   /a⌐no pe⌐n̄/
9. A⌐no pe⌐n̄ wa ⌐do⌐o desu ka⌐   /A⌐no pe⌐n̄ wa/ da⌐me⌐ desu.
    /da⌐me⌐/
10. Do⌐no zi⌐biki⌐ ḡa i⌐rima⌐su   So⌐no zibiki⌐ ḡa irimasu.
    ka⌐   /so⌐no zibiki⌐/

G. Response Drill (based on Grammatical Notes 1 and 2)

1. Zi⌐biki⌐ (ḡa) a⌐rima⌐su ka⌐   E⌐e, /zi⌐biki⌐ (ḡa)/ arimasu.
    /E⌐e./
2. Zi⌐biki⌐ (ḡa) a⌐rima⌐su ka⌐   Iie, /zi⌐biki⌐ (wa)/ a⌐rimase⌐n̄.
    /Iie./
3. Zi⌐biki⌐ desu ka⌐   /Iie./   Iie, zi⌐biki⌐ zya a⌐rimase⌐n̄.
4. Hu⌐rosiki (ḡa) gozaima⌐su   Ha⌐a, /hu⌐rosiki (ḡa)/ gozaima⌐su.
    ka⌐   /Ha⌐a./
5. Hu⌐rosiki (ḡa) gozaima⌐su   Iie, /hu⌐rosiki (wa)/ gozaimase⌐n̄.
    ka⌐   /Iie./
6. Hu⌐rosiki de⌐su ka⌐   /Iie./   Iie, hu⌐rosiki zya arimase⌐n̄.
7. Ha⌐iza⌐ra (ḡa) a⌐rima⌐su   E⌐e, /ha⌐iza⌐ra (ḡa)/ arimasu.
    ka⌐   /E⌐e./
8. Ha⌐iza⌐ra (ḡa) a⌐rima⌐su   Iie, /ha⌐iza⌐ra (wa)/ a⌐rimase⌐n̄.
    ka⌐   /Iie./
9. Ha⌐iza⌐ra desu ka⌐   /Iie./   Iie, ha⌐iza⌐ra zya a⌐rimase⌐n̄.

---

[1] Particles ordinarily designated as optional are not so marked in this exercise because drill on the particles is the purpose of the exercise.

H. Expansion Drill

1. Please show [it to me].   Mi˥sete kudasai.
    Please show [me] a furo-   Hu˺rosiki (o) mi˥sete kudasai.
    shiki.
    Please show [me] that furo-   A˥no hurosiki (o) mi˥sete kudasai.
    shiki.
    Say, please show [me] that   Tyo˥tto, a˥no hurosiki (o) mi˥sete ku-
    furoshiki.   dasai.

2. I need [it].   I˺rima˥su.
    I need a small one.   Ti˺isa˥i no (ḡa) irimasu.
    I need a little smaller one.   Mo˺o suko˥si ti˺isa˥i no (ḡa) iri-
                                               masu.
    I need a little smaller one   Mo˺o suko˥si ti˺isa˥i no (ḡa) i˥ri-
    but [do you have one?]   ma˥su ḡa＿

3. I'd like [it].   O˺neḡai-sima˥su.
    I'd like a red one too.   A˺ka˥i no mo oneḡai-simasu.
    I'd like this red one, too.   Kono a˺ka˥i no mo oneḡai-simasu.
    And I'd like this red one,   Sore kara, kono a˺ka˥i no mo oneḡai-
    too.   simasu.

4. [He] bought [it].   Ka˺ima˥sita.
    [He] bought a dictionary.   Zi˺biki˥ (o) ka˥ima˥sita.
    [He] bought a magazine and   Za˺ssi to zibiki˥ (o) ka˥ima˥sita.
    a dictionary.
    Mr. Tanaka bought a maga-   Tanaka-sañ (wa) za˺ssi to zibiki˥ (o)
    zine and a dictionary.   ka˥ima˥sita.

5. Aren't there any?   A˺rimase˥ñ ka＿
    Aren't there any ashtrays?   Ha˺iza˥ra (wa) a˥rimase˥ñ ka＿
    Aren't there any cheap ash-   Ya˺su˥i ha˥iza˥ra (wa) a˥rimase˥ñ
    trays?   ka＿
    Aren't there any ashtrays   Mo˺o suko˥si ya˺su˥i ha˥iza˥ra (wa)
    that are a little cheaper?   a˥rimase˥ñ ka＿

6. It's a dictionary.   Zi˺biki˥ desu.
    Is it a dictionary?   Zi˺biki˥ desu ka＿
    Is it a new dictionary?   A˺tarasi˥i zi˺biki˥ desu ka＿
    Which one is a new dic-   Do˥re ḡa a˥tarasi˥i zi˥biki˥ desu ka＿
    tionary?

SHORT DIALOGUE PRACTICE

1. Do you have a match?   Ma˥tti (ḡa) a˥rima˥su ka＿
      No, I haven't.   Iie, a˺rimase˥ñ.
    How about a lighter?   Ra˥itaa wa?
      I don't have a lighter   Ra˥itaa mo a˥rimase˥ñ.
      either.

2. Do you have magazines?   Za˺ssi (ḡa) arima˥su ka＿
      No, we haven't.   Iie, a˺rimase˥ñ.

How about papers?	Siñbuñ wa?
Papers we have.	Si⌐ñbuñ wa arima⌐su.

3. Do you have a pencil?   E⌐ñpitu (g̃a) gozaima⌐su ka⌐
   Yes, I have.   Ha⌐a, go⌐zaima⌐su.
   How about a pen?   Pe⌐ñ wa?
   I have a pen, too.   Pe⌐ñ mo gozaimasu.

4. Do you have a cigarette?   Ta⌐bako (g̃a) arima⌐su ka⌐
   Yes, I have.   E⌐e, a⌐rima⌐su.
   How about a match?   Ma⌐tti wa?
   A match I don't have.   Ma⌐tti wa aˡrimase⌐ñ.

5. Did you buy a book?   Ho⌐ñ (o) kaˡima⌐sita ka⌐
   Yes, I did (buy).   E⌐e, ka⌐ima⌐sita.
   How about a magazine?   Zassi wa?
   I bought a magazine, too.   Za⌐ssi mo kaima⌐sita.

6. Did you buy a pen?   Pe⌐ñ (o) kaˡima⌐sita ka⌐
   No, I didn't.   Iie, ka⌐imase⌐ñ desita.
   How about a pencil?   Eñpitu wa?
   I didn't buy a pencil either. E⌐ñpitu mo kaimase⌐ñ desita.

7. Did you buy a paper?   Si⌐ñbuñ (o) kaima⌐sita ka⌐
   Yes, I did.   E⌐e, ka⌐ima⌐sita.
   How about a magazine?   Zassi wa?
   A magazine I didn't buy.   Za⌐ssi wa kaimase⌐ñ desita.

8. Did you buy a book?   Ho⌐ñ (o) kaˡima⌐sita ka⌐
   No, I didn't.   Iie, ka⌐imase⌐ñ desita.
   How about a dictionary?   Zi⌐biki⌐ wa?
   A dictionary I bought.   Zi⌐biki⌐ wa kaˡima⌐sita.

9. Did you buy cigarettes and   Ta⌐bako to ma⌐tti (o) kaˡima⌐sita ka⌐
   matches?
   Cigarettes I bought but   Ta⌐bako wa kaima⌐sita g̃a, ma⌐tti wa
   matches I didn't buy.   ka⌐imase⌐ñ desita.

10. Did you buy a magazine?   Za⌐ssi (o) kaima⌐sita ka⌐
    A magazine I didn't buy but   Za⌐ssi wa kaimase⌐ñ desita g̃a, siñ-
    I bought a paper.   buñ (o) kaima⌐sita.

11. Do you need a pen and pen-   Pe⌐ñ to e⌐ñpitu (g̃a) irimaˡsu ka⌐
    cil?
    A pen I need but a pencil   Pe⌐ñ wa iˡrimaˡsu g̃a, eñpitu wa
    I don't need.   irimase⌐ñ.

12. Do you need a pen?   Pe⌐ñ (g̃a) iˡrimaˡsu ka⌐
    A pen I don't need but I   Pe⌐ñ wa iˡrimase⌐ñ g̃a, e⌐ñpitu (g̃a)
    need a pencil.   irima⌐su.

SUPPLEMENTARY CONVERSATIONS

1. Smith (calling a clerk): Oˤnegai-simaˡsu. Soˤno peˡñ o ˥miᴶsete kudasai.
   Clerk: Iˤrassyaˡi. Doˡno ˥peᴶñ desu ka˻
   Smith: Sono kuˤroˡi no desu.
   Clerk: Doˡozo.
   Smith: Iˡkura desu ka˻
   Clerk: Niˤseñ- eñ deˡsu.
   Smith: Tyoˡtto taˤkaˡi desu ˤneˡe. Moˤo sukoˡsi yaˤsuˡi no wa aˤrimaseˡñ ka˻
   Clerk: Kono aˤkaˡi no wa i˥kaᴶga desu ka. Seˤñ-eñ deˡsu ga˼
   Smith: Soˡo desu ˤneˡė. Sore mo ˤtyoˡtto˼
   Clerk: Aˡa, koˤre wa ikaˡga desu ka˻ Seˤñ nihyakuˡ-eñ desu.
   Smith (trying it out): Aˡa, koˤre wa iˡi ˥peᴶñ desu ˤneˡe. Koˤre o kudasaˡi.
   Clerk: Aˤriˡgatoo gozaimasu. Eˤñpitu mo ikaˡga desu ka˻
   Smith: Eˤñpitu wa irimaseˡñ. (Handing over money) Seˤñ gohyakuˡ- eñ. Haˡi.
   Clerk: Syoˡosyoo o˥mati-kudasaᴶi.

   Clerk (returning with package and change): Oˤmatase-itasimaˡsita. Saˤñ-byakuˡ-eñ desu. Maˤido ariˡgatoo gozaimasu. Maˤta doˡozo.

2. Smith: Tyoˡtto.
   Clerk: Iˤrassyaimaˡse.
   Smith: Are wa ˤnaˡñ desu ka˻
   Clerk: Aˤre deˡsu ka˻ Haˤizaˡra desu.
   Smith: Soˡo desu ka. Kiˤree desu ˤneˡe. Tyoˡtto ˥miᴶsete kudasai.
   Clerk: Kiˤiroˡi no desu ka˻
   Smith: Eˡe.
   Clerk: Doˡozo.
   Smith: Ano aˤkaˡi no mo ˥miᴶsete kudasai.
   Clerk: Kaˤsikomarimaˡsita.
   Smith: Iˡkura desu ka˻
   Clerk: Kiˤiroˡi no wa saˤñbyakuˡ-eñ desu. Aˤkaˡi no wa ˤsaˤñbyaku goˤzyuˡu-eñ desu.
   Smith: Oˤnazi zya arimaseˡñ ˤneˡe.
   Clerk: Haˡa. Kiˤiroˡi no wa ˤtyoˡtto tiˤisaˡi desu.
   Smith: Aˡa, soˤo desu ka. Aˤkaˡi no o ku˥dasaᴶi.
   Clerk: Aˤriˡgatoo gozaimasu.
   Smith: Tyoˡtto ˥maᴶtte kudasai. Kiˤiroˡi no mo onegai-simasu.
   Clerk: Kaˤsikomarimaˡsita. Hoˤka ni naˡni ka?
   Smith: Soˤre dakeˡ desu.
   Clerk: Roˤppyaku gozyuˡu-eñ desu.
   Smith: Señ-eñ. Haˡi.
   Clerk: Syoˡosyoo o˥mati-kudasaimaᴶse.

   Clerk: Oˤmatase-itasimaˡsita. Saˤñbyaku goˤzyuˡu - eñ desu. Doˡo mo a˥riᴶgatoo gozaimasita.

English Equivalents

1. Smith: Would you wait on me? Please show me that pen.
   Clerk: (Welcome.) Which pen do you mean?
   Smith: (It's) that black one.
   Clerk: Here you are.
   Smith: How much is it?
   Clerk: It's ¥2000.
   Smith: It's a little expensive, isn't it. Don't you have a little cheaper one?
   Clerk: How about this red one? It's ¥1000. . . .
   Smith: Hmmm. I'm afraid that one won't do either.
   Clerk: Oh, how about this one? It's ¥1200.
   Smith: Oh, this is a good pen, isn't it. I'll take this one.
   Clerk: Thank you. How about a pencil, too?
   Smith: I don't need any pencils. Here you are. ¥1500.
   Clerk: Just a moment, please.

                         .   .   .

   Clerk: I'm sorry to have kept you waiting. [Your change] is ¥300. Thank you. Please come again.

2. Smith: Say there!
   Clerk: (Welcome.)
   Smith: What are those things?
   Clerk: Those? They're ashtrays.
   Smith: Oh? Aren't they pretty. Let me have a look.
   Clerk: Do you mean a yellow one?
   Smith: Yes.
   Clerk: Here you are.
   Smith: Let me see that red one, too.
   Clerk: Certainly.
   Smith: How much are they?
   Clerk: The yellow one is ¥300. The red one is ¥350.
   Smith: They're not the same, are they.
   Clerk: No (i.e. that's right). The yellow one is a little small[er].
   Smith: Oh? I'll take the red one.
   Clerk: Thank you.
   Smith: Just a minute. I'd like the yellow one, too.
   Clerk: Certainly. Anything else?
   Smith: That's all.
   Clerk: (It's) ¥650.
   Smith: Here you are. ¥1000.
   Clerk: Just a moment, please.

                         .   .   .

   Clerk: I'm sorry to have kept you waiting. [Your change] is ¥350. Thank you very much.

EXERCISES

1. Mr. Smith asks the clerk: The clerk replies:

    a. to show him that big   Which one do you mean?
       book.
    b. if he has any small dic-   I do, but they aren't very good.
       tionaries.
    c. for that.   Here you are.
    d. for cigarettes and   Anything else?
       matches.
    e. how much that red   It's ¥ 350.
       furoshiki is.
    f. if that blue ashtray is   No, it's ¥ 500.
       ¥ 400.

2. Mr. Smith has just entered a stationery store.

    a. The clerk greets Mr. Smith.
    b. Mr. Smith asks if they have any pens.
    c. The clerk answers that they do.
    d. Mr. Smith asks the clerk to show him a black pen.
    e. The clerk shows him one and says that it is a fine pen.
    f. Mr. Smith asks the price.
    g. The clerk answers that it is ¥ 2500.
    h. Mr. Smith remarks that it is very expensive. He asks if they have
       any that are a little cheaper.
    i. The clerk answers that they have, but they aren't black. He suggests
       a blue one. It costs ¥ 1500.
    j. Mr. Smith thinks the blue pen is pretty. He remarks that it isn't very
       expensive. He decides to buy it.
    k. The clerk thanks Mr. Smith and asks if he wants anything else.
    l. Mr. Smith says that that's all he wants, and gives the clerk ¥ 2000.
    m. The clerk asks him to wait a moment. When he returns, he apolo-
       gizes for having kept Mr. Smith waiting and gives him ¥ 500 change.
       He thanks Mr. Smith and invites him to come again.
    n. Mr. Smith says goodbye.

3. Practice the Basic Dialogues with variations and appropriate props.

Lesson 5. Shopping (cont.)

(a)

Smith

more	mo⌐tto
1. Do you have more of these? (Lit. As for these, are there more?)	Kore (wa) ⌐mo⌐tto a⌐rima⌐su ka˩

Clerk

much or many	ta⌐kusa⌐ñ
2. Yes, we have lots of those. (Lit. As for those, there are many.)	Ha⌐a, sore wa ta⌐kusañ gozaima⌐su.

Smith

one unit	hi⌐to⌐-tu
two units	hu⌐ta-tu⌐
three units	mi-⌐ttu⌐
four units	yo-⌐ttu⌐
five units	i⌐tu⌐-tu
six units	mu-⌐ttu⌐
seven units	na⌐na⌐-tu
eight units	ya-⌐ttu⌐
nine units	ko⌐ko⌐no-tu
ten units	to⌐o
eleven units	zyu⌐uiti⌐
twelve units	zyu⌐uni⌐

3. I'd like five.   I⌐tu⌐-tu onegai-simasu.

4. And then give me three of those white ones, too.   Sore kara, sono si⌐ro⌐i no mo mi-⌐ttu kudasa⌐i.

Clerk

I'm sorry but	su⌐mimase⌐ñ ḡa
5. I'm sorry but that is all we have of the white ones. (Lit. As for the white ones, it's just that.)	Su⌐mimase⌐ñ ḡa, si⌐ro⌐i no wa so⌐re dake⌐ desu.

Smith

three units more	mo⌐o mi-ttu⌐
6. Then give me three more of these.	Zya⌐a, kore (o) mo⌐o mi-ttu kudasa⌐i.

57

(b)

Smith

how many units?   i˥kutu or
                                          oikutu +

7. How many of these do you   Kore (wa) ˥i˥kutu aʳrima˥su ka⌐
    have? (Lit. As for these, how
    many are there?)

Clerk

8. We have five (but) . . .   I˥tu˥-tu goʳzaima˥su ḡa⌐

Smith

    just three units   mi-˥ttu dake˥
9. I'd like just three.   Mi-˥ttu dake oneḡai-sima˥su.

    one long, cylindrical unit   i˥p-poñ
    two long, cylindrical units   ni˥-hoñ
    three long, cylindrical units   sa˥ñ-boñ
10. And then give me three of those   Sore kara, sono eñpitu mo ˥sa˥ñ-boñ
    pencils, too.   kudasai.

Clerk

    color   i˥ro˥
    what (kind of) color?   do˥ñna iro
    is good or fine   yorosii /-ku/
11. What color would you like?   Do˥ñna i˥ro˥ ḡa yoʳrosi˥i desu ka⌐
    (Lit. What kind of color is
    good?)

Smith

12. I'd like one red one and two   A˥ka˥i no (o) ˥i˥p-poñ to, a˥o˥i no (o)
    blue ones.   ˥ni˥-hoñ oneḡai-simasu.

(c)

Smith

    paper   ka˥mi˥
    this kind of paper   ko˥ñna kami˥
    one thin, flat unit   i˥ti˥-mai
    two thin, flat units   ni˥-mai
    three thin, flat units   sa˥ñ-mai
13. How much is one sheet of this   Ko˥ñna kami˥ (wa) i˥ti˥-mai ˥i˥kura
    kind of paper?   desu ka⌐

Clerk

14. It's ¥20.   Ni˥zyuu-eñ desu.

Smith

15. Give me two sheets of the red   A˥ka˥i no (o) ʳni˥-mai to, si˥ro˥i no
    and three sheets of the white.   (o) ˥sa˥ñ-mai kudasai.

one bound unit (as, a book, magazine, etc.)	i⌐s-satu⌐
two bound units	ni⌐-satu
three bound units	sa⌐ñ-satu

16. And then I'd like two of these small dictionaries, too.

Sore kara, kono ti⌐isa⌐i zi⌐biki⌐ mo ⌐ni⌐-satu onegai-simasu.

(d)

Tanaka

17. What are you going to buy?

Na⌐ni (o) ka⌐ima⌐su ka⌐

Smith

I <u>or</u> me

watakusi <u>or</u> bo⌐ku (man's word; has unaccented alternant)

18. (Do you mean) me?

Wa⌐takusi de⌐su ka⌐ <u>or</u> Bo⌐ku desu ka⌐

map

ti⌐zu

19. I'm going to buy a map.

Ti⌐zu (o) kaimasu.

(to the clerk)

Tokyo

Tookyoo

map of Tokyo

To⌐okyoo no ti⌐zu

20. Say! Do you have maps of Tokyo?

Tyo⌐tto. To⌐okyoo no ti⌐zu (ga) a⌐rima⌐su ka⌐

Clerk

both big ones and small ones

o⌐oki⌐i no mo ti⌐isa⌐i no mo

21. Yes. We have (both) big ones and small ones (but) . . .

Ha⌐a. O⌐oki⌐i no mo ti⌐isa⌐i no mo go⌐zaima⌐su ga—

Smith

just

tyo⌐tto

22. (Just) let me have a look.

Tyo⌐tto ⌐mi⌐sete kudasai.

. . . . .

23. Oh, this one is fine.

A⌐a, ko⌐re ga i⌐i desu.

24. Give me two.

Ni⌐-mai kudasai.

(e)

Smith

today's newspaper

kyo⌐o no siñbuñ

25. Don't you have today's paper?

Kyo⌐o no siñbuñ (wa) a⌐rimase⌐ñ ka⌐

Clerk

yesterday's newspaper

kinoo no siñbuñ

26. No (i.e. that's right). This is yesterday's paper.

E⌐e, kore wa ki⌐noo no siñbuñ de⌐su.

as for today's (one) or today's (one), comparatively speaking	kyo⌐o no wa
soon or any minute or right away	su⌐g̃u
come	ki⌐ma⌐su

27. Today's (one) will come any   Kyo⌐o no wa ⌐su⌐g̃u ki⌐ma⌐su yo⌣
     minute.

ADDITIONAL PLACE NAMES

Japan	Ni⌐ho⌐n or Ni⌐ppo⌐n	England	Ig̃irisu or Eekoku
Fukuoka	Hu⌐ku⌐oka	London	Ro⌐ndon
Hokkaido	Ho⌐kka⌐idoo	France	Hurañsu
Honshu	Ho⌐ñsyuu	Paris	Pa⌐rii
Kobe	Ko⌐obe	Germany	Do⌐itu
Kyushu	Kyu⌐usyuu	Berlin	Beruriñ
Nara	Na⌐ra	U. S. S. R.	So⌐reñ or So⌐bie⌐to
Nikko	Ni⌐kkoo		
Osaka	Oosaka	Moscow	Mosukuwa
Sapporo	Sapporo	India	I⌐ñdo
Shikoku	Si⌐ko⌐ku	Korea	Tyo⌐ose⌐ñ
Yokohama	Yokohama	China	Tyu⌐ug̃oku
U. S. A.	Amerika or Beekoku	Formosa (Communist China	Ta⌐iwa⌐ñ Tyuukyoo)[1]
New York	Nyu⌐uyo⌐oku		
San Francisco	Sa⌐ñhurañsi⌐suko		
Washington	Wa⌐si⌐ñton		

NOTES ON THE BASIC DIALOGUES

8. 'We have five but—how many do you want? or is that enough? or did you want more than that? or I hope that is enough (etc.)'

11. Yorosii resembles i⌐i in meaning and general usage, but is a more polite word. It occurs in the negative only under special circumstances.

18. Bo⌐ku occurs in men's speech and is less polite than watakusi, which is used by both men and women. Watakusi is often contracted to watasi by men and women, and to atasi by women.

21. 'We have big ones and small ones but—which kind did you want?'

22. Tyo⌐tto 'just' is not interchangeable with su⌐ko⌐si.

27. The gerund of ki⌐ma⌐su is ki⌐te⌐.

---

[1] This name has become obsolete.

GRAMMATICAL NOTES

1. Numerals: Series II

The numerals of Series I (i⌐ti⌐, ni⌐, sañ, etc.) were introduced in Lesson 3. The second numeral series, of native Japanese origin, is introduced in this lesson:

hi⌐to⌐-	'1'	mu-	'6'
huta-	'2'	na⌐na⌐-	'7'
mi-	'3'	ya-	'8'
yo-	'4'	ko⌐ko⌐no-	'9'
i⌐tu⌐-	'5'	to- or to⌐o-	'10'

This second series goes only as far as 10; beyond 10, Series I (zyu⌐uiti⌐, zyu⌐uni⌐, etc.) is used.

The numerals of Series I occur both as independent words (for example, in mathematics) and in number compounds (for example, combined with -eñ to count yen); but the numerals of Series II usually occur only in number compounds. Combined with -/t/tu 'unit,'[1] the numerals of Series II are used to count unit objects which are inanimate (see the list preceding Basic Sentence 3 in this lesson; note that in to⌐o '10 units,' the longer alternant for 10 occurs, without the -/t/tu which occurs in the equivalents of '1 unit' through '9 units'). To count the number of units beyond 10, the numerals of Series I are used independently.

Thus, '1' in reply to the question 'What is 3 minus 2?' is i⌐ti⌐, but '1' in reply to the question 'How many chairs do you need?' is hi⌐to⌐-tu; '11' in reply to both of the questions 'What is 21 minus 10?' and 'How many chairs do you need?' is zyu⌐uiti⌐.

The question word corresponding to the hi⌐to⌐-tu, hu⌐ta-tu⌐ series is i⌐kutu (polite, oikutu) 'how many units?' Oikutu is used more commonly, but not exclusively, by women.

Single units of some objects are always counted with the hi⌐to⌐-tu, hu⌐ta-tu⌐ series; some things are never counted with it (i.e. they use a specialized counter); and units of some objects are counted either with the hi⌐to⌐-tu, hu⌐ta-tu⌐ series or with a specialized counter (with some variation among individual speakers).[2]

---

[1] They also enter into other combinations, some of which will be introduced later. Examples: hi⌐to⌐-bañ '1 night'; hi⌐to⌐-kumi '1 set'; hi⌐to⌐-asi '1 pace.'

[2] In the last case there may be a difference of meaning, depending on whether the hi⌐to⌐-tu, hu⌐ta-tu⌐ series or a specialized counter is used. For example, in reference to tabako, i⌐p-poñ, ni⌐-hoñ, etc. refer only to individual cigarettes, but hi⌐to⌐-tu, hu⌐ta-tu⌐ etc. may also be used to count packages of cigarettes.

2. Counters: -hon̄, -mai, -satu

Single units of objects which are thin and flat in shape—sheets, blankets, furoshiki, handkerchiefs, plates, boards, rugs, leaves, etc.—are counted with the counter -mai, which combines with numerals of Series I. Numbers from 1 to 10 are:

i⌈ti⌉-mai	'1 thin, flat unit'	ro⌈ku⌉-mai	'6 thin, flat units'
ni⌉-mai	'2 thin, flat units'	na⌈na⌉-mai or	
sa⌉n̄-mai	'3 thin, flat units'	si⌈ti⌉-mai	'7 thin, flat units'
yo⌉n̄-mai or		ha⌈ti⌉-mai	'8 thin, flat units'
yo-mai	'4 thin, flat units'	kyu⌉u-mai	'9 thin, flat units'
go-mai	'5 thin, flat units'	zyu⌉u-mai	'10 thin, flat units'

Question word: na⌉n̄-mai 'how many thin, flat units?'

Single units of objects which are long and cylindrical in shape—pens, pencils, cigarettes, bottles, arms, legs, trees, poles, cut flowers, etc.—are counted with the counter -hon̄, which combines with numerals of Series I. Some combinations of numeral + counter in this series undergo assimilation: namely, '1,' '3,' '6,' '8,' '10.' The numbers from one to ten are:

i⌉p-pon̄	'1 long, cylindrical unit'
ni⌉-hon̄	'2 long, cylindrical units'
sa⌉n̄-bon̄	'3 long, cylindrical units'
yo⌉n̄-hon̄ or si⌉-hon̄	'4 long, cylindrical units'
go-hon̄	'5 long, cylindrical units'
ro⌉p-pon̄	'6 long, cylindrical units'
na⌈na⌉-hon̄ or si⌈ti⌉-hon̄	'7 long, cylindrical units'
ha⌉p-pon̄ or ha⌈ti⌉-hon̄	'8 long, cylindrical units'
kyu⌉u-hon̄	'9 long, cylindrical units'
zi⌉p-pon̄ or zyu⌉p-pon̄	'10 long, cylindrical units'

Question word: na⌉n̄-bon̄ 'how many long, cylindrical units?'

Single units of bound objects—books, magazines, albums, etc.—are counted with the counter -satu, which combines with numerals of Series I. Some combinations of numeral + counter in this series undergo assimilation: namely, '1,' '8,' '10.' The numbers from one to ten are:

i⌈s-satu⌉	'1 bound unit'	ro⌈ku-satu⌉	'6 bound units'
ni⌉-satu	'2 bound units'	na⌈na⌉-satu or	
sa⌉n̄-satu	'3 bound units'	si⌈ti-satu⌉	'7 bound units'
yo⌉n̄-satu	'4 bound units'	ha⌈s-satu⌉	'8 bound units'
go-⌈satu⌉	'5 bound units'	kyu⌉u-satu	'9 bound units'
		zi⌈s-satu⌉ or	
		zyu⌈s-satu⌉	'10 bound units'

Question word: na⌉n̄-satu 'how many bound units?'

Numbers are nominals and accordingly occur in the same kinds of patterns as nominals. They occur frequently in the nominal pattern described in the following note.

3. Extent

A Japanese word or phrase which asks or answers the question 'how many?' 'how much?' 'how far?' or 'how long?' with reference to an inflected expression, regularly occurs without a following particle.[1] Compare:

Peˡñ o kudasai. 'Please give me a pen.' (tells WHAT I want)
Suˡkoˡsi kudasai. 'Please give me a little (or a few).' (tells HOW MUCH or HOW MANY I want)
Huˡrosiki ḡa arimaˡsu. 'I have a furoshiki.' (tells WHAT I have)
Iˡtiˡ-mai arimasu. 'I have one (thin, flat object).' (tells HOW MANY I have)

Hurosiki (ḡa) iˡtiˡ-mai arimasu. 'I have one furoshiki.' (lit. 'There are furoshiki to the extent of one thin, flat unit.') contains the information of the last two sentences. In Japanese, the WHAT occurs as the subject or object or topic followed by particle ḡa, o, or wa, and the HOW MANY or HOW MUCH occurs as an extent expression, without a following particle.

When the WHAT is apparent from the context, it is regularly omitted. For example, in Zyuˡu-eñ kudasaˡi. 'Please give me ¥ 10.' zyuu-eñ tells HOW MUCH I want; the WHAT (i.e. money) is apparent from the counter and is not explicitly stated.

Examples:

Kore (o) ˡmoˡtto oneḡai-simasu. 'I'd like more of this.' (Lit. 'I'd like this to a greater extent.')
Sore (o) ˡzeˡñbu siˡmaˡsita. 'I did all of that.' (Lit. 'I did that to the extent of the whole thing.')
Haˡizaˡra (ḡa) taˡkusañ irimaˡsu. 'I need lots of ashtrays.' (Lit. 'Ashtrays are needed to the extent of many.')
Eñpitu (ḡa) ˡnaˡñ-boñ aˡrimaˡsu ka⌐ 'How many pencils are there? ' (Lit. 'There are pencils to the extent of how many long, cylindrical units?')
Haˡizaˡra (o) mi-ˡttu kaimaˡsita. 'I bought three ashtrays.' (Lit. 'I bought ashtrays to the extent of three units.')

The hiˡtoˡ-tu, huˡta-tuˡ series is regularly used to count all the many inanimate unit objects for which there are no specialized counters. It is also frequently used alternatively with specialized counters for counting inanimate unit objects which do have specialized counters. This series, then, is safer for the beginning student to use until his stock of specialized counters is enlarged. For example, if a student didn't know the counter -satu and said Hoˡñ o huˡta-tu kaimaˡsita 'I bought two books,' a Japanese would have no difficulty understanding him, whereas if he substituted the mathematical niˡ without a counter, most Japanese listeners would be baffled.

---

[1] Irrespective of formality. This is different from the optional omission of ḡa, wa, and o in conversation.

The order of the WHAT preceding the quantity expression in the above examples is the usual one. The reverse order also exists, however, with no difference in basic structure but only in emphasis. Thus: Ta⌐kusa⌐n ha⌐iza⁻ra g̃a irimasu. 'I need LOTS of ashtrays.'

The particle to 'and' may occur with extent patterns. A common pattern consists of—

> nominal being counted or measured (+ particle wa, g̃a, or o)
> + extent expression
> + to,
> + nominal being counted or measured (+ particle wa, g̃a, or o)
> + extent expression

Thus:

> Ka⌐mi⌐ (o) ⌐ni⁻-mai to, eñpitu (o) ⌐sa⌐ñ-boñ ka⌐ima⁻sita. 'I bought two sheets of paper and three pencils.'

See also Basic Sentences 12 and 15.

4. Particle no

The particle no occurs between nominals with the meaning 'the preceding nominal describes the following nominal'—that is to say, A no B is an A kind of B. For example:

To⌐okyoo no ti⌐zu	'Tokyo map(s)' or 'map(s) of Tokyo'
Amerika no tabako	'American cigarettes' or 'cigarettes in America'
asita no siñbuñ	'tomorrow's newspaper(s)' or 'newspaper(s) tomorrow'
Tookyoo no siñbuñ	'Tokyo newspaper(s)' or 'Tokyo's newspaper(s)' or 'newspapers in Tokyo'
Tookyoo no Tanaka-sañ	'Mr. Tanaka from Tokyo' or 'Mr. Tanaka in Tokyo'
a⌐na⌐ta no zibiki	'your dictionary'
wa⌐takusi no ho⌐ñ	'my book'

There is no single word in English which is exactly equivalent to no. Sometimes (by no means always) it corresponds to English 'of.' A nominal + no sequence may indicate possession, location, origin, or other things; but in every instance, it is descriptive.

An adjectival or demonstrative describing a nominal has no connecting particle; but a nominal describing a nominal is regularly followed by no. Compare:

> a⌐tarasi⌐i zassi 'new magazine'
> kono zassi 'this magazine'
> Nihoñ no zassi 'Japanese magazine'

When a nominal has more than one describing word or phrase, a nominal + <u>no</u> sequence may be separated from the nominal it describes by another descriptive word or phrase.[1] Thus:

Tookyoo no oˈokiˈi ˈtiˈzu 'a big map of Tokyo'
   (tiˈzu described by <u>Tookyoo</u> and <u>oˈokiˈi</u>)

Tanaka-sañ no soˈno hoˈñ 'that book of Mr. Tanaka's'
   (hoˈñ described by <u>Tanaka-sañ</u> and <u>sono</u>)

Tanaka-sañ no Toˈokyoo no tiˈzu 'Mr. Tanaka's map of Tokyo'
   (tiˈzu described by <u>Tanaka-sañ</u> and <u>Tookyoo</u>)

It is also possible for the nominal of a nominal + <u>no</u> sequence to be described:[2]

aˈtarasiˈi zaˌssi no kami   'the paper in new magazines'
                                    (kaˈmiˈ described by <u>zassi</u>,
                                       which is described by <u>aˈtarasiˈi</u>)

soˈno zibˌikiˈ no kami   'the paper in that dictionary'
                                    (kaˈmiˈ described by <u>ziˈbikiˈ</u>,
                                       which is described by <u>sono</u>)

Niˈhoñ no hoˈñ no kami[3]   'the paper in Japanese books'
                                    (kaˈmiˈ described by <u>hoˈñ</u>,
                                       which is described by <u>Niˈhoñ</u>)

In some special cases, a nominal describes another nominal directly without an intervening <u>no</u> (for example: moˈo sukoˈsi 'a little more'). Such combinations should be memorized as they occur.

When particle <u>no</u> immediately precedes the nominal <u>no</u> 'one(s),' the two <u>no</u> are contracted to a single <u>no</u>: that is, <u>x no no</u> is contracted to <u>x no</u>[4] (with <u>no</u> accented if <u>x</u> is unaccented). The contraction occurs in the same kinds of patterns as nominals. Compare:

---

[1] In such cases, the two descriptive words or phrases are usually not in the same accent phrase.

[2] In such cases, the descriptive words or phrases are usually in the same accent phrase.

[3] With different intonation, these three phrases could mean 'new paper in (or for) magazines,' 'that paper in (or for) dictionaries,' 'Japanese paper in (or for) books.' With these meanings, the final nominal in each case has two modifiers (cf. the examples in the preceding group above).

[4] <u>x no</u> (in which <u>no</u> = particle) and <u>x no</u> (the contraction of <u>x no no</u>) are distinguished by context: the former must be followed by a nominal which it describes.

Ta⌐naka-sañ de⌐su. 'It's Mr. Tanaka.'
Ta⌐naka-sañ no ho⌐ñ desu. 'It's Mr. Tanaka's book.'
Ta⌐naka-sañ no⌐ desu. 'It's Mr. Tanaka's (one).'
  (Tanaka-sañ no 'Mr. Tanaka's' + no 'one' = Ta⌐naka-sañ no⌐ 'one belonging to Mr. Tanaka')

Tookyoo wa o⌐oki⌐i desu. 'Tokyo is big.'
To⌐okyoo no ti⌐zu wa o⌐oki⌐i desu. 'The map of Tokyo is big.'
To⌐okyoo no⌐ wa o⌐oki⌐i desu. 'The one of Tokyo is big.'
  (Tookyoo no 'of Tokyo' + no 'one' = To⌐okyoo no⌐ 'the one of Tokyo')

A⌐tarasi⌐i To⌐okyoo no ti⌐zu wa o⌐oki⌐i desu. 'The new map of Tokyo is big.'
A⌐tarasi⌐i To⌐okyoo no⌐ wa o⌐oki⌐i desu. 'The new one of Tokyo is big.' (No 'one' modified by a⌐tarasi⌐i and by Tookyoo no, with no + no contracted to a single no)

5. koñna, soñna, añna, do⌐ñna

Koñna 'this kind (of),' soñna and añna 'that kind (of),' and do⌐ñna 'what kind (of)?' modify nominals directly, without an intervening particle. The nominals may or may not be preceded by other descriptive words or phrases. The spatial and relational meanings of this series are parallel to those of the kore and kono series.

Examples:

koñna eñpitu 'this kind of pencil'
so⌐ñna ti⌐zu 'that kind of map'
a⌐ñna waru⌐i ⌐ho⌐ñ 'a bad book like that'
do⌐ñna a⌐tarasi⌐i ⌐pe⌐ñ 'what kind of new pen?'

The Japanese equivalent of 'what color?' is do⌐ñna iro (lit. 'what kind of color?') or the compound word naniiro.

6. moo ~ mo⌐tto

Mo⌐tto means 'more.' It occurs as an extent expression with verbals (mo⌐tto ka⌐ima⌐sita 'I bought more'), adjectivals (mo⌐tto ⌐i⌐i 'it's better'), and a nominal + √de⌐su (mo⌐tto ⌐ki⌐ree desu 'it's prettier').

Moo means 'more' IF FOLLOWED IMMEDIATELY WITHIN THE SAME ACCENT PHRASE BY A NUMBER OR INDEFINITE QUANTITY EXPRESSION.[1]

---

[1] Ta⌐kusa⌐ñ 'many' or 'much' does not occur in this pattern.

Examples:

> moo iti-do 'one time more'
> mo⌐o iti⌐-mai 'one thin, flat unit more'
> mo⌐o hyaku⌐-eñ ' ¥ 100 more'
> mo⌐o suko⌐si 'a little more'

7. dake

A nominal followed by dake 'just,' 'only,' 'no more than' may occur as an extent expression without a following particle.

Examples:

> Ta⌐naka-sañ dake ikima⌐sita. 'Just Mr. Tanaka went.'
> Su⌐ko⌐si dake onegai-simasu. 'I'd like just a little.'
> O⌐mosiro⌐i zassi wa ko⌐re dake⌐ desu.[1] 'This is the only interesting magazine.' (Lit. 'As for interesting magazines, it's just this.')

8. ── mo ── mo

x mo y mo, in which x and y are subject or object nominals (with or without preceding descriptive expressions), means 'both x and y' or 'x AND y.' With a negative, it means 'neither x nor y,' 'not x OR y.'

Examples:

> Pe⌐ñ mo e⌐ñpitu mo arima⌐su. 'There are pens AND pencils.'
> Ti⌐isa⌐i ⌐ti⌐zu mo o⌐oki⌐i ⌐ti⌐zu mo ku⌐dasa⌐i. 'Give me the small map AND the big map.'
> A⌐na⌐ta no mo Ta⌐naka-sañ no⌐ mo onegai-simasu. 'I'd like both yours (lit. your one) and Mr. Tanaka's (one).'
> Pe⌐ñ mo e⌐ñpitu mo arimase⌐ñ. 'I don't have a pen OR a pencil.'

DRILLS

A. Substitution Drill

1. I'd like one of those.   Sore (o) hi⌐to⌐-tu onegai-simasu.
2. I'd like two of those (thin,   Sore (o) ⌐ni⌐-mai onegai-simasu.
   flat objects).
3. I'd like three of those (bound   Sore (o) ⌐sa⌐ñ-satu onegai-simasu.
   objects).
4. I'd like four of those (long,   Sore (o) ⌐yo⌐ñ-hoñ onegai-simasu.
   cylindrical objects).

---

[1] Dake is regularly accented (da⌐ke⌐) in its occurrences before √desu.

5. I'd like more of that.   Sore (o) ⌐mo̊tto onegai-simasu.
6. I'd like a little more of that.   Sore (o) mo⌐o sukȯsi onegai-simasu.
7. I'd like one more of those.   Sore (o) mo⌐o hito⌐-tu onegai-simasu.
8. I'd like all of that.   Sore (o) ⌐ze⌐ñbu onegai-simasu.
9. I'd like just a little of that.   Sore (o) su⌐ko⌐si dake onegai-simasu.
10. I'd like ten of those.   Sore (o) to⌐o onegai-sima⌐su.

B. Substitution Drill

1. I bought lots of cigarettes.   Tabako (o) ta⌐kusañ kaima⌐sita.
2. I bought one ashtray.   Ha⌐iza⌐ra (o) hi⌐to⌐-tu ka⌐ima⌐sita.
3. I bought three maps.   Ti⌐zu (o) ⌐sa⌐n-mai ka⌐ima⌐sita.
4. I bought a little paper.   Ka⌐mi⌐ (o) su⌐ko⌐si ka⌐ima⌐sita.
5. I bought ten pencils.   Eñpitu (o) ⌐zyu⌐p-poñ ka⌐ima⌐sita.
6. I bought two dictionaries.   Zi⌐biki⌐ (o) ⌐ni⌐-satu ka⌐ima⌐sita.
7. I bought three furoshiki.   Hurosiki (o) ⌐sa⌐ñ-mai ka⌐ima⌐sita.
8. I bought one pen.   Pe⌐ñ (o) ⌐i⌐p-poñ ka⌐ima⌐sita.
9. I bought one book.   Ho⌐ñ (o) i⌐s-satu kaima⌐sita.
10. I bought five sheets of paper.   Ka⌐mi⌐ (o) go-⌐mai kaima⌐sita.

C. Substitution Drill

1. I have both a newspaper and   Si⌐ñbuñ mo zassi mo arima⌐su.
    a magazine. [1]
2. I have neither a newspaper   Si⌐ñbuñ mo zassi mo arimase⌐ñ.
    nor a magazine.
3. I bought both a newspaper   Si⌐ñbuñ mo zassi mo kaima⌐sita.
    and a magazine.
4. I forgot both the newspaper   Si⌐ñbuñ mo zassi mo wasurema⌐sita.
    and the magazine.
5. I have both a newspaper and   Si⌐ñbuñ mo zassi mo gozaima⌐su.
    a magazine.
6. I have neither a newspaper   Si⌐ñbuñ mo zassi mo gozaimase⌐ñ.
    nor a magazine.
7. I'd like both a newspaper   Si⌐ñbuñ mo zassi mo onegai-sima⌐su.
    and a magazine.
8. Please give me both a news-   Si⌐ñbuñ mo zassi mo kudasa⌐i.
    paper and a magazine.
9. Please show me both the   Si⌐ñbuñ mo zassi mo mi⌐sete kudasai.
    newspaper and the magazine.

D. Substitution Drill

1. That's all there are of ash-   Ha⌐iza⌐ra wa so⌐re dake⌐ desu.
    trays.

---

[1] In any given situation, the use of 'a' or 'the' in the English equivalents would be determined by the context in which the Japanese sentence occurred.

2. That's all there are of dictionaries.　Zi⌐biki⌐ wa so⌐re dake⌐ desu.

3. That's all there are of this kind (of one).　Ko⌐nna no⌐ wa so⌐re dake⌐ desu.

4. That's all there are of new ones.　A⌐tarasi⌐i no wa so⌐re dake⌐ desu.

5. That's all there are of good ones.　I⌐i no wa so⌐re dake⌐ desu.

6. That's all there are of red ones.　A⌐ka⌐i no wa so⌐re dake⌐ desu.

7. That's all there are of maps of America.　A⌐merika no ti⌐zu wa so⌐re dake⌐ desu.

8. That's all there are of today's papers.　Kyo⌐o no siñbuñ wa so⌐re dake⌐ desu.

9. That's all there are of yesterday's (ones).　Ki⌐no⌐o no wa so⌐re dake⌐ desu.

10. That's all there are of English ones.　I⌐girisu no⌐ wa so⌐re dake⌐ desu.

E. Substitution Drill

1. What (kind of) color would you like? (Lit. What kind of color is good?)　Do⌐nna i⌐ro⌐ ḡa yo⌐rosi⌐i desu ka⌐

2. Which one would you like?　Do⌐re ḡa yo⌐rosi⌐i desu ka⌐

3. What would you like?　Na⌐ni ḡa yo⌐rosi⌐i desu ka⌐

4. Which map would you like?　Do⌐no ⌐ti⌐zu ḡa yo⌐rosi⌐i desu ka⌐

5. What kind of map would you like?　Do⌐nna ⌐ti⌐zu ḡa yo⌐rosi⌐i desu ka⌐

6. Would you like this kind of paper?　Ko⌐nna kami⌐ ḡa yo⌐rosi⌐i desu ka⌐

7. Would you like that kind of magazine?　So⌐nna zassi ḡa yorosi⌐i desu ka⌐

8. Would you like that map?　A⌐no ti⌐zu ḡa yo⌐rosi⌐i desu ka⌐

F. Substitution Drill (based on Grammatical Note 4)

(Insert the substitution item in the model sentence as a modifier of pe⌐ñ with or without a following particle as required.)

1. Please show me that pen.　So⌐no pe⌐ñ (o) ⌐mi⌐sete kudasai.

2. Please show me your pen.　A⌐na⌐ta no ⌐pe⌐ñ (o) ⌐mi⌐sete kudasai.

3. Please show me a good pen.　I⌐i ⌐pe⌐ñ (o) ⌐mi⌐sete kudasai.

4. Please show me this kind of pen.　Ko⌐nna pe⌐ñ (o) ⌐mi⌐sete kudasai.

5. Please show me a black pen.　Ku⌐ro⌐i ⌐pe⌐ñ (o) ⌐mi⌐sete kudasai.

6. Please show me an American pen.　A⌐merika no pe⌐ñ (o) ⌐mi⌐sete kudasai.

7. Please show me Mr. Tanaka's pen.　Ta⌐naka-sañ no pe⌐ñ (o) ⌐mi⌐sete kudasai.

8. Please show me that pen over there.　A⌐no pe⌐ñ (o) ⌐mi⌐sete kudasai.

9. Please show me a blue pen.   Aˡoˡi ˥peˈñ (o) ˥miˈsete kudasai.
10. Please show me a Japanese   Niˡhoñ no peˈñ (o) ˥miˈsete kudasai.
    pen.

G. Grammar Drill (based on Grammatical Note 4)

   Tutor: Toˡokyoo no tiˈzu desu. 'It's a map of Tokyo.'
   Student: Toˡokyoo noˈ desu. 'It's one of Tokyo.'

1. Siˡñbuñ no kamiˈ desu ka⏘   Siˡñbuñ noˈ desu ka⏘
2. Oˡokiˈi ˥tiˈzu (o) kaˡimaˈsi-   Oˡokiˈi no (o) kaˡimaˈsita.
   ta.
3. Taˡnaka-sañ no raˈitaa desu   Taˡnaka-sañ noˈ desu ka⏘
   ka⏘
4. Aˡnaˈta no ˥hoˈñ desu ka⏘   Aˡnaˈta no desu ka⏘
5. Kyoˈo no siñbuñ (wa) ˡsuˈḡu   Kyoˈo no (wa) ˡsuˈḡu kimasu.
   kimasu.
6. Aˡmerika no peˈñ (o) ˥miˈ-   Aˡmerika noˈ (o) ˥miˈsete kudasai.
   sete kudasai.
7. Waˡtakusi no siñbuñ deˈsu   Waˡtakusi noˈ desu yo⏘
   yo⏘
8. Aˡkai eñpitu (o) oneḡai-   Aˡkaˈi no (o) oneḡai-simasu.
   simaˈsu.

H. Expansion Drill

1. I'd like [it].   Oˡneḡai-simaˈsu.
   I'd like three.   Mi-ˈttu oneḡai-simaˈsu.
   I'd like three white ones,   Siˡroˈi no mo mi-ˈttu oneḡai-simaˈsu.
   too.
   I'd like three of those white   Sono siˡroˈi no mo mi-ˈttu oneḡai-si-
   ones, too.   maˈsu.

2. I bought [it].   Kaˡimaˈsita.
   I bought two (long cylin-   Niˈ-hoñ kaˡimaˈsita.
   drical units).
   I bought two pencils.   Eñpitu (o) ˡniˈ-hoñ kaˡimaˈsita.
   I bought one pen and two   Peˈñ (o) ˥iˈp-poñ to, eñpitu (o) ˡniˈ-
   pencils.   hoñ kaˡimaˈsita.

3. How much is [it]?   Iˈkura desu ka⏘
   How much is one (thin, flat   Iˡtiˈ-mai ˡiˈkura desu ka⏘
   unit)?
   How much is one sheet of   Kaˡmiˈ (wa) iˡtiˈ-mai ˡiˈkura desu ka⏘
   paper?
   How much is one sheet of   Koˡñna kamiˈ (wa) iˡtiˈ-mai ˡiˈkura
   this kind of paper?   desu ka⏘

4. Do you have [any]?   Goˡzaimaˈsu ka⏘
   Do you have maps too?   Tiˈzu mo goˡzaimaˈsu ka⏘

Do you have maps of
America too?

A⌐merika no ti˥zu mo go╘zaima˦su
ka⌟

Do you have maps of Eng-
land AND maps of Amer-
ica?

I⌐g̃irisu no ti˥zu mo A⌐merika no ti˥-
zu mo go╘zaima˦su ka⌟

5. It's a dictionary.

Zi⌐biki˥ desu.

It's a new dictionary.

A⌐tarasi˥i zi╘biki˦ desu.

It's my new dictionary.

Bo˥ku no a⌐tarasi˥i zi╘biki˦ desu.

This is my new dictionary.

Kore wa ⌐bo˥ku no a⌐tarasi˥i zi╘biki˦
desu.

6. I don't want [it]!

I⌐rimase˥n̄ yo⌟

I don't want any books!

Ho˥n̄ wa i⌐rimase˥n̄ yo⌟

I don't want any dull books!

Tu⌐mara˥nai ╘ho˦n̄ wa i⌐rimase˥n̄
yo⌟

I don't want any dull books
like that!

So⌐n̄na tumara˥nai ╘ho˦n̄ wa i⌐rima-
se˥n̄ yo⌟

SUPPLEMENTARY CONVERSATIONS

1. Smith: Sore o to⌐o kudasa˥i.
   Clerk: To˥o desu ka⌟ Ha˥i.
   Smith: A˥a, tyo˥tto ╘ma˦tte kudasai. Zyu⌐uni oneg̃ai-sima˥su.
   Clerk: Mo⌐o huta-tu˥ desu ka⌟
   Smith: E˥e, so˥o desu.
   Clerk: Ka⌐sikomarima˥sita. A⌐ri˥g̃atoo gozaimasu.

2. Smith: Sono a⌐o˥i ha╘iza˦ra o mu-⌐ttu kudasa˥i.
   Clerk: Su⌐mimase˥n̄ g̃a, kore wa i⌐tu˥-tu da⌐ke˥ desu g̃a⌐
   Smith: So˥o desu ka⌐ Ano ki⌐iro˥i no wa?
   Clerk: A⌐re mo itu˥-tu da╘ke˦ desu. Do˥o mo su╘mimase˦n̄.

English Equivalents

1. Smith: Give me ten of those.
   Clerk: Ten? All right.
   Smith: Oh, wait a minute. I'd like twelve.
   Clerk: Two more?
   Smith: Yes, that's right.
   Clerk: Certainly. Thank you.

2. Smith: Give me six of those blue ashtrays.
   Clerk: I'm sorry but there are only five of these (lit. as for these, it's just
   five). . .
   Smith: Oh? How about those yellow ones?
   Clerk: There are (lit. It is) just five of those, too. I'm very sorry.

EXERCISES

1. Ask for each of the following:

    a. one cigarette
    b. two of those dictionaries
    c. three red pencils
    d. ten sheets of this kind of white paper
    e. five of those small ashtrays
    f. one of those magazines
    g. two of these blue furoshiki
    h. a few of these
    i. all of that
    j. more of those
    k. a little more of that
    l. one more of those (i.e. ashtrays)
    m. one more of those (i.e. pens)
    n. one more of those (i.e. furoshiki)
    o. one more of those (i.e. books)
    p. one sheet of white paper and two sheets of blue paper
    q. two red pencils and three black ones

2. Practice the Basic Dialogues with variations and appropriate props.

Lesson 6. Locating People and Things

BASIC DIALOGUES: FOR MEMORIZATION

(a)

Tanaka

that place or there	soko
embassy	ta⌐isi⌐kañ
American Embassy	A⌐merika-taisi⌐kañ
1. Is that (place) the American Embassy?	Soko (wa) A⌐merika-taisi⌐kañ desu ka⌐

Smith

consulate	ryo⌐ozi⌐kañ
2. No, it's the consulate.	Iie, ryo⌐ozi⌐kañ desu yo⌐

Tanaka

what place? or where?	do⌐ko
3. Where's the embassy?	Ta⌐isi⌐kañ wa ⌐do⌐ko desu ka⌐

Smith

in Tokyo	Tookyoo ni
4. It's in Tokyo.	To⌐okyoo ni arima⌐su.
this place or here	koko
as for in this place or in this place, comparatively speaking	ko⌐ko ni⌐ wa
5. There isn't [one] here.	Ko⌐ko ni⌐ wa a⌐rimase⌐ñ.

(b)

Smith (pointing)

station	e⌐ki
Tokyo Station	To⌐okyo⌐o-eki
this one (of two) or this way or hereabouts or here	kotira
side or direction or alternative	ho⌐o
this side or this direction	ko⌐tira no ho⌐o
6. Is Tokyo Station this way?	To⌐okyo⌐o-eki (wa) ko⌐tira de⌐su ka⌐
or Is Tokyo Station in this direction or on this side?	To⌐okyo⌐o-eki (wa) ko⌐tira no ho⌐o desu ka⌐

73

Stranger

building (Western style)	bi⌐ru
beyond or over there or the far side	mukoo
beyond the building	bi⌐ru no mŭkoo

7. Yes. It's beyond that big building.   E⌐e. Ano o⌐oki⌐i ⌐bi⌐ru no mu⌐koo de⌐su.

Smith

8. I see. Thank you.   Wa⌐karima⌐sita. A⌐ri̇̄gatoo gozaima-sita.

(c)

Smith

that place over there or	asoko or
over there	asuko
hotel (Western style)	ho⌐teru
it's probably a hotel	ho⌐teru desyoo

9. Do you suppose that (place) is a hotel?   Asuko (wa) ⌐ho⌐teru desyoo ka.

Yamamoto

hmm	sa⌐a

10. I wonder. . . .   Sa⌐a. Do⌐o desyoo ka ⌐ne⌐e.

Tanaka

11. Oh, that IS a hotel.   A⌐a, ho⌐teru desu yo↲

Smith

12. It's probably expensive, isn't it. or It must be expensive!   Ta⌐ka⌐i desyoo ⌐ne⌐e.

Yamamoto

13. It must be (that way)!   So⌐o desyoo ⌐ne⌐e.

(d)

Smith

be in a place (of animate beings)	i⌐ma⌐su or o⌐rima⌐su ↓ or i⌐rassyaima⌐su ↑

14. Is Mr. Tanaka [in]?   Tanaka-sañ (wa) i⌐ma⌐su ka↲   or Tanaka-sañ (wa) i⌐rassyaima⌐su ka↲

Yamamoto

15. No, he isn't.   Iie, i⌐mase⌐ñ. or Iie, o⌐rimase⌐ñ. or Iie, i⌐rassyaimase⌐ñ.

Smith

which one (of two)? or	do˺tira
which way? or	
whereabouts? or where?	
in what place? or where?	do˺ko ni or
	do˺tira ni
16. Where is he?	Do˺ko ni i⊦ma˧su ka⌐ or
	Do˺tira ni i⊦rassyaima˧su ka⌐

Yamamoto

in Kyoto	Kyo˺oto ni
17. He's in Kyoto.	Kyo˺oto ni imasu. or
	Kyo˺oto ni orimasu. or
	Kyo˺oto ni irassyaimasu.

(e)

Smith

in this area or around here	kono heñ ni
telephone	deñwa or
	o⌐de˺ñwa +
18. Is(n't) there a telephone around here?	Kono heñ ni deñwa (wa) arimase˺ñ ka⌐

Tanaka

front	ma˺e
front of the station	e˺ki no ⌐ma˺e
side	yoko
both in front and at the side	ma˺e ni mo yo⌐ko ni˺ mo
19. There is (indeed). There's [one] in front of the station AND at the side.	A⌐rima˺su yo⌐ E˺ki no ⌐ma˺e ni mo yo⌐ko ni˺ mo arimasu.
department store	de⌐pa˺ato
in the department store too	de⌐pa˺ato ni mo
20. And then there's [one] in that department store, too.	Sore kara, sono de⌐pa˺ato ni mo arimasu.

Smith

building	ta⌐temo˺no
21. Which building is the department store?	De⌐pa˺ato (wa) ⌐do˺no ta⊦temo˧no desu ka⌐ or
	Do˺no ta⊦temo˧no ḡa de⊦pa˧ato desu ka⌐

Tanaka

next door or adjoining	tonari
next door to the station	e˺ki no to˺nari
22. It's next door to the station.	E˺ki no to⌐nari de˺su.

(f)

Smith

post office	yu⌐ubi⌐ŋkyoku
the post office here or	ko⌐ko no yuubi⌐ŋkyoku
the post office in this place	
23. Where's the post office in this place?	Ko⌐ko no yuubi⌐ŋkyoku (wa) ⌐do⌐ko ni a⌐rima⌐su ka⌐

Tanaka

vicinity	so⌐ba
immediate vicinity	su⌐gu ⌐so⌐ba
right near the station	e⌐ki no ⌐su⌐gu ⌐so⌐ba
24. The post office? It's right near the station.	Yu⌐ubi⌐ŋkyoku desu ka⌐ E⌐ki no ⌐su⌐gu ⌐so⌐ba ni arimasu.
bank	giñkoo
next door to the bank	giñkoo no tŏnari
the building next door to the bank	giñkoo no to⌐nari no bi⌐ru
25. It's [the building] next door to the big bank.	O⌐oki⌐i giñkoo no to⌐nari [no bi⌐ru] desu.[1]

(g)

Smith

inquire	u⌐kaḡaima⌐su ↓
I'm just going to ask [you something] (but)	tyo⌐tto u⌐kaḡaima⌐su ḡa
Imperial Hotel	Te⌐ekoku-ho⌐teru
26. Excuse me but where is the Imperial Hotel?	Tyo⌐tto u⌐kaḡaima⌐su ḡa, Te⌐ekoku-ho⌐teru (wa) ⌐do⌐ko desyoo ka.

Stranger

ahead	saki
a little further ahead	mo⌐o suko⌐si saki
27. The Imperial Hotel? It's a little further ahead.	Te⌐ekoku-ho⌐teru desu ka⌐ Mo⌐o suko⌐si saki desu.

Smith

left	hidari
the left side or toward the left	hi⌐dari no ho⌐o
28. Is it [on] the left side?	Hi⌐dari no ho⌐o desu ka⌐

---

[1] Accent of short alternant: de⌐su.

Stranger

right	miɡi
the right side or	mi⌐ɡi no ho⌐o
toward the right	
29. No, it's [on] the right side.	Iie, mi⌐ɡi no ho⌐o desu.

Smith

Nikkatsu Building	Ni⌐kkatu⌐-biru[1]
beyond the Nikkatsu	Ni⌐kkatu⌐-biru no mŭkoo
Building	
30. Is it beyond the Nikkatsu Build-	Ni⌐kkatu⌐-biru no mu⌐koo de⌐su ka⌐⌐
ing?	

Stranger

this side	temae
31. No, it's this side [of it].	Iie, te⌐mae de⌐su.

ADDITIONAL VOCABULARY[2]

bookstore	ho⌐ñya
cigar store	tabakoya
drugstore	kusuriya
fish market	sakanaya
flower shop	ha⌐na⌐ya
inn (Japanese style)	ryokañ
meat market	ni⌐ku⌐ya
park	kooeñ
school	gakkoo
store or shop (small)	mi⌐se⌐
theater	gekizyoo
toilet	be⌐ñzyo⌐ [3] or
	te⌐a⌐rai or
	o⌐tea⌐rai [+4] or
	to⌐iretto
vegetable store	yaoya

NOTES ON THE BASIC DIALOGUES

1. Words like A⌐merika-taisi⌐kañ, To⌐okyo⌐o-eki (sentence 6), Te⌐ekoku-ho⌐te-ru (sentence 26), and Nikkatu - biru (sentence 30) are single, compound

---

[1] Has unaccented alternant.

[2] Practice these words as substitutes for deñwa in Basic Sentence 18 (cf. Drill G, page 86.

[3] Man's word.

[4] Woman's word.

nominals, w h i c h name specific buildings o r organizations. Compare Tŏokyŏo-eki 'Tokyo Station' and Tŏokyoo no eki 'station(s) in Tokyo' — i.e. any one(s) at all.

7. Remember that an A no B combination (in which A and B are nominals) refers to a kind of B.   Thus, bi⌐ru no mukoo is a kind of mukoo, i.e. 'the far side described by the building' or 'beyond the building.' Mu⌐koo no bi⌐ru, on the other hand, is a kind of bi⌐ru, i.e. 'the building described by the far side' or 'the building over there.'

8. Wa⌐karima⌐sita often means 'I have understood what you just said (i.e. the information you just gave me, or what you just told me to do).'

18. The negative here occurs as a less direct — and slightly more polite — alternative. It does not mean that the speaker expects a negative reply.

21. Ta⌐temo⌐no is the general word for 'building,' but bi⌐ru is commonly used only in reference to large, Western-style buildings. The f i r s t alternative of sentence 21 means literally ' As for the department store, which building is it? '

23. Koko here refers to 'this place' meaning 'this town' or 'this village' or 'this particular section.' Ko⌐ko no yuubi⌐ñkyoku is another example of the particle no between nominals the first of which describes the second.

24. Su⌐g̃u ⌐so⌐ba is an example of one nominal describing another without the intervening particle no. Only certain nominals occur in this pattern.

26. √U⌐kag̃aima⌐su (gerund ukag̃atte) is a humble polite verbal. Tyo⌐tto u⌐kag̃aima⌐su g̃a and su⌐mimase⌐ñ g̃a are both common Japanese equivalents of English 'excuse me but': the former is used when the speaker is about t o request information, and the latter is an apology for interrupting, bothering, etc. Thus, in stopping a stranger on the street to ask for directions, either one may be used; in asking someone to do something, however, the former does not occur.

27. Saki usually means ' ahead — on the same street or route,' whereas mukoo 'beyond,' 'over there' is a word of more general meaning.

GRAMMATICAL NOTES

1. C o p u l a :   T e n t a t i v e

De⌐syo⌐o is the less positive, less direct equivalent of de⌐su. It will hereafter be called the TENTATIVE of de⌐su. Compare:

Ho⌐ñ desu. 'It's a book.'
Ho⌐ñ desyoo. 'It's probably a book,' 'I think it's a book,' 'It must be
a book,' etc.

Both de⌐su and de⌐syo⌐o are formal.

Like de⌐su, de⌐syo⌐o may refer to present or future time, and it follows nominals and adjectivals. (Other uses will be introduced later.) It is unaccented when the preceding word or phrase is accented.

Examples:

Ta⌐naka-san desyo⌐o. 'It probably is (or will be) Mr. Tanaka.'
I⌐i desyoo. 'I guess it's all right.'
So⌐o desyoo. 'I guess that's right.'
O⌐mosiro⌐i desyoo. 'It's probably interesting.'

In questions, the less direct de⌐syo⌐o is slightly more polite than de⌐su.
Compare:

Do⌐ko desu ka⌐ 'Where is it?'
Do⌐ko desyoo ka. 'Where would it be?' 'Where do you suppose it is?'
etc.— or simply 'Where is it?'

The indicated difference in intonation is common.

Both de⌐syo⌐o statements and de⌐syo⌐o ka questions are often followed by
exclamatory ne⌐e (Lesson 1, Grammatical Note 4). Thus:

Da⌐me⌐ desyoo ⌐ne⌐e. 'It must be out of order!' 'I guess it is out of
order, isn't it.'
Ya⌐su⌐i desyoo ⌐ne⌐e. 'It must be cheap!' 'I guess it is cheap, isn't
it.'
Na⌐n desyoo ka ⌐ne⌐e. 'What DO you suppose it is!' 'I'm wondering
what it is,' 'What is it indeed!'
Do⌐o desyoo ka ⌐ne⌐e. 'I wonder [about what you said],' 'I wonder
how [what you said] would be,' 'How WOULD it be!'

WARNING: Be sure to distinguish between the pronunciation of de⌐syo⌐o
(de-⌐syo⌐-o) and de⌐su yo (de⌐-su-yo). The former indicates doubt, probability,
indefiniteness, indirectness, etc., whereas the latter indicates certainty, assurance, emphasis, etc.

2. do⌐ko desu ka ~ do⌐ko ni a⌐rima⌐su ka

X de⌐su (in which X is a nominal) has two basic meanings: '[it] is X' or '[it]
is described by X.' Accordingly, depending on context, To⌐okyoo de⌐su means
either '[it] is Tokyo' or '[it] is described by—i.e. has something to do with—
Tokyo.' Compare:

Koko wa To⌐okyoo de⌐su. 'This (place) is Tokyo.'
and:
Ta⌐isi⌐kan wa To⌐okyoo de⌐su. 'The embassy is described by Tokyo'
—i.e. 'The embassy is in Tokyo.'

In other words, if √de⌐su is preceded by a place word (or phrase), the combination may signify equivalence or it may describe the location of something
or someone. Accordingly, do⌐ko desu ka, depending on context, means either
'what place is it?' or 'what place describes it?'—i.e. 'where is it?'

Examples:

Koko wa ⌐do⌐ko desu ka⌐ 'What place is this (place)?'
Tanaka-san wa ⌐do⌐ko desu ka⌐ 'Mr. Tanaka is described by what
place?'—i.e. 'Where is Mr. Tanaka?'

Koko wa Oᶠosaka deˀsu. 'This (place) is Osaka.'
Aᶜno hoˀteru wa Oᶠosaka deˀsu. 'That hotel is described by Osaka'—
i.e. 'That hotel is in Osaka.'

There is a second construction, used only in describing location:

$$\text{Place expression} + \underline{ni} + \begin{cases} \sqrt{a^r ima^1 su} \\ \sqrt{i^r ma^1 su} \end{cases}$$

Aᶜrimaˀsu in its location meaning refers to inanimate objects and iᶜmaˀsu refers to the location of animate beings. The particle ni follows the place expression which tells where something or someone is.

Examples:

Taᶜisiˀkañ wa Toᶜokyoo ni arimaˀsu. 'The embassy is located in Tokyo.'

Tanaka-sañ wa ᶜdoˀko ni iᶜmaˀsu ka⌐ 'Where (i.e. in what place) is Mr. Tanaka located?'

Aᶜno hoˀteru wa Oᶠosaka ni arimaˀsu. 'That hotel is located in Osaka.'

To sum up: Place expression + deˀsu means either '[it] is the place' or '[it] is described by the place.' In the latter meaning, it is used more or less interchangeably with a pattern consisting of place expression + ni + aᶜrimaˀsu ~ iᶜmaˀsu. '[something or somebody] is located in the place.' Thus, the equivalent of 'it is the front' is maˀe desu; the equivalent of 'it is in front' is maˀe desu or maˀe ni arimasu.

3. iᶜmaˀsu ~ oᶜrimaˀsu ~ iᶜrassyaimaˀsu

These three verbals all occur with the same lexical meaning: 'an animate object is located in a place.' They differ only in politeness.

Iᶜmaˀsu belongs to the plain level—the level of aᶜrimaˀsu, waᶜkarimaˀsu, kaᶜrimaˀsu, etc.

Like goᶜzaimaˀsu, oᶜrimaˀsu and iᶜrassyaimaˀsu are polite words, but goᶜzaimaˀsu is neutrally polite (+), whereas oᶜrimaˀsu is humble (↓) and iᶜrassyaimaˀsu is honorific (↑).

Oᶜrimaˀsu is used most commonly in reference to oneself, members of one's own family, and one's own close friends, or in any situation where the speaker wishes to talk politely without exalting the position of the subject to which the verbal refers. Iᶜrassyaimaˀsu, on the other hand, exalts the position of its subject and, accordingly, is NEVER USED IN REFERENCE TO ONESELF. Compare:

{ Employee: Taᶜnaka-sañ irassyaimaˀsu ka⌐ 'Is Mr. Tanaka (i.e. the boss) in?'
  Tanaka's Secretary: Haˀa, iᶜrassyaimaˀsu. 'Yes, he is.'

{ Visitor: Taᶜnaka-sañ irassyaimaˀsu ka⌐ 'Is Mr. Tanaka in?'
  Tanaka's co-worker: Haˀa, oᶜrimaˀsu. 'Yes, he is.'

Oᵣimaˈsu and iᵣrassyaimaˈsu, like many other polite words introduced previously, are used more commonly—though by no means exclusively—by women.

4. Particle _ni_ of Location

The particle _ni_ 'in,' 'on,' 'at' follows a nominal of place which indicates the location of something animate or inanimate, and is followed by √aᵣrimaˈsu or √iᵣmaˈsu or a more polite equivalent (cf. Note 2 above).

Examples:

Aᵣsoko ni arimaˈsu. 'It's over there (lit. in that place).'
Asoko ni koᵣoeñ ḡa arimaˈsu. 'Over there there's a park.'
Gaᵣkkoo no maˈe ni imasu. '[He] is in front of the school.'
Teᵣekoku-hoˈteru ni orimasu. 'I'm at the Imperial Hotel.'

Note that particle _ni_ is not ordinarily used in _desu_ sentences. Compare:

Tonari wa giᵣñkoo deˈsu. 'Next door is a bank.'

but:

Tonari ni giᵣñkoo ḡa arimaˈsu. '(In the place) next door there's a bank.'

5. Multiple Particles

In Japanese there are many occurrences of multiple particles—sequences of more than one consecutive particle. That is to say, a particle may follow a sequence that ends with a particle. Study the following examples:

waᵣtakusi no hoˈñ ni 'in my book'
waᵣtakusi no hoˈñ ni mo 'in my book too,' as in—
Taᵣnaka-sañ no hoˈñ ni arimasu. . . . Waᵣtakusi no hoˈñ ni mo arimasu. 'It's in Mr. Tanaka's book. . . . It's in my book, too.'
koko ni 'in this place'
koᵣko niˈ wa[1] 'in this place, comparatively speaking,' as in—
Doᵣko ni aᵏrimaˈsu ka˩ . . . Toᵣokyoo ni arimaˈsu. Koᵣko niˈ wa aᵣrimaseˈñ. 'Where is it? . . . It's in Tokyo. It isn't here.'

Particles _wa_ and _mo_ may follow _ni_ and various other particles which will be introduced later; but they replace, rather than follow, _ḡa_ and _o_. Compare the following groups:

Koᵣko ni arimaˈsu. 'It's here.'
Soᵣko niˈ wa aᵣrimaseˈñ. 'It isn't there.'
Aᵣsoko niˈ mo aᵏrimaseˈñ. 'It isn't over there either.'

---

[1] Particle _ni_ acquires an accent when it follows an unaccented word and is followed by an unaccented particle.

{ Ta⌐bako g̅a arima⌐su. 'There are cigarettes.'
   Ma⌐tti mo arimasu. 'There are matches, too.'
   Ra⌐itaa wa a⌐rimase⌐n̄. 'There isn't a lighter.'

{ Ho⌐n̄ o ka⌐ima⌐sita. 'I bought a book.'
   Za⌐ssi mo kaima⌐sita. 'I bought a magazine, too.'
   Sin̄bun̄ wa ka⌐imase⌐n̄ desita. 'A paper I didn't buy.'

6. Place-Word Series

koko	kotira	ko⌐tti⌐
soko	sotira	so⌐tti⌐
asoko	atira	a⌐tti⌐
do⌐ko	do⌐tira	do⌐tti

The above words — all nominals — bear an obvious resemblance to the kore,
kono, and kon̄na series.

The first group (koko, soko, etc.) refer specifically to place:

koko 'this place' or 'here'
soko 'that place' or 'there'
asoko[1] 'that place over there' or 'over there'
do⌐ko 'what place?' or 'where?'

The words of the second group (kotira, sotira, etc.) have several meanings:

(1) they refer to one alternative out of two possibilities.[2]

Compare: Do⌐re desu ka⌣ . . . Ko⌐re de⌐su. 'Which one (of three or
more) is it? . . . It's this one.'

and: Do⌐tira desu ka⌣ . . . Ko⌐tira de⌐su. 'Which one (of two) is
it? . . . It's this one.'

(2) they have a directional meaning. In a different context—for example,
pointing to a fork in the road—the last example above would have a different meaning:

Do⌐tira desu ka⌣ . . . Ko⌐tira de⌐su. 'Which way is it? . . .
It's this way.'

(3) they have an indefinite locational meaning: 'hereabouts,' 'thereabouts,'
'whereabouts.' The indirect and vague, as mentioned before, is more
polite in Japanese than the direct and specific; accordingly, the kotira
series with meaning (3) often occurs as a polite equivalent of the koko

---

[1] Asuko is an alternant of asoko. It is particularly common in rapid speech.

[2] The kore series more commonly refers to inanimate objects, but the kotira series in meaning (1) refers equally to animate beings and to objects.

series. Thus, in asking a stranger for the location of something, do˥tira desyoo ka [lit.] 'whereabouts would it be?' is simply a more indirect—and therefore m o r e polite—way of saying 'where is it?' Similarly, with polite √go˥zaima˥su a n d √i˥rassyaima˥su, the kotira series is more common than the koko series. Do˥tira ni i˥rassyaima˥su ka is a more polite way of saying do˥ko ni i˥ma˥su ka 'where is he?'

One further use of the kotira series will be introduced later.

Summary: kotira 'this one (of two),' 'this way,' 'hereabouts,' 'here'

sotira and atira[1] 'that way (of two),' 'that way,' 'thereabouts,' 'there'

do˥tira 'which one (of two)?' 'which way?' 'whereabouts?' 'where?'

The ko˥tti˥ series in an informal, contracted equivalent of the kotira series. Its members have the same meanings but they are used in less formal speech.

7. -ya

Product name + -ya means 'place where the product is sold' or 'dealer in the product.' Thus:

tabako 'cigarette' or 'tobacco'   tabakoya 'cigar store' or 'tobacco dealer'
ho˥ñ 'book'   ho˥ñya 'bookstore' or 'book dealer'
ha˥na˥ 'flower'   ha˥na˥ya 'flower shop' or 'florist'
kusuri 'medicine'   kusuriya 'drugstore' or 'druggist'
ni˥ku˥ 'meat'   ni˥ku˥ya 'meat market' or 'butcher'
sakana 'fish'   sakanaya 'fish market' or 'fish man'

The dealer is often addressed with the appropriate -ya word + -sañ. For example:

Ku˥suriyasañ de˥su ka⌐ 'Are you the druggist?'

DRILLS

A. Substitution Drill

1. Where is that?   Sore (wa) ˥do˥ko desu ka⌐
2. Which one (of three or   Sore (wa) ˥do˥re desu ka⌐
   more) is that?
3. How is that? or   Sore (wa) ˥do˥o desu ka⌐
   How about that?

[1] The differences between the two words are parallel to the differences between sore and are (cf. Lesson 2, Grammatical Note 3).

4. What is that?   Sore (wa) ⌐naˉn̄ desu ka⌐

5. Which way (or which of   Sore (wa) ⌐doˉtira desu ka⌐
    two, or whereabouts) is
    that?

6. Which building is that?   Sore (wa) ⌐doˉno ꜔biꜛru desu ka⌐

7. How is that? or   Sore (wa) i⌐kaˉḡa desu ka⌐
    How about that?

8. How much is that?   Sore (wa) ⌐iˉkura desu ka⌐

9. How many yen is that?   Sore (wa) ⌐naˉn̄-en̄ desu ka⌐

10. Which way (or which of   Sore (wa) ⌐doˉtti desu ka⌐
    two, or whereabouts) is
    that?

B. Substitution Drill

1. It's beyond the embassy.   Ta⌐isiˉkan̄ no mu⌐koo deˉsu.
2. It's in front of the embassy.   Ta⌐isiˉkan̄ no ⌐maˉe desu.
3. It's at the side of the em-   Ta⌐isiˉkan̄ no yo⌐ko deˉsu.
    bassy.
4. It's next door to the em-   Ta⌐isiˉkan̄ no to⌐nari deˉsu.
    bassy.
5. It's near the embassy.   Ta⌐isiˉkan̄ no ⌐soˉba desu.
6. It's right near the embassy.   Ta⌐isiˉkan̄ no ⌐suˉḡu ꜔soˉba desu.
7. It's up ahead, past the em-   Ta⌐isiˉkan̄ no sa⌐ki deˉsu.
    bassy.
8. It's this side of the em-   Ta⌐isiˉkan̄ no te⌐mae deˉsu.
    bassy.
9. It's to the right of the em-   Ta⌐isiˉkan̄ no mi⌐ḡi deˉsu.
    bassy.
10. It's to the left of the em-   Ta⌐isiˉkan̄ no hi⌐dari deˉsu.
    bassy.

C. Substitution Drill

1. It's the store over there.   Mu⌐koo no miseˉ desu.
2. It's the store in front.   Ma⌐e no mi꜔seˉ desu.
3. It's the store at the side.   Yo⌐ko no miseˉ desu.
4. It's the store next door.   To⌐nari no miseˉ desu.
5. It's the store right near.   Su⌐ḡu ꜔soˉba no mi꜔seˉ desu.
5. It's the store up ahead.   Sa⌐ki no miseˉ desu.
7. It's the store on the right.   Mi⌐ḡi no miseˉ desu.
8. It's the store on the left.   Hi⌐dari no miseˉ desu.
9. It's a store in Tokyo.   To⌐okyoo no miseˉ desu.
10. It's a store in America.   A⌐merika no miseˉ desu.

D. Substitution Drill

(The Japanese sentences with the intonations as marked correspond to English sentences having the emphasis on the final word or words.)

1. It's the school next door   Ko⌐oen̄ no tonari no gakkoo deˉsu.
    to the park.

2. It's the park next (door) to the school.

Ga⌐kkoo no tonari no kooeñ deˈsu.

3. It's the vegetable store next door to the florist.

Ha⌐naˈya no toᴴnari no yaoya deᴧsu.

4. It's the florist next door to the vegetable store.

Ya⌐oya no tonari no hanaˈya desu.

5. It's the cigar store next door to the bookstore.

Hoˈñya no toᴴnari no tabakoya deᴧsu.

6. It's the bookstore next door to the cigar store.

Ta⌐bakoya no tonari no hoˈñya desu.

7. It's the drugstore next door to the meat market.

Ni⌐kuˈya no toᴴnari no kusuriya deᴧsu.

8. It's the meat market next door to the drugstore.

Ku⌐suriya no tonari no nikuˈya desu.

9. It's the post office next door to the bank.

Gi⌐ñkoo no tonari no yuubiˈñkyoku desu.

10. It's the bank next door to the post office.

Yu⌐ubiˈñkyoku no toᴴnari no giñkoo deᴧsu.

E. Substitution Drill

1. The park is next (door) to the school. [1]

Kooeñ wa ga⌐kkoo no tonari deˈsu.

2. The school is next door to the park.

Gakkoo wa ko⌐oeñ no tonari deˈsu.

3. The florist is next door to the vegetable store.

Ha⌐naˈya wa ya⌐oya no tonari deˈsu.

4. The vegetable store is next door to the florist.

Yaoya wa ha⌐naˈya no toᴴnari deᴧsu.

5. The bookstore is next door to the cigar store.

Hoˈñya wa ta⌐bakoya no tonari deˈsu.

6. The cigar store is next door to the bookstore.

Tabakoya wa ⌐hoˈñya no toᴴnari deᴧsu.

7. The meat market is next door to the drugstore.

Ni⌐kuˈya wa ku⌐suriya no tonari deˈsu.

8. The drugstore is next door to the meat market.

Kusuriya wa ni⌐kuˈya no toᴴnari deᴧsu.

9. The bank is next door to the post office.

Giñkoo wa yu⌐ubiˈñkyoku no toᴴnari deᴧsu.

10. The post office is next door to the bank.

Yu⌐ubiˈñkyoku wa gi⌐ñkoo no tonari deˈsu.

---

[1] In order to correspond to the Japanese sentences, the emphasis of the English sentences in this drill must fall on the second half of the sentence. After mastering the drill in its present form, go through it again replacing every wa with ga; now the emphasis in the English shifts to the first half of the sentence.

F. Substitution Drill

1. Next (door) to the school
    is a park.[1]

    Gakkoo no tonari wa ko⌐oeñ de˥su.

2. Next door to the park is a
    school.

    Kooeñ no tonari wa ga⌐kkoo de˥su.

3. Next door to the vegetable
    store is a florist.

    Yaoya no tonari wa ha⌐na˥ya desu.

4. Next door to the florist is
    a vegetable store.

    Ha⌐na˥ya no tonari wa ya⌐oya de˥su.

5. Next door to the cigar store
    is a bookstore.

    Tabakoya no tonari wa ⌐ho˥ñya desu.

6. Next door to the bookstore
    is a cigar store.

    Ho˥ñya no tonari wa ta⌐bakoya de˥su.

7. Next door to the drugstore
    is a meat market.

    Kusuriya no tonari wa ni⌐ku˥ya desu.

8. Next door to the meat mar-
    ket is a drugstore.

    Ni⌐ku˥ya no tonari wa ku⌐suriya de˥su.

9. Next door to the post office
    is a bank.

    Yu⌐ubi˥ñkyoku no tonari wa gi⌐ñkoo de˥su.

10. Next door to the bank is a
    post office.

    Giñkoo no tonari wa yu⌐ubi˥ñkyoku desu.

G. Substitution Drill

1. Is(n't) there a telephone
    around here?

    Kono heñ ni de⌐ñwa (wa) arimase˥ñ ka↲

2. Is(n't) there a station around
    here?

    Kono heñ ni ⌐e˥ki (wa) a˥rimase˥ñ ka↲

3. Is(n't) there a hotel around
    here?

    Kono heñ ni ⌐ho˥teru (wa) a˥rimase˥ñ ka↲

4. Is(n't) there a department
    store around here?

    Kono heñ ni de⌐pa˥ato (wa) a˥rimase˥ñ ka↲

5. Is(n't) there a bank around
    here?

    Kono heñ ni gi⌐ñkoo (wa) arimase˥ñ ka↲

6. Is(n't) there a consulate
    around here?

    Kono heñ ni ryo⌐ozi˥kañ (wa) a˥rimase˥ñ ka↲

7. Is(n't) there an embassy
    around here?

    Kono heñ ni ta⌐isi˥kañ (wa) a˥rimase˥ñ ka↲

8. Is(n't) there a post office
    around here?

    Kono heñ ni yu⌐ubi˥ñkyoku (wa) a˥rimase˥ñ ka↲

----

[1] In order to correspond to the Japanese sentences, the emphasis of the English sentences in this drill must fall on the second half of the sentence. After mastering the drill in its present form, go through it again replacing every wa with ğa; now the emphasis in the English shifts to the first half of the sentence.

H. Substitution Drill

1. Excuse me, but where is   Tyo˺tto u˥kaḡaima˩su ḡa, A˥merika-
    the American Embassy?   taisi˺kañ (wa) ˹do˺ko desyoo ka.

2. Excuse me, but where is   Tyo˺tto u˥kaḡaima˩su ḡa, To˹okyo˺o-
    Tokyo Station?   eki (wa) ˹do˺ko desyoo ka.

3. Excuse me, but where is   Tyo˺tto u˥kaḡaima˩su ḡa, Te˹ekoku-
    the Imperial Hotel?   ho˺teru (wa) ˹do˺ko desyoo ka.

4. Excuse me, but where is   Tyo˺tto u˥kaḡaima˩su ḡa, Nikkatu-
    the Nikkatsu Building?   biru (wa) ˹do˺ko desyoo ka.

5. Excuse me, but where is   Tyo˺tto u˥kaḡaima˩su ḡa, Ni˹hoñ-
    the Bank of Japan?   gi˺ñkoo (wa) ˹do˺ko desyoo ka.

6. Excuse me, but where is   Tyo˺tto u˥kaḡaima˩su ḡa, E˹ekoku-
    the British Embassy?   taisi˺kañ (wa) ˹do˺ko desyoo ka.

7. Excuse me, but where is   Tyo˺tto u˥kaḡaima˩su ḡa, To˹okyoo-
    the Tokyo Hotel?   ho˺teru (wa) ˹do˺ko desyoo ka.

8. Excuse me, but where is   Tyo˺tto u˥kaḡaima˩su ḡa, A˥merika-
    the Bank of America?   gi˺ñkoo (wa) ˹do˺ko desyoo ka.

I. Grammar Drill (based on Grammatical Note 5)

Tutor: Ko˹ko ni arima˺su. /soko/ 'It's here.' /'there'/
Student: So˹ko ni˺ mo arimasu. 'It's there, too.'

1. E˹ki no ˹ma˺e ni arimasu.   E˹ki no yo˹ko ni˺ mo arimasu.
    /yoko/

2. Tanaka-sañ (wa) To˹okyoo   Ya˹mamoto-sañ mo Tookyoo ni ima˺su.
    ni ima˺su. /Yamamoto-
    sañ/

3. Tookyoo ni ryo˹ozi˺kañ (ḡa)   Ko˹obe ni mo ryo˥ozi˺kañ (ḡa) arima-
    arimasu. /Ko˹obe/   su.

4. Koko (wa) o˹tea˺rai desu.   A˹suko mo otea˺rai desu.
    /asuko/

5. Koko ni o˹tea˺rai (ḡa)   A˹suko ni˺ mo o˥tea˩rai (ḡa) arima-
    arimasu. /asuko/   su.

6. Zi˺syo (o) ka˥ima˩sita.   Si˹ñbuñ mo kaima˺sita.
    /siñbuñ/

7. Ta˹bako (o) oneḡai-sima˺su.   Ra˹itaa mo oneḡai-simasu.
    /ra˹itaa/

8. Kono heñ ni ni˹ku˺ya (wa)   Kono heñ ni sa˹kanaya mo arimase˺ñ.
    a˥rimase˩ñ. /sakanaya/

J. Grammar Drill (based on Grammatical Note 1)

Tutor   Pe˺ñ desu. 'It's a pen.'
Student: Pe˺ñ desyoo. 'It's probably a pen.'

1. Hu˹ru˺i desu.   Hu˹ru˺i desyoo.
2. Ga˹kkoo de˺su.   Ga˹kkoo desyo˺o.
3. So˺o desu.   So˺o desyoo.
4. Na˺ñ desu ka⌐   Na˺ñ desyoo ka.
5. Ta˹naka-sañ no˺ desu.   Ta˹naka-sañ no˺ desyoo.
6. So˺o desu ˥ne˩e.   So˺o desyoo ˥ne˩e.

7. Ta⌐ka⌐i desu ⌐ne⌐e.   Ta⌐ka⌐i desyoo ⌐ne⌐e.
8. Do⌐ko desu ka⌐.   Do⌐ko desyoo ka.

K. Response Drill (based on Grammatical Note 2)

(Give the answer in the same basic form as the question.)

1. Koko (wa) ⌐do⌐ko desu ka⌐   Ko⌐obe desu.
    /Ko⌐obe/
2. A⌐merika-taisi⌐kañ (wa)   To⌐okyoo ni arima⌐su.
    ⌐do⌐ko ni arimasu ka⌐
    /Tookyoo/
3. Asoko ni ⌐na⌐ni (ḡa) arimasu   Ko⌐oeñ (ḡa) arima⌐su.
    ka⌐ /kooeñ/
4. Kooeñ (wa) ⌐do⌐ko ni arima-   A⌐soko ni arima⌐su.
    su ka⌐ /asoko/
5. Kooeñ (wa) ⌐do⌐ko desu ka⌐   A⌐soko de⌐su.
    /asoko/
6. Tanaka-sañ (wa) ⌐do⌐ko ni   A⌐soko ni ima⌐su.
    imasu ka⌐   /asoko/
7. Te⌐ekoku-ho⌐teru no ⌐ma⌐e   Ko⌐oeñ de⌐su.
    (wa) ⌐na⌐ñ desu ka⌐
    /kooeñ/
8. Te⌐ekoku-ho⌐teru no ⌐ma⌐e   Ko⌐oeñ (ḡa) arima⌐su.
    ni ⌐na⌐ni (ḡa) arimasu
    ka⌐ /kooeñ/
9. Kooeñ (wa) ⌐do⌐ko desu ka⌐   Te⌐ekoku-ho⌐teru no ⌐ma⌐e desu.
    /Te⌐ekoku-ho⌐teru no
    ⌐ma⌐e/
10. Kooeñ (wa) ⌐do⌐ko ni ari-   Te⌐ekoku-ho⌐teru no ⌐ma⌐e ni ari-
    masu ka⌐ /Te⌐ekoku-   masu.
    ho⌐teru no ⌐ma⌐e/

L. Level Drill[1]

1. Ta⌐naka-sañ ima⌐su ka⌐   Ta⌐naka-sañ irassyaima⌐su ka⌐
2. Ta⌐bako arima⌐su ka⌐   Ta⌐bako gozaima⌐su ka⌐
3. Tyo⌐tto ⌐ma⌐tte kudasai.   Syo⌐osyoo o⌐mati-kudasa⌐i.
4. Tanaka-sañ (wa) ⌐do⌐ko ni   Tanaka-sañ (wa) ⌐do⌐tira ni i⌐rassyai-
    i⌐ma⌐su ka⌐   ma⌐su ka⌐
5. I⌐kura desu ka⌐   O⌐ikura de⌐su ka⌐
6. I⌐kutu a⌐rima⌐sita ka⌐   O⌐ikutu gozaima⌐sita ka⌐
7. Ge⌐ñki desu ka⌐   O⌐ge⌐ñki desu ka⌐

_____

[1] The sentences on the right are more polite equivalents of the sentences on the left.

8. Ta⌐naka ima⌐su ka⌐ ¹   Ta⌐naka orima⌐su ka⌐
9. Kono heñ ni yu⌐ubi⌐ñkyoku   Kono heñ ni yu⌐ubi⌐ñkyoku (wa) go⌐za-
   (wa) a⌐rimase⌐ñ ka⌐   imase⌐ñ ka⌐
10. Tanaka-sañ (wa) i⌐mase⌐ñ   Tanaka-sañ (wa) i⌐rassyaimase⌐ñ de-
    desita ka⌐   sita ka⌐

M. Expansion Drill

1. [It]'s beyond.   Mu⌐koo de⌐su.
   [It]'s beyond the post office.   Yu⌐ubi⌐ñkyoku no mu⌐koo de⌐su.
   [It]'s beyond the big post of-   O⌐oki⌐i yu⌐ubi⌐ñkyoku no mu⌐koo
   fice.   de⌐su.
   [It]'s beyond that big post   Ano o⌐oki⌐i yu⌐ubi⌐ñkyoku no mu⌐koo
   office.   de⌐su.
   Tokyo Station is beyond that   To⌐okyo⌐o-eki (wa) ano o⌐oki⌐i yu⌐u-
   big post office.   bi⌐ñkyoku no mu⌐koo de⌐su.

2. [It]'s probably expensive.   Ta⌐ka⌐i desyoo.
   [It] must be expensive!   Ta⌐ka⌐i desyoo ⌐ne⌐e.
   The inn must be expensive!   Ryokañ (wa) ta⌐ka⌐i desyoo ⌐ne⌐e.
   The new inn must be expen-   A⌐tarasi⌐i ryokañ (wa) ta⌐ka⌐i desyoo
   sive!   ⌐ne⌐e.
   A new inn like that must be   So⌐ñna atarasi⌐i ryokañ (wa) ta⌐ka⌐i
   expensive!   desyoo ⌐ne⌐e.

3. There is.   A⌐rima⌐su.
   There's a toilet.   To⌐iretto (ğa) arimasu.
   There's a toilet over there,   A⌐soko ni⌐ mo ⌐to⌐iretto (ğa) arima-
   too.   su.
   There's a toilet here AND   Ko⌐ko ni⌐ mo a⌐soko ni⌐ mo ⌐to⌐iret-
   over there.   to (ğa) arimasu.

4. There is.   A⌐rima⌐su.
   Where is [it]?   Do⌐ko ni a⌐rima⌐su ka⌐
   Where is the hotel?   Ho⌐teru (wa) ⌐do⌐ko ni a⌐rima⌐su ka⌐
   Where is the new hotel?   A⌐tarasi⌐i ⌐ho⌐teru (wa) ⌐do⌐ko ni a⌐ri-
                                    ma⌐su ka⌐
   Where is the new hotel in   Oosaka no a⌐tarasi⌐i ⌐ho⌐teru (wa)
   Osaka?   ⌐do⌐ko ni a⌐rima⌐su ka⌐

5. There isn't [any].   A⌐rimase⌐ñ.
   Isn't there [any]?   A⌐rimase⌐ñ ka⌐
   Is(n't) there an inn?   Ryo⌐kañ (wa) arimase⌐ñ ka⌐
   Is(n't) there a good inn?   I⌐i ryo⌐kañ (wa) arimase⌐ñ ka⌐
   Is(n't) there a good inn   Kono heñ ni ⌐i⌐i ryo⌐kañ (wa) arima-
   around here?   se⌐ñ ka⌐

---

¹ Spoken for example by a relative of Mr. Tanaka's.

6. What is [it]?
   What is the big building?
   What is the big building on
   the right?
   What is the big building to
   the right of the station?

   Na⌉n desyoo ka.
   O⌐oki⌉i ⌐bi⌐ru (wa) ⌐na⌉n desyoo ka.
   Miḡi no o⌐oki⌉i ⌐bi⌐ru (wa) ⌐na⌉n de-
   syoo ka.
   E⌉ki no miḡi no o⌐oki⌉i ⌐bi⌐ru (wa)
   ⌐na⌉n desyoo ka.

7. [It]'s a florist.
   Is [it] a florist?
   Is [it] a new florist?
   Is [it] that new florist?
   Which shop is that new
   florist?

   Ha⌐na⌉ya desu.
   Ha⌐na⌉ya desu ka⌐
   A⌐tarasi⌉i ha⌐na⌐ya desu ka⌐
   Sono a⌐tarasi⌉i ha⌐na⌐ya desu ka⌐
   Do⌉no mi⌐se⌐ ḡa sono a⌐tarasi⌐i
   ha⌐na⌐ya desu ka⌐

8. There's a drugstore.
   There's a big drugstore.
   [Up] ahead there's a big
   drugstore.
   A little ahead there's a big
   drugstore.
   A little further ahead there's
   a big drugstore.

   Ku⌐suriya (ḡa) arima⌉su.
   O⌐oki⌉i ku⌐suriya (ḡa) arima⌐su.
   Saki ni o⌐oki⌉i ku⌐suriya (ḡa) arima⌐-
   su.
   Su⌐ko⌉si saki ni o⌐oki⌉i ku⌐suriya (ḡa)
   arima⌐su.
   Mo⌐o suko⌉si saki ni o⌐oki⌉i ku⌐suri-
   ya (ḡa) arima⌐su.

SHORT SUPPLEMENTARY DIALOGUES

1. A: Wa⌐takusi no zi⌉syo ⌐do⌉ko desu ka⌐
   B: Ko⌐ko de⌉su yo⌐

2. A: Kyo⌉o no siñbuñ ko⌐ko de⌉su yo⌐
   B: Wa⌐karima⌉sita. Do⌉o mo.

3. A: Ta⌐naka-sañ to Yamamoto-sañ ima⌉su ka⌐
   B: Ta⌐naka-sañ wa ima⌉su ḡa, Ya⌐mamoto-sañ wa imase⌉ñ.

4. Visitor: Ta⌐naka-sañ irassyaima⌉su ka⌐
   Secretary: Ha⌐a, i⌐rassyaima⌉su. Syo⌐osyoo o⌐mati-kudasa⌐i.

5. Mrs. Tanaka (calling her husband's office): Ta⌐naka orima⌉su ka⌐
   Secretary: Ha⌐a, i⌐rassyaima⌉su. Syo⌐osyoo o⌐mati-kudasaima⌐se.

6. A: Be⌐ñzyo⌉ ko⌐tti⌉ desu ka⌐
   B: Iie, so⌐tti⌉ desu yo.

7. A: So⌐ñna ho⌉ñ (wa) ta⌐ka⌉i desyoo ⌐ne⌐e.
   B: So⌉o desyoo ⌐ne⌐e.

8. A: Sore wa ⌐na⌉ñ desyoo ka.
   B: Na⌉ñ desyoo ka ⌐ne⌐e.

9. A: Soko wa ga⌐kkoo desyo⌉o ka.
   B: Sa⌉a. Do⌉o desyoo ka ⌐ne⌐e.

10. A: I⌉i desu ka⌐
    B: Ma⌉a ⌐i⌐i desyoo.

English Equivalents

1. A: Where's my dictionary?
    B: Here it is!

2. A: Today's paper is [over] here!
    B: I see. Thanks.

3. A: Are Mr. Tanaka and Mr. Yamamoto in?
    B: Mr. Tanaka is (in) but Mr. Yamamoto isn't (in).

4. Visitor: Is Mr. Tanaka in?
    Secretary: Yes, he is (in). Just a moment, please.

5. Mrs. Tanaka: Is [Mr.] Tanaka in?
    Secretary: Yes, he is (in). Just a moment, please.

6. A: Is the toilet this way?
    B: No, it's that way.

7. A: A book like that must be expensive!
    B: It must be!

8. A: What do you suppose that is?
    B: What DO you suppose it is! (or What is it, indeed!)

9. A: Would that (place) be a school?
    B: I wonder . . .

10. A: Is it all right?
    B (reluctantly): I guess it probably is (all right).

—oOo—

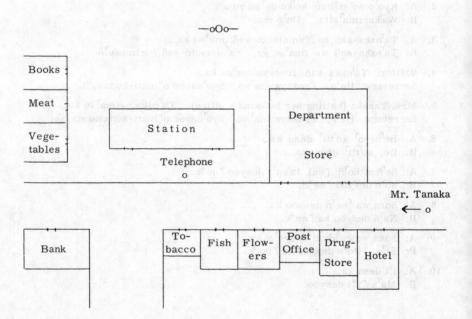

EXERCISES

1. Answer the following on the basis of the diagram on page 92.

   a. True – False

      (1) E⌐ki no ⌐ma⌐e ni de⌐ñwa ḡa arima⌐su.
      (2) E⌐ki no tonari wa de⌐pa⌐ato desu.
      (3) Ga⌐kkoo wa arima⌐su ḡa, gi⌐ñkoo wa arimase⌐ñ.
      (4) Yu⌐ubi⌐ñkyoku no tonari ni sa⌐kanaya ḡa arima⌐su.
      (5) E⌐ki no yoko ni mi⌐se⌐ ḡa arimasu.

   b. Answer the following questions for Mr. Tanaka, who is facing in the di-
      rection of the arrow.

      (1) Giñkoo wa sa⌐ki de⌐su ka⌐.
      (2) E⌐ki wa ⌐do⌐tira desyoo ka⌐.
      (3) Kono heñ ni ⌐ho⌐ñya wa a⌐rimase⌐ñ ka⌐.
      (4) Do⌐ñna mi⌐se⌐ ḡa ⌐e⌐ki no yo⌐ko ni arima⌐su ka⌐.
      (5) Yaoya wa ⌐e⌐ki no te⌐mae de⌐su ka⌐.

2. Using the diagram on page 92, other similar diagrams, photographs, or
   models, take turns asking and answering questions about the identity and
   location of the buildings. Always use 'left' and 'right' relative to a position facing the front of a building.

3.

You ask a stranger:	The stranger replies:
a. where the American Embassy is.	It's that way.
b. where the Imperial Hotel is.	It's near the Nikkatsu Building.
c. where Tokyo Station is.	It's beyond that big building.
d. where the British Consulate is.	It's this side of that white building.
e. if there is(n't) a telephone around here.	There's [one] in front of the station.
f. if that is the Nikkatsu Hotel.	No, it's the Imperial Hotel.
g. if Tokyo is in this direction.	No, it's that way.
h. if there is(n't) a post office around here.	There is. It's next to that big bank.
i. if the Imperial Theater is on the left.	No, it's on the right.

4. Practice the Basic Dialogues with variations and appropriate props.

Lesson 7. Around Town

BASIC DIALOGUES: FOR MEMORIZATION

(a)

Smith

now	iˈma
to what place?	doˈko e or
	doˈko ni or
	doˈtira e or
	doˈtira ni
go	iˈkimaˈsu or
	maˈirimaˈsu ↓ or
	iˈrassyaimaˈsu ↑

1. Where are you going to go now?

I̐ma ˈdoˈko │e/ni│ iˈkimaˈsu ka↲ or

I̐ma ˈdoˈtira │e/ni│ iˈrassyaimaˈsu ka↲

Tanaka

movie theater	eˈeḡaˈkañ
to a movie theater	eˈeḡaˈkañ e or
	eˈeḡaˈkañ ni

2. I'm going to go to a movie (theater).

Eˈeḡaˈkañ │e/ni│ ikimasu. or

Eˈeḡaˈkañ │e/ni│ mairimasu.

3. Won't you go too? or
   Wouldn't you [like to] go too?

Aˈnaˈta mo iˈkimaseˈñ ka↲ or
Aˈnaˈta mo iˈrassyaimaseˈñ ka↲

Smith

4. Thank you but I'm afraid I can't [just] now.

Aˈriˈḡatoo gozaimasu ḡa, iˈma wa ˈtyoˈtto↲

(b)

Smith

Marunouchi Building (in Tokyo)	Maru-biru
to the Maru-biru	Maru-biru e or
	Maru-biru ni
want to go or would like to go	ikitai /-ku/
street or road or way	miti

94

5. I want to go to the Maru-biru   Ma⌐ru‐biru │ e │ ikita⌐i n̄ desu ḡa,
    but I don't know the way (lit.   │ ni │
    the road isn't clear).   mi⌐ti ḡa wakarimase⌐n̄.

    write or draw   ka⌐kima⌐su
    would you write (or draw)   ka⌐ite ku⌐dasaimase⌐n̄ ka
        for me
6. Would you (just) draw a map   Tyo⌐tto, ti⌐zu (o) ⌐ka⌐ite ku⌐dasai-
    for me?   mase⌐n̄ ka⌐

                    Tanaka

    avenue or wide street   to⌐ori⌐
7. A map? The Maru-biru is a   Ti⌐zu desu ka⌐ Maru-biru (wa) ko⌐no
    little further along this street toori⌐ no mo⌐o suko⌐si sa⌐ki de⌐su
    (but)...   ḡa⌐

                    Smith

8. Then I don't need a map, do I.   Zya⌐a, ti⌐zu wa i⌐rimase⌐n̄ ⌐ne⌐e.

                    (c)

                    Smith

    (a section between Tokyo   Kawasaki
        and Yokohama)
    to Kawasaki   Kawasaki e or
                                      Kawasaki ni
    teach or inform   o⌐siema⌐su
    would you teach (or in-   o⌐siete kudasaimase⌐n̄ ka
        form) me?
9. I want to go to Kawasaki. Would   Ka⌐wasaki │ e │ ikita⌐i n̄ desu ḡa,
    you show me the way?   │ ni │
                                      mi⌐ti (o) osiete kudasaimase⌐n̄ ka⌐

                    Tanaka

    space between   aida
    between Tokyo and Yoko-   Tookyoo to Yokohama no aida
        hama
10. Kawasaki? Why, it's between   Ka⌐wasaki de⌐su ka⌐ To⌐okyoo to
    Tokyo and Yokohama.   Yokohama no aida de⌐su yo⌐

                    Smith

11. Oh? Then, it's that road,   So⌐o desu ka. Zya⌐a, so⌐no miti de⌐su
    isn't it.   ⌐ne⌐e.

                    Tanaka

12. That's right.   So⌐o desu yo⌐

                    (d)

                    Smith

    policeman   zyuñsa[1]

----
[1] Alternate accent: zyu͞ñsa.

13. Is(n't) there a policeman around   Kono heñ ni zyu⌐ñsa (wa) imase˥ñ ka⌐
    here?

Tanaka

    police box   koobañ
14. There's a police box over there.   Asoko ni ko⌐obañ ḡa arima˥su yo⌐

Smith (to policeman)

    hospital   byooiñ
    St. Luke's Hospital   Se⌐eroka-byo˥oiñ
15. Say! Where (or which way) is   Tyo˥tto. Se⌐eroka-byo˥oiñ (wa) ⌐do˥-
    St. Luke's Hospital?   tira desu ka⌐

Policeman

    up ahead from here   kono saki
16. St. Luke's Hospital? Why, it's   Se⌐eroka-byo˥oiñ desu ka⌐ Kono saki
    the big building on the left side   no hi⌐dari no ho˥o no o⌐oki˥i ta˥te-
    up ahead (from here).   mo˥no desu yo⌐

Smith

17. I see. Thank you very much.   Wa⌐karima˥sita.   Do˥o mo a˥ri˥ḡa-
                                         too gozaimasita.

(e)

Tanaka

    by means of what?   na˥ñ de
    let's go   i⌐kimasyo˥o   or
                                         ma⌐irimasyo˥o ↓
    shall we go?   i⌐kimasyo˥o ka   or
                                         ma⌐irimasyo˥o ka
18. How shall we go?   Na˥ñ de i⌐kimasyo˥o ka.   or
                                         Na˥ñ de ma⌐irimasyo˥o ka.

Smith

    taxi   ta˥kusii
    by taxi   ta˥kusii de
19. Let's go by taxi.   Ta˥kusii de i⌐kimasyo˥o. or
                                         Ta˥kusii de ma⌐irimasyo˥o.

. . .

Driver

20. Where to?   Do˥tira |e / ni| ?

Tanaka

    as far as Tokyo Station   To⌐okyo˥o-eki made
    please go   i⌐tte kudasa˥i
21. (Go as far as) Tokyo Station,   To⌐okyo˥o-eki made (i⌐tte kudasa˥i).
    please.

. . .

Smith

be in a hurry	i⌐soḡima¬su
please don't hurry	i⌐soḡa¬nai de kudasai

22. Please don't go so fast.   Añmari i⌐soḡa¬nai de kudasai.

. . .

Driver

23. [This] is Tokyo Station (but). . .   To⌐okyo¬o-eki desu ḡa_

Tanaka

automobile	zi⌐do¬osya
car or cart	kuruma
back or rear	usiro
at the back	usiro de
bring to a halt	to⌐mema¬su
please bring to a halt	to⌐mete kudasa¬i

24. Please stop in back of that black car.   Ano ku⌐ro¬i kuruma no u⌐siro de tomete kudasa¬i.

(f)

Passenger

(section of Tokyo)	Giñza
1-chome	i ⌐t-tyoome¬
2-chome	ni- ⌐tyoome¬
as far as 4-chome	yo⌐ñ-tyoome¬ made

25. (Go as far as) Ginza 4-chome, please. . . .   Gi⌐ñza yoñ-tyoome¬ made (i⌐tte kudasa⌐i). . . .

is dangerous	abunai /-ku/

26. Oh! Look out!   A. Abunai.

Driver

safe or all right	da⌐izyo¬obu

27. It's all right! . . .   Da⌐izyo¬obu desu yo. . . .

28. [This] is 4-chome (but). . .   Yo⌐ñ-tyoome¬ desu ḡa_

Passenger

next	tu⌐ḡi¬
street corner	ka⌐do
next corner	tu⌐ḡi¬ no ⌐ka⌐do
make a turn	ma⌐ḡarima¬su
turn a corner	ka⌐do o ma⌐ḡarima⌐su
turn to the right	mi⌐ḡi e maḡarima¬su or mi⌐ḡi ni maḡarima¬su
please turn	ma⌐ḡatte kudasa¬i

29. Please turn right at the next corner. (Lit. Please turn the next corner to the right.) . . .   Tu⌐ḡi¬ no ⌐ka⌐do (o) mi⌐ḡi |e/ni| maḡatte kudasa¬i. . . .

straight	ma⌐ssu⌐gu
going straight along this street	kono miti o ma⌐ssu⌐gu itte
end of a street <u>or</u> corridor	tukiatari
turn at the end <u>of</u> the street	tu⌐kiatari o ma̅garima⌐su

30. Please go straight along this street, and turn (to the) left at the end. . . .

Kono miti (o) ma⌐ssu⌐gu itte, tuki-atari (o) hi⌐dari |e / ni| ma̅gatte kuda-sa⌐i. . . .

at that place over there	asoko de

31. Please stop over there. . . .   A⌐soko de tomete kudasa⌐i. . . .

go back	mo̅dorima⌐su
please go back	mo̅do⌐tte kudasai

32. Please back up a little. . . .   Tyo⌐tto mo┕do┐tte kudasai. . . .

33. Here we are! Thanks (for your trouble).

Ko⌐ko de⌐su yo˩ Go⌐ku⌐roosama.

NOTES ON THE BASIC DIALOGUES

1. I⌐ma 'now' is a nominal (i⌐ma desu 'it's now'; i⌐ma zya a┕rimase┐ñ 'it isn't now'). I⌐ma with a non-past verbal refers to immediate future, and with a past verbal to immediate past: I⌐ma simasu 'I'll do [it] now'; i⌐ma si┕ma┐sita 'I just did [it].'

5. Remember that √wa⌐karima⌐su is never preceded by particle o. Both the person who understands and the thing which is clear are followed by g̅a or wa, depending upon emphasis.

7. 'It's a little further along this street but—if you want a map, I'll draw one.' To⌐ori⌐ usually refers to a broad avenue, whereas miti is any street or road. As the second part of a compound, to⌐ori⌐ becomes -doori: thus, Ya⌐esu - do⌐ori 'Yaesu Avenue,' Na⌐miki-do⌐ori 'Namiki Avenue.'

9. Mi⌐sema⌐su means 'show—i.e. let someone see'; o⌐siema⌐su means 'show —i.e. explain.' Note particle g̅a connecting a statement of fact with a related question or request.

14. Koobañ 'police boxes' are booths located at frequent intervals throughout Japanese cities where one or more policemen are on duty at all times.

16. Ta⌐temo⌐no has three modifiers in this sentence: kono saki, hi⌐dari no ho⌐o, and o⌐oki⌐i. The first two are nominal modifiers, each followed by particle no. O⌐oki⌐i, an adjectival modifier, takes no connecting particle.

21. Itte here is the gerund of i⌐kima⌐su 'go.' This itte is not to be confused with the itte of mo⌐o iti-do⌐ itte kudasa⌐i 'please say it once more,' the gerund of i⌐ima⌐su ' say.' The two gerunds sound alike; they are distinguished only by context in the spoken language.

22. The gerund of i⌐so̅gima⌐su is i⌐so⌐ide. This is the first example of a

gerund ending in -de instead of the more common -te.

23. 'This is Tokyo Station but— where shall I go from here?   or where do you want to get out?'

24. 'Stop' here means 'stop the taxi,' 'bring the taxi to a halt.'

26. Note the use of the informal adjectival.   The formal equivalent would be a⌐buna⌐i desu.

27. Da⌐izyo⌐obu, a nominal, has many English equivalents: 'safe,' 'all right,' 'O.K.,' 'don't worry,' 'I can manage,' etc.   The underlying meaning is one of safety or security or lack of concern.

28. See 23 above.

GRAMMATICAL NOTES

1.   Adjectivals Ending in -tai 'want to —'

Take a verbal in its -ma⌐su form: replace -ma⌐su with -tai, and the result is an ADJECTIVAL meaning 'want to (or would like to) do so-and-so.'[1] For example:

ka⌐kima⌐su	'[I] write'	ka⌐kita⌐i	'[I] want to write'
i⌐kima⌐su	'[I] go'	ikitai	'[I] want to go'
ka⌐ima⌐su	'[I] buy'	kaitai	'[I] want to buy'
si⌐ma⌐su	'[I] do'	sitai	'[I] want to do'

Like all other adjectivals, a -tai form alone is informal. The formal equivalent is the informal + de⌐su—in this case, yielding -ta⌐i desu—and the formal negative is the derived -ku form + a⌐rimase⌐n. Compare:

> ti⌐isa⌐i desu '[it] is small' : ti⌐isaku a⌐rimase⌐n '[it] is not small'
> i⌐kita⌐i desu '[I] want to go' : i⌐kitaku arimase⌐n '[I] don't want to go'

A common formal pattern, frequently followed by ḡa 'but,' is -ta⌐i n̄ desu— an example of the pattern adjectival + nominal + de⌐su (cf. ti⌐isa⌐i ⌐ho⌐n̄ desu 'it is a small book'). N̄[2] is a nominal meaning something like 'matter,' 'fact,' 'case,' and i⌐kita⌐i n̄ desu means literally 'it is a wanting-to-go matter.'

The adjectival + n̄ desu pattern is not limited to -tai adjectivals; any other adjectival may occur in the same construction. Thus:

---

[1] Whether or not a -tai word is accented depends on the verbal root from which it is derived. But all adjectivals—and therefore all -tai words—are accented in their occurrences before √de⌐su.

[2] N̄ is the contraction of a nominal no, which occurs in more formal, precise speech.

aᶝbunaˀi ñ desu 'it is dangerous' (lit. 'it is a matter of being dangerous')

iˀi ñ desu ' it's fine' (lit. 'it is a matter of being fine')

The alternative with ñ is considered softer and less abrupt than the alternative without ñ. More will be said about this pattern later.

The particle g̱a 'but' frequently follows a -tai pattern. In final position it serves to qualify and/or soften the preceding: 'I'd like to do so-and-so but—do you mind?' or 'is it all right?' or 'I don't know how to proceed' or 'I can't,' etc. (Cf. Lesson 4, Grammatical Note 5.)

In statements, -tai patterns usually refer to the speaker, and in questions, to the person addressed.

-Tai words have one special characteristic: the direct object (followed by particle o) of a verbal often becomes the subject (followed by particle g̱a) of the adjectival -tai derivative. Thus:

Siᶝñbuñ o kaimaˀsu. 'I am going to buy a newspaper.'

but:

Siᶝñbuñ g̱a kaitaˀi ñ desu g̱a_ 'I want to buy a newspaper but. . . '

Siñbuñ o kaitai also occurs and has the same meaning. With many -tai words the g̱a alternant is more common, but with some o is more usual. Observe individual examples as they occur.

WARNING: A -tai question means 'do you WANT to do so-and-so?' 'is so-and-so what you want to do?' in a literal sense. It does not carry the same connotation as English questions beginning 'would you like to do so-and-so?'; these are invitations, and the usual Japanese equivalent is a negative question. Example:

Aᶝsita kimaseˀñ ka_ 'Won't you come tomorrow?' 'Would(n't) you like to come tomorrow?' etc.

Compare also Basic Sentence 3 in this lesson.

2.   Verbal Tentative

The tentative of a formal verbal is made by changing the -maˀsu ending to -masyoˀo (compare deˀsu and deᶝsyoˀo). One English equivalent is 'let's do so-and-so' or, in a question, 'shall we do so-and-so?'; another will be introduced in a later lesson.

Examples:

Soᶝo simasyoˀo. 'Let's do that.' or 'Let's do [it] that way.'
Iᶝsog̱imasyoˀo. 'Let's hurry.'
Iᶝkimasyoˀo ka. 'Shall we go?'

In polite speech, the humble form—not the honorific—is used:

Maᶝirimasyoˀo ka. 'Shall we go?'
Maᶝirimasyoˀo. 'Let's go.'

Note: The use of the assertive sentence particle yo following the formal tentative—for example, iˈkimasyoˈo yo 'let's go!'—is typical of women's speech.

3. Particles e 'to,' ni 'to,' maˈde 'as far as,' de 'at,' de 'by means of,' o 'through'

    a. e and ni

      A nominal of place followed by particle e 'to' modifies an inflected expression directly or is followed by another particle; it indicates a goal. When a phrase ending in e modifies a nominal, it is regularly followed by no. Examples:

> Doˈko e iˈkimasyoˈo ka. 'Where (lit. to what place) shall we go?'
> Tanaka-sañ wa Toˈokyoo e kimaˈsu ka⌣ 'Is Mr. Tanaka coming to Tokyo?'
> Koˈoeñ eˈ mo iˈkimaˈsita. 'I went to the park, too.'
> Kyoˈoto e wa iˈkimaseˈñ desita. 'I didn't go to Kyoto (in comparison with other places).'
> Toˈokyoo e no miti deˈsu ka. 'Is it the road to Tokyo?'

      In this pattern, ni 'to' may usually be used instead of e. For example, the first two sentences cited just above could be changed to Doˈko ni iˈkimasyoˈo ka. and Tanaka-sañ wa Toˈokyoo ni kimaˈsu ka⌣ with no significant difference in meaning. This ni must not be confused with ni meaning 'in'; the two particles are distinguished by the immediate context, particularly the accompanying verbal. Compare:

> Kyoˈoto ni arimasu. 'It's in Kyoto.'
> Kyoˈoto ni ikimasu. 'I'm going to Kyoto.'
> Gaˈkkoo ni imaseˈñ desita. '[He] wasn't in school.'
> Gaˈkkoo ni kimaseˈñ desita. '[He] didn't come to school.'

Sometimes a larger context is required. For example, iˈrassyaimaˈsu has been introduced as the honorific equivalent of both iˈmaˈsu and iˈkimaˈsu. Therefore, depending on context, gaˈkkoo ni irassyaimaˈsu might mean 'he is in school' or 'he is going to go to school.'

    b. maˈde

      A nominal of place followed by maˈde 'as far as,' 'up to and including but not beyond' occurs as a modifier of inflected expressions directly or followed by another particle, and indicates how far something proceeds. When a phrase ending in maˈde modifies a nominal, it is regularly followed by no. Maˈde normally loses its accent when it follows an accented word.

    Examples:

> Doˈko made iˈkimaˈsita ka⌣ 'How far (lit. as far as what place) did you go?'
> Koˈko maˈde siˈmaˈsita. 'I did [it] as far as this point' (indicating a place in the lesson, for example).

A⌐merika e⌐ wa[1] i˧kima˦sita g̃a, Nyu⌐uyo⌐oku made wa[1] i˧kimase˦ñ
desita.   'I did go to America, but I didn't go as far as New York.'
To⌐okyoo ma⌐de no mi˧ti de˦su ka⌐ 'Is it the road [that goes] as
far as Tokyo?'

c. de 'at,' 'in'

A nominal of place followed by particle de occurs as a modifier of inflected expressions directly or followed by another particle, and indicates the
place where something happens. This is in contrast with the pattern consisting
of a place word + ni + √ a⌐rima⌐su or √ i⌐ma⌐su meaning 'something or someone
is statically located in a place.' Examples:

A⌐soko de tomete kudasa⌐i. 'Please stop [the car] over there.'
De⌐pa⌐ato de ka˧ima˦sita. 'I bought [it] at a department store.'
Ho⌐ñya de wa[1] ka˧imase˦ñ desita. 'I didn't buy [it] at a bookstore.'
Ga⌐kkoo de kakima⌐sita. 'I wrote [it] at school.'
Do⌐ko de si˧masyo˦o ka. 'Where shall we do [it]?'

d. de 'by means of'

A nominal + de 'by means of' occurs as a modifier of an inflected expression directly or followed by another particle and indicates the means by
which an action is accomplished. Examples:

Ta⌐kusii de ki˧ma˦sita. 'I came by taxi.'
E⌐ñpitu de kakima⌐sita. 'I wrote with a pencil.'
Pe⌐ñ de wa[1] ka˧kimase˦ñ desita. 'I didn't write with a pen.'
Ma⌐tti de si˧ma˦sita. 'I did [it] with a match.'

e. o 'through,' 'along'

A nominal of place + o followed by a word of motion indicates the place
through which the motion takes place. Examples:

A⌐no miti o ikimasyo⌐o. 'Let's go along that street.'
Tu⌐gi⌐ no ˧ka˦do o ma⌐gatte kudasa⌐i. 'Please turn the next corner.'
(Lit. 'Please make a turn through the next corner.')

Like particle o which follows a direct object (for example, ho⌐ñ o ka˧ima˦sita
'I bought a book'), this o is often omitted in conversation.

4. Verbal Gerund + ku⌐dasaimase⌐ñ ka

Reread Grammatical Note 3 of Lesson 4.

The gerund (i. e. the -te or -de form) of a verbal + ku⌐dasaimase⌐ñ ka—lit.
'won't you [be kind enough to] give me?'—is a very polite request, softer and

----

[1] Wa = the wa of comparison.

less direct than one consisting of a gerund + the imperative ku⌐dasa⌐i. Examples:

> Ma⌐tte ku⌐dasaimase⌐n̄ ka⌐ 'Would you be kind enough to wait for me?' (Lit. 'Won't you [be kind enough to] give me waiting?')
>
> Mi⌐sete ku⌐dasaimase⌐n̄ ka⌐ 'Would you be kind enough to show me?' (Lit. 'Won't you [be kind enough to] give me showing?')
>
> O⌐siete kudasaimase⌐n̄ ka⌐ 'Would you be kind enough to instruct me?' (Lit. 'Won't you [be kind enough to] give me instructing?')

5. . . . <u>ma⌐ssu⌐ḡu itte</u> . . . <u>ma⌐ḡatte kudasa⌐i</u>

Observe the following four pairs of independent sentences:

1. (a) Kono miti (o) ma⌐ssu⌐ḡu i⌐tte kudasa⌐i. 'Please go straight along this street.'
   (b) Tukiatari (o) hi⌐dari e māḡatte kudasa⌐i. 'Please turn left at the end.'

2. (a) Kono miti (o) ma⌐ssu⌐ḡu ikimasu. '[I] go (<u>or</u> will go) straight along this street.'
   (b) Tukiatari (o) hi⌐dari e māḡarima⌐su. '[I] turn (<u>or</u> will turn) left at the end.'

3. (a) Kono miti (o) ma⌐ssu⌐ḡu i⌐kima⌐sita. '[I] went straight along this street.'
   (b) Tukiatari (o) hi⌐dari e māḡarima⌐sita. '[I] turned left at the end.'

4. (a) Kono miti (o) ma⌐ssu⌐ḡu i⌐kimasyo⌐o. 'Let's go straight along this street.'
   (b) Tukiatari (o) hi⌐dari e māḡarimasyo⌐o. 'Let's turn left at the end.'

Each pair can be combined into a single, complex sentence, meaning 'A and [then] B,' simply by replacing the inflected word or phrase at the end of the first sentence with its corresponding gerund.[1] The gerund regularly ends with comma intonation, and the next word begins a new accent phrase. Thus:

1. Kono miti (o) ma⌐ssu⌐ḡu itte, tukiatari (o) hi⌐dari e māḡatte kudasa⌐i. 'Please go straight along this street, and turn left at the end.'

2. Kono miti (o) ma⌐ssu⌐ḡu itte, tukiatari (o) hi⌐dari e māḡarima⌐su. '[I] go (<u>or</u> will go) straight along this street, and turn left at the end.'

3. Kono miti (o) ma⌐ssu⌐ḡu itte, tukiatari (o) hi⌐dari e māḡarima⌐sita. '[I] went straight along this street and turned left at the end.'

4. Kono miti (o) ma⌐ssu⌐ḡu itte, tukiatari (o) hi⌐dari e māḡarimasyo⌐o. 'Let's go straight along this street, and turn left at the end.'

---

[1] When three or more sentences are combined in this way, the inflected word or phrase at the end of every sentence except the last is replaced by the corresponding gerund.

Note that regardless of whether the sentence final is past, non-past, tentative, imperative, etc., the gerund is used in the middle. In other words, the
time and mode of complex sentences like these are determined only by the time
and mode of the inflected forms at the end of the sentence and by context—unless, of course, a time word like 'today,' 'tomorrow,' etc. furnishes additional
time evidence.

6. iˈkimaˈsu ~ maˈirimaˈsu ~ iˈrassyaimaˈsu

Iˈkimaˈsu 'go' is a plain formal verbal, and maˈirimaˈsu and iˈrassyaimaˈsu
are polite formal verbals with the same meaning. Maˈirimaˈsu, a humble
verbal, is used in polite speech in reference to oneself or members of one's
own family, while iˈrassyaimaˈsu, an honorific, is used in reference to persons
other than the speaker, in an exalting sense.

The following is a chart of the verbals introduced thus far that have polite
equivalents:

Meaning	Plain Formal	Polite Formal		
		Neutral +	Humble ↓	Honorific ↑
'be located (inanimate) or have'	aˈrimaˈsu	goˈzaimaˈsu		
'be located (animate)'	iˈmaˈsu		oˈrimaˈsu	iˈrassyaimaˈsu
'go'	iˈkimaˈsu		maˈirimaˈsu	iˈrassyaimaˈsu

7. kono saki

Kono saki means 'up ahead, from here,' and sono saki means 'up ahead,
from there,' 'further (along the road) than that.' Words of the kono series plus
other nominals of place have parallel meanings. For example:

koˈno maˈe 'in front of this'
sono usiro 'in back of that'
ano mukoo 'beyond that'
kono tonari 'next door to this [place]'
soˈno soˈba 'near that'

8. -tyoome 'chome'

With the exception of the names of a few main arteries, street names are
rarely used in Japan. Addresses are usually given in terms of location within

particular sections, and directions are regularly given in terms of landmarks
—hence the common use of maps and diagrams and the frequent stops at police
boxes for instructions.

One of the divisions into which some sections of a city are divided is the
-tyoome. While it is one of the smallest divisions, its size is not fixed, and
there may be considerable variation among the -tyoome of a given section.
The numerals of Series I (i⌐ti⌐, ni⌐, sañ, etc.) combine with -tyoome to name
(not count!) the -tyoome. Study the following list, noting particularly the forms
for '1,' '8,' and '10':

i⌐t-tyoome⌐	' 1-chome' [1]	ro⌐ku-tyoome⌐	' 6-chome'
ni-⌐tyoome⌐	' 2-chome'	na⌐na-tyoome⌐	' 7-chome'
sa⌐ñ-tyoome⌐	' 3-chome'	ha⌐t-tyoome⌐	' 8-chome'
yo⌐ñ-tyoome⌐	' 4-chome'	kyu⌐u-tyoome⌐	' 9-chome'
go-⌐tyoome⌐	' 5-chome'	zi⌐t-tyoome⌐ or	
		zyu⌐t-tyoome⌐	' 10-chome'

na⌐ñ-tyoome⌐ 'what number chome?'

The lower numbers occur more frequently.

DRILLS

A. Substitution Drill

(Insert no whenever appropriate.)

1. Please turn the next corner. Tu⌐gi⌐ no ˥ka˧do (o) ma⌐gatte kuda-
    sa˥i.

2. Please turn that corner. A⌐no ka˥do (o) ma⌐gatte kudasa˥i.

3. Please turn the corner Ga⌐kkoo no ka˥do (o) ma⌐gatte kuda-
    where the school is. sa˥i.

4. Please turn the corner De⌐pa˥ato no ˥ka˧do (o) ma⌐gatte ku-
    where the department store dasa˥i.
    is.

5. Please turn the corner Ko⌐obañ no ka˥do (o) ma⌐gatte kuda-
    where the police box is. sa˥i.

6. Please turn the corner Byo⌐oiñ no ka˥do (o) ma⌐gatte kuda-
    where the hospital is. sa˥i.

7. Please turn the corner Ku⌐suriya no ka˥do (o) ma⌐gatte ku-
    where the drugstore is. dasa˥i.

8. Please turn the corner Ta⌐bakoya no ka˥do (o) ma⌐gatte ku-
    where the cigar store is. dasa˥i.

---

[1] This is the usual English equivalent, although 'chome 1' or '1st chome'
would be more accurate.

B. Substitution Drill

1.	It's between Tokyo and Yo-kohama.	Tookyoo to Yoᵣkohama no aida deˡsu.
2.	It's between Japan and America.	Niᶠhoˡn̄ to Aᵣmerika no aida deˡsu.
3.	It's between a bank and a department store.	Giñkoo to deᵣpaˡato no aᵗida deˡsu.
4.	It's between a bookstore and a flower shop.	Hoˡn̄ya to haᶠnaˡya no aᵗida deˡsu.
5.	It's between the embassy and the consulate.	Taᶠisiˡkañ to ryoᵣoziˡkañ no aᶠida deˡsu.
6.	It's between the books and the magazines.	Hoˡn̄ to zaᵣssi no aida deˡsu.
7.	It's between Mr. Tanaka and Mr. Yamamoto.	Tanaka-sañ to Yaᵣmamoto-sañ no ai-da deˡsu.
8.	It's between the car and the taxi.	Kuruma to ᵣtaˡkusii no aᵗida deˡsu.

C. Substitution Drill

1.	MR. TANAKA went.	Taᶠnaka-sañ ḡa ikimaˡsita.
2.	Mr. Tanaka (compared with the others) went.	Taᶠnaka-sañ wa ikimaˡsita.
3.	Mr. Tanaka went, too.	Taᶠnaka-sañ mo ikimaˡsita.
4.	He went by cab.	Taˡkusii de iᵗkimaˡsita.
5.	He went along that street.	Soᶠno miti (o) ikimaˡsita.
6.	He went to the bank.	Giᶠñkoo e ikimaˡsita.
7.	He went to the bank.	Giᶠñkoo ni ikimaˡsita.
8.	He went as far as the bank.	Giᶠñkoo maˡde iᵗkimaˡsita.

D. Substitution Drill

1.	Please stop here.	Koᶠko de tomete kudasaˡi.
2.	Please wait here.	Koᶠko de maˡtte kudasai.
3.	Please write here.	Koᶠko de kaˡite kudasai.
4.	Please do [it] here.	Koᶠko de site kudasaˡi.
5.	Please buy [it] here.	Koᶠko de katte kudasaˡi.
6.	Please say [it] here.	Koᶠko de itte kudasaˡi.

E. Grammar Drill (based on Grammatical Note 2)

Tutor: Aᵣsoko e ikimaˡsu. 'I'm going to go there.'
Student: Aᵣsoko e ikimasyoˡo. 'Let's go there.'

1.	Eᵣeḡaˡkañ e maᵗirimaˡsu.	Eᵣeḡaˡkañ e maᵗirimasyoˡo.
2.	Tiˡzu (o) kaᵗkimaˡsu.	Tiˡzu (o) kaᵗkimasyoˡo.
3.	Iᵣsoḡimaˡsu.	Iᵣsoḡimasyoˡo.
4.	Gaᶠkkoo no maˡe de toᵗme-maˡsu.	Gaᶠkkoo no maˡe de toᵗmemasyoˡo.
5.	Tuᶠḡiˡ no ᵗkaˡdo (o) maᵗḡa-rimaˡsu.	Tuᶠḡiˡ no ᵗkaˡdo (o) maᵗḡarimasyoˡo.

6. Ka⌐do made mo⌐dorima⌐su.   Ka⌐do made mo⌐dorimasyo⌐o.
7. Kyo⌐o no si⌐ñbuñ (o) kai-   Kyo⌐o no si⌐ñbuñ (o) kaimasyo⌐o.
   ma⌐su.
8. So⌐o sima⌐su.   So⌐o simasyo⌐o.

F. Grammar Drill (based on Grammatical Note 1)

   Tutor: Ma⌐ru-biru e ikima⌐su. 'I'm going to go to the Maru-biru.'
   Student: Maru-biru e i⌐kita⌐i ñ desu ḡa＿   'I'd like to go to the Maru-
            biru (but). . . '

   1. A⌐sita⌐ mo i⌐kima⌐su.   A⌐sita⌐ mo i⌐kita⌐i ñ desu ḡa＿
   2. E⌐ñpitu de kakima⌐su.   Eñpitu de ka⌐kita⌐i ñ desu ḡa＿
   3. E⌐eḡa⌐kañ no ⌐ka⌐do (o)   E⌐eḡa⌐kañ no ⌐ka⌐do (o) ma⌐ḡarita⌐i
      ma⌐ḡarima⌐su.   ñ desu ḡa＿
   4. Ze⌐ñbu si⌐ma⌐su.   Ze⌐ñbu si⌐ta⌐i ñ desu ḡa＿
   5. Yu⌐ubi⌐ñkyoku e i⌐kima⌐su.   Yu⌐ubi⌐ñkyoku e i⌐kita⌐i ñ desu ḡa＿
   6. A⌐tarasi⌐i ku⌐ruma (o) kai-   A⌐tarasi⌐i kuruma (o) ka⌐ita⌐i ñ desu
      ma⌐su.   ḡa＿
   7. Tyo⌐tto u⌐kaḡaima⌐su ḡa＿   Tyo⌐tto u⌐kaḡaita⌐i ñ desu ḡa＿
   8. A⌐soko de tomema⌐su.   Asoko de to⌐meta⌐i ñ desu ḡa＿

G. Grammar Drill (based on Grammatical Note 4)

   Tutor: A⌐na⌐ta no siñbuñ (o) ⌐mi⌐sete kudasai.'Please show me your
            paper.'
   Student: A⌐na⌐ta no siñbuñ (o) ⌐mi⌐sete ku⌐dasaimase⌐ñ ka＿ 'Would
            you be kind enough to show me your paper?'

   1. Pe⌐ñ de ⌐ka⌐ite kudasai.   Pe⌐ñ de ⌐ka⌐ite ku⌐dasaimase⌐ñ ka＿
   2. Ko⌐ko de tomete kudasa⌐i.   Ko⌐ko de tomete kudasaimase⌐ñ ka＿
   3. Ka⌐do made mo⌐do⌐tte kuda-   Ka⌐do made mo⌐do⌐tte ku⌐dasaima-
      sai.   se⌐ñ ka＿
   4. A⌐sita⌐ mo i⌐tte kudasa⌐i.   A⌐sita⌐ mo i⌐tte kudasaimase⌐ñ ka＿
   5. Mi⌐ti (o) osiete kudasa⌐i.   Mi⌐ti (o) osiete kudasaimase⌐ñ ka＿
   6. Mo⌐o iti-do itte kudasa⌐i.   Mo⌐o iti-do itte kudasaimase⌐ñ ka＿
   7. Tu⌐ḡi⌐ no ⌐ka⌐do (o) ma-   Tu⌐ḡi⌐ no ⌐ka⌐do (o) ma⌐ḡatte kudasa-
      ⌐ḡatte kudasa⌐i.   imase⌐ñ ka＿
   8. Koko de ⌐ma⌐tte kudasai.   Koko de ⌐ma⌐tte ku⌐dasaimase⌐ñ ka＿

H. Grammar Drill (based on Grammatical Note 5)

   Tutor: Ko⌐no miti (o) itte kudasa⌐i. Tu⌐ḡi⌐ no ⌐ka⌐do (o) ma⌐ḡatte
            kudasa⌐i. 'Please go along this street. Please turn at the
            next corner.' (2 sentences)
   Student: Kono miti (o) itte, tu⌐ḡi⌐ no ⌐ka⌐do (o) ma⌐ḡatte kudasa⌐i.
            'Please go along this street and turn at the next corner.'
            (1 complex sentence)

   1. Ka⌐do made mo⌐dorima⌐sita.   Ka⌐do made mo⌐do⌐tte, so⌐ko de to-
      So⌐ko de tomema⌐sita.   mema⌐sita.
   2. To⌐okyo⌐o-eki no ⌐ma⌐e de   To⌐okyo⌐o-eki no ⌐ma⌐e de tomete,
      to⌐mete kudasa⌐i.   soko de ⌐ma⌐tte kudasai.
      Soko de ⌐ma⌐tte kudasa⌐i.

3. Tu⌐g̅i⌐ no ⌐ka⁺do (o) mi⌐g̅i   Tu⌐g̅i⌐ no ⌐ka⁺do (o) mi̅g̅i e ma-
   e mag̅arima⌐su.   g̅atte, ano miti (o) tu⌐kiatari ma⌐de
   Ano miti (o) tu⌐kiatari ma⌐de   ikimasu.
   ikimasu.

4. Ho⌐ñya e i⁺kimasyo⁺o.   Ho⌐ñya e itte, a⌐tarasi⌐i zi⁺biki⁺ (o)
   A⌐tarasi⌐i zi⁺biki⁺ (o) ka⁺i-   ka⁺imasyo⁺o.
   masyo⁺o.

I. Grammar Drill

Tutor: Wa⌐karima⌐su.   'It's clear.' (affirmative)
Student: Wa⌐karimase⌐ñ.   'It isn't clear.' (negative)

1. A⌐buna⌐i desu.   A⌐bunaku arimase⌐ñ.
2. Gi⌐ñkoo no ma⌐e desu.   Gi⌐ñkoo no ma⌐e zya a⁺rimase⁺ñ.
3. Ma⌐g̅arima⌐sita.   Ma⌐g̅arimase⌐ñ desita.
4. Ma⌐ssu⌐g̅u desu.   Ma⌐ssu⌐g̅u zya a⁺rimase⁺ñ.
5. I⌐kita⌐i desu.   I⌐kitaku arimase⌐ñ.
6. To⌐mema⌐su.   To⌐memase⌐ñ.
7. E⌐eg̅a⌐kañ desita.   E⌐eg̅a⌐kañ zya a⁺rimase⁺ñ desita.
8. A⌐o⌐i desu.   A⌐oku a⁺rimase⁺ñ.

J. Level Drill[1]

1. Ta⌐bako (g̅a) arima⌐su ka⌐   Ta⌐bako (g̅a) gozaima⌐su ka⌐
2. I⌐ma i⁺kimasyo⁺o.   I⌐ma ma⁺irimasyo⁺o.
3. Ta⌐naka ima⌐su ka⌐   Ta⌐naka orima⌐su ka⌐
4. Tanaka-sañ (wa) ⌐do⌐ko ni   Tanaka-sañ (wa) ⌐do⌐tira ni i⁺rassya-
   i⁺kima⁺su ka⌐   ima⁺su ka⌐
5. Tanaka-sañ (wa) ⌐do⌐ko ni   Tanaka-sañ (wa) ⌐do⌐tira ni i⁺rassya-
   i⁺ma⁺su ka⌐   ima⁺su ka⌐
6. Tyo⌐tto ⌐ma⁺tte kudasai.   Syo⌐osyoo o⁺mati-kudasa⁺i.
7. I⌐kutu a⁺rima⁺sita ka⌐   O⌐ikutu gozaima⌐sita ka⌐
8. Watakusi (wa) i⌐kimase⌐ñ   Watakusi (wa) ma⁺irimase⌐ñ desita.
   desita.

K. Expansion Drill

1. I'm not going to go.   I⌐kimase⌐ñ.
   Wouldn't you [like to] go?   I⌐kimase⌐ñ ka⌐
   Wouldn't you [like to] go   E⌐eg̅a⌐kañ e i⁺kimase⁺ñ ka⌐
   to a movie (theater)?
   Wouldn't you [like to] go   A⌐na⌐ta mo e⌐eg̅a⌐kañ e i⁺kimase⁺ñ
   to a movie (theater), too?   ka⌐

---

[1] In each case, the sentence on the right is the polite equivalent of the sentence on the left.

2. I don't understand.   Wa⌐karimase⌐n̄.

I don't know the way.   Mi⌐ti ḡa wakarimase⌐n̄.

I want to go, but I don't know the way.   I⌐kita⌐i n̄ desu ḡa, mi⌐ti ḡa wakarimase⌐n̄.

I want to go to Yokohama, but I don't know the way.   Yo⌐kohama e ikita⌐i n̄ desu ḡa, mi⌐ti ḡa wakarimase⌐n̄.

3. Would(n't) you give [it] to me?   Ku⌐dasaimase⌐n̄ ka⌐

Would you be kind enough to teach me?   O⌐siete kudasaimase⌐n̄ ka⌐

Would you be kind enough to show me the way?   Mi⌐ti (o) osiete kudasaimase⌐n̄ ka⌐

I'd like to go. Would you be kind enough to show me the way?   I⌐kita⌐i n̄ desu ḡa, mi⌐ti (o) osiete kudasaimase⌐n̄ ka⌐

I'd like to go to the Imperial Theater. Would you be kind enough to show me the way?   Te⌐ekoku-ge⌐kizyoo e i⌐kita⌐i n̄ desu ḡa, mi⌐ti (o) osiete kudasaimase⌐n̄ ka⌐

4. It's a building.   Ta⌐temo⌐no desu.

It's a big building.   O⌐oki⌐i ta⌐temo⌐no desu.

It's a big building on the right.   Mi⌐gi no ho⌐o no o⌐oki⌐i ta⌐temo⌐no desu.

It's a big building on the right up ahead.   Saki no mi⌐gi no ho⌐o no o⌐oki⌐i ta⌐temo⌐no desu.

It's a big building on the right up ahead of that hospital.   Sono byooin̄ no saki no mi⌐gi no ho⌐o no o⌐oki⌐i ta⌐temo⌐no desu.

5. Let's go.   I⌐kimasyo⌐o.

Shall we go?   I⌐kimasyo⌐o ka.

Shall we go by cab?   Ta⌐kusii de i⌐kimasyo⌐o ka.

Shall we go to the station by cab?   E⌐ki e ⌐ta⌐kusii de i⌐kimasyo⌐o ka.

6. I brought [it] to a halt.   To⌐mema⌐sita.

I brought the car to a halt.   Ku⌐ruma (o) tomema⌐sita.

I stopped the car in front.   Ma⌐e de ku⌐ruma (o) tomema⌐sita.

I stopped the car in front of the school.   Ga⌐kkoo no ma⌐e de ku⌐ruma (o) tomema⌐sita.

7. Please make a turn.   Ma⌐gatte kudasa⌐i.

Please make a turn to the right.   Mi⌐gi e maḡatte kudasa⌐i.

Please go as far as the end of the street and turn to the right.   Tu⌐kiatari ma⌐de itte, mi⌐gi e maḡatte kudasa⌐i.

Please go along this street as far as the end, and turn to the right.   Kono miti (o) tu⌐kiatari ma⌐de itte, mi⌐gi e maḡatte kudasa⌐i.

8. Please stop. [1]   To゛mete kudasa゛i.
    Please stop there.   So゛ko de tomete kudasa゛i.
    Please back up and stop   Mo゛do゛tte, so゛ko de tomete kudasa゛i.
    there.
    Please back up as far as   Ka゛do made mo゛do゛tte, so゛ko de to-
    the corner and stop   mete kudasa゛i.
    there.

SUPPLEMENTARY CONVERSATIONS

1. Cab driver: Do゛tira made?
   Smith: Go゛tañda゛[2]-eki made.
   Cab driver: Ha゛i wa゛karima゛sita.
   Smith: Añmari i゛soḡa゛nai de kudasai⌐
   Cab driver: Da゛izyo゛obu desu yo. . . .   Ko゛ko ḡa Gotañda゛-eki desu ḡa⌐
   Smith: Ko゛no e゛ki no ゛so゛ba no byo゛oiñ e ikita゛i ñ desu ḡa, kono heñ
                ni ko゛obañ wa arimase゛ñ ka⌐   Byo゛oiñ wa koobañ no usiro
                de゛su ḡa⌐
   Cab driver: A゛soko ni koobañ ḡa arima゛su yo⌐   Ho゛ñya no mi゛ḡi no ho゛o
                desu.
   Smith: A゛a, so゛o desu ゛ne゛e.   So゛no koobañ no ka゛do o hi゛dari e ma-
                ḡatte kudasa゛i.
   Cab driver: Ha゛i.
   Smith: Mo゛o suko゛si sa゛ki ma゛de i゛tte kudasa゛i. A. Ko゛ko de゛su yo⌐
                Go゛ku゛roosama. I゛kura desu ka⌐
   Cab driver: Ni゛hyaku゛-eñ desu. A゛ri゛ḡatoo gozaimasu.

2. Smith: Tyo゛tto u゛kaḡaima゛su ḡa, To゛okyoo-gi゛ñkoo ko゛no heñ de゛su
                ka⌐
   Stranger: To゛okyoo-gi゛ñkoo desu ka⌐   Ni゛hoñ-gi゛ñkoo zya a゛rimase゛ñ
                ka⌐   Ni゛hoñ-gi゛ñkoo wa so゛no depa゛ato no to゛nari de゛su ḡa⌐
   Smith: To゛okyoo-gi゛ñkoo desu ḡa⌐
   Stranger: So゛o desu ka. Ko゛no heñ ni゛ wa a゛rimase゛ñ yo⌐

English Equivalents

1. Cab driver: Where to? (lit. How far?)
   Smith: (As far as) Gotanda Station.
   Cab driver: All right.
   Smith: Don't go so fast.
   Cab driver: Don't worry! . . . Here's Gotanda Station (but) . . .
   Smith: I want to go to a hospital near this station. Is(n't) there a po-

---

[1] Lit. 'bring something to a halt.'

[2] Section of Tokyo.

lice box around here? The hospital is behind the police box
(but). . . [1]

Cab driver: There's a police box over there! It's to the right of the book-
              store.
Smith: Oh, that's right. Turn left at the corner where that police box
              is.
Cab driver: All right.
Smith: Go a little further ahead. Oh, this is the place! Thanks (for
              your trouble). How much is it?
Cab driver: (It's) ¥ 200. Thank you.

2. Smith: Excuse me but is the Bank of Tokyo around here?
   Stranger: The Bank of Tokyo? Don't you mean the Bank of Japan? The
              Bank of Japan is next door to that department store (but). . .
   Smith: It's the Bank of Tokyo [I'm looking for] (but). . . [2]
   Stranger: Oh? It's not around here.

EXERCISES

1. Give the following instructions to the taxi driver:

    a. Imperial Hotel, please.
    b. American Embassy, please.
    c. St. Luke's Hospital, please.
    d. Please hurry.
    e. Please don't go so fast.
    f. Turn right.
    g. Turn left.
    h. Go straight.
    i. Turn right at the next corner.
    j. Turn left at the corner where the bank is.
    k. Stop here.
    l. Stop in front of the department store.
    m. Stop in back of that taxi.
    n. Back up a little.
    o. Back up to the corner.
    p. Look out!

2. Using a detailed street map of any area—real or imaginary—practice con-
    versations between a taxi driver and his customer by choosing particular
    destinations and giving explicit directions.

---

[1] 'but—where is the police box?'
[2] 'but—maybe it isn't around here.'

3. Practice conversations between Mr. Smith and a Japanese stranger, asking
    how to reach particular destinations.

4. Practice the Basic Dialogues with appropriate variations and props.

Lesson 8. Time

BASIC DIALOGUES: FOR MEMORIZATION

(a)

Tanaka

what time?
1. What time is it (now)?

naˀn̄-zi
Iˀma ˹naˀn̄-zi desu ka˩ or
Iˀma ˹naˀn̄-zi?

Yamamoto

one o'clock
2. It's one o'clock.

iˈtiˀ-zi
Iˈtiˀ-zi (desu).

Tanaka

exactly
3. Is it exactly one o'clock?

tyoodo
Tyo˹odo itiˀ-zi desu ka˩ or
Tyo˹odo itiˀ-zi?

Yamamoto

two minutes or minute
   two[1]
minute two past or after
4. No. It's 1:02. or No. It's
two minutes after one.

niˀ-hun̄
ni-˹huˀn̄-suḡi
Iie. Iˈtiˀ-zi ˹niˀ-hun̄ (desu). or
Iie. Iˈtiˀ-zi ni-˹huˀn̄-suḡi (desu).

Tanaka

clock or watch
5. This watch is out of order.

tokee
Kono tokee (wa) daˈmeˀ (desu).

ten minutes or minute
   ten
minute ten before the
   hour
6. It says (lit. is) ten minutes
before.

ziˀp-pun̄ or
zyuˀp-pun̄
zi˹p-puˀn̄-mae
Zi˹p-puˀn̄-mae (desu).

(b)

Tanaka

first day of the month
7. Is today the first?

tuˈitatiˀ
Kyoˀo (wa) tuˈitatiˀ desu ka˩

---

[1] I.e. 'minute two of a sixty-minute hour.'

113

Smith

second day of the month or two days	hutu-ka
8. Why no, it's the second.	Iie. Hu⌐tu-ka de⌐su yo⌐

Tanaka

Monday	getuyoo[1] or ge⌐tuyo⌐obi
9. It isn't Monday?	Ge⌐tuyoo zya arimase⌐ñ ka⌐

Smith

Tuesday	ka⌐yo⌐o(bi)[2]
Wednesday	su⌐iyo⌐o(bi)[2]
Thursday	mo⌐kuyo⌐o(bi)[2]
Friday	ki⌐ñyo⌐o(bi)[2]
Saturday	do⌐yo⌐o(bi)[2]
Sunday	nitiyoo or ni⌐tiyo⌐obi
10. No (i.e. that's right). It's Tuesday.	E⌐e, ka⌐yo⌐o desu yo⌐

Tanaka

11. Oh, that's right!	A⌐a, so⌐o desu ⌐ne⌐e.

(c)

Tanaka

when	i⌐tu
come	ki⌐ma⌐su or ma⌐irima⌐su↑ or i⌐rassyaima⌐su↑
12. When did you come here?	I⌐tu ko⌐ko e kima⌐sita ka⌐ or I⌐tu ko⌐tira e irassyaima⌐sita ka⌐

Smith

three years or the year three	sañ-neñ
three years before or ago at a time three years ago	sa⌐ñ-neñ ma⌐e sa⌐ñ-neñ ma⌐e ni
13. I came three years ago.	Sa⌐ñ-neñ ma⌐e ni ki⌐ma⌐sita. or Sa⌐ñ-neñ ma⌐e ni ma⌐irima⌐sita.
Meiji Era (1868–1912) Taisho Era (1912–1926) Showa Era (1926–)	me⌐ezi taisyoo syoowa

---

[1] Alternate accented form: ge⌐tuyo⌐o.

[2] Short form has unaccented alternant.

58885

          32 years or the year 32   sa⌐nzyuu ⌐ni⌐-neñ
14. That was Showa 32.   Sore wa syōowa ⌐sa⌐nzyuu ⌐ni⌐-neñ
                                               desita.

                              Tanaka

    airplane   hi⌐ko⌐oki
15. Did you come by plane?   Hi⌐ko⌐oki de ki⌐ma⌐sita ka⌐   or
                                               Hi⌐ko⌐oki de i⌐rassyaima⌐sita ka⌐

                               Smith

    ship   hu⌐ne
16. No. I came by ship.   Iie, hu⌐ne de ki⌐ma⌐sita.   or
                                               Iie, hu⌐ne de ma⌐irima⌐sita.

                              Tanaka

    about how long?   dono-ḡurai
    be required or take   ka⌐karima⌐su
17. About how long did it take?   Do⌐no-ḡurai kakarima⌐sita ka⌐

                               Smith

    two weeks   ni-⌐syu⌐ukañ
    about two weeks   ni-⌐syuukañ-ḡu⌐rai
18. It took about two weeks.   Ni-⌐syuukañ-ḡu⌐rai ka⌐karima⌐sita.

                                (d)

                              Tanaka

    day before yesterday   o⌐toto⌐i
19. Say, I went to Nikko the day   Ototoi ⌐Ni⌐kkoo e i⌐kima⌐sita yo⌐
    before yesterday.

                               Smith

20. Oh? How was it?   So⌐o desu ka. Do⌐o desita ka⌐

                              Tanaka

    exceedingly or very   totemo   or
                                               tottemo
21. It was very pretty. Wouldn't   To⌐ttemo ki⌐ree desita. A⌐na⌐ta mo
    you [like to] go too?   i⌐kimase⌐ñ ka⌐

                               Smith

    from here   koko kara
22. I'd like to go some (lit. one)   Iti-do i⌐kita⌐i ñ desu ga, ko⌐ko kara
    time. About how long does   Ni⌐kkoo made do⌐no-ḡurai kakari-
    it take from here to Nikko?   ma⌐su ka⌐

                              Tanaka

    electric train or street car   de⌐nsya[1]

----
[1] Has unaccented alternant.

(steam) train	ki⌐sya⌐
bus	ba˺su
three hours	sa⌐ñ-zi˺kañ
three hours and a half	sa⌐ñ-zikañ-ha˺ñ
about three hours and a half	sa⌐ñ-zikañ-hañ-g̃u˺rai

23. I went by electric train. It took about three hours and a half.

Watakusi wa ⌐de˺ñsya de iᵏkima˄sita g̃a, sa⌐ñ- zikañ- hañ- g̃u˺rai kaᵏkarima˄sita.

(e)

Smith

vacation or holiday or time off	ya⌐sumi˺ or oyasumi ꜛ

24. When is your vacation?

Oyasumi (wa) ⌐i˺tu desu ka⌐

Tanaka

this year	kotosi
August	ha⌐ti-g̃atu˺
about August	ha⌐ti-g̃atu-g̃o˺ro

25. This year it will be about August (but). . .

Kotosi wa ha⌐ti-g̃atu-g̃o˺ro desu ḡa_

Smith

one month	i⌐k-ka˺g̃etu

26. Will it be a month?

I⌐k-ka˺g̃etu desu ka⌐

Tanaka

27. Heavens no!

To˺ñde mo arimase˺ñ.

ten days or tenth of the month	too-ka

28. It will be ten days.

To⌐o-ka de˺su yo⌐

NOTES ON THE BASIC DIALOGUES

1. The Japanese equivalent WITH i⌐ma and the English equivalent WITHOUT 'now' are more usual.

5. Tokee is the general term for 'timepiece,' covering all kinds of clocks and watches. There are more specific terms which can be used when it is necessary to distinguish among different kinds of timepieces.

9, 10. The shorter forms of the days of the week, without -bi, are less formal, and common in conversation.

12. Particle e maybe replaced here by particle ni (cf. Lesson 7, Grammatical Note 3 a).

14. The Japanese regularly count years according to eras, which in recent times have coincided with the reigns of their emperors. Each era, or reign, has its own name. When a new emperor takes the throne, a new

era begins; the remainder of the current calendar year is the year 1
(ga⌐nneñ) of that era, the next calendar year is the year 2, and so on.
Thus 1926—the end of the Taisho Era—began as Taisho 15 (the 15th year
of Taisho) but, with the accession of a new emperor, became Showa 1;
1927 was Showa 2.   To distinguish the Western system, seereki is used
to designate the Christian Era: syoowa 35, for example, corresponds to
seereki 1960.

17. Ka⌐karima¬su (gerund ka⌐ka¬tte) means 'take' or 'require,' as in 'take
time,' 'take money.'   Like wa⌐karima¬su, i⌐rima¬su, and a⌐rima¬su,
ka⌐karima¬su may occur with particles ḡa and/or wa, but never with particle o.   Ka⌐karima¬su frequently occurs with extent constructions, as in
the present instance, with no particle.

19. See Note 12 above.

21. Tottemo is the more emphatic alternant of totemo.   Intensifying words
like totemo and zu¬ibuñ have a complicated distribution, and students can
learn where they occur only by observing how native speakers use them.
For example, before ta⌐ka¬i, both totemo and zu¬ibuñ occur frequently,
but before i¬i, only totemo is common.   Distinguishing among the meanings of these intensifying words is something like trying to distinguish
among degrees of intensity of English 'it is very difficult,' 'it is extremely
difficult,' 'it is terribly difficult,' 'it is exceedingly difficult,' 'it is awfully difficult,' etc.
Note the use of negative + ka as an invitation.

22. Note the use of particle ḡa connecting a statement with a related question.

23. Here the particle ḡa connects a qualification with the direct answer to a
question.   The answer to the question 'how long does it take?' is 'it took
about three hours and a half,' but this answer is subject to the immediately
preceding qualification—'I went by electric train.'

25. 'but—why do you ask?'

27. To⌐nde mo arimase¬ñ is an emphatic rejection of what has been said and,
accordingly, must be used with caution.   Common English equivalents are
'Ridiculous!' 'Far from it!' 'Nothing of the kind!' 'Don't be silly!' 'Never happen!'

28. The same sentence in a different context could mean 'It is (or will be) the
tenth (of the month).'

GRAMMATICAL NOTES

1. T i m e   C o u n t e r s : -huñ, -zi, -zikañ, -ka/-niti, -syuukañ, -ḡatu, -ka-
ḡetu, -neñ

The above counters can be divided into three groups:

A. those that combine with numerals to NAME:
   (1) -zi—to name the o'clocks
   (2) -ḡatu—to name the calendar months

B. those that combine with numerals to COUNT:

    (1) -zikañ—to count the number of hours

    (2) -syuukañ—to count the number of weeks

    (3) -kaḡetu—to count the number of months

C. those that combine with numerals to NAME AND COUNT:

    (1) -huñ—to name the minute of a sixty-minute hour and count the number of minutes

    (2) -ka/-niti—to name the days of the month[1] and count the number of days

    (3) -neñ—to name the years[2] and count the number of years

With the exception of -ka/-niti, all the above counters combine with numerals of Series I (i⌐ti⌐, ni⌐, sañ, etc.). -Ka/-niti combines with some numerals of Series I and some of Series II (the hi⌐to⌐, huta, mi series), and there are some irregular forms.

Study the following lists, noting particularly the assimilated forms (for example, ro⌐ku⌐ + -huñ = ro⌐p-puñ) and the irregular forms (for example, hutu-ka, nano-ka, etc.).

-huñ		-zi		-zikañ	
i⌐p-puñ	'1 minute' or 'minute 1'	i⌐ti⌐-zi	'1 o'clock'	i⌐ti-zi⌐kañ	'1 hour'
ni⌐-huñ	'2 minutes' or 'minute 2'	ni⌐-zi	'2 o'clock'	ni-⌐zi⌐kañ	'2 hours'
sa⌐ñ-puñ	'3 minutes' or 'minute 3'	sa⌐ñ-zi	'3 o'clock'	sa⌐ñ-zi⌐kañ	'3 hours'
yo⌐ñ-puñ	'4 minutes' or 'minute 4'	yo⌐-zi	'4 o'clock'	yo-⌐zi⌐kañ	'4 hours'
go⌐-huñ	'5 minutes' or 'minute 5'	go⌐-zi	'5 o'clock'	go-⌐zi⌐kañ	'5 hours'
ro⌐p-puñ	'6 minutes' or 'minute 6'	ro⌐ku⌐-zi	'6 o'clock'	ro⌐ku-zi⌐kañ	'6 hours'
na⌐na⌐-huñ or si⌐ti⌐-huñ	'7 minutes' or 'minute 7'	si⌐ti⌐-zi	'7 o'clock'	na⌐na-zi⌐kañ or si⌐ti-zi⌐kañ	'7 hours'
ha⌐ti⌐-huñ or ha⌐p-puñ	'8 minutes' or 'minute 8'	ha⌐ti⌐-zi	'8 o'clock'	ha⌐ti-zi⌐kañ	'8 hours'
kyu⌐u-huñ	'9 minutes' or 'minute 9'	ku⌐-zi	'9 o'clock'	ku-⌐zi⌐kañ	'9 hours'
zi⌐p-puñ or zyu⌐p-puñ	'10 minutes' or 'minute 10'	zyu⌐u-zi	'10 o'clock'	zyu⌐u-zi⌐kañ	'10 hours'
na⌐ñ-puñ	'how many minutes?' or 'what minute?'	na⌐ñ-zi	'what time?'	na⌐ñ-zi⌐kañ	'how many hours?'

---

[1] Except the first day of the month, for which there is the special word tu⌐itati⌐.

[2] Except the year 1. See the note on sentence 14 above. There are also counters -neñkañ and -kaneñkañ, which combine with numerals to count (but not name) years and hence belong in Group B above.

-ka/-niti

(tu⌐itati¬	'the first day of the month')		
i⌐ti-niti¬	'one day'		
hutu-ka	'the second'	or	'2 days'
mi-kka	'the third'	or	'3 days'
yo-kka	'the fourth'	or	'4 days'
itu-ka	'the fifth'	or	'5 days'
mu-ika	'the sixth'	or	'6 days'
nano-ka	'the seventh'	or	'7 days'
yoo-ka	'the eighth'	or	'8 days'
ko⌐kono-ka¬	'the ninth'	or	'9 days'
too-ka	'the tenth'	or	'10 days'
zyu⌐uiti-niti¬	'the eleventh'	or	'11 days'
zyu⌐uni-niti¬	'the twelfth'	or	'12 days'
zyu¬usañ-niti	'the thirteenth'	or	'13 days'
zyu¬uyo-kka	'the fourteenth'	or	'14 days'
zyu¬ugo-niti	'the fifteenth'	or	'15 days'
zyu⌐uroku-niti¬	'the sixteenth'	or	'16 days'
zyu⌐usiti-niti¬	'the seventeenth'	or	'17 days'
zyu⌐uhati-niti¬	'the eighteenth'	or	'18 days'
zyu¬uku-niti	'the nineteenth'	or	'19 days'
hatu-ka	'the twentieth'	or	'20 days'
ni¬zyuu i⌐ti-niti¬	'the twenty-first'	or	'21 days'
ni¬zyuu ni-⌐niti¬	'the twenty-second'	or	'22 days'
ni¬zyuu ⌐sa¬ñ-niti	'the twenty-third'	or	'23 days'
ni¬zyuu yo-kka	'the twenty-fourth'	or	'24 days'
ni¬zyuu ⌐go¬-niti	'the twenty-fifth'	or	'25 days'
ni¬zyuu ro⌐ku-niti¬	'the twenty-sixth'	or	'26 days'
ni¬zyuu si⌐ti-niti¬	'the twenty-seventh'	or	'27 days'
ni¬zyuu ha⌐ti-niti¬	'the twenty-eighth'	or	'28 days'
ni¬zyuu ⌐ku¬-niti	'the twenty-ninth'	or	'29 days'
sa⌐ñzyu¬u-niti	'the thirtieth'	or	'30 days'
sa¬ñzyuu i⌐ti-niti¬	'the thirty-first'	or	'31 days'
na¬ñ-niti	'what date?'	or	'how many days?'

-syuukañ

i⌐s-syu¬ukañ	'1 week'
ni-⌐syu¬ukañ	'2 weeks'
sa⌐ñ-syu¬ukañ	'3 weeks'
yo⌐ñ-syu¬ukañ	'4 weeks'
go-⌐syu¬ukañ	'5 weeks'
ro⌐ku-syu¬ukañ	'6 weeks'
na⌐na-syu¬ukañ or	
si⌐ti-syu¬ukañ	'7 weeks'
ha⌐s-syu¬ukañ	'8 weeks'
kyu⌐u-syu¬ukañ	'9 weeks'
zi⌐s-syu¬ukañ or	
zyu⌐s-syu¬ukañ	'10 weeks'
na⌐ñ-syu¬ukañ	'how many weeks?'

-ḡatu		-kaḡetu	
i⌐ti-ḡatu¬	'January'	i⌐k-ka¬ḡetu	'1 month'
ni-⌐ḡatu¬	'February'	ni-⌐ka¬ḡetu	'2 months'
sa¬n̄-ḡatu¬	'March'	sa⌐n̄-ka¬ḡetu	'3 months'
si-⌐ḡatu¬	'April'	yo⌐n̄-ka¬ḡetu	'4 months'
go¬-ḡatu	'May'	go-⌐ka¬ḡetu	'5 months'
ro⌐ku-ḡatu¬	'June'	ro⌐k-ka¬ḡetu	'6 months'
si⌐ti-ḡatu¬	'July'	si⌐ti-ka¬ḡetu or	
ha⌐ti-ḡatu¬	'August'	na⌐na-ka¬ḡetu	'7 months'
ku¬-ḡatu	'September'	ha⌐ti-ka¬ḡetu or	
zyu⌐u-ḡatu¬	'October'	ha⌐k-ka¬ḡetu	'8 months'
zyu⌐uiti-ḡatu¬	'November'	ku-⌐ka¬ḡetu or	
zyu⌐uni-ḡatu¬	'December'	kyu⌐u-ka¬ḡetu	'9 months'
		zi⌐k-ka¬ḡetu or	
na¬n̄-ḡatu	'what month?'	zyu⌐k-ka¬ḡetu	'10 months'
		na⌐n̄-ka¬ḡetu	'how many
			months?'

-nen̄		
i⌐ti¬-nen̄	'1 year'	
(ga¬n̄nen̄	'the year 1')	
ni¬-nen̄	'2 years'	or 'the year 2'
san̄-nen̄	'3 years'	or 'the year 3'
yo-nen̄	'4 years'	or 'the year 4'
go-nen̄	'5 years'	or 'the year 5'
ro⌐ku¬-nen̄	'6 years'	or 'the year 6'
si⌐ti¬-nen̄ or		
na⌐na¬-nen̄	'7 years'	or 'the year 7'
ha⌐ti¬-nen̄	'8 years'	or 'the year 8'
ku-nen̄ or		
kyu¬u-nen̄	'9 years'	or 'the year 9'
zyu¬u-nen̄	'10 years'	or 'the year 10'

na¬n̄-nen̄   'how many years?'   or 'what year?'

The regular order of Japanese dates is year—month—day, with the smaller unit always following the larger. The units are usually joined without intervening particles. [1] Examples:

---

[1] But they can be joined by particle no. Ni-ḡatu kŏkono-ka might be compared to 'February 9th,' and ni-⌐ḡatu no kokono-ka¬ to 'the 9th of February [rather than of another month].'

[syoowa] ⌐zyu┐uku-neñ ⌐sa┐ñ-g̃atu mi̅-kka 'March 3, 19 *[Showa]*
(= A. D. 1944)'
[seereki] ⌐se┐ñ ʰkyuᐟuhyaku go⌐zyu┐u-neñ ha̅ti-g̃atu mu̅-ika
'August 6, 1950 *[Christian era]* '

-Ha┐ñ added to a number means 'a half added to the preceding':

       i⌐ti-zi-ha┐ñ '1:30'
       i⌐ti-zikañ-ha┐ñ 'one hour and a half'
       ni-⌐neñ-ha┐ñ 'two years and a half'

But hañ- + counter means 'a half of one counter unit' (not all counters occur in
this combination):

       ha⌐ñ-zi┐kañ 'a half hour'
       ha⌐ñ-niti┐ 'a half day'

2. Telling Time

For telling time in terms of the hour only, a numeral + counter -zi is used.
Thus:

       Yo┐-zi desu. 'It's 4 o'clock.'

To indicate time before the hour, ma┐e is added, and to indicate time after the
hour, su⌐g̃i┐ is added. Thus:

       Si⌐ti-zi ma┐e desu. 'It's before 7.'
       Ku-⌐zi sug̃i┐ desu. 'It's after 9.'

To tell time in terms of hours and minutes, two patterns are used. The
simpler pattern consists of the o'clock + the minute. This corresponds to the
English pattern of '2:10,' '8:15,' '10:45,' etc. Thus:

       Ni┐-zi ⌐zyu┐p-puñ desu. 'It's 2:10.' (Lit. 'It's 2 o'clock minute 10.')
       Ha⌐ti┐-zi ⌐zyu┐ugo-huñ desu. 'It's 8:15.'
       Zyu┐u-zi ⌐yo┐ñzyuu ʰgo┐-huñ desu. 'It's 10:45.'

The alternate pattern consists of (a) the o'clock + the minute before + -mae
'before' (when the minute hand is in the left half of the clock; compare English
'5 of 2,' '20 minutes to 3,' 'a quarter of 8,' etc.); and (b) the o'clock + the minute after + -sug̃i 'beyond' (when the minute hand is in the right half of the clock;
compare English ' 10 after 2,' 'a quarter past 3,' etc.). The accent of the
minute expression shifts to the first syllable of the counter. Thus:

       Ni┐-zi go-⌐hu┐ñ-mae desu. 'It's 5 of 2.' (Lit. 'It's 2 o'clock minute 5
       before.')
       Ha⌐ti┐-zi zyu⌐ugo-hu┐ñ-mae desu. 'It's a quarter of 8.'
       Ni┐-zi zi⌐p-pu┐ñ-sug̃i desu. 'It's 10 after 2.'
       Sa┐ñ-zi zyu⌐ugo-hu┐ñ-sug̃i desu. 'It's a quarter after 3.'

In all the above examples, -huñ occurs as a naming counter (cf. Group C of
the preceding grammatical note), telling WHICH minute of the hour. -Huñ also
occurs as an enumerating counter, telling HOW MANY minutes, before ma┐e
'ago,' 'before' and also in various other expressions. Compare the following:

Zi⌐p-pu⌉ñ-mae desita. 'It was 10 of.' (i. e. it was 10 minutes before
the hour)

Zi⌉p-puñ ⌐ma⁺e desita.
      or   } 'It was 10 minutes ago.'
Zi⌐p-puñ ma⁺e desita.

Sentences like those in the groups above are differentiated by accent. Else-
where, context determines whether -huñ is naming or counting.

3. Informal Speech

The subject of speech levels has already been introduced in connection with
the occurrence of parallel pairs such as a⌐rima⌉su and go⌐zaima⌉su, i⌐kima⌉su
and i⌐rassyaima⌉su, ge⌉ñki and o⌐ge⌉ñki, i⌐kura and oikura. In general, we
can speak of two major levels: the POLITE and the PLAIN. The polite includes NEUTRAL POLITE (like go⌐zaima⌉su⁺), HUMBLE (like ma⌐irima⌉su↓),
and HONORIFIC (like i⌐rassyaima⌉su↑). In addition to politeness levels, there
are formality levels—the FORMAL and the INFORMAL. A given verbal may
be formal polite, informal polite, formal plain, or informal plain. Verbals
ending in -ma⌉su and all of its derived forms (-ma⌉sita, -mase⌉ñ, -mase⌉ñ desita, and -masyo⌉o) and copula forms de⌉su, de⌉sita, and de⌐syo⌉o are all
formal forms. Thus, a⌐rima⌉su is formal plain style, whereas go⌐zaima⌉su
is formal polite; i⌐kima⌉su is formal plain, but ma⌐irima⌉su and i⌐rassyaima⌉su
are formal polite. [1]

In general, a sentence is assigned to the level of its final (or only) inflected
word—provided, of course, that it has an inflected word. Other features of the
sentence may make it a more or less formal and/or polite degree of that major
level. A speech sequence is said to belong to the level which characterizes
most of its sentences.

The ability to choose the appropriate level for any given situation requires
a thorough knowledge of Japanese social structure. In general, the informal
style of speech is used most commonly in addressing friends and in speaking to
social inferiors in informal situations; formal speech is used in addressing
strangers, casual acquaintances, and superiors, and in speaking to social inferiors in formal situations; polite words are usually used in reference to persons of equal or superior social standing; the plain level is usually used in
reference to persons of equal or inferior social standing; women use polite and
formal speech more commonly than men. This is at best an oversimplification;
one of the most complicated phases of the problem for a foreigner is to determine the bases for social inferiority and superiority in the Japanese system,
and to know when a formal, comparatively stiff style of speech is appropriate
and when it is fitting to be informal.

---

[1] Informal equivalents will be introduced later.

The following are two patterns typical of the informal style of speech:[1]

a. Adjectivals and nominals occur at the end of statements without the de⌐su which follows them in formal speech.

Examples:

Formal	Informal
O⌐oki⌐i desu. 'It's big.'	O⌐oki⌐i. 'It's big.'
Pe⌐ñ desu. 'It's a pen.'	Pe⌐ñ. 'A pen.'

Note that the only difference between an adjectival + desu and an adjectival alone is in the formality; an adjectival in its -i form has tense and is a complete, major—but informal—sentence when it occurs alone. A nominal, on the other hand, has no tense and occurs as a sentence by itself only in fragments (cf. Lesson 4, Grammatical Note 5) similar to English sentences like these: 'A book.' 'Some bread.' 'That ashtray.' etc.

b. Adjectivals and nominals occur with question-mark intonation in questions, without the de⌐su + ka which occurs in formal speech.

Examples:

Formal	Informal
O⌐oki⌐i desu ka⌐ 'Is it big?'	O⌐oki⌐i? 'Is it big?'
Pe⌐ñ desu ka⌐ 'Is it a pen?'	Pe⌐ñ? 'A pen?'

But note the following:

Formal	Informal[2]
So⌐o desu ka⌐ 'Is that right?'	So⌐o? 'Really?'
So⌐o desu ka. 'Is that right.'	A⌐a ⌐so⌐o. 'Oh.' or 'Oh?'
So⌐o desu ⌐ne⌐e. 'That's right, isn't it.'	So⌐o. 'Right.'
So⌐o desu. 'That's right.'	So⌐o. 'Right.'

The first form in each column is more animated than the second and shows livelier interest. The difference between So⌐o. occurring as the informal equivalent of So⌐o desu. and of So⌐o desu ⌐ne⌐e. is determined by context.

Additional informal patterns and forms will be introduced later.

---

[1] But these are by no means the only informal equivalents of the given formal patterns.

[2] Again, each informal expression mentioned here is only one of several possibilities; others will be described later.

4. Particles: <u>kara</u> 'from,' <u>ni</u> (time when)

a. <u>kara</u> 'from'

The particle <u>kara</u> following a nominal means 'from.' A phrase ending with <u>kara</u> may modify an inflected expression directly, or it may be followed by another particle. When a <u>kara</u> phrase describes a nominal it is followed by <u>no</u>. Examples:

KyoꞋoto kara kiⵉmaˑsita. 'I came from Kyoto.'
Asita ꞋkuꞋ-zi kara koꞋko ni imaꞋsu.   'I'll be here from 9 o'clock [on] tomorrow.'
TaꞋnaka-sañ kara wa kimaseꞋñ desita. 'It didn't come from Tanaka [but where it did come from I don't know].'
Are wa ꞋNiꞋkkoo kara no ⵉbaˑsu desu kaꓹ 'Is that the bus from Nikko?'

Compare also <u>sore kara</u> 'from that' (i.e. 'after that' or 'next').

b. <u>ni</u> 'in,' 'on,' 'at'

Time expressions modifying an inflected expression, and indicating the time at which something happens, a r e divided into two main groups: those which occur without a following particle, and those which are followed by <u>ni</u>. (Compare the English use of 'on' with days of the week, 'in' with months and years, 'at' with hours of the day, and no preposition with 'today,' 'tomorrow,' 'yesterday,' etc.) In general, time words whose meaning is relative to the time of usage—for example, iꞋma 'now,' kyoꞋo 'today,' aꞋsitaꞋ 'tomorrow,' and kiꞋnoꞋo 'yesterday'—occur without a following particle, while other time expressions are more apt to take <u>ni</u>, but the rule is not hard and fast.

Some time expressions—for example, those ending with -ḡoꞋro (cf. the following note)—occur both with or without <u>ni</u> in this kind of construction.

Examples:

IꞋtu iⵉkimaˑsu kaꓹ 'When are you going to go?'
AꞋsita simaꞋsu. 'I'll do [it] tomorrow.'
IꞋma kaⵉkimaˑsita. 'I just wrote [it].'
KuꞋ-zi ꞋzyuꞋugohuñ ni kiⵉmaˑsita. 'I came at 9:15.'
SiꞋti-ḡatuꞋ ni iⵉkimasyoˑo. 'Let's go in July.'
ToꞋo-ka ni kaimaꞋsita. 'I bought [it] on the tenth.'

Such time expressions, both those with <u>ni</u> and those without <u>ni</u>, may be followed by particles <u>wa</u> or <u>mo</u>:

KyoꞋo wa iⵉkimaˑsu ḡa_ 'Today (in comparison with other times) I'll go but . . .'
SiꞋti-ḡatuꞋ ni wa iⵉkimaˑsu ḡa_   'In July (in comparison with other times) I'll go but . . .'
AꞋsitaꞋ mo kimasu. 'I'll come tomorrow, too.'
ToꞋo-ka niꞋ mo kimasu. 'I'll come on the tenth, too.'

All the preceding applies only when the time expression tells when

something occurs. Time expressions also occur in other nominal constructions. Compare the following pairs of examples:

1. (a) Sore (wa) ⌐na˥ñ desu ka⌐ 'What is that?'
   (b) Kyo˥o (wa) na⌐ñyo˥obi desu ka⌐ 'What day is today?'

2. (a) Na˥ni ḡa ˥i˦i desyoo ka. 'What would be good?'
   (b) Na⌐ñyo˥obi ḡa ˥i˦i desyoo ka. 'What day would be good?'

3. (a) A⌐merika no zido˥osya desu. 'It's an American car.'
   (b) Ro⌐kuzyu˥u-neñ no zi˥do˦osya desu. 'It's a '60 car.'

5. -ḡo˥ro ~ -ḡu˥rai 'about'

-Ḡo˥ro is added to time expressions which ask or answer the question
'when?'; it means 'approximate point of time.'

-Ḡu˥rai 'approximate quantity' is added to quantity expressions which ask
or answer the questions 'how much?' 'how many?' 'how far?' or 'how long?'
and to kono, sono, ano, and do˥no.

An expression ending with -ḡo˥ro is always a nominal time expression but
one ending with -ḡu˥rai may be any kind of nominal quantity expression.

Speaking in terms of the time counter groups introduced in Grammatical
Note 1 above, those in Group A (-zi and -ḡatu) may be followed by -ḡo˥ro; those
in Group B (-zikañ, -syuukañ, and -kaḡetu) may be followed by -ḡu˥rai; and
those in Group C (-huñ, -ka/-niti, and -neñ) may be followed by -ḡo˥ro when
naming a time and by -ḡu˥rai when counting time.

Before -ḡo˥ro and -ḡu˥rai, an accented word regularly loses its accent; and
in some combinations, -ḡo˥ro and -ḡu˥rai also lose their accents (note examples
below).

Examples:

itu-ḡoro 'about when?'
sa⌐ñ-zi-ḡo˥ro 'about 3 o'clock'
sa⌐ñ-zi zi˥p-puñ-ḡo˥ro 'about 3:10'
go-⌐huñ-mae-ḡo˥ro 'about five minutes before [the hour]'
go-⌐huñ-suḡi-ḡo˥ro 'about 5 minutes after [the hour]'
do⌐yoobi-ḡo˥ro 'about Saturday'
to⌐o-ka-ḡo˥ro 'about the 10th of the month'
se⌐ñ ˥kyu˦uhyaku go˥zyuu-neñ-ḡo˦ro 'about 1950'
dono-ḡurai 'about how much?'
kono-ḡurai 'about this much'
zi⌐p-puñ-ḡu˥rai 'about 10 minutes'
sa⌐ñ-zikañ-ḡu˥rai 'about 3 hours'
to⌐o-ka-ḡu˥rai 'about 10 days'
yo⌐ñ-kaḡetu-ḡu˥rai 'about 4 months'
zyu⌐u-neñ-ḡu˥rai 'about 10 years'
to⌐o-ḡu˥rai 'about 10 (units)'
hya⌐ku-eñ-ḡu˥rai 'about ¥ 100'

When a phrase ending in -ḡo˥ro tells the approximate time at which something happens, it may occur with particle ni, but more commonly occurs without it (cf. Grammatical Note 4b above). Compare English 'I'm going [at] about 4 o'clock.'

Examples:

Sa⌐ñ-zi-ḡo˥ro [ni] i˥kimasyo˥o. 'Let's go [at] about 3 o'clock.'
Sa⌐ñ-ḡatu-ḡo˥ro [ni] ki˥ma˦sita. 'He came [in] about March.'
So⌐no ho˥ñ wa syóowa zyu⌐u-neñ-ḡo˥ro [ni] ka⌐kima˦sita. 'That book he wrote [in] about Showa 10.'

6. ki⌐ma˥su ～ ma⌐irima˥su ～ i⌐rassyaima˥su

Ki⌐ma˥su 'come' is a plain formal verbal; ma⌐irima˥su and i⌐rassyaima˥su are polite formal verbals with the same meaning. Ma⌐irima˥su, a humble verbal, refers to the actions of the speaker (or members of his own family), in polite speech. I⌐rassyaima˥su, an honorific verbal, refers to the actions of persons other than the speaker, whose position is being elevated or exalted, in polite speech.

Three meanings for i⌐rassyaima˥su and two for ma⌐irima˥su have now been introduced. Study the following chart:

	Plain Formal	Polite Formal	
		Humble	Honorific
'be located (animate)'	i⌐ma˥su	o⌐rima˥su	i⌐rassyaima˥su
'go'	i⌐kima˥su	ma⌐irima˥su	i⌐rassyaima˥su
'come'	ki⌐ma˥su	ma⌐irima˥su	i⌐rassyaima˥su

Ki⌐ma˥su regularly means motion toward—and i⌐kima˥su motion away from—the speaker's position. Thus, the Japanese equivalent of 'I'm not coming to school tomorrow' said, for example, during a telephone conversation from outside, with someone at the school, would be A⌐sita˥ wa ga⌐kkoo e ikimase˦ñ lit. 'I'm not going to school tomorrow.' A⌐sita˥ wa ga⌐kkoo e kimase˦ñ would be said only by someone actually at the school.

DRILLS

A. Substitution Drill

1. It took 2 hours.   Ni-⌐zi˥kañ ka⌐karima˦sita.
2. It took 2 minutes.   Ni˥-huñ ka⌐karima˦sita.
3. It took 2 days.   Hu⌐tu-ka kakarima˥sita.
4. It took 2 years.   Ni˥-neñ ka⌐karima˦sita.
5. It took 2 months.   Ni-⌐ka˥ḡetu ka⌐karima˦sita.
6. It took 2 weeks.   Ni-⌐syu˥ukañ ka⌐karima˦sita.
7. It took 2½ years.   Ni-⌐neñ-ha˥ñ ka⌐karima˦sita.

8. It took 2½ hours.   Ni-⌈zikañ-ha⌉ñ ka⌐karima⌐sita.
9. It took a half day.   Ha⌈ñ-niti kakarima⌉sita.
10. It took a half hour.   Ha⌈ñ-zi⌉kañ ka⌐karima⌐sita.

B. Substitution Drill

1. I did [it] at 2 o'clock.   Ni⌉-zi ni si⌐ma⌐sita.
2. I did [it] 2 days ago.   Hu⌈tu-ka ma⌉e ni si⌐ma⌐sita.
3. I did [it] in Showa 2.   Syoowa ⌈ni⌉-neñ ni si⌐ma⌐sita.
4. I did [it] in February.   Ni-⌈ḡatu⌉ ni si⌐ma⌐sita.
5. I did [it] at 2:30.   Ni-⌈zi-ha⌉ñ ni si⌐ma⌐sita.
6. I did [it] on Tuesday.   Ka⌈yo⌉obi ni si⌐ma⌐sita.
7. I did [it] 2 hours ago.   Ni-⌈zikañ ma⌉e ni si⌐ma⌐sita.
8. I did [it] on the second.   Hu⌈tu-ka ni sima⌉sita.

C. Substitution Drill

1. I went to the station by   Kyo⌉o ⌈e⌉ki e ⌈ba⌉su de i⌐kima⌐sita.
   bus today.
2. I went to the station by   Kinoo ⌈e⌉ki e ⌈ba⌉su de i⌐kima⌐sita.
   bus yesterday.
3. I went to the hospital by   Kinoo byóoiñ e ⌈ba⌉su de i⌐kima⌐sita.
   bus yesterday.
4. I went to the hospital by   Kinoo byóoiñ e ⌈ta⌉kusii de i⌐kima⌐si-
   taxi yesterday.   ta.
5. I came to the hospital by   Kinoo byóoin e ⌈ta⌉kusii de ki⌐ma⌐sita.
   taxi yesterday.
6. I came to the hospital by   Ototoi byóoiñ e ⌈ta⌉kusii de ki⌐ma⌐si-
   taxi the day before yes-   ta.
   terday.
7. I came to school by taxi   Ototoi ḡákkoo e ⌈ta⌉kusii de ki⌐ma⌐si-
   the day before yesterday.   ta.
8. I came to school by elec-   Ototoi ḡákkoo e ⌈de⌉ñsya de ki⌐ma⌐si-
   tric train the day before   ta.
   yesterday.
9. I came here by electric   Ototoi kóko e ⌈de⌉ñsya de ki⌐ma⌐sita.
   train the day before yes-
   terday.
10. I came here by plane the   Ototoi kóko e hi⌈ko⌉oki de ki⌐ma⌐si-
    day before yesterday.   ta.
11. I came here by plane this   Kotosi kóko e hi⌈ko⌉oki de ki⌐ma⌐si-
    year.   ta.
12. I came here by ship this   Kotosi kóko e ⌈hu⌉ne de ki⌐ma⌐sita.
    year.

D. Substitution Drill

1. I came 10 years ago.   Zyu⌈u-neñ ma⌉e ni ki⌐ma⌐sita.
2. I came 5 minutes ago.   Go-⌈huñ ma⌉e ni ki⌐ma⌐sita.
3. I came 1 hour ago.   I⌈ti-zikañ ma⌉e ni ki⌐ma⌐sita.
4. I came 10 days ago.   To⌈o-ka ma⌉e ni ki⌐ma⌐sita.

5. I came 6 months ago.   Ro˥k-kaḡetu ma˥e ni ki˩ma˥sita.
6. I came 3 weeks ago.   Sañ-syuukañ ma˥e ni ki˩ma˥sita.
7. I came a little (while) ago.   Su˥ko˥si ˩ma˥e ni ki˩ma˥sita.
8. I came a little (while) ago.   Tyo˥tto ˩ma˥e ni ki˩ma˥sita.

E. Substitution Drill

1. When is that?   Sore (wa) ˥i˥tu desu ka⌐
2. What is that?   Sore (wa) ˥na˥ñ desu ka⌐
3. Which one is that?   Sore (wa) ˥do˥re desu ka⌐
4. Where is that?   Sore (wa) ˥do˥ko desu ka⌐
5. How is that?   Sore (wa) ˥do˥o desu ka⌐
6. What month is that?   Sore (wa) ˥na˥ñ-ḡatu desu ka⌐
7. What time is that?   Sore (wa) ˥na˥ñ-zi desu ka⌐
8. What day is that?   Sore (wa) na˥ñyo˥obi desu ka⌐
9. How much is that?   Sore (wa) ˥i˥kura desu ka⌐
10. How many yen is that?   Sore (wa) ˥na˥ñ-eñ desu ka⌐

F. Substitution Drill

1. I went from the hotel.   Ho˥teru kara i˩kima˥sita.
2. I went by train.   Ki˥sya˥ de i˩kima˥sita.
3. I went as far as the station. E˥ki made i˩kima˥sita.
4. I went on the third.   Mi-˥kka ni ikima˥sita.
5. I went along that road.   So˥no miti (o) ikima˥sita.
6. I went.   Wa˥takusi˥ ḡa ikima˥sita.
7. I (in comparison with oth-   Wa˥takusi wa ikima˥sita.
    ers) went.
8. I went the day before yes-   O˥totoi ikima˥sita.
    terday.
9. I went about 9 o'clock.   Ku-˥zi-ḡo˥ro i˩kima˥sita.
10. I went to the consulate.   Ryo˥ozi˥kañ e i˩kima˥sita.

G. Grammar Drill (based on Grammatical Note 5)

        Tutor: Yo˥-zi desu. 'It's 4 o'clock.'
        Student: Yo-˥zi-ḡo˥ro desu. 'It's about 4 o'clock.'

1. To˥o-ka ima˥sita.   To˥o-ka-ḡu˥rai i˩ma˥sita.
2. To˥o-ka ni ima˥sita.   To˥o-ka-ḡo˥ro i˩ma˥sita.
3. Ku˥-ḡatu desu.   Ku-˥ḡatu-ḡo˥ro desu.
4. Mo˥kuyo˥o ni i˩kimasyo˥o. Mo˥kuyoo-ḡo˥ro i˩kimasyo˥o.
5. Go-˥neñ ima˥sita.   Go-˥neñ-ḡu˥rai i˩ma˥sita.
6. Go-˥neñ ni ima˥sita.   Go-˥neñ-ḡo˥ro i˩ma˥sita.
7. Zyu˥s-syu˥ukañ desita.   Zyu˥s-syuukañ-ḡu˥rai desita.
8. Zi˥p-puñ ka˩karima˥sita.   Zi˥p-puñ-ḡu˥rai ka˩karima˥sita.

H. Level Drill (The sentences on the right are the plain equivalents of the po-
    lite sentences on the left.)

1. I˥tu ko˩tira e irassyaima˥si-   I˥tu ko˩ko e kima˥sita ka⌐
    ta ka⌐

2. Ya⌐mamoto orima˥su ka⌐   Ya⌐mamoto ima˥su ka⌐
3. I˥ma ma⌐irimasyo˥o ka.   I˥ma i⌐kimasyo˥o ka.

4. Ta⌐naka-sañ irassyaima˥su   Ta⌐naka-sañ | ima˥su |
   ka⌐ | kima˥su | ka⌐
                                                | ikima⌐su |

5. Ra˥itaa go⌐zaima˦su ka⌐   Ra˥itaa a⌐rima˦su ka⌐
6. Ni˥-neñ ⌐ma˦e ni ko⌐tira   Ni˥-neñ ⌐ma˦e ni ko⌐ko e kima˦sita.
   e mairima˦sita.
7. Do˥tira e i⌐rassyaima˦su   Do˥ko e i⌐kima˦su ka⌐
   ka⌐
8. To⌐ñde mo gozaimase˥ñ.   To⌐ñde mo arimase˥ñ.

I. Level Drill (The sentences on the right are informal equivalents of the sentences on the left.)

1. Kyo˥o tu⌐itati˥ desu ka⌐   Kyo˥o tu̅itati?
2. Tyo⌐odo yo˥-zi desu.   Tyo⌐odo yo˥-zi.
3. A˥a, so˥o desu ka.   A˥a, so˥o.
4. To⌐ttemo i˥i desu.   To⌐ttemo i˥i.
5. Yo⌐rosi˥i desu ka⌐   Yorosii?
6. Sore ⌐na˥ñ desu ka⌐   Sore ⌐na˥ni?

J. Expansion Drill

1. [He] went.   I⌐kima˥sita.
   [He] went to France.   Hu⌐rañsu e ikima˥sita.
   [He] went to France six   Ro⌐k-kaḡetu ma˥e ni Hu⌐rañsu e iki-
     months ago.   ma˥sita.
   Mr. Tanaka went to France   Tanaka-sañ (wa) ro⌐k-kaḡetu ma˥e ni
     six months ago.   Hu⌐rañsu e ikima˥sita.

2. I came.   Ki˥ma˥sita.
   I came on the 24th.   Ni˥zyuu yo-⌐kka ni kima˥sita.
   I came on August 24th.   Hati-ḡatu ⌐ni˥zyuu yo-⌐kka ni kima˥si-
                                      ta.
   I came on August 24, 35 (i.e.   Sa˥ñzyuu go-neñ hăti-ḡatu ⌐ni˥zyuu yo-
     of the Showa Era).   ⌐kka ni kima˥sita.

3. About how many days does it   Na⌐ñ-niti-ḡu˥rai ka⌐karima˦su ka⌐
     take?
   About how many days does it   Hu˥ne de na⌐ñ-niti-ḡu˥rai ka⌐karima˦-
     take by ship?   su ka⌐
   About how many days does it   A⌐merika ma˥de ⌐hu˥ne de na⌐ñ-niti-ḡu˥-
     take by ship, as far as   rai ka⌐karima˦su ka⌐
     America?
   About how many days does it   Ni⌐ho˥ñ kara A⌐merika ma˥de ⌐hu˥ne de
     take from Japan as far as   na⌐ñ-niti-ḡu˥rai ka⌐karima˦su ka⌐
     America by ship?

4.	I'd like to go...	I⌈kita⌉i n̄ desu ḡa_
	I'd like to go by car...	Zi⌈do⌉osya de i⊢kita⊣i n̄ desu ḡa_
	I'd like to go to Nikko by car...	Ni⌉kkoo e zi⌈do⌉osya de i⊢kita⊣i n̄ desu ḡa_
	I'd like to go to Nikko by car some (lit. one) time...	Iti-do ⌈Ni⌉kkoo e zi⌈do⌉osya de i⊢kita⊣i n̄ desu ḡa_
5.	It will probably be about July.	Si⌈ti-ḡatu-ḡo⌉ro desyoo.
	[His] vacation will probably be about July.	Oyasumi (wa) si⌈ti-ḡatu-ḡo⌉ro desyoo.
	[His] vacation this year will probably be about July.	Kotosi no oyasumi (wa) si⌈ti-ḡatu-ḡo⌉ro desyoo.
	Mr. Tanaka's vacation this year will probably be about July.	Tanaka-san̄ no kōtosi no oyasumi (wa) si⌈ti-ḡatu-ḡo⌉ro desyoo.
6.	[They]'re good!	I⌉i desu yo⌋
	[They]'re very good!	To⌉ttemo i⌉i desu yo⌋
	The new hotels are very good!	A⌈tarasi⌉i ⊢ho⊣teru (wa) to⌉ttemo i⌉i desu yo⌋
	The new hotels in Tokyo are very good!	Tookyoo no a⌈tarasi⌉i ⊢ho⊣teru (wa) to⌉ttemo i⌉i desu yo⌋

QUESTION SUPPLEMENT

Answer the following questions, using a calendar when necessary:

1. I⌈ti-zi⌉kan̄ wa ⌈na⌉n̄-pun̄ desu ka⌋
2. I⌈ti-niti⌉ wa na⌈n̄-zi⌉kan̄ desu ka⌋
3. I⌈s-syu⌉ukan̄ wa ⌈na⌉n̄-niti desu ka⌋
4. I⌈k-ka⌉ḡetu wa na⌈n̄-niti-ḡu⌉rai desu ka⌋
5. I⌈k-ka⌉ḡetu wa na⌈n̄-syuukan̄-ḡu⌉rai desu ka⌋
6. I⌈ti⌉-nen̄ wa ⌈na⌉n̄-niti desu ka⌋
7. I⌈ti⌉-nen̄ wa na⌈n̄-syu⌉ukan̄ desu ka⌋
8. I⌈ti⌉-nen̄ wa na⌈n̄-ka⌉ḡetu desu ka⌋
9. Kyo⌉o wa na⌈n̄yo⌉obi desu ka⌋
10. A⌈sita⌉ wa ⌈na⌉n̄-niti desu ka⌋
11. Ki⌈no⌉o wa ⌈na⌉n̄-niti na⌈n̄yo⌉obi desita ka⌋
12. O⌈toto⌉i wa ni⌈tiyoo de⌉sita ka⌋
13. Kotosi no īti-ḡatu hātu-ka wa na⌈n̄yo⌉obi desu ka⌋
14. Kotosi no ⌈go⌉-ḡatu mi-kka wa na⌈n̄yo⌉obi desu ka⌋
15. Kotosi no sīti-ḡatu ⌈ni⌉zyuu si⊢ti-niti⊣ wa na⌈n̄yo⌉obi desu ka⌋
16. Kotosi no hāti-ḡatu hūtu-ka wa na⌈n̄yo⌉obi desu ka⌋
17. Ko⌈tosi no Kurisu⌉masu ['Christmas'] wa na⌈n̄yo⌉obi desu ka⌋
18. Watakusi wa ha⌈n̄-zikan̄ ma⌉e ni ki⊢ma⊣sita. Na⌈n̄-zi ni ki⊢ma⊣sita ka⌋
19. Watakusi wa tyōodo sa⌈n̄-kaḡetu ma⌉e ni ⌈Ni⌉kkoo e i⊢kima⊣sita. Na⌈n̄-ḡatu ⌈na⌉n̄-niti ni i⊢kima⊣sita ka⌋

20. Watakusi wa tyóodo i⌐s-syuukañ ma⌐e ni ko⌐no kuruma o kaima⌐sita.
    Na⌐ñ-niti ni ka⌐ima⌐sita ka↲

21. Syoowa ⌐zyu⌐u-neñ wa séereki ⌐na⌐ñ-neñ desita ka↲

22. Me⌐ezi ⌐ga⌐ñneñ wa séereki ⌐na⌐ñ-neñ desita ka↲

23. Kotosi wa ⌐na⌐ñ-neñ desu ka↲

EXERCISES

1. Mr. Tanaka has asked what time it is. Give the following answers:

    a. It's 4 o'clock.
    b. It's just 7:30.
    c. It's 10 after 6.
    d. It's 10:45.
    e. It's 5:15.
    f. It's about 7 o'clock.
    g. It's about a quarter to eight.
    h. It's 2:28.
    i. It's one minute after 1.
    j. It's 10 to 12.
    k. It's 20 to 11.
    l. It's probably about 9.

2. Mr. Tanaka has just asked you when you came here. Tell him that you
   came:

    a. In 1955.
    b. In January.
    c. In March, 1953.
    d. On April 14th.
    e. In Showa 29.
    f. About six months ago.
    g. About two years ago.
    h. About ten weeks ago.

3. Using a calendar, practice asking and answering questions pertaining to
   dates and days of the week.

4. Practice asking and answering questions on how long it takes from one
   given geographical point to another by a given mode of transportation. The
   geographical points may include everything from countries to buildings
   within a city. Timetables are useful as the basis for some questions.

5. Practice the Basic Dialogues with appropriate variations.

Lesson 9. Time (cont.)

BASIC DIALOGUES: FOR MEMORIZATION

(a)

Tanaka

every day	ma⁷initi
return home	ka⌐erima⁷su or
	o⌐kaeri ni narima⁷su ⁺
1. What time do you go home every day?	Ma⁷initi ⌐na⁷ñ-zi ni ka⁺erima⁴su ka⌐
	or
	Ma⁷initi ⌐na⁷ñ-zi ni o⌐kaeri ni narima⁴su ka⌐

Smith

usually	taitee
sometimes	to⌐kidoki⁷
2. I usually go home at 5:30, but sometimes I go home about 6.	Taitee go-⌐zi-ha⁷ñ ni ka⌐erima⁷su ḡa, tokidoki ro⌐ku-zi-ḡo⁷ro kaerimasu.

Tanaka

morning	a⁷sa
home	uti or
	otaku ⁺
go out or leave	de⌐ma⁷su or
	o⌐de ni narima⁷su ⁺
3. What time do you leave home in the morning?	A⁷sa ⌐na⁷ñ-zi ni u⁺ti (o) dema⁴su ka⌐
	or
	A⁷sa ⌐na⁷ñ-zi ni o⁺taku (o) ode ni narima⁴su ka⌐

Smith

always	i⁷tu mo
a little after 8	ha⌐ti⁷-zi tyo⌐tto suḡi⁷
4. I always leave at a little after 8.	I⁷tu mo ha⌐ti⁷-zi tyo⌐tto suḡi⁷ ni demasu.
going out or leaving	de⁷te
business office	zi⌐mu⁷syo
arrive	tu⌐kima⁷su
5. I leave the house about 8, and arrive at the office about 9.	Ha⌐ti-zi-ḡo⁷ro u⁺ti (o) de⁴te, ku-⌐zi-ḡo⁷ro zi⌐mu⁷syo ni tukimasu.

132

(b)

Tanaka

6. (About) when are you going
back to America?

I⌐tu-ḡoro Amerika ni kaerima⌐su ka↲
or
I⌐tu-ḡoro Amerika ni okaeri ni narima⌐su ka↲

Smith

by October
7. I'd LIKE to go back by October (but) . . .

zyu⌐u-ḡatu⌐ made ni
Zyu⌐u-ḡatu⌐ made ni ka⌐erita⌐i ñ desu ḡa↲

Tanaka

be possible or can do

de⌐kima⌐su or
o⌐deki ni narima⌐su↑

8. Can't you?

De⌐kimase⌐ñ ka↲
or
O⌐deki ni narimase⌐ñ ka↲

Smith

9. Hmm. I wonder.

Sa⌐a. Do⌐o desyoo ka ⌐ne⌐e.

(c)

At a government office

Employee

tomorrow morning
please come

a⌐sita no a⌐sa
ki⌐te⌐ kudasai or
i⌐rassya⌐tte↑ kudasai or
i⌐ra⌐site↑ kudasai

10. Please come again tomorrow morning.

A⌐sita no a⌐sa ma⌐ta kite⌐ kudasai.
or
A⌐sita no a⌐sa ma⌐ta irassya⌐tte kudasai.
or
A⌐sita no a⌐sa ma⌐ta ira⌐site kudasai.

Tanaka

I guess I'll come

ki⌐masyo⌐o or
ma⌐irimasyo⌐o↑

shall I come?

ki⌐masyo⌐o ka or
ma⌐irimasyo⌐o ka↑

11. What time shall I come?

Na⌐ñ-zi ni ki⌐masyo⌐o ka.
or
Na⌐ñ-zi ni ma⌐irimasyo⌐o ka.

Employee

by 9 o'clock

ku⌐-zi made ni

12. Please come by 9 o'clock.   Ku˺-zi made ni kiˡteˉ kudasai.
                                            or
                                            Ku˺-zi made ni iˡrassyaˉtte kudasai.
                                            or
                                            Ku˺-zi made ni iˡraˉsite kudasai.

                    Tanaka

    is fast or early   haˊya˺i /-ku/
13. That's early!   Haˊya˺i desu ˊne˺e.

    be(come) distressing or   koˊmarima˺su
    troublesome or annoy-
    ing or inconvenient or
    perplexing
14. I'm afraid that will be a bit   Tyo˺tto koˊmarima˺su ḡa_
    inconvenient. . .

                    Employee

15. Well then, how about 10   Zya˺a, zyu˺u-zi wa ˡdoˉo desu ka.
    o'clock?   or
                                            Zya˺a, zyu˺u-zi wa iˡkaˉḡa desu
                                            ka.

                    Tanaka

    fine   ke˺kkoo+
    by 10 o'clock   zyu˺u-zi made ni
16. That's fine. I'll come by   I˺i desu yo_ Zyu˺u-zi made ni kima-
    10.   su.
                                            or
                                            Ke˺kkoo desu. Zyu˺u-zi made ni ma-
                                            irimasu.

                    (d)

                    Secretary

    until what time?   na˺ñ-zi made
    how long? (i.e. from   na˺ñ-zi kara ˊna˺ñ-zi made
        what time until
        what time?)
    I guess I'll be or stay   iˊmasyo˺o or
                                            oˊrimasyo˺o ˉ
    shall I be or stay?   iˊmasyo˺o ka or
                                            oˊrimasyo˺o ka ˉ
17. How long shall I stay here   Asita ˊna˺ñ-zi kara ˊna˺ñ-zi made ko-
    tomorrow?   ˡko ni orimasyoˉo ka_

                    Smith

    afternoon or p.m.   go˺ḡo
    until 3 o'clock   sa˺ñ-zi made
    please be or stay   iˊte kudasa˺i or
                                            iˊrassya˺tteˉ kudasai   or
                                            iˊra˺siteˉ kudasai

18. Please be [here] from 9 in the
morning until 3 in the afternoon.

A꜒sa ꜒kuˬzi kara ꜒go꜒go ꜒sa꜒ñ-zi made
iꜛte kudasaꜛi.

Secretary

19. Certainly. I'll be here (lit.
come) by 9.

Ka꜒sikomarima꜒sita. Ku꜒-zi made ni
mairimasu.

(e)
Smith

this morning

20. Did you go to the bank this
morning?

ke꜒sa

Ke꜒sa giꜛñkoo e ikima꜒sita kaˬ

Tanaka

make no difference <u>or</u>
    be all right

21. No, I'm going later. Is that
all right?

ka꜒maimase꜒ñ

Iie, a꜒to de iꜛkimaꜛsu ga, ka꜒maima-
se꜒ñ kaˬ

Smith

until 3 o'clock

22. The bank closes at (lit.
is until) 3, you know.

sa꜒ñ-zi made

Giñkoo (wa) ꜒sa꜒ñ-zi made desu yoˬ

Tanaka

well then <u>or</u> then
    I guess I'll go

23. Oh, of course! Then I guess
I'll go now.

zya
i꜒kimasyo꜒o <u>or</u>
ma꜒irimasyo꜒o ꜛ

A. ꜒So꜒o ꜛsoꜛo. Zya, i꜒ma iꜛkima-
syoꜛo.

NOTES ON THE BASIC DIALOGUES

1. <u>Ma꜒initi</u>: compare also <u>ma꜒iasa</u> 'every morning,' <u>maisyuu</u> 'every week,'
<u>maituki</u> or <u>maiḡetu</u> 'every month,' and <u>maitosi</u> or <u>maineñ</u> 'every year.'
All are time nominals and all occur without particle <u>ni</u> indicating time
when something happens.

Ka꜒erima꜒su means 'return to a place where one habitually spends time—
one's own home, office, native land, etc.' The gerund (-<u>te</u> form) of <u>ka꜒e-
rima꜒su</u> is <u>ka꜒ette</u>.

2. Remember that after -<u>ḡo꜒ro</u>, time particle <u>ni</u> is optional but more often
omitted. <u>Ni</u> does not occur after <u>taitee</u> and <u>toꜛkidoki꜒</u>.

3. <u>A꜒sa</u> is another time word which indicates time when something happens,
without a following particle.

Note these expressions: Place word + <u>o</u> + <u>de꜒ma꜒su</u> 'leave a place'; place
word + <u>kara</u> + <u>de꜒ma꜒su</u> 'leave from a place.'

5. De⌐te is the gerund (-te form) of de⌐ma⌐su. The gerund of tu⌐kima⌐su is tu⌐ite. Zi⌐mu⌐syo ni tukimasu may be replaced by zi⌐mu⌐syo e tukimasu without significant difference in meaning.

6. Amerika e or Amerika ni. Compare the preceding note.

7. 'I'd like to, but—I don't know whether I can or not.'

8. Like √wa⌐karima⌐su, √a⌐rima⌐su, √i⌐rima⌐su, and √ka⌐karima⌐su, √de⌐kima⌐su does not occur with particle o. Both the person who can and the thing which is possible are followed by particles wa or ḡa, depending on emphasis. The gerund (-te form) of de⌐kima⌐su is de⌐kite.

10. Note the difference between a⌐sita no a⌐sa ki⌐te⌐ kudasai (in which a⌐sita describes a⌐sa) 'please come tomorrow morning' and asita ⌐a⌐sa ki⌐te⌐ kudasai (in which both a⌐sita and a⌐sa tell 'time when' and modify ki⌐te⌐ kudasai) 'please come tomorrow, in the morning.'

   Ki⌐te⌐ is the gerund (-te form) of ki⌐ma⌐su. I⌐rassya⌐tte and i⌐ra⌐site are alternate gerunds of the honorific i⌐rassyaima⌐su 'come,' 'go,' or 'be,' with i⌐ra⌐site the less stiff and more conversational of the two.

13. Like all adjectivals, ha⌐ya⌐i occurs in its adverbial (-ku) form when it modifies an inflected expression. Thus: ha⌐yaku a⌐rimase⌐ñ 'it isn't fast or early,' ha⌐yaku si⌐te kudasa⌐i 'do [it] quickly or early,' ha⌐yaku ki⌐⌐ma⌐sita 'I came early or quickly,' etc. Compare: Ha⌐ya⌐i ⌐ta⌐kusii de ki⌐ma⌐sita 'I came in a fast taxi' and ha⌐yaku ⌐ta⌐kusii de ki⌐ma⌐sita 'I came quickly by taxi.'

14. Ko⌐marima⌐su and ko⌐marima⌐sita have many varied English equivalents: 'Oh, dear!' 'What am I going to do?' 'What a mess I'm in!' 'This is a bad situation'; etc. The -ma⌐su form usually refers to a general or future situation, while the -ma⌐sita form indicates either that the difficult situation has taken place (i. e. I'm affected now) or did take place. Both what is troublesome and the person affected are followed by particles wa or ḡa depending on emphasis. The gerund of ko⌐marima⌐su is ko⌐ma⌐tte.

   The final ḡa qualifies the statement politely: 'It will be a bit inconvenient but—I don't like to insist on your making a change' or 'I don't like to mention it,' etc. Basic Sentence 14 is a close equivalent of English 'I'm afraid it will be a bit inconvenient. . . '

16. The nominal ke⌐kkoo is a polite word which usually occurs in affirmative statements. Like adjectivals i⌐i and yorosii, it refers to situations which are 'fine,' 'good,' 'all right,' and also to those which are 'fine as they are—nothing more needed.' Accordingly, in some contexts the closest English equivalent is 'never mind.'

18. Go⌐ḡo is used both as a conversational term for 'afternoon' and as a technical term corresponding to English p.m. In the latter meaning, its opposite is go⌐zeñ 'a.m.,' while the conversational word for morning is a⌐sa. Go⌐ḡo occurs both with and without following particle ni in indicating time when something happens.

   Ite is the gerund (-te form) of i⌐ma⌐su.

20. Ke⌐sa occurs without a following particle in indicating time when something happens.

21. Ka⌐maimase⌉ñ, a verbal negative whose corresponding affirmative is comparatively rare, has many English equivalents: 'It makes no difference'; 'It doesn't matter'; 'I don't care'; 'I don't mind'; 'It doesn't bother me'; 'It's all right'; etc. Ko⌐marima⌉su usually occurs as its opposite. Thus: Ko⌐marima⌉su ka⌴ 'Will it be inconvenient?' . . . 'Iie, ka⌐maimase⌉ñ. 'No, it doesn't matter.'

23. Repeated so⌉o is emphatic. So⌉o here is the informal equivalent of so⌉o desu ⌐ne⌉e. Zya is a more clipped, terse alternant of zya⌉a.

GRAMMATICAL NOTES

1. Verbals: More About the Tentative

In Lesson 7, Grammatical Note 2, the tentative of verbals was introduced, meaning 'let's do so-and-so' in statements, and 'shall we do so-and-so?' in questions. Thus:

I⌐kimasyo⌉o ka. 'Shall we go?'
E⌉e, i⌐kimasyo⌉o. 'Yes, let's go.'

The verbal tentative has a second use, distinguished from the first only by context. It may indicate a suggestion by the speaker directed to himself alone: 'I guess I'll do so-and-so'; and in its more common use — in questions — this second kind of tentative is an offer: 'Shall I do so-and-so?' In such cases, the affirmative reply is an appropriate imperative, or o⌐negai-sima⌉su, or another request expression. Possible negative replies include i⌉i desu and the more polite ke⌉kkoo desu meaning 'never mind.'

Examples:

Ti⌉zu (o) ka⌐kimasyo⌉o ka. 'Shall I draw a map?'
E⌉e, ka⌉ite kudasai. 'Yes, please (draw).' or
E⌉e, o⌐negai-sima⌉su. 'Yes, please do.'

Ta⌐bako (o) kaimasyo⌉o ka. 'Shall I buy some cigarettes?'
Iie, i⌉i desu yo. or
Iie, ke⌉kkoo desu. } 'No, never mind.'

2. Verbals: Honorific Equivalents Ending in √na⌐rima⌉su

The polite verbals previously introduced (√go⌐zaima⌉su, √i⌐rassyaima⌉su, etc.) were words which had to be memorized along with their plain equivalents because structurally they were unrelated. Such polite verbals are limited in number. Far more common are those having the same root as their plain equivalents.

One of the most common types of honorific (†) consists of the polite o- prefixed to the stem of a plain verbal (the stem is the -ma⌉su form minus -ma⌉su) + particle ni + √na⌐rima⌉su. (√Na⌐rima⌉su as an independent verbal means 'become,' 'come to be'; it will occur in later lessons.) The form of √na⌐rima⌉su shows whether the combination is non-past or past, affirmative or negative, etc. The accent of the combination occurs on √na⌐rima⌉su. The combination is the honorific equivalent of the corresponding plain verbal.

Examples:

Plain	(Stem)	Honorific (†) Equivalent
ka⌐erima⌐su	(ka⌐eri)	o⌐kaeri ni narima⌐su '[he] returns (or will return) home'
de⌐ma⌐sita	(de⌐)	o⌐de ni narima⌐sita '[he] went out'
tu⌐kimase⌐ñ	(tu⌐ki)	o⌐tuki ni narimase⌐ñ '[he] doesn't (or won't) arrive or hasn't arrived'
de⌐kimase⌐ñ desita	(de⌐ki)	o⌐deki ni narimase⌐ñ desita '[he] couldn't do it'

The gerund of the honorific is o- + verbal stem + ni + na⌐tte.

The corresponding form for √i⌐ma⌐su, √i⌐kima⌐su, and √ki⌐ma⌐su is irregular: o⌐ide ni √narima⌐su. Like √i⌐rassyaima⌐su, it occurs as the honorific equivalent of all three plain verbals.

Like all honorifics, these are used only in reference to persons other than the speaker, in polite speech. The plain equivalent is used as a corresponding non-honorific form. Thus:

A: Tanaka-sañ (wa) o⌐wakari ni narima⌐su ka⌐
'Does Mr. Tanaka understand?'

B: Ha⌐a, o⌐wakari ni narima⌐su.
'Yes, he understands.'

A: A⌐na⌐ta mo o⌐wakari ni narima⌐su ka⌐
'Do you understand too?'

B: Ha⌐a, wa⌐takusi mo wakarima⌐su.
'Yes, I understand too.'

WARNING: Don't try to make up o-⌐(stem) ni √narima⌐su honorific equivalents for all plain verbals. As always, let the usage of native speakers be your guide.

3. Particles: ma⌐de 'until,' ma⌐de ni 'by'

a. ma⌐de 'until'

Reread Lesson 7, Grammatical Note 3b.

The particle ma⌐de after a time expression means 'until'—i.e. 'up to and including part or all of.'

Examples:

a⌐sita⌐ made 'until tomorrow'
i⌐tu made 'until when?'

i⌐ti-g̃atu ma⌐de[1] 'until January'
i⌐ma ma⌐de[1] 'until now'

b. ma⌐de ni 'by'

The particle sequence ma⌐de ni preceded by a time expression means 'at a point in the time until,' i.e. 'by' the given time. It regularly occurs with an inflected expression which indicates action.

Examples:

A⌐sita⌐ made ni kimasu. 'He'll come by tomorrow.'
I⌐ti-g̃atu ma⌐de ni tukimasu. 'He'll arrive by January.'
I⌐ma ma⌐de ni de⌐ma⌐sita. 'It has left by now.'
Ku⌐-zi ma⌐de ni⌐ wa kaerimasu. 'By 9 (comparatively speaking) I'll be home (lit. return home).'

4. √de⌐su Following a Particle

Besides occurring after adjectivals and nominals, √de⌐su also occurs immediately after phrases which end in some particles—for example, it may follow kara and ma⌐de but it rarely follows wa, g̃a, or o directly. √De⌐su is accented if the preceding phrase is unaccented.

Examples:

Sa⌐ñ-zi made desu. 'It is until 3'—i.e. 'it lasts until 3' or 'it ends at 3' or 'it closes at 3' or 'it is open until 3.'

Sa⌐ñ-zi kara desu. 'It is from 3'—i.e. 'it begins at 3' or 'it opens at 3.'

The negative equivalent of a sequence ending in particle + √de⌐su ends in particle + zya a⌐rimase⌐ñ:

Sa⌐ñ-zi kara zya a⌐rimase⌐ñ. 'It isn't from 3 o'clock'—i.e. 'it doesn't begin at 3' or 'it doesn't open at 3.'

DRILLS

A. Substitution Drill

1. I usually come by bus.   Taitee ⌐ba⌐su de kimasu.
2. I sometimes come by bus.   Tokidoki ⌐ba⌐su de kimasu.
3. I always come by bus.   I⌐tu mo ⌐ba⌐su de kimasu.
4. I come by bus a good deal. Yo⌐ku ⌐ba⌐su de kimasu.
5. I come by bus every day.   Ma⌐initi ⌐ba⌐su de kimasu.

---

[1] Note the irregular accent of this phrase.

6. I come by bus in the afternoon.   Go⌐go ⌐ba⌐su de kimasu.

7. I come by bus in the morning.   A⌐sa ⌐ba⌐su de kimasu.

8. I come by bus every morning.   Ma⌐iasa ⌐ba⌐su de kimasu.

B. Substitution Drill

1. Mr. Tanaka HAS LEFT.   Tanaka-sañ (wa) de⌐ma⌐sita.
2. MR. TANAKA left.   Ta⌐naka-sañ ḡa dema⌐sita.
3. He left the office.   Zi⌐mu⌐syo (o) de⌐ma⌐sita.
4. He left from the office.   Zi⌐mu⌐syo kara de⌐ma⌐sita.
5. He left today.   Kyo⌐o de⌐ma⌐sita.
6. He left in the afternoon.   Go⌐go /ni/ de⌐ma⌐sita.
7. He left at 8 o'clock.   Ha⌐ti⌐-zi ni de⌐ma⌐sita.
8. He left by 8 o'clock.   Ha⌐ti⌐-zi made ni de⌐ma⌐sita.
9. I left, too.   Wa⌐takusi mo dema⌐sita.

C. Substitution Drill

1. Please come again tomorrow.   Asita ma⌐ta kite⌐ kudasai.

2. Please come again in the afternoon.   Go⌐go ma⌐ta kite⌐ kudasai.

3. Please come again on Monday.   Ge⌐tuyo⌐obi ni ma⌐ta kite⌐ kudasai.

4. Please come again in April.   Si-⌐ḡatu⌐ ni ma⌐ta kite⌐ kudasai.

5. Please come again about 4.   Yo-⌐zi-ḡo⌐ro ma⌐ta kite⌐ kudasai.

6. Please come again at 7:30.   Si⌐ti-zi-ha⌐ñ ni ma⌐ta kite⌐ kudasai.

7. Please come again tomorrow morning.   A⌐sita no a⌐sa ma⌐ta kite⌐ kudasai.

8. Please come again tomorrow about 10.   Asita zyu⌐u-zi-ḡo⌐ro ma⌐ta kite⌐ kudasai.

D. Substitution Drill

1. I'm going later. Is that all right?   A⌐to de i⌐kima⌐su ḡa, ka⌐maimase⌐ñ ka⌐

2. I'm not coming tomorrow. Is that all right?   A⌐sita kimase⌐ñ ḡa, ka⌐maimase⌐ñ ka⌐

3. I'd like to go home early. Is that all right?   Ha⌐yaku ka⌐erita⌐i ñ desu ḡa, ka⌐maimase⌐ñ ka⌐

4. I'm going to leave from the office. Is that all right?   Zi⌐mu⌐syo kara de⌐ma⌐su ḡa, ka⌐maimase⌐ñ ka⌐

5. I'll arrive about 10. Is that all right?   Zyu⌐u-zi-ḡo⌐ro tu⌐kima⌐su ḡa, ka⌐maimase⌐ñ ka⌐

6. I'll be [here] until afternoon. Is that all right?   Go⌐go made i⌐ma⌐su ḡa, ka⌐maimase⌐ñ ka⌐

7. I bought a cheap furoshiki.   Ya⌐su⌐i hu⌐rosiki (o) kaima⌐sita g̃a,
    Is that all right?   ka⌐maimase⌐ñ ka⌐

8. There aren't any cigarettes.   Ta⌐bako (wa) arimase⌐ñ g̃a, ka⌐mai-
    Is that all right?   mase⌐ñ ka⌐

9. This one is a little different.   Kore (wa) su⌐ko⌐si ti⌐g̃aima⌐su g̃a,
    Is that all right?   ka⌐maimase⌐ñ ka⌐

10. It's a little expensive. Is   Su⌐ko⌐si ta⌐ka⌐i desu g̃a, ka⌐maima-
    that all right?   se⌐ñ ka⌐

E. Substitution Drill

1. I was here from morning   A⌐sa kara ⌐go⌐g̃o made ko⌐ko ni ima⌐-
    until afternoon.   sita.

2. I was in the office from 9   Ku⌐-zi kara ⌐go⌐-zi made zi⌐mu⌐syo ni
    until 5.   i⌐ma⌐sita.

3. I was at home from Friday   Ki⌐ñyo⌐o kara ni⌐tiyoo ma⌐de u⌐ti ni ima⌐-
    until Sunday.   sita.

4. I was at the hospital from   Si-⌐g̃atu⌐ kara ha⌐ti-g̃atu⌐ made byo⌐oiñ
    April until August.   ni ima⌐sita.

5. I was in school from the   Sa⌐ñzyu⌐u-neñ kara ko⌐tosi ma⌐de ga⌐k-
    year 30 until this year.   koo ni ima⌐sita.

6. I was in the park from   Zyu⌐u-zi-g̃o⌐ro kara zyu⌐uiti-zi-hañ-
    about 10 until about 11:30.   g̃o⌐ro made ko⌐oeñ ni ima⌐sita.

7. I was at that hotel from the   Tu⌐itati⌐ kara to⌐o-ka ma⌐de a⌐no ho⌐-
    first until the tenth.   teru ni i⌐ma⌐sita.

8. I was at an inn in Kyoto   O⌐toto⌐i kara ki⌐no⌐o made ⌐Kyo⌐oto no
    from the day before yes-   ryo⌐kañ ni ima⌐sita.
    terday until yesterday.

9. I was in the post office   Zyu⌐u-zi zyu⌐p-pu⌐ñ-mae kara go-⌐hu⌐ñ-
    from 10 to 10 until 5 af-   sug̃i made yu⌐ubi⌐ñkyoku ni i⌐ma⌐si-
    ter.   ta.

10. I was at Mr. Tanaka's   Ki⌐noo no a⌐sa kara ⌐ke⌐sa made Ta⌐na-
    house from yesterday   ka-sañ no otaku ni ima⌐sita.
    morning until this morn-
    ing.

F. Substitution Drill

1. I am always at home about   I⌐tu mo ha⌐ti-zi-g̃o⌐ro u⌐ti ni ima⌐su.
    8.

2. I usually am at home about   Taitee ha⌐ti-zi-g̃o⌐ro u⌐ti ni ima⌐su.
    8.

3. I usually am at home at   Taitee tyo⌐odo ku⌐-zi ni u⌐ti ni ima⌐su.
    exactly 9.

4. I usually am in the office   Taitee tyo⌐odo ku⌐-zi ni zi⌐mu⌐syo ni
    at exactly 9.   imasu.

5. I usually arrive at the of-   Taitee tyo⌐odo ku⌐-zi ni zi⌐mu⌐syo ni
    fice at exactly 9.   tukimasu.

6. Every day I arrive at the   Ma⌐initi tyo⌐odo ku⌐-zi ni zi⌐mu⌐syo ni
    office at exactly 9.   tukimasu.

7. Every day I arrive at the   Ma⌐initi ⌐ku⌐-zi ⌐tyo⌐tto ⌐ma⌐e ni zi-
    office at a little before 9.   ⌐mu⌐syo ni tukimasu.

8. Every day I arrive at school   Ma⌐initi ⌐ku⌐-zi ⌐tyo⌐tto ⌐ma⌐e ni ga⌐k-
    at a little before 9.   koo ni tukima⌐su.

9. Every day I go to school at   Ma⌐initi ⌐ku⌐-zi ⌐tyo⌐tto ⌐ma⌐e ni ga⌐k-
    a little before 9.   koo ni ikima⌐su.

G. Grammar Drill

    Tutor: I⌐ma desu ka⌐ 'Is it now?' (affirmative)
    Student: I⌐ma zya a⌐rimase⌐ñ ka⌐ 'Isn't it now?' (negative)

1. Ma⌐initi desu ka⌐   Ma⌐initi zya a⌐rimase⌐ñ ka⌐
2. O⌐wakari ni narima⌐su ka⌐   O⌐wakari ni narimase⌐ñ ka⌐
3. Ke⌐sa desita yo⌐   Ke⌐sa zya a⌐rimase⌐ñ desita yo⌐
4. Sa⌐ñ-zi kara desu ka⌐   Sa⌐ñ-zi kara zya a⌐rimase⌐ñ ka⌐
5. Kinoo o⌐kaeri ni narima⌐si-   Kinoo o⌐kaeri ni narimase⌐ñ desita
    ta ka⌐   ka⌐
6. Ha⌐ya⌐i desu ka⌐   Ha⌐yaku a⌐rimase⌐ñ ka⌐
7. Yo⌐-zi made desu ka⌐   Yo⌐-zi made zya a⌐rimase⌐ñ ka⌐
8. De⌐kima⌐sita ka⌐   De⌐kimase⌐ñ desita ka⌐
9. A⌐na⌐ta mo o⌐de ni nari-   A⌐na⌐ta mo o⌐de ni narimase⌐ñ ka⌐
    ma⌐su ka⌐
10. Ta⌐naka-sañ no⌐ desu yo⌐   Ta⌐naka-sañ no⌐ zya a⌐rimase⌐ñ yo⌐

H. Response Drill[1]

    Tutor: I⌐kimasyo⌐o ka. 'Shall I go?' (an offer)
    Student: E⌐e, i⌐tte kudasa⌐i. 'Yes, please (go).' (affirmative answer)

1. Ti⌐zu (o) ka⌐kimasyo⌐o ka.   E⌐e, ka⌐ite kudasai.
2. Ma⌐timasyo⌐o ka.   E⌐e, ma⌐tte kudasai.
3. Wa⌐takusi mo mairimasyo⌐o   Ha⌐a, i⌐ra⌐site kudasai.
    ka.
4. A⌐sita⌐ mo ki⌐masyo⌐o ka.   E⌐e, ki⌐te⌐ kudasai.
5. Ko⌐re (o) simasyo⌐o ka.   E⌐e, si⌐te kudasa⌐i.
6. Mo⌐o iti-do iimasyo⌐o ka.   E⌐e, i⌐tte kudasa⌐i.
7. Ro⌐ku⌐-zi made i⌐masyo⌐o   E⌐e, i⌐te kudasa⌐i.
    ka.
8. Si⌐ñbuñ mo kaimasyo⌐o ka.   E⌐e, ka⌐tte kudasa⌐i.

---

[1] Based on Grammatical Note 1. After practicing the drill in its given
form, practice it with o⌐negai-sima⌐su as an alternate affirmative reply, and
with i⌐i desu and ke⌐kkoo desu as negative replies.

I. Level Drill[1]

1. I⌐tu-g̃oro kaerima⌐su ka⌟   I⌐tu-g̃oro okaeri ni narima⌐su ka⌟
2. Wa⌐surema⌐sita ka⌟   O⌐wasure ni narima⌐sita ka⌟
3. To⌐kee (g̃a) arima⌐su ka⌟   To⌐kee (g̃a) gozaima⌐su ka⌟
4. Na⌐ñ-zi ni u⌐ti (o) dema⁴su   Na⌐ñ-zi ni o⌐taku (o) ode ni narima⁴su
    ka⌟   ka⌟

5. Go⌐g̃o made i⌐ma⁴su ka⌟   Go⌐g̃o made $\begin{vmatrix} i⌐rassyaima⁴su \\ o⌐ide ni narima⁴su \end{vmatrix}$ ka⌟

6. I⌐tu ko⌐ko ni kima⁴sita ka⌟   I⌐tu ko⌐tira ni $\begin{vmatrix} irassyaima⁴sita \\ oide ni narima⁴sita \end{vmatrix}$ ka⌟

7. Wa⌐karima⌐sita ka⌟   O⌐wakari ni narima⌐sita ka⌟
8. Na⌐ñ-niti-g̃o⌐ro tu⌐kima⁴su   Na⌐ñ-niti-g̃o⌐ro o⌐tuki ni narima⁴su ka⌟
    ka⌟

J. Expansion Drill

1. I guess I'll come.   Ki⌐masyo⌐o.
    Shall I come?   Ki⌐masyo⌐o ka.
    Shall I come again?   Ma⌐ta kimasyo⌐o ka.
    Shall I come again tomor-   A⌐sita mata kimasyo⌐o ka.
      row?

2. I go back.   Ka⌐erima⌐su.
    I go back to Kyoto.   Kyo⌐oto ni kaerimasu.
    I go back to Kyoto in June.   Ro⌐ku-g̃atu⌐ ni ⌐Kyo⌐oto ni kaerimasu.
    I usually go back to Kyoto   Taitee ro⌐ku-g̃atu⌐ ni ⌐Kyo⌐oto ni kae-
      in June.   rimasu.

3. I'm [here].   I⌐ma⌐su.
    I'm in the office.   Zi⌐mu⌐syo ni imasu.
    I'm in the office until 5:30.   Go-⌐zi-ha⌐ñ made zi⌐mu⌐syo ni imasu.
    I'm in the office from 9   Ku⌐-zi kara go-⌐zi-ha⌐ñ made zi⌐mu⌐-
      until 5:30.   syo ni imasu.
    I'm in the office every day   Ma⌐initi ⌐ku⌐-zi kara go-⌐zi-ha⌐ñ made
      from 9 to 5:30.   zi⌐mu⌐syo ni imasu.

4. [He] arrived.   Tu⌐kima⌐sita.
    [He] arrived in America.   A⌐merika ni tukima⌐sita.
    [He] arrived in America   Ni-⌐syuukañ-g̃u⌐rai ⌐ma⁴e ni A⌐meri-
      about 2 weeks ago.   ka ni tukima⌐sita.
    Mr. Tanaka arrived in   Tanaka-sañ (wa) ni-⌐syuukañ-g̃u⌐rai
      America about 2 weeks   ⌐ma⁴e ni A⌐merika ni tukima⌐sita.
      ago.

---

[1] In each case the sentence on the right is the polite equivalent of the sentence on the left.

5. Is it all right?
   I'd like to leave. Is it
   all right?
   I'd like to leave here. Is
   it all right?
   I'd like to leave here by 3
   o'clock. Is it all right?

Ka⌐maimase⌐ñ ka⌐
De⌐ta⌐i ñ desu ḡa, ka⌐maimase⌐ñ ka⌐
Ko⌐ko (o) deta⌐i ñ desu ḡa, ka⌐maima-
se⌐ñ ka⌐
Sa⌐ñ-zi made ni ko⌐ko (o) deta⌐i ñ de-
su ḡa, ka⌐maimase⌐ñ ka⌐

6. I arrived.
   I arrived in Japan.
   I arrived in Japan on the
   15th.
   I left America on the 1st
   and arrived in Japan on
   the 15th.

Tu⌐kima⌐sita.
Ni⌐ho⌐ñ ni tu⌐kima⌐sita.
Zyu⌐ugo-niti ni Ni⌐ho⌐ñ ni tu⌐kima⌐si-
ta.
Tu⌐itati⌐ ni A⌐merika (o) de⌐te, zyu⌐u-
go-niti ni Ni⌐ho⌐ñ ni tu⌐kima⌐sita.

7. I can't do [it].
   I can't do [it] (I tell you).
   All of it, I can't do (I tell
   you).
   I can do a little but I can't
   do all of it (I tell you).

De⌐kimase⌐ñ.
De⌐kimase⌐ñ yo⌐
Ze⌐ñbu wa de⌐kimase⌐ñ yo⌐
Su⌐ko⌐si wa de⌐kima⌐su ḡa, ze⌐ñbu wa
de⌐kimase⌐ñ yo.

8. It's troublesome.
   It's troublesome (I tell you).
   It's a little troublesome (I
   tell you).
   This is a little troublesome
   (I tell you).
   That doesn't matter, but
   this is a little troublesome
   (I tell you).

Ko⌐marima⌐su.
Ko⌐marima⌐su yo⌐
Tyo⌐tto ko⌐marima⌐su yo⌐
Kore wa ⌐tyo⌐tto ko⌐marima⌐su yo⌐
So⌐re wa kamaimase⌐ñ ḡa, kore wa
⌐tyo⌐tto ko⌐marima⌐su yo⌐

SUPPLEMENTARY CONVERSATIONS
(with questions)

1. Yamamoto (a visitor): Ta⌐naka-sañ irassyaima⌐su ka⌐
   Secretary: Ta⌐naka-sañ de⌐su ka⌐ Yo⌐kohama e irassyaima⌐sita ḡa⌐
   Yamamoto: So⌐o desu ka. Na⌐ñ-zi-ḡo⌐ro o⌐kaeri ni narima⌐su ka⌐
   Secretary: Yo⌐ku wa⌐karimase⌐ñ ḡa, ni-⌐zi-ḡo⌐ro desyoo.
   Yamamoto: So⌐o desu ka. Zya⌐a, ma⌐ta a⌐to de ma⌐irimasyo⌐o. Do⌐o mo
   a⌐ri⌐ḡatoo gozaimasita.
   Secretary: Do⌐o itasimasite.

Questions (Answer in Japanese on the basis of the above conversation.)

   1. Tanaka-sañ wa i⌐ma⌐su ka⌐
   2. Tanaka-sañ wa ⌐do⌐ko ni i⌐ma⌐su ka⌐
   3. Tanaka-sañ wa ⌐i⌐tu ka⌐erima⌐su ka⌐

4. Yamamoto-sañ wa ⌐do⌐o si⌐ma⌐su ka⌐[1]

2. Mr. Smith: A⌐sita⌐ kara[2] Ka⌐makura[3] e ikima⌐su ḡa, a⌐na⌐ta mo iti-do i⌐ki-
                mase⌐ñ ka⌐

    Tanaka: A⌐ri⌐ḡatoo gozaimasu ḡa⌐

    Smith: Tu⌐ḡi⌐ no ni⌐tiyo⌐obi wa ⌐do⌐o desu ka.

    Tanaka: A⌐ri⌐ḡatoo gozaimasu. Tu⌐ḡi⌐ no ni⌐tiyo⌐obi ⌐na⌐ñ-niti desyoo
                ka.

    Smith: Ha⌐tu-ka de⌐su ḡa⌐   Do⌐o desu ka. I⌐kimase⌐ñ ka⌐

    Tanaka: A⌐ri⌐ḡatoo gozaimasu. Ka⌐maimase⌐ñ ka⌐

    Smith: E⌐e, do⌐ozo ⌐do⌐ozo. Na⌐ñ de i⌐kima⌐su ka⌐

    Tanaka: So⌐o desu ⌐ne⌐e. De⌐ñsya de i⌐kima⌐su ḡa⌐

    Smith: Na⌐ñ-zi-ḡo⌐ro tu⌐kima⌐su ka⌐   Tookyoo kara tyóodo i⌐ti-zi⌐kañ
                ka⌐karima⌐su ḡa⌐

    Tanaka: Zya⌐a, zyu⌐u-zi-ḡo⌐ro Ka⌐makura-e⌐ki e tu⌐kimasyo⌐o ka.

    Smith: I⌐i desu yo⌐   Bo⌐ku wa ⌐zyu⌐u-zi made ni ⌐e⌐ki e itte, e⌐ki no
                ⌐ma⌐e ni imasu.

    Tanaka: A⌐ri⌐ḡatoo gozaimasu. Do⌐ozo o⌐neḡai-sima⌐su.

    Smith: Zya⌐a mata.

    Tanaka: Sayonara.

    Smith: Sayonara.

Questions:

1. Su⌐misu-sañ wa a⌐sita⌐ kara ⌐do⌐ko e i⌐kima⌐su ka⌐
2. Ta⌐naka-sañ mo asita ikima⌐su ka⌐
3. Tanaka-sañ wa na⌐ñyo⌐obi ni i⌐kima⌐su ka⌐
4. Tanaka-sañ wa ⌐na⌐ñ-niti ni i⌐kima⌐su ka⌐
5. Tanaka-sañ wa ⌐na⌐ñ de i⌐kima⌐su ka⌐
6. Tanaka-sañ wa ⌐na⌐ñ-zi ni Ka⌐makura e tukima⌐su ka⌐
7. To⌐okyoo kara Kamakura ma⌐de ⌐de⌐ñsya de do⌐no-ḡurai kakarima⌐su
    ka⌐
8. Su⌐misu-sañ wa tu⌐ḡi⌐ no ni⌐tiyo⌐obi no ⌐na⌐ñ-zi ni Ka⌐makura-e⌐ki
    e i⌐kima⌐su ka⌐
9. Kamakura wa ⌐do⌐ko desu ka.

---

[1] 'What (lit. how) will Mr. Yamamoto do?'

[2] Lit. 'I go from tomorrow' —i.e. 'I go tomorrow and stay on.'

[3] A resort city near Yokohama.

English Equivalents of Conversations

1. Yamamoto: Is Mr. Tanaka in?
    Secretary: Mr. Tanaka? He went to Yokohama but [is there anything I
                 can do for you?]
    Yamamoto: Oh. (About) what time will he be back?
    Secretary: I'm not sure but it will probably be about 2 o'clock.
    Yamamoto: Oh. Then I guess I'll come again later. Thank you very
                 much.
    Secretary: Not at all.

2. Mr. Smith: I'm going to Kamakura tomorrow to stay for a while. Won't
                 you come (lit. go[1]) too some (lit. one) time?
    Tanaka: Thank you but . . .
    Smith: How about next Sunday?
    Tanaka: Thank you. What date is next Sunday?
    Smith: It's the 20th. . . . How about it? Won't you come?
    Tanaka: Thank you. (Hesitantly) Will it be all right?
    Smith: Yes. Please [come]! How will you come?
    Tanaka: Let's see. I'll come by electric train but [will that be con-
                 venient?]
    Smith: About what time will you arrive? It takes just an hour from
                 Tokyo . . .
    Tanaka: Well then, shall I arrive at Kamakura Station about 10?
    Smith: That will be fine. I'll go to the station by 10, and I'll be in
                 front (of the station).
    Tanaka: Thank you. Would you do that [i.e. meet me]?
    Smith: Well then, [I'll see you] again.
    Tanaka: Goodbye.
    Smith: Goodbye.

EXERCISES

1. You ask Mr. Tanaka: Mr. Tanaka replies:

    a. to come again tomorrow   Certainly.
        afternoon.
    b. if you should come again   Please do.
        tomorrow afternoon.
    c. how long (i.e. until what   Until 5:30.
        time) he will be here.
    d. what time he goes home.   Usually at 5:00.
    e. if he always goes home at   No. Sometimes I go home at
        about 5:00.   about 6:00.

---

[1] Reread Lesson 8, Grammatical Note 6, last paragraph.

f.	what time you should come on Saturday.	By 10:30.
g.	what time he is coming on Saturday.	At 10:30.
h.	how late the post office is open.	I think it's until about 5:30.
i.	to wait until 4:30.	I'm sorry but I can't.
j.	to stay here from 12:00 to 1:00.	All right.
k.	if Mr. Yamamoto has gone home.	Yes, he went home at 5:00.
l.	when he is returning to Tokyo.	I'd like to go back tomorrow.
m.	to come here by 6:30.	I'm afraid that's a bit inconvenient.
n.	if you should draw a map.	No, never mind.
o.	if he is coming here again tomorrow morning.	Yes, at 8:45.
p.	if he is coming here again on the 19th.	No, on the 20th.
q.	if he will be here until 6:00.	No, I'm going home at 5:00.
r.	if he will be in Tokyo until March.	No, I'm returning to Osaka in February.
s.	if you should turn this corner to the left.	No, to the right.
t.	if you should back up a little.	It doesn't matter.
u.	what time he leaves home in the morning.	Usually, at 7:45.
v.	when he arrived in Kyoto.	I came here in March of this year.

2. Using a timetable, real or made up, practice asking and answering questions like the following:

   (Time) ni (place) o de⌐ma⌐sita. ⌐Na⌐ñ-zi ni (another place) ni tu⌐kima⌐sita ka?

   (Time) ni (place) ni tu⌐kima⌐sita. Na⌐ñ-zi ni (another place) o de⌐ma⌐sita ka?

3. Practice asking and answering questions like the following:

   Ge⌐tuyo⌐o kara ki⌐ñyo⌐o made ⌐na⌐ñ-niti a⌐rima⌐su ka⌐
   Sa⌐ñ-zi kara ku-⌐zi-ha⌐ñ made na⌐ñ-zi⌐kañ a⌐rima⌐su ka⌐
   Si-g̃atu tu⌐itati⌐ kara, ⌐go⌐-g̃atu ⌐sa⌐ñzyuu i⌐ti-niti⌐ made, na⌐ñ-ka⌐g̃etu a⌐rima⌐su ka⌐

4. Practice the Basic Dialogues with appropriate variations.

Lesson 10. Meeting People

BASIC DIALOGUES: FOR MEMORIZATION

(a)

Smith

female	oꜛñnaꜜ
person	hiꜛtoꜜ or kaꜛtaꜜ ꜜ
woman	oꜛñna no hitoꜜ or oꜛñna no kataꜜ ꜜ
who?	daꜜre or doꜜnata ꜜ

1. Who is that woman?

    Ano oꜛñna no hitoꜜ (wa) ꜛdaꜜre desu ka⌐

    or

    Ano oꜛñna no kataꜜ (wa) ꜛdoꜜnata desu ka⌐

    or

    Ano oꜛñna no kataꜜ (wa) ꜛdoꜜnata de (i)rassyaimasu ka⌐

Tanaka

an American	aꜛmerikaꜜziñ

2. Do you mean the American?

    Aꜛmerikaꜜziñ desu ka⌐

Smith

a Japanese	niꜛhoñziꜜñ

3. No, I mean the Japanese.

    Iie, niꜛhoñziꜜñ desu.

Tanaka

4. Oh, that (person) is Miss (or Mrs.) Yamada.

    Aꜜa, aꜜno hito wa Yaꜛmada-sañ deꜜsu.

    or

    Aꜜa, aꜜno kataꜜ wa Yaꜛmada-sañ deꜜsu.

    or

    Aꜜa, aꜜno kataꜜ wa Yaꜛmada-sañ de (i)rassyaimaꜜsu.

Smith

friend	tomodati or otomodati ꜜ

5. Is she a friend?

    Toꜛmodati deꜜsu ka⌐

    or

    Oꜛtomodati deꜜsu ka⌐

    or

    Oꜛtomodati de (i)rassyaimaꜜsu ka⌐

148

Tanaka

name   namae or
                              onamae †
know   si⌐tte (i)ma˥su or
                              si⌐tte orima˥su † or
                              si⌐tte (i)rassyaima˥su †

6. No, she isn't a friend, but I   Iie, to⌐modati zya arimase˥ñ ḡa,
   know her name.   na⌐mae wa sitte (i)ma˥su.

                                    or

                                    Iie, to⌐modati de˥ wa go˪zaimase˥ñ
                                    ḡa, o⌐namae wa sitte orima˥su.

(b)

Smith

rudeness or rude   si⌐tu˥ree
it is rude [of me] but   si⌐tu˥ree desu ḡa or
                              si⌐tu˥ree de gozaimasu ḡa

7. Excuse me [for asking] but   Si⌐tu˥ree desu ḡa, onamae wa?
   [what is] your name?
                                   or

                                   Si⌐tu˥ree de gozaimasu ḡa,   onamae
                                   wa?

Sato

8. I'm Yukio Sato.   Sa˥too Yu⌐kio de˥su.

                                   or

                                   Sa˥too Yu⌐kio de gozaima˥su.

Smith

work   siḡoto or
                              o⌐si˥ḡoto †

9. What do you do? (Lit. As   O⌐si˥ḡoto wa?
   for your work?)

Sato

for the American Em-   A⌐merika-taisi˥kañ ni
  bassy
become employed   tu⌐tomema˥su
be employed   tu⌐to˥mete (i)masu or
                              tu⌐to˥mete orimasu † or
                              tu⌐to˥mete (i)rassyaimasu †

10. I'm working for the American   A⌐merika-taisi˥kañ ni tu⌐to˥mete
    Embassy.   (i)masu.

                                   or

                                   A⌐merika-taisi˥kañ ni tu⌐to˥mete
                                   orimasu.

(c)

Smith

marry   ke⌐kkoñ-sima˥su

be married	ke⌐kkoñ-site (i)ma⌐su <u>or</u>
	ke⌐kkoñ-site orima⌐su⌐ <u>or</u>
	ke⌐kkoñ-site (i)rassyaima⌐su⌐

11. Excuse me [for asking] but   Si⌐tu⌐ree desu ḡa, ke⌐kkoñ-site (i)ma⌐-
    are you married?   su ka⌐

                                   <u>or</u>

                                   Si⌐tu⌐ree de gozaimasu ḡa, ke⌐kkoñ-
                                   site (i)rassyaima⌐su ka⌐

                        Tanaka

    single   hi⌐to⌐ri <u>or</u>
                                   ohitori⌐

12. No, I'm single. How about   Iie, hi⌐to⌐ri desu. A⌐na⌐ta wa?
    you?
                                   <u>or</u>

                                   Iie, hi⌐to⌐ri de gozaimasu. A⌐na⌐ta wa?

                        Smith

13. I'm married.   Ke⌐kkoñ-site (i)ma⌐su.

                                   <u>or</u>

                                   Ke⌐kkoñ-site orima⌐su.

                        Tanaka

    child   kodomo <u>or</u>
                                   okosañ⌐

14. (a) Do you have any   Ko⌐domo (ḡa) arima⌐su ka⌐
        children?
                                   <u>or</u>
    <u>or</u>
                                   O⌐kosañ (ḡa) gozaima⌐su ka⌐

    (b) Are there any children   Ko⌐domo (ḡa) ima⌐su ka⌐
        [in your family]?
                                   <u>or</u>

                                   O⌐kosañ (ḡa) irassyaima⌐su ka⌐

                        Smith

    1 person   hi⌐to⌐-ri
    2 people   hu⌐ta-ri⌐
    3 people   sa⌐ñ-ni⌐ñ
15. (a) Yes, I have two.   E⌐e, hu⌐tari arima⌐su.

    <u>or</u>   <u>or</u>

                                   E⌐e, hu⌐tari gozaima⌐su.

    (b) Yes, there are two.   E⌐e, hu⌐tari ima⌐su.

                                   <u>or</u>

                                   E⌐e, hu⌐tari orima⌐su.

                        Tanaka

    how old?   i⌐kutu <u>or</u>
                                   oikutu⌐

16. How old are they?   I⌐kutu desu ka⌐

                                   <u>or</u>

                                   O⌐ikutu de⌐su ka⌐

                                   <u>or</u>

                                   O⌐ikutu de (i)rassyaima⌐su ka⌐

Smith

1 year old	hiˈtoˈ-tu
2 years old	huˈta-tuˈ
being 12 years old	zyuˈuniˈ de
this month	koñɡetu
become	naˈrimaˈsu
become 8 years old	ya-ˈttuˈ ni narimasu

17. One is 12 and the other (lit. one more person) will be 8 this month.
    Hiˈtoˈ-ri wa zyuˈuniˈ de, moˈo hitoˈ-ri wa kóñɡetu ya-ˈttuˈ ni narimasu.

Tanaka

both	doˈtira mo[1]
male	oˈtokoˈ
boy	oˈtokoˈ no ko or
	oˈtokoˈ no okosañ †

18. Are both boys?
    Dotira mo oˈtokoˈ no ko desu ka⌣

    or

    Dotira mo oˈtokoˈ no oˈkosañ de (i)rassyaimaˈsu ka⌣

Smith

over or top or topmost or oldest	ue
under or below or bottom or youngest	sita
being a boy	oˈtokoˈ no ko de
girl	oˈñnaˈ no ko or
	oˈñnaˈ no okosañ †

19. No. The older is a boy and the younger is a girl.
    Iie. Uˈe wa otokoˈ no ko de, sita wa oˈñnaˈ no ko desu.

    or

    Iie. Uˈe wa otokoˈ no ko de, sita wa oˈñnaˈ no ko de gozaimasu.

(d)

Smith

that child	aˈnoˈ ko or
	ano okosañ †
child of what place (i.e. what household)?	doˈko no ko or
	doˈtira no okosañ †

---

[1] Has unaccented alternant (cf. sentence following).

20. Whose child is that? (Lit.   A⌐no⌐ ko (wa) ⌐do⌐ko no ko ⌐de⌐su ka⌐
    That child is the child of   or
    what place?)   Ano okosañ (wa) ⌐do⌐tira no o⌐kosañ
                                        de gozaima⌐su ka⌐

                            Tanaka

    belonging or pertaining   uti no or
    to one's household   otaku no ⌐
21. Why, that's our Taro.   Uti no ⌐Ta⌐roo desu yo⌐
                                                    or
                                        Uti no ⌐Ta⌐roo de gozaimasu yo⌐

                            Smith

    Master Taro   Ta⌐roo-tyañ
22. (Is he) your Taro?   Otaku no ⌐Ta⌐roo-tyañ desu ka.
                                                    or
                                        Otaku no ⌐Ta⌐roo-tyañ de (i)rassyai-
                                        masu ka.

    become big   o⌐okiku narimasu or
                                        o⌐okiku o⌐nari ni narima⌐su⌐
23. Hasn't he grown!   * O⌐okiku na⌐rima⌐sita ⌐ne⌐e.
                                                    or
                                        * O⌐okiku o⌐nari ni narima⌐sita ⌐ne⌐e.

ADDITIONAL NATIONALITIES

(All the following words refer to people only.[1])

Japanese	ni⌐hoñzi⌐ñ or
	ni⌐ppoñzi⌐ñ
American	a⌐merika⌐ziñ or
	be⌐ekoku⌐ziñ
Korean	tyo⌐oseñzi⌐ñ
	(or ka⌐ñkoku⌐ziñ[2])
Chinese	tyu⌐ugoku⌐ziñ
	(or si⌐na⌐ziñ[3])
Englishman	i⌐girisu⌐ziñ or
	e⌐ekoku⌐ziñ

----

[1] Compare:
Ni⌐hoñzi⌐ñ desu. 'He's Japanese.'
Ni⌐hoñ no⌐ desu. 'It's Japanese.'

[2] Refers to South Koreans only. Preferred by them to preceding older
term, which refers to all Koreans.

[3] Formerly a commonly used word, now considered insulting by many
Chinese.

Frenchman	hu⌐ranˢu⌐zin
German	do⌐itu⌐ziñ
Russian	ro⌐sia⌐ziñ
Indian (from India)	i⌐ñdo⌐ziñ
what nationality?	na⌐ni⌐ziñ

NOTES ON THE BASIC DIALOGUES

Sentences for which alternate forms are given are in the order of increasing politeness. Polite alternants are used more commonly, but not exclusively, by women.

5. The polite otomodati usually refers to someone else's friend(s), but some women use it in reference to their own friends as well—i.e. as a polite neutral (+) word.

6. Si⌐tte ima⌐su 'know' implies knowledge, whereas wa⌐karima⌐su 'understand,' 'can tell,' 'be clear' implies understanding or recognition by the senses. For example, I know (si⌐tte ima⌐su) Mr. Tanaka—perhaps because I have been introduced to him—but I can tell (wa⌐karima⌐su) who Mr. Tanaka is— perhaps because he is the only Japanese in the room.

The wa following namae is the wa of comparison: i.e. 'even if I don't know her well, her name I know.'

7. The nominal si⌐tu⌐ree + desu (or de go⌐zaima⌐su) ga is common before questions of a personal nature. It is also used to introduce an interruption.

8. Remember that -sañ is not used with one's own name.

The family name precedes the given name in Japanese. When -sañ is used with the full name, it comes last, after the given name (for example, Sa⌐too Yŭkio - sañ). -Sañ may also be used with the given name alone.

Additional examples of family names:

Aoyama	Ikeda	Ueda
Gotoo	Kimura	Watanabe
Hasimoto	Oota	Yamada
Hatoyama	Ta⌐mura	Yosida

Additional examples of given names:

Men's		Women's	
Haruo	Siğeru	Ha⌐nako	Ma⌐sako
Hi⌐rosi	Syo⌐ozi	Ha⌐ru	Mi⌐dori
Masao	Ta⌐roo	Harue	Si⌐ğe
Masaru	Yosio	Ha⌐ruko	Yo⌐siko
Sa⌐buro⌐o	Zi⌐roo	Haruyo	Yu⌐kiko

11. Ke⌐kkoñ-sima⌐su is one of a vast number of verbals consisting of a nomi-
     nal compounded with the verbal √si⌐ma⌐su 'make' or 'do.' Kekkoñ is a
     nominal meaning 'marriage.'

14. √A⌐rima⌐su occurs with both animate and inanimate subjects (correspond-
     ing to objects in English) when it means 'have'; thus, ko⌐domo g̃a √arima⌐su
     (polite √go⌐zaima⌐su) 'have children.' In the given context, 14 (a) and (b)
     and 15 (a) and (b) are used almost interchangeably, except for differences
     of politeness.

18. Do⌐tira mo is used in reference to inanimate objects as well as living be-
     ings.

19. Compare: u⌐e no ho⌐ñ 'top book' and ho⌐ñ no ue 'top of the book'; si⌐ta no
     ho⌐ñ 'bottom book' and ho⌐ñ no sita 'under the book.'

22. -Tyañ is added to boys' and girls' given names. It is polite, but less
     formal than -sañ. While it is used in talking TO one's own children, it is
     not ordinarily used in talking ABOUT them to those outside the family or
     circle of very close friends.

GRAMMATICAL NOTES

1. √de⌐su: Polite Equivalents

    √de⌐su ~ √de go⌐zaima⌐su ~ √de (i)⌐rassyaima⌐su

The polite neutral (+) equivalent of de⌐su following a nominal or a particle
is de go⌐zaima⌐su (de = the gerund of de⌐su). The past is de go⌐zaima⌐sita, and
the tentative de go⌐zaimasyo⌐o.

Examples:

	Plain	Polite +
'It's a book.'	Ho⌐ñ desu.	Ho⌐ñ de gozaimasu.
'It's that one.'	So⌐re de⌐su.	So⌐re de gozaima⌐su.
'It was pretty.'	Ki⌐ree desita.	Ki⌐ree de gozaimasita.
'It's probably the same.'	O⌐nazi desyo⌐o.	O⌐nazi de gozaimasyo⌐o.
'It's until tomorrow.'	A⌐sita⌐ made desu.	A⌐sita⌐ made de gozaimasu.

WARNING: Do not confuse the above with:

'There's a book.' or   Ho⌐ñ (g̃a) arimasu.   Ho⌐ñ (g̃a) gozaimasu.
'I have a book.'

The negative equivalent of de go⌐zaima⌐su following a nominal or a particle
is de⌐[1] wa go⌐zaimase⌐ñ (past, de⌐ wa go⌐zaimase⌐ñ desita).

_____

[1] De is accented before wa, unless an accented word or phrase precedes.

Examples:

	Plain	Polite [+]
'It isn't a book.'	Ho⌐n zya a⌐rimase⌐ñ.	Ho⌐ñ de wa go⌐zaimase⌐ñ.
'It isn't that.'	So⌐re zya arimase⌐ñ.	So⌐re de⌐ wa go⌐zaimase⌐ñ.
'It wasn't a taxi.'	Ta⌐kusii zya a⌐rimase⌐ñ desita.	Ta⌐kusii de wa go⌐zaimase⌐ñ desita.
'It doesn't start at 3 o'clock.'	Sa⌐ñ-zi kara zya a⌐rimase⌐ñ.	Sa⌐ñ-zi kara de wa go⌐zaimase⌐ñ.

Actually, zya is the contracted equivalent of de⌐ wa, and the two can be used interchangeably anywhere, with only a difference of formality.

If a nominal (with or without following particle) + de⌐su refers to a PERSON other than the speaker, it has a second polite equivalent which is honorific (†) —namely, nominal + de (i)⌐rassyaima⌐su[1] (past, de (i)⌐rassyaima⌐sita; tentative, de (i)⌐rassyaimasyo⌐o; negative, de⌐ wa i⌐rassyaimase⌐ñ; past negative, de⌐ wa i⌐rassyaimase⌐ñ desita).

Thus:

	Plain	Polite
'He is Mr. Sato.'	Sa⌐too-sañ desu.	(Neutral) Sa⌐too-sañ de gozaimasu. or (Honorific) Sa⌐too-sañ de (i)rassyaimasu.
But:		
'I am Mr. Sato.'	Sa⌐too desu.	Sa⌐too de gozaimasu.

The de go⌐zaima⌐su alternative represents simply a polite style of speech, whereas the de (i)⌐rassyaima⌐su alternative exalts the person under discussion besides being a polite style of speech. Of the two, the latter is more common—unless, of course, the speaker is talking politely about himself, a member of his own family, or someone of inferior social status.

WARNING: De⌐su following an adjectival (for example, ta⌐ka⌐i) is NOT replaced by de go⌐zaima⌐su or de (i)⌐rassyaima⌐su in the polite style.

---

[1] The form without i- is a contracted form, very common in conversation. Compare the end of Note 2 following.

2. Verbal Gerund + √i⌐ma⌐su

The non-past of a verbal usually refers to repeated or future punctual[1] occurrence.

A present or future durative[1] action or state is regularly indicated by a verbal gerund + i⌐ma⌐su. This pattern means either (a) 'an action is now or will be taking place over a period of time' or (b) 'the state resulting from an action now exists, or will exist, over a period of time.' Meaning (b) is more common among verbals which never take a direct object — particularly among verbals indicating motion from one place to another and among those which basically mean 'become so-and-so.' Depending on the individual verbal, the subject may be animate or inanimate.

Examples:

Non-Past	Gerund + i⌐ma⌐su

Meaning (a)

si⌐ma⌐su '[someone] does' or '[someone] will do'	si⌐te ima⌐su '[someone] is doing' or '[someone] will be doing'
ka⌐kima⌐su '[someone] writes' or '[someone] will write'	ka⌐ite imasu '[someone] is writing' or '[someone] will be writing'
ka⌐ima⌐su '[someone] buys' or '[someone] will buy'	ka⌐tte ima⌐su '[someone] is buying' or '[someone] will be buying'

Meaning (b)

ke⌐kkoñ-sima⌐su '[someone] gets married' or '[someone] will get married'	ke⌐kkoñ-site ima⌐su '[someone] is married' or '[someone] will be married (i.e. in a married state)'
tu⌐tomema⌐su '[someone] becomes employed' or '[someone] will become employed'	tu⌐to⌐mete imasu '[someone] is employed' or '[someone] will be employed (i.e. in an employed state)'
i⌐kima⌐su '[someone] goes' or '[someone] will go'	i⌐tte ima⌐su[2] '[someone] is gone' or '[someone] will be gone'

---

[1] PUNCTUAL indicates simple occurrence without any reference to duration of time, whereas DURATIVE indicates occurrence over a period of time, during which something else may happen. Compare: 'I wrote a letter' (punctual) and 'I was writing a letter' (durative).

[2] Also occurs with meaning (a): '[Someone] is going (i.e. repeatedly, over a period of time)' as in 'He is going to that school.'

Gerund + i⌐ma⌐su may also indicate an action or state which began in the past and is still continuing.   A time expression + particle kara tells when the action or state began and a time expression without following particle tells how long the action or state has been continuing.   Thus:

Kyo⌐neñ kara ⌐ma⌐tte imasu. 'I have been waiting since last year.' (Lit. 'I am waiting from last year.')

Ni⌐-neñ ⌐ma⌐e kara tu⌐to⌐mete imasu. 'I have been employed for the last two years.' (Lit. 'I am employed from two years ago.')

Sa⌐ñ-neñ-ḡu⌐rai o⌐siete ima⌐su. 'I have been teaching for about three years.'

Si⌐tte ima⌐su, meaning literally '[someone] is in a state of having come to know'—i.e. '[someone] knows'—is another example of the gerund + i⌐ma⌐su pattern. The opposite is si⌐rimase⌐ñ '[someone] doesn't know' (lit. '[someone] has not come to know'). [1]

Following a gerund, √i⌐ma⌐su and its more polite equivalents √o⌐rima⌐su and √i⌐rassyaima⌐su may occur in the affirmative or negative, non-past or past, etc., with corresponding equivalents. Thus:

ma⌐tte orimasu 'I'm waiting'
ke⌐kkoñ-site irassyaimase⌐ñ '[he] is not married'
ka⌐ite i⌐ma⌐sita '[I] was writing'
ka⌐ette i⌐mase⌐ñ desita '[I] wasn't back (home)'

In rapid speech, the initial i- of √i⌐ma⌐su and √i⌐rassyaima⌐su is regularly dropped after a gerund. Thus:

ke⌐kkoñ-site rassyaimase⌐ñ
ka⌐ite masita
ka⌐ette ma⌐se⌐ñ desita

3. √de⌐su: Gerund

The gerund of √de⌐su is de.   Preceded by a nominal or particle, it occurs in the middle of sentences, coordinate with what follows (cf. Lesson 7, Grammatical Note 5). Thus:

2 sentences: A⌐merika⌐ziñ desu. 'I'm an American.'
              A⌐merika-taisi⌐kañ ni tu⌐to⌐mete imasu. 'I work for the American Embassy.'

1 sentence: A⌐merika⌐ziñ de, A⌐merika-taisi⌐kañ ni tu⌐to⌐mete imasu.
             'I'm an American and I work for the American Embassy.'

---

[1] WARNING: Do not attempt to use the corresponding negative of si⌐tte ima⌐su (i.e. ~ i⌐mase⌐ñ) or the corresponding -ma⌐su affirmative of si⌐rimase⌐ñ.

Additional examples:

Ue wa zyuʳuniˀ de, sita wa ya-ʳttuˀ desu. 'The older one is 12 and the younger one is 8.'

Dotira mo ōnazi de, dotira mo daʳmeˀ desu. 'They're both the same and they're both no good.'

Sono kuruma wa Iʳgirisu noˀ de, toʳttemo takaˀi desu yo. 'That car is a British one and it's very expensive.'

4. Adjectival + √naʳrimaˀsu ~ Nominal + ni + √naʳrimaˀsu

An adjectival modifying an inflected expression is regularly in its adverbial (-ku) form:

Yoˀku na⊢rima⊣sita. '[It] has become good.' or '[It] has improved.'

Taˀkaku narimasu. '[It] gets (or is going to get) expensive.'

Oˀokiku na⊢rimase⊣ñ. '[It] doesn't (or won't) get big.' or '[It] hasn't grown big.'

Yaˀsuku na⊢rimase⊣ñ desita. '[It] didn't get cheap.'

Iʳkitaku narimaˀsita. 'I've reached the point where I want to go.' (Lit. 'I've become wanting to go.')

When the goal of √naʳrimaˀsu is a nominal, the nominal is followed by the goal particle ni: X ni √naʳrimaˀsu 'become X,' 'get to be X.'

Deʳpaˀato ni na⊢rima⊣sita. '[It] has become a department store.'

Daʳmeˀ ni narimasu. '[It] gets (or will get) bad.'

Toʳmodati niˀ wa[1] na⊢rita⊣ku aʳrimase⊣ñ. 'I don't want to become a friend.'

Oʳnazi niˀ wa[1] na⊢rimase⊣ñ desita. '[It] didn't become the same.'

Note the regular difference in usage between:

Iˀkura desu ka⌣ 'How much is it?' (i.e. one item)

and:

Iˀkura ni na⊢rima⊣su ka⌣ 'How much does it (or will it) come to?' (i.e. several items purchased)

Naʳrimaˀsu frequently corresponds to an English future, provided a change in situation is involved. Compare:

'It will be cheap tomorrow' (i.e. it isn't today): Aʳsitaˀ wa ʳyaˀsuku narimasu.

'It will be cheap tomorrow, too' (i.e. as it is today; no change): Aʳsitaˀ mo ya⊢su⊣i desu.

---

1 The wa of comparison.

5. Counting People and Their Ages

The counter for people has two shapes, -ri for '1' and '2' and -niñ for higher numerals. -Ri combines with the numerals of Series II and -niñ with the numerals of Series I. Thus:

hi⌐to⌐-ri '1 person'   ro⌐ku⌐-niñ '6 people'
hu⌐ta-ri⌐ '2 people'   si⌐ti⌐-niñ '7 people'
sa⌐ñ-ni⌐ñ '3 people'   ha⌐ti⌐-niñ '8 people'
yo-⌐ni⌐ñ '4 people'   ku-⌐ni⌐ñ '9 people'
go-⌐ni⌐ñ '5 people'   zyu⌐u-niñ '10 people'

na⌐ñ-niñ 'how many people?'

The numbers used in counting people's ages are identical with those used in counting unit objects (hi⌐to⌐-tu, hu⌐ta-tu⌐, mi-⌐ttu⌐, etc.; see Lesson 5, Grammatical Note 1), except for the special word ha⌐tati '20 years old.' '20 units' is ni⌐zyuu.

Compare the following examples:

Hi⌐to⌐ri no kodomo wa o⌐ñna⌐ no ko desu. 'One child is a girl.'
Hi⌐to⌐tu no kodomo wa o⌐ñna⌐ no ko desu. 'The one-year-old child is a girl.'

DRILLS

A. Substitution Drill

1. Who is your friend?   Otomodati (wa) ⌐do⌐nata desu ka⌐
2. Where is your friend?   Otomodati (wa) ⌐do⌐ko desu ka⌐
3. How is your friend?   Otomodati (wa) i⌐ka⌐ga desu ka⌐
4. How old is your friend?   Otomodati (wa) o⌐ikutu de⌐su ka⌐
5. Is your friend English?   Otomodati (wa) i⌐girisu⌐ziñ desu ka⌐
6. Is your friend single?   Otomodati (wa) o⌐hitori de⌐su ka⌐
7. Which one (lit. person) is   Otomodati (wa) ⌐do⌐no ka⌐ta⌐ desu ka⌐
    your friend?
8. What kind of person is your   Otomodati (wa) ⌐do⌐ñna ka⌐ta⌐ desu
    friend?   ka⌐

B. Substitution Drill

1. A woman has come.   O⌐ñna no hito⌐ (ga) ki⌐ma⌐sita.
2. A man has come.   O⌐toko no hito⌐ (ga) ki⌐ma⌐sita.
3. A little girl has come.   O⌐ñna⌐ no ko (ga) ki⌐ma⌐sita.
4. A little boy has come.   O⌐toko⌐ no ko (ga) ki⌐ma⌐sita.
5. A friend (i.e. a lady) has   O⌐ñna no tomodati (ga) kima⌐sita.
    come.
6. A friend (i.e. a man) has   O⌐toko no tomodati (ga) kima⌐sita.
    come.

C. Substitution Drill

1. I'm working for the American Embassy.	A⌐merika-taisi⌐kañ ni tu⌐to⌐mete (i)-masu.
2. I'm working for the British Consulate.	E⌐ekoku-ryoozi⌐kañ ni tu⌐to⌐mete (i)-masu.
3. I'm working for the Bank of Japan.	Ni⌐hoñ-gi⌐ñkoo ni tu⌐to⌐mete (i)masu.
4. I'm working for the Yokohama Post Office.	Yo⌐kohama-yuubi⌐ñkyoku ni tu⌐to⌐mete (i)masu.
5. I'm working for a Tokyo department store.	To⌐okyoo no depa⌐ato ni tu⌐to⌐mete (i)masu.
6. I'm working for a Kyoto hotel.	Kyo⌐oto no ⌐ho⌐teru ni tu⌐to⌐mete (i)-masu.
7. I'm working for St. Luke's Hospital.	Se⌐eroka-byo⌐oiñ ni tu⌐to⌐mete (i)ma-su.
8. I'm working for an American school.	A⌐merika no gakkoo ni tuto⌐mete (i)-masu.

D. Substitution Drill

1. Who did [it]?	Da⌐re ḡa si⌐ma⌐sita ka ⌐
2. Who doesn't understand?	Da⌐re ḡa wa⌐karimase⌐ñ ka ⌐
3. Who wants to go?	Da⌐re ḡa i⌐kita⌐i ñ desu ka ⌐
4. Who is here?	Da⌐re ḡa i⌐ma⌐su ka ⌐
5. Who wrote [it]?	Da⌐re ḡa ka⌐kima⌐sita ka ⌐
6. Who bought [it]?	Da⌐re ḡa ka⌐ima⌐sita ka ⌐
7. Who needs [it]?	Da⌐re ḡa i⌐rima⌐su ka ⌐
8. Who is waiting?	Da⌐re ḡa ⌐ma⌐tte (i)masu ka ⌐
9. Who isn't here?	Da⌐re ḡa i⌐mase⌐ñ ka ⌐
10. Who didn't come?	Da⌐re ḡa ki⌐mase⌐ñ desita ka ⌐

E. Substitution Drill

1. One (person) is 12 and the other is 10.	Hi⌐to⌐-ri wa zyu⌐uni⌐ de, mo⌐o hito⌐-ri wa ⌐to⌐o desu.
2. One (person) is 8 and the other is 4.	Hi⌐to⌐-ri wa ya-⌐ttu⌐ de, mo⌐o hito⌐-ri wa yo-⌐ttu⌐ desu.
3. One (person) is 20 and the other is 21.	Hi⌐to⌐-ri wa ⌐ha⌐tati de, mo⌐o hito⌐-ri wa ⌐ni⌐zyuu i⌐ti⌐ desu.
4. One (person) is French and the other is German.	Hi⌐to⌐ri wa hu⌐rañsu⌐ziñ de, mo⌐o hito⌐-ri wa do⌐itu⌐ziñ desu.
5. One (person) is a boy and the other is a girl.	Hi⌐to⌐-ri wa o⌐toko⌐ no ko de, mo⌐o hito⌐-ri wa o⌐ñna⌐ no ko desu.
6. One (person) is a man and the other is a woman.	Hi⌐to⌐-ri wa o⌐toko no hito⌐ de, mo⌐o hito⌐-ri wa o⌐ñna no hito⌐ desu.
7. One (person) is a policeman and the other is a druggist.	Hi⌐to⌐-ri wa zyu⌐ñsa de, mo⌐o hito⌐-ri wa ku⌐suriya de⌐su.
8. One (person) is a book dealer and the other is a florist.	Hi⌐to⌐-ri wa ⌐ho⌐ñya de, mo⌐o hito⌐-ri wa ha⌐na⌐ya desu.

F. Substitution Drill

1.	One woman came.	Oˉʼñna no hitoˈ (g̃a) hiˈtoˈ-ri kiˈmaˈsi-ta.
2.	Two friends came.	Tomodati (g̃a) huˈta-ri kimaˈsita.
3.	Three children came.	Kodomo (g̃a) saˈñ-niñ kimaˈsita.
4.	Four policemen came.	Zyuñsa (g̃a) yo-ˈniñ kimaˈsita.
5.	Five Koreans came.	Tyoˈoseñziˈñ (g̃a) go-ˈniñ kimaˈsita.
6.	Six Russians came.	Roˈsiaˈziñ (g̃a) roˈkuˈ-niñ kiˈmaˈsita.
7.	Seven Indians came.	Iˈñdoˈziñ (g̃a) siˈtiˈ-niñ kiˈmaˈsita.
8.	Eight Chinese came.	Tyuˈug̃okuˈziñ (g̃a) haˈtiˈ-niñ kiˈmaˈ-sita.

G. Substitution Drill

1.	I'm doing [it] now.	Iˈma siˈte (i)maˈsu.
2.	I've been doing [it] for the last 10 minutes.	Ziˈp-puñ ˈmaˈe kara siˈte (i)maˈsu.
3.	I've been waiting for the last 10 minutes.	Ziˈp-puñ ˈmaˈe kara ˈmaˈtte (i)ma-su.
4.	I've been waiting since last year.	Kyoˈneñ[1] kara ˈmaˈtte (i)masu.
5.	I've been teaching since last year.	Kyoˈneñ kara oˈsiete (i)maˈsu.
6.	I've been teaching for about 10 years.	Zyuˈu-neñ-g̃uˈrai oˈsiete (i)maˈsu.
7.	I've been employed for about 10 years.	Zyuˈu-neñ-g̃uˈrai tuˈtoˈmete (i)masu.
8.	I'm employed now.	Iˈma tuˈtoˈmete (i)masu.

H. Grammar Drill (based on Grammatical Note 4)

Tutor: Oˈokiˈi desu. '[It] is big.'
Student: Oˈokiku naˈrimaˈsita. '[It] has become big.'

1.	Aˈkaˈi desu.	Aˈkaku narimaˈsita.
2.	Geˈñki desu.	Geˈñki ni naˈrimaˈsita.
3.	Tuˈmaraˈnai desu.	Tuˈmaraˈnaku naˈrimaˈsita.
4.	Iˈi desu.	Yoˈku naˈrimaˈsita.
5.	Haˈtati desu.	Haˈtati ni naˈrimaˈsita.
6.	Oˈmosiroˈi desu.	Oˈmosiroˈku naˈrimaˈsita.
7.	Toˈmodati deˈsu.	Toˈmodati ni narimaˈsita.
8.	Waˈruˈi desu.	Waˈruku naˈrimaˈsita.
9.	Daˈmeˈ desu.	Daˈmeˈ ni naˈrimaˈsita.
10.	Aˈbunaˈi desu.	Aˈbunaku narimaˈsita.

I. Grammar Drill (based on Grammatical Note 3)

Tutor: Ue wa oˈtokoˈ no ko desu. Sita wa oˈñnaˈ no ko desu. 'The oldest is a boy. The youngest is a girl.' (2 sentences)

Student: Ue wa oˈtokoˈ no ko de, sita wa oˈñnaˈ no ko desu. 'The oldest is a boy and the youngest is a girl.' (1 sentence)

---

[1] Kyoˈneñ 'last year'

1. Tomodati wa niˈhoñziˈñ
   desu.
   Aˈmerika-giˈñkoo ni tuˈtoˈ-
   mete (i)masu.

   Tomodati wa niˈhoñziˈñ de, Aˈmerika-
   giˈñkoo ni tuˈtoˈmete (i)masu.

2. Taˈroo-tyañ wa koˈkoˈno-tu
   desu.
   Haˈruko-tyañ wa naˈnaˈ-tu
   desu.

   Taˈroo-tyañ wa koˈkoˈno-tu de, Haˈruko-tyañ wa naˈnaˈ-tu desu.

3. Niˈhoˈñ de keˈkkoñ-simaˈ-
   sita.
   Aˈmerika e kaerimaˈsita.

   Niˈhoˈñ de kekkoñ-site, Aˈmerika e
   kaerimaˈsita.

4. Kore wa waˈtakusi noˈ desu.
   Sore wa ˈtomodai noˈ desu.

   Kore wa waˈtakusi noˈ de, sore wa to-
   ˈmodati noˈ desu.

5. Aˈno kaˈdo ni moˈdoˈtte
   kudasai.
   Miˈḡi e maḡatte kudasaˈi.

   Aˈno kaˈdo ni moˈdoˈtte, miˈḡi e maḡatte kudasaˈi.

6. Kono hurosiki wa niˈhyakuˈ-eñ desu.
   Sore wa saˈñbyakuˈ-eñ
   desu.

   Kono hurosiki wa niˈhyakuˈ-eñ de, sore wa saˈñbyakuˈ-eñ desu.

7. Tuˈitatiˈ wa geˈtuyoˈo desu.
   Nano-ka wa niˈtiyoo deˈsu.

   Tuˈitatiˈ wa geˈtuyoˈo de, nano-ka wa
   niˈtiyoo deˈsu.

8. Haˈtiˈ-zi ni uˈti (o) demaˈ-
   sita.
   Roˈku-zi-ḡoˈro kaˈerimaˈ-
   sita.

   Haˈtiˈ-zi ni uˈti (o) deˈte, roˈku-zi-
   ḡoˈro kaˈerimaˈsita.

J. Response Drill

(Give the corresponding negative reply—same politeness level—to each
question.)

1. Toˈmodati deˈsu ka⏌
   Toˈmodati zya arimaseˈñ.

2. Siˈmaˈsu ka⏌
   Siˈmaseˈñ.

3. Siˈte (i)maˈsu ka⏌
   Siˈte (i)maseˈñ.

4. Gaˈkkoo de gozaimaˈsu ka⏌
   Gaˈkkoo deˈ wa goˈzaimaseˈñ.

5. Oˈtotoˈi de goˈzaimaˈsita
   ka⏌
   Oˈtotoˈi de wa goˈzaimaseˈñ desita.

6. Soˈno kataˈ (wa) aˈmerikaˈziñ
   de (i)rassyaimasu ka⏌
   Soˈno kataˈ (wa) aˈmerikaˈziñ de wa
   iˈrassyaimaseˈñ.

7. Tanaka-sañ (wa) tuˈtoˈmete
   (i)rassyaimasu ka⏌
   Tanaka-sañ (wa) tuˈtoˈmete (i)ˈras-
   syaimaseˈñ.

8. Siˈtuˈree desu ka⏌
   Siˈtuˈree zya aˈrimaseˈñ.

9. Siˈtte (i)maˈsu ka⏌
   Siˈrimaseˈñ.

10. Aˈbunaˈi desu ka⏌
    Aˈbunaku arimaseˈñ.

K. Level Drill (The sentences on the right are the polite equivalents of those
on the left.)

1. Doˈko desu ka⏌
   Doˈtira de gozaimasu ka⏌

2. Iˈtu desu ka⏌
   Iˈtu de gozaimasu ka⏌

3. Aˈsitaˈ desu.
   Aˈsitaˈ de gozaimasu.

4. Ko⌐re de¬su.   Ko⌐re de gozaima¬su.
5. U⌐siro de¬su.   U⌐siro de gozaima¬su.
6. Ya⌐sumi¬ desu ka˩   O⌐yasumi de gozaima¬su ka˩
7. Ra¬itaa desu.   Ra¬itaa de gozaimasu.
8. Ga⌐kkoo de¬su.   Ga⌐kkoo de gozaima¬su.

L. Level Drill (The sentences on the right are the polite equivalents of those on the left.)

1. Na¬ñ desu ka˩   Na¬ñ de gozaimasu ka˩
2. A⌐na¬ta (wa) Ta⌐naka-sañ   A⌐na¬ta (wa) Ta⌐naka-sañ de (i)ras-
   de¬su ka˩   syaima¬su ka˩
3. Wa⌐surema¬sita ka˩   O⌐wasure ni narima¬sita ka˩
4. Ko⌐domo (ḡa) ima¬su ka˩   O⌐kosañ (ḡa) $\begin{vmatrix} \text{irassyaima}¬\text{su} \\ \text{oide ni narima}¬\text{su} \end{vmatrix}$ ka˩

5. Na¬ñ-zi ni ki˫ma˦sita   Na¬ñ-zi ni $\begin{vmatrix} \text{i˫rassyaima˦sita} \\ \text{o˫ide ni narima˦sita} \end{vmatrix}$ ka˩
   ka˩
6. O⌐tomodati de¬su ka˩   O⌐tomodati de (i)rassyaima¬su ka˩
7. Ko⌐domo (ḡa) arima¬su   O⌐kosañ (ḡa) gozaima¬su ka˩
   ka˩
8. Do¬ko ni tu˫to˦mete (i)ma-   Do¬tira ni tu˫to˦mete (i)rassyaimasu
   su ka˩   ka˩
9. Na¬ni (ḡa) i˫rima˦su ka˩   Na¬ni (ḡa) o˫iri ni narima˦su ka˩
10. Watakusi wa ke⌐kkoñ-site   Watakusi wa ke⌐kkoñ-site orimase¬ñ.
    imase¬ñ.

M. Expansion Drill

1. I don't know.   Si⌐rimase¬ñ.
   The name I don't know.   Na⌐mae wa sirimase¬ñ.
   He's employed but I don't   Tu⌐to¬mete (i)masu ḡa, na⌐mae wa si-
   know his name.   rimase¬ñ.
   He's employed here (lit. for   Ko⌐ko ni tuto¬mete (i)masu ḡa, na⌐mae
   this place) but I don't know   wa sirimase¬ñ.
   his name.

2. Are you working (lit. doing   Si⌐goto (o) site (i)ma¬su ka˩
   work)?
   What kind of work are you   Do¬ñna si˫goto (o) site (i)ma˦su ka˩
   doing?
   What kind of work are you   I¬ma ⌐do¬ñna si˫goto (o) site (i)ma˦su
   doing now?   ka˩
   Excuse me [for asking],   Si⌐tu¬ree desu ḡa, i¬ma ⌐do¬ñna si˫go-
   but what kind of work are   to (o) site (i)ma˦su ka˩
   you doing now?

3. [They]'re in America.   A⌐merika ni ima¬su.
   Both are in America.   Do¬tira mo A⌐merika ni ima¬su.
   I have two (people) but both   Hu˫ta-ri arima¬su ḡa, do¬tira mo A⌐me-
   are in America.   rika ni ima¬su.
   I have two children but both   Kodomo ḡa hu˫ta-ri arima¬su ḡa, do¬ti-
   are in America.   ra mo A⌐merika ni ima¬su.

4. It's become expensive.   Ta⌐kaku na⊦rima⌐sita.
   It's become awfully expen-   Zu⌐ibuñ ⌐ta⌐kaku na⊦rima⌐sita.
   sive.
   It's become awfully expen-   Kotosi ⌐zu⌐ibuñ ⌐ta⌐kaku na⊦rima⌐sita.
   sive this year.
   Meat has become awfully   Ni⌐ku⌐ wa ko̐tosi ⌐zu⌐ibuñ ⌐ta⌐kaku na-
   expensive this year.   ⊦rima⌐sita.
   Meat has become awfully   Ni⌐ku⌐ wa ko̐tosi ⌐zu⌐ibuñ ⌐ta⌐kaku na-
   expensive this year,   ⊦rima⌐sita ⌐ne⌐e.
   hasn't it!

5. Would you be kind enough   Ka⌐ite ku⊦dasaimase⌐ñ ka⌐
   to write [it]?
   Would you be kind enough   Pe⌐ñ de ⊦ka⌐ite ku⊦dasaimase⌐ñ ka⌐
   to write [it] with a pen?
   Would you be kind enough   Onamae o ⌐pe⌐ñ de ⊦ka⌐ite ku⊦dasa-
   to write your name with   imase⌐ñ ka⌐
   a pen?
   I'm sorry but would you   Su⌐mimase⌐ñ ğa, onamae o ⌐pe⌐ñ de
   be kind enough to write   ⊦ka⌐ite ku⊦dasaimase⌐ñ ka⌐
   your name with a pen?

6. How old is [he]?   O⌐ikutu de (i)rassyaima⌐su ka⌐
   How old is Taro?   Ta⌐roo-tyañ (wa) o⌐ikutu de (i)rassya-
                           ima⌐su ka⌐
   How old is your Taro?   O⌐taku no Ta⌐roo-tyañ (wa) o⌐ikutu de
                           (i)rassyaima⌐su ka⌐
   Excuse me [for asking],   Si⌐tu⌐ree desu ğa, o⌐taku no Ta⌐roo-
   but how old is your   tyañ (wa) o⌐ikutu de (i)rassyaima⌐-
   Taro?   su ka⌐

SUPPLEMENTARY SELECTIONS

(with questions)

(Give precise answers for each group of questions according to the information contained in the statements that precede them.)

1. Ko⌐domo ğa sañ-niñ ima⌐su. Ha⌐ruko ğa ŭe no ko de, ⌐to⌐o desu. Tu⌐ği⌐ wa
   ⌐Ta⌐roo de, na⌐na⌐-tu desu. Zi⌐roo ğa si̐ta no ko de, si-⌐ğatu⌐ ni yo-⌐ttu⌐ ni
   narimasu.

   Kodomo ğa ⌐na⌐ñ-niñ i⊦ma⌐su ka⌐
   Ue no ko no namae wa ⌐na⌐ñ desu ka⌐
   Ue wa o⌐toko⌐ no ko desu ka⌐
   Da⌐re ğa ⊦to⌐o desu ka⌐
   Ta⌐roo-tyañ wa ⌐i⌐kutu desu ka⌐
   Sita wa o⌐ñna⌐ no ko desu ka⌐
   Zi⌐roo-tyañ wa ⌐i⌐ma ⌐i⌐kutu desu ka⌐
   Ue no ko ğa si-⌐ğatu⌐ ni yo-⌐ttu⌐ ni na⊦rima⌐su ka⌐

2. Ke˺sa a˺merika˺ziñ to i˺g̃irisu˺ziñ g̃a wa˺takusi no zimu˺syo e ki⊦ma˺sita.
A˺merika˺ziñ wa o˺toko no hito˺ de, A˺merika-gi˺ñkoo ni tu⊦to˺mete imasu.
I˺g̃irisu˺ziñ wa o˺ñna no hito˺ de, E˺ekoku-taisi˺kañ ni tu⊦to˺mete imasu.
A˺merika˺ziñ no namae wa ˹Su˺misu de, i˺g̃irisu˺ziñ no namae wa ˹Zyo˺oñzu
desu.

       Na˺ñ-niñ wa⊦takusi no zimu˺syo e ki⊦ma˺sita ka﹈
       Do˺tira mo a⊦merika˺ziñ desu ka﹈
       Do˺tira g̃a o⊦ñna no hito˺ desu ka﹈
       Do˺tira g̃a ta⊦isi˺kañ ni tu⊦to˺mete imasu ka﹈
       Do˺tira g̃a ⊦Su˺misu-sañ desu ka﹈

3. Yamamoto-sañ wa go-˹neñ ma˺e ni ke⊦kkoñ-sima˺sita.   Tanaka-sañ wa
kŏtosi zyu˺uni-g̃atu˺ ni ke⊦kkoñ-sima˺su.

       Do˺tira g̃a ⊦i˺ma ke⊦kkoñ-site ima˺su ka﹈
       So˹no˺ hito wa ˹na˺ñ-neñ ni ke⊦kkoñ-sima˺sita ka﹈
       So˹no˺ hito wa ˹na˺ñ-neñ kara ke⊦kkoñ-site ima˺su ka﹈
       So˹no˺ hito wa ˹na˺ñ-neñ ⊦ma˺e kara ke⊦kkoñ-site ima˺su ka﹈
       So˹no˺ hito wa ˹na˺ñ-neñ ke⊦kkoñ-site ima˺su ka﹈
       Do˺tira g̃a ko⊦tosi kekkoñ-sima˺su ka﹈

EXERCISES

1. Using pictures of familiar people, practice asking and answering questions
about their names, nationalities, marital status, and age.

2. You ask Mr. Tanaka: Mr. Tanaka replies:

    a. what his name is.   I'm Taro Tanaka.
    b. to write his name.   I'm sorry but I don't have a pencil.
    c. how old he is.   I'm 52.
    d. what kind of work he does.   I work for the Bank of Japan.
    e. if he is married.   Yes, I am.
    f . if he has any children.   Yes, I have three.
    g. who that is.   That's Yukio Sato.
    h. who that Japanese is.   He's a friend.
    i. who that woman is.   I don't know her name but she works
                                       for the embassy.

    j. if Mr. Jones is American.   No, he's English.

3. Practice the Basic Dialogues with appropriate variations.

Lesson 11. Meeting People (cont.)

BASIC DIALOGUES: FOR MEMORIZATION

(a)

(Mr. and Mrs. Tanaka meet Mr. Smith)

Mr. Tanaka

a while (long or short)
si⌐ba⌐raku

1. Mr. Smith! It's been a long time [since I last saw you].
Su⌐misu-sañ. Si⌐ba⌐raku desita.

Mr. Smith

2. Oh, Mr. Tanaka! It has been a long time.
A⌐a, Tanaka-sañ. Si⌐ba⌐raku desita ┌ne┐e.

Mr. Tanaka

everyone or everything
everyone
miñna
mi⌐na⌐sañ

3. Is everyone well?
Mi⌐na⌐sañ o⌐ge⌐ñki desu ka⌐

Mr. Smith

4. Yes, thank you. Is everyone at your house [well], too?
E⌐e, okaḡesama de. O⌐taku no mi-na⌐sañ mo?

Mr. Tanaka

5. Yes, thank you.
E⌐e, a⌐ri⌐ḡatoo gozaimasu.

wife
ka⌐nai or o⌐kusañ

6. Mr. Smith, this is my wife.
Su⌐misu-sañ. Kore (wa) ka⌐nai de-su.

(addressing his wife)

this person
kotira

7. This is Mr. Smith from the American Embassy.
Kotira (wa) A⌐merika-taisi⌐kañ no ┌Su⌐misu-sañ desu.

Mr. Smith

the first time
ha⌐zi⌐mete

meet or see (a person)
o⌐me ni kakarima⌐su

how do you do
ha⌐zimema⌐site or

how do you do (lit. I meet you for the first time)
ha⌐zi⌐mete ome ni kakarimasu

8. Are you Mrs. [Tanaka]? I'm [Mr.] Smith. How do you do.
O⌐kusañ desu ka⌐ Su⌐misu desu. Ha-┌zimema⌐site.

166

Mrs. Tanaka

9. I'm [Mrs.] Tanaka. How do
   you do. I'm glad to meet
   you.

Ta⌐naka de gozaima⌐su. Ha⌐zi⌐mete
ome ni kakarimasu. Do⌐ozo yŏrosiku.

    Japanese language

nihoñḡo or
nippoñḡo

10. You can [speak] Japanese very
    well, can't you!

Nihoñḡo (ḡa) ⌐yo⌐ku o⌐deki ni nari-
ma⌐su ⌐ne⌐e.

Mr. Smith

    study
    be studying

be⌐ñkyoo-sima⌐su
beñkyoo-site (i)ru (informal) or
be⌐ñkyoo-site (i)ma⌐su

    because [I] am studying
    or [I] am studying, so

be⌐ñkyoo-site (i)ru⌐ kara or
be⌐ñkyoo-site (i)ma⌐su kara

11. Oh, no! I am studying so I can
    [speak it] a little but. . .

Do⌐o itasimasite. Be⌐ñkyoo-site (i)ru⌐
kara, su⌐ko⌐si wa de⌐kima⌐su ḡa_
    or
Do⌐o itasimasite. Be⌐ñkyoo-site (i)-
ma⌐su kara, su⌐ko⌐si wa de⌐kima⌐su
ḡa_

    considerably or more
    than expected
    is difficult

nakanaka

muzukasii /-ku/

12. It's quite difficult, isn't it—
    Japanese.

Na⌐kanaka muzukasi⌐i desu ⌐ne⌐e—nihoñḡo wa.

Mrs. Tanaka

    foreign language
    is easy

gaikokuḡo
yasasii /-ku/

13. Foreign languages aren't easy,
    are they!

Ga⌐ikokuḡo wa yasasiku gozaimase⌐ñ
⌐ne⌐e.

(b)

Smith

14. Whose is this?

Kore (wa) ⌐da⌐re no desu ka_

Tanaka

15. It's Mr. Kobayashi's, isn't
    it?

Ko⌐bayasi-sañ no⌐ desyoo?

Smith

16. It isn't yours?

A⌐na⌐ta no zya a⌐rimase⌐ñ ka_

Tanaka

17. No (i.e. that's right). It's
    his.

E⌐e, a⌐no⌐ hito no desu.

Smith

18. What about yours?

A⌐na⌐ta no wa?

Tanaka

19. Hmm. I wonder where it is.   Sa⌐a. Do⌐ko desyoo ka ⌐ne⌐e. Ko⌐ko
It <u>was</u> here but . . .   ni arima⌐sita ḡa_

(c)

Smith

is late <u>or</u> slow   osoi /-ku/
become late   o⌐soku na⌐ru (informal) <u>or</u>
o⌐soku narima⌐su

because it becomes late   o⌐soku na⌐ru kara <u>or</u>
or it becomes late so   o⌐soku narima⌐su kara
20. Well, <u>it</u>'s getting late so if   Zya⌐a, o⌐soku na⌐ru kara, si⌐tu⌐ree.
you'll excuse me . . .   <u>or</u>
Zya⌐a, o⌐soku narima⌐su kara, si⌐tu⌐-
ree-simasu.

Tanaka

meet <u>or</u> see a person   a⌐ima⌐su
21. Well, I'll see you again. Goodbye.   Zya⌐a, ma⌐ta (aimasyo⌐o). Sayonara_

Smith

to everyone   mi⌐na⌐sañ ni ¹
22. Give my regards to everyone.   Mi⌐na⌐sañ ni yo⌐rosiku. Sayonara_
Goodbye.

(d)

Smith

why?   na⌐ze
why? <u>or</u> how?   do⌐o site
23. Why aren't you going to go?   Na⌐ze i⌐kimase⌐ñ ka_ <u>or</u>
Do⌐o site i⌐kimase⌐ñ ka_

Tanaka

father   ti⌐ti⌐ <u>or</u> o⌐to⌐osañ ¹
sickness <u>or</u> sick   byooki <u>or</u> gobyooki ¹
is sick   byooki da (informal) <u>or</u>
byo⌐oki de⌐su

because [he] is sick <u>or</u>   byo⌐oki da⌐ kara <u>or</u>
[he] is sick so   byo⌐oki de⌐su kara
24. Because my father is sick.   Ti⌐ti⌐ ḡa byo⌐oki da⌐ kara.
<u>or</u>
Ti⌐ti⌐ ḡa byo⌐oki de⌐su kara.

Smith

25. He's sick?   Go⌐byooki de⌐su ka.

26. That's too bad.   I⌐kemase⌐ñ ⌐ne⌐e.

27. Take care.   Odaizi ni.

Tanaka

28. Thank you.   A⌐ri⌐ḡatoo gozaimasu.

(e)

Smith

last night	yu⌐ube⌐
Foreign Office	ga⌐imu⌐syoo
meet or see Mr. Yamada	Ya⌐mada-sañ ni aima⌐su

29. You know, I saw Mr. Yamada from the Foreign Office last night.

Yuube ga⌐imu⌐syoo no Ya⌐mada-sañ ni aima⌐sita yo◡

Tanaka

30. You did? Was it the first time?

So⌐o desu ka. Ha⌐zi⌐mete desita ka◡

Smith

31. Yes, that's right.

E⌐e, so⌐o desu.

Tanaka

32. He's a fine man, isn't he?

I⌐i ka⌐ta⌐ desyoo?

Smith

33. Yes, very.

E⌐e, tottemo.

FAMILY TERMS [1]

	Plain or Humble[†] Word	Polite Honorific [†] Word
family	ka⌐zoku	go⌐ka⌐zoku
grandfather	so⌐hu	o⌐zi⌐isañ [2]
grandmother	so⌐bo	o⌐ba⌐asañ [3]
parent	o⌐ya⌐	oyag̃osañ
both parents	ryo⌐osiñ	go⌐ryo⌐osiñ
father	ti⌐ti⌐	o⌐to⌐osañ
mother	ha⌐ha	o⌐ka⌐asañ
son	musuko	musukosañ or bo⌐ttyañ
daughter	mu⌐sume⌐	musumesañ or o⌐zyo⌐osañ
husband	syu⌐ziñ	go⌐syu⌐ziñ
wife	ka⌐nai	o⌐kusañ

---

[1] Practice these words according to the pattern of Drill I. page 185.

[2] Also means 'old man.'

[3] Also means 'old woman.'

	Plain or Humble ⁺ Word	Polite Honorific ⁺ Word
uncle	ozi	ozisañ ¹
aunt	oba	obasañ ²
brothers and/or sisters³	kyoˀodai	goˈkyoˀodai
older brother	aˀni	niˀisañ or oˈniˀisañ
older sister	ane	neˀesañ or oˈneˀesañ
younger brother	oˈtootoˀ	otootosañ
younger sister	iˈmootoˀ	imootosañ or oimotosañ
cousin	iˈtoˀko	oitokosañ
nephew	oi	oiḡosañ
niece	meˀe	meeḡosañ
grandchild	maˈḡoˀ	omaḡosañ

ADDITIONAL LANGUAGE NAMES ⁴

(All the following words refer to languages only)

English	eeḡo
French	hurañsuḡo
German	doituḡo
Russian	rosiaḡo
Korean	tyooseñḡo
Chinese	tyuuḡokuḡo (or sinaḡo⁵)
Spanish	supeiñḡo

NOTES ON THE BASIC DIALOGUES

3. For Americans from the South, miˈnaˀsañ is the most common equivalent of 'you-all.'

---

¹ Also an informal word for 'man' used especially commonly by children and in talking to children; often used in reference to a close friend of the family.

² Also means 'woman'; its usage parallels that of ozisañ.

³ I.e. 'siblings.'

⁴ Practice these words as substitutes for nihoñḡo in Basic Sentence 10 (cf. Drill A, page 181.

⁵ Formerly a commonly used word, now considered insulting by many Chinese.

7. The <u>kotira</u> series is frequently used in reference to people. In this usage, it is polite (+). <u>Kotira</u>, depending on context, means either 'this person — close to me' or 'this person—i.e. myself.' Similarly, <u>sotira</u> means 'that person—not far away' or 'the person I'm addressing—i.e. you.'

8, 9. In Japanese, it is customary to repeat one's own name according to the patterns of Basic Sentences 8 and 9, immediately upon being introduced.

Ha⌐zi⌐mete is a nominal: ha⌐zi⌐mete desu 'it's the first time'; ha⌐zi⌐mete zya a⌐rimase⌐ň 'it's not the first time.' Its formal equivalent ha⌐zimema⌐site is used only in introductions as a shorter equivalent of humble-polite ha⌐zi⌐mete ome ni kakarimasu.

<u>Yorosiku</u> is the adverbial (-<u>ku</u> form) of the adjectival <u>yorosii</u>. Do⌐ozo yorosiku means 'please [treat our acquaintance] favorably.' A person who is being introduced regularly says ha⌐zimema⌐site OR ha⌐zi⌐mete ome ni kakarimasu AND/OR do⌐ozo yorosiku.

Note the use of polite speech by Mrs. Tanaka in addressing Mr. Smith— typical in the given situation. Mr. Smith may use plain or polite speech, depending on circumstances of position, age, etc.

10. In reference to a language, √de⌐kima⌐su 'be possible' or 'can do' means 'know' or 'can speak.' Remember that both the thing that is possible and the person to whom it is possible are followed by particles ḡa and/or <u>wa</u>.

11. √Be⌐ňkyoo-sima⌐su is a compound verbal (like √ke⌐kkoň-sima⌐su) made up of the nominal <u>beňkyoo</u> 'study (noun)' + √si⌐ma⌐su 'do.'

The <u>wa</u> here is the <u>wa</u> of comparison: 'A little I can speak it but—not very well.'

13. <u>Gaikoku</u> means 'foreign country' and <u>gaikokuḡo</u> is the language of a foreign country. <u>Gaikokuziň</u> means 'foreigner'; this word frequently occurs in the abbreviated form <u>gaiziň</u>, which now usually refers to Westerners.

Ya⌐sasiku gozaimase⌐ň is the polite (+) equivalent of ya⌐sasiku arimase⌐ň. Remember that √a⌐rima⌐su can regularly be replaced by the appropriate form of √go⌐zaima⌐su to form a polite equivalent.

14–18. Note the contraction of particle <u>no</u> + nominal <u>no</u> into a single <u>no</u>.

19. 'It was here but—I don't know where it is now.'

20. O⌐soku narima⌐sita 'it has become late' is often used as an apology for being late.

21. A⌐ima⌐su is a formal plain verbal, and o⌐me ni kakarima⌐su (sentence 9 above) is its humble (↓) equivalent. The honorific (↑) equivalent is o⌐ai ni narima⌐su. These verbals usually mean 'meet' or 'see' in the sense 'meet up with and talk to,' not 'catch sight of' or 'look at.' The person seen or met is followed by particle <u>ni</u> (sentence 29 below).

Ma⌐ta aimasyo⌐o means '(I guess) I'll see you again' or 'let's meet again.'

23. As an equivalent of 'why?' do⌐o site (literally 'doing how?') is softer and less direct than na⌐ze.

26. I⌐kemase⌐ň is a verbal negative which has taken on a specialized meaning

(compare su⌜mimase⌝ñ). It is used to prohibit ('it won't do,' 'you mustn't do that'), and with ne⌝e, it occurs as an expression of sympathy in regard to a matter of not too serious a nature.

27. Odaizi ni is an admonition to 'treat yourself—or someone close to you—carefully.' Daizi (polite odaizi↑) is a nominal meaning 'important,' 'valuable.'

Family terms:

The plain words in the list of family terms, besides being used as general terms without reference to any particular individuals, are used in talking about members of one's own family, whereas the polite words are used in polite reference to members of the families of others. O⌜zi⌝isañ, o⌜ba⌝asañ, o⌜to⌝osañ, o⌜ka⌝asañ, ozisañ, obasañ, ni⌝isañ, and ne⌝esañ are also used in addressing one's own relatives. Thus:

ti⌜ti⌝ 'my father,' 'a father'
o⌜to⌝osañ 'your father,' 'his father,' etc., and 'Father!'

In reference to someone else's young son and daughter, bo⌝ttyañ and o⌜zyo⌝osañ are more polite than musukosañ and musumesañ; but the latter terms are regularly used in reference to someone else's adult son and daughter. Bo⌝ttyañ may also be used in addressing boys and o⌜zyo⌝osañ in addressing girls and young ladies, not related to the speaker.

O⌝kusañ is the regular polite way to address married women—including strangers. It is the Japanese equivalent of 'madam' and 'Mrs. ——.'

To distinguish among different members of a given family, kinship terms are regularly used preceded by the family name + no. Thus:

Ta⌜naka-sañ no gosyu⌝ziñ 'Mr. Tanaka'
Ta⌜naka-sañ no o⌝kusañ 'Mrs. Tanaka'
Ta⌜naka-sañ no ozyo⌝osañ 'Miss Tanaka'
Ta⌜naka-sañ no bo⌝ttyañ 'Master Tanaka'

GRAMMATICAL NOTES

1. Verbals: Informal Non-past, Stem, and Gerund

A verbal ending in -ma⌝su is formal, non-past, and affirmative. Its informal equivalent—i.e. informal, non-past, affirmative—introduced in this lesson for the first time, is the form regularly listed in dictionaries and will hereafter be referred to as the CITATION FORM. A verbal stem (the -ma⌝su form minus -ma⌝su) and gerund (the -te form) are related to the citation form according to regular patterning.

Toward the end of this note is a chart listing the informal non-past affirmative (i.e. the citation form; other informal forms will be introduced later), stem, gerund, and English equivalent of verbals introduced thus far. Study the chart carefully while noting the following points:

(1) Informal Non-past Affirmative (Citation Form)

Henceforth, all new verbals will be cited in this form when they first occur.

THIS FORM IS IDENTICAL IN MEANING WITH THE -MAˈSU FORM EXCEPT THAT IT IS LESS FORMAL.   Don't make the very common mistake of equating it with the English infinitive and then translating it 'to do so-and-so.'   Just as Waˈkarimaˈsu. may occur as a complete sentence meaning 'It's clear.' 'I understand.' so Waˈkaˈru. occurs with the same meanings, as its informal equivalent.

Verbals may be divided into 4 groups:

(a) The -RU GROUP includes verbals which have -ru in the informal (citation form) corresponding to -maˈsu in the formal. In all such verbals, the vowel preceding -ru is e or i.

Example: deˈru/deˈmaˈsu 'go out'

(b) The -U GROUP includes verbals which have -u in the informal (citation form) corresponding to -imaˈsu in the formal. In all such verbals, the -u is preceded by one of 8 consonants—t, r, s, k, g̃, b, m, or n—or by a vowel other than e.

Example: kaˈeru/kaˈerimaˈsu 'return (home)'

(c) The -ARU GROUP includes verbals which have -aru in the informal (citation form) corresponding to -aimaˈsu in the formal. This group includes only 5 verbals, all of which are polite.

Example: kuˈdasaˈru/kuˈdasaimaˈsu 'give me'

(d) The IRREGULAR GROUP includes only 2 verbals:

suru/siˈmaˈsu 'do'
kuˈru/kiˈmaˈsu 'come'

In subsequent lessons, a new verbal will be identified at its first appearance according to its group.   For example:

kaˈkeˈru /-ru/

(2) Stem

The stem is the -maˈsu form minus -maˈsu. [1] It is the form to which the

---

[1] The stem is accented if the citation form is accented.   The accent of the citation form must be learned for each verbal.   A -maˈsu form is regularly accented on the ma syllable except in environments where the accent is lost.

adjectival -tai ending, meaning 'want to do so-and-so,' is added (for example, KAItai 'want to buy,' IKItai 'want to go,' etc.).[1] The polite nominals which are derived from verbals and which occur in polite patterns consist of the polite prefix o- plus the stem[2] (for example, o⌐DEKI ni narima⌐su ka 'can you do it?'; o⌐KAERI ni narima⌐su ka 'are you going to go home?'). Other uses of the stem will be introduced later.

To determine the stem, given the citation form:

(a) for verbals of the -ru group, drop the -ru ending.

Example: wasureru 'forget,' stem wasure

(b) for verbals of the -u group, change final -u to -i.

Example: kau 'buy,' stem kai

(c) for verbals of the -aru group, change final -aru to -ai.

Example: go⌐za⌐ru 'be,' 'have,' stem go⌐za⌐i

(d) irregular:

suru 'do,' stem si
ku⌐ru 'come,' stem ki⌐

(3) Gerund (the -te form)

The gerund has been introduced in the following patterns:

O⌐namae o KA⌐ITE kudasai. 'Please write your name.'
O⌐namae o KA⌐ITE ku⌐dasaimase⌐ñ ka⌐ 'Would you be kind enough to
    write your name?'
So⌐re o KA⌐ITE, ka⌐erima⌐sita. 'I wrote it and went home.'
Na⌐mae o KA⌐ITE (i)masu. 'I'm writing my name.'

Other uses will be introduced later.

To determine the gerund, given the citation form:

(a) for -ru verbals, change the final -ru to -te.

Example: wasureru 'forget' : wasurete

---

[1] When -tai is added to an accented stem, the combination is accented on syllable ta; when it is added to an unaccented stem, the combination is also unaccented.

[2] The combination is an unaccented word.

(b) for -u verbals: change final—

-tu to -tte	Example: ma˥tu 'wait' : ma˥tte
-ru to -tte	ka˥eru 'return' : ka˥ette
vowel + -u to vowel + -tte	kau 'buy' : katte
-su to -site	ha⌐na˥su 'speak' : ha⌐na˥site
-ku to -ite	ka˥ku 'write' : ka˥ite
-g̅u to -ide	i⌐so˥g̅u 'hurry' : i⌐so˥ide
-bu to -ñde	yobu[1] 'call' : yoñde
-mu to -ñde	yo˥mu[1] 'read' : yo˥ñde
-nu to -ñde	sinu[1] 'die' : siñde (unique example)

(c) for -aru verbals, change the final -aru to -atte, but note also the alternate forms in the chart below.

   Example: i⌐rassya˥ru 'go,' 'come,' 'be': i⌐rassya˥tte
                                    (and i⌐ra˥site)

(d) irregular:

   suru 'do' : site
   ku˥ru 'come' : ki⌐te˥

A stem and gerund are accented only if the informal non-past (citation) form from which they are derived is accented. In the -ru group, the accent of the stem and gerund occurs one syllable nearer the beginning of the word than the accent of the citation form, unless that accent is on the first syllable (example: non-past mi⌐se˥ru, stem mi˥se, gerund mi˥sete); elsewhere, the accent of the stem and gerund regularly occurs on the same syllable as the accent of the citation form (example: non-past ka˥ku, stem ka˥ki, gerund ka˥ite). [2]

Once you have learned the five -aru and two irregular verbals, any other verbal not ending in -eru or -iru must belong to the -u group. A verbal ending in -eru or -iru may belong to the -ru group or the -u group; this cannot be determined unless other inflected forms of the word are known or unless the word is specifically identified as to group. Compare:

   iru (-ru) 'be in a place (animate)':

      stem i
      formal i⌐ma˥su
      gerund ite

   iru (-u) 'be needed':

      stem iri
      formal i⌐rima˥su
      gerund itte

---

[1] These verbals and others ending in -bu and -mu will occur in later lessons. They are mentioned here only for the sake of completeness.

[2] The accent of ki⌐te˥, gerund of ku˥ru, is irregular.

VERBALS

Informal Non-past (Citation Form)	Stem	Gerund	English Equivalent
-RU Group:			
de⌐ki'ru	de⌐ki	de'kite	'be possible'
de'ru	de'	de'te	'go out'
iru[1]	i	ite	'be in a place (animate)'
mi⌐se'ru	mi⌐se	mi'sete	'show'
osieru	osie	osiete	'teach,' 'inform'
tomeru	tome	tomete	'bring to a halt'
tu⌐to'me'ru	tu⌐to'me	tu⌐to'mete	'become employed'
wasureru	wasure	wasurete	'forget'
-U Group:			
-tu			
ma'tu	ma'ti	ma'tte	'wait'
-ru			
a'ru	a'ri	a'tte	'be in a place (inanimate),' 'have'
iru	iri	itte	'be needed'
ka'eru	ka'eri	ka'ette	'return home'
ka⌐ka'ru	ka⌐ka'ri	ka⌐ka'tte	'be required' (ome ni ∼ ↓ 'meet')
ko⌐ma'ru	ko⌐ma'ri	ko⌐ma'tte	'be upsetting'
maḡaru	maḡari	maḡatte	'make a turn'
ma'iru ↓	ma'iri	ma'itte	'come,' 'go'
mo⌐do'ru	mo⌐do'ri	mo⌐do'tte	'go back,' 'back up'
na'ru	na'ri	na'tte	'become' (o- + stem ni ∼ = honorific)
o'ru ↓	o'ri	o'tte	'be in a place (animate)'
siru	siri	sitte	'come to know'
wa⌐ka'ru	wa⌐ka'ri	wa⌐ka'tte	'be comprehensible'
-Vowel + u			
a'u	a'i	a'tte	'meet,' 'see (a person)'

---

[1] (i)ru, (i), (i)te following a gerund.

	iu[1]	ii	itte	'say'
	kau	kai	katte	'buy'
	tiḡau	tiḡai	tiḡatte	'be different'
	ukaḡau ↓	ukaḡai	ukaḡatte	'inquire'
-su	ha⌐na⌐su	ha⌐na⌐si	ha⌐na⌐site	'talk'
-ku	ka⌐ku	ka⌐ki	ka⌐ite	'write,' 'draw'
	tu⌐ku	tu⌐ki	tu⌐ite	'arrive'
	iku	iki	itte[2]	'go'
-ḡu	i⌐so⌐ḡu	i⌐so⌐ḡi	i⌐so⌐ide	'be in a hurry'

-ARU Group:	go⌐za⌐ru⁺ [3]	go⌐za⌐i	—	'be in a place (inanimate),' 'have'
	i⌐rassya⌐ru ↓	i⌐rassya⌐i	i⌐rassya⌐tte or i⌐ra⌐site	'go,' 'come,' 'be in a place (animate)'
	ku⌐dasa⌐ru ↓	ku⌐dasa⌐i	ku⌐dasa⌐tte or ku⌐dasu⌐tte	'give to me'

Irregular Group:	ku⌐ru	ki⌐	ki⌐te⌐	'come'
	suru	si	site	'make,' 'do' (benkyoo-~ 'study,' kekkon-~ 'marry,' etc.)

In informal speech, used most commonly in addressing close friends, relatives, or inferiors, the majority of inflected forms that occur are informal. They occur at the end of sentences as well as within longer sentences, in the informal speech of both men and women—but with specific differences. Remember that it is possible to be polite and informal at the same time, for example with forms like i⌐rassya⌐ru ↓. Informal speech will be discussed in greater detail in later lessons.

Even in formal speech, informal inflected forms frequently occur as non-final inflected forms, in some patterns. (There is no difference here between the speech of men and women except that men use informal forms more frequently.) For one such pattern, see Note 3 below.

---

[1] The combination i + u is regularly pronounced yuu. The spelling iu is preferred here because it helps the student determine the other inflected forms.

[2] Itte, the gerund of iku, is an irregular form, but since it is the only irregular form, iku is not listed among the irregular verbs.

[3] This form is rare in conversational Japanese.

2.   Copula: Informal Non-past <u>da</u>

The informal equivalent of de⌐su is <u>da</u>, which will hereafter be designated
as the citation form of the copula. It occurs after nominals and particles.

Examples:

> so⌐o da 'that's right'
> sa⌐ñ-zi made da 'it's until 3 o'clock'

<u>De</u>, the gerund of the copula, has already been introduced. The copula has
no form corresponding to a verbal stem.

WARNING: Remember that the informal equivalent of an adjectival + de⌐su
is the adjectival alone. Thus: ta⌐ka⌐i desu 'it's expensive' (formal); ta⌐ka⌐i
'it's expensive' (informal).

Study the following chart:

Affirmative Non-past Inflectional Patterns

	Formal	Informal
Verbal Pattern	Verbal ending in -<u>ma⌐su</u> (wa⌐karima⌐su)	Verbal ending in -<u>[r]u</u> (wa⌐ka⌐ru)
Adjectival Pattern	Adjectival ending in -i + de⌐su (o⌐oki⌐i desu)	Adjectival ending in -<u>i</u> (o⌐oki⌐i)
Nominal[1] Pattern	Nominal[1] + de⌐su (ho⌐ñ desu)	Nominal[1] + <u>da</u> (ho⌐ñ da)

3.   Particle <u>kara</u> 'so'

The particle <u>kara</u> following a nominal and meaning 'from' was described in
Lesson 8, Grammatical Note 4.

Following an inflected expression (verbal, adjectival, or copula) in the non-
past or past or tentative, affirmative or negative, <u>kara</u> means 'so,' 'therefore,' or 'because,' with the following differences in word order: x kara y
'x so y,' 'x therefore y,' or 'because x y.' In this pattern, <u>kara</u> usually ends
with comma intonation.

Examples:

> A⌐sita ikima⌐su kara, kyo⌐o wa i⌐kimase⌐ñ.
> 'I'm going tomorrow, so today I'm not going to go.'

---

[1] With or without following particle.

Wa⌐karimase⌐ñ desita kara, mo⌐o iti-do itte kudasa⌐i.
'I didn't understand so please say it again.'
Ta⌐ka⌐i desyoo kara, ka⌐imase⌐ñ.
'It's probably expensive so I'm not going to buy it.'
Ta⌐kaku a⌐rimase⌐ñ kara, mo⌐o hito⌐-tu ka⌐imasyo⌐o.
'They're not expensive so let's buy one more.'
Tanaka-sañ wa byo⌐oki de⌐su kara, ki⌐mase⌐ñ.
'Mr. Tanaka isn't going to come because he's sick.'

An informal inflected expression before kara has the same meaning (except for formality) as its formal equivalent in the same position. Before kara, a normally unaccented verbal or nominal-plus-da expression acquires an accent on its final syllable, and a non-past adjectival on its next-to-last syllable.

A⌐sita iku⌐ kara, kyo⌐o wa i⌐kimase⌐ñ. [1]
Ta⌐ka⌐i kara, ka⌐imase⌐ñ. 'It's expensive so I'm not going to buy it.'
Tanaka-sañ wa byo⌐oki da⌐ kara, ki⌐mase⌐ñ. [1]

A major sentence as a whole is assigned to the level of its final inflected form. That form is as formal as, or more formal than, inflected forms occurring earlier in the sentence. [2]

Compare:

    (a) Be⌐ñkyoo-site (i)ru⌐ kara, su⌐ko⌐si wa⌐ka⌐ru.
    (b) Be⌐ñkyoo-site (i)ru⌐ kara, su⌐ko⌐si wakarimasu.
    (c) Be⌐ñkyoo-site (i)ma⌐su kara, su⌐ko⌐si wakarimasu.

All three sentences mean 'I am studying so I understand a little.' Sentence (a) is said to be informal because final wa⌐ka⌐ru is informal, and sentences (b) and (c) are both said to be formal because of final wa⌐karima⌐su, which is formal. Within the formal style, sentence (c) is more formal than (b) because its non-final inflected form (i)⌐ma⌐su is also formal.

A sentence (i. e. a fragment) may consist of a sequence ending with kara if the over-all meaning is clear from the context. For example:

    (To a taxi driver) I⌐sog̃ima⌐su kara_ 'I'm in a hurry so [please go fast].'
    Ta⌐kusii de i⌐kima⌐su ka_ . . . Iie. Ku⌐ruma g̃a arima⌐su kara_
    'Are you going by taxi? . . . No. I have a car so [I don't need a cab].'

---

[1] The English equivalent is the same as for the corresponding sentence just above.

[2] G̲a 'but' is one of the few particles which is usually preceded only by an inflected form of the same level as the final one in the sentence. An informal inflected form before g̲a occurs only in men's informal speech.

Do⌐o site i⌐kimase⌐ñ ka⌐ . . . Ki⌐noo ikima⌐sita kara. 'Why aren't you going to go? . . . Because I went yesterday [I'm not going to go].'
Na⌐ze ka⌐imase⌐ñ ka⌐ . . . Ta⌐ka⌐i kara. 'Why aren't you going to buy it? . . . Because it's expensive [I'm not going to buy it].'

A minor sentence like the last, ending with an informal form + kara, may occur in both informal and formal speech (determined by the formality of final inflected forms in surrounding sentences), but one ending with a formal form + kara occurs only in formal speech.

4. d e s y o o ?

Sentence-final desyoo with question-mark intonation indicates a question which anticipates agreement from the person addressed. Thus:

Koñna tokee wa ta⌐ka⌐i desyoo? 'Watches like these a r e expensive, aren't they?'
Kore to are wa onazi desyoo? 'This one and that one are the same, aren't they?'
Koko no giñkoo wa ⌐sa⌐ñ-zi made desyoo? 'The banks here are [open] until 3, aren't they?'

Desyoo? in sentence-final position is always unaccented. It often occurs with shortening of the final vowel (desyo?).

5. I n v e r t e d S e n t e n c e s

Na⌐kanaka muzukasi⌐i desu ⌐ne⌐e — nihoñgo wa

The above is an example of a Japanese INVERTED SENTENCE. If the order of the first part (na⌐kanaka muzukasi⌐i desu ⌐ne⌐e) and the second part (nihoñgo wa) is reversed, the result is a standard Japanese sentence of identical meaning except that it is more formal. Inverted sentences are common in conversation.

Examples:

Standard	Inverted
Sore wa ⌐na⌐ñ desu ka.	Na⌐ñ desu ka — sore wa. [1]
'What is that?'	'What is [it] — that thing?'
So⌐ko e ikima⌐sita yo.	I⌐kima⌐sita yo — soko e.
'You know, I went there.'	'You know, I went — to that place.'

---

[1] For the dash, see Introduction, page xli.

Standard	Inverted

Si⌐ñbuñ o kaima⌐sita ⌐ne⌐e.   Ka⌐imasita ⌐ne⌐e — siñbuñ o.
'You bought the news-   'You bought [it], didn't you — the
paper, didn't you.'   newspaper.'
So⌐re wa i⌐i desu yo⌐   I⌐i desu yo⌐ — sore wa.
'Why, that's fine.'   'It's fine — that.'

What normally occurs as a kind of sentence-final intonation occurs within an inverted sentence at the end of the first part, with the initial word of the second part pronounced as if it were part of the same accent phrase. An intonation other than period intonation is indicated by its regular symbol, preceding the dash (cf. the last example above).

DRILLS

A. Substitution Drill

1. You can [speak] Japanese   Nihoñgo (ga) ⌐yo⌐ku de⌐kima⌐su ⌐ne⌐e.
   very well, can't you!

2. You can [speak] English   Eego (ga) ⌐yo⌐ku de⌐kima⌐su ⌐ne⌐e.
   very well, can't you!

3. You can [speak] French   Huransugo (ga) ⌐yo⌐ku de⌐kima⌐su
   very well, can't you!   ⌐ne⌐e.

4. You can [speak] Chinese   Tyuugokugo (ga) ⌐yo⌐ku de⌐kima⌐su
   very well, can't you!   ⌐ne⌐e.

5. You can [speak] Spanish   Supeiñgo (ga) ⌐yo⌐ku de⌐kima⌐su ⌐ne⌐e.
   very well, can't you!

6. You can [speak] German   Doitugo (ga) ⌐yo⌐ku de⌐kima⌐su ⌐ne⌐e.
   very well, can't you!

7. You can [speak] Russian   Rosiago (ga) ⌐yo⌐ku de⌐kima⌐su ⌐ne⌐e.
   very well, can't you!

8. You can [speak] foreign   Gaikokugo (ga) ⌐yo⌐ku de⌐kima⌐su
   languages very well,   ⌐ne⌐e.
   can't you!

B. Substitution Drill

1. You know, I met Mr. Yamada   Yuube ga⌐imu⌐syoo no Ya⌐mada-sañ ni
   from the Foreign Office last   aima⌐sita yo⌐
   night.

2. You know, I met Mr. Yamada   Ha⌐zi⌐mete ga⌐imu⌐syoo no Ya⌐mada-
   from the Foreign Office for   sañ ni aima⌐sita yo⌐
   the first time.

3. You know, I met Mr. Yamada   Ha⌐zi⌐mete Ni⌐hoñ-gi⌐ñkoo no Ya⌐ma-
   from the Bank of Japan for   da-sañ ni aima⌐sita yo⌐
   the first time.

4. You know, I met your (old-   Ha⌐zi⌐mete Ni⌐hoñ-gi⌐ñkoo no o⌐ni⌐isañ
   er) brother from the Bank of   ni a⌐ima⌐sita yo⌐
   Japan for the first time.

5. You know, I met your (old-   Ha⌐zi⌐mete Ni⌐hoñ-gi⌐ñkoo no o⌐ni⌐isañ
   er) brother from the Bank   ni o⌐me ni kakarima⌐sita yo⌐
   of Japan for the first time.
6. You know, I met your (old-   Ototoi Ni⌐hoñ-gi⌐ñkoo no o⌐ni⌐isañ ni
   er) brother from the Bank   o⌐me ni kakarima⌐sita yo⌐
   of Japan the day before
   yesterday.

C. Grammar Drill (based on Grammatical Note 4)

   Tutor: Ta⌐ka⌐i desu. 'It's expensive.'
   Student: Ta⌐ka⌐i desyoo? 'It's expensive, isn't it?'

1. Mi⌐ñna onazi de⌐su.   Miñna onazi desyoo?
2. Koñna siḡoto (wa) mu⌐zu-   Koñna siḡoto (wa) mu⌐zukasi⌐i desyoo?
   kasi⌐i desu.
3. Gakkoo (wa) ⌐ku⌐-zi kara   Gakkoo (wa) ⌐ku⌐-zi kara desyoo?
   desu.
4. Gekizyoo no tonari (wa)   Gekizyoo no tonari (wa) kŭsuriya de-
   ku⌐suriya de⌐su.   syoo?
5. A⌐no ba⌐su (wa) Yo⌐koha-   A⌐no ba⌐su (wa) Yo⌐kohama ma⌐de de-
   ma ma⌐de desu.   syoo?
6. Ko⌐ñna huru⌐i kuruma (wa)   Ko⌐ñna huru⌐i kuruma (wa) o⌐so⌐i de-
   o⌐so⌐i desu.   syoo?
7. A⌐no zibiki⌐ (wa) Tānaka-   A⌐no zibiki⌐ (wa) Tānaka-sañ no ⌐bo⌐t-
   sañ no ⌐bo⌐ttyañ no desu.   tyañ no desyoo?
8. Yokohama (wa) a⌐no toori⌐   Yokohama (wa) a⌐no toori⌐ desyoo?
   desu.

D. Grammar Drill (based on Grammatical Note 5)

   Tutor: I⌐i desu ⌐ne⌐e— sore wa. 'Isn't it nice— that!' (inverted or-
            der)
   Student: Sore wa ⌐i⌐i desu ⌐ne⌐e. 'That's nice, isn't it!' (standard or-
            der)

1. Yo⌐ku wa⌐karima⌐su ⌐ne⌐e—   Nihoñḡo ḡa ⌐yo⌐ku wa⌐karima⌐su ⌐ne⌐e.
   nihoñḡo ḡa.
2. Mu⌐zukasi⌐i desu yo⌐ — koñ-   Koñna siḡoto wa mu⌐zukasi⌐i desu yo⌐
   na siḡoto wa.
3. Ya⌐sasi⌐i desu ⌐ne⌐e— kore   Kore wa ya⌐sasi⌐i desu ⌐ne⌐e.
   wa.
4. Ka⌐ima⌐sita yo⌐ — a⌐tara-   A⌐tarasi⌐i kuruma o ka⌐ima⌐sita yo⌐
   si⌐i kuruma o.
5. Yu⌐ube ikima⌐sita ⌐ne⌐e—   Te⌐ekoku-ge⌐kizyoo ni yu⌐ube ikima⌐si-
   Te⌐ekoku-ge⌐kizyoo ni.   ta ⌐ne⌐e.
6. O⌐kaeri ni narima⌐su ka⌐   I⌐ma o⌐kaeri ni narima⌐su ka⌐
   — i⌐ma.
7. O⌐okiku na⌐rima⌐sita ⌐ne⌐e   Bo⌐ttyañ wa ⌐o⌐okiku na⌐rima⌐sita
   — bo⌐ttyañ wa.   ⌐ne⌐e.
8. A⌐rimase⌐ñ yo⌐ — tabako   Tabako ḡa a⌐rimase⌐ñ yo⌐
   ḡa.

Drills   183

E. Grammar Drill (based on Grammatical Note 3)

   (Retain the formal level before <u>kara</u>)

   Tutor: Be⌐ñkyoo-site (i)ma⌐su. Wa⌐karima⌐su. 'I'm studying. I understand.'
   Student: Be⌐ñkyoo-site (i)ma⌐su kara, wa⌐karima⌐su. 'I'm studying so I understand.'

1. I⌐ma be⌐ñkyoo-site (i)mase⌐ñ.
    Mi⌐ñna wasurema⌐sita.

    I⌐ma be⌐ñkyoo-site (i)mase⌐ñ kara, mi⌐ñna wasurema⌐sita.

2. Tyo⌐oseñḡo (ḡa) dekimase⌐ñ.
    Wa⌐karimase⌐ñ desita.

    Tyo⌐oseñḡo (ḡa) dekimase⌐ñ kara, wa⌐karimase⌐ñ desita.

3. Sa⌐ñ-zi suḡi⌐ desu.
    U⌐ti e kaerimasyo⌐o.

    Sa⌐ñ-zi suḡi⌐ desu kara, u⌐ti e kaerimasyo⌐o.

4. Ha⌐zi⌐mete desu.
    A⌐ñmari wakarimase⌐ñ.

    Ha⌐zi⌐mete desu kara, a⌐ñmari wakarimase⌐ñ.

5. Ta⌐kusii wa ta⌐ka⌐i desu.
    De⌐ñsya de i⌐kimasyo⌐o.

    Ta⌐kusii wa ta⌐ka⌐i desu kara, de⌐ñsya de i⌐kimasyo⌐o.

6. I⌐soḡima⌐su.
    Ha⌐yaku site kudasai.

    I⌐soḡima⌐su kara, ha⌐yaku site kudasai.

7. A⌐ñmari ki⌐ree zya a⌐rimase⌐ñ desita.
    Ka⌐imase⌐ñ desita.

    A⌐ñmari ki⌐ree zya a⌐rimase⌐ñ desita kara, ka⌐imase⌐ñ desita.

8. Hu⌐ne wa o⌐so⌐i desu.
    Hi⌐ko⌐oki de i⌐kima⌐sita.

    Hu⌐ne wa o⌐so⌐i desu kara, hi⌐ko⌐oki de i⌐kima⌐sita.

9. Hu⌐ruku na⌐rima⌐sita.
    A⌐tarasi⌐i no (ḡa) ka⌐ita⌐i ñ desu ḡa_

    Hu⌐ruku na⌐rima⌐sita kara, a⌐tarasi⌐i no (ḡa) ka⌐ita⌐i ñ desu ḡa_

10. Byo⌐oki ni narima⌐sita.
    Kyo⌐o wa de⌐kimase⌐ñ.

    Byo⌐oki ni narima⌐sita kara, kyo⌐o wa de⌐kimase⌐ñ.

F. Level Drill[1]

   Tutor: A⌐sita ikima⌐su kara. (formal verbal) } 'Because I'm going to go tomorrow.'
   Student: A⌐sita iku⌐ kara. (informal verbal) }

1. Tanaka-sañ (ḡa) ⌐yo⌐ku de⌐kima⌐su kara.

    Tanaka-sañ (ḡa) ⌐yo⌐ku de⌐ki⌐ru kara.

2. Sa⌐ñ-ḡatu ni Tóokyoo de ke⌐kkoñ-sima⌐su kara.

    Sa⌐ñ-ḡatu ni Tóokyoo de ke⌐kkoñ-suru⌐ kara.

---

[1] This drill is based on Grammatical Notes 1 and 3. After practicing it in its given form, reverse the procedure, with the tutor giving the sentence on the right and the student the sentence on the left.

3. Iˈtu mo tuˈitatiˈ ni koˈko ni tukimaˈsu kara.
   Iˈtu mo tuˈitatiˈ ni koˈko ni tuˈku ka-ra.

4. Kaˈmiˈ g̃a taˈkusañ iri-maˈsu kara.
   Kaˈmiˈ g̃a taˈkusañ iruˈ kara.

5. Zyuˈu-neñ ˈmaˈe kara tuˈtoˈmete (i)ˈmaˈsu kara.
   Zyuˈu-neñ ˈmaˈe k a r a tuˈtoˈmete (i)ˈruˈ kara.

6. Aˈsa haˈtiˈ-zi wa ˈtyoˈtto koˈmarimaˈsu kara.
   Aˈsa haˈtiˈ-zi wa ˈtyoˈtto koˈmaˈru ka-ra.

7. Tuˈg̃iˈ no ˈkaˈdo (o) maˈg̃arimaˈsu kara.
   Tuˈg̃iˈ no ˈkaˈdo (o) maˈg̃aruˈ kara.

8. Maˈiniti roˈku-zi-g̃oˈro ziˈmuˈsyo (o) deˈmaˈsu kara.
   Maˈiniti roˈku-zi-g̃oˈro ziˈmuˈsyo (o) ˈdeˈru kara.

9. Koñg̃etu Aˈmerika e okae-ri ni narimaˈsu kara.
   Koñg̃etu Aˈmerika e okaeri ni naˈru kara.

10. Tookyoo (o) ˈyoˈku siˈtte (i)maˈsu kara.
   Tookyoo (o) ˈyoˈku siˈtte (i)ruˈ kara.

11. Koko kara yo-ˈzikañ-g̃uˈ-rai kaˈkarimaˈsu kara.
   Koko kara yo-ˈzikañ-g̃uˈrai kaˈkaˈru kara.

12. Tanaka-sañ mo ˈNiˈkkoo e iˈrassyaimaˈsu kara.
   Tanaka-sañ mo ˈNiˈkkoo e iˈrassyaˈ-ru kara.

G.　Level Drill[1]

Tutor:　Byoˈoki deˈsu kara.　(formal inflected word) ⎫　‘Because I'm
Student: Byoˈoki daˈ kara.　(informal inflected word) ⎭　sick.'

1. Dotira mo daˈmeˈ desu kara.
   Dotira mo daˈmeˈ da kara.

2. Aˈtarasiˈi kuruma (wa) ta-ˈkaˈi desu kara.
   Aˈtarasiˈi kuruma (wa) taˈkaˈi kara.

3. Koñna miti (wa) aˈbunaˈi desu kara.
   Koñna miti (wa) aˈbunaˈi kara.

4. Aˈnoˈ hito (wa) zyuˈñsa deˈsu kara.
   Aˈnoˈ hito (wa) zyuˈñsa daˈ kara.

5. Aˈno miseˈ (wa) haˈnaˈya desu kara.
   Aˈno miseˈ (wa) haˈnaˈya da kara.

6. Koˈñna hoˈñ (wa) oˈmosi-roˈi desu kara.
   Koˈñna hoˈñ (wa) oˈmosiroˈi kara.

7. Kyoˈo go-ˈzi maˈe ni kaˈeritaˈi desu kara.
   Kyoˈo go-ˈzi maˈe ni kaˈeritaˈi kara.

8. Tanaka-sañ (wa) ˈiˈi to-ˈmodati deˈsu kara.
   Tanaka - sañ (wa) ˈiˈi toˈmodati daˈ kara.

---

[1] This drill is based on Grammatical Note 2. Again, practice it both in its given form and in reverse.

H. Level Drill[1]

1. Naň-zi-ǧo⌐ro ka┌erima┐su
ka⌐

Naň-zi-ǧo⌐ro o┌kaeri ni narima┐su
ka⌐

2. O⌐kusañ desu ka⌐

O⌐kusañ de (i)┌rassyaima┐su ka⌐

3. A┌sita┐ mo ki┌te┐ kudasai.

A┌sita┐ mo | i┌rassya┐tte / o┌ide ni na┐tte | kudasai.

4. Mi┌na┐sañ o┌ge┐ňki desu
ka⌐

Mi┌na┐sañ o┌ge┐ňki de (i)┌rassyaima┐su
ka⌐

5. Ha┌zi┐mete desyoo?

Ha┌zi┐mete de gozaimasyoo?

6. Si┌ba┐raku desita.

Si┌ba┐raku de gozaimasita.

7. Kore (wa) ┌da┐re no desu
ka⌐

Kore (wa) ┌do┐nata no de go┌zaima┐su
ka⌐

8. Ni┌hoňǧo (o) beňkyoo-site
(i)ma┐su ka⌐

Ni┌hoňǧo (o) beňkyoo-site (i)rassyai-
ma┐su ka⌐

I. Response Drill

Tutor: O⌐kusañ desu ka⌐ 'Is it your wife?'
Student: E┐e, ka┐nai desu. 'Yes, it's my wife.'

1. Ni┐isañ desu ka⌐

E┐e, a┐ni desu.

2. O┌zyo┐osañ desu ka⌐

E┐e, mu┌sume┐ desu.

3. O┌ka┐asañ desu ka⌐

E┐e, ha┐ha desu.

4. Bo┐ttyañ desu ka⌐

E┐e, mu┌suko de┐su.

5. Ne┐esañ desu ka⌐

E┐e, a┐ne de┐su.

6. O┌to┐osañ desu ka⌐

E┐e, ti┌ti┐ desu.

7. O┌iǧosañ de┐su ka⌐

E┐e, o┌i de┐su.

8. Go┌syu┐ziñ desu ka⌐

E┐e, syu┐ziñ desu.

J. Expansion Drill

1. [He] can do it, can't he!

O┌deki ni narima┐su ┌ne┐e.

[He] can do it very well,
can't he!

Yo⌐ku o┌deki ni narima┐su ┌ne┐e.

[He] can [speak] English
very well, can't he!

Eeǧo (ǧa) ┌yo┐ku o┌deki ni narima┐su
┌ne┐e.

Mr. Tanaka can [speak]
English very well, can't
he!

Tanaka-sañ (wa) éeǧo (ǧa) ┌yo┐ku o-
┌deki ni narima┐su ┌ne┐e.

Mr. Tanaka at the Foreign
Office can [speak] Eng-
lish very well, can't he!

Ga┌imu┐syoo no Tānaka-sañ (wa) eeǧo
(ǧa) ┌yo┐ku o┌deki ni narima┐su ┌ne┐e.

---

[1] In each case, the sentence on the right is a more polite equivalent of the sentence on the left.

2. [They]'re good, aren't they!   I⌐i desu ⌐ne⊣e.
   [They]'re quite good, aren't Na⌐kanaka i⌐i desu ⌐ne⊣e.
   they!
   They're quite good, aren't Na⌐kanaka i⌐i desu ⌐ne⊣e—A⊢merika
   they—American pens!   no pe⊣n̄ wa.
   They're quite good, aren't Na⌐kanaka i⌐i desu ⌐ne⊣e—ko⊢n̄na Ame-
   they—American pens like   rika no pe⊣n̄ wa.
   this!

3. It's interesting, isn't it?   O⌐mosiro⌐i desyoo?
   It's quite interesting, isn't Na⌐kanaka omosiro⌐i desyoo?
   it?
   The work is quite interest- Siḡoto (wa) na⌐kanaka omosiro⌐i de-
   ing, isn't it?   syoo?
   This kind of work is quite Kon̄na siḡoto (wa) na⌐kanaka omosiro⌐i
   interesting, isn't it?   desyoo?

4. I'm not going to go.   I⌐kimase⌐n̄.
   Today I'm not going to go. Kyo⌐o wa i⌐kimase⌐n̄.
   [She]'s sick so today I'm   Byo⌐oki da⌐ kara, kyo⌐o wa i⌐kimase⌐n̄.
   not going to go.
   My wife is sick too, so   Ka⌐nai mo byo⌐oki da⌐ kara, kyo⌐o wa
   today I'm not going to go. i⌐kimase⌐n̄.
   My mother AND my wife   Ha⌐ha mo ⌐ka⌐nai mo byo⌐oki da⌐ kara,
   are sick so today I'm not kyo⌐o wa i⌐kimase⌐n̄.
   going to go.

5. Please study.   Be⊢n̄kyoo-site kudasa⊣i.
   Please study some more.   Mo⌐tto be⊢n̄kyoo-site kudasa⊣i.
   It will get interesting so O⌐mosi⌐roku ⊢na⊣ru kara, mo⌐tto be-
   please study some more.   ⊢n̄kyoo-site kudasa⊣i.
   From this point [on] it will Kore kara o⌐mosi⌐roku ⊢na⊣ru kara,
   get interesting so please mo⌐tto be⊢n̄kyoo-site kudasa⊣i.
   study some more.
   Japanese will get interest- Nihon̄ḡo wa ko̅re kara o⌐mosi⌐roku
   ing from this point [on] so ⊢na⊣ru kara, mo⌐tto be⊢n̄kyoo-site
   please study some more.   kudasa⊣i.

6. You know, I met [her].   A⌐ima⌐sita yo⌐
   You know, I met [his]   O⌐kusan̄ ni a⌐ima⌐sita yo⌐
   wife.
   You know, I met Mrs. Ko- Ko⌐bayasi-san̄ no o⌐kusan̄ ni a⌐ima⌐-
   bayashi.   sita yo⌐
   You know, I met Mrs. Ko- Ha⌐zi⌐mete Ko⌐bayasi-san̄ no o⌐kusan̄
   bayashi for the first   ni a⊢ima⊣sita yo⌐
   time.
   You know, I met Mrs. Ko- Te⌐ekoku-ge⌐kizyoo de ha⌐zi⌐mete Kobayashi for the first   ⌐bayasi-san̄ no o⌐kusan̄ ni a⊢ima⊣si-
   time, at the Imperial   ta yo⌐
   Theater.
   You know, I met Mrs. Ko- Yuube Te⌐ekoku-ge⌐kizyoo de ha⌐zi⌐-

bayashi for the first   mete Ko⌐bayasi-sañ no o⌐kusañ ni
time, at the Imperial   a⌐ima⌐sita yo⌐
Theater last night.

SHORT SUPPLEMENTARY DIALOGUES

(The following are commonly occurring exchanges at meeting or parting.)

1. Guest: De⌐ wa, si⌐tu⌐ree-simasu.
   Host [ess]:   Sayoonara. Ma⌐ta do⌐ozo. O⌐kusañ ni yŏrosiku.
   Guest: A⌐ri⌐gatoo gozaimasu. Sayoonara.

2. Tanaka: O⌐soku na⌐ru kara, si⌐tu⌐ree.
   Yamamoto: Zya⌐a, mata.
   Tanaka: Sayonara.

3. Watanabe: Kore wa ti⌐ti⌐ desu. Ko⌐no kata⌐ wa A⌐merika - ryoozi⌐kañ no
                 ⌐Su⌐misu-sañ desu.
   Father: Wa⌐tanabe de⌐su. Do⌐ozo yŏrosiku.
   Smith: Su⌐misu desu. Ha⌐zimema⌐site.

4. Tanaka: Kore wa ⌐ha⌐ha de gozaimasu.   Kotira wa Nyu⌐uyo⌐oku no
                 ⌐Zyo⌐oñzu-sañ de irassyaimasu.
   Mother: Ta⌐naka de gozaima⌐su. Ha⌐zi⌐mete ome ni kakarimasu.
   Jones: Zyo⌐oñzu de gozaimasu. Ha⌐zimema⌐site. Do⌐ozo yŏrosiku.

5. Tanaka: A⌐a, Kobayasi-sañ. Si⌐ba⌐raku.
   Kobayashi: Si⌐ba⌐raku. Mi⌐na⌐sañ o⌐ge⌐ñki?
   Tanaka: E⌐e, okagesama de. Otaku mo?
   Kobayashi: E⌐e. A⌐ri⌐gatoo.

6. Employee: Zya⌐a, si⌐tu⌐ree-simasu.
   Employer: Go⌐ku⌐roosama. Sayonara.

7. Yamamoto: Ka⌐nai ga byo⌐oki de⌐su kara, kyo⌐o wa ⌐ha⌐yaku ka⌐erita⌐i ñ
                 desu ga⌐
   Watanabe: Go⌐byooki de⌐su ka⌐ I⌐kemase⌐ñ ⌐ne⌐e. Odaizi ni.
   Yamamoto: A⌐ri⌐gatoo gozaimasu.

8. Visitor: Ta⌐naka-sañ irassyaima⌐su ka⌐
   Secretary: Ha⌐a irassyaimasu. Syo⌐osyoo o⌐mati-kudasa⌐i.

English Equivalents

1. Guest: Well, I must be leaving.
   Host [ess]:   Goodbye. Please come again. Regards to your wife.
   Guest: Thank you. Goodbye.

2. Tanaka: It's getting late so if you'll excuse me . . .
   Yamamoto: Well, [I'll see you] again.
   Tanaka: Goodbye.

3. Watanabe: This is my father. This is Mr. / Mrs. / Miss Smith from the
                 American Consulate.
    Father: (I'm Watanabe.) I'm glad to meet you.
    Smith: (I'm Smith.) How do you do.

4. Tanaka: This is my mother. This is Mr. / Mrs. / Miss Jones from New
                 York.
    Mother: (I'm Tanaka.) How do you do?
    Jones: (I'm Jones.) How do you do? I'm glad to meet you.

5. Tanaka: Oh, Mr. / Mrs. / Miss Kobayashi! I h a v e n ' t seen you for
                 ages.
    Kobayashi: It <u>has</u> been a long time. Is everyone well?
    Tanaka: Yes, thank you. [Everyone at] your house too?
    Kobayashi: Yes, thanks.

6. Employee: Well, I'll be leaving.
    Employer: (Thanks for your trouble.) Goodbye.

7. Yamamoto: My wife is sick so today I'd like to go home early . . .
    Watanabe: She's sick? That's too bad. Take care.
    Yamamoto: Thank you.

8. Visitor: Is Mr. Tanaka in?
    Secretary: Yes, he is. Just a moment, please.

EXERCISES

1. On the basis of the following family tree, answer the questions below.

        (M = Male; F = Female; Number = Age)

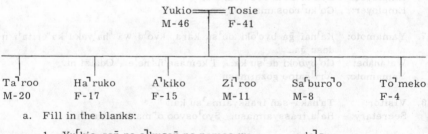

        a. Fill in the blanks:

        1. Yu⌐kio-sañ no o⌐kusañ no namae wa _____ de⌐su.
        2. Yu⌐kio-sañ to Tosie-sañ no ozyo⌐osañ no namae wa _____ to _____
            to _____ desu.
        3. Yukio-sañ wa ⌐Ta⌐roo-sañ no _____ desu.
        4. Ta⌐roo-sañ no o⌐ka⌐asañ no namae wa _____ de⌐su.
        5. Yukio-sañ wa To⌐sie-sañ no _____ desu.
        6. Yu⌐kio-sañ to Tosie-sañ no _____ wa ⌐Ta⌐roo-sañ to ⌐Zi⌐roo-sañ to
            Sa⌐buro⌐o-sañ desu.

7. _____ to _____ to _____ wa oˊtokoˀ de, _____ to _____ to _____
   wa oˊñnaˀ desu.
8. _____ wa ˹haˀtati desu.

b. Answer the following questions:

1. Yukio-sañ to Tosie-sañ wa o̅kosañ g̅a ˹naˀñ-niñ imasu ka⌐
2. Boˀttyañ g̅a ˹naˀñ-niñ imasu ka⌐
3. Taˀroo-sañ to ˹Ziˀroo-sañ to Saˊburoˀo-sañ wa oˊikutu deˀsu ka⌐
4. Tosie-sañ wa oˊtokoˀ desu ka⌐
5. Toˀmeko-sañ wa ya-˹ttuˀ desu ka⌐
6. Yuˊkio-sañ no oˀkusañ wa oˊikutu deˀsu ka⌐
7. Koˊno kaˀzoku wa ˹naˀñ-niñ desu ka⌐

c. Determine whether the following statements are true or false:

1. Aˀkiko-sañ wa ˹Haˀruko-sañ no muᵗsumesañ deˀsu.
2. Yukio-sañ wa ˹Toˀmeko-sañ no oᵗtoˀosañ desu.
3. Taˀroo-sañ wa huˊta-tuˀ desu.
4. Toˀmeko-sañ wa Yu̅kio-sañ to Tosie-sañ no uˊe no ozyoˀosañ desu.
5. Haˀruko-sañ wa zyuˊusitiˀ de, Aˀkiko-sañ wa ˹zyuˀugo de, doˊtira mo
   otokoˀ no ko desu.
6. Yukio-sañ to Tosie-sañ wa oˊzyoˀosañ g̅a go-˹niñ arimaˀsu.

2. Within the framework of the vocabulary and sentence patterns you have
   learned, practice asking and answering questions concerning families, and
   on the basis of the information acquired, draw family trees similar to the
   above.

3. Practice introductions. Take turns performing introductions and being introduced.

4. (a) Give the single Japanese word which is the equivalent of each of the
       following:

   (Example: kodomo no kodomo   Answer: maˊgoˀ)

   1. tiˀtiˀ to ˹haˀha
   2. oˊya no haˀha
   3. oya no oˀtoko no kyoˀodai
   4. oñna no kodomo
   5. kyoˀodai no oˊñnaˀ no ko

   (b) For each of the following words, give a defining phrase:

   (Example: musuko   Answer: otoko no kodomo)

   1. soˀhu
   2. oba
   3. haˀha
   4. oi
   5. iˊtoˀko

5. Practice the Basic Dialogues with appropriate variations.

Lesson 12. Telephoning

BASIC DIALOGUES: FOR MEMORIZATION

(a)

Smith

to Mr. Hashimoto	Hasimoto-sañ ni
telephone (verb)	de⌐ñwa o kake⌐ru /-ru/
number	ba⌐ñḡo⌐o
telephone number	de⌐ñwaba⌐ñḡoo
what number?	na⌐ñ-bañ

1. I'd like to telephone Mr. Hashimoto. What (number) is his telephone number?
   Ha⌐simoto-sañ ni deñwa (o) kaketa⌐i ñ desu ḡa, de⌐ñwaba⌐ñḡoo (wa) ⌐na⌐ñ-bañ desyoo ka.

Tanaka

business company or company office	kaisya

2. Do you mean his home('s), or his office('s)?
   O⌐taku no⌐ desu ka, ka⌐isya no⌐ desu ka◡

Smith

3. I mean his office('s).
   Ka⌐isya no⌐ desu.

Tanaka

4. I don't know either. . . .
   Wa⌐takusi mo sirimase⌐ñ ḡa◡

Smith

telephone book	deñwatyoo
see or look at	mi⌐ru /-ru/

5. Then would you look it up in (lit. look at) the phone book?
   Zya⌐a, de⌐ñwatyoo (o) mi⌐te ku⌐dasaimase⌐ñ ka◡

Yamamoto

6. Are you talking about Mr. Hashimoto's telephone [number]?
   Ha⌐simoto-sañ no deñwa de⌐su ka◡

number 21	ni⌐zyuu i⌐ti⌐-bañ or hu⌐ta⌐zyuu i⌐ti⌐-bañ

7. It's 481-7921.
   Yo⌐ñhyaku ha⌐ti⌐zyuu i⌐ti⌐ no, na-⌐na⌐señ ⌐kyu⌐uhyaku hu⌐ta⌐zyuu i⌐ti⌐-bañ desu.

Smith

extension	naiseñ

8. How about the extension?
   Naiseñ wa?

190

Yamamoto

9. The extension I don't know. . . .   Na⌐iseñ wa sirimase⌐ñ ḡa_

Smith

    telephone operator (i.e.   ko⌐oka⌐ñsyu
      central or switchboard)
    ask a question or listen   kiku /-u/
      or hear
    ask the operator   ko⌐oka⌐ñsyu ni kiku
10. Then would you ask the oper-   Zya⌐a, ko⌐oka⌐ñsyu ni ki┕ite kudasa-
    ator?   imase┑ñ ka_

(b)

(On the telephone)

Smith

11. Hello (on the telephone) or   Mo⌐simosi.
    Say there!

Operator

12. Hello. (This is the) Bank   Mo⌐simosi.   Ni⌐hoñ-gi⌐ñkoo de go-
    of Japan.   zaimasu.

Smith

    number 10   zyu⌐u-bañ or
                                  to⌐o-bañ
13. Extension 210, please.   Naiseñ ni̅hyaku ⌐to⌐o-bañ |e/ni| onegai-
                                  simasu.

                                  or

                                  Naiseñ ni̅hyaku ⌐to⌐o-bañ (o) onegai-
                                  simasu.

14. Hello. Is Yoshio Hashi-   Mo⌐simosi.   Ha⌐simoto Yosio - sañ
    moto there?   ima⌐su ka_

Secretary

    the person addressed   sotira
      who?   do⌐tirasama †
15. Who is calling, please?   Sotira (wa) ⌐do⌐tirasama de (i)┕ras-
    (Lit. Who are you?)   syaima┑su ka_

Smith

16. This is [Mr.] Smith of the   A⌐merika-taisi⌐kañ no ⌐Su⌐misu desu
    American Embassy. . . .   ḡa_

Secretary

    seat or assigned place   se⌐ki or
                                  o⌐se⌐ki †
    be at one's place   se⌐ki ni iru
17. Mr. Hashimoto isn't at his   Hasimoto - sañ (wa) ⌐i̅⌐ma o⌐se⌐ki ni
    desk (lit. place) [just] now. . . .   i┕rassyaimase⌐ñ ḡa_

Smith

later
make a telephone call

nótihodo
deñwa-suru or
o⌐de⌐ñwa-suru⁺

18. Well then, I'll call again later
    (so). . .

Zya⌐a, ma⌐ta notihodo ode⌐ñwa - simasu kara⌐

Secretary

19. Thank you very much.

Do⌐o mo su⌐mimase⌐ñ.

(c)

(On the telephone)

Smith

the Yoshida residence
20. Is this the Yoshida resi-
    dence?

Yosida-sañ no otaku ⌐
Sotira (wa) Yo⌐sida-sañ no otaku de
(i)rassyaima⌐su ka⌐

Maid

that way or thus or so
21. Yes, that's right.

sayoo
Ha⌐a, sa⌐yoo de gozaima⌐su.

Smith

master
mistress

da⌐ñnasa⌐ma ⌐
o⌐kusañ ⌐ or
o⌐kusama ⌐

22. Is Mr. Yoshida (lit. the mas-
    ter) in?

Da⌐ñnasa⌐ma i⌐rassyaima⌐su ka⌐

Maid

away from home

ru⌐su or
o⌐ru⌐su ⌐

23. He's out [just] now. . . .

I⌐ma o⌐ru⌐su de gozaimasu ḡa⌐

Smith

24. About what time will he be
    back?

Na⌐ñ-zi-ḡo⌐ro o⌐kaeri ni narima⌐su
ka⌐

Maid

he probably returns (or
will return) home
25. He will probably be back by
    about 6 o'clock. . . .

ka⌐eru desyoo or
o⌐kaeri ni na⌐ru desyoo ⌐
Ro⌐ku-zi-ḡo⌐ro ma⌐de ni⌐ wa o⌐ka-
eri ni na⌐ru desyoo ḡa⌐

Smith

excuse me (i.e. for breaking away or interrupting)
26. I see. Goodbye.

go⌐meñ-kudasa⌐i or
go⌐meñ-kudasaima⌐se
Wa⌐karima⌐sita. Go⌐meñ-kudasa⌐i.

Maid

27. Goodbye.

Go⌐meñ-kudasaima⌐se.

(d)

(On the telephone)

Yamamoto

zero	re⌐e or
	ze⌐ro
number 4	yo⌐n̄-ban̄

28. Hello. Is this 080-0704?   Mo⌐simosi. Sotira (wa) ⌐re⌐e ha⌐ti-zyu⌐u no, re⌐e na⌐na⌐hyaḳu ⌐yo⌐n̄-ban̄ desu ka↲

Secretary

29. Yes, that's right. . . .   Ha⌐a, sa⌐yoo de gozaima⌐su ḡa↲

Yamamoto

30. Is Mr. Yamada in?   Ya⌐mada-san̄ ima⌐su ka↲

Secretary

in the middle of work	siḡoto-tyuu or
	osiḡoto-tyuu ↑

31. He's busy [just] now. . . .   I⌐ma o⌐siḡoto-tyuu de (i)rassyaima⌐su ḡa↲

Yamamoto

the person speaking	kotira
Japan Travel Bureau	ko⌐otuuko⌐osya
free time or leisure	hima or
	ohima ↑
time or occasion	to⌐ki⌐
at a free time	hi⌐ma na toki⌐ /ni/

32. This is [Mr.] Yamamoto of the Japan Travel Bureau. Please give me a call when he is free.   Kotira (wa) ko⌐otuuko⌐osya no Ya-⌐mamoto de⌐su ḡa, o⌐hima na toki⌐ /ni/ o⌐de⌐n̄wa (o) kudasai.

Secretary

33. Certainly.   Ka⌐sikomarima⌐sita.

Yamamoto

34. Goodbye.   Sayonara.

Secretary

35. Goodbye.   Go⌐men̄-kudasaima⌐se.

NOTES ON THE BASIC DIALOGUES

1. The ni following Hasimoto-san̄ is the ni of goal: 'I want to make a telephone call TO Mr. Hashimoto.' Compare Yo⌐kohama ni ikima⌐sita 'I went to Yokohama.' Following a place expression, both goal particles—ni and

e — occur, but following a person, only <u>ni</u> is used.

Ba⌐ngo⌐o means 'number' in the sense of 'assigned number' or 'serial number' — not 'mathematical numeral.' Similarly, na⌐ñ-bañ means 'what assigned number?' or 'what serial number?'

2. <u>Kaisya</u> 'private company' is also commonly used in reference to the office of such a company. While zi⌐mu⌐syo 'business office' has a broader meaning (it includes a private individual's office, an embassy, etc.), it is used less commonly than <u>kaisya</u> in situations where <u>kaisya</u> applies. As the second part of a compound, <u>kaisya</u> often becomes -g̃aisya (for example, ga⌐sug̃a⌐isya 'gas company').

4. 'I don't know either but—is there any way I can help you?'

5. <u>Mi⌐ru</u> more commonly refers to seeing or looking at things. When used with a personal object, it means 'look at': for example, it is used in reference to a doctor's looking at a patient. When 'see a person' corresponds to 'meet and talk to,' the Japanese equivalent is a⌐u.

9. 'The extension I don't know but—is there any way I can help you?'

10. Note the following particles which occur with <u>kiku</u>: the person who asks, listens, or hears is followed by particle g̃a (or <u>wa</u>); the thing asked, listened to, or heard is followed by particle o (or <u>wa</u>); the person asked or listened to is followed by particle <u>ni</u>; the person from whom something is heard is followed by particle <u>kara</u> or <u>ni</u>.

11. Mo⌐simosi is the most common way of saying hello on the telephone. It is also a polite way of attracting attention (in this usage it is similar to, but more polite than, tyo⌐tto)—particularly when addressing strangers.

When making a telephone call in Japan, it is the person who places the call who usually says <u>mo⌐simosi</u> first; he speaks when he hears a click at the other end of the line.

13. The first alternant means 'I'd like [to be connected] to extension 210.' The second alternant means 'I'd like extension 210.'

15. Do⌐tirasama and do⌐natasama are honorific words, more polite than <u>do⌐nata</u> alone. <u>Do⌐tirasama</u> is especially common in telephone conversations.

16. 'This is Mr. Smith but—may I speak to Mr. Hashimoto?'

17. 'Mr. Hashimoto isn't at his desk but—is there anything I can do?'

18. 'I'll call later so—you won't have to do anything.'

<u>Notihodo</u> is a formal equivalent of a⌐to de.

21. <u>Sa⌐yoo de gozaima⌐su</u> is the polite equivalent of so⌐o desu.

22. Da⌐ñnasa⌐ma is used commonly by servants and in conversations with servants. It is also sometimes used as a synonym for go⌐syu⌐ziñ.

<u>O⌐kusama</u> is a more polite equivalent of <u>o⌐kusañ</u>. Compare also the very polite words o⌐to⌐osama 'father,' o⌐ka⌐asama 'mother,' go⌐syu⌐ziñsama 'husband,' o⌐zyo⌐osama 'daughter,' etc.; the comparable form for bo⌐ttyañ

'son' is o⌐bo⌐ttyama.   Note also that -sama is added to proper names as a more polite equivalent of -sañ (for example, Tanaka-sama).

25. 'He'll probably be back . . . but—I can't be sure.'

The wa is the wa of comparison.

26. Go⌐meñ-kudasa⌐i is also used when entering a house or a shop, to attract attention.   Compare English 'Hello there!' and 'Is anybody home?'

Go⌐meñ-kudasaima⌐se is the formal equivalent of gomeñ-kudasai, used most commonly by women, and by men who are employees of shops, restaurants, hotels, etc.

29. 'That's right but—what can I do for you?'

32. Koosya (as in ko⌐otuuko⌐osya) refers to a public corporation, whereas kaisya is a private company.

GRAMMATICAL NOTES

A Japanese telephone number consisting of two numerical parts—for example, 481-5021—is regularly read in one of the following ways:

1) The first number (i.e. the exchange number) is read in terms of individual digits and is followed by particle no; the second number is also read as individual digits. In this system '4' is regularly yo⌐ñ (not si⌐), '7' is na⌐na (not si⌐ti⌐), '9' is kyu⌐u (not ku⌐); '2' has a special alternant ni⌐i, and '5' go⌐o; '0' is ze⌐ro or re⌐e and is regularly included in reading. Thus:

yo⌐ñ hati i⌐ti⌐ no, go⌐o ⌐ze⌐ro ⌐ni⌐i iti
'(lit.) five zero two one of four eight one'

or

2) The exchange number is read as an independent number (in terms of hundreds, tens, and units, if it consists of three digits) and is followed by particle no; the following four-digit number is read in terms of thousands, hundreds, tens, and digits, plus counter -bañ 'number.' An initial zero in the exchange number is read re⌐e or ze⌐ro; otherwise it is often omitted in this style of reading. Thus:

yo⌐ñhyaku ha⌐tizyu⌐u i⌐ti⌐ no, go⌐se⌐ñ [⌐re⌐e/ ni⌐zyuu i⌐ti⌐-bañ
'(lit.) number five thousand twenty-one of four hundred eighty-one'

In this system, '4', '7', and '9' have the same alternants as above; '2' is ni⌐ or hu⌐ta⌐, and '10' is zyu⌐u or to⌐o.
Formerly, the second type of reading described above (i.e. the style used in Dialogue A of this lesson) was more common, but recently the first type has become more prevalent.
The numerals of Series I (with alternants for '2' and '10' from Series II)

combine with the counter -bañ to name telephone numbers, seat numbers, license numbers, etc. The numbers from 1 to 10 are:

i⌐ti¬-bañ	'number 1'	ro⌐ku¬-bañ	'number 6'
ni¬-bañ or		na⌐na¬-bañ	'number 7'
hu⌐ta¬-bañ	'number 2'	ha⌐ti¬-bañ	'number 8'
sañ-bañ	'number 3'	kyu¬u-bañ	'number 9'
yo¬ñ-bañ	'number 4'	zyu¬u-bañ or	
go-bañ	'number 5'	to¬o-bañ	'number 10'
	na¬ñ-bañ	'what number?'	

2. desyoo Following a Non-past Verbal

Desyoo, the formal tentative of da indicating probability or uncertainty, has been introduced previously as occurring after an adjectival ending in -i, a nominal, or a phrase ending with a particle:

Ta⌐ka¬i desyoo. 'It's probably expensive.'
Da⌐me¬ desyoo. 'It's probably no good.'
Tanaka-sañ kara desyoo? 'It's from Mr. Tanaka, isn't it?'

Desyoo also occurs after non-past[1] verbals, informal or formal. Since desyoo is formal, the combination is always classified as formal; but a formal verbal + desyoo is more formal than an informal verbal + desyoo.

When it follows an accented verbal, desyoo is unaccented:

Ku¬ru desyoo.

A normally unaccented verbal + desyoo is accented according to one of two possible patterns, depending upon the speaker; either the verbal acquires an accent on its final syllable, or desyoo is accented on its next-to-last syllable:

I⌐ku¬ desyoo.
or
I⌐ku desyo¬o.

Desyoo following a verbal indicates probability or uncertainty or indirectness, just as it does after words of other classes:

I⌐ku desyo¬o. 'He probably goes (or probably will go).'
Be⌐ñkyoo-site (i)ru desyo¬o. 'He's probably studying (or probably will be studying).'
Wa⌐karima¬su desyoo? 'It's clear, isn't it?'
A¬ni ni ⌐a⌐u desyoo ka. 'Do you suppose you'll see my older brother?'

---

[1] Desyoo occurs after past forms also. These patterns, as well as all informal negatives, will be taken up later.

Ta⌐roo-tyañ wa ⌐na⌐ni o si⌐te (i)ru desyo⌐o ka. 'What do you suppose
Taro is doing?'
Si⌐tte (i)ru desyo⌐o ka ⌐ne⌐e. 'I wonder if he does know!'
Ka⌐maimase⌐ñ desyoo? 'It doesn't matter, does it?'

Do not confuse a verbal + <u>desyoo</u> with a tentative verbal, which indicates a
suggestion:[1]

Ka⌐u desyo⌐o. '[Someone] probably buys (<u>or</u> will probably buy) [it].'
Ka⌐imasyo⌐o. 'Let's buy [it].' <u>or</u> 'I guess I'll buy [it].'

3. Alternate Questions

Two questions occurring within a sentence with the pattern A ka B ka are
alternate questions—'is it A, or is it B?'

Examples:

Ko⌐marima⌐su ka, ka⌐maimase⌐ñ ka. 'Is it inconvenient, or doesn't it
matter?'
O⌐mosiro⌐i desu ka, tu⌐mara⌐nai desu ka. 'Is it interesting, or is it
dull?'
O⌐nazi de⌐su ka, ti⌐gaima⌐su ka. 'Is it the same or is it different?'
Ma⌐e desu ka, u⌐siro de⌐su ka. 'Is it in front, or is it in back?'

4. na

Prior to this lesson, words or phrases used as descriptions of nominals
have been of four kinds:

1. An adjectival (or a sequence ending with an adjectival)

Examples: ta⌐ka⌐i zi⌐do⌐osya 'expensive car'
to⌐temo i⌐i hito 'a very nice person'

2. A demonstrative

Example: kono tokee 'this watch'

3. A nominal + <u>no</u> or a nominal phrase (consisting of a nominal preceded
by descriptive words and/or followed by particles) + <u>no</u>

Examples: a⌐na⌐ta no ⌐ho⌐ñ 'your book'
o⌐mosiro⌐i ⌐ho⌐ñ no namae 'the name of an interesting
book'
A⌐merika kara no hu⌐ne 'a ship from America'

---

[1] In the standard spoken language, a verbal + <u>desyoo</u> may refer to first,
second, or third person, but a tentative verbal regularly refers to the first
person.

4. A nominal alone (in special combinations only)

> Examples: su⌐gu ⌐so⌐ba 'immediate vicinity'
> tyo⌐tto ⌐ma⌐e 'a little before'

Within the class of nominals, there is a subclass having the following special characteristic: when they describe another nominal, they are followed by na.

Examples:

> hi⌐ma na toki⌐ 'time of leisure'
> ki⌐ree na uti 'a pretty house'
> si⌐tu⌐ree na hito 'a rude person'

All na-nominals describe qualities; but since not all quality nominals take na, they must be memorized as they occur. Ge⌐ñki 'healthy,' 'peppy,' for example, is a na-nominal, but byooki 'sick' is not:

> ge⌐ñki na kodomo 'a healthy child'
> byooki no kodomo 'a sick child'

Among the n o m i n a l s introduced up to this point, the following are na-nominals:

> (o)⌐ge⌐ñki 'healthy,' 'peppy'
> da⌐me⌐ 'no good'
> ki⌐ree 'pretty,' 'clean'
> da⌐izyo⌐obu 'safe'
> ke⌐kkoo 'fine'
> si⌐tu⌐ree 'rude'
> (o)hima 'free (of time)'
> da⌐izi 'important,' 'valuable'

In the lessons that follow, all na-nominals will be so designated when they are first introduced.

Besides being followed by na when describing another nominal, na-nominals regularly occur before various forms of √da, and before particle ni (as in da⌐me⌐ ni na⌐rima⌐sita 'it went bad' [lit. 'it became no good']).

DRILLS

A. Substitution Drill

1. When you are free, please give me a call.

   O⌐hima na toki⌐ ni o⌐de⌐ñwa (o) kudasai.

2. When you are free, please come again.

   O⌐hima na toki⌐ ni ma⌐ta kite⌐ kudasai.

3. When you are free, please look at this.

   O⌐hima na toki⌐ ni ko⌐re (o) mi⌐te kudasai.

4. When you are free, please let me see that.

   O⌐hima na toki⌐ ni a⌐re (o) mi⌐sete kudasai.

5. When you are free, please show me the way.

   O⌐hima na toki⌐ ni mi⌐ti (o) osiete kudasa⌐i.

6. When you are free, please draw a map.

O⌐hima na toki⌐ ni ⌐ti⌐zu (o) ⌐ka⌐ite kudasai.

7. When you are free, please come to see me (lit. come to my house).

O⌐hima na toki⌐ ni u⌐ti e ira⌐site kudasai.

8. When you are free, please telephone Mr. Tanaka.

O⌐hima na toki⌐ ni Ta⌐naka-sañ ni deñwa (o) ka⌐kete kudasai.

B. Substitution Drill

1. I saw [it] at that school.

A⌐no gakkoo de mima⌐sita.

2. I asked at that school.

A⌐no gakkoo de kikima⌐sita.

3. I telephoned at that school.

A⌐no gakkoo de deñwa-sima⌐sita.

4. I saw [him] at that school.

A⌐no gakkoo de aima⌐sita.

5. I studied at that school.

A⌐no gakkoo de beñkyoo-sima⌐sita.

6. I wrote [it] at that school.

A⌐no gakkoo de kakima⌐sita.

7. I bought [it] at that school.

A⌐no gakkoo de kaima⌐sita.

8. I did [it] at that school.

A⌐no gakkoo de sima⌐sita.

C. Substitution Drill

1. I asked (or heard [it] or listened).

Wa⌐takusi ḡa kikima⌐sita.

2. I (comparatively speaking) asked (or heard [it] or listened).

Wa⌐takusi wa kikima⌐sita.

3. I too asked (or heard [it] or listened).

Wa⌐takusi mo kikima⌐sita.

4. I asked (or heard [it] from) a friend.

To⌐modati ni kikima⌐sita.

5. I heard [it] from a friend.

To⌐modati kara kikima⌐sita.

6. I asked (or heard or listened to) that.

So⌐re o kikima⌐sita.

7. That I asked (or heard or listened to).

So⌐re wa kikima⌐sita.

8. I asked (or heard or listened to) that, too.

So⌐re mo kikima⌐sita.

9. I asked (or heard [it] or listened) at the Japan Travel Bureau.

Ko⌐otuuko⌐osya de ki⌐kima⌐sita.

10. I asked (or heard [it] or listened) at 3 o'clock.

Sa⌐ñ-zi ni ki⌐kima⌐sita.

D. Substitution Drill

1. I'd like to telephone a friend. . . .

To⌐modati ni deñwa (o) kaketa⌐i ñ desu ḡa_

2. I'd like to telephone my home. . . .

U⌐ti │ ni │ deñwa (o) kaketa⌐i ñ desu
        │ e │
ḡa_

3. I'd like to telephone a cousin in Osaka. . . .

Oˀosaka no itoˀko ni deˀñwa (o) kaketaˀi ñ desu ḡa_

4. I'd like to telephone my uncle in Kyoto. . . .

Kyoˀoto no oˀzi ni deñwa (o) kaketaˀi ñ desu ḡa_

5. I'd like to telephone Mrs.
Hashimoto. . . .

Haˀsimoto-sañ no oˀkusañ ni deˀñwa
(o) kaketaˀi ñ desu ḡa_

6. I'd like to telephone Miss
Kobayashi. . . .

Koˀbayasi-sañ no ozyoˀosañ ni deˀñwa (o) kaketaˀi ñ desu ḡa_

7. I'd like to telephone my
child's school. . . .

Koˀdomo no gakkoo $\begin{vmatrix} ni \\ e \end{vmatrix}$ deñwa (o)
kaketaˀi ñ desu ḡa_

8. I'd like to telephone the
Japan Travel Bureau. . . .

Koˀotuukoˀosya $\begin{vmatrix} ni \\ e \end{vmatrix}$ deˀñwa (o) kaketaˀi ñ desu ḡa_

9. I'd like to telephone (our)
Jiro. . . .

Uˀti no Ziˀroo ni deˀñwa (o) kaketaˀi ñ desu ḡa_

10. I'd like to telephone Mr.
Tanaka at the Foreign
Office. . . .

Gaˀimuˀsyoo noTaˀnaka-sañ ni deñwa (o) kaketaˀi ñ desu ḡa_

E. Substitution Drill

1. He'll probably return home
by about 6 o'clock.

Roˀku-zi-ḡoˀro made ni wa oˀkaeri
ni naˀru desyoo.

2. He'll probably return home
by tomorrow.

Aˀsita maˀde ni wa oˀkaeri ni naˀru
desyoo.

3. He'll probably come (or go)
by tomorrow.

Aˀsita maˀde ni wa iˀrassyaˀru desyoo.

4. He'll probably come (or go)
by Wednesday.

Suˀiyoˀo made ni wa iˀrassyaˀru desyoo.

5. He'll probably arrive by
Wednesday.

Suˀiyoˀo made ni wa oˀtuki ni naˀru
desyoo.

6. He'll probably arrive by
April.

Si-ˀḡatuˀ made ni wa oˀtuki ni naˀru
desyoo.

7. He'll probably be able to
do [it] by April.

Si-ˀḡatuˀ made ni wa oˀdeki ni naˀru
desyoo.

8. He'll probably be able to
do [it] by the first.

Tuˀitatiˀ made ni wa oˀdeki ni naˀru
desyoo.

9. He'll probably leave by the
first.

Tuˀitatiˀ made ni wa oˀde ni naˀru
desyoo.

10. He'll probably leave by a
quarter after.

Zyuˀugo-huˀñ-suḡi made ni wa oˀde
ni naˀru desyoo.

F. Grammar Drill (based on Grammatical Note 2)

(Use the informal verbal before desyoo.)

Tutor: Asita ˀNiˀkkoo ni ikimasu.   '[He] is going to go to Nikkoo tomorrow.'

Student: Asita ˀNiˀkkoo ni iˀku desyoˀo. '[He] is probably going to
go to Nikkoo tomorrow.'

1. Ma⌐ta asita aima⌐su.   Ma⌐ta asita a⌐u desyoo.
2. So⌐re wa komarima⌐su.   So⌐re wa koma⌐ru desyoo.
3. U⌐ti no usiro de tomema⌐su.   U⌐ti no usiro de tomeru desyo⌐o.
4. Ko⌐nna siḡoto wa dekima⌐su.   Ko⌐nna siḡoto wa deki⌐ru desyoo.
5. Ni⌐hoñḡo to eeḡo wa wakari-   Ni⌐hoñḡo to eeḡo wa waka⌐ru desyoo.
   ma⌐su.
6. Ko⌐re to sore wa tiḡaima⌐-   Ko⌐re to sore wa tiḡau desyo⌐o.
   su.
7. Hi⌐ma na toki⌐ ni mi⌐ma⌐su.   Hi⌐ma na toki⌐ ni ⌐mi⌐ru desyoo.
8. Asoko ni tabako (ḡa) ⌐mo⌐t-   Asoko ni tabako (ḡa) ⌐mo⌐tto ⌐a⌐ru
   to arimasu.   desyoo.
9. Go⌐ḡo made u⌐ti ni ima⌐su.   Go⌐ḡo made u⌐ti ni iru desyo⌐o.
10. A⌐sita Yokohama ni tuki-   A⌐sita Yokohama ni tu⌐ku desyoo.
    ma⌐su.

G. Grammar Drill (based on Grammatical Note 3)

   Tutor: I⌐kima⌐su. I⌐kimase⌐ñ. 'I'll go. I won't go.' (2 statements)
   Student: I⌐kima⌐su ka, i⌐kimase⌐ñ ka↵ 'Are you going, or aren't you
            going?' (alternate questions)

1. Ryo⌐kañ de⌐su. Ho⌐teru   Ryo⌐kañ de⌐su ka, ho⌐teru desu ka↵
   desu.
2. Si⌐tte (i)ma⌐su. Si⌐rima-   Si⌐tte (i)ma⌐su ka, si⌐rimase⌐ñ ka↵
   se⌐ñ.
3. Mu⌐zukasi⌐i desu. Ya⌐sa-   Mu⌐zukasi⌐i desu ka, ya⌐sasi⌐i desu
   si⌐i desu.   ka↵
4. Bo⌐ttyañ no desu. O⌐zyo⌐o-   Bo⌐ttyañ no desu ka, o⌐zyo⌐osañ no
   sañ no desu.   desu ka↵
5. Ki⌐no⌐o desita. O⌐toto⌐i   Ki⌐no⌐o desita ka, o⌐toto⌐i desita ka↵
   desita.
6. Ke⌐kkoñ-site ima⌐su. O⌐hi-   Ke⌐kkoñ-site (i)ma⌐su ka, o⌐hitori
   tori de⌐su.   de⌐su ka↵
7. De⌐kima⌐sita. De⌐kimase⌐ñ   De⌐kima⌐sita ka, de⌐kimase⌐ñ desita
   desita.   ka↵
8. Sa⌐ñ-zi made desu. Yo⌐-zi   Sa⌐ñ-zi made desu ka, yo⌐-zi made
   made desu.   desu ka↵

H. Grammar Drill (based on Grammatical Note 4)

   Tutor: Ko⌐no ho⌐ñ (wa) ta⌐ka⌐i desu ⌐ne⌐e. 'This book is expensive,
          isn't it.'
   Student: Kore (wa) ta⌐ka⌐i ⌐ho⌐ñ desu ⌐ne⌐e. 'This is an expensive
            book, isn't it.'

1. Ano kodomo (wa) ⌐ge⌐ñki   Are (wa) ⌐ge⌐ñki na ko⌐domo de⌐su
   desu ⌐ne⌐e.   ⌐ne⌐e.
2. Ko⌐no ba⌐su (wa) o⌐so⌐i desu Kore (wa) o⌐soi ba⌐su desu ⌐ne⌐e.
   ⌐ne⌐e.
3. So⌐no mise⌐ (wa) sa⌐ki de-   Sore (wa) sa⌐ki no mise⌐ desyoo?
   syoo?

4. Kono siḡoto (wa) ⌐ma⌐initi   Kore (wa) ⌐ma⌐initi no siḡoto de-
   desyoo?   syoo?
5. O⌐zyo⌐osañ (wa) ⌐ki⌐ree desu   Ki⌐ree na o⌐zyo⌐osañ desu ⌐ne⌐e.
   ⌐ne⌐e.
6. So⌐no ka⌐do (wa) tu⌐gi⌐ de-   Sore (wa) tu⌐gi⌐ no ⌐ka⌐do desyoo?
   syoo?
7. A⌐no zido⌐osya (wa) hu⌐ru⌐i   Are (wa) hu⌐ru⌐i zi⌐do⌐osya desu
   desu ⌐ne⌐e.   ⌐ne⌐e.
8. Ano zyuñsa (wa) si⌐tu⌐ree   Are (wa) si⌐tu⌐ree na zyu⌐ñsa de⌐si-
   desita ⌐ne⌐e.   ta ⌐ne⌐e.
9. Kono miti (wa) a⌐buna⌐i   Kore (wa) a⌐bunai miti de⌐su ⌐ne⌐e.
   desu ⌐ne⌐e.

I. Expansion Drill

1. [He] didn't know.   Si⌐rimase⌐ñ desita.
   I asked, but [he] didn't   Ki⌐kima⌐sita ḡa, si⌐rimase⌐ñ desita.
   know.
   I asked the telephone num-   De⌐ñwaba⌐ñḡoo (o) ki⌐kima⌐sita ḡa,
   ber, but [he] didn't know.   si⌐rimase⌐ñ desita.
   I asked the telephone num-   Ga⌐imu⌐syoo no de⌐ñwaba⌐ñḡoo (o)
   ber of the Foreign Office,   ki⌐kima⌐sita ḡa, si⌐rimase⌐ñ de-
   but [he] didn't know.   sita.
   I asked my friend the tele-   Tomodati ni ga⌐imu⌐syoo no de⌐ñwa-
   phone number of the For-   ba⌐ñḡoo (o) ki⌐kima⌐sita ga, si⌐ri-
   eign Office, but [he]   mase⌐ñ desita.
   didn't know.

2. I'll probably see [him].   A⌐u desyoo.
   I'll probably see your   O⌐tomodati ni a⌐u desyoo.
   friend.
   I'm going to go, so I'll   I⌐kima⌐su kara, o⌐tomodati ni a⌐u
   probably see your   desyoo.
   friend.
   I'm going to go to the Ja-   Ko⌐otuuko⌐osya e i⌐kima⌐su kara,
   pan Travel Bureau, so   o⌐tomodati ni a⌐u desyoo.
   I'll probably see your
   friend.
   I'm going to go to the Ja-   I⌐ma ko⌐otuuko⌐osya e i⌐kima⌐su ka-
   pan Travel Bureau now,   ra, o⌐tomodati ni a⌐u desyoo.
   so I'll probably see your
   friend.

3. You know, I saw [it].   Mi⌐ma⌐sita yo⌐
   You know, I saw [it] for the   Ha⌐zi⌐mete mi⌐ma⌐sita yo⌐
   first time.
   You know, I saw the house   Uti (o) ha⌐zi⌐mete mi⌐ma⌐sita yo⌐
   for the first time.
   You know, I saw a pretty   Ki⌐ree na uti (o) ha⌐zi⌐mete mi⌐ma⌐-
   house for the first   sita yo⌐
   time.

You know, I saw your son's pretty house for the first time.	Musukosañ no ⌐ki⌐ree na uti (o) ha-⌐zi⌐mete mi⌐ma⌐sita yo⌐
You know, I saw your son's pretty house for the first time last night.	Yuube mūsukosañ no ⌐ki⌐ree na uti (o) ha⌐zi⌐mete mi⌐ma⌐sita yo⌐

4. Did you ask?   Ki⌐kima⌐sita ка⌐

   Did you ask the operator?   Ko⌐oka⌐ñsyu ni ki⌐kima⌐sita ka⌐

   Did you see [it] or did you ask the operator?   Mi⌐ma⌐sita ka, ko⌐oka⌐ñsyu ni ki⌐kima⌐sita ka⌐

   Did you look at the phone book or did you ask the operator?   De⌐ñwatyoo (o) mima⌐sita ka, ko⌐oka⌐ñsyu ni ki⌐kima⌐sita ka⌐

5. Is it number 2?   Hu⌐ta⌐-bañ desu ka⌐

   Is it number 22?   Hu⌐ta⌐zyuu hu⌐ta⌐-bañ desu ka⌐

   Is it number 422?   Yo⌐ñhyaku hu⌐ta⌐zyuu hu⌐ta⌐-bañ desu ka⌐

   Is it number 0422?   Re⌐e ⌐yo⌐ñhyaku hu⌐ta⌐zyuu hu⌐ta⌐-bañ desu ka⌐

   Is it (number) 081-0422?   Re⌐e ha⌐tizyu⌐u i⌐ti⌐ no, re⌐e ⌐yo⌐ñ-hyaku hu⌐ta⌐zyuu hu⌐ta⌐-bañ desu ka⌐

   Is this (i.e. the person I'm addressing) (number) 081-0422?   Sotira (wa) ⌐re⌐e ha⌐tizyu⌐u i⌐ti⌐ no, re⌐e ⌐yo⌐ñhyaku hu⌐ta⌐zyuu hu⌐ta⌐-bañ desu ka⌐

SUPPLEMENTARY CONVERSATIONS

1. Smith: Ki⌐mura-sañ no deñwaba⌐ñgoo o si⌐tte ma⌐su ka⌐
   Tanaka: Tyo⌐tto ⌐ma⌐tte kudasai⌐ . . . Go⌐hyaku nana⌐zyuu i⌐ti⌐ no, sa⌐ñze⌐ñ ⌐yo⌐ñzyuu i⌐ti⌐-bañ desu yo⌐
   Smith: Ma⌐e wa so⌐no bañgo⌐o desita ga, i⌐ma wa ⌐so⌐o zya a⌐rimase⌐ñ yo.
   Tanaka: A⌐a, so⌐o desu ka⌐ Zya⌐a, kinoo Ha⌐simoto-sañ ga Kimura-sañ ni deñwa-sima⌐sita kara, Ha⌐simoto-sañ wa sitte ru⌐ de-syoo.
   Smith: Zya⌐a, Ha⌐simoto-sañ ni kikimasyo⌐o. Do⌐o mo su⌐mimase⌐ñ.
   Tanaka: Iie.

2. Mr. Tanaka: Mo⌐simosi⌐
   Maid: Mo⌐simosi⌐
   Mr. Tanaka: Ya⌐mada-sañ no otaku de⌐su ka⌐
   Maid: Ha⌐a, sa⌐yoo de gozaima⌐su.
   Mr. Tanaka: Yu⌐kio-sañ ima⌐su ka⌐
   Maid: Bo⌐ttyañ wa ⌐i⌐ma ga⌐kkoo de gozaima⌐su ga, do⌐tira-sama de i⌐rassyaima⌐su ka⌐

Mr. Tanaka: Azabu[1] no Ta⌐naka de⌐su ḡa, na⌐ñ-zi-ḡo⌐ro ka⌐erima⌐su ka⌐

Maid: Kyo⌐o wa do⌐yo⌐o desu kara i⌐ti-zi-ḡo⌐ro o⌐kaeri ni narima⌐su
             ḡa, notihodo ko⌐tira kara ode⌐ñwa si⌐masyo⌐o ka.

Mr. Tanaka: Iie. Ma⌐ta a⌐to de ⌐bo⌐ku ḡa de⌐ñwa suru⌐ kara.

Maid: Sa⌐yoo de gozaima⌐su ka⌐

Mr. Tanaka: Zya⌐a, sayonara.

Maid: Go⌐meñ-kudasaima⌐se.

3. Smith: Tyo⌐tto de⌐ñwa (o) kaketa⌐i ñ desu ḡa⌐

   Tanaka: Ko⌐no deñwa do⌐ozo.

   Smith: A⌐ri⌐ḡatoo. De⌐ñwaba⌐ñḡoo si⌐rimase⌐ñ ḡa⌐

   Tanaka: De⌐ñwatyoo arima⌐su yo⌐ Do⌐nata ni ka⌐keta⌐i ñ desu ka⌐

   Smith: Ki⌐mura Yosio de⌐su.

   Tanaka: Ki⌐mura Yosio de⌐su ka⌐ Tyo⌐tto ⌐ma⌐tte kudasai⌐ A⌐a, A⌐o⌐-
             yama[1] ro⌐ku-tyoome⌐ no Ki⌐mura-sañ de⌐su ka⌐

   Smith: E⌐e, so⌐o desu.

   Tanaka: Yo⌐ñhyaku ha⌐tizyu⌐u i⌐ti⌐ no, yo⌐ñse⌐ñ happyaku ⌐to⌐o-bañ de-
             su yo.

   Smith: Tyo⌐tto ⌐ma⌐tte kudasai—ka⌐kima⌐su kara.

   Tanaka: Do⌐ozo. E⌐ñpitu arima⌐su ka⌐

   Smith: E⌐e, a⌐rima⌐su. Su⌐mimase⌐ñ ḡa, mo⌐o iti-do itte kudasaima-
             se⌐ñ ka⌐

   Tanaka: Yo⌐ñhyaku ha⌐tizyu⌐u i⌐ti⌐ no, yo⌐ñse⌐ñ happyaku ⌐to⌐o-bañ de-
             su yo.

   Smith: Do⌐o mo su⌐mimase⌐ñ desita.

   Tanaka: Do⌐o itasimasite.

English Equivalents

1. Smith: Do you know Mr. Kimura's telephone number?

   Tanaka: Just a minute. It's 571-3041.

   Smith: It was that number before, but it isn't that now.

   Tanaka: Oh? Well then, Mr. Hashimoto telephoned Mr. Kimura yes-
              terday so Mr. Hashimoto probably knows.

   Smith: Well then, I'll ask Mr. Hashimoto. Thanks very much.

   Tanaka: Not at all.

2. Mr. Tanaka: Hello.

   Maid: Hello.

   Mr. Tanaka: Is this the Yamada residence?

   Maid: Yes, it is.

   Mr. Tanaka: Is Yukio there?

---

[1]
A section of Tokyo.

Maid: He (lit. the young master) is [at] school now.   Who is calling, please?

Mr. Tanaka: This is Mr. Tanaka in Azabu.   About what time will he be home?

Maid: Today is Saturday so he'll be home about 1.   Do you want him to call you later? (Lit. Shall we call later from this side?)

Mr. Tanaka: No. (Because) I'll call again later.

Maid: Oh.

Mr. Tanaka: Well, goodbye.

Maid: Goodbye.

3. Smith: I'd (just) like to make a telephone call. . . .

Tanaka: Here, [use] this telephone.

Smith: Thanks.   I don't know the telephone number. . . .

Tanaka: I have a telephone book.   Who is it you want to call?

Smith: It's Yoshio Kimura.

Tanaka: Yoshio Kimura?   Just a minute. . . .   Oh, is it Mr. Kimura in Aoyama 6-chome?

Smith: Yes, that's right.

Tanaka: It's 481-4810.

Smith: Just a minute—because I'm going to write it [down].

Tanaka: Certainly.   Do you have a pencil?

Smith: Yes, I have.   I'm sorry but would you say it again?

Tanaka: It's 481-4810.

Smith: Thanks very much.

Tanaka: You're welcome.

EXERCISES

1. Read the following telephone numbers aloud in Japanese:

   a. 371-3923   f. 251-0360
   b. 481-1333   g. 622-2011
   c. 047-3092   h. 996-0520
   d. 891-1510   i. 291-5272, extension 607
   e. 611-6161   j. 631-0044, extension 941

2. Mr. Tanaka has just telephoned and asked for Mr. Yamamoto.   Give the following answers, practicing different levels, if appropriate:

   a. Just a moment, please.
   b. Mr. Yamamoto isn't at his desk just now. . . .
   c. Mr. Yamamoto is busy just now.   Would you like him to call later? (Lit. Shall we call later from this side?)
   d. Mr. Yamamoto is in Osaka.   He'll be back tomorrow.
   e. Who is calling, please?
   f. Mr. Yamamoto is in Mr. Sato's office just now.   It's extension 243.
   g. Mr. Yamamoto is away from home just now.   He'll be back on the first of the month. (Mrs. Yamamoto speaking)

h. Mr. Yamamoto is at the office. He'll be back at about 6:00. (Mrs. Yamamoto speaking)

i. Mr. Yamamoto will be away from home until Saturday. (Maid speaking)

j. Do you mean Yosio Yamamoto, or Yukio Yamamoto?

3. Practice the Basic Dialogues with appropriate variations.

Lesson 13. Telephoning (cont.)

BASIC DIALOGUES: FOR MEMORIZATION

(a)

Sakamoto

1. Hello. Is Mr. Smith there?　　　Moˈsimosi ‿　Suˈmisu - sañ iˈras-
　　　　　　　　　　　　　　　　　　　　syaimaˈsu ka‿

Secretary

　　set out or go out　　　　　　　dekakeru /-ru/
2. No. He stepped out for a　　　Iie, tyoˈtto deˈkakemaˈsita ḡa‿
　　minute. . . .

Sakamoto

　　message or the giving　　　　kotozuke　or
　　　of a message　　　　　　　　okotozuke +
　　make or do　　　　　　　　　itasu⁺ /-u/
　　request　　　　　　　　　　　neˈḡaˈu⁺/-u/　　or
　　　　　　　　　　　　　　　　　oˈneḡai-itasimaˈsu ⁺
3. Well then, I'd like to leave a　Zyaˈa, Suˈmisu - sañ ni oˈkotozuke
　　message for Mr. Smith.　　　　(o) oneḡai-itasimaˈsu.

Secretary

4. Certainly.　　　　　　　　　　Doˈozo.

Sakamoto

　　university　　　　　　　　　daiḡaku
　　Tokyo University　　　　　　Toˈokyoo-daˈiḡaku　or
　　　　　　　　　　　　　　　　Toodai
5. This is [Mr.] Sakamoto at　　Kotira (wa) Tōodai no Saˈkamoto de
　　Tokyo University. . . .　　　gozaimaˈsu ḡa‿

Secretary

6. Yes.　　　　　　　　　　　　Haˈa.

Sakamoto

　　this evening or tonight　　　koˈñbañ
　　say　　　　　　　　　　　　oˈssyaˈru⁺/-aru/
　　say that or say [it] that　　soˈo ossyaˈru
　　　way
7. Please tell him that I will be　Koˈñbañ siˈtiˈ - zi ni Maˈru-biru no
　　waiting in front of the Maru-　maˈe de ˈmaˈtte orimasu kara, soˈo
　　biru at 7 o'clock this evening.　ossyaˈtte kudasai.
　　(Lit. I'll be waiting in front of
　　the Maru-biru at 7 o'clock this
　　evening so please say [it] that
　　way.)

207

Secretary

report or communicate   tutaeru /-ru/ or
or convey a message   o⌐tutae-itasima⌐su ┤
8. I understand. I'll give him your   Wa⌐karima⌐sita. O⌐tutae-itasima⌐-
message.   su.

(b)

Tanaka

9. Hello.   Mo⌐simosi.

Yamamoto

10. Hello. . . . Hello.   Mo⌐simosi_ . . . Mo⌐simosi.

Tanaka (in a louder voice)

is far   tooi /-ku/
have trouble hearing (on   deñwa ḡa tooi
the phone)
voice   ko⌐e
with a loud voice   o⌐oki⌐i ┌ko┘e de or
o⌐oki na ┌ko┘e de
speak or talk   ha⌐na⌐su /-u/
11. Hello. Say, I can't hear so   Mo⌐simosi⌐ Tyo⌐tto, deñwa ḡa to-
please talk in a little louder   ┌oi⌐ desu kara ne? Mo⌐o suko⌐si ⌐o⌐o-
voice.   ki na ┌ko┘e de ha┌na┘site kudasai.

Yamamoto (still louder)

be audible or can hear   kikoeru /-ru/
12. Hello. Hello. Can you hear   Mo⌐simosi_ Mo⌐simosi_ Ki⌐koe-
[me]?   ma⌐su ka⌐

Tanaka (shouting)

cut or cut off or hang   ki⌐ru /-u/
up (the telephone)
13. It's no good so I'll hang up now   Da⌐me⌐ desu kara ne? I⌐ma ┌ki┘tte
and call again later.   ne? Ma┌ta a⌐to de de┌ñwa-sima┘su
yo.

(c)

Smith

know   go⌐zo⌐ñzi desu ┤
14. Do you know Mr. Ito's tele-   Itoo-sañ no deñwa (o) go⌐zo⌐ñzi desu
phone [number]?   ka⌐

Tanaka

don't know   zo⌐ñzimase⌐ñ ┤
15. No, I don't know [it]. . . .   Iie, zo⌐ñzimase⌐ñ ḡa_

Yoshida

know   zo⌐ñzite orimasu ┤

name card <u>or</u> calling   meesi
card

16. I know—because I have Mr.   Wa⌐takusi wa zo⌐ñzite o r i m a s u _
Ito's card.   I⌐too-sañ no meesi g̱a gozaima⌐su
kara.

Smith

read   yo⌐mu /-u/
17. Would you read it for me?   Yo⌐ñde ku⌐dasaimase⌐ñ ka⌐

slowly   yu⌐kku⌐ri
18. I'm going to write it [down]   Ka⌐kima⌐su kara yu⌐kku⌐ri onegai-
so [read it] slowly, please.   simasu.

(d)

Secretary

make <u>or</u> do   na⌐sa⌐ru † /-aru/
make a telephone call   o⌐de⌐ñwa-nasaru †

19. Did you telephone the school?   Gakkoo $\begin{vmatrix} ni \\ e \end{vmatrix}$ o⌐de⌐ñwa-nasaimasita
ka⌐

Smith

talking <u>or</u> a talk <u>or</u>   hanasi <u>or</u>
a story   ohanasi †
in the middle of talking   hanasi-tyuu <u>or</u>
ohanasi-tyuu †
nobody   dare mo /+ negative/
answer (the telephone)   de⌐ru /-ru/
20. Five minutes ago the line was   Go - ⌐huñ ma⌐e ni wa ha⌐nasi-tyuu
busy but now no one answers.....   de⌐sita g̱a, i⌐ma wa da⌐re mo demase⌐ñ g̱a _

Secretary

strange   he⌐ñ /na/
21. Isn't that strange!   He⌐ñ desu ⌐ne⌐e.

(e)

Tanaka

22. Hello. Is this Tokyo Uni-   Mo⌐simosi_ To⌐odai de⌐su ka⌐
versity?

Stranger

23. Wrong number.   Ti⌐g̱aima⌐su.

Tanaka

24. Oh, I'm sorry. (Lit. I   A. Si⌐tu⌐ree-simasita.
committed a rudeness.)

(f)

Husband

out of order	kosyoo
25. This telephone is out of order.	Kono deñwa kōsyoo da yo⌣

Wife (testing phone)

do what? or act how?	do⌐o suru
26. It is, isn't it. What are you going to do?	Hoñtoo ⌐ne⌐e. Do⌐o suru?

Husband

borrow or rent	kariru /-ru/
say to the operator or tell the operator	ko⌐oka⌐ñsyu ni iu
27. I'm going to borrow the telephone next door and tell the operator.	Tonari no deñwa karite, ko⌐oka⌐ñsyu ni i⌐u⌐ yo.

(On the telephone)

say! or hey there!	ano ne
fix or repair	na⌐o⌐su /-u/
28. Say! 401-5602 is out of order so please fix it.	Ano ne? Yo⌐ñhyaku i⌐ti⌐ no ne? Go-⌐se⌐ñ rōppyaku ⌐ni⌐-bañ wa ne? Ko-⌐syoo da⌐ kara ne? Na⌐o⌐site kudasai.

(g)

Mr. Tanaka

(Mr.) Sato	Sa⌐too-kuñ
is busy	i⌐sogasi⌐i /-ku/ or o⌐isogasi⌐i ↑ /-ku/
29. Sato, are you busy?	Sa⌐too-kuñ, i⌐sogasi⌐i?

Mr. Sato

30. No, not especially.	Iie, betu ni⌣ [1]

Mr. Tanaka

call or summon	yobu /-u/

---

[1] Regularly followed by the negative in longer sentences.

31. Call Okada—because he has   Okada-kuñ yoñde— deʰñwa daˈkara.
    (lit. it is) a phone call.

                          Mr. Sato

32. Where is Okada now?   Okada-kuñ ˈiˈma ˈdoˈko?

                          Mr. Tanaka

        room   heˈyaˈ or
                                       oheya ↑
33. He's in the next room.   Toˈnari no heyaˈ ni iru yo⌐

NOTES ON THE BASIC DIALOGUES

Dialogue (a): Sakamoto uses polite speech in talking to Smith's secretary
as a sign of respect for Smith.

2. 'He stepped out but— is there anything I can do?'

    Dekakeru means 'go out' or 'set out' or 'start out,' whereas deˈru means
    'go out' or 'leave' or 'emerge.'

3. Itasu is the polite humble (↓) equivalent of suru, both as an independent
    word and as part of compounds like beñkyoo- suru (humble, beñkyoo-
    itasu).

7. Oˈssyaˈru is the polite honorific equivalent of iu, used as an exalting
    form in reference to people other than the speaker, in polite speech. It
    belongs to the same subclass of verbals as iˈrassyaˈru, kuˈdasaˈru, and
    goˈzaˈru: its stem is oˈssyaˈi and its -maˈsu form oˈssyaimaˈsu.

11. The opposite of oˈokiˈi (or oˈoki na) ˈkoˈe is tiˈisaˈi (or tiˈisa na) ˈkoˈe
     'low voice.'

     Remember that verbals ending in -su in their citation form have gerunds
     ending in -site.

12. Kikoeru is another verbal which does not occur with particle o. Both the
     thing which is audible and the person who can hear are followed by particle
     wa or g̃a.

13. Kiˈru, like iru 'be necessary,' is a verbal ending in -iru but belonging to
     the -u class of verbals: stem ki˥ri; -maˈsu form, kiˈrimaˈsu; gerund,
     kiˈtte.

14, 15, 16. The verbal zoˈñziˈru ↓ (-ru) 'come to know' is not included in the
     lists of this book. It will occur only in the following forms:

        zoˈñzite (i)masu and zoˈñzite orimasu 'I know (humble equivalents of
          siˈtte (i)maˈsu and siˈtte orimaˈsu)

        zoˈñzimaseˈñ 'I don't know' (humble equivalent of siˈrimaseˈñ)

        goˈzoˈñzi desu (desita, desyoo, etc.) '[you] know (knew, probably know,
          etc.)' (honorific equivalent of siˈtte [i]maˈsu [(i)maˈsita, etc.])

15. 'No, I don't know it but— is there anything I can do?'

16. Meesi are used in Japan in professional circles to a much greater extent than calling cards are used in America. They are regularly exchanged by new acquaintances. They usually include name, title, business affiliation, address, and telephone number.

17. Verbals ending in -mu in their citation form have gerunds ending in -ňde.

18. Yuᴿkku�nori means 'slowly,' 'without hurrying,' 'in a relaxed way.' Unlike the adjectival osoi, it has no connotation of lateness.

19. Naᴿsa�0ru is the polite honorific equivalent of suru, both as an independent word and as part of compounds like beňkyoo-suru (honorific, beᴿňkyoo-nasa�0ru). Compare:

                        'Did you study?'   'Yes, I studied.'

        Plain: Beᴿňkyoo-sima�0sita ka⌐   E�8e, beᴿňkyoo-sima�0sita.
        Polite: Beᴿňkyoo-nasaima�0sita ka⌐   Ha�8a, beᴿňkyoo-itasima�0sita.

Naᴿsa�0ru, like oᴿssya�0ru above (sentence 7), belongs to the same subclass of verbals as iᴿrassya�0ru, kuᴿdasa�0ru, and goᴿza�0ru: its stem is naᴿsa�8i and its gerund naᴿsa�0tte (alternant: naᴿsu�8tte). These five verbals are the only members of the -aru subclass.

20. 'Now no one answers but—I wonder why.' The two wa's in this sentence are wa of comparison.

25. Note also: kosyoo-suru 'break down.'

28. Ano ne is a less polite equivalent of tyo�8tto 'say there!' It does not ordinarily occur in polite c o n v e r s a t i o n, but is used most commonly in addressing close friends and inferiors. It is usually wise to avoid it when speaking to strangers whose position is not known.

29. -Kuň, like -sañ, is added to the family or given names of persons other than the speaker. However, it is a man's word, and is usually used by men in reference to men. It is an informal word and implies familiarity. It may be compared to the English use of a last name without 'Mr.' as a term of address.

30. When betu ni occurs alone, it implies an appropriate negative. Here, it means betu ni iᴿsoga�8siku aᵏrimase�8ň 'I'm not especially busy.'

31. Verbals ending in -bu in their citation form have gerunds ending in -ňde. Note the difference in accent between yo�0ňde 'reading' and yoňde 'calling.'

GRAMMATICAL NOTES

1. ne? and the Explicit Style

Ne? occurs at the end of sentences and means 'are you following me?' or 'do you understand me?' or 'do you agree with me?' It must not be confused with confirming or exclamatory ne�8e. Ne? is an actual question, inviting agreement or acknowledgment. Compare:

Ta⌈ka⌉i desu ⌈ne⌉e. 'Isn't it expensive!' 'It's expensive, isn't it.'
Ta⌈ka⌉i desu ne? 'It's expensive, don't you think so?'

The latter is similar to: <u>Ta⌈ka⌉i desyoo?</u>

When speaking explicitly, or when speaking in a situation where there is some question of the comprehension of the listener (for example, when talking on the telephone, or when giving complicated instructions or explanations, or when talking to an inferior, etc.), it is common to break up a long sentence into a series of shorter sentences ending in <u>ne?</u> The shorter the sentences, the more explicit they are. The listener usually replies to each of these sentences with <u>ha⌉i</u>, <u>e⌉e</u>, <u>ha⌉a</u>, <u>so⌉o</u>, etc.— or with a nod— indicating that he is following the conversation.

However, the frequent occurrence of <u>ne</u> in ordinary, non-explicit conversation is usually a sign of informality and familiarity; to use it appropriately and naturally is very difficult for a foreigner. Beginning students of Japanese should use it sparingly except in the situations described above.

Compare:

  Ordinary style:

    Asita tyo⌈odo ku⌉-zi ni ko⌈ko e kite⌉ kudasai.
    'Please come here tomorrow at 9 sharp.'

  Explicit style:

    Asita ne? 'Tomorrow—understand?'
    Ha⌉i. 'Yes.'
    Tyo⌈odo ku⌉-zi ni ne? 'At 9 sharp—understand?'
    Ha⌉i. 'Yes.'
    Ko⌈ko e kite⌉ kudasai. 'Come here.'
    Ha⌉i. Ka⌈sikomarima⌉sita. 'Yes. Certainly.'

Compare also sentences 11, 13, and 28 in the Basic Dialogues.

2. More About Informal Speech

In informal speech, informal inflected forms occur in sentence-final position and before sentence particles as well as within longer sentences. The following are a few of the common patterns:

(a) Informal verbals and adjectivals occur in sentence-final position in statements and questions, in the speech of men and women. [1]

---

[1] But informal honorific verbals in this position are typical of women's speech. Example: I⌈rassya⌉ru? 'Are you going (<u>or</u> coming)?' or 'Will you be here?'

	Formal	Informal
'It's clear.'	Wa⌐karima⌐su.	Wa⌐ka⌐ru.
'Is it clear?'	Wa⌐karima⌐su ka␣	Wa⌐ka⌐ru?
'It's expensive.'	Ta⌐ka⌐i desu.	Ta⌐ka⌐i.
'Is it expensive?'	Ta⌐ka⌐i desu ka␣	Ta⌐ka⌐i?

(b) Both men and women use nominals in sentence-final position in statements and questions as the informal equivalents of nominal + de⌐su or
de⌐su ka (cf. Lesson 8, Grammatical Note 3); but the occurrence of a
nominal + informal da in statement-final position is typical only of
men's speech.

	Formal	Informal	
		Men	Women
'It's true.'	Hoⁿtoo de⌐su.	Hoñtoo.	Hoñtoo.
		or	
		Hoñtoo da.	
'Is it true?'	Hoⁿtoo de⌐su ka␣	Hoñtoo?	Hoñtoo?

(c) Informal verbals and adjectivals occur before sentence particle yo and
before ne⌐[e] predominantly in informal men's speech.

	Formal	Informal— Men
'It is clear (I tell you).'	Wa⌐karima⌐su yo␣	Wa⌐ka⌐ru yo␣
'It is expensive (I tell you).'	Ta⌐ka⌐i desu yo␣	Ta⌐ka⌐i yo␣
'It's clear, isn't it?'	Wa⌐karima⌐su ne?	Wa⌐ka⌐ru ne?
'It's expensive, isn't it!'	Ta⌐ka⌐i desu ⌐ne⌐e.	Ta⌐ka⌐i ⌐ne⌐e.

(d) As the informal equivalent of a nominal + de⌐su + yo or ne⌐[e], men
regularly use nominal + da + yo or ne⌐[e], while women use nominal +
yo or ne⌐[e].

	Formal	Informal	
		Men	Women
'It is true (I tell you).'	Hoⁿtoo de⌐su yo␣	Hoñtoo da yo␣	Hoñtoo yo␣
'It's true, isn't it!'	Hoⁿtoo de⌐su ⌐ne⌐e.	Hoñtoo da ⌐ne⌐e.	Hoñtoo ⌐ne⌐e.

Basic Dialogues (f) and (g) in this lesson are informal. Sentences 25, 27,
and 33 are typical of men's informal speech, and Hoñtoo ⌐ne⌐e. in 26 is typical
of women's informal speech.   The remaining sentences of these two dialogues
occur in the speech of both men and women, except that -kuñ of sentences 29,
31, and 32 would ordinarily be replaced by -sañ in women's speech.

Grammatical Notes

215

3. Gerunds As Informal Requests

The gerund of a verbal may occur in sentence-final position, or pre-final before a particle, as an informal request. It is normally used in addressing an equal who is well known to the speaker, or an inferior.

Examples:

So⌐re o mi⌐sete. 'Show me that.'
Tyo⌐tto ⌐ma⌐tte yo. 'Wait a minute!'
Yu⌐kku⌐ri ha⌐na⌐site ne? 'Speak slowly, would you?'

The gerund of an honorific is also often used in this way by women, in informal but polite requests.

Examples:

Ko⌐tti⌐ e i⌐ra⌐site. 'Come here.'
Tyo⌐tto o⌐mati ni na⌐tte. 'Wait a minute.'
Yu⌐kku⌐ri o⌐hanasi ni na⌐tte ne? 'Speak slowly, would you?'

4. Verbals: Humble Equivalents in √-suru and √-itasu

A compound verbal consisting of the polite prefix o- + a verbal stem + √suru (or its humble equivalent √itasu) is a humble equivalent of the verbal, used in reference to oneself, members of one's own family, etc. The form with √itasu is more humble than the corresponding form with √suru. Study the following chart:

Plain (Citation Form)	Polite (Citation Form)	
	Humble ↓	Honorific ↑
yobu 'call'	oyobi-suru or oyobi-itasu	o⌐yobi ni na⌐ru
ha⌐na⌐su 'speak'	ohanasi-suru or ohanasi-itasu	o⌐hanasi ni na⌐ru
tutaeru 'report'	otutae-suru or otutae-itasu	o⌐tutae ni na⌐ru

A corresponding humble form does NOT exist for all verbals. Some verbals have only special humble equivalents with unrelated roots (for example, iku and ku⌐ru have the humble equivalent ma⌐iru; iru has o⌐ru; etc.), and some have no commonly occurring humble equivalents.

In general, honorific (↑) verbals are more common than humble (↓) verbals.

Humbling oneself represents a greater degree of politeness in Japanese than exalting others. Accordingly, it is not unusual to use a plain verbal in reply to an honorific question (cf. Lesson 9, Grammatical Note 2):

> O⌐yobi ni narima¬sita ka⌐⌐ 'Did you call?'
> E¬e, yo⌐bima¬sita. 'Yes, I did (call).'

The use of o⌐yobi-sima¬sita (or o⌐yobi-itasima¬sita) in the above reply would be an indication of considerable deference.

However, some humble polite verbals are extremely common. O⌐neḡai-sima¬su and o⌐neḡai-itasima¬su are humble polite equivalents of ne⌐ḡaima¬su (informal, ne⌐ḡa¬u¹). In this case, the humble polite forms probably occur more commonly than the plain form.

Another commonly occurring example of a polite humble verbal is o⌐matase-itasima¬sita, based on the plain verbal ma⌐tase¬ru /-ru/ 'make [someone] wait.'

5. o⌐oki¬i ∼ o¬oki na

A few adjectivals —for example, o⌐oki¬i and ti⌐isa¬i —have a derived nominal which is a na-nominal (see Lesson 12, Grammatical Note 4). It is formed by dropping the final -i of the adjectival and moving the accent toward the beginning of the word (o⌐oki¬i ∼ o¬oki, ti⌐isa¬i ∼ ti¬isa). These nominals are used in combination with na to describe a following nominal: o¬oki na ⌐ho¬ñ 'big book,' ti¬isa na zibiki 'small dictionary,' etc.

Thus, o⌐oki¬i MODIFYING A FOLLOWING NOMINAL is interchangeable with o¬oki na, and ti⌐isa¬i with ti¬isa na.

DRILLS

A. Substitution Drill

1. Who is reading [it]?	Da¬re ḡa ⌐yo¬ñde (i)masu ka⌐⌐
2. Who is calling?	Da¬re ḡa yo⌐ñde (i)ma¬su ka⌐⌐
3. Who is fixing [it]?	Da¬re ḡa na⌐o¬site (i)masu ka⌐⌐
4. Who is speaking?	Da¬re ḡa ha⌐na¬site (i)masu ka⌐⌐
5. Who is saying [it]?	Da¬re ḡa i⌐tte (i)ma¬su ka⌐⌐
6. Who is renting (or borrowing) [it]?	Da¬re ḡa ka⌐rite (i)ma¬su ka⌐⌐
7. Who is listening (or asking)?	Da¬re ḡa ki⌐ite (i)ma¬su ka⌐⌐

---

¹ This verbal, in all its forms, is usually used only in reference to the speaker.

8. Who is cutting [it]?   Da⌐re ḡa ⌐ki⌐tte (i)masu ka⌐
9. Who is looking at [it]?   Da⌐re ḡa ⌐mi⌐te (i)masu ka⌐
10. Who is waiting?   Da⌐re ḡa ⌐ma⌐tte (i)masu ka⌐

B. Substitution Drill

1. Whom are you calling?   Da⌐re o yo⌐nde (i)ma⌐su ka⌐
2. Whom are you waiting for?   Da⌐re o ⌐ma⌐tte (i)masu ka⌐ [1]
3. Whom are you looking at?   Da⌐re o ⌐mi⌐te (i)masu ka⌐
4. What are you looking at?   Na⌐ni o ⌐mi⌐te (i)masu ka⌐
5. What are you reading?   Na⌐ni o ⌐yo⌐nde (i)masu ka⌐
6. What are you fixing?   Na⌐ni o na⌐o⌐site (i)masu ka⌐
7. What are you saying?   Na⌐ni o i⌐tte (i)ma⌐su ka⌐
8. What are you listening to?   Na⌐ni o ki⌐ite (i)ma⌐su ka⌐
9. What are you cutting?   Na⌐ni o ⌐ki⌐tte (i)masu ka⌐
10. What are you writing?   Na⌐ni o ⌐ka⌐ite (i)masu ka⌐

C. Substitution Drill

1. I'm going to read this   Ke⌐sa ko⌐no siñbuñ (o) yomima⌐su.
    paper this morning.
2. I'm reading this paper   Ke⌐sa ko⌐no siñbuñ (o) yo⌐nde (i)ma-
    this morning.   su.
3. I was reading this paper   Ke⌐sa ko⌐no siñbuñ (o) yo⌐nde (i)ma-
    this morning.   sita.
4. I read this paper this   Ke⌐sa ko⌐no siñbuñ (o) yomima⌐sita.
    morning.
5. Let's read this paper   Ke⌐sa ko⌐no siñbuñ (o) yomimasyo⌐o.
    this morning.
6. He's probably going to   Ke⌐sa ko⌐no siñbuñ (o) yo⌐mu desyoo.
    read this paper this
    morning.
7. He's probably reading   Ke⌐sa ko⌐no siñbuñ (o) yo⌐nde (i)⌐ru
    this paper this morn-   desyo⌐o.
    ing.
8. Do you suppose he's   Ke⌐sa ko⌐no siñbuñ (o) yo⌐nde (i)⌐ru
    reading this paper this   desyo⌐o ka.
    morning?
9. Shall we (or I) read this   Ke⌐sa ko⌐no siñbuñ (o) yomimasyo⌐o
    paper this morning?   ka.
10. Please read this paper   Ke⌐sa ko⌐no siñbuñ (o) yo⌐nde kuda-
    this morning.   sai.

---

[1] Note: X o ⌐ma⌐tu 'wait for X,' 'await X.'

D. Substitution Drill

1. I'm not especially busy.   Betu ni i⌐soḡa⌐siku a⌐rimase⌐ǹ.
2. I don't especially want to   Betu ni i⌐kitaku arimase⌐ǹ.
    go.
3. It doesn't especially mat-   Betu ni ka⌐maimase⌐ǹ.
    ter.
4. I'm not in any special   Betu ni i⌐soḡimase⌐ǹ.
    hurry.
5. It isn't especially strange.   Betu ni ⌐he⌐ǹ zya a⌐rimase⌐ǹ.
6. It isn't especially far.   Betu ni to⌐oku arimase⌐ǹ.
7. It isn't especially difficult.   Betu ni mu⌐zukasiku arimase⌐ǹ.
8. It isn't especially rude.   Betu ni si⌐tu⌐ree zya a⌐rimase⌐ǹ.

E. Substitution Drill

1. Nobody answers.   Da⌐re mo demase⌐ǹ.
2. Nobody knows. or I don't   Da⌐re mo sirimase⌐ǹ.
    know anybody.
3. Nobody understands.   Da⌐re mo wakarimase⌐ǹ.
4. Nobody can.   Da⌐re mo dekimase⌐ǹ.
5. Nobody is here.   Da⌐re mo imase⌐ǹ.
6. Nobody wants to do [it].   Da⌐re mo sitaku arimase⌐ǹ.
7. Nobody is busy.   Da⌐re mo isoḡa⌐siku a⌐rimase⌐ǹ.
8. Nobody is sick.   Da⌐re mo byooki zya arimase⌐ǹ.
9. Nobody is out (of the   Da⌐re mo ru⌐su zya a⌐rimase⌐ǹ.
    house).
10. Nobody has free time.   Da⌐re mo hima ḡa arimase⌐ǹ.

F. Substitution Drill

1. I know—because I have   Wa⌐takusi wa zo⌐ǹzite orimasu—
    Mr. Ito's card.   I⌐too-sañ no meesi (ḡa) gozaima⌐-
                                       su kara.

2. I know—because I read the   Wa⌐takusi wa zo⌐ǹzite orimasu—si-
    paper.   ⌐ǹbuñ (o) yomima⌐sita kara.

3. I know—because I looked at   Wa⌐takusi wa zo⌐ǹzite orimasu—de-
    the phone book.   ⌐ǹwatyoo (o) mima⌐sita kara.

4. I know—because I heard [it]   Wa⌐takusi wa zo⌐ǹzite orimasu—to-
    from a friend.   ⌐modati kara kikima⌐sita kara.

5. I know—because I studied   Wa⌐takusi wa zo⌐ǹzite orimasu—
    hard.   ⌐yo⌐ku be⌐ǹkyoo-sima⌐sita kara.

6. I know—because I asked a   Wa⌐takusi wa zo⌐ǹzite orimasu—
    policeman.   zyu⌐ǹsa ni kikima⌐sita kara.

7. I know—because I go there   Wa⌐takusi wa zo⌐ǹzite orimasu—
    a good deal.   ⌐yo⌐ku a⌐soko e mairima⌐su ka-
                                       ra.

8. I know—because I telephone   Wa⌐takusi wa zo⌐ǹzite orimasu—
    him every day.   a⌐no⌐ hito ni ⌐ma⌐initi de⌐ǹwa
                                       (o) kakema⌐su kara.

9. I know—because I come (or go) by car.

Wa˥takusi wa zo˥ñzite orimasu—ku-˥ruma de mairima˥su kara.

10. I know—because I was able to hear well.

Wa˥takusi wa zo˥ñzite orimasu—˥yo˥ku ki˥koema˥sita kara.

G. Substitution Drill

1. Call Mr. Okada—because he has a phone call.

Okada-kuñ (o) yoñde—de˥ñwa da˥ kara.

2. Call Mr. Okada—because this won't do.

Okada-kuñ (o) yoñde—ko˥ma˥ru kara.

3. Call Mr. Okada—because I want to see [him].

Okada-kuñ (o) yoñde—a˥ita˥i kara.

4. Call Mr. Okada—because I'm in a hurry.

Okada-kuñ (o) yoñde—i˥so˥ḡu kara.

5. Call Mr. Okada—because I want to talk [to him].

Okada-kuñ (o) yoñde—ha˥nasita˥i kara.

6. Call Mr. Okada—because it's out of order.

Okada-kuñ (o) yoñde—ko˥syoo da˥ kara.

7. Call Mr. Okada—because I'm going out for a minute.

Okada-kuñ (o) yoñde—tyo˥tto de-˥kakeru˥ kara.

8. Call Mr. Okada—because it's no good.

Okada-kuñ (o) yoñde—da˥me˥ da kara.

H. Substitution Drill

1. Please tell him that I'll be waiting in front of the Maru-biru. [1]

Ma˥ru-biru no ma˥e de ˥ma˥tte (i)ru kara, so˥o itte kudasa˥i.

2. Please tell him that I want to talk [to him] at (lit. from) about 3:30.

Sa˥ñ-zi-hañ-ḡo˥ro kara ha˥nasita˥i ka-ra, so˥o itte kudasa˥i.

3. Please tell him that I want to go home early today.

Kyo˥o ˥ha˥yaku ka˥erita˥i kara, so˥o itte kudasa˥i.

4. Please tell him that I'll tele-phone again later.

Ma˥ta a˥to de de˥ñwa-suru˥ kara, so˥o itte kudasa˥i.

5. Please tell him that I'm go-ing to the office by bus to-day.

Kyo˥o ka̅isya e ˥ba˥su de i˥ku˥ kara, so˥o itte kudasa˥i.

6. Please tell him that I'll be studying at home tonight.

Ko˥ñbañ u˥ti de beñkyoo-site (i)ru˥ ka-ra, so˥o itte kudasa˥i.

7. Please tell him that our car is out of order.

Uti no kuruma (wa) ko˥syoo da˥ kara, so˥o itte kudasa˥i.

---

[1] Lit. 'I'll be waiting in front of the Maru-biru so please say [it] that way.'

8. Please tell him that I'll   A⌐sita⌐ made i⌐soḡasi⌐i kara, so⌐o it-
    be busy through tomorrow.   te kudasa⌐i.
9. Please tell him that school   Ga⌐kkoo (wa) yo⌐-zi made da kara,
    lasts (lit. is) until 4.   so⌐o itte kudasa⌐i.
10. Please tell him that Mr. Ta-   Ta⌐naka-sañ (wa) koñḡetu yasumi⌐ da
    naka is on vacation this   kara, so⌐o itte kudasa⌐i.
    month.

I. Response Drill

    1. To⌐oi⌐ desu ka↵   Iie, to⌐oku arimase⌐ñ.
    2. He⌐ñ desu ka↵   Iie, he⌐ñ zya a⌐rimase⌐ñ.
    3. I⌐soḡasi⌐i desu ka↵   Iie, i⌐soḡa⌐siku a⌐rimase⌐ñ.
    4. A⌐na⌐ta (wa) ko⌐re (o) go⌐zo⌐-   Iie, zo⌐ñzimase⌐ñ.
       ñzi desu ka↵
    5. A⌐no ka⌐ta (wa) ko⌐re (o) go-   Iie, go⌐zo⌐ñzi zya a⌐rimase⌐ñ. [1]
       ⌐zo⌐ñzi desu ka↵
    6. Ko⌐syoo de⌐su ka↵   Iie, ko⌐syoo zya arimase⌐ñ.

J. Level Drill [2]

    1. Yu⌐kku⌐ri neḡaimasu.   Yu⌐kku⌐ri oneḡai-{ simasu.
                                                     { itasimasu.

    2. Yo⌐bimasyo⌐o ka.   O⌐yobi-{ simasyo⌐o } ka.
                                         { itasimasyo⌐o }

    3. Si⌐rimase⌐ñ.   Zo⌐ñzimase⌐ñ.
    4. Ke⌐sa da⌐iḡaku e ikima⌐sita.   Ke⌐sa da⌐iḡaku e mairima⌐sita.
    5. Si⌐tu⌐ree-simasita.   Si⌐tu⌐ree-itasimasita.
    6. Ta⌐naka-sañ ni aima⌐sita. Ta⌐naka-sañ ni ome ni kakarima⌐si-
                                 ta.
    7. O⌐de⌐ñwa si⌐masyo⌐o ka.   O⌐de⌐ñwa i⌐tasimasyo⌐o ka.
    8. So⌐o tutaema⌐su.   So⌐o otutae-{ sima⌐su.
                                             { itasima⌐su.

K. Level Drill [3]

    1. Kosyoo da ne?   (M)   Ko⌐syoo de⌐su ne?

---

[1] Compare the preceding humble answer (referring to the speaker) with this
honorific answer (referring to someone else).

[2] In each case, sentences on the right are humble equivalents of the sentences on the left.

[3] Based on Grammatical Note 2. In each case, the sentence on the right is
a formal equivalent of the sentence on the left. Informal sentences marked (M)
occur predominantly in men's speech and those marked (W) predominantly in
women's speech.

2. I⌐soḡasi⌐i?   I⌐soḡasi⌐i desu ka↲
3. He⌐ñ ⌐ne⌐e.   (W)   He⌐ñ desu ⌐ne⌐e.
4. I⌐ma ⌐tyo⌐tto dekakeru   (M)   I⌐ma ⌐tyo⌐tto de⌐kakema⌐su yo↲
   yo↲
5. Kikoeru?   Ki⌐koema⌐su ka↲
6. Wa⌐ru⌐i yo↲   (M)   Wa⌐ru⌐i desu yo↲
7. Do⌐re (o) ⌐yo⌐mu?   Do⌐re (o) yo⌐mima⌐su ka↲
8. So⌐o yo↲   (W)   So⌐o desu yo↲
9. Na⌐ñ de ⌐ki⌐ru?   Na⌐ñ de ki⌐rima⌐su ka↲
10. Zu⌐ibuñ tooi yo↲   (M)   Zu⌐ibuñ to⌐oi⌐ desu yo↲

L. Expansion Drill

1. Telephone. [1]   Deñwa-site.
   YOU telephone.   A⌐na⌐ta ḡa deñwa-site.
   [I] am busy so YOU tele-   I⌐soḡasi⌐i kara, a⌐na⌐ta ḡa deñwa-si-
   phone.   te.
   [I] am very busy so YOU   To⌐ttemo isoḡasi⌐i kara, a⌐na⌐ta ḡa
   telephone.   deñwa-site.
   I am very busy so YOU   Bo⌐ku wa to⌐ttemo isoḡasi⌐i kara,
   telephone.   a⌐na⌐ta ḡa deñwa site.

2. Would you speak?   Ha⌐na⌐site ku⌐dasaimase⌐ñ ka↲
   Would you speak in a loud   O⌐oki na ⌐ko⌐e de ha⌐na⌐site ku⌐da-
   voice?   saimase⌐ñ ka↲
   Would you speak in a louder   Mo⌐tto ⌐o⌐oki na ⌐ko⌐e de ha⌐na⌐site
   voice?   ku⌐dasaimase⌐ñ ka↲
   I can't hear so would you   Ki⌐koemase⌐ñ kara, mo⌐tto ⌐o⌐oki na
   speak in a louder voice?   ⌐ko⌐e de ha⌐na⌐site ku⌐dasaima-
                                           se⌐ñ ka↲
   I can't hear very well so   Yo⌐ku ki⌐koemase⌐ñ kara, mo⌐tto
   would you speak in a   ⌐o⌐oki na ⌐ko⌐e de ha⌐na⌐site ku-
   louder voice?   ⌐dasaimase⌐ñ ka↲

3. It's all right (I tell you).   Da⌐izyo⌐obu desu yo↲
   Now it's all right (I tell   I⌐ma wa da⌐izyo⌐obu desu yo↲
   you).
   It was out of order but   Ko⌐syoo de⌐sita ḡa, i⌐ma wa da⌐i-
   now it's all right (I   zyo⌐obu desu yo↲
   tell you).
   Yesterday it was out of   Ki⌐no⌐o wa ko⌐syoo de⌐sita ḡa, i⌐ma
   order but now it's all   wa da⌐izyo⌐obu desu yo↲
   right (I tell you).

---

[1] This English sentence and its Japanese equivalent are equally abrupt.

4. It can't be heard, can   Ki⌐koemase⌝n̄ ⌐ne⁴e.
    it!
    [He] speaks in a low voice,   Ti⌝isa na ⌐ko⁴e de ha⌐na⁴su kara,
    so you can't hear [him]   ki⌐koemase⌝n̄ ⌐ne⁴e.
    (isn't that so)!
    [He] always speaks in a low   I⌝tu mo ⌐ti⌝isa na ⌐ko⁴e de ha⌐na⁴su
    voice so you can't hear   kara, ki⌐koemase⌝n̄ ⌐ne⁴e.
    [him] (isn't that so)!
    He always speaks in a low   A⌐no⌝ hito (wa) ⌐i⌝tu mo ⌐ti⌝isa na
    voice so you can't hear   ⌐ko⁴e de ha⌐na⁴su kara, ki⌐koe-
    [him] (isn't that so)!   mase⌝n̄ ⌐ne⁴e.

5. I'll convey [the message].   O⌐tutae-sima⌝su.
    I'll convey [it] all.   Ze⌝n̄bu otutae-simasu.
    I'll convey all of that.   Sore (o) ⌐ze⌝n̄bu otutae-simasu.
    I'll convey all of that by   Den̄wa de sóre (o) ⌐ze⌝n̄bu otutae-
    telephone.   simasu.
    I'll convey all of that by   I⌝ma dén̄wa de sóre (o) ⌐ze⌝n̄bu otu-
    telephone now.   tae-simasu.

6. Would you say [it]?   O⌐ssya⌝tte ku⌐dasaimase⁴n̄ ka↵
    Would you say [it] once   Mo⌐o iti-do ossya⌝tte ku⌐dasaima-
    more?   se⁴n̄ ka↵
    I didn't understand so would   Wa⌐karimase⌝n̄ desita kara, mo⌐o
    you say [it] once more?   iti-do ossya⌝tte ku⌐dasaimase⁴n̄
                                   ka↵
    I didn't understand your   O⌐namae (ḡa) wakarimase⌝n̄ desita
    name so would you say   kara, mo⌐o iti-do ossya⌝tte ku⌐da-
    [it] once more?   saimase⁴n̄ ka↵
    I'm sorry but I didn't under- Su⌐mimase⌝n̄ ḡa; o⌐namae (ḡa) waka-
    stand your name so would   rimase⌝n̄ desita kara, mo⌐o iti-do
    you say it once more?   ossya⌝tte ku⌐dasaimase⁴n̄ ka↵

SHORT INFORMAL DIALOGUES

(M = man; W = woman; X = either)

1. X(1): Iku?
    X(2): Iku.

2. X: I⌝i?
    M: Da⌐me⌝ da yo.

3. W: Ki⌝ree ⌐ne⌝e.
    M: So⌝o da ⌐ne⌝e.

4. X: Wa⌐ka⌝ru?
    M: Wa⌐ka⌝ru yo↵

5. X: Kosyoo?
    W: So⌝o yo↵

6. M: He⁷n da ˥ne⁴e.
   W: So⁷o ˥ne⁴e.

7. X: Sore ⌐do⁷o?
   M: O⌐mosiro⁷i yo⌐

8. M(1): Sore ⌐na⁷ni?
   M(2): A⌐tarasi⁷i deñwatyoo.
   M(1): Tyo⁷tto ˥mi⁴sete. . . . O⌐oki⁷i ⌐ne⁷e.
   M(2): So⁷o da ⌐ne⁷e.

9. M(1): Tyo⁷tto, ta⁷kusii yo˥bu⁴ kara, koko de ⌐ma⁷tte te.¹
   M(2): Bo⌐ku ḡa deñwa-suru⁷ kara.
   M(1): I⁷i yo. Boku ḡa suru yo.

10. X: Su⁷misu-sañ sítte ru?
    M: E⁷e, yo⁷ku.
    X: A⌐no⁷ hito nǐhoñḡo de⌐ki⁷ru?
    M: Na⌐kanaka yo⁷ku de˥ki⁴ru yo⌐ Yo-⌐neñ-ḡu⁷rai ˥ma⁴e kara be˥ñkyoo
       site ru⁴ kara.

SUPPLEMENTARY TELEPHONE CONVERSATIONS

1. Jones: Mo⁷simosi⌐
   Secretary: Ni⌐hoñḡo-ga⁷kkoo de gozaimasu.
   Jones: Ta⌐isi⁷kañ no ⌐Zyo⁷oñzu desu ḡa; kyo⁷o wa ga⌐kkoo e iki-
                mase⁷ñ ² kara, Sa⁷too-sañ ni so⁷o itte kudasa⁷i.
   Secretary: Wa⌐karima⁷sita. Do⁷o mo a⌐ri⁷ḡatoo gozaimasita.
   Jones: O⌐neḡai-sima⁷su. Sayonara.

2. Mr. Matsumoto: Mo⁷simosi⌐ Ta⁷mura-sañ no o˥taku de⁴su ka⌐
   Mrs. Tamura: Ha⁷i. Sa⌐yoo de gozaima⁷su.
   Mr. Matsumoto: Kotira wa Ma⁷tumoto de⁷su ḡa; su⌐mimase⁷ñ ḡa, otonari
                  no ⌐U⁷eno ⌐Ha⁷ruko- sañ o yo˥ñde kudasaimase⁷ñ ka⌐
   Mrs. Tamura: Ha⁷i. Syo⁷osyoo o˥mati-kudasaima⁷se.

   Miss Ueno: Mo⁷simosi. O⌐matase-itasima⁷sita.
   Mr. Matsumoto: Aa, Ha⌐ruko-sañ? Bo⁷ku desu. O⌐ge⁷ñki?
   Miss Ueno: E⁷e. A⌐na⁷ta mo?

---

¹ Matte (i)te 'be waiting,' 'stay here and wait.'

² Compare Japanese gakkoo e IKIMASEN (lit. 'I'm not going to school') and
English 'I'm not COMING to school (where you are).'

Mr. Matsumoto: Ko⌐ñbañ o̅hima?
Miss Ueno: E⌐e. Hi⌐ma de⌐su g̅a⌐
Mr. Matsumoto: Ni⌐tig̅eki[1] e ikimase⌐ñ ka⌐
Miss Ueno: A⌐ri⌐g̅atoo. Na⌐ñ-zi kara?
Mr. Matsumoto: Go-⌐zi-ha⌐ñ kara. Go⌐-zi ni o⌐taku e ikima⌐su yo.
Miss Ueno: Zya⌐a, ma⌐tte masu kara, o⌐neg̅ai-sima⌐su.
Mr. Matsumoto: Zya⌐a, ma⌐ta a⌐to de.
Miss Ueno: E⌐e. Notihodo ne? Do⌐o mo a⌐ri⌐g̅atoo.
Mr. Matsumoto: Sayonara.
Miss Ueno: Sayonara.

3. Mr. Yamada: Mo⌐simosi⌐
    Maid: Mo⌐simosi⌐   Ya⌐mada de gozaima⌐su. [2]
    Mr. Yamada: Yo⌐si-sañ?
    Maid: Ha⌐a, sa⌐yoo de gozaima⌐su. Da⌐ñnasa⌐ma de irassyai-
                  masu ka⌐
    Mr. Yamada: E⌐e, bo⌐ku. O⌐kusañ iru?
    Maid: Iie, tyo⌐tto o⌐dekake ni narima⌐sita g̅a⌐
    Mr. Yamada: A⌐a, so⌐o. Ano ne? Ko⌐ñbañ ne?
    Maid: Ha⌐a.
    Mr. Yamada: A⌐merika-taisi⌐kañ no ⌐Su⌐misu-sañ no o⌐taku e iku⌐ ka-
                  ra ne?
    Maid: Ha⌐a.
    Mr. Yamada: O⌐kusañ ni so⌐o itte⌐ yo.
    Maid: Ha⌐a, o⌐tutae-itasima⌐su. Na⌐ñ-zi-g̅o⌐ro o⌐kaeri ni nari-
                  ma⌐su ka⌐
    Mr. Yamada: Zyu⌐uiti-zi sug̅i⌐ ni ⌐na⌐ru yo.
    Maid: Ha⌐a, wa⌐karima⌐sita.
    Mr. Yamada: Zya⌐a.
    Maid: Go⌐meñ-kudasaima⌐se.

English Equivalents

1. Jones: Hello.
    Secretary: This is the Japanese Language School.
    Jones: This is [Mr.] Jones from the Embassy. Please tell Mr.
                 Sato that I'm not coming to school today.
    Secretary: Certainly. Thank you very much [for calling].
    Jones: Please take care of this for me. Goodbye.

---

[1] Abbreviated name of Nihoñ-gekizyoo, a theater in Tokyo.

[2] A maid usually answers the telephone with the name of her employer.

2. Mr. Matsumoto: Hello. Is this the Tamura residence?
   Mrs. Tamura: Yes, it is.
   Mr. Matsumoto: This is [Mr.] Matsumoto. I'm sorry to bother you but would you call Miss Haruko Ueno (who lives) next door?
   Mrs. Tamura: Yes. Just a moment, please.

   . . . . .

   Miss Ueno: Hello. (I'm sorry to have kept you waiting.)
   Mr. Matsumoto: Oh, Haruko? It's me. How are you?
   Miss Ueno: Fine. And you?
   Mr. Matsumoto: Are you free tonight?
   Miss Ueno: Yes, I'm free but [why do you ask?]
   Mr. Matsumoto: Would you like to go to the Nichigeki?
   Miss Ueno: Thanks. (From) what time?
   Mr. Matsumoto: (From) 5:30. I'll come to your house at 5.
   Miss Ueno: Well, I'll be waiting so do [come].
   Mr. Matsumoto: Well, [I'll talk to you] again later.
   Miss Ueno: Yes, later (right?). Thanks very much.
   Mr. Matsumoto: Goodbye.
   Miss Ueno: Goodbye.

3. Mr. Yamada: Hello.
   Maid: Hello. This is the Yamada residence.
   Mr. Yamada: Yoshi?
   Maid: Yes. Is this Mr. [Yamada]?
   Mr. Yamada: Yes, it's me. Is Mrs. [Yamada] in?
   Maid: No. She went out for a while but [is there anything I can do?]
   Mr. Yamada: Oh. Say! Tonight—
   Maid: Yes.
   Mr. Yamada: I'm going to the home of Mr. Smith from the American Embassy so—
   Maid: Yes.
   Mr. Yamada: Tell Mrs. [Yamada] (that).
   Maid: Yes. I'll give her the message. About what time will you be home?
   Mr. Yamada: It will be after 11.
   Maid: I understand.
   Mr. Yamada: Well then. . . .
   Maid: Goodbye.

EXERCISES

1. Make the following telephone calls:

   a. Call the Tanaka home and ask if Mrs. Tanaka is in.
   b. Call the American Embassy and leave a message for Mr. Smith that you are not coming today.
   c. Call your home and tell the maid that you are going to the Satos' house and will be home about 11:30.

    d. Call a friend and ask her to go to the Nichigeki with you. Tell her you'll come to her house at 2:30.

    e. Call Mr. Sato's house and ask Mr. Sato to call (i.e. summon) Mr. Yoshio Ito who lives next door. [1]

    f. Call Mr. Yamamoto's house and ask when Mr. Yamamoto is returning to Tokyo.

    g. Report that Extension 636 is out of order and request that it be fixed.

2. Leave the following telephone messages for Mr. Yoshida:

    a. You'll be waiting in front of the Nichigeki at 6 this evening.

    b. You want to see him before 3 o'clock today.

    c. You are leaving the office early today because your wife is sick.

    d. You'll telephone him from Osaka tomorrow morning at about 10:30.

    e. You'll be at Tokyo University today until 5:30.

    f. Your new office telephone number is 481-7600.

    g. Mr. Smith arrived at Yokohama last night and is now at the Imperial Hotel.

3. Practice the conversations preceding the Exercises, using other politeness and/or formality levels.

4. Practice the Basic Dialogues with appropriate variations.

---

[1] This is normal procedure when someone does not have a telephone.

Lesson 14. Eating and Drinking

BASIC DIALOGUES: FOR MEMORIZATION

(a)

(Tanaka has taken Smith to a restaurant)

Waitress

already or yet or now   mo⌐o /+ affirmative/
already or soon now
place an order   tyuumoñ-suru or
                                   tyuumoñ-itasu ⌐ or
                                   go⌐tyuumoñ-nasa⌐ru↑
1. Have you ordered yet?   Mo⌐o go⌐tyuumoñ-nasaima⌐sita ka⌐

Tanaka

it is yet [to happen]   ma⌐da da
not yet   ma⌐da /+ negative/
2. No, not yet.   Iie, ma⌐da desu.
                              or
No, I haven't (ordered yet). Iie, ma⌐da tyu⌐umoñ-simase⌐ñ.

Waitress

into what?   na⌐ñ ni or
                                 na⌐ni ni
3. What would you like?   Na⌐ñ ni i⌐tasimasyo⌐o ka.
    (Lit. Into what shall I make
    [it]?)

Tanaka (to Smith)

thing   mo⌐no⌐
eat   ta⌐be⌐ru /-ru/ or
                                itadaku ↑ /-u/ or
                                mesiaḡaru↑ /-u/
4. What (kind of things) shall   Do⌐ñna mo⌐no⌐ (o) ta⌐bemasyo⌐o
    we eat?   ka.

Smith

5. What WOULD be good?   Na⌐ni ḡa yo⌐rosi⌐i desyoo ka ⌐ne⌐e.

Waitress

tempura (kind of Japa-   teñpura
    nese food)
6. How about tempura?   Teñpura (wa) i⌐ka⌐ḡa de go⌐zaima-
                                syo⌐o ka.

Tanaka (to Smith)

into tempura   teñpura ni
make it tempura or   teñpura ni suru
    decide on tempura
7. Shall we decide on tempura?   Te⌐ñpura ni simasyo⌝o ka.

Smith

8. That will be fine!   Ke⌝kkoo desu ⌐ne⌝e.

Tanaka (to waitress)

9. Then let's make [it] that   Zya, so⌐o simasyo⌝o.
    (way).

    Japanese rice wine   sake or
                                           osake +
    bring (of things)   mo⌐tte ku⌝ru
10. And please bring some sake   Sore kara, sa⌐ke mo motte⌝ kite
    too.   kudasai.

(to Smith)

is cold (of weather)   sa⌐mu⌝i /-ku/
is hot   a⌐tu⌝i /-ku/
is delicious   oisii /-ku/
11. It's cold so hot sake will   Sa⌐mu⌝i kara, a⌐tu⌝i sake (wa) o⌐i-
    probably taste good, won't   si⌝i desyoo ne?
    it?

(b)

(Tanaka has invited Smith to have something to drink with him)

Tanaka

beer   bi⌝iru
drink   no⌝mu /-u/ or
                                           itadaku⌐/-u/   or
                                           mesiaḡaru⌐/-u/
12. Will you have some beer?   Bi⌝iru (o) me⌐siaḡarima⌐su ka⌐

Smith

13. Thank you. I will (drink).   A⌐ri⌝ḡatoo gozaimasu. I⌐tadakima⌝-
                                           su.

Tanaka (to waitress)

14. Two bottles of beer, please.   Bi⌝iru (o) ⌐ni⌝-hoñ oneḡai-simasu.
    (Lit. I'd like beer to the ex-
    tent of two long, cylindrical
    units.)

Tanaka (when beer is brought)

15. Here you are.   Do⌝ozo.

Smith

16. (I'll have some.)   I⌐tadakima⌐su.

    is cold   tumetai /-ku/
17. Isn't it delicious—cold   O⌐isi⌐i desu ⌐ne⌐e—tu⌐metai bi⌐iru
    beer!   wa.

. . .

Tanaka

    one glassful <u>or</u> cupful   i⌐p-pai
18. How about another glass?   Mo⌐o i⌐p-pai i⌐ka⌐g̃a desu ka⌐

Smith

    half   ha⌐n̄bu⌐n̄
19. Well, just half, please.   Zya⌐a, ha⌐n̄buñ dake onegai-sima⌐su.

. . .

Tanaka

20. Won't you have a little   Mo⌐o suko⌐si me⌐siag̃arimase⌐n̄
    more?   ka⌐

Smith

21. No, thank you. (Lit. No,   Iie, mo⌐o ta⌐kusa⌐n̄ desu.
    already it's a lot <u>or</u> fine.)   <u>or</u>
                                          Iie, mo⌐o ⌐ke⌐kkoo desu.

    a feast <u>or</u> delicious   gotisoo   <u>or</u>
    food and/or drink   gotisoosama[+]
22. It was delicious.   Go⌐tisoosama de⌐sita.

(c)

(Smith and Yamamoto meet on the street)

Yamamoto

    is pale   a⌐o⌐i /-ku/
    face <u>or</u> expression   kao
    be pale   a⌐o⌐i kao o suru
23. Mr. Smith. You're pale!   Su⌐misu-sañ. A⌐o⌐i ka⌐o (o) site
                                          (i)ma⌐su yo⌐

24. What happened?   Do⌐o simasita ka.

Smith

    shrimp <u>or</u> prawn   ebi
    shrimp tempura   ebi no teñpura
    become spoiled   i⌐ta⌐mu /-u/
    became spoiled (informal)   i⌐ta⌐n̄da
    spoiled shrimp   i⌐ta⌐n̄da ebi
    it was shrimp (informal)   e⌐bi da⌐tta
25. Last night I ate shrimp tem-   Yuube Gin̄za de e⌐bi no teñpura (o)
    pura in the Ginza (but) I got   tabema⌐sita g̃a; i⌐ta⌐n̄da e⌐bi da⌐tta
    sick because it was bad   kara, byo⌐oki ni narima⌐sita yo.
    shrimp.

Yamamoto

26. That's too bad.   I⌐kemase⌐n̄ ⌐ne⌐e.

Smith

medicine   kusuri
take (of medicine)   no⌐mu /-u/
get well or recover   na⌐o⌐ru /-u/
27. I took some medicine but   Ku⌐suri (o) nomima⌐sita ḡa, ma⌐da
    I'm not better (lit. I have-   na⌐orimase⌐n̄.
    n't recovered) yet.

Yamamoto

28. Take care of yourself.   Odaizi ni.

(d)

(Tanaka and Smith are in a tea shop)

Smith

make a request or   ta⌐no⌐mu /-u/
  place an order
requested or ordered   ta⌐no⌐nda
  (informal)
probably requested or or-   ta⌐no⌐nda desyoo
  dered
29. You ordered a long time ago,   Zu⌐ibun̄ ⌐ma⌐e ni ta⌐no⌐nda desyoo?
    didn't you?

Tanaka

30. Yes. I ordered about ten   E⌐e. Mo⌐o zyu⌐p-pun̄-ḡu⌐rai ⌐ma⌐e
    minutes ago (already) but   ni ta⌐nomima⌐sita ḡa, ma⌐da mo⌐tte
    they haven't brought [it]   kimase⌐n̄ ⌐ne⌐e.
    yet, have they!

Smith

31. They'll probably bring it   Mo⌐o mo⌐tte ku⌐ru desyoo ḡa, o⌐so⌐i
    soon now but they are   desu ⌐ne⌐e.
    slow, aren't they!

(e)

(Two friends are talking)

Tanaka

ate (informal)   ta⌐beta
32. Did you eat that?   A⌐re ta⌐beta?

Yamamoto

too much or so much   an̄mari / + affirmative/
is spicy or salty   ka⌐ra⌐i /-ku/
was spicy or salty (in-   ka⌐rakatta
  formal)
33. No, because it was too spicy.   Iie, an̄mari ⌐ka⌐rakatta kara.

Tanaka

34. It was spicy?   Ka⌐rakatta?

Yamamoto

 yeah   ñ [1]
 is bad-tasting   ma⌐zu⌐i /-ku/
 was bad-tasting (in-   ma⌐zukatta
  formal)
35. Yeah. It tasted awful!   N̄. To⌐ttemo ma⌐zukatta yo.

(f)

Tanaka

36. How about a cigarette?   Ta⌐bako do⌐o desu ka↵

Smith

 smoke   no⌐mu /-u/ or
              suu /-u/
37. No, I don't smoke.   Iie, no⌐mimase⌐ñ.

Tanaka

38. You don't smoke? Since   No⌐mimase⌐ñ ka↵ I⌐tu kara desu
 when?   ka↵

Smith

 last month   se⌐ñḡetu
 quit or give up   yameru /-ru/
39. Why, I quit last month.   Se⌐ñḡetu ya⌐mema⌐sita yo.

ADDITIONAL EATING AND DRINKING VOCABULARY [2]

1. Shall we eat at a Ginza   Gi⌐ñza no teñpuraya de tabemasyo⌐o
 tempura shop?   ka.

  dining room   syokudoo
  noodle shop   so⌐ba⌐ya or osobaya +
  restaurant (Japanese style)   ryo⌐ori⌐ya
  restaurant (Western style)   re⌐sutorañ

---

[1] Man's word, informal.

[2] Drill on the new words by substituting them for the underlined word in the
pattern sentence.

sushi shop	su⌐si⌐ya or osusiya +
tearoom	kissateñ [1]

2. I'd like a little more
   shrimp.

   Ebi (o) mo⌐o suko⌐si oneḡai-
   simasu.

fish	sakana or osakana +
meat	ni⌐ku⌐ or o⌐ni⌐ku +
fowl or chicken	tori
egg	ta⌐ma⌐ḡo
vegetable	yasai or o⌐ya⌐sai +
fruit	ku⌐da⌐mono
cooked rice or food	go⌐hañ
uncooked rice	ko⌐me⌐ or okome +
bread and butter	pa⌐ñ to ⌐ba⌐ta
toast	to⌐osuto
cake or sweets	o⌐ka⌐si +
noodles	so⌐ba or o⌐so⌐ba +
sashimi (raw fish)	sa⌐simi⌐ or osasimi +
sushi (rice with fish, sea-weed, egg, etc.)	su⌐si or o⌐su⌐si +
sukiyaki (stew of vegetables with meat or chicken or fish)	sukiyaki
tempura (batter-fried fish and vegetables)	teñpura
sugar	sa⌐to⌐o or osatoo +
salt	si⌐o⌐ or o⌐si⌐o +
pepper	ko⌐syo⌐o
soy sauce	syooyu or osyooyu +

3. Please bring some sake.

   Sa⌐ke (o) motte⌐ kite kudasai.

cold water	mizu or omizu +
hot water	oyu +
coffee	ko⌐ohi⌐i
tea	otya +
black tea	kootya
milk	mi⌐ruku or gyuunyuu
ice	koori

4. Don't you want a knife?

   Na⌐ihu wa i⌐rimase⌐ñ ka⌐

fork	ho⌐oku
spoon	su⌐pu⌐uñ

---

[1] With kissateñ, substitute no⌐mimasyo⌐o for ta⌐bemasyo⌐o in the pattern sentence. Alternate accent: ki⌐ssa⌐teñ.

chopsticks	ha˺si or o˹ha˺si +
dish	sara or osara +
bowl	wañ or owañ +
napkin	na˺pukiñ
tray	oboñ +
glass for drinking	koppu
cup or small bowl (Japanese style)	tyawañ or o˹tya˺wañ +
cup (with handles)	ko˹ohiizya˺wañ

5. It's so spicy that it doesn't taste good. — A˺ñmari kara˺i kara, o˹isiku arimase˺ñ.

is weak or thin (of liquids) or is light (of colors)	usui /-ku/
is strong or thick (of liquids) or is dark (of colors)	ko˺i /-ku/
is sweet or sugary or insufficiently salted	amai /-ku/
is bitter	ni˹ga˺i /-ku/
is acid or sour	su˹ppa˺i /-ku/

NOTES ON THE BASIC DIALOGUES

1. Tyuumoñ (honorific, gotyuumoñ †) is a c o m m o n l y occurring nominal. Example: Gotyuumoñ wa? 'Your order?'

4. Mo˹no˺ refers to things that are tangible.

   Ta˹be˺ru 'eat' has a second honorific equivalent, o˹tabe ni na˺ru, which is less common than—and not quite as polite as—mesiaḡaru. Both honorific equivalents are, of course, used only in polite speech, in reference to the action of someone other than the speaker. Conversely, the humble equivalent refers to the action of the speaker, in polite speech.

10. Mo˹tte ku˺ru means literally 'come holding' or 'come carrying.' Mo˺tte is the gerund of the verbal mo˺tu 'hold,' 'have,' 'own.' Note also motte iku 'take (something somewhere)' (lit. 'go holding'). The polite equivalents of these words are: humble (†), mo˹tte ma˺iru honorific (†), mo˹tte irassya˺ru and mo˹tte oide ni na˺ru.

12. No˺mu 'drink' has a second honorific equivalent, o˹nomi ni na˺ru, which is not quite as polite as mesiaḡaru. See the note on Sentence 4 above.

16. A guest always says i˹tadakima˺su (or an equivalent) just before beginning to eat or drink.

17. Tumetai is the general term meaning 'is cold,' but it is rarely used in reference to weather or atmosphere. Sa˹mu˺i, on the other hand, refers only to weather and a t m o s p h e r e . A˺tu˺i is the opposite of b o t h words.

21. The second alternative is more polite. Both are refusals of second or later helpings. Ke⌐kkoo desu (without mo⌐o) is a commonly occurring polite refusal of a first offering. I⌐i and yorosii are also used as refusals in the same kinds of patterns.

22. Go⌐tisoosama (de⌐sita) is regularly said, upon finishing eating or drinking, by a guest to his host, or by a person served to the person who prepared or served the food and/or drink.   It is also said by a guest at the conclusion of a visit during which refreshments were served.

29. Ta⌐no⌐mu 'make a request' is a verbal of more general meaning than tyuumoñ-suru 'place an order for something.' The thing requested is followed by particle o (or wa); the person of whom the request is made is followed by particle ni (i.e. the request is made TO someone). Compare:

I asked Mr. Tanaka (= I asked him a question):
   Ta⌐naka-sañ ni kikima⌐sita.
and
I asked Mr. Tanaka (= I asked him to do something):
   Ta⌐naka-sañ ni tanomima⌐sita.

Ta⌐no⌐mu [yo] is used by men as a plain informal equivalent of o⌐neḡai-sima⌐su.

Eating and Drinking Vocabulary:

In general, where alternate forms are given, women almost invariably use the polite alternant, whereas men use either, depending on the level of politeness being used.   In a few cases—for example, otya 'tea' (the drink) and oyu 'hot water'—the polite form is regularly used by both men and women.

GRAMMATICAL NOTES

1. Verbals: Informal Past

The informal past of a verbal is made by changing the final -e of the gerund to -a. Thus, the informal past always ends in -ta or -da. It is the exact equivalent of the -ma⌐sita form except that it is informal. The informal past and the gerund regularly have the same accent. Examples:

Informal Non-past (Citation Form)	Gerund	Informal Past	Formal Past
(-ru): ta⌐be⌐ru 'eat'	ta⌐bete	ta⌐beta	ta⌐bema⌐sita
mi⌐ru 'see'	mi⌐te	mi⌐ta	mi⌐ma⌐sita
(-u): ma⌐tu 'wait'	ma⌐tte	ma⌐tta	ma⌐tima⌐sita
ka⌐eru 'return'	ka⌐ette	ka⌐etta	ka⌐erima⌐sita
kau 'buy'	katte	katta	ka⌐ima⌐sita
ha⌐na⌐su 'talk'	ha⌐na⌐site	ha⌐na⌐sita	ha⌐nasima⌐sita
ka⌐ku 'write'	ka⌐ite	ka⌐ita	ka⌐kima⌐sita
iku 'go'	itte (irreg.)	itta	i⌐kima⌐sita

i⌐so⌐gu 'be in a hurry'	i⌐so⌐ide	i⌐so⌐ida	i⌐sogima⌐sita
yobu 'call'	yoñde	yoñda	yo⌐bima⌐sita
yo⌐mu 'read'	yo⌐ñde	yo⌐ñda	yo⌐mima⌐sita
(-aru): o⌐ssya⌐ru † 'say'	o⌐ssya⌐tte	o⌐ssya⌐tta	o⌐ssyaima⌐sita
(Ir-reg.): ku⌐ru 'come	ki⌐te⌐	ki⌐ta 1	ki⌐ma⌐sita
suru 'do'	site	sita	si⌐ma⌐sita

2. Adjectivals: Informal and Formal Past

The informal past of an adjectival is made by dropping the final -i of the non-past and adding -katta. If the non-past is unaccented, the past is regularly accented on the syllable immediately preceding the -katta; if the non-past is accented, the past is also accented but usually on an earlier syllable. 2

Examples:

Informal Non-past (Citation Form)	Informal Past
amai 'is sweet'	a⌐ma⌐katta 'was sweet'
a⌐tu⌐i 'is hot'	a⌐tukatta 'was hot'
hu⌐ru⌐i 'is old'	hu⌐rukatta 'was old'
muzukasii 'is difficult'	mu⌐zukasi⌐katta 'was difficult'
ti⌐isa⌐i 'is small'	ti⌐isakatta 'was small'
ikitai 'wants to go'	i⌐kita⌐katta 'wanted to go'

The comparatively rare formal past consisting of an adjectival in its -i form + formal desita (for example, ta⌐ka⌐i desita 'it was expensive') has already been mentioned in Lesson 3, Grammatical Note 3(c). Another formal past adjectival pattern consists of an informal past adjectival ending in -katta + formal desu.

Examples:

	Informal Past	Formal Past
'was sweet'	a⌐ma⌐katta	a⌐ma⌐katta desu
'was hot'	a⌐tukatta	a⌐tukatta desu
'was old'	hu⌐rukatta	hu⌐rukatta desu
'was difficult'	mu⌐zukasi⌐katta	mu⌐zukasi⌐katta desu

---

1 Note the difference in accent between this form and the gerund.

2 However, an accented -tai word is accented on the -ta- syllable in both the non-past and the past: ta⌐beta⌐i 'want to eat,' ta⌐beta⌐katta 'wanted to eat.'

3. Copula: Informal Past

The past of <u>da</u> is da⌐tta. It is the informal equivalent of de⌐sita, but like
<u>da</u>, it follows nominals and particles but does NOT occur immediately after
verbals or adjectivals. It regularly loses its accent following an accented
word or phrase.

Examples:

Informal Non-past	Informal Past	Formal Past
tomodati da 'it's a friend'	to⌐modati da⌐tta 'it was a friend'	to⌐modati de⌐sita
tomodati kara da 'it's from a friend'	to⌐modati kara da⌐tta 'it was from a friend'	to⌐modati kara de⌐sita

Now study the following chart:

	Affirmative Past Inflectional Patterns	
	Formal	Informal
Verbal Pattern	Verbal ending in -ma⌐sita (wa⌐karima⌐sita)	Verbal ending in -ta (wa⌐ka⌐tta)
Adjectival Pattern	Adjectival ending in: -katta + desu (o⌐okikatta desu) or -i + desita (o⌐oki⌐i desita)	Adjectival ending in: -katta (o⌐okikatta)
Nominal[1] Pattern	Nominal + de⌐sita (ho⌐ñ desita)	Nominal + da⌐tta (ho⌐ñ datta)

4. Uses of the Informal Past

In informal speech, the uses of verbal and adjectival informal past forms
parallel the uses of corresponding non-past forms, but there are some differences between the uses of non-past <u>da</u> and past da⌐tta.

The following are past equivalents of the non-past examples in Lesson 13,
Grammatical Note 2. Compare and study them carefully.

---

[1] With or without following particle.

	Formal	Informal— Men and Women
'It was clear.'	Waꜞkarimaꜞsita.	Waꜞkaꜞtta.
'Was it clear?'	Waꜞkarimaꜞsita ka⌣	Waꜞkaꜞtta?
'It was expensive.'	Taꜞkakatta desu.	Taꜞkakatta.
	(or Taꜞkaꜞi desita.)	
'Was it expensive?'	Taꜞkakatta desu ka⌣	Taꜞkakatta?
	(or Taꜞkaꜞi desita ka⌣)	
'It was true.'	Hoꜞntoo deꜞsita.	Hoꜞntoo daꜞtta.
'Was it true?'	Hoꜞntoo deꜞsita ka⌣	Hoꜞntoo daꜞtta?

		Informal — Men
'It was clear (I tell you).'	Waꜞkarimaꜞsita yo⌣	Waꜞkaꜞtta yo⌣
'It was clear, wasn't it?'	Waꜞkarimaꜞsita ne?	Waꜞkaꜞtta ne?
'It was expensive (I tell you).'	Taꜞkakatta desu yo⌣	Taꜞkakatta yo⌣
	(or Taꜞkaꜞi desita yo⌣)	
'It was expensive, wasn't it!'	Taꜞkakatta desu ꜛneꜛe.	Taꜞkakatta ꜛneꜛe.
	(or Taꜞkaꜞi desita ꜛneꜛe.)	
'It was true (I tell you).'	Hoꜞntoo deꜞsita yo⌣	Hoꜞntoo daꜞtta yo⌣
'It was true, wasn't it!'	Hoꜞntoo deꜞsita ꜛneꜛe.	Hoꜞntoo daꜞtta ꜛneꜛe.

In formal speech, the use of verbal and adjectival informal past forms before deꜞsyoꜞo, and of verbal, adjectival, and copula informal past forms before particle kara 'so' is parallel to that of corresponding non-past forms. The accentuation is also parallel. Thus:

> Informal (or formal[1]) past + formal tentative deꜞsyoꜞo = 'it probably happened or was true' or 'it probably has happened or has been true' (formal)

Examples:

> Iꜞtta desyoꜞo. 'He probably went.'
> Yoꜞnde (i)ta desyoo. 'He was probably reading.'
> Waꜞkarimaꜞsita desyoo? 'You understood, didn't you?'
> Taꜞkakatta desyoo? 'It was expensive, wasn't it?'
> Miꜞtaꜞkatta desyoo. 'He probably wanted to see [it].'
> Waꜞkaꜞtta desyoo ka. 'Do you suppose he understood?' or 'Did you understand?' (indirect)

---

[1] A formal verbal may also occur before formal deꜞsyoꜞo. The combination is more formal than an informal verbal + deꜞsyoꜞo. See the third example following.

Informal (or formal[1]) past + <u>kara</u> 'so' = 'so-and-so happened (<u>or</u> was true) so' or 'so-and-so has happened (<u>or</u> has been true) so'

Examples:

Kinoo ⌐yo⌐ku be⌐ñkyoo-sita⌐ kara, kyo⌐o wa ⌐yo⌐ku wakarimasu. 'I studied hard yesterday so today I understand well.'

Ta⌐kakatta kara, ka⌐imase⌐ñ desita. 'It was expensive so I didn't buy [it].'

Ma⌐zu⌐i ku⌐da⌐mono datta kara, a⌐ñmari tabemase⌐ñ desita. 'It was awful fruit so I didn't eat very much.'

In addition, the informal past <u>da⌐tta</u> (or, less commonly, formal <u>de⌐sita</u>) following a nominal or particle may occur before the formal tentative <u>de⌐syo⌐o</u> with the meaning 'it probably was <u>or</u> has been so-and-so.'

Thus:

Formal Non-past Tentative	Formal Past Tentative
To⌐modati desyo⌐o. 'He's probably a friend.'	To⌐modati da⌐tta desyoo. 'He was probably a friend.'
To⌐modati kara desyo⌐o. 'It's probably from a friend.'	To⌐modati kara da⌐tta desyoo. 'It was probably from a friend.'
Ho⌐ñtoo desyo⌐o. 'It's probably true.'	Ho⌐ñtoo de⌐sita desyoo? 'It was true, wasn't it?'

5. <u>mo⌐o</u> + Affirmative; <u>ma⌐da</u> + Negative

<u>Mo⌐o</u> plus an affirmative means 'already' or 'yet,' or 'now already,' 'now—after a change has taken place,' 'soon now.'

<u>Ma⌐da</u> plus a negative means 'not yet.' The non-past negative indicates that something has not happened up to the present moment (cf. Lesson 1, Grammatical Note 1).

<u>Ma⌐da</u> occurs in the <u>iie</u> answer to a <u>mo⌐o</u> question, and <u>mo⌐o</u> occurs in the <u>iie</u> answer to a <u>ma⌐da</u> question:

Tanaka-sañ wa ⌐mo⌐o ki⌐ma⌐sita ka⌐ 'Has Mr. Tanaka come already?'
Ha⌐i, mo⌐o ki⌐ma⌐sita. 'Yes, he's come already.'
Iie, ⌐ma⌐da ki⌐mase⌐ñ. 'No, he hasn't come yet.'

Tanaka-sañ wa ⌐ma⌐da ki⌐mase⌐ñ ka⌐ 'Hasn't Mr. Tanaka come yet?'
Ha⌐i, ⌐ma⌐da ki⌐mase⌐ñ. 'That's right. He hasn't come yet.'
Iie, ⌐mo⌐o ki⌐ma⌐sita. 'That's not right. He's already come.'

---

[1] A formal inflected form may also occur before <u>kara</u> in formal speech, as a more formal alternant. Many examples have already occurred.

Ma⌐da desu, meaning literally 'It is yet [to happen],' is the closest Japanese equivalent of English 'It hasn't happened yet'; 'Not yet.'

WARNING: Do not confuse the mo⌐o described above with moo (unaccented) occurring with immediately following numbers and indefinite quantity words, meaning 'more.' Compare the following examples:

      Mo⌐o su⌐ko⌐si ta⌐bema⌐sita. 'I've eaten a little, already.'

      Mo⌐o suko⌐si ta⌐bema⌐sita. 'I ate a little more.'

6. Goal Patterns with √suru

A nominal X + particle ni of goal + √suru[1] means 'make [something] into X,' 'make it X,' 'decide on X.' Compare the following pairs:

> A⌐sita simasyo⌐o. 'Let's do [it] tomorrow.'
> (Tells when we should do something)
>
> A⌐sita⌐ ni si⌐masyo⌐o. 'Let's make [it] tomorrow.' or
>   ' Let's decide on tomorrow.'
> (Tells what day we should decide on)

> So⌐o sima⌐sita. 'We did [it] that way.'
> So⌐re ni sima⌐sita. 'We decided on that one.'

> Hi⌐to⌐-tu si⌐masyo⌐o. 'Let's do one.'
>
> Hi⌐to⌐-tu ni si⌐masyo⌐o. 'Let's make [it] into one' (for example, several sentences into one lesson, or several small packages into one bundle, or all the dough into one cake, etc.)

Similarly, a waitress asks Na⌐ñ ni (i⌐ta)simasyo⌐o ka '(Into) what shall I make [your order]?'

Now reread Lesson 10, Grammatical Note 4.

If √na⌐ru, preceded by nominal + ni, or the -ku form of an adjectival, is replaced by the corresponding form of √suru, the English equivalent changes from 'become X' to 'make [it] X.' Study the following pairs:[2]

---

[1] Or, of course, a more polite alternative.

[2] The subjects and objects of the English equivalents will vary, as always, depending on the context.

{ Oʳnazi ni narimaˈsita.   'They have become the same.'
{ Oʳnazi ni simaˈsita.   'I made them the same.'

{ Naʳniiro ni narimaˈsita ka⌐   'What color did it become?'
{ Naʳniiro ni simaˈsita ka⌐   'What color did you make it?'

{ Oˈokiku naᵗrimaᵗsita.   'It has become big.'
{ Oˈokiku siᵗmaᵗsita.   'I made it big.'

{ Aˈtuku narimasu.   'It will become hot.'
{ Aˈtuku simasu.   'I will make it hot.'

7.   Counter -<u>hai</u>

Glassfuls and cupfuls are counted with the counter -<u>hai</u>, which combines with numerals of Series I. Numbers from one to ten are:

iˈp-pai '1 glassful <u>or</u> cupful'
niˈ-hai '2 glassfuls <u>or</u> cupfuls'
saˈñ-bai '3 glassfuls <u>or</u> cupfuls'
yoˈñ-hai '4 glassfuls <u>or</u> cupfuls'
go-hai '5 glassfuls <u>or</u> cupfuls'
roˈp-pai '6 glassfuls <u>or</u> cupfuls'
naʳnaˈ-hai <u>or</u> siᵗtiˈ-hai '7 glassfuls <u>or</u> cupfuls'
haˈp-pai <u>or</u> haᵗtiˈ-hai '8 glassfuls <u>or</u> cupfuls'
kyuˈu-hai '9 glassfuls <u>or</u> cupfuls'
ziˈp-pai <u>or</u> zyuˈp-pai '10 glassfuls <u>or</u> cupfuls'

naˈñ-bai 'how many glassfuls <u>or</u> cupfuls?'

DRILLS

A. Substitution Drill

1. Shall we decide on tem- pura?[1]	Teˈñpura ni simasyoˈo ka.
2. Shall we decide on suki- yaki?	<u>Su</u>ʳkiyaki ni simasyoˈo ka.
3. Shall we decide on sushi?	Oʳsuˈsi ni siᵗmasyoᵗo ka.
4. Shall we decide on noodles?	Oʳsoˈba ni siᵗmasyoᵗo ka.
5. Shall we decide on rice wine?	Saʳke ni simasyoˈo ka.

---

[1] Or 'Shall we (<u>or</u> I) make it tempura?'

6. Shall we decide on sa-
   shimi?
7. Shall we decide on beer?
8. Shall we decide on coffee?
9. Shall we decide on chick-
   en?
10. Shall we decide on fish?

Sa⌐simi⌐ ni si┝masyo┫o ka.

Bi˥iru ni si┝masyo┫o ka.
Ko⌐ohi˥i ni si┝masyo┫o ka.
To⌐ri ni simasyo˥o ka.

Sa⌐kana ni simasyo˥o ka.

B. Substitution Drill

1. Shall I make [it] hot?
2. It got hot.
3. It got cold.
4. I'll make [it] cold.
5. I'm going to make [it] into
   a school.
6. It has become a school.
7. It has become a company.
8. He'll probably make [it]
   into a company.
9. He'll probably make [it]
   cheap.
10. It will probably get cheap.

A˥tuku si┝masyo┫o ka.
A˥tuku na┝rima┫sita.
Tu⌐metaku narima˥sita.
Tu⌐metaku sima˥su yo⌐
Ga⌐kkoo ni sima˥su yo⌐

Ga⌐kkoo ni narima˥sita.
Ka⌐isya ni narima˥sita.
Ka⌐isya ni suru desyo˥o.

Ya˥suku su┝ru desyo┫o.

Ya˥suku ┝na┫ru desyoo.

C. Substitution Drill

1. I've been eating here for
   about two years now (already).
2. I've been eating here for
   about six months now.
3. I've been buying here for
   about six months now.
4. I've been buying here for
   about two weeks now.
5. I've been studying here
   for about two weeks now.
6. I've been studying here for
   about four hours now.
7. I've been reading here for
   about four hours now.
8. I've been reading here for
   about twenty minutes now.
9. I've been waiting here for
   about twenty minutes now.

Mo˥o ni-⌐neñ-g̃u˥rai kŏko de ⌐ta˥bete
(i)masu yo⌐
Mo˥o ro⌐k-kag̃etu-g̃u˥rai kŏko de
⌐ta˥bete (i)masu yo⌐
Mo˥o ro⌐k-kag̃etu-g̃u˥rai kŏko de
ka˥tte (i)ma˥su yo⌐
Mo˥o ni-⌐syuukañ-g̃u˥rai kŏko de ka-
⌐tte (i)ma˥su yo⌐
Mo˥o ni-⌐syuukañ-g̃u˥rai kŏko de be-
⌐ñkyoo-site (i)ma˥su yo⌐
Mo˥o yo-⌐zikañ-g̃u˥rai kŏko de be⌐ñ-
kyoo-site (i)ma˥su yo⌐
Mo˥o yo-⌐zikañ-g̃u˥rai kŏko de ⌐yo˥-
ñde (i)masu yo⌐
Mo˥o ni⌐zip-puñ-g̃u˥rai kŏko de ⌐yo˥-
ñde (i)masu yo⌐
Mo˥o ni⌐zip-puñ-g̃u˥rai kŏko de ⌐ma˥-
tte (i)masu yo⌐

D. Substitution Drill

1. I (compared with others)
   ate [it].

Wa⌐takusi wa tabema˥sita.

2. The sashimi (compared   Sa˥simi˥ wa ta˩bema˥sita.
   with other things) [I] ate.

3. [I] ate sashimi.   Sa˥simi˥ o ta˩bema˥sita.

4. I ate [it].   Wa˥takusi ga̱ tabema˥sita.

5. I ate [it], too.   Wa˥takusi mo tabema˥sita.

6. [I] ate sashimi, too.   Sa˥simi˥ mo ta˩bema˥sita.

7. [I] ate with chopsticks.   O˥ha˥si de ta˩bema˥sita.

8. [I] ate at home.   U˥ti de tabema˥sita.

9. [I] ate at eight.   Ha˥ti˥-zi ni ta˩bema˥sita.

10. [I] ate starting at eight.   Ha˥ti˥-zi kara ta˩bema˥sita.

E. Substitution Drill

1. It's delicious, isn't it—   O˥isi˥i desu ˥ne˥e—ko˥no bi˥iru wa.
   this beer.

2. It's hot, isn't it—this tea.   A˥tu˥i desu ˥ne˥e—kono otya wa.

3. It's cold, isn't it—this   Sa˥mu˥i desu ˥ne˥e—ko˥no heya˥ wa.
   room.

4. It's cold, isn't it—this   Tu˥meta˥i desu ˥ne˥e—ko˥no mi˥ru-
   milk.   ku wa.

5. It's awful(-tasting), is-   Ma˥zu˥i desu ˥ne˥e—kono sakana wa.
   n't it—this fish.

6. It's sour, isn't it—this   Su˥ppa˥i desu ˥ne˥e—ko˥no kuda˥mo-
   fruit.   no wa.

7. It's bitter, isn't it—this   Ni˥g̱a˥i desu ˥ne˥e—ko˥no koohi˥i wa.
   coffee.

8. It's spicy, isn't it—this   Ka˥ra˥i desu ˥ne˥e—ko˥no osu˥si wa.
   sushi.

9. It's sweet, isn't it—this   A˥ma˥i desu ˥ne˥e—ko˥no oka˥si wa.
   cake.

10. It's strong, isn't it—this   Ko˥i desu ˥ne˥e—kono kootya wa.
    (black) tea.

F. Substitution Drill

1. Please bring two bottles   Sake (o) ˥ni˥-hoñ mo˥tte˥ kite kuda-
   of sake.   sai.

2. Please bring two glasses   Bi˥iru (o) ˥ni˥-hai mo˥tte˥ kite ku-
   of beer.   dasai.

3. Please bring three knives.   Na˥ihu (o) ˥sa˥ñ-boñ mo˥tte˥ kite ku-
                                  dasai.

4. Please bring three pieces   To˥osuto (o) ˥sa˥ñ-mai mo˥tte˥ kite
   of toast.   kudasai.

5. Please bring three glasses   Mi˥ruku (o) ˥sa˥ñ-bai mo˥tte˥ kite
   of milk.   kudasai.

6. Please bring one fork.   Ho˥oku (o) ˥i˥p-poñ mo˥tte˥ kite ku-
                                  dasai.

7. Please bring one glass of   Mizu (o) ˥i˥p-pai mo˥tte˥ kite kuda-
   water.   sai.

8. Please bring a little more   Go˥hañ (o) mo˥o suko˥si mo˥tte˥ kite
   rice.   kudasai.

9. Please bring two cups.   <u>Tyawañ</u> (o) <u>hu⌐tatu</u> motte⌐ kite kudasai.

10. Please bring two cups of   <u>Otya</u> (o) ⌐ni⌐-hai mo⌐tte⌐ kite kuda-
tea.   sai.

G. Response Drill

(Reply in the negative.)

1. Ya⌐sai de⌐su ka⌐   Iie, ya⌐sai zya arimase⌐ñ.
2. A⌐ma⌐i desu ka⌐   Iie, a⌐maku arimase⌐ñ.
3. Ya⌐mema⌐sita ka⌐   Iie, ya⌐memase⌐ñ desita.
4. Syo⌐kudoo de⌐su ka⌐   Iie, syo⌐kudoo zya arimase⌐ñ.
5. O⌐sobaya kara de⌐su ka⌐   Iie, o⌐sobaya kara zya arimase⌐ñ.
6. Ku⌐suri de⌐sita ka⌐   Iie, ku⌐suri zya arimase⌐ñ desita.
7. Su⌐ppa⌐i desu ka⌐   Iie, su⌐ppa⌐ku a⌐rimase⌐ñ.
8. Ko⌐i desu ka⌐   Iie, ko⌐ku a⌐rimase⌐ñ.

H. Response Drill (based on Grammatical Note 5)

1. Mo⌐o ta⌐bema⌐sita ka⌐ /iie/   Iie, ma⌐da ta⌐bemase⌐ñ.
2. Ma⌐da na⌐orimase⌐ñ ka⌐   Iie, mo⌐o na⌐orima⌐sita.
/iie/
3. Mo⌐o ku⌐suri (o) nomima⌐si-   E⌐e, mo⌐o ku⌐suri (o) nomima⌐sita.
ta ka⌐ /e⌐e/
4. Ma⌐da ta⌐nomimase⌐ñ ka⌐   E⌐e, ma⌐da ta⌐nomimase⌐ñ.
/e⌐e/
5. Mo⌐o de⌐kima⌐sita ka⌐ /iie/   Iie, ma⌐da de⌐kimase⌐ñ.
6. Ma⌐da ka⌐erimase⌐ñ ka⌐   Iie, mo⌐o ka⌐erima⌐sita.
/iie/
7. Mo⌐o ku⌐ruma (o) naosima⌐si-   E⌐e, mo⌐o ku⌐ruma (o) naosima⌐sita.
ta ka⌐ /e⌐e/
8. Ma⌐da a⌐imase⌐ñ ka⌐ /e⌐e/   E⌐e, ma⌐da a⌐imase⌐ñ.
9. Mo⌐o wa⌐karima⌐sita ka⌐   Iie, ma⌐da wa⌐karimase⌐ñ.
/iie/
10. Ma⌐da de⌐ñwa-simase⌐ñ ka⌐   Iie, mo⌐o de⌐ñwa-sima⌐sita.
/iie/

I. Level Drill (based on Grammatical Notes 1 and 4)

Tutor: Mo⌐o i⌐kima⌐sita kara.
        (formal verbal)

Student: Mo⌐o i⌐tta⌐ kara.   'Because I already went.'
         (informal verbal)

1. Sa⌐ke (o) yamema⌐sita kara.   Sa⌐ke (o) yameta⌐ kara.
2. Miti de to⌐modati ni aima⌐si-   Miti de to⌐modati ni a⌐tta kara.
ta kara.
3. I⌐sogima⌐sita kara.   I⌐so⌐ida kara.
4. Mo⌐o i⌐ti-neñ-ḡu⌐rai ⌐ma⌐e   Mo⌐o i⌐ti-neñ-ḡu⌐rai ⌐ma⌐e ni ⌐yo⌐ñ-
ni yo⌐mima⌐sita kara.   da kara.

5. Ka⌐nai mo kŏdomo mo   Ka⌐nai mo kŏdomo mo byo⌐oki ni na⌐-
    byo⌐oki ni narima⌐sita   tta kara.
    kara.

6. Hu⌐ru⌐i sa⌐kana (o) tabe-   Hu⌐ru⌐i sa⌐kana (o) ta⌐beta kara.
    ma⌐sita kara.

7. Kinoo ⌐yo⌐ku be⌐ñkyoo-   Kinoo ⌐yo⌐ku be⌐ñkyoo-sita⌐ kara.
    sima⌐sita kara.

8. To⌐modati kara karima⌐-   To⌐modati kara karita⌐ kara.
    sita kara.

9. Ti⌐isa na ⌐ko⌐e de ha⌐na-   Ti⌐isa na ⌐ko⌐e de ha⌐na⌐sita kara.
    sima⌐sita kara.

10. Yuube ⌐bi⌐iru (o) ta⌐kusañ   Yuube ⌐bi⌐iru (o) ta⌐kusañ no⌐ñda
    nomima⌐sita kara.   kara.

J.   Grammar Drill (based on Grammatical Notes 1, 2, 3, and 4)

        Tutor: I⌐ku desyo⌐o. 'He'll probably go.' (non-past)
        Student: I⌐tta desyo⌐o. 'He probably went.' (past)

1. Kyo⌐o de⌐ñwa (o) nao⌐su   Kyo⌐o de⌐ñwa (o) nao⌐sita desyoo.
    desyoo.

2. Ze⌐ñbu tu⌐taeru desyo⌐o.   Ze⌐ñbu tu⌐taeta desyo⌐o.

3. Koñna sara (wa) ta⌐ka⌐i   Koñna sara (wa) ⌐ta⌐kakatta desyoo.
    desyoo.

4. Byo⌐oki desyo⌐o.   Byo⌐oki da⌐tta desyoo.

5. Kyo⌐o to⌐temo isoḡasi⌐i   Kyo⌐o to⌐temo isoḡa⌐sikatta desyoo.
    desyoo.

6. Ha⌐yaku na⌐o⌐ru desyoo.   Ha⌐yaku na⌐o⌐tta desyoo.

7. Sono siḡoto (wa) tu⌐mara⌐-   Sono siḡoto (wa) tu⌐mara⌐nakatta de-
    nai desyoo.   syoo.

8. Ko⌐no koohi⌐i (wa) ma⌐zu⌐i   Ko⌐no koohi⌐i (wa) ⌐ma⌐zukatta de-
    desyoo.   syoo.

9. Sono tori (wa) o⌐isi⌐i de-   Sono tori (wa) o⌐isi⌐katta desyoo.
    syoo.

10. Ha⌐nasi-tyuu desyo⌐o.   Ha⌐nasi-tyuu da⌐tta desyoo.

K.   Level Drill [1]

1. Ko⌐marima⌐sita ⌐ne⌐e.   Ko⌐ma⌐tta ⌐ne⌐e. (M)

2. So⌐re (wa) yo⌐katta desu.   So⌐re (wa) yo⌐katta.

3. So⌐no⌐ hito no ⌐ko⌐e (wa)   So⌐no⌐ hito no ⌐ko⌐e (wa) ⌐he⌐ñ datta
    ⌐he⌐ñ desita yo↵   yo↵ (M)

_____

[1] In each case, the sentence on the right is the informal equivalent of the
sentence on the left. M = more typical of men's speech; W = more typical of
women's speech.

4. A⌐no kissa⌐teñ no o⌐ka⌐si
   (wa) o⌐isi⌐katta desu ⌐ne⌐e.

   A⌐no kissa⌐teñ no o⌐ka⌐si (wa) o⌐isi⌐-
   katta ⌐ne⌐e.   (M)

5. Mo⌐o o⌐kaeri ni narima⌐si-
   ta ka↲

   Mo⌐o o⌐kaeri ni na⌐tta?   (W)

6. Sono miti (wa) da⌐izyo⌐obu
   desita ka↲

   Sono miti (wa) da⌐izyo⌐obu datta?

7. So⌐no ho⌐ñ (wa) to⌐temo
   omosi⌐rokatta desu.

   So⌐no ho⌐ñ (wa) to⌐temo omosi⌐rokat-
   ta.

8. Na⌐ni (o) go⌐tyuumoñ-
   nasaima⌐sita ka↲

   Na⌐ni (o) go⌐tyuumoñ-nasa⌐tta?   (W)

9. Sono sakana (wa) da⌐me⌐
   desita.

   Sono sakana (wa) da⌐me⌐ datta.

10. Mo⌐o zi⌐p-puñ-ḡu⌐rai ⌐ma⌐e
    ni de⌐kakema⌐sita yo↲

    Mo⌐o zi⌐p-puñ-ḡu⌐rai ⌐ma⌐e ni dēka-
    keta yo↲   (M)

L. Expansion Drill

1. They haven't brought it.
   They haven't brought it yet.
   I ordered but they haven't
   brought it yet.
   I ordered coffee but they
   haven't brought it yet.
   I ordered coffee about fifteen minutes ago but they
   haven't brought it yet.
   I ordered coffee about fifteen minutes ago (al-
   ready) but they haven't
   brought it yet.

   Mo⌐tte kimase⌐ñ yo↲
   Ma⌐da mo⌐tte kimase⌐ñ yo↲
   Tyu⌐umoñ-sima⌐sita ḡa, ma⌐da mo-
   ⌐tte kimase⌐ñ yo↲
   Ko⌐ohi⌐i (o) tyu⌐umoñ-sima⌐sita ḡa,
   ma⌐da mo⌐tte kimase⌐ñ yo↲
   Zyu⌐ugo-huñ-ḡu⌐rai ⌐ma⌐e ni ko⌐o-
   hi⌐i (o) tyu⌐umoñ-sima⌐sita ḡa,
   ma⌐da mo⌐tte kimase⌐ñ yo↲
   Mo⌐o zyu⌐ugo-huñ-ḡu⌐rai ⌐ma⌐e ni
   ko⌐ohi⌐i (o) tyu⌐umoñ-sima⌐sita
   ḡa, ma⌐da mo⌐tte kimase⌐ñ yo↲

2. I got sick.
   Because it was bad, I got
   sick.
   Because that fish was bad,
   I got sick.
   I ate fish. Because the fish
   was bad, I got sick.

   I ate fish at a cheap dining
   room. Because the fish
   was bad, I got sick.

   The day before yesterday
   I ate fish at a cheap dining room. Because the
   fish was bad, I got sick.

   Byo⌐oki ni narima⌐sita yo.
   Da⌐me⌐ datta kara, byo⌐oki ni nari-
   ma⌐sita yo.
   Sono sakana wa da⌐me⌐ datta kara,
   byo⌐oki ni narima⌐sita yo.
   Sa⌐kana (o) tabema⌐sita ḡa; sono
   sakana wa da⌐me⌐ datta kara, byo-
   ⌐oki ni narima⌐sita yo.
   Ya⌐su⌐i syokudoo de sa⌐kana (o) ta-
   bema⌐sita ḡa; sono sakana wa da-
   ⌐me⌐ datta kara, byo⌐oki ni nari-
   ma⌐sita yo.
   Ototoi ya⌐su⌐i syokudoo de sa⌐kana
   (o) tabema⌐sita ḡa; sono s a k a n a
   wa da⌐me⌐ datta kara, byo⌐oki ni
   narima⌐sita yo.

3. [They] eat.
   [They] eat with chopsticks.

   Ta⌐bema⌐su.
   Ha⌐si de tabemasu.

Japanese eat with chop-   Ni⌐hoñzi⌐ñ wa ⌐ha⌐si de tabemasu.
sticks.

Americans eat with knives   A⌐merika⌐ziñ wa ⌐na⌐ihu to ⌐ho⌐oku
and forks, but Japanese   de ta⌐bema⌐su ḡa, ni⌐hoñzi⌐ñ wa
eat with chopsticks.   ⌐ha⌐si de tabemasu.

4. He has probably arrived. . . .   Tu⌐ita desyoo ḡa_

    He has probably arrived   O⌐taku ni tu⌐ita desyoo ḡa_
    home. . . .

    He has probably arrived   Mo⌐o o⌐taku ni tu⌐ita desyoo ḡa_
    home already. . . .

    He left about an hour ago   I⌐ti-zikañ-ḡu⌐rai ⌐ma⌐e ni ⌐de⌐ta ka-
    so he has probably ar-   ra, mo⌐o o⌐taku ni tu⌐ita desyoo
    rived home already. . . .   ḡa_

    He left the office about an   I⌐ti-zikañ-ḡu⌐rai ⌐ma⌐e ni zi⌐mu⌐syo
    hour ago so he has prob-   (o) ⌐de⌐ta kara, mo⌐o o⌐taku ni tu⌐-
    ably arrived home al-   ita desyoo ḡa_
    ready. . . .

5. Let's make it tomorrow.   A⌐sita⌐ ni si⌐masyo⌐o.

    I'm busy so let's make it   I⌐soḡasi⌐i kara, a⌐sita⌐ ni si⌐ma-
    tomorrow.   syo⌐o.

    I'm very busy so let's   To⌐ttemo isoḡasi⌐i kara, a⌐sita⌐ ni
    make it tomorrow.   si⌐masyo⌐o.

    Today I'm very busy so   Kyo⌐o wa to⌐ttemo isoḡasi⌐i kara,
    let's make it tomorrow.   a⌐sita⌐ ni si⌐masyo⌐o.

6. I telephoned.   De⌐ñwa-sima⌐sita.

    I telephoned his home.   O⌐taku e deñwa-sima⌐sita.

    I wanted to talk so I tele-   Ha⌐nasita⌐katta kara, o⌐taku e deñ-
    phoned his home.   wa-sima⌐sita.

    I didn't see him but I   A⌐imase⌐ñ desita ḡa; ha⌐nasita⌐katta
    wanted to talk to him so   kara, o⌐taku e deñwa-sima⌐sita.
    I telephoned his home.

    I didn't see him at the of-   Kaisya de a⌐imase⌐ñ desita ḡa; ha-
    fice but I wanted to talk   ⌐nasita⌐katta kara, o⌐taku e deñwa-
    to him so I telephoned   sima⌐sita.
    his home.

SUPPLEMENTARY CONVERSATION

(Two friends, Mr. Tanaka and Mr. Sato, sit down in a restaurant and are ap-
proached by a waitress)

Waitress: I⌐rassyaima⌐se. Na⌐ñ ni i⌐tasimasyo⌐o ka.
Tanaka: Mo⌐o hito⌐-ri ⌐ku⌐ru kara, tyo⌐tto ⌐ma⌐tte kudasai.
Waitress: Ha⌐a.
Tanaka: (to Sato)   Osoi ⌐ne⌐e — Yosida-kuñ wa.
Sato: So⌐o da ⌐ne⌐e. Na⌐ñ ni suru?
Tanaka: Tori wa?

Sato: Yosida-kuñ wa tŏri wa dame.
Tanaka: So⌐o ⌐so⌐o. Te⌐ñpura wa do⌐o? Te⌐ñpura wa ta⌐beta ne? — boku no
            uti de.
Sato: So⌐o datta ⌐ne⌐e.

            (Mr. Yoshida arrives)

Yoshida: O⌐soku narima⌐sita. Su⌐mimase⌐ñ.
Tanaka ⎫
Sato   ⎭ : Iie.
Tanaka: Na⌐ñ ni suru?
Sato: Te⌐ñpura do⌐o?
Yoshida: A⌐a, i⌐i ⌐ne⌐e.
Sato: Zya⌐a, te⌐ñpura tano⌐mu yo. (To waitress) Tyo⌐tto_
Waitress: Ha⌐a. Na⌐ñ ni i⌐tasimasyo⌐o ka.
Sato: Teñpura mi-⌐ttu onegai-sima⌐su.
Waitress: Ha⌐a, ka⌐sikomarima⌐sita.
Tanaka: (to Yoshida and Sato) Bi⌐iru mo ⌐no⌐mu?
Yoshida: No⌐mu yo_ — tu⌐meta⌐i no o.
Sato: (to waitress) Zya⌐a, bi⌐iru mo. A⌐rima⌐su ka_ — tu⌐meta⌐i no ḡa.
Waitress: Ha⌐a gozaimasu. O⌐bi⌐iru 1 mo⌐tte mairimasyo⌐o ka.
Sato: O⌐negai-sima⌐su.

                    . . .

Waitress: O⌐matase-itasima⌐sita. Do⌐ozo. Te⌐ñpura wa notihodo motte mai-
            rima⌐su.
Tanaka: (to Yoshida and Sato) Tu⌐metai bi⌐iru wa ŏisii ⌐ne⌐e.

                    . . .

Yoshida: O⌐isi⌐katta ⌐ne⌐e — ko⌐no bi⌐iru wa.
Sato: Mo⌐tto ta⌐no⌐mu?
Yoshida: Mo⌐o takusañ. Zu⌐ibuñ ⌐no⌐ñda yo_
Tanaka: (to Sato) Mo⌐o suko⌐si ⌐do⌐o?
Sato: Boku mo ⌐mo⌐o ⌐zu⌐ibuñ ⌐no⌐ñda kara_
Waitress: O⌐matase-itasima⌐sita. Do⌐ozo. Go⌐hañ mo mo⌐tte mairimasyo⌐o
            ka.
Tanaka: O⌐negai-sima⌐su.
Waitress: Ka⌐sikomarima⌐sita.

Yoshida: O⌐tya onegai-sima⌐su.
Waitress: Ha⌐a ⌐ha⌐a.
Tanaka: (to Yoshida and Sato) O⌐isi⌐katta ⌐ne⌐e.

---

1 The polite o⌐bi⌐iru+ is regularly used by restaurant and hotel personnel.

Sato: Saᴿkana g̃a ataraˈsikatta kara, oᴿisiˈkatta ᴸneᴸe.
Yoshida: Oᴿisii teñpura daˈtta kara, taᴿkusañ taˈbeta yo⌐
Tanaka: (to waitress) Tyoˈtto_ Iˈkura?
Waitress: Aᴿrig̃atoo gozaimasu. Seˈñ happyaku roᴿkuzyuˈu-eñ de gozaimasu.
Yoshida: Kyoˈo wa ᴿboˈku g̃a_
Tanaka: Iie, boku g̃a_
Sato: Niseñ-eñ. Haˈi.

                            . . .

Waitress: Maᴸido ariˈg̃atoo gozaimasu. Hyaku yoᴿñzyuˈu-eñ. Doˈozo. Maᴸta
              doˈozo.

Tanaka }:   (to Sato) Doˈo mo suᴸmimaseᴸñ. Gotisoosama.
Yoshida }
Sato: Iie iie.

                       English Equivalent

Waitress: (Welcome.) What would you like?
Tanaka: One more is coming so just a minute.
Waitress: Certainly.
Tanaka: (to Sato) He's late, isn't he— Yoshida.
Sato: He is, isn't he. What are you going to have (lit. decide on)?
Tanaka: How about chicken?
Sato: Chicken is out for Yoshida.
Tanaka: That's right. How about tempura? Tempura he ate, didn't he— at
              my house?
Sato: He did, didn't he.
Yoshida: (joining his friends) I'm sorry I'm late.
Tanaka }:   Not at all.
Sato }
Tanaka: What are you going to have?
Sato: How about tempura?
Yoshida: Oh, fine!
Sato: Then I'll order tempura. (Calling waitress) Miss!
Waitress: Yes. What would you like?
Sato: We'd like three [orders of] tempura.
Waitress: Yes, certainly.
Tanaka: (to Yoshida and Sato) Are you going to have beer, too?
Yoshida: I'll have some— some that's cold.
Sato: (to waitress) Well then, beer too. Do you have some— some that's
              cold?
Waitress: Yes, we have. Shall I bring beer?
Sato: Yes, please.

                            . . .

Waitress: I'm sorry to have kept you waiting. Here you are. The tempura
              I'll bring later.
Tanaka: (to Yoshida and Sato) Isn't cold beer good!

Yoshida: Wasn't it good—this beer!
Sato: Do you want more?
Yoshida: No, thank you. I had an awful lot.
Tanaka: (to Sato) How about a little more?
Sato: I've had an awful lot already too so. . . .
Waitress: (bringing the tempura) I'm sorry to have kept you waiting. Here you are. Shall I bring some rice too?
Tanaka: Yes, please.
Waitress: Certainly.

. . .

Yoshida: We'd like some tea.
Waitress: Certainly.
Tanaka: (to Yoshida and Sato) Wasn't it good!
Sato: The fish was fresh so it WAS good, wasn't it!
Yoshida: It was delicious tempura so I ate a lot.
Tanaka: (to waitress) Miss! How much?
Waitress: (Thank you.) It's ¥1860.
Yoshida: Today I [will pay the check].
Tanaka: No, I [will pay].
Sato: (paying) Here. ¥2000.
Waitress: (Returning with change) Thank you. Here you are, ¥140. Please come again.
Tanaka }
Yoshida }: (to Sato) Thank you very much. It was delicious.
Sato: Not at all.

EXERCISES

1. Tell the waitress:

    a. to bring 2 (portions of) sashimi.
    b. to bring some water.
    c. to bring more sake.
    d. that your tea is cold.
    e. that your coffee is weak.
    f. that the fish tastes bad.
    g. that you haven't ordered yet.
    h. that you want a little more rice.
    i. that you don't want any cake.
    j. that you enjoyed your meal.

2. Ask your guest: Your guest replies:

    a. what he will have to eat.   I'll have some sushi.
    b. if he will have some sake.   Yes, thank you.
    c. if he will have some more beer.   No, thank you.

       d. if he will have some   Just half, please.
           more coffee.
       e. if he would like sugar.   Just a little, please.

3. Turn back to Level Drill I on pages 243–44. Make up questions for which
the sentences of this drill would be appropriate answers. For example,
using the model sentence M$\overline{o}$o i⌐tta⌐ kara., an appropriate question would be:
D$\overline{o}$o site g⌐iñkoo e ikimase⌐ñ ka⌣ 'Why aren't you going to go to the bank?'
Then drill on the questions together with their answers (informal alternants).

4. Practice the Basic Dialogues using appropriate variations.

Lesson 15. Eating and Drinking (cont.)

BASIC DIALOGUES: FOR MEMORIZATION

(a)

At the office

Smith

together	issyo
dining or a meal	syokuzi or
	osyokuzi [1]
dine or eat a meal	syokuzi o suru
dine together	issyo ni syokuzi o suru
1. Shall we have lunch [1] together?	I⌐ssyo ni syokuzi (o) simasyo⌐o ka.

Tanaka

2. Haven't you eaten yet?	Ma⌐da ta˧bemase˧n ka⌐
doesn't know (informal)	siranai
didn't know (informal)	si⌐rana⌐katta
with Mr. Saito	Saitoo-sañ to
together with Mr. Saito	Saitoo-sañ to issyo
eat together	i⌐ssyo ni tabe⌐ru
3. I didn't know so today I ate early (already) with Mr. Saito. . . .	Si⌐rana⌐katta kara, kyo⌐o wa ⌐mo⌐o Saitoo-sañ to issyo ni ⌐ha⌐yaku ta-˧bema˧sita ḡa⌐

Smith

other or another	hoka
day	hi⌐
another day	ho⌐ka no hi⌐
4. Well then, let's make it another day.	Zya⌐a, ho⌐ka no hi⌐ ni si˧masyo˧o.

Tanaka

whatever day of the week it is or any day of the week at all	na⌐ñyo⌐o(bi) de mo
5. Yes. Any day at all will be fine.	E⌐e. Na⌐ñyo⌐o de mo ˧i˧i desu yo⌐

---

[1] Or breakfast or dinner.

251

(b)

In a restaurant

Tanaka

	which alternative	do⌐tira no ⌐ho⌐o
6.	Which [alternative] would be better, noodles or sushi?	So⌐ba to ⌐su⌐si to, do⌐tira [no ⌐ho⌐o] ḡa ⌐i⌐i desyoo ka.

Smith

	whichever of two it is or either one	do⌐tira de⌐ mo
7.	Either one is fine, but let's make it sushi, shall we?	Do⌐tira de mo i⌐i desu ḡa, su⌐si ni si⌐masyo⌐o ne?

Tanaka (to waitress)

	one portion	iti-niñmae
8.	We'd like two portions of sushi.	Su⌐si (o) ni-⌐niñmae oneḡai-sima⌐su.

. . .

	bill or accounting or check	kaikee or okaikee +
9.	Check, please.	Ka⌐ikee (o) oneḡai-sima⌐su.
10.	How much does it come to?	I⌐kura ni na⌐rima⌐su ka⌐

Waitress

11.	It's ¥150 for one portion so it comes to ¥300. Thank you.

Iti-niñmae hya⌐ku gozyu⌐u-eñ de go-⌐zaima⌐su kara, sa⌐ñbyaku⌐-eñ ni narimasu.   Ma⌐ido ari⌐ḡatoo gozai-masu.

(c)

Mrs. Smith (arriving home)

	noon meal	hi⌐rugo⌐hañ or o⌐hirugo⌐hañ +
	stomach	onaka
	become empty	suku /-u/
12.	I had lunch early so I'm hungry. (Lit. Lunch was early so my stomach has become empty.)	O⌐hirugo⌐hañ (ḡa) ⌐ha⌐yakatta kara, o⌐naka ḡa sukima⌐sita yo⌐

	a meal	go⌐hañ
	come into being or be(come) completed	de⌐ki⌐ru /-ru/
13.	Is dinner ready?	Go⌐hañ (ḡa) de⌐kima⌐sita ka⌐

Maid

	soon now or any minute now	mo⌐o su⌐ḡu

14. It will be ready any minute
now. . . .

Mo⌐o su⌐ḡu de⌐kima⌐su ḡa_

(d)

Mr. Tanaka

pleasing

su⌐ki⌐ /na/   or
osuki⌐ /na/

15. Which /alternative/ do you
prefer— sukiyaki or sushi?

Sukiyaki to ⌐su⌐si to, do⌐tira /no
⌐ho⌐o/ ḡa o⌐suki de⌐su ka_

Mr. Smith

the alternative of suki-
yaki

su⌐kiyaki no ho⌐o

16. Me, I prefer sukiyaki.

Boku wa su⌐kiyaki /no ho⌐o/ ḡa su-
⌐ki⌐ desu yo. [1]

Mr. Tanaka

more than sukiyaki
the alternative of sushi

su⌐kiyaki yo⌐ri
su⌐si no ⌐ho⌐o

17. Oh? I like sushi more than
sukiyaki.

So⌐o desu ka. Boku wa su⌐kiyaki
yo⌐ri ⌐su⌐si /no ⌐ho⌐o/ ḡa su⌐ki⌐
desu.

however or but
to the highest degree
the one that's most pleasing

si⌐ka⌐si
i⌐ti⌐bañ
i⌐tibañ suki⌐ na no

18. But what I like best is tempura.

Si⌐ka⌐si, i⌐tibañ suki⌐ na no wa te⌐ñ-
pura de⌐su yo.

Mr. Smith

19. Oh, tempura?

A⌐a, te⌐ñpura de⌐su ka.

20. I like tempura best, too.

Bo⌐ku mo te⌐ñpura ḡa itibañ suki⌐
desu yo.

to the extent of tempura
or as much as tem-
pura

te⌐ñpura hodo

21. I like sukiyaki too, but not
so much as tempura.

Su⌐kiyaki mo suki⌐ desu ḡa, te⌐ñpura
hodo zya arimase⌐ñ yo.

(e)

Tanaka

for dining or for a
meal

syokuzi ni

---

[1] Accent of short alternant: suki⌐.

being fish and meat and
fowl

sakana to ni⌐ku⌐ to tŏri de

[being] among fish and
meat and fowl

sakana to ni⌐ku⌐ to tŏri no uti
[de]

22. Mr. Smith is coming to our
house for dinner. Which do
you suppose he would like
best, fish, meat, or fowl?

Su⌐misu - sañ (ḡa) u⌐ti e syokuzi ni
irassyaima⌐su ḡa; sakana to ni⌐ku⌐

to tŏri $\begin{vmatrix} \text{de} \\ \text{no uti } [de] \end{vmatrix}$, do⌐re ḡa i⌐ti-
bañ osuki desyo⌐o ka.

Jones

isn't meat (informal)

ni⌐ku⌐ zya ⌐na⌐i

it probably isn't meat

ni⌐ku⌐ zya ⌐na⌐i desyoo

wouldn't it be meat?

ni⌐ku⌐ zya ⌐na⌐i desyoo ka

23. Hmm. I'm not sure but would-
n't it be meat?

Sa⌐a, yo⌐ku wa⌐karimase⌐ñ ḡa; ni-
⌐ku⌐ zya ⌐na⌐i desyoo ka.

Tanaka

24. I suppose so.

So⌐o desyoo ⌐ne⌐e.

Jones

whichever (of three or
more) it is or any
one at all

do⌐re de mo

most Americans

ta⌐itee no Amerika⌐ziñ

25. I guess any one (of the three
alternatives) would be fine,
but sashimi most Americans
don't like very much. . . .

Ma⌐a, do⌐re de mo ⌐i⌐i desyoo ḡa;
sa⌐simi wa ta⌐itee no Amerika⌐ziñ
wa a⌐ñmari suki⌐ zya a⌐rimase⌐ñ ḡa_

Tanaka

26. That's right, isn't it.

So⌐re wa so⌐o desu ⌐ne⌐e.

(f)

Mr. Tanaka

27. Which do you like better—
beer or sake?

Bi⌐iru to săke to, do⌐tti *[no ⌐ho⌐o]*
ḡa suki?

Mr. Yamamoto

the alternative of beer

bi⌐iru no ⌐ho⌐o

by far

zutto

a drink *or* beverage

no⌐mi⌐mono

displeasing

kirai */na/*

28. I like beer much more—
since I hate hot drinks.

Bi⌐iru *[no ⌐ho⌐o]* ḡa zu⌐tto suki⌐ da
yo—a⌐tu⌐i no⌐mi⌐mono (wa) ki⌐rai
da⌐ kara.

Mr. Tanaka

29. Tea too?

Otya mo?

Mr. Yamamoto

    of course _or_ to be sure   mo⌐ti˥roñ
    very pleasing   da˥isuki /na/
30. Oh, tea is different. Of course   A˥a, otya wa tiḡau. Mo⌐ti˥roñ ⌐da˥i-
    I like it a lot!   suki da yo.

(g)

Mr. Tanaka

    throat   no˥do
    become dry   ka⌐wa˥ku /-u/
31. I'm thirsty. (Lit. My throat   No˥do (ḡa) ka⌐wa˧ita.
    has become dry.)

Mr. Yamamoto

32. What do you want to drink?   Na˥ni (ḡa) nomitai?

Mr. Tanaka

    no matter what it is   na⌐ñ de˥ mo
      _or_ anything at all
33. Anything will be fine.   Na⌐ñ de mo i˥i yo.

(h)

At a restaurant

Tanaka

34. Is this coffee?   Kore ko⌐ohi˥i?

Yamamoto

35. Yes, that's right.   E˥e, so˥o.

Tanaka

    isn't strange (informal)   he˥ñ zya ˥na˧i
36. Doesn't it taste funny? (Lit.   He˥ñ zya nai?
    Isn't it strange?)

Yamamoto (after tasting it)

    isn't delicious   o⌐isiku na˥i
37. It isn't good, is it!   O⌐isiku na˥i ⌐ne˥e.

NOTES ON THE BASIC DIALOGUES

3. 'but—if I had known, I would have waited for you.'

4. Compare : <u>hoka no zassi</u> 'another magazine' or 'other magazines'; <u>zassi
    no hoka</u> 'other than magazines,' 'besides magazines.'

12. Hi⌐ru˥ means 'noon' or 'daytime.'

    Compare also a⌐sago˥hañ 'breakfast' and ba⌐ñgo˥hañ 'dinner,' 'evening
    meal.'

Note also the following, all of which are in common use: o⌐naka ga⌐ (or wa) sukimase⌐ṅ 'I'm not hungry' (lit. 'my stomach hasn't become empty'); o⌐naka ga⌐ suite (i)ma⌐su 'I'm hungry' (lit. 'my stomach is in a state of having become empty'); o⌐naka ga⌐ (or wa) suite (i)mase⌐ṅ 'I'm not hungry' (lit. 'my stomach is not in a state of having become empty').

14. 'but—will that be all right?'

15. Both the thing which is pleasing and the person to whom it is pleasing are followed by particles ga⌐ or wa (depending upon emphasis). Note that su⌐ki⌐ is a na-nominal: thus, su⌐ki⌐ na mono 'pleasing things,' 'things [I] like'; o⌐suki na mono⌐ 'things pleasing to someone else,' 'things [you] like.'

16. Wa here is the wa of comparison: 'I, for my part.'

17. See the immediately preceding note.

18. Si⌐ka⌐si occurs at the beginning of sentences.

No is the nominal no 'one,' referring here to a kind of food.

22. Ni here is the ni of goal.

25. 'but—they like most other things.'

26. Wa here is the wa of comparison.

28. Zutto: note also zu⌐tto ma⌐e 'a long time before or ago,' zutto usiro 'way in back,' etc.

No⌐mi⌐mono: compare ta⌐bemo⌐no 'food,' 'edibles.'

Kirai is the opposite of su⌐ki⌐ and enters into the same kinds of patterns (except that it does not have a polite equivalent). Ki⌐rai de⌐su is a stronger, less tactful expression than su⌐ki⌐ zya a⌐rimase⌐ṅ '[I] don't like [it],' '[I] don't care for [it].'

30. Da⌐isuki is an informal word.

31. Nŏdo ga⌐ ka⌐wa⌐ku occurs in the same kinds of patterns as onaka ga⌐ suku. See the note on Sentence 12 above.

32. Compare: Na⌐ni o ⌐no⌐mu? 'What are you going to drink?' but Na⌐ni ga⌐ (or, less commonly, o) nomitai? 'What do you want to drink?' See Lesson 7, Grammatical Note 1.

28, 30, 33, and 37 contain informal non-past or past inflected words followed directly by yo or nee. Such combinations occur more commonly in men's speech.

GRAMMATICAL NOTES

1. Informal Negatives, Non-past and Past

The informal equivalent of a formal non-past negative ending in -mase┐n is an ADJECTIVAL ending in -[a]nai.

To make the informal negative adjectival from the citation form of a verbal:

-ru group: drop -ru and add -nai

Example: ta┐be┐ru 'eat'—ta┐be┐nai 'doesn't eat'

-u group: drop -u and add -anai

Example: no┐mu 'drink'—no┐ma┐nai 'doesn't drink'

but: for -u verbals ending in a vowel + -u, drop -u and add -wanai

Example: kau 'buy'—kawanai 'doesn't buy'

Note: The informal negative of a┐ru 'be (inanimate),' 'have' is na┐i.

-aru group: change -aru to -aranai [1]

Example: ku┌dasa┐ru 'give me'—ku┌dasara┐nai 'doesn't give me'

Note: A corresponding informal negative does not exist for go┌za┐ru.

Irregular group:

suru 'do'—sinai 'doesn't do'
ku┐ru 'come'—ko┐nai 'doesn't come'

An unaccented verbal has an unaccented informal negative equivalent; an accented verbal has an accented informal negative equivalent, with the accent occurring on the syllable immediately preceding the -nai ending.

The past informal negative ends in -nakatta; like all adjectival past informal forms, it is made by replacing the final -i of the non-past with -katta. It is accented on syllable na if derived from an unaccented non-past negative, and on the syllable immediate preceding -nakatta if derived from an accented non-past negative.

Examples:

---

[1] Or, worded differently: drop -u and add -anai.

AFFIRMATIVE	NEGATIVE	
Verbal Non-past Informal (Citation Form)	Non-past: Informal/Formal	Past: Informal/Formal
(-ru Group)		
deꞌru 'go out'	deꞌnai/deꞌmaseꞌñ	deꞌnakatta/deꞌmaseꞌñ desita
miꞌru 'see'	miꞌnai/miꞌmaseꞌñ	miꞌnakatta/miꞌmaseꞌñ desita
(-u Group)		
maꞌtu 'wait'	maꞌtaꞌnai/maꞌtimaseꞌñ	maꞌtaꞌnakatta/maꞌtimaseꞌñ desita
kaꞌeru 'return'	kaꞌeraꞌnai/kaꞌerimaseꞌñ	kaꞌeraꞌnakatta/kaꞌerimaseꞌñ desita
iu 'say'	iwanai/iꞌimaseꞌñ	iꞌwanaꞌkatta/iꞌimaseꞌñ desita
haꞌnaꞌsu 'talk'	haꞌnasaꞌnai/haꞌnasimaseꞌñ	haꞌnasaꞌnakatta/haꞌnasimaseꞌñ desita
kiku 'ask,' 'listen,' 'hear'	kikanai/kiʳkimaseꞌñ	kiʳkanaꞌkatta/kiʳkimaseꞌñ desita
iꞌsoḡu 'be in a hurry'	iꞌsoḡaꞌnai/iꞌsoḡimaseꞌñ	iꞌsoḡaꞌnakatta/iꞌsoḡimaseꞌñ desita
yobu 'call'	yobanai/yoʳbimaseꞌñ	yoʳbanaꞌkatta/yoʳbimaseꞌñ desita
yoꞌmu 'read'	yoʳmaꞌnai/yoʳmimaseꞌñ	yoʳmaꞌnakatta/yoʳmimaseꞌñ desita
(-aru Group)		
naʳsaꞌru 'do'	naʳsaraꞌnai/naʳsaimaseꞌñ	naʳsaraꞌnakatta/naʳsaimaseꞌñ desita
(Irregular Group)		
kuꞌru 'come'	koꞌnai/kiꞌmaseꞌñ	koꞌnakatta/kiꞌmaseꞌñ desita
suru 'do,' 'make'	sinai/siꞌmaseꞌñ	siꞌnaꞌkatta/siꞌmaseꞌñ desita

The occurrences of non-negative adjectival forms like taʳkaꞌi/taʳkakatta (i.e. informal non-past and past forms) parallel the occurrences of negative adjectivals.

Examples:

Informal sentences

Siranai. 'I don't know.'
Ikanai yo⌣ 'I'm not going!' (men's speech)

Ma¹da de⌐ki⁴nai ⌐ne¹e. 'It hasn't been finished yet, has it.' (men's
speech)
Saitoo-sañ wa ⌐ma¹da ⌐ko⁴nai? 'Hasn't Mr. Saito come yet?'
Wa⌐kara¹nakatta. 'I didn't understand.'
Da⌐re mo de¹nakatta yo⌐ 'Nobody answered (the telephone)!' (men's
speech)
Pa¹ñ ka⌐wana¹katta? 'Didn't you buy any bread?'

Formal Sentences:

So⌐ñna hito¹ wa de⌐ki¹nai desyoo. 'That kind of person probably can't
do it.'
Tanaka-sañ wa i⌐rassyara¹nai desyoo ka. 'Do you suppose Mr. Tanaka
isn't in?'
So⌐o iwana¹katta desyoo. 'He probably didn't say that.'
Wa⌐kara¹nai kara, mo⌐o iti-do itte kudasa¹i. 'I don't understand so
please say it again.'
I⌐kana¹katta kara, mi⌐mase¹ñ desita. 'I didn't go so I didn't see it.'

However, note this difference: a formal equivalent of a non-negative adjectival
like ta⌐ka¹i/ta¹kakatta is ta⌐ka¹i desu/ta¹kakatta desu. While a corresponding
formal negative pattern does exist—for example, na¹i desu / na¹katta desu are
frequently occurring forms—the more usual formal negative pattern is the
-mase¹ñ / -mase¹ñ desita pattern derived from the corresponding formal affirmative verbal.

Note, now, the following patterns:

Non-past Negative

	Formal	Informal
Verbal Pattern	-mase¹ñ form (or negative adjectival ending in -[a] nai + desu) (wa⌐karimase¹ñ or wa⌐kara¹nai desu)	Negative adjectival ending in -[a] nai (wa⌐kara¹nai)
Adjectival Pattern	Adjectival ending in -ku + a⌐rimase¹ñ or + na¹i desu (ta¹kaku a⌐rima-se⁴ñ or ta¹kaku ⌐na⁴i desu)	Adjectival ending in -ku + na¹i (ta¹kaku ⌐na⁴i)
Nominal Pattern	Nominal + zya a⌐ri-mase¹ñ or + zya na¹i desu (ho¹ñ zya a⌐rima-se⁴ñ or ho¹ñ zya ⌐na⁴i desu)	Nominal + zya ⌐na¹i (ho¹ñ zya ⌐na⁴i)

To form the corresponding past forms of the above:
    (a) Add desita to -mase¹ñ forms.
    (b) Change -nai to -nakatta and -nai desu to -nakatta desu.

An adjectival modifying a verbal occurs in its -ku form (cf. Lesson 10, Grammatical Note 4). For negative adjectivals, occurrence before na⌐ru 'become' is the most common example of this pattern:

> de⌐ki⌐naku ⌐na⌐ru 'become unable'
> wa⌐kara⌐naku ⌐na⌐ru 'reach the point of not understanding'

The accent of a -naku form is the same as that of the corresponding -nai form.

2.   Comparison of Two Items; Particles yori and hodo

X to Y to, do⌐tira —— asks: 'of X and Y, which is [more] ——?'[1] X and Y are both nominals (which may be preceded by descriptive words or phrases and/or followed by particles). Following do⌐tira is an appropriate particle— usually ḡa (if do⌐tira is the subject) or o (if do⌐tira is the object)—and an inflected expression.

Study the following examples:

(a) Kore to sore to, do⌐tira ḡa ⌐ki⌐ree desu ka⌣
      'Which is prettier—this or that?'
(b) O⌐oki⌐i no to ti⌐isa⌐i no to, do⌐tira ḡa ⌐i⌐i desyoo ka.
      'Which would be better—the big one or the small one?'
(c) Tanaka-sañ no okosañ to o⌐taku no⌐ to, do⌐tira ḡa o⌐oki⌐i desu ka⌣
      'Who is bigger—the Tanakas' child or yours?'
(d) Ko⌐no oka⌐si to so⌐no oka⌐si to, do⌐tti ḡa a⌐ma⌐i desu ka⌣
      'Which is sweeter—this cake or that cake?'
(e) Tanaka-sañ to Yamamoto-sañ to, do⌐tira o ⌐yo⌐ku si⌐tte ima⌐su ka⌣
      'Which one do you know better—Mr. Tanaka or Mr. Yamamoto?'

In examples of this kind, do⌐tira no ⌐ho⌐o 'which alternative?' is inter- changeable with do⌐tira 'which one?'

In the replies, the word or phrase which answers the question is followed by the same particle that followed the interrogative word or phrase in the question. Ho⌐o 'alternative' may or may not be included in the answer.

Study the following answers to the questions above:

(a) Ko⌐re ḡa ki⌐ree desu.   or   Ko⌐no ho⌐o ḡa ⌐ki⌐ree desu.
      'This is prettier.'
(b) O⌐oki⌐i no ḡa ⌐i⌐i desu.   or   O⌐oki⌐i ⌐ho⌐o ḡa ⌐i⌐i desu.
      'The big one is better.'
(c) Ta⌐naka-sañ no okosañ ḡa ooki⌐i desu.   or
      Ta⌐naka-sañ no okosañ no ho⌐o ḡa o⌐oki⌐i desu.
      'The Tanakas' child is bigger.'

---

[1] For an alternate pattern, see Note 3 below.

(d) So⌐no oka⌐si ḡa a⌐ma⁺i desu.   or
    So⌐no oka⌐si no ⌐ho⁺o ḡa a⌐ma⁺i desu.
    'That cake is sweeter.'
(e) Ya⌐mamoto-sañ o yo⌐ku sitte imasu.   or
    Ya⌐mamoto-sañ no ho⌐o o ⌐yo⁺ku sitte imasu.
    'I know Mr. Yamamoto better.'

Yo⌐ri (yori after an accented word) 'more than' follows the nominal with which another nominal is being compared. Again, the nominals may be preceded by descriptive words or phrases and/or followed by particles.

Study the following examples, noting the particles:

(a) So⌐re yo⌐ri ko⌐re ḡa ki⌐ree desu.   or   So⌐re yo⌐ri ko⌐no ho⌐o ḡa ⌐ki⁺ree desu.
    'THIS is prettier than that.' (Lit. 'More than that, THIS [or THIS ALTERNATIVE] is pretty.')
(b) Ti⌐isa⌐i no yori o⌐oki⌐i no ḡa ⌐i⁺i desu.   or   Ti⌐isa⌐i no yori o⌐oki⌐i ⌐ho⁺o ḡa ⌐i⁺i desu.
    'A BIG ONE is better than a small one.' (Lit. 'More than a small one, a BIG ONE [or ALTERNATIVE] is good.')
(c) Ta⌐naka-sañ yo⌐ri Ya⌐mamoto-sañ o yo⌐ku sitte imasu.   or   Ta⌐naka-sañ yo⌐ri Ya⌐mamoto-sañ no ho⌐o o ⌐yo⁺ku sitte imasu.
    'I know MR. YAMAMOTO better than Mr. Tanaka.' (Lit. 'More than Mr. Tanaka I know MR. YAMAMOTO [or the alternative of MR. YAMAMOTO] well.')

In the above examples, the phrase ending with yori may occur after the ḡa or o phrase without any difference in meaning other than a slight change in emphasis.

Examples of the pattern X wa Y yori —— also occur; here, X is already under discussion or is being compared, and the emphasis is on what follows.

Hodo 'to the extent of' occurs in negative comparisons: X wa Y hodo /+ negative/ 'X is not as —— as Y.'

Study the following examples:

(a) Sore wa kőre hodo ⌐ki⌐ree zya a⁺rimase⁺ñ.
    'That is not as pretty as this.' (Lit. 'That is not pretty to the extent of this.')
(b) Ti⌐isa⌐i no wa o⌐oki⌐i no hodo ⌐yo⌐ku a⁺rimase⁺ñ.
    'A small one is not as good as a big one.' (Lit. 'A small one is not good to the extent of a big one.')
(c) Tanaka-sañ wa Yắmamoto-sañ hodo ⌐yo⌐ku si⁺rimase⁺ñ.
    'Mr. Tanaka I don't know as well as Mr. Yamamoto.' (Lit. 'Mr. Tanaka I don't know well to the extent of Mr. Yamamoto.')
         or
    'Mr. Tanaka doesn't know as well as Mr. Yamamoto.' (Lit. 'Mr. Tanaka doesn't know well to the extent of Mr. Yamamoto.')

3.   Comparison of Three or More Items; i⌐ti⌐bañ

I⌐ti⌐bañ[1] 'to the greatest degree' occurs with verbals, adjectivals, nominals,
and the copula:

> Ta⌐naka-sañ ḡa itibañ dekima⌐su.   'Mr. Tanaka is the most capable.'
> I⌐tibañ taka⌐i no wa so⌐re de⌐su.   'The most expensive one is that one.'
> So⌐no sara ḡa itibañ ki⌐ree desyoo ne?   'I guess that plate is the pret-
> tiest, isn't it?'
> So⌐re mo i⌐i desu ḡa, ko⌐re ḡa iti⌐bañ desu.   'That's good too, but this
> is the best.'

The two most common Japanese patterns for asking ' of X and Y and Z,
which is most —— ?' are:

> X to Y to Z de, do⌐re + particle + i⌐ti⌐bañ ——
> Lit. 'being X and Y and Z, which to the greatest extent —— ?'

and

> X to Y to Z no uti[2] /de/, do⌐re + particle + i⌐ti⌐bañ ——
> Lit. '/ being/ among X and Y and Z, which to the greatest extent —
> ——?'

X, Y, and Z are nominals (which may be preceded by descriptive words or
phrases and/or followed by particles); following do⌐re is an appropriate particle. These patterns are used when three or more items are specifically
mentioned.   A cover phrase such as ko⌐no mi-ttu⌐ /no uti/ /de/ '/being/
/among/ these three things,' Nihoñ no yasai /no uti/ /de/ '/being/ /among/
Japanese vegetables,' etc., may be used instead of naming the specific items.
Also, question words other than do⌐re may be used when they are appropriate.

Statements involving the same kind of comparison have the same general
pattern as questions.

Examples:

> Gaiziñ wa, sukiyaki to teñpura to ⌐su⌐si no uti de, taitee ⌐do⌐re o i⌐ti-
> bañ yo⌐ku ta⌐bema⌐su ka⌐ 'Which do Westerners usually eat most
> often— sukiyaki or tempura or sushi?'
> Ko⌐obe to Oosaka to Yokohama de, do⌐ko ḡa i⌐tibañ ooki⌐i desu ka⌐
> 'Which is the biggest place— Kobe or Osaka or Yokohama?'
> So⌐no sañ-ni⌐ñ no uti de, da⌐re ḡa ni⌐hoñḡo ḡa itibañ yo⌐ku wa⌐kari-
> ma⌐su ka⌐ 'Of those 3 people, who understands Japanese best?'
> Ko⌐no yo-ttu⌐ no uti de, ko⌐re ḡa itibañ suki⌐ desu kara; ko⌐re ni sima⌐-
> sita. 'Of these 4 I like this one best so I decided on this one.'

---

[1] I⌐ti⌐bañ is regularly accented in isolation and immediately before √da.

[2] Uti (nominal) 'among'; other meanings will be introduced later.

Eeḡo to nīhoñḡo to hǔrañsuḡo de, i꜕tibañ hana꜖su no wa ni꜕hoñḡo de꜖su.
'Of English and Japanese and French, the one I speak most is Japanese.'

In comparing two alternatives, X̲ to Y̲ de ꜕do꜖tira —— 'being X̲ and Y̲, which one —— ?' is sometimes used as an alternant of X̲ to Y̲ to ꜕do tira ——, the pattern introduced in Note 2 above.   Here too, a covering phrase may be used instead of mentioning specific items: ko꜕no huta-tu꜖ de ꜕do꜖tira —— 'being these two things, which one —— ?'

4. Interrogative + de꜖ mo

An interrogative word or phrase (na꜖n̄, do꜖re, do꜖tira, i꜖tu, do꜕ko, na꜖n̄-zi, do꜕no ⊦ho꜕n̄, etc.) + de (the gerund of da) + particle mo 'even' means '——ever it is,' 'no matter —— it is,' 'any —— at all' (lit. 'even being ——'). Thus:[1]

da꜕re de꜖ mo 'whoever it is,' 'no matter who it is,' 'anyone at all'

do꜕ko de꜖ mo 'wherever it is,' 'no matter what place it is,' 'any place at all'

i꜕tu de꜖ mo 'whenever it is,' 'no matter when it is,' 'any time at all'

i꜕ku-tu de꜖ mo 'any number (of units) at all,' 'however many it is,' 'no matter how many it is'

na꜕n̄-niñ de꜖ mo 'any number of people at all,' 'however many people it is,' 'no matter how many people it is'

The interrogative may be followed by any of the particles which normally precede √da:

do꜕ko kara de꜖ mo   'wherever it is from,' 'no matter where it is from'

Examples:

Da꜕re de꜖ mo de⊦ki⊣ru desyoo.   'Anyone at all can probably do it.'
I꜕tu de꜖ mo ⊦i⊣i desu yo⌐ 'Any time at all will be all right.'
So꜕no꜖ hito wa na꜕n̄ de꜖ mo tabemasu. 'He eats anything at all.'
Na꜕n̄-zi kara de꜖ mo ka⊦maimase⊣n̄. 'No matter what time it starts (lit. even being from what time), it makes no difference.'

---

[1] There is considerable variation in the accent of such combinations. The original accent of the interrogative is sometimes retained, but is more often lost.

5.　M a n n e r

To indicate how or in what manner something is done, the following patterns occur:

(a)　a verbal gerund

Example: i⌐so⌐ide ⌐ka⌐ku 'write in a hurry'

(b)　an adverbial adjectival (i.e. the -ku form)[1]

Example: o⌐mosi⌐roku ⌐ka⌐ku 'write interestingly'

(c)　a nominal + particle ni of manner

Examples: i⌐ssyo ni ka⌐ku 'write together'
　　　　　 ki⌐ree ni ⌐ka⌐ku 'write beautifully'

(d)　a nominal alone

Examples: so⌐o ka⌐ku 'write thus'
　　　　　 yu⌐kku⌐ri ⌐ka⌐ku 'write slowly'

Na-nominals are among those regularly followed by ni in patterns of manner. Otherwise, it is impossible to know which nominals are followed by ni and which may occur alone, except by observing the usage of native speakers.

6.　P a r t i c l e to ' w i t h '

To, the particle of accompaniment, following a nominal means 'with.' A phrase ending in to may modify an inflected word directly or it may be followed by other particles:

　　　ni⌐hoñzi⌐ñ to kekkoñ-suru 'marry (with) a Japanese'
　　　to⌐modati to hana⌐su 'talk with a friend'
　　　to⌐modati to⌐ mo ha⌐na⌐su 'talk with a friend, too'

It may also modify certain nominals directly:

　　　tomodati to issyo 'together with a friend'

But as a description of nominals, it is regularly followed by particle no:

　　　a⌐merika⌐ziñ to no kekkoñ 'marriage with an American'
　　　a⌐ni to no hanasi 'a talk with my (older) brother'

The particle to 'and' introduced in Lesson 4, Grammatical Note 1(e), joins coordinate nominals. Compare:

---

[1] This is another example of an adjectival in its -ku form modifying an inflected word—a constantly recurring pattern.

Tanaka-sañ to Yamamoto-sañ wa ha⌐nasima⌐sita.   'Mr. Tanaka and
Mr. Yamamoto talked. '

and :

Tanaka-sañ wa Ya⌐mamoto-sañ to hanasima⌐sita.   'Mr. Tanaka talked
with Mr. Yamamoto.'

WARNING :   To never means 'with' in the sense of 'the means by which an
action is performed.'   Compare :

To⌐modati to hanasima⌐sita.   'I talked with a friend.'

and :

Ha⌐si de ta⌐bema⌐sita.   'I ate with chopsticks.'

For de 'by means of,' see Lesson 7, Grammatical Note 3 (d).

7.   Counter -niñmae

The counter -niñmae combines with the numerals of Series I to count portions or servings—of a single item or of everything eaten by a single person:

iti-niñmae	'1 portion'	roku-niñmae	'6 portions'
ni-niñmae	'2 portions'	siti-niñmae or nana-niñmae	'7 portions'
sañ-niñmae	'3 portions'	hati-niñmae	'8 portions'
yo-niñmae	'4 portions'	kyuu-niñmae or ku-niñmae	'9 portions'
go-niñmae	'5 portions'	zyuu-niñmae	'10 portions'

nañ-niñmae   'how many portions?'

DRILLS

A.   Substitution Drill (based on Grammatical Note 4)

1. Anything at all will be
   fine.   Na⌐ñ de mo i⌐i desu yo⌐

2. Either one will be fine.   Do⌐tira de mo i⌐i desu yo⌐

3. Any one (of a group of 3   Do⌐re de mo i⌐i desu yo⌐
   or more) at all will be
   fine.

4. Any time at all will be   I⌐tu de mo i⌐i desu yo⌐
   fine.

5. Anybody at all will be   Da⌐re de mo i⌐i desu yo⌐
   fine.

6. Any place at all will be   Do⌐ko de mo i⌐i desu yo⌐
   fine.

7. Any hour at all will be   Na⌐ñ-zi de mo i⌐i desu yo⌐
   fine.

8. Any number of people at   Na⌐ñ-niñ de mo i⌐i desu yo⌐
   all will be fine.

9. Any number of things (or   I⌐ku-tu de mo i⌐i desu yo⌐
   any age) at all will be fine.

10. Any book at all will be   Do⌐no hoñ de mo ⌐i⌐i desu yo⌐
    fine.
11. No matter whose it is,   Da⌐re no de mo i⌐i desu yo⌐
    it will be fine.
12. No matter what time it   Na⌐ñ-zi kara de mo i⌐i desu yo⌐
    starts, it will be fine.

B. Substitution Drill

1. How much is it for one   Iti-niñmae ⌐i⌐kura desu ka⌐
    portion?
2. How much is it for one   I⌐p-pai ⌐i⌐kura desu ka⌐
    glass (ful)?
3. How much is it for one   I⌐p-poñ ⌐i⌐kura desu ka⌐
    bottle? [1]
4. How much is it for one   I⌐ti⌐-mai ⌐i⌐kura desu ka⌐
    (thin, flat object)?
5. How much is it for one   Is-satu ⌐i⌐kura desu ka⌐
    book?
6. How much is it for one   I⌐ti-zi⌐kañ ⌐i⌐kura desu ka⌐
    hour?
7. How much is it for one   Iti-niti ⌐i⌐kura desu ka⌐
    day?
8. How much is it for one   I⌐k-ka⌐ḡetu ⌐i⌐kura desu ka⌐
    month?
9. How much is it for one   Hi⌐to⌐-ri ⌐i⌐kura desu ka⌐
    person?
10. How much is it for one   Hi⌐to⌐-tu ⌐i⌐kura desu ka⌐
    (thing)?

C. Substitution Drill (based on Grammatical Note 5)

1. They talked slowly.   Yu⌐kku⌐ri ha⌐nasima⌐sita.
2. They talked [in] simple   Ya⌐sasiku hanasima⌐sita.
    [language].
3. They talked together.   I⌐ssyo ni hanasima⌐sita.
4. They talked in a hurry.   I⌐so⌐ide ha⌐nasima⌐sita.
5. They talked that way.   So⌐o hanasima⌐sita.
6. They talked quickly.   Ha⌐yaku ha⌐nasima⌐sita.
7. They talked in the same   O⌐nazi ni hanasima⌐sita.
    way.
8. They talked [in] difficult   Mu⌐zukasiku hanasima⌐sita.
    [language].

---

[1] Or any long, cylindrical object.

D. Substitution Drill (based on Grammatical Note 6)

1. Last night I had dinner with a friend.
Yuube to⌐modati to issyo ni syokuzi (o) sima⌐sita.

2. Last night I went [there] with my mother.
Yuube ⌐ha⌐ha to issyo ni i⌐kima⌐si-ta.

3. Last night I went out with my father.
Yuube ti⌐ti⌐ to issyo ni de⌐kakema⌐-sita.

4. Last night I studied with my cousin.
Yuube i⌐to⌐ko to issyo ni be⌐ñkyoo-sima⌐sita.

5. Last night I came here with my parents.
Yuube ⌐ryo⌐osiñ to issyo ni ki⌐ma⌐-sita.

6. Last night I returned home with my children.
Yuube ko⌐domo to issyo ni kaerima⌐-sita.

7. Last night I saw [it] with my wife.
Yuube ⌐ka⌐nai to issyo ni mi⌐ma⌐si-ta.

8. Last night I ate with my aunt.
Yuube o⌐ba to issyo ni tabema⌐sita.

E. Substitution Drill (based on Grammatical Note 2)

1. Which do you like better, this one or that one?
Kore to are to ⌐do⌐tira /no ⌐ho⌐o/ ḡa o⌐suki de⌐su ka⌐

2. Which is more expensive, this one or that one?
Kore to are to ⌐do⌐tira /no ⌐ho⌐o/ ḡa ta⌐ka⌐i desu ka⌐

3. Which is bigger, this one or that one?
Kore to are to ⌐do⌐tira /no ⌐ho⌐o/ ḡa o⌐oki⌐i desu ka⌐

4. Which tastes better, this one or that one?
Kore to are to ⌐do⌐tira /no ⌐ho⌐o/ ḡa o⌐isi⌐i desu ka⌐

5. Which is better, this one or that one?
Kore to are to ⌐do⌐tira /no ⌐ho⌐o/ ḡa ⌐i⌐i desu ka⌐

6. Which is easier, this one or that one?
Kore to are to ⌐do⌐tira /no ⌐ho⌐o/ ḡa ya⌐sasi⌐i desu ka⌐

7. Which is newer, this one or that one?
Kore to are to ⌐do⌐tira /no ⌐ho⌐o/ ḡa a⌐tarasi⌐i desu ka⌐

8. Which is more difficult, this one or that one?
Kore to are to ⌐do⌐tira /no ⌐ho⌐o/ ḡa mu⌐zukasi⌐i desu ka⌐

9. Which is more interesting, this one or that one?
Kore to are to ⌐do⌐tira /no ⌐ho⌐o/ ḡa o⌐mosiro⌐i desu ka⌐

F. Substitution Drill (based on Grammatical Note 3)

(Insert na where required)

1. The one I like best is tempura.
I⌐tibañ suki⌐ na no wa te⌐ñpura de⌐su yo.

2. The worst one is this paper.
I⌐tibañ waru⌐i no wa ko⌐no siñbuñ de⌐-su yo.

3. The peppiest one is that child.
I⌐tibañ ge⌐ñki na no wa a⌐no kodomo de⌐su yo.

4. The oldest one is our car.
I⌐tibañ huru⌐i no wa u⌐ti no kuruma de⌐su yo.

5. The prettiest one is Miss
    Tanaka.

I⌐tibañ ki⌐ree na no wa Ta⌐naka-sañ
no ozyo⌐osañ desu yo.

6. The slowest one is that
    bus.

I⌐tibañ oso⌐i no wa a⌐no ba⌐su desu
yo.

7. The strangest one is that
    name.

I⌐tibañ he⌐ñ na no wa a⌐no namae desu yo.

8. The busiest one is that
    company.

I⌐tibañ isoḡasi⌐i no wa a⌐no kaisya
de⌐su yo.

9. The coldest one is the next
    room.

I⌐tibañ samu⌐i no wa to⌐nari no heya⌐
desu yo.

10. The most delicious (one) is
     the sushi at that place.

I⌐tibañ oisi⌐i no wa a⌐soko no osu⌐si
desu yo.

G. Substitution Drill (based on Grammatical Note 3)

1. Which is most expensive—
    this one, that one, or the
    one over there?

Kore to sore to are de, do⌐re ḡa
i⌐tibañ taka⌐i desu ka⌟

2. Which is most expensive—
    the blue one, the red one,
    or the black one?

A⌐o⌐i no to a⌐ka⌐i no to ku⌐ro⌐i no de,
do⌐re ḡa i⌐tibañ taka⌐i desu ka⌟

3. Which is most expensive—
    this store, that store, or
    the store over there?

Ko⌐no mise⌐ to so⌐no mise⌐ to a⌐no
mise⌐ de, do⌐re ḡa i⌐tibañ taka⌐i
desu ka⌟

4. Which is most expensive—
    train, airplane, or ship?

Ki⌐sya⌐ to hi⌐ko⌐oki to ⌐hu⌐ne no uti
de, do⌐re ḡa i⌐tibañ taka⌐i desu
ka⌟

5. Which is most expensive of
    those three things?

A⌐no mittu⌐ no uti de, do⌐re ḡa i⌐ti-
bañ taka⌐i desu ka⌟

6. Which is most expensive of
    these four (long, cylindrical
    objects)?

Ko⌐no yo⌐ñ-hoñ no uti de, do⌐re ḡa
i⌐tibañ taka⌐i desu ka⌟

7. Which is most expensive—
    meat, fish, or fowl?

Ni⌐ku⌐ to sākana to to̅ri de, do⌐re
ḡa i⌐tibañ taka⌐i desu ka⌟

8. Which is most expensive—
    tea, coffee, or milk?

Otya to ko⌐ohi⌐i to ⌐mi⌐ruku no uti,
do⌐re ḡa i⌐tibañ taka⌐i desu ka⌟

H. Grammar Drill (based on Grammatical Note 2)

Tutor: Kore wa āre hodo ⌐yo⌐ku a⌐rimase⌐ñ. 'This one is not as
         good as that one.'
Student: Are wa ko⌐re yo⌐ri ⌐i⌐i desu. 'That one is better than this
         one.'

1. Ki⌐sya⌐ wa hi⌐ko⌐oki hodo
    ⌐ha⌐yaku a⌐rimase⌐ñ.

Hi⌐ko⌐oki wa ki⌐sya⌐ yori ha⌐ya⌐i desu.

2. Tookyoo wa Sapporo hodo
    ⌐sa⌐muku a⌐rimase⌐ñ.

Sapporo wa To⌐okyoo yo⌐ri sa⌐mu⌐i
desu.

3. Bi⌐iru wa sāke hodo a⌐maku
    arimase⌐ñ.

Sake wa ⌐bi⌐iru yori a⌐ma⌐i desu.

4. Ro⌐ku-g̃atu⌐ wa ha⌐ti-g̃atu⌐   Ha⌐ti-g̃atu⌐ wa ro⌐ku-g̃atu⌐ yori a⌐tu⌐i
   hodo ⌐a⌐tuku a⌐rimase⌐ñ.   desu.
5. O⌐re⌐ñzi[1] wa rémoñ[2] hodo   Remoñ wa o⌐re⌐ñzi yori su⌐ppa⌐i desu.
   su⌐ppa⌐ku a⌐rimase⌐ñ.
6. Ba⌐su wa ki⌐sya⌐ hodo ⌐ta⌐-   Ki⌐sya⌐ wa ⌐ba⌐su yori ta⌐ka⌐i desu.
   kaku a⌐rimase⌐ñ.
7. Nihoñg̃o wa éeg̃o hodo   Eeg̃o wa ni⌐hoñg̃o yo⌐ri ⌐yo⌐ku wa⌐ka-
   ⌐yo⌐ku wa⌐karimase⌐ñ.   rima⌐su.
8. Ko⌐ohi⌐i wa ótya hodo   Otya wa ko⌐ohi⌐i yori su⌐ki⌐ desu.
   su⌐ki⌐ zya a⌐rimase⌐ñ.

I. Grammar Drill (based on Grammatical Note 1)

Tutor: A⌐ñmari wakarimase⌐ñ.   'He doesn't understand very much.'
Student: A⌐ñmari wakara⌐nai desyoo?   'He doesn't understand very
         much, does he?'

1. Ma⌐da so⌐no ho⌐ñ (o) yo-   Ma⌐da so⌐no ho⌐ñ (o) yo⌐ma⌐nai de-
   ⌐mimase⌐ñ.   syoo?
2. Da⌐re mo kaimase⌐ñ desi-   Da⌐re mo kawana⌐katta desyoo?
   ta.
3. Be⌐tu ni oisiku arimase⌐ñ.   Be⌐tu ni oisiku na⌐i desyoo?
4. Ni⌐hoñg̃o de iimase⌐ñ de-   Ni⌐hoñg̃o de iwana⌐katta desyoo?
   sita.
5. Da⌐re mo demase⌐ñ desi-   Da⌐re mo de⌐nakatta desyoo?
   ta.
6. Ta⌐naka-sañ no o⌐kusañ   Ta⌐naka-sañ no o⌐kusañ (wa) ta⌐ba-
   (wa) ta⌐bako (o) suimase⌐ñ.   ko (o) suwana⌐i desyoo?
7. A⌐tarasi⌐i sakana zya a⌐ri-   A⌐tarasi⌐i sakana zya ⌐na⌐katta de-
   mase⌐ñ desita.   syoo?
8. Bi⌐iru to sáke wa no⌐mi-   Bi⌐iru to sáke wa no⌐ma⌐nai desyoo?
   mase⌐ñ.
9. E⌐eg̃o (o) beñkyoo-site (i)-   E⌐eg̃o o beñkyoo-site (i)na⌐i desyoo?
   mase⌐ñ.
10. Ta⌐isi⌐kañ ni tu⌐to⌐mete   Ta⌐isi⌐kañ ni tu⌐to⌐mete (i)⌐rassya-
    (i)⌐rassyaimase⌐ñ.   ra⌐nai desyoo?

J. Response Drill

Tutor: Sore (wa) ⌐na⌐ñ desyoo ka. /hurosiki/ 'What do you suppose
         that is?' /furoshiki/
Student: Yo⌐ku wa⌐karimase⌐ñ g̃a, hu⌐rosiki zya na⌐i desyoo ka.   'I
         can't tell for sure but isn't it a furoshiki?'

---

[1] 'Orange.'

[2] 'Lemon.'

1. Are (wa) ⌐na⌐ñ desyoo   Yo⌐ku wa⌐karimase⌐ñ g̃a, ku⌐suri
   ka.   /kusuri/   zya na⌐i desyoo ka.

2. Koko (wa) ⌐do⌐ko desyoo   Yo⌐ku wa⌐karimase⌐ñ g̃a, Siñbasi
   ka.   /Siñbasi[1]/   zya na⌐i desyoo ka.

3. I⌐ma ⌐na⌐ñ-zi desyoo ka.   Yo⌐ku wa⌐karimase⌐ñ g̃a, sañ-zi-
   /sa⌐ñ-zi-g̃o⌐ro/   g̃o⌐ro zya ⌐na⌐i desyoo ka.

4. A⌐no⌐ hito (wa) ⌐da⌐re de- Yo⌐ku wa⌐karimase⌐ñ g̃a, Ta⌐naka-
   syoo ka.   /Ta⌐naka-sañ   sañ no oto⌐osañ zya ⌐na⌐i desyoo
   no oto⌐osañ/   ka.

5. Sore (wa) na⌐ñyo⌐obi de-   Yo⌐ku wa⌐karimase⌐ñ g̃a, do⌐yo⌐obi
   syoo ka.   /do⌐yo⌐obi/   zya ⌐na⌐i desyoo ka.

6. Sore (wa) ⌐i⌐kura desyoo   Yo⌐ku wa⌐karimase⌐ñ g̃a, sañbya-
   ka.   /sa⌐ñbyaku⌐-eñ/   ku⌐-eñ zya ⌐na⌐i desyoo ka.

7. Ta⌐naka-sañ no ho⌐ñ (wa)   Yo⌐ku wa⌐karimase⌐ñ g̃a, ku⌐ro⌐i
   ⌐do⌐re desyoo ka.   /ku⌐ro⌐i   no zya ⌐na⌐i desyoo ka.
   no/

8. Are (wa) ⌐do⌐no da⌐ig̃aku Yo⌐ku wa⌐karimase⌐ñ g̃a, To⌐odai
   desyo⌐o ka.   /Toodai/   zya na⌐i desyoo ka.

K. Response Drill (based on Grammatical Note 2)

> Tutor: Kore (wa) a⌐re yo⌐ri ⌐i⌐i desu ka.   'Is this one better than
> that one?'
> Student: Iie, a⌐re hodo yo⌐ku a⌐rimase⌐ñ yo.   'Why no, it isn't as
> good as that one.'

1. Kono miti (wa) a⌐no miti   Iie, a⌐no miti hodo abunaku arima-
   yo⌐ri a⌐buna⌐i desu ka.   se⌐ñ yo.

2. Kono kusuri (wa) a⌐no ku-   Iie, a⌐no kusuri hodo ni⌐g̃aku a⌐ri-
   suri yo⌐ri ni⌐g̃a⌐i desu ka.   mase⌐ñ yo.

3. Ko⌐no koohi⌐i (wa) a⌐no koo- Iie, a⌐no koohi⌐i hodo ⌐ko⌐ku a⌐ri-
   hi⌐i yori ⌐ko⌐i desu ka.   mase⌐ñ yo.

4. Ko⌐no ho⌐ñ (wa) a⌐no ho⌐ñ   Iie, a⌐no ho⌐ñ hodo ⌐ya⌐suku a⌐ri-
   yori ya⌐su⌐i desu ka.   mase⌐ñ yo.

5. Kono tokee (wa) a⌐no tokee   Iie, a⌐no tokee hodo ya⌐suku a⌐ri-
   yo⌐ri ya⌐su⌐i desu ka.   mase⌐ñ yo.

6. Kono uti (wa) a⌐no uti yo⌐ri Iie, a⌐no uti hodo ki⌐ree zya a⌐ri-
   ⌐ki⌐ree desu ka.   mase⌐ñ yo.

7. Ko⌐no oka⌐si (wa) a⌐no oka⌐si Iie, a⌐no oka⌐si hodo o⌐isiku arima-
   yori o⌐isi⌐i desu ka.   se⌐ñ yo.

8. Ko⌐no iro⌐ (wa) a⌐no iro⌐ yo- Iie, a⌐no iro⌐ hodo u⌐suku arimase⌐ñ
   ri u⌐su⌐i desu ka.   yo.

9. Kono o⌐su⌐si (wa) a⌐no osu⌐- Iie, a⌐no osu⌐si hodo ⌐ka⌐raku a⌐ri-
   si yori ka⌐ra⌐i desu ka.   mase⌐ñ yo.

10. Ko⌐no⌐ ko (wa) a⌐no⌐ ko   Iie, a⌐no⌐ ko hodo ⌐ge⌐ñki zya a⌐ri-
    yori ⌐ge⌐ñki desu ka.   mase⌐ñ yo.

---

[1] Section of Tokyo.

L. Level Drill (based on Grammatical Note 1)

> Tutor: A⌐ñmari wakarimase⌐ñ kara. (Formal)
> Student: A⌐ñmari wakara⌐nai kara. (Informal)
> 'Because I don't understand very much.'

1. So⌐re wa sirimase⌐ñ kara.   So⌐re wa sirana⌐i kara.
2. O⌐oki na ⌐ko⁴e de ha⌐nasi-   O⌐oki na ⌐ko⁴e de ha⌐nasa⌐nakatta
   mase⌐ñ desita kara.   kara.
3. Ko⌐ñna iro⌐ (wa) su⌐ki⌐ zya   Ko⌐ñna iro⌐ (wa) su⌐ki⌐ zya ⌐na⌐i
   a⌐rimase⌐ñ kara.   kara.
4. Ma⌐da ka⌐wakimase⌐ñ kara.   Ma⌐da ka⌐waka⌐nai kara.
5. Kinoo i⌐rassyaimase⌐ñ de-   Kinoo i⌐rassyara⌐nakatta kara.
   sita kara.
6. Ki⌐ree na uti zya a⌐rima-   Ki⌐ree na uti zya ⌐na⌐katta kara.
   se⌐ñ desita kara.
7. Ko⌐ñna ho⌐ñ (wa) o⌐mosi⌐-   Ko⌐ñna ho⌐ñ (wa) o⌐mosi⌐roku ⌐na⌐i
   roku a⌐rimase⌐ñ kara.   kara.
8. Kinoo da⌐re mo kimase⌐ñ   Kinoo da⌐re mo ko⌐nakatta kara.
   desita kara.
9. Kyo⌐o no siḡoto (wa) mu⌐zu-   Kyo⌐o no siḡoto wa mu⌐zukasiku na⌐-
   kasiku arimase⌐ñ desita   katta kara.
   kara.
10. Go⌐hañ (wa) ⌐ma⌐da de⌐ki-   Go⌐hañ wa ⌐ma⌐da de⌐ki⌐nai kara.
    mase⌐ñ kara.

M. Expansion Drill

1. Is it fast? (Indirect)   Ha⌐ya⌐i desyoo ka.
   Which is faster?   Do⌐tira no ⌐ho⁴o ḡa ha⌐ya⁴i desyoo
                                        ka.

   Which is faster—bus or   Ba⌐su to deñsya to, do⌐tira no ⌐ho⁴o
   electric train?   ḡa ha⌐ya⁴i desyoo ka.

2. It isn't ready. . . .   De⌐kimase⌐ñ ḡa_
   It isn't ready yet. . . .   Ma⌐da de⌐kimase⌐ñ ḡa_
   The toast isn't ready yet. . . .   To⌐osuto wa ⌐ma⌐da de⌐kimase⌐ñ ḡa_
   The eggs are ready but the   Ta⌐ma⌐ḡo wa ⌐mo⁴o de⌐kima⁴sita
   toast isn't ready yet. . . .   ḡa, to⌐osuto wa ⌐ma⌐da de⌐kimase⌐ñ
                                         ḡa_

3. Please come.   I⌐ra⌐site kudasai.
   Please come to see us (lit.   U⌐ti e ira⌐site kudasai.
   to our house).
   Do please come to see us.   Do⌐ozo u⌐ti e ira⌐site kudasai.
   Any time will be fine but do   I⌐tu de mo ⌐ti⁴i desu ḡa, do⌐ozo u⌐ti
   please come to see us.   e ira⌐site kudasai.

4. You know, it has grown   Su⌐kima⌐sita yo.
   empty.
   You know, I'm hungry.   O⌐naka ḡa sukima⌐sita yo.

You know, I'm hungry already.	Mo˺o o˹naka g̃a sukima˺sita yo.
You know, I didn't eat so I'm hungry already.	Ta˹be˺nakatta kara, mo˺o o˹naka g̃a sukima˺sita yo.
You know, I didn't eat breakfast so I'm hungry already.	A˹sago˺hañ o ta˹be˺nakatta kara, mo˺o o˹naka g̃a sukima˺sita yo.

5. I went to the JTB. [1]

I went to the JTB. [1]	Ko˹otuuko˺osya e i˥kima˧sita.
We went to the JTB together.	Issyo ni ko˹otuuko˺osya e i˥kima˧sita.
I went to the JTB (together) with a friend.	Tomodati to issyo ni ko˹otuuko˺osya e i˥kima˧sita.
I went to the JTB (together) with a Japanese friend.	Ni˹hoñzi˺ñ no tomodati to issyo ni ko˹otuuko˺osya e i˥kima˧sita.
I went to the JTB (together) with a Japanese friend this morning.	Ke˹sa ni˹hoñzi˺ñ no tomodati to issyo ni ko˹otuuko˺osya e i˥kima˧sita.

6.

I don't like them.	Su˹ki˺ zya a˥rimase˧ñ.
I don't like them as much as ships.	Hu˺ne hodo su˥ki˧ zya a˥rimase˧ñ.
I like [them] but I don't like them as much as ships.	Su˹ki˺ desu g̃a, hu˺ne hodo su˥ki˧ zya a˥rimase˧ñ.
I like [them] more than airplanes, but I don't like them as much as ships.	Hi˹ko˺oki yori su˥ki˧ desu g̃a, hu˺ne hodo su˥ki˧ zya a˥rimase˧ñ.
Trains I like more than airplanes, but I don't like them as much as ships.	Ki˹sya˺ wa hi˹ko˺oki yori su˥ki˧ desu g̃a, hu˺ne hodo su˥ki˧ zya a˥rimase˧ñ.

SHORT SUPPLEMENTARY DIALOGUES

(with questions)

1. Smith (host): O˹nomi˺mono wa ˹na˺ni o me˥siag̃arima˧su ka˩
   Tanaka (guest): O˹sake mo bi˺iru mo i˥tadakimase˧ñ kara, zyu˺usu[2] o oneg̃ai-itasimasu.

   a. Tanaka-sañ wa ˹do˺ñna no˥mi˧mono o ta˥nomima˧su ka˩
   b. Do˺o site so˥re o tanomima˧su ka˩

---

[1] 'Japan Travel Bureau.'

[2] 'Juice.'

2. Tanaka: Kyo˥o wa ki⌐no˥o hodo ⌐a˥tuku ⌐na˥i ⌐ne˥e.
   Yamamoto: Kyo˥o wa tyo⌐odo i˥i ⊢ne˦e.

   a. Kyo˥o to ki⌐no˥o to, ⌐do˥tira g̃a a⊢tu˦i desu ka⌟
   b. Tanaka-sañ to Yamamoto-sañ wa o⌐toko˥ desyoo ka, o⌐ñna˥ desyoo ka⌟

3. Tanaka: Su˥misu-sañ no nihoñg̃o ⌐do˥o?
   Yamamoto: A⌐no˥ hito na⌐ñ de mo waka˥ru yo⌟

   a. Su˥misu-sañ wa ni⌐hoñg̃o g̃a yo˥ku wa⊢karima˦su ka, a⌐ñmari waka-rimase˥ñ ka.
   b. Da˥re g̃a so⊢o iima˦su ka⌟

4. Tanaka: Su˥misu-sañ mo ko⌐otuuko˥osya e i⌐rassyaima˥sita ka⌟
   Yamamoto: I⌐rassyara˥nakatta desyoo. Tyo˥tto ⊢ma˦e ni zi⌐mu˥syo ni i⊢ra-ssya˦tta kara.

   a. Su˥misu-sañ wa ko⌐otuuko˥osya e i⌐kima˥sita ka⌟
   b. Yamamoto-sañ wa ⌐do˥o site wa⊢karima˦su ka⌟

5. Smith: De⌐ñwa-sima˥sita ka⌟
   Tanaka: E˥e, si⌐ma˥sita g̃a; da⌐re mo de˥nakatta kara, ma˥ta a˥to de kake-masu.

   a. Ta⌐naka-sañ wa deñwa-sima˥sita ka⌟
   b. Do˥o site ma⊢ta a˥to de ka⊢kema˦su ka⌟

SUPPLEMENTARY CONVERSATION

(Mr. Saito is telephoning a restaurant to arrange for a dinner party.)

Saito: Mo˥simosi.
Restaurant Employee: Mo˥simosi. Su⌐ehiro[1] de gozaima˥su.
Saito: Kotira wa To⌐okyoo-gi˥ñkoo no Sa⌐itoo de˥su g̃a⌟
R. E.: Ma⌐ido ari˥g̃atoo gozaimasu.
Saito: Ko˥ñbañ ro⌐ku-zi-g̃o˥ro i⊢ku˦ kara, o˥neg̃ai-sima˥su.
R. E.: Ha˥a, ka⌐sikomarima˥sita. Ko˥ñbañ wa ⌐na˥ñ-niñ-sama[2] de go⊢zaima˦-su ka⌟
Saito: Go-⌐ni˥ñ desu yo.
R. E.: Ha˥a. Kyo˥o wa ⌐do˥ñna mo⊢no˦ ni i⊢tasimasyo˦o ka.
Saito: Do˥ñna mo⊢no˦ g̃a ⊢i˦i desyoo ka ⌐ne˥e. Kyo˥o wa ni⌐ku˥ to sakana to do˥tti g̃a ii?

---

[1] A restaurant name.

[2] Polite equivalent of nañ-niñ used commonly by restaurant and hotel personnel.

R. E.: Sa⌐yoo de gozaima⌐su ⌐ne⌐e. Kyo⌐o wa a⌐tarasi⌐i o⌐sakana ḡa gozai-
        ma⌐su kara, osasimi wa i⌐ka⌐ḡa de gozaimasu ka⌐
Saito: A⌐a, i⌐i desyoo.
R. E.: I⌐i to⌐ri mo gozaima⌐su kara, tori no sukiyaki mo i⌐ka⌐ḡa de gozaima-
        syoo ka.
Saito: A⌐a, ke⌐kkoo. So⌐re go-niñmae oneḡai-sima⌐su. Hoka ni ya̅sai to ku-
        ⌐da⌐mono su⌐ko⌐si oneḡai-simasu.
R. E.: Ha⌐a, ka⌐sikomarima⌐sita. O⌐nomi⌐mono wa o⌐sake to obi⌐iru to ⌐do⌐tira
        ḡa yo⌐rosi⌐i desyoo ka.
Saito: Tu⌐metai bi⌐iru oneḡai-simasu.
R. E.: Ha⌐a ⌐ha⌐a.
Saito: Iti-niñmae i⌐kura-ḡu⌐rai?
R. E.: Sa⌐yoo de gozaima⌐su ⌐ne⌐e. Iti-niñmae se⌐ñ-eñ-ḡu⌐rai de gozaimasu
        ḡa⌐ O⌐bi⌐iru wa hya⌐ku rokuzyu⌐u-eñ de gozaimasu.
Saito: Ke⌐kkoo. Zya⌐a oneḡai-simasu.
R. E.: Ka⌐sikomarima⌐sita. Ro⌐ku⌐-zi de gozaimasu ne? A⌐ri⌐ḡatoo gozai-
        masu.

English Equivalent

Saito: Hello.
Restaurant Employee: Hello. (This is the) Suehiro (Restaurant).
Saito: This is [Mr.] Saito at the Bank of Tokyo (but) . . .
R. E.: (Thank you for coming here often.)
Saito: Tonight I'm coming (lit. going) at about 6 so will you take care of us?
R. E.: Certainly. How many people will it be tonight?
Saito: It will be 5.
R. E.: Certainly. What kind of things would you like today?
Saito: I w o n d e r what (kind of things) would be good. . . . Which is better
        today—meat or fish?
R. E.: Let me see. We have fresh fish today so how about sashimi?
Saito: Oh, that would be fine.
R. E.: I have some good chicken too, so how about chicken sukiyaki (too)?
Saito: Oh, fine. I'd like 5 portions of that. In addition, I'd like a few vege-
        tables and some fruit.
R. E.: Certainly. For drinks, which would be better— sake or beer?
Saito: I'd like cold beer.
R. E.: All right.
Saito: About how much [will it be] per person?
R. E.: Let me see. . . . It will be about ¥1000 per person but [will that be all
        right?] The beer will be ¥160 [i.e. extra].
Saito: Fine. Well then, please take good care of us!
R. E.: Certainly. Six o'clock, isn't it? Thank you.

EXERCISES

1. Using appropriate magazine pictures, photographs, or line drawings, prac-
    tice comparisons: 'Which is more —— , X or Y?'; 'X is more —— than Y';
    'Y is not as —— as X.'

2. You have taken some Japanese friends to a restaurant for dinner as your guests. Find out what each one wants, place the orders, and make any complaints that are necessary (for example: 'I ordered beer but you brought sake,' 'I ordered rice but you haven't brought it,' etc.), and at the end, take care of the check.

3. Telephone the Suehiro Restaurant and order dinner. Include the following information:

   a. who you are
   b. how many will be in your party
   c. when you are coming
   d. what you would like to eat and drink
   e. the price per person

4. Turn back to Drill L on page 271. Make up questions for which the sentences of Drill L would be appropriate answers (cf. Lesson 14, Exercise 3), and then drill on the questions with their answers (informal alternants).

5. Practice the Basic Dialogues, using appropriate variations.

Lesson 16. At Home

BASIC DIALOGUES: FOR MEMORIZATION

(a)

Smith

teacher or doctor	se⌐nse⌐e
Teacher Wada or Dr. Wada	Wa⌐da-sense⌐e
next week	raisyuu
next Friday	ra⌐isyuu no kiñyo⌐obi

1. Dr. Wada, won't you come to our house for dinner (lit. a meal) next Friday?

⌐Wa⌐da-sense⌐e. Ra⌐isyuu no kiñyo⌐-obi ni úti e syo⌐kuzi ni irassyaima-se⌐ñ ka⌐

Dr. Wada

reply to invitation

take pleasure in	yo⌐roko⌐bu /-u/
gladly or with pleasure	yo⌐roko⌐ñde
visit or call on	ukagau ⌐ /-u/

2. Next Friday? I'll be glad to come.

⌐Raisyuu no ki⌐ñyo⌐obi desu ka⌐ Yo-⌐roko⌐ñde ukaḡaimasu.

residence	su⌐mai or o⌐su⌐mai⌐

3. Where do you live? (Lit. Where is your residence?)

⌐O⌐su⌐mai (wa) ⌐do⌐tira desyoo ka.

Formal

Smith

(a section of Tokyo)	A⌐ka⌐saka
apartment house	a⌐pa⌐ato
Harris (Apartment) House	Ha⌐risu-apa⌐ato

4. I live in (lit. it is) Harris House in Akasaka. You probably know it, don't you?

⌐A⌐ka⌐saka no Ha⌐risu-apa⌐ato desu ḡa, go⌐zo⌐ñzi desyoo ne?

Dr. Wada

5. Yes, I do (know).

⌐E⌐e, zo⌐ñzite orimasu.

what floor? or how many floors?	nañ-ḡai

6. What floor is your apartment?

⌐Otaku (wa) na⌐ñ-ḡai desyo⌐o ka.

Smith

first floor or one floor	ik-kai
third floor or three floors	sañ-ḡai

7. It's number 306 on the third floor.

    Sañ-ḡai no ⌐sa⌐ñbyaku ro⌐ku⌐-bañ desu.

Dr. Wada

8. I see.

    Wa⌐karima⌐sita.

9. What time shall I come?

    Na⌐ñ-zi ni u⌐kaḡaimasyo⌐o ka.

Smith

    night or night-time   yo⌐ru

10. How would about 7:30 in the evening be?

    Yo⌐ru no si⌐ti-zi-hañ-ḡo⌐ro i⌐ka⌐ḡa desyoo ka.

Dr. Wada

11. That will be fine. I'll come at 7:30. Thank you very much.

    Ke⌐kkoo desu. Si⌐ti-zi-ha⌐ñ ni ukaḡaimasu. Do⌐o mo a⌐ri⌐ḡatoo gozaimasu.

(b)

Tanaka

    gray   haiiro
    blue or green   a⌐o
    a gray and blue car   haiiro to ⌐a⌐o no kuruma

12. Is that gray and blue car yours?

    Ano haiiro to ⌐a⌐o no kuruma (wa) o⌐taku no⌐ desu ka⌐

Smith

13. No. That's the doctor's (or teacher's), isn't it?

    Iie. Are wa se⌐ñse⌐e no desyoo?

    brown   tyairo

14. Ours is brown.

    U⌐ti no⌐ wa tya⌐iro de⌐su yo.

(c)

Mr. Tanaka

    door   to
    [something] closes or shuts   si⌐ma⌐ru /-u/
    be closed or be shut   si⌐ma⌐tte (i)ru or si⌐ma⌐tte ⌐o⌐ru+

15. Is the door closed?

    To (ḡa) si⌐ma⌐tte (i)ru?

Maid

    close or shut [something]   si⌐me⌐ru /-ru/

16. Yes. I just closed it. . . .

    E⌐e, i⌐ma si⌐mema⌐sita ḡa⌐

Mr. Tanaka

    key   ka⌐gi⌐
    [something] locks   ka⌐gi⌐ ḡa ka⌐ka⌐ru /-u/

be locked	ka⌐gi˥ ḡa ka˫ka˧tte (i)ru or ka⌐gi˥ ḡa ka˫ka˧tte oru+
17. Is it locked too?	Ka⌐gi˥ mo ka˫ka˧tte (i)ru?

Maid

lock [something]	ka⌐gi˥ o ka˫ke˧ru /-ru/
18. No. Shall I lock it?	Iie. Ka⌐kemasyo˥o ka.

Mr. Tanaka

yes	a˥a [1]
19. Yes. Lock it, will you?	A˥a, ka˥kete ne?

(d)

Mrs. Tanaka

window	ma˥do
[something] opens	aku /-u/
be open	aite (i)ru or a⌐ite oru+
20. Are the windows open?	Ma˥do (ḡa) aite (i)ru?

Maid

have been closed or shut	si˥mete ˫a˧ru
21. The ones over there are open, but the ones here have been shut. . .	Mu⌐koo no˥ wa a˫ite orima˧su ḡa, ko⌐tira no˥ wa ⌐si˥mete arimasu.
open [something]	akeru /-ru/
22. Shall I open them?	A⌐kemasyo˥o ka.

Mrs. Tanaka

23. Yes. It's a little hot.	E˥e. Tyo˥tto a⌐tu˥i wa⌣

(e)

Mr. Tanaka

heater	su⌐to˥obu
[something] becomes attached or turned on	tu˥ku /-u/
be attached or be turned on	tu˥ite (i)ru or tu˥ite ˫o˧ru+
24. Is the heater on?	Su⌐to˥obu (ḡa) ⌐tu˥ite (i)ru?

Maid

attach or turn on [something]	tu⌐ke˥ru /-ru/

---

[1] Informal, man's word.

25. It's not on. Shall I turn it   ⌈Tu⌐ite o⌐rimase⌐n̄. Tu⌐kemasyo⌐o ka.
    on?

Mr. Tanaka

          no   i⌐ya [1]
          being that condition   so⌐no mama⌐ de
          is warm   a⌐tataka⌐i /-ku/ or
                                       a⌐ttaka⌐i /-ku/

26. No, it's fine as it is. (Since)   ⌈I⌐ya, so⌐no mama⌐ de ⌐i⌐i yo. Mo⌐o
    it's warm already.   ⌊a⌐ttaka⌐i kara.

(f)

Tanaka

          television   te⌐rebi
          electricity or electric   de⌐n̄ki
            light
          turn off or extinguish   kesu /-u/   ⌐⌐ .
            or erase [something]

27. I'm going to watch television   ⌈Te⌐rebi (o) ⌐mi⌐ru kara, de⌐n̄ki (o)
    so turn off the light.   ⌊ke̱site.

Maid

          have been turned off   ke⌐site a⌐ru   or
                                        ke⌐site gozaima⌐su +

28. The ones here have all been   ⌈Ko⌐ko no⌐ (wa) mi⌐n̄na ke̱site gozai-
    turned off. . . .   ma⌐su ḡa_

Tanaka

          entry hall   ge⌐n̄kan̄
29. How about the one in the   ⌈Ge⌐n̄kan̄ no wa?
    entry hall?

Maid

30. Oh, that one is on, isn't it.   ⌈A⌐a, a⌐re wa tu⌐ite orimasu ⌐ne⌐e.
    I'll turn it off [right] now.   ⌊I⌐ma ke⌐sima⌐su.

(g)

Maid

          radio   ra⌐zio
          make small or turn   ti⌐isaku suru   or
            down   ti⌐isaku i⌐tasima⌐su +
31. Shall I turn down the radio a   ⌈Ra⌐zio (o) mo⌐o suko⌐si ti⌐isaku i⌐ta-
    little more?   simasyo⌐o ka.

---

[1] Informal, man's word.

Mr. Tanaka

being big or loud, as
it is
door (Western style)

o⌐oki⌐i ma⌐ma⌐ de

do⌐a   *doesn't matter*

32. No, it doesn't matter if it's
loud but close that door,
will you? — because Taro
is studying in there.

I⌐ya, o⌐oki⌐i ma⌐ma⌐ de ka⌐mawa⌐nai
ğa, sono ⌐do⌐a (o) ⌐si⌐mete ne? —
⌐Ta⌐roo (ğa) mu⌐koo de beñkyoo-
site (i)ru⌐ kara.

(h)

Mrs. Tanaka

women's speech

is dirty

ki⌐tana⌐i /-ku/

33. Hasn't this place gotten
dirty!

Koko (wa) ki⌐tana⌐ku ⌐na⌐tta wa
⌐ne⌐e.

clean (verb)
after cleaning
straighten up

soozi-suru
so⌐ozi-site⌐ kara
vt. ka⌐tazuke⌐ru /-ru/

34. Clean it up, will you? Then
after you clean it, straighten
up the entry hall.

So⌐ozi-site⌐ ne? Sore kara, so⌐ozi-
site⌐ kara, ge⌐ñkañ (o) ka⌐tazu⌐ke-
te.

Maid

preparation

sitaku

35. What about getting dinner
ready? (Lit. As for meal
preparations?)

Osyokuzi no sitaku wa?

Mrs. Tanaka

after straightening up

ka⌐tazu⌐kete kara

36. Do it after you straighten
up, will you?

Ka⌐tazu⌐kete kara si⌐te⌐ ne?

informal

NOTES ON THE BASIC DIALOGUES

1. Se⌐ñse⌐e means 'teacher,' and 'doctor' in both the medical and non-
medical sense. It is the regular term of address for such persons, always
implying respect and deference on the part of the speaker. As a term of
address, it may be affixed to the family name or used independently.

   Raisyuu 'next week': compare also raineñ 'next year' and ra⌐iğetu 'next
month.'

2. Yo⌐roko⌐bu is not used in reference to the speaker except in its gerund
form, when describing the manner in which something is done (cf. Lesson
15, Grammatical Note 5). In this latter pattern, it may be used in reference to any subject. Thus: yo⌐roko⌐bu desyoo '[someone other than the
speaker] will probably enjoy it or be glad'; but yo⌐roko⌐ñde simasu '[some-
one] will gladly do it.'

6. A⌐pa⌐ato is an apartment house. An apartment within an apartment house

is one's household—uti or otaku.

12. Otaku no means 'your(s),' i.e. '(the one) belonging to your household.'

14. Uti no means 'our(s),' i.e. '(the one) belonging to our household.'

16. 'but— is that all right?'

17-18. Note: X ⌐no kaḡi¬ ḡa ka⌐ka¬ru 'X locks';
         X ⌐no kaḡi¬ o ka⌐ke¬ru 'lock X'

21. 'but— how do you want them?'

26. Lit. 'Being that condition, it's fine.' The nominal ma⌐ma¬ refers to an existing condition defined by the descriptive word or sequence which always precedes it.

A⌐tataka¬i, and contracted a⌐ttaka¬i, mean 'warm'— i.e. 'nice and warm.' Typical days of spring, and unseasonably w a r m days of winter, a r e⋅ a⌐tataka¬i.

28. 'but— is there anything else I can do?'

32. Lit. 'Even being its loud condition, it doesn't matter.'

An informal inflected word before ḡa 'but' occurs in the informal speech of men.

To (Sentence 15 above) is the general term for door and can refer to doors of any style. Do¬a, on the other hand refers only to Western-style doors.

35. Note: sitaku o suru 'make preparations,' 'prepare'; X no sitaku o suru 'make preparations for X,' 'prepare for X.'

GRAMMATICAL NOTES

 Verbals: Transitive and Intransitive; Gerund + √⌐a¬ru

A verbal which may be preceded by a direct object + particle o is said to be TRANSITIVE. A verbal which never so occurs is said to be INTRANSITIVE. Thus, kau 'buy' is transitive (za⌐ssi o kaima¬sita 'I bought a magazine') but wa⌐ka¬ru 'be comprehensible' is intransitive (e⌐eḡo¬ ḡa wakarima¬su 'I understand English').

Some other transitive verbals are: ta⌐be¬ru 'eat,' no⌐mu 'drink,' mi¬ru 'see,' mi⌐se¬ru 'show,' wasureru 'forget'; some other intransitive verbals are: iru 'be needed,' ka⌐ka¬ru 'be required,' kikoeru 'be audible,' a¬ru 'be (inanimate,' 'have,' iku 'go.'

In Japanese, there are many pairs of verbals whose stems resemble each other phonetically, one member of which is transitive and the other intransitive. Several examples occur in this lesson:

Transitive	Intransitive
akeru 'open [something]'	aku '[something] opens'
(Do˥a o a˩kema˥sita.	(Do˥a ga a˩kima˥sita.
'I opened the door.')	'The door opened.')
si˩me˩ru 'close [something]'	si˩ma˩ru '[something] closes'
(Do˥a o si˩mema˥sita.	(Do˥a ga si˩marima˥sita.
'I closed the door.')	'The door closed.')
tu˩ke˩ru 'attach [something]'	tu˩ku '[something] becomes attached'
(De˥ñki o tu˩kema˥sita. tsukete	(De˥ñki ga tu˩kima˥sita. tsuite
'I turned on the light.')	'The light went on.')

A pair introduced previously is:

na˩o˩su 'make [something or	na˩o˩ru '[something or someone]
someone] better'	gets better'

Note also the following pair:

kesu 'turn [something] off'	kieru /-ru/ '[something] goes out
	or becomes extinguished'

A verbal gerund + (i)ru means that an action is now going on, or that the result of a previous action now exists (cf. Lesson 10, Grammatical Note 2). Usually the gerund of a transitive verbal + (i)ru has the former meaning, whereas the gerund of an intransitive + (i)ru has the latter meaning:

now going on Transitive   now exists Intransitive

Do˥a o a˩kete (i)ma˥su.	Do˥a ga a˩ite (i)ma˥su.
'I'm opening the door.'	'The door is open.'
Do˥a o ˩si˩mete (i)masu.	Do˥a ga si˩ma˥tte (i)masu.
'I'm closing the door.'	'The door is closed.'
De˥ñki o tu˩ke˥te (i)masu.	De˥ñki ga ˩tu˩ite (i)masu.
'I'm turning on the light.'	'The light is on.'

The subject of a gerund + √(i)ru pattern may be animate or inanimate. When the subject is inanimate, √(i)ru is replaced by √o˩ru (formal: √o˩rima˥su) in polite speech, [1] but never by √i˩rassya˩ru, an honorific which refers only to people.

A new combination appears in this lesson: the gerund of a TRANSITIVE verbal + √a˩ru 'so-and-so has been done.' [2] Like an intransitive gerund + √(i)ru, it indicates the existing result of a previous action, and the combination is itself intransitive; however, a transitive gerund + √a˩ru always implies the result of an action that HAS BEEN DONE BY SOMEONE. Thus:

use transitive verb form

---

[1] The combination is polite neutral (+), not humble (+).

[2] This pattern includes transitive verbals in general—not only those having an intransitive partner.

Do¹a ḡa a⊢kete arima⁴su. 'The door has been opened.'
Do¹a ḡa ⊢si⁴mete arimasu. 'The door has been closed.'
De⁷ñki ḡa tu⊢ke⁴te arimasu. 'The light has been turned on.'
Ti¹zu ḡa ⊢ka⁴ite arimasu. 'The map has been drawn.'
Si⁷ñbuñ ḡa katte arima⁷su. 'The newspaper has been bought.'

Compare these examples with one like Do¹a ḡa a⊢ite ima⁴su, which means simply 'The door is open'; whether it was opened by someone or whether it opened by itself is not made clear by the pattern which uses the intransitive gerund.

The object of a transitive verbal becomes the subject of the corresponding gerund + √a⁷ru: *(√te arimasu*

Sa⊢kana o tabema⁷sita. 'I ate the fish.'
Sa⊢kana ḡa ta⁷bete arimasu. 'The fish has been eaten.'

The subject of a gerund + √a⁷ru pattern is always inanimate.

In the informal negative, the contracted form of a transitive gerund + √iru may coincide with the transitive gerund + √a⁷ru, namely in those environments where the accent of the two forms is the same:

ta⁷bete iru '[I] am eating'
ta⁷bete inai, contracted ta⁷bete nai '[I] am not eating';
ta⁷bete ⊢na⁴i kara 'because [I] am not eating'

ta⁷bete ⊢a⁴ru '[it] has been eaten'
ta⁷bete ⊢na⁴i '[it] has not been eaten'
ta⁷bete ⊢na⁴i kara 'because [it] has not been eaten'

The coinciding forms are distinguished only by context.

② Verbal Gerund + <u>kara</u>

A verbal gerund (-<u>te</u>/-<u>de</u> form) + <u>kara</u> means 'after doing so-and-so' or 'since doing so-and-so.' A regularly unaccented gerund acquires an accent on its final syllable when it occurs before <u>kara</u>. Thus:

ta⁷bete kara 'after eating'
ka⁷ette kara 'after returning home'
mi⁷te kara 'after seeing'
i⊢tte⁷ kara 'after going' <u>or</u> 'after saying'

A gerund + <u>kara</u> combination regularly modifies an inflected expression without a following particle; but when it describes a nominal, it is followed by <u>no</u>.

Examples:

Ta⁷bete kara, ka⊢isya e kaerima⁷sita.
'After eating, I went back to the office.'
Yo⊢sida-sañ to hana⁷site kara, ma⊢ta koko e kite⁷ kudasai.
'After talking with Mr. Yoshida, please come back here.'
Si⊢ñbuñ o yo⁷ñde kara, so⁷no zassi o mima⁷su.
'After I read the paper, I'm going to look at that magazine.'
Hu⁷ne ḡa ⊢de⁴te kara, To⊢okyoo e kaerima⁷sita.
'After the ship left, I returned to Tokyo.'

Ko⌐ko e kite⌐ kara, mo⌐o ro⌐k-ka⌐ḡetu ni narimasu.
'It is almost 6 months since I came here.'
(Lit. 'Since coming here, it will become 6 months already.')
Sore wa zi⌐mu⌐syo o ⌐de⌐te kara no siḡoto desu.
'That is work [to be done] after leaving the office.'

WARNING: Be sure to distinguish between the gerund + <u>kara</u> and the informal
past + <u>kara</u>, which are easily confused by a beginner. Thus:

si⌐te⌐ kara 'after doing'   <u>but</u> si⌐ta⌐ kara 'because [I] did'
ki⌐ite⌐ kara 'after asking'   <u>but</u> ki⌐ita⌐ kara 'because [I] asked'
si⌐mete kara 'after shutting'   <u>but</u> si⌐meta kara 'because [I] shut'

3.   Color Words

<u>Akai</u>, <u>a⌐o⌐i</u>, <u>kiiroi</u>, <u>si⌐ro⌐i</u>, and <u>ku⌐ro⌐i</u> are color words which are adjectivals.
Thus:

a. a⌐kai ho⌐n̄ 'a red book'
b. akai 'it's red' (informal)
c. a⌐ka⌐i desu 'it's red' (formal)
d. a⌐ka⌐katta 'it was red' (informal)
e. a⌐ka⌐katta desu (or a⌐ka⌐i desita) 'it was red' (formal)
f. a⌐kaku narima⌐sita 'it's become red' (formal)
g. a⌐kaku arimase⌐n̄ 'it isn't red' (formal)
h. a⌐kaku na⌐i 'it isn't red' (informal)

<u>Tyairo</u> and <u>haiiro</u> are color words which are nominals. Thus:

a. tya⌐iro no ho⌐n̄ 'a brown book'
b. tyairo da 'it's brown' (informal)
c. tya⌐iro de⌐su 'it's brown' (formal)
d. tya⌐iro da⌐tta 'it was brown' (informal)
e. tya⌐iro de⌐sita 'it was brown' (formal)
f. tya⌐iro ni narima⌐sita 'it's become brown' (formal)
g. tya⌐iro zya arimase⌐n̄ 'it isn't brown' (formal)
h. tya⌐iro zya na⌐i 'it isn't brown' (informal)

Some other color words which are nominals are: <u>mu⌐ra⌐saki</u> 'purple,' <u>momo-</u>
<u>iro</u> 'pink,' <u>mi⌐dori</u> 'green.'

<u>A⌐ka</u>, <u>a⌐o</u>, <u>kiiro</u>, <u>si⌐ro</u>, and <u>ku⌐ro</u> are nominal alternants of the adjectival
color words listed above. While they are often used interchangeably with their
adjectival counterparts, they also have various special uses which distinguish
them from the adjectivals, including the following:

a. Only the nominals are used to NAME the colors. Thus:

A⌐o ḡa su⌐ki⌐ desu. 'I like blue (i.e. the color blue).'
but:
A⌐o⌐i no ḡa su⌐ki⌐ desu. 'I like the blue one (i.e. an object that is
blue).'

b. Only the nominals are used when one object is described by several
colors. Thus:

a⌐o⌐i ha⌐iza⌐ra 'a blue ashtray'
and:
si⌐ro⌐i ha⌐iza⌐ra 'a white ashtray'
but:
a⌐o to ⌐si⌐ro no ha⌐iza⌐ra 'a blue and white ashtray'

c. Only the nominals are themselves described by adjectivals. Thus:

a⌐o⌐i ha⌐iza⌐ra 'a blue ashtray'
but:
u⌐sui a⌐o no ha⌐iza⌐ra 'a light blue ashtray'

akai kuruma 'a red car'
but:
ko⌐i ⌐a⌐ka no kuruma 'a dark red car'

 Sentence Particle wa

The sentence particle wa[1] occurs as a sentence final, or pre-final before yo, nee, and ne, IN THE SPEECH OF WOMEN. It regularly follows non-past and past inflected words in the informal style,[2] plain and polite. It is a particle which indicates friendliness and assertiveness—in a gentle way—and some familiarity. Whereas So⌐o da. is abrupt and masculine, So⌐o da wa⌐ is friendly and feminine.[3]

Informal patterns consisting of an informal non-past or past directly followed by yo, ne⌐e, and ne are more typical of men's speech (cf. Lesson 13, Grammatical Note 2). If sentence particle wa is inserted before yo, ne⌐e, and ne in such sequences they become typical of women's speech. However, the most frequently occurring women's equivalents of sentences ending in da yo, da ⌐ne⌐e, and da ne simply omit the da.

	Men's Speech	Women's Speech
'I understand.'	Wa⌐ka⌐ru yo⌐	Wa⌐ka⌐ru wa yo⌐
'I understood.'	Wa⌐ka⌐tta yo⌐	Wa⌐ka⌐tta wa yo⌐
'Isn't it expensive!'	Ta⌐ka⌐i ⌐ne⌐e.	Ta⌐ka⌐i wa ⌐ne⌐e.
'Wasn't it expensive!'	Ta⌐kakatta ⌐ne⌐e.	Ta⌐kakatta wa ⌐ne⌐e.
'That's right, isn't it?'	So⌐o da ne?	So⌐o ne?
'It was strange, wasn't it?'	He⌐ñ datta ne?	He⌐ñ datta wa ne?

[1] It is best to consider this wa and the particle wa introduced previously as different words.

[2] It also occurs with the formal style, but less frequently.

[3] In some dialects of Japanese, sentence particle wa occurs in men's speech, but in standard Tokyo Japanese, it is a feminine particle.

Comparisons of some informal patterns which have already been introduced are shown in the following chart:

	Men and Women	Men	Women
'I understand.'	Wa⌐ka⌐ru.		Wa⌐ka⌐ru wa‿
'It's expensive.'	Ta⌐ka⌐i.		Ta⌐ka⌐i wa‿
'That's right.'	So⌐o.	So⌐o da.	So⌐o da wa‿
'That's right!'		So⌐o da yo‿	So⌐o yo‿
'That's right, isn't it!'		So⌐o da ⌐ne⌐e.	So⌐o ⌐ne⌐e.
'That's right, isn't it?'		So⌐o da ne?	So⌐o ne?

5. Counter -kai 'floor'

The counter -kai combines with the numerals of Series I to count and to name the floors of a building. Numbers from one to ten are:

ik-kai	'1 floor'	or	'1st floor'
ni-kai	'2 floors'	or	'2d floor'
san-gai	'3 floors'	or	'3d floor'
yon-kai	'4 floors'	or	'4th floor'
go-kai	'5 floors'	or	'5th floor'
rok-kai	'6 floors'	or	'6th floor'
nana-kai	'7 floors'	or	'7th floor'
hati-kai or hak-kai	'8 floors'	or	'8th floor'
kyuu-kai	'9 floors'	or	'9th floor'
zik-kai or zyuk-kai	'10 floors'	or	'10th floor'
nan-gai	'how many floors?'	or	'what floor?'

Nikai (polite, onikai[+]) occurs as the equivalent of 'upstairs' when 'upstairs' refers to the second floor of a two-story building. The equivalent of 'downstairs' is sita ('below,' 'under').

DRILLS

A. Substitution Drill

1. Shall I turn down the radio?
   Ra⌐zio (o) ⌐ti⌐isaku si⌐masyo⌐o ka.

2. Shall I turn up the television?
   Te⌐rebi (o) ⌐o⌐okiku si⌐masyo⌐o ka.

3. Shall I heat the tea?
   Otya (o) ⌐a⌐tuku si⌐masyo⌐o ka.

4. Shall I chill the beer?
   Bi⌐iru (o) tu⌐metaku simasyo⌐o ka.

5. Shall I warm this room?
   Ko⌐no heya⌐ (o) a⌐ttaka⌐ku si⌐masyo⌐o ka.

6. Shall I make the coffee strong?
   Ko⌐ohi⌐i (o) ⌐ko⌐ku si⌐masyo⌐o ka.

7. Shall I make the (black) tea weak?
   Kootya (o) u⌐suku simasyo⌐o ka.

B. Substitution Drill (based on Grammatical Note 3) *colors*

1. It's a gray and blue car.	Haiiro to ᒥaᒣo no kuᒪruma deᒣsu.
2. It's a black and white ashtray.	Kuᒪro to ᒥsiᒣro no haᒪizaᒣra desu.
3. It's a green and yellow electric train.	Miᒣdori to kiᒥiro no deñsya deᒣsu.
4. It's a gray and black ship.	Haiiro to ᒪkuᒣro no ᒪhuᒣne desu.
5. It's a red and blue plate.	Aᒣka to ᒥaᒣo no (saᒥra) deᒣsu.
6. It's a black and red tray.	Kuᒪro to ᒥaᒣka no (oᒪboñ) deᒣsu.
7. It's a pink and white cake.	Momoiro to ᒥsiᒣro no (oᒪkaᒣsi) desu.
8. It's dark blue paper.	Koᒣi ᒪaᒣo no kaᒪmiᒣ desu.
9. It's a light brown pen.	Uᒪsui tyairo no peᒣñ desu.
10. It's a dark purple fu-roshiki.	Koᒣi muᒪraᒣsaki no huᒪrosiki deᒣsu.

C. Substitution Drill (based on Grammatical Note 1)

Practice this drill in two ways: (1) Omit the particles in parentheses; (2) Include the particles in parentheses with the student supplying them on the basis of what verbals occur.

1. Did you lock the door?	Toᒥno kagiᒣ (o) kaᒪkemaᒣsita kaᒧ
2. Is the door locked?	Toᒥno kagiᒣ (ga) kaᒪkaᒣtte (i)masu ga⌐
3. Is the window locked?	Maᒣdo no kaᒪgiᒣ (ga) kaᒪkaᒣtte (i)masu kaᒧ
4. Shall I lock the window?	Maᒣdo no kaᒪgiᒣ (o) kaᒪkemasyoᒣo kaᒧ
5. Shall I lock the car?	Kuᒪruma no kagiᒣ (o) kaᒪkemasyoᒣo kaᒧ
6. Please lock the car.	Kuᒪruma no kagiᒣ (o) ᒥkaᒣkete kudasai.
7. Please lock the entry hall.	Geᒣñkañ no kaᒪgiᒣ (o) ᒥkaᒣkete kudasai.
8. Has the entry hall been locked?	Geᒣñkañ no kaᒪgiᒣ (ga) ᒥkaᒣkete arima-su kaᒧ

D. Grammar Drill

Tutor: Kiᒥtanaᒣi desu yoᒧ 'It's dirty!'
Student: Kiᒥtanaᒣku naᒪrimaᒣsita yoᒧ 'It's gotten dirty!'

ku - adjs.

1. Kuᒥroᒣi desu yoᒧ	Kuᒪroku naᒪrimaᒣsita yoᒧ
2. Haᒥiiro deᒣsu yoᒧ	Haᒥiiro ni narimaᒣsita yoᒧ
3. Aᒥttakaᒣi desu yoᒧ	Aᒥttaᒣkaku naᒪrimaᒣsita yoᒧ
4. Seᒢnseᒣe desu yoᒧ	Seᒣnseᒣe ni naᒪrimaᒣsita yoᒧ
5. Aᒥoᒣi desu yoᒧ	Aᒣoku naᒪrimaᒣsita yoᒧ
6. Geᒣñki desu yoᒧ	Geᒣñki ni naᒪrimaᒣsita yoᒧ
7. Aᒥbunaᒥi desu yoᒧ	Aᒥbunaku narimaᒣsita yoᒧ
8. Miᒣdori desu yoᒧ	Miᒣdori ni naᒪrimaᒣsita yoᒧ

E. Grammar Drill (based on Grammatical Note 1)

> Tutor: Ma⌐do o a⌐kema⌐sita.   'I opened the window.'
> Student: Ma⌐do ḡa a⌐kima⌐sita. 'The window opened.'

trans.

1. De⌐ńki o tu⌐kema⌐sita.   De⌐ńki ḡa tu⌐kima⌐sita.
2. To⌐o simema⌐sita.   To⌐ḡa simarima⌐sita.
3. So⌐re o naosima⌐sita.   So⌐re ḡa naorima⌐sita.
4. Su⌐to⌐obu o ke⌐sima⌐sita.   Su⌐to⌐obu ḡa ki⌐ema⌐sita.
5. To⌐no kaḡi⌐ o ka⌐kema⌐si-   To⌐no kaḡi⌐ ḡa ka⌐karima⌐sita.
   ta.

intrans.

F. Grammar Drill (based on Grammatical Note 1)

quiz on xlon.

> Tutor: Ma⌐do o a⌐kema⌐sita ka⌐   'Did you open the window?'
> Student: Ma⌐do ḡa a⌐kete arima⌐su ka⌐ 'Has the window been opened?'

1. Kuruma o na⌐osima⌐sita   Kuruma ḡa na⌐o⌐site a⌐rima⌐su ka⌐
   ka⌐
2. Ti⌐zu o ka⌐kima⌐sita ka⌐   Ti⌐zu ḡa ka⌐ite a⌐rima⌐su ka⌐
3. Su⌐to⌐obu o ke⌐sima⌐sita   Su⌐to⌐obu ḡa ke⌐site arima⌐su ka⌐
   ka⌐
4. A⌐tarasi⌐i zi⌐biki⌐ o   A⌐tarasi⌐i zi⌐biki⌐ ḡa ga⌐kkoo e mot-
   ga⌐kkoo e motte ikima⌐si-   te i⌐tte a⌐rima⌐su ka⌐
   ta ka⌐
5. Do⌐a o si⌐mema⌐sita ka⌐   Do⌐a ḡa si⌐mete a⌐rima⌐su ka⌐
6. Te⌐rebi o tu⌐kema⌐sita   Te⌐rebi ḡa tu⌐ke⌐te a⌐rima⌐su ka⌐
   ka⌐
7. Ku⌐ruma no kaḡi⌐ o ka⌐ke-   Ku⌐ruma no kaḡi⌐ ḡa ka⌐kete a⌐ri-
   ma⌐sita ka⌐   ma⌐su ka⌐
8. Pa⌐ń o ka⌐ima⌐sita ka⌐   Pa⌐ń ḡa ka⌐tte arima⌐su ka⌐

G. Grammar Drill (based on Grammatical Note 2)

> Tutor: Ta⌐bema⌐sita. Sore kara, ka⌐erima⌐sita.
>   'I ate. After that, I went home.'
> Student: Ta⌐bete kara, ka⌐erima⌐sita.
>   'After eating, I went home.'

1. To⌐(o) simema⌐sita. Sore   To⌐(o) si⌐mete kara, ma⌐do mo mi⌐ń-
   kara, ma⌐do mo mi⌐ńna si-   na simema⌐sita.
   mema⌐sita.
2. De⌐ńki (o) mi⌐ńna kesima⌐si-   De⌐ńki (o) mi⌐ńna kesite⌐ kara, te⌐re-
   ta. Sore kara, te⌐rebi (o)   bi (o) tu⌐kema⌐sita.
   tu⌐kema⌐sita.
3. U⌐ti (o) katazukema⌐sita.   U⌐ti (o) katazu⌐kete kara, de⌐kakema⌐-
   Sore kara, de⌐kakema⌐si-   sita.
   ta.
4. So⌐ozi-sima⌐sita. Sore   So⌐ozi-site⌐ kara, syo⌐kuzi no sitaku
   kara, syo⌐kuzi no sitaku   (o) sima⌐sita.
   (o) sima⌐sita.

5. Siⁿbuñ (o) yomimaˈsi-   Siⁿbuñ (o) yoˈñde kara, kaˈisya ni i-
    ta. Sore kara, kaˈisya   kimaˈsita.
    ni ikimaˈsita.

6. Niˈhoñziˈñ to keˈkkoñ-   Niˈhoñziˈñ to keˈkkoñ-siteˈ kara,
    simaˈsita. Sore kara,   Aˈmerika e kaerimaˈsita.
    Aˈmerika e kaerimaˈsi-
    ta.

7. Soˈo iimaˈsita. Sore   Soˈo itteˈ kara, heˈyaˈ (o) deˈmaˈsi-
    kara, heˈyaˈ (o) deˈmaˈ-   ta.
    sita.

8. Deˈñwa (o) (kirimaˈsita.)   Deˈñwa (o) kiˈtte kara, maˈta suˈgu
    Sore kara, maˈta suˈgu   kaˈkemaˈsita.
    kaˈkemaˈsita.

9. Byoˈoki ni narimaˈsita.   Byoˈoki ni naˈtte kara, oˈsake to ta-
    Sore kara, oˈsake to   bako (o) yamemaˈsita.
    tabako (o) yamema si-   Stop
    ta.

10. Zyuⁿsa ni kikimaˈsita.   ~~kkkk~~ cop
    Sore kara, suˈgu miˈti   Zyuⁿsaˈni kiiteˈ kara, suˈgu miˈti
    ga wakarimaˈsita.   ga wakarimaˈsita.

H. Response Drill

    (Give the _iie_ answer, same politeness and formality level, for each of
    the following.)

1. Aˈkimaˈsu ka⌐   Iie, aˈkimaseˈñ.
2. Aˈite (i)maˈsu ka⌐   Iie, aˈite (i)maseˈñ.
3. Miˈdori?   Iie, miˈdori zyaˈ ˈnaˈi.
4. Yoˈru desu ka⌐   Iie, yoˈru zya aˈrimaseˈñ.
5. Kiˈete orimaˈsu ka⌐   Iie, kiˈete orimaseˈñ.
6. Kiˈtanaˈi?   ?   Iie, kiˈtanaˈku ˈnaˈi.
7. Aˈnaˈta wa seˈñseˈe de   Iie, seˈñseˈe de wa goˈzaimaseˈñ.
    (i)ˈrassyaimaˈsu ka⌐
8. Aˈtatakaˈi desu ka⌐   Iie, aˈtataˈkaku aˈrimaseˈñ.
9. Naˈoˈsite (i)ru?   Iie, naˈoˈsite (i)nai.
10. Naˈoˈsite ˈaˈru?   Iie, naˈoˈsite ˈnaˈi.
11. Aˈoˈi desu ka⌐   Iie, aˈoku aˈrimaseˈñ.
12. Aˈo desu ka⌐   Iie, aˈo zya aˈrimaseˈñ.

I. Response Drill

    Tutor: Oˈokiku siˈmasyoˈo ka. 'Shall I make it loud?'

                                     ⎰ˈiˈ desu yo⌐   ⎱
             Student: Iie, tiˈisaˈi maˈmaˈ de ⎱ yoˈrosiˈi desu yo⌐ ⎰ (Practice all
                                     ⎰ˈkeˈkkoo desu yo⌐ ⎱ 4 for each
                                     ⎱ kaˈmaimaseˈñ yo⌐ ⎰ answer)
                      'No, it's all right soft, as it is.'

1. Tiˈisaku siˈmasyoˈo ka.   Iie, oˈokiˈi maˈmaˈ de ˈiˈi desu yo⌐
2. Aˈtuku siˈmasyoˈo ka.   Iie, tuˈmetai mamaˈ de ˈiˈi desu yo⌐

dark (handwritten)   _light_ (handwritten)

3. Ko⌐ku si⌐masyo⌐o ka.   Iie, u⌐sui mama⌐ de ⌐i⌐i desu yo⌐

4. Ki⌐ree ni si⌐masyo⌐o ka.   Iie, ki⌐tana⌐i ma⌐ma⌐ de ⌐i⌐i desu
                                       yo⌐

5. Ya⌐sasiku simasyo⌐o ka.   Iie, mu⌐zukasii mama⌐ de ⌐i⌐i desu
                                       yo⌐

6. U⌐suku simasyo⌐o ka.   Iie, ko⌐i ma⌐ma⌐ de ⌐i⌐i desu yo⌐

7. Ka⌐raku si⌐masyo⌐o ka.   Iie, a⌐mai mama⌐ de ⌐i⌐i desu yo⌐

spicy, salty (handwritten)   _sweet_ (handwritten)

J. Expansion Drill

or kiete (handwritten)

1. Have [they] been turned   Ke⌐site arima⌐su ka⌐
   off?

   Are [they] on, or have   Tu⌐ite (i)⌐ma⌐su ka, ke⌐site arima⌐-
   they been turned off?   su ka⌐

   Are the lights on, or   De⌐ñki wa ⌐tu⌐ite (i)⌐ma⌐su ka, ke-
   have they been turned   ⌐site arima⌐su ka⌐
   off?

   Are the upstairs lights   Ni⌐kai no de⌐ñki wa ⌐tu⌐ite (i)⌐ma⌐su
   on, or have they been   ka, ke⌐site arima⌐su ka ⌐
   turned off?

2. It's grown cold. . . .[1]   Sa⌐muku na⌐rima⌐sita ḡa⌐

   It's grown very cold. . . .   To⌐ttemo sa⌐muku na⌐rima⌐sita ḡa⌐

   It's gone out so it's   Ki⌐ete (i)ru⌐ kara, to⌐ttemo sa⌐muku
   grown very cold. . . .   na⌐rima⌐sita ḡa⌐

   The heater is off so it's   Su⌐to⌐obu (ḡa) ki⌐ete (i)ru⌐ kara, to-
   grown very cold. . . .   ⌐ttemo sa⌐muku na⌐rima⌐sita ḡa⌐

3. Hasn't it grown warm!   A⌐tta⌐kaku na⌐rima⌐sita ⌐ne⌐e.

   Hasn't the room grown   He⌐ya⌐ (ḡa) a⌐tta⌐kaku na⌐rima⌐sita
   warm!   ⌐ne⌐e.

   Since turning [it] on,   Tu⌐ke⌐te kara, he⌐ya⌐ (ḡa) a⌐tta⌐kaku
   hasn't the room grown   na⌐rima⌐sita ⌐ne⌐e.
   warm!

   Since turning on the heater,   Su⌐to⌐obu (o) tu⌐ke⌐te kara, he⌐ya⌐
   hasn't the room grown   (ḡa) a⌐tta⌐kaku na⌐rima⌐sita
   warm!   ⌐ne⌐e.

   Hasn't the room grown   Ha⌐ruko-sañ (ḡa) su⌐to⌐obu (o) tu⌐ke⌐-
   warm since Haruko   te kara, he⌐ya⌐ (ḡa) a⌐tta⌐kaku na⌐ri-
   turned on the heater!   ma⌐sita ⌐ne⌐e.

4. Because I don't like it.   Su⌐ki⌐ zya a⌐rimase⌐ñ kara.

   Because I don't like it very   A⌐ñmari suki⌐ zya a⌐rimase⌐ñ kara.
   much.

---

[1] 'but— can anything be done about it?'

Because I don't like sweet things very much.	A⌐mai mono⌐ (wa) a⌐ñmari suki⌐ zya a⌐rimase⌐ñ kara.
That's fine– because I don't like sweet things very much.	Ke⌐kkoo desu yo— a⌐mai mono⌐ (wa) a⌐ñmari suki⌐ zya a⌐rimase⌐ñ ka- ra.
It's fine <u>sour</u>—as it is— because I don't like sweet things very much.	<u>Su⌐ppa⌐i ma⌐ma⌐ de</u> ⌐ke⌐kkoo desu yo — a⌐<u>mai</u> mono⌐ (wa) a⌐ñmari suki⌐ zya a⌐rimase⌐ñ kara.

5. It's pretty, isn't it? — Ki⌐ree desyoo?

The furoshiki is pretty, isn't it? — Hurosiki (wa) ⌐ki⌐ree desyoo?

The purple furoshiki is pretty, isn't it? — Mu⌐ra⌐saki no hurosiki (wa) ⌐ki⌐ree desyoo?

The yellow and purple furoshiki is pretty, isn't it? — Kiiro to mu⌐ra⌐saki no hurosiki (wa) ⌐ki⌐ree desyoo?

That yellow and purple furoshiki is pretty, isn't it? — Ano kiiro to mu⌐ra⌐saki no hurosiki (wa) ⌐ki⌐ree desyoo?

6. I understood. — Wa⌐karima⌐sita.

After seeing [it] I understood. — Mi⌐te kara, wa⌐karima⌐sita.

After seeing his name card I understood. — Me⌐esi (o) mi⌐te kara, wa⌐karima⌐sita.

I couldn't hear but after seeing his name card I understood. — Ki⌐koemase⌐ñ desita g̃a; me⌐esi (o) mi⌐te kara, wa⌐karima⌐sita.

I couldn't hear his name but after seeing his name card I could tell [what it was]. — Namae (wa) ki⌐koemase⌐ñ desita g̃a; me⌐esi (o) mi⌐te kara, wa⌐karima⌐ sita.

SUPPLEMENTARY SELECTIONS

(with questions)

1. Ke⌐sa to⌐temo sa⌐mukatta kara, su⌐to⌐obu o tu⌐kema⌐sita g̃a; su⌐g̃u ki⌐e- ma⌐sita.   To⌐nari no heya⌐ kara ho⌐ka no⌐ o mo⌐tte⌐ kite tu⌐ke⌐te kara, he⌐ya⌐ g̃a a⌐tata⌐kaku na⌐rima⌐sita.

     a. I⌐tu su⌐to⌐obu o tu⌐kema⌐sita ka↲
     b. Na⌐ze su⌐to⌐obu o tu⌐kema⌐sita ka↲
     c. Su⌐to⌐obu o hu⌐ta-tu tukema⌐sita g̃a, do⌐tira mo ko⌐syoo de⌐sita ka↲
     d. Na⌐ni o si⌐te⌐ kara he⌐ya⌐ g̃a a⌐tta⌐kaku na⌐rima⌐sita ka↲

2. Kyo⌐o uti g̃a ⌐zu⌐ibuñ ki⌐tana⌐ku ⌐na⌐tte ita kara, go⌐g̃o no ⌐sa⌐ñ-zi made so⌐ozi-sima⌐sita. So⌐ozi o site⌐ kara ótya o ⌐i⌐p-pai ⌐no⌐ñde; sore kara,

sa⌐kanaya ni deñwa o ka⌐kete, o⌐sasimi n o sakana o tyuumoñ-sima⌐sita.
Go⌐-zi kara ro⌐ku⌐-zi made syo⌐kuzi no sitaku o sima⌐sita. Ro⌐ku-zi-ha⌐ñ
ni ⌐syu⌐ziñ ḡa kāisya kara ⌐ka⌐ette kite;[1] sore kara, i⌐ssyo ni syokuzi o si-
ma⌐sita.

    a. Do⌐o site u⌐ti o soozi-sima⌐sita ka⌐

    b. Na⌐ñ-zi made so⌐ozi-sima⌐sita ka⌐

    c. So⌐ozi-site⌐ kara ⌐su⌐ḡu ⌐na⌐ni o si⌐ma⌐sita ka⌐

    d. Da⌐re ni de⌐ñwa o kakema⌐sita ka⌐

to order e. Na⌐ni o tyu⌐umoñ-sima⌐sita ka⌐

    f. Go⌐-zi kara ro⌐ku⌐-zi made ⌐na⌐ni o si⌐ma⌐sita ka⌐

    g. Go⌐syu⌐ziñ wa ⌐na⌐ñ-zi ni kāisya kara ⌐ka⌐ette ki⌐ma⌐sita ka⌐

3. Ke⌐kkoñ-site⌐ kara ⌐mo⌐o ⌐ni⌐-neñ ni narimasu. A⌐merika de kekkoñ-si-
ma⌐sita ḡa, ke⌐kkoñ-site⌐ kara ⌐su⌐ḡu Ni⌐ho⌐ñ e ki⌐ma⌐sita. Watakusi wa
A⌐merika-taisi⌐kañ ni tu⌐to⌐mete ite, ka⌐nai wa Ni⌐ho⌐ñ no gākkoo de e⌐eḡo
o osiete ima⌐su. Mo⌐o su⌐ḡu ka⌐erima⌐su ḡa; Ni⌐ho⌐ñ ḡa to⌐temo suki⌐ desu
kara, ka⌐erita⌐ku a⌐rimase⌐ñ.

ⁿi
narimashita
came to like Jpn.

    a. I⌐ma ⌐do⌐ko ni i⌐ma⌐su ka⌐

    b. Na⌐ñ-neñ ni ke⌐kkoñ-sima⌐sita ka⌐

    c. Na⌐ñ-neñ ma⌐e ni ke⌐kkoñ-sima⌐sita ka⌐

    d. Do⌐ko de ke⌐kkoñ-sima⌐sita ka⌐

    e. Ke⌐kkoñ-site⌐ kara ⌐do⌐ko e i⌐kima⌐sita ka⌐

    f. Go⌐syu⌐ziñ wa ⌐do⌐ñna si⌐ḡoto o site ima⌐su ka⌐

    g. O⌐kusañ wa ⌐do⌐ñna si⌐ḡoto o site ima⌐su ka⌐

    h. I⌐tu ka⌐erima⌐su ka⌐

    i. Do⌐o site ka⌐erita⌐ku a⌐rimase⌐ñ ka⌐

SUPPLEMENTARY CONVERSATION

(In an office building)

Smith (to receptionist):   Go-⌐kai e ikita⌐i ñ deṣu ḡa⌐

Receptionist: Zya⌐a, asoko ni e⌐rebe⌐eta[2] ḡa gozaimasu.

Smith: Do⌐o mo.

Elevator operator: U⌐e e mairima⌐su. Na⌐na-kai ma⌐de mairimasu.

Smith: Go-⌐kai oneḡai-sima⌐su.

Other passenger: Sañ-ḡai.

Elevator operator: Ka⌐sikomarima⌐sita. . . . Sa⌐ñ-ḡai de gozaima⌐su.

Other passenger: Do⌐o mo.

Elevator operator: Tu⌐ḡi⌐ wa go-⌐kai de gozaima⌐su. . . . O⌐matase-itasima⌐si-
ta. Go-⌐kai de gozaima⌐su.

Smith: A⌐ri⌐ḡatoo.

---

[1] ka⌐ette ⌐ku⌐ru 'come back.'
[2] 'Elevator.'

English Equivalent

Smith: I want to go to the fifth floor. . . .
Receptionist: (In that case) there's an elevator over there.
Smith: Thanks.
Elevator operator: Going up. [This car] goes to the seventh floor.
Smith: Five, please.
Other passenger: Three.
Elevator operator: Certainly. . . . Third floor.
Other passenger: Thanks.
Elevator operator: Fifth floor next. . . . (I'm sorry to have kept you waiting.)
　　Fifth floor.
Smith: Thanks.

EXERCISES

1. You ask Mr. Tanaka where he lives. He answers:
    immediate vicinity
　　a. In Akasaka.
　　b. Near Kamakura Station. *Sugu soba desu, sugu tonari desu*
　　c. Right near the American Embassy.
　　d. In an apartment in Shibuya.

2. Ask the salesgirl to show you:
　　a. that green pen. *midori iro no ~~El~~ pen*
　　b. that yellow ashtray. *kiiro no haizara*
　　c. those gray teacups. ~~haiiro~~ *haiiro no*
　　d. those brown and white dishes.
　　e. those red chopsticks.
　　f. that red and blue pencil.
　　g. that red and black tray.
　　h. that pink paper.
　　i. that light purple furoshiki.
　　j. that dark blue book. *koi ao no hon*
　　　　Kon - navy blue

3. Tell Haruko to:
　　a. open the door.
　　b. shut the window.
　　c. turn on the light. *tsukete*
　　d. turn off the heater. *keshite*
　　e. turn the radio down.
　　f. make the television louder.
　　g. clean this room.
　　h. straighten up the next room.
　　i. get dinner ready.
　　j. lock the door in the entry hall.
　　k. take this upstairs.
　　l. turn off the upstairs heater.

4. Indicate whether each of the following is M (more typical of men's speech),
   W (more typical of women's speech), or MW (used by men and women). If
   you are a man, give an M or MW equivalent for all sentences marked W; if
   you are a woman, give a W or MW equivalent for all sentences marked M.

   a. O⌐su⌐mai ⌐do⌐tira?
   b. Yameta yo↲
   c. Hoñtoo ⌐ne⌐e.
   d. Ki⌐ree da.
   e. Si⌐rana⌐katta?
   f. Abunai.
   g. So⌐o yo.
   h. Ze⌐ñbu wa⌐ka⌐tta?
   i. De⌐kita wa↲
   j. O⌐naka ḡa suita⌐ wa yo↲
   k. He⌐ñ da ⌐ne⌐e.
   l. Ki⌐koena⌐katta yo↲

5. Practice the Basic Dialogues with appropriate variations.

Lesson 17. At Home (cont.)

BASIC DIALOGUES: FOR MEMORIZATION

(The Smiths have just moved into a new house. Masao-sañ and
Fumiko-sañ are helping them.)

(a)

Smith (to Masao)

	help or lend a hand	te˩tuda˩u /-u/
1.	Give me a hand, will you?	Te˩tuda˩tte ne?
	things like books and magazines	ho˩ñ ya zássi
	study (i.e. a room)	syosai
	desk	tukue
	onto the desk	tukue ni
	top of the desk	tu˩kue no ue˩
	onto the top of the desk	tu˩kue no ue˩ ni
	put or place	oku /-u/
2.	Put these books and magazines and things on [top of] the desk in the study.	Kono ˩ho˩ñ ya zássi (o) syo˩sai no tukue [no ue˩] ni oite. [1]
	bookshelf	ho˩ñdana
	onto the bookshelf	ho˩ñdana ni
	put away or store	simau /-u/
3.	(Because) I'll put them (away) on the bookshelves later.	A˩to de ˩ho˩ñdana ni si˩mau˩ kara.
	is small or fine or detailed	ko˩maka˩i /-ku/
	drawer	hikidasi
	into the drawer	hikidasi ni
	inside	na˩ka
	inside the drawer	hi˩kidasi no na˩ka
	into the inside of the drawer	hi˩kidasi no na˩ka ni
	insert or put in	ireru /-ru/

---

[1] Accent of short alternant: syósai.

295

4. Then put all those little things in⌈side⌋ the desk drawer.

⌈Sore kara, ano ko⌈maka⌉i mo⌈no⌉(o) ⌈ze⌉ñbu tu⌈kue no hikidasi ⌈no na⌉ka⌋ ni irete.[1]

. . .

Masao

finish putting in	irete simau
following or subsequent	a⌉to

5. I finished putting everything in.   What shall I do next?

⌈Mi⌈ñna irete simaima⌉sita ḡa, a⌉to ⌈na⌉ni (o) si⌈masyo⌉o ka.

Smith

dog	i⌈nu⌉
hindrance or bother	zyama /na/ or ozyama⁺
become a bother or get in the way	zya⌈ma ni na⌉ru
outside	so⌉to
to the outside	so⌉to ni
put out or send out or take out	da⌉su /-u/

6. The dog gets in the way so put him outside.

⌈I⌈nu⌉ ḡa zya⌈ma ni na⌉ru kara, so⌉to ni dasite.

(calling after Masao)

give	yaru /-u/

7. Say! Give him some water too, will you?

⌈Ano ne! Mi⌈zu mo yatte⌉ ne?

(b)

Masao

8. What shall I do with these dishes?

⌈Kono sara (wa) ⌈do⌉o simasyoo ka.

Smith

soap	sekkeñ
wash	arau /-u/
receive or get	morau /-u/
have Fumiko wash	Hu⌈miko-sañ ni a̅ratte morau

9. Those—have Fumiko wash with soap and hot water.

⌈Sore (wa) ⌈Hu⌉miko-sañ ni sekkeñ to oyu de a̅ratte moratte.

---

[1] Accent of short alternant: tŭkue.

	cupboard (with shelves)	todana
	into the cupboard	todana ni
10.	(Because) I'll put them (away) in the dining-room closet later.	A⌐to de syo⌐kudoo no todana ni simau⌐ kara. *shimaimasu*

. . .

Smith

	on top of this	kono ue
	take up or take away	to⌐ru /-u/
11.	Say, take away the things on top of this.	Tyo⌐tto, ko⌐no ue no mono⌐ (o) ⌐to⌐t-te.

	table	teeburu
	kitchen	daidokoro
	into the kitchen	daidokoro ni
12.	(Because) I'm going to take this table into the kitchen.	Kono teeburu (o) da⌐idokoro ni motte i⌐ku kara.

Masao

13.	Shall I help you?	O⌐te⌐tudai-simasyoo ka⌐

Smith

	alone (lit. being one person)	hi⌐to⌐ri de
14.	No, I can manage alone.	Iie, hi⌐to⌐ri de da⌐izyo⌐obu.

(c)

Masao

	throw away	suteru /-ru/
15.	These old newspapers— shall I throw them away?	Kono hu⌐ru⌐i siñbuñ (wa) su⌐temasyo⌐o ka.

Smith

	corner (of a room)	su⌐mi
	into the corner	su⌐mi ni
	put for the time being	oit(e) oku
16.	No, I need them so put them in that corner for the time being.	Iie, i⌐ru⌐ kara, a⌐no su⌐mi ni o⌐it(e) o⌐ite.

. . .

	be careful	ki⌐otuke⌐ru /-ru/
	[something] spills	ko⌐bore⌐ru /-ru/
	be spilt	ko⌐bo⌐rete (i)ru
17.	Oh, be careful! (Because) something's spilt.	A, ki⌐otuke⌐te. Na⌐ni ka ko⌐bo⌐rete (i)ru kara.

	wipe	huku /-u/
	have Fumiko wipe	Hu⌐miko-sañ ni hu⌐ite morau

18. Have Fumiko wipe it up!   Hu˺miko-sañ ni hu˹ite moratte˺ yo.

Masao

19. What'll she wipe it up   Na˺ñ de hu˹kimasyo˺o ka.
     with?

Smith

box	hako
into the box	hako ni
cleaning rag	zookiñ
dishrag or dish cloth	hu˹ki˺ñ
or cloth	
things like rags and	zo˹okiñ ya huki˺ñ
cloths	
go in or enter	ha˺iru /-u/
be in or be entered	ha˺itte (i)ru

20. Clean rags and cloths and   Ano hako ni ˹ki˺ree na zo˹okiñ ya hu-
     things are in that box   ki˺ñ (ḡa) ˺ha˺itte (i)ru kara—
     (so. . .)

. . .

become tired	tu˹kare˺ru˞-/-ru/
become tired out or	tu˹ka˺rete simau or
exhausted	tu˹ka˺retyau /-u/
rest	ya˹su˺mu /-u/

21. You're (lit. You've become)   Tu˹ka˺rete si˺matta˺ desyoo? Tyo˺-
     tired out, aren't you? Let's   tto ya˹sumimasyo˺o.
     rest for a minute.

(d)

(Smith is talking to his friend Tanaka, who has
dropped in to see how things are coming along)

Smith

head	a˹tama˺
is painful	i˹ta˺i /-ku/

22. You know, I have a terrible   To˹temo atama˺ (ḡa) i˹ta˺i ñ desu
     headache.   yo.

Tanaka

give (you)	aḡeru /-ru/

23. I have medicine. Would you   Ku˹suri ḡa arima˺su ḡa, a˹ḡemasyo˺o
     like some? (Lit. Shall I   ka⏌
     give you some?)

Smith

receive from Fumiko	Hu˺miko-sañ ni morau or
	Hu˺miko-sañ kara morau
same as this	kore to onazi
same medicine	onazi kusuri

24. I already got this from Fu-
    miko. Is it the same medi-
    cine as this?

Hu⌐miko-sañ $\left|\begin{array}{l}\text{ni}\\\text{kara}\end{array}\right|$ ⌐mo⌐o ko⌐re (o)
moraima⌐sita ḡa, kore to o⌐nazi ku-
suri de⌐su ka↲

                                   Tanaka

       be different from that   sore to tiḡau
25. No, it's different from that.   Iie, so⌐re to⌐ wa ti⌐ḡaima⁴su.

     is strong   tu⌐yo⌐i /-ku/
26. It's a much stronger kind   So⌐re yo⌐ri zu⌐tto tuyo⌐i no desu ḡa↲
    (lit. one) than that. . . .   than

                                   Smith

27. Then may I have some?   Zya⌐a o⌐neḡai-sima⁴su.

                              Tanaka

28. Aren't you hungry?   O⌐naka ḡa suita⌐ desyoo?

     order for you   tyuumoñ-site aḡeru
29. Shall I order something for   Deñwa de ⌐na⌐ni ka tyu⌐umoñ-site
    you by telephone?   aḡemasyo⌐o ka.

                                   Smith

       give me   kureru /-ru/
       request or order for   ta⌐no⌐ñde kureru
         me
30. Thank you but Fumiko al-   A⌐ri⌐ḡatoo gozaimasu ḡa, Hu⌐miko-
    ready ordered for me   sañ ḡa ⌐mo⌐o ta⌐no⌐ñde ku⌐rema⁴si-
    (so . . .)   ta kara↲

ADDITIONAL VOCABULARY

1. Where is the stairway in   Kono uti no kaidañ (wa) ⌐do⌐ko desyoo
   this house?   ka.

       washroom or lavatory   señmeñzyo
       bathroom   hu⌐roba⌐ or ohuroba⁺
       family room (Japanese   tyanoma
         style)

2. That I saw in the bedroom.   Sore (wa) si⌐ñsitu de mima⌐sita.

       living room   i⌐ma⌐
       hall or corridor   rooka
       garden   niwa or oniwa⁺

3. Where did you buy that furni-   So⌐no ka⌐ḡu (wa) ⌐do⌐ko de ka⌐ima⁴si-
   ture?   ta ka↲

       bed   be⌐tto[1] or siñdai
       chair   isu
       couch or sofa   naḡaisu
       lamp   sutañdo

---

[1] Obsolete.

4. Put that in the refrigerator, will you?

Sore (o) re⌐ezo⌐oko ni irete ne?

  chest of drawers
  closet (for clothing,
    quilts, etc.)

  tañsu
  osiire

5. The sink is dirty!

Na⌐ḡasi⌐ (ḡa) ki⌐tana⌐i desu yo⌐

  wash basin
  stove (for cooking)
  shelf

  se⌐ñme⌐ñki
  re⌐ñzi
  tana

6. There's a cat over there!

Asuko ni ⌐ne⌐ko (ḡa) i⌐ma⌐su yo⌐

  horse
  bull or cow
  goat
  rabbit
  pig

  u⌐ma⌐ or ñ⌐ma⌐
  usi
  ya⌐ḡi
  usaḡi
  buta

7. What kind of animals are there in Japan?

Ni⌐ho⌐ñ ni ⌐do⌐ñna do⌐obutu ḡa ima⌐su ka⌐

  bird
  snake

  tori or kotori
  he⌐bi

8. My ear hurts!

Mi⌐mi⌐ (ḡa) i⌐ta⌐i ñ desu yo.

  tooth
  nose
  mouth
  eye
  neck
  arm
  hand
  finger
  leg or foot
  chest
  back
  lower back
  body

  ha⌐
  hana
  kuti
  me⌐
  kubi
  u⌐de⌐
  te⌐
  yu⌐bi⌐
  a⌐si⌐
  mu⌐ne⌐
  senaka
  kosi
  karada

NOTES ON THE BASIC DIALOGUES

2. Particle underline{ni} here, and in Basic Sentences 3, 4, 6, 10, 12, 16, and 20, is the underline{ni} of goal or destination (cf. Lesson 7, Grammatical Note 3; Lesson 10, Note 4; and Lesson 14, Note 6).

4. Ko⌐maka⌐i means 'occurring in small pieces.' For example, in reference to an explanation, it indicates a detailed one.

6. Note also zyama-suru 'bother.' O⌐zyama-sima⌐sita (or -itasima⌐sita) is a common apology: 'I'm sorry to have bothered you.'

  Da⌐su is the transitive partner of intransitive de⌐ru: X ḡa ⌐de⌐ru 'X goes out'; X o ⌈da⌉su 'make X go out,' 'put X out.' Da⌉su occurs as the opposite of both ireru 'put in' and simau 'put away.'

11. Kono ue: compare kono saki in Lesson 7, Basic Sentence 16.   Other
     equivalents of to⌉ru: 'pick up,' 'remove,' 'hand [me],' 'pass [me].'
     To⌉ru occurs as the opposite of oku 'put,' 'place.'

13. O⌈te⌉tudai-suru (or -itasu) is the humble equivalent of te⌈tuda⌉u (cf. Lesson 13, Grammatical Note 4).

15. Note the use of particle wa. Primary interest is in what follows: 'about these old papers — shall I throw them away [or what shall I do with them]?'

17. The transitive partner of intransitive ko⌈bore⌉ru is ko⌈bo⌉su: X o ko⌈bo⌉su 'spill X'; X ḡa ko⌈bore⌉ru 'X spills.'

20. A zookiñ would be used to wipe up the floor, but a hu⌈ki⌉ñ to wipe a table or a dish.

     Ha⌉iru is the intransitive partner of transitive ireru (Sentence 4 above):
     X ḡa ⌈ha⌉iru 'X goes in,' X o ireru 'put X in.' Ha⌉iru may refer to a person's entering a room or building in general; a hospital, as a patient; a school, as a student; a company, as an employee; etc.

22. N̄ is the nominal meaning something like 'matter' or 'case' (cf. Lesson 7, Grammatical Note 1).

24. The nominal onazi 'same' (onazi da 'it's the same'; o⌈nazi zya na⌉i 'it isn't the same'; o⌈nazi ni na⌉ru 'become the same') occurs directly before a nominal without particle no: onazi kusuri 'the same medicine.'

24, 25. Note the use of particle to 'with' with onazi and tiḡau: X to onazi 'same as X,' X to tiḡau 'different from X.'

25. Wa, here, is the wa of comparison: 'From that it is different.'

26. 'but — would you like to try some?'

Supplementary Vocabulary:

     Hu⌈roba⌉ refers only to the place for bathing, in a Japanese house or inn. It is not to be confused with be⌈ñzyo⌉ or te⌈a⌉rai.

     Pieces of furniture like beds, chairs, etc., though commonly found in Japan, are Western style — not native Japanese style.

GRAMMATICAL NOTES

1.   Verbals of Giving and Receiving

     The following four verbals all mean 'give,' with specific differences in usage:

     Aḡeru means 'someone gives to an equal or a superior, or to anyone present to whom one is being polite.' It NEVER means 'give to the speaker.' i.e. 'give to me.'

Yaru means 'someone gives to an inferior or [in plain, informal speech] to an equal.' It is regularly used for giving to animals or to things (as in 'give water to the flowers'). Like aḡeru, it NEVER means 'give to the speaker,' i.e. 'give to me.'

Ku⌐dasa⌐ru means 'someone gives to me.'[1] It implies either that the speaker's position is inferior to that of the giver, or that the speaker is deferring to persons present for the sake of politeness.

Kureru means 'someone gives to me.' It implies that the giver is the speaker's equal or inferior. Sometimes it means 'he, she, or they give to you'—i.e. 'a third person gives to the person addressed,' if the giver and recipient are more or less equal.[2]

Particles (with all four verbals above): If expressed, the giver is followed by ḡa or wa, the thing given by particle o or wa, and the recipient by particle ni.

Examples:

    (a) A⌐ḡemasyo⌐o ka. 'Shall I give it to you?'
    (b) Se⌐ñse⌐e ni a⌐ḡema⌐sita ka↵ 'Did you give it to the teacher?'
    (c) U⌐ti no Ta⌐roo wa se⌐ñse⌐e ni ⌐ho⌐ñ o a⌐ḡema⌐sita. 'Our Taro gave the teacher a book.'
    (d) Musuko ni ⌐pe⌐ñ o ya⌐rima⌐sita. 'I gave my son a pen.'
    (e) Ko⌐oka⌐ñsyu ni a⌐tarasi⌐i de⌐ñwatyoo o yarima⌐sita ka↵ 'Did you give the operator a new phone book?'
    (f) Se⌐ñse⌐e wa ⌐ma⌐initi ko⌐domo ni ku⌐da⌐mono o yarimasu. 'The teacher gives the children some fruit every day.'
    (g) Kore wa ⌐o⌐kusañ ḡa ku⌐dasaima⌐sita. 'This your wife gave me.'
    (h) Ta⌐bako o kudasa⌐i. 'Please give me a cigarette.'
    (i) Kore wa to⌐modati ḡa kurema⌐sita. 'This a friend gave me.'
    (j) Da⌐re ḡa /a⌐na⌐ta ni/ kureta? 'Who gave it to you?'

Situations involving giving can also be described from the point of view of receiving. The Japanese equivalent of 'receive' is morau. This verbal may refer to receiving by or from the speaker, the person addressed, or a third person. Its polite honorific equivalent is o⌐morai ni na⌐ru (↑) and its humble equivalent is itadaku (↓).

Particles: If expressed, the person who receives is followed by ḡa or wa, the thing received by particle o or wa, and the person from whom it is received by particle kara or ni.

----

[1] Or to person(s) closely associated with me—for example, a member of my family.

[2] Be careful of this usage. To rate a third party (not present) the equal of the person addressed would, in some circumstances, be insulting.

Examples:

    (k) Tomodati kara o⌐ka⌐si o mo⌐raima⌐sita. 'I received some candy
        from a friend.'
    (l) Kore wa ⌐da⌐re ni mo⌐raima⌐sita ka⌐ 'From whom did you get
        this?'
    (m) Kore wa ⌐da⌐re ḡa mo⌐raima⌐sita ka⌐ 'Who received this?'
    (n) Tanaka-sañ kara ⌐na⌐ni o o⌐morai ni narima⌐sita ka⌐ 'What did
        you receive from Mr. Tanaka?'
    (o) O⌐kusama ni ⌐ki⌐ree na hu⌐rosiki o itadakima⌐sita. 'I received
        a beautiful furoshiki from your wife.'

A situation in which one person does something for another is indicated in
Japanese by a verbal gerund, followed immediately in the same phrase by the
appropriate verbal of giving or receiving. For example:

    ka⌐ite aḡeru and ka⌐ite yaru 'write for someone' (lit. 'give writing')
    ka⌐ite ku⌐dasa⌐ru 'write for me' (lit. 'give me writing')
    ka⌐ite kureru 'write for me [or you]' (lit. 'give me [or you] writing')
    ka⌐ite morau 'have someone write' (lit. 'receive writing')

The differences in usage of the verbals of giving and receiving described
above apply equally to the combination of one of these verbals preceded by a
gerund. The particles are also the same, except that the person by whom
someone has something done is followed by particle ni but not kara. Also, the
gerund preceding the verbal of giving or receiving may have its own direct object, goal phrase, etc. [1] Study the following examples carefully, comparing
them with the corresponding examples above:

    (a) Yo⌐ñde a⌐ḡemasyo⌐o ka. 'Shall I read it for you?'
    (b) Se⌐ñse⌐e ni ⌐ka⌐ite a⌐ḡema⌐sita ka⌐ 'Did you write it for the
        teacher?'
    (c) U⌐ti no Ta⌐roo wa se⌐ñse⌐e ni ⌐ho⌐ñ o tyu⌐umoñ-site aḡema⌐sita.
        '(Our) Taro ordered a book for the teacher.'
    (d) Musuko ni ⌐pe⌐ñ o ka⌐tte yarima⌐sita. 'I bought a pen for my
        son.'
    (e) Ko⌐oka⌐ñsyu ni a⌐tarasi⌐i de⌐ñwatyoo o tano⌐ñde ya⌐rima⌐sita
        ka⌐ 'Did you ask for a new telephone book for the operator?'
    (f) Se⌐ñse⌐e wa ⌐ma⌐initi kŏdomo ni ku⌐da⌐mono o ki⌐tte⌐ yarimasu.
        'The teacher cuts the fruit for the children every day.'

---

[1] Without sufficient context, some examples are ambiguous. For example,
Ta⌐naka-sañ ni kiite moraima⌐sita. may mean 'I had Mr. Tanaka ask [him]' or
'I had [him] ask Mr. Tanaka.' If both 'Mr. Tanaka' and 'him' are expressed,
the order determines the difference:

    Tanaka-sañ ni a⌐no⌐ hito ni ki⌐ite moraima⌐sita. 'I had Mr. Tanaka
    ask him.'
    A⌐no⌐ hito ni Ta⌐naka-sañ ni kiite moraima⌐sita. 'I had him ask Mr.
    Tanaka.'

(g) Kore wa ⌈o⌉kusañ ḡa a⌐kete (or o⌐ake ni na⁴tte ⁱ) kudasaima⁴sita.
    'This your wife opened for me.'
(h) Ta⌐bako o motte⌉ kite kudasai. 'Please bring the cigarettes (for
    me).'
(i) Kore wa to⌐modati ḡa nao⌉site ku⌐rema⁴sita. 'This my friend
    fixed for me.'
(j) Da⌉re ḡa ⌠a⌐na⁴ta ni⌡ site kureta? 'Who did it for you?'
(k) Tomodati ni o⌐ka⌉si o mo⌐tte⁴ kite mo⌐raima⁴sita. 'I had my
    friend bring some candy.'
(l) Kore wa ⌈da⌉re ni ⌐mi⁴sete mo⌐raima⁴sita ka⌟   'Who showed
    you this?' (Lit. 'As for this, by whom did you receive show-
    ing?')
(m) Kore wa ⌈da⌉re ḡa si⌐te moraima⁴sita ka⌟   'For whom was
    this done?' (Lit. 'As for this, who received the doing?')
(n) Tanaka-sañ ni ⌈na⌉ni o ka⌐tte omorai ni narima⁴sita ka⌟ 'What
    did Mr. Tanaka buy for you?' (Lit. 'You received the buying of
    what by Mr. Tanaka?')
(o) O⌐kusama ni ⌈ki⌉ree na hu⌐rosiki o katte (or okai ni na⁴tte ⁱ)
    itadakima⁴sita. 'Your wife bought a beautiful furoshiki for me.'
    (Lit. 'I received the buying of a beautiful furoshiki by your wife.')

A gerund + moraitai (or itadakitai) is an indirect request— 'I want to have
something done by someone.'   Compare this with a direct request— '(you) do
something.' For example:

> Mi⌉te moraitai. 'I want to have it looked at.'   But:
> Mi⌉te. 'Look at it!'

> A⌐ratte moraita⌉i ñ desu. 'I want to have it washed.'   But:
> A⌐ratte kudasa⌉i. 'Please wash it.'

> A⌐kete itadakita⌉i ñ desu. 'I'd like to have it opened.'   But:
> A⌐kete kudasaimase⌉ñ ka⌟ 'Would you be kind enough to open it?'

A gerund + √morau sequence occurs as a request when someone is directly
asked to have something done by someone.

> Mi⌉te moratte. 'Have it looked at.'
> A⌐ratte moratte kudasa⌉i. 'Please have it washed.'
> A⌐kete moratte kudasaimase⌉ñ ka⌟ 'Would you be kind enough to have
>   it opened?'

2. Verbal Gerund + √simau

A verbal gerund + √simau means 'do so-and-so completely' or 'finish doing
so-and-so' or 'end up by doing so-and-so.' Examples:

> Wa⌐surete simaima⌉sita. 'I've forgotten [it] completely.'
> Kodomo ḡa o⌐ka⌉si o ⌈ta⌉bete si⌐maima⁴sita. 'The children finished
>   eating the candy.' or 'The children ate up the candy.'
> I⌐kitaku na⌉katta desyoo ḡa, i⌐tte simaima⌉sita. 'He probably didn't
>   want to go but he ended up by going.'

In this pattern, √simau follows the verbal gerund immediately in the same phrase without pause. Compare:

Sa⌐ra o aratte simaima⌐sita. 'I finished washing the dishes.'
Sara o aratte, si⌐maima⌐sita. 'I washed the dishes and put them away.'

In conversational Japanese, a gerund + √simau is very commonly contracted:

----te √simau > √----tyau
----de √simau > √----zyau

Examples:

Uncontracted	Contracted
ta⌐bete simau	ta⌐betyau
no⌐nde simatte	no⌐nzyatte
wasurete simatta	wasuretyatta
a⌐ratte simaima⌐su	a⌐rattyaima⌐su
i⌐tte simaima⌐sita	i⌐ttyaima⌐sita

3. Verbal Gerund + √oku

A verbal gerund followed immediately in the same phrase without pause by √oku [1] means 'do so-and-so and put aside,' or 'do so-and-so in advance,' or 'do so-and-so for future use or benefit,' or 'do so-and-so for the time being.' Examples:

Tomodati ḡa ⌐su⌐ḡu ⌐ku⌐ru kara, do⌐a o a⌐kete o⌐ite kudasai. 'A friend is coming very soon so please open the door (for future benefit).'
A⌐sita iru⌐ kara, kyo⌐o ka⌐tte okima⌐sita. 'I'll need it tomorrow so I bought it (in advance) today.'
Sono zassi o ⌐a⌐to de ⌐yo⌐mu kara, tu⌐kue no ue⌐ ni o⌐ite o⌐ite kudasai. 'I'm going to read that magazine later so please put it on top of the desk for the time being.'

In conversational Japanese, the final -e of the gerund is dropped before those forms of √oku which begin oi-. Examples:

Uncontracted	Contracted
a⌐kete o⌐ita	a⌐keto⌐ita
o⌐ite o⌐ite	o⌐ito⌐ite
yo⌐nde oite	yo⌐ndoite

---

[1] The past oita and gerund oite, among other forms, acquire a first-syllable accent when they follow an unaccented gerund.

4.   Particle ya

The particle ya occurs between nominals A and B meaning 'A and B and others of the same kind,' 'A and B and so on,' 'A and B among others,' 'things like A and B.' Thus:

> oᵗoᵗosañ to oᵏkaᵃasañ 'your father and mother'
> but:
> oᵗoᵗosañ ya oᵏkaᵃasañ 'your father and mother and others in your family'
>
> oᵗtya to koohiᵗi 'tea and coffee'
> but:
> oᵗtya ya koohiᵗi 'tea and coffee and other similar drinks'

There may be more than two nominals in the series:

> hoᵗñ ya zassi ya siñbuñ 'books and magazines and newspapers and the like'

A series of two or more nominals joined by ya occurs in the same kinds of patterns as a nominal alone.

Examples:

> Hoᵗñ ya zassi wa ᵈoᵗo simasyoo ka.   'What shall I do with the books and magazines and such things?'
> Peᵗñ ya eᵏñpitu ḡa irimaᵃsu.   'I need things like pens and pencils.'
> Yaᵗsai ya kudaᵗmono o kaᵗimaᵃsita.   'I bought vegetables and fruit among other things.'

DRILLS

A. Substitution Drill

1. I finished putting in the dishes. What shall I do next?	Saᵗra (o) irete simaimaᵗsita ḡa, aᵗto ᵗnaᵗni (o) siᵏmasyoᵃo ka.
2. I finished putting away the little things. What shall I do next?	Koᵗmakaᵗi moᵗnoᵃ (o) siᵏmatte sima-imaᵗsita ḡa, aᵗto ᵗnaᵗni (o) siᵏmasyoᵃo ka.
3. I finished washing the glasses. What shall I do next?	Koᵗppu (o) aratte simaimaᵗsita ḡa, aᵗto ᵗnaᵗni (o) siᵏmasyoᵃo ka.
4. I finished cleaning the kitchen. What shall I do next?	Daᵗidokoro (o) soozi-site simaimaᵗsita ḡa, aᵗto ᵗnaᵗni (o) siᵏmasyoᵃo ka.
5. I finished straightening up the study. What shall I do next?	Syoᵗsai (o) katazuᵗkete siᵏmaimaᵃsita ḡa, aᵗto ᵗnaᵗni (o) siᵏmasyoᵃo ka.
6. I finished turning on all the heaters. What shall I do next?	Suᵗtoᵗobu (o) miᵗñna tukeᵗte siᵏmai-maᵗsita ḡa, aᵗto ᵗnaᵗni (o) siᵏma-syoᵃo ka.

7. I finished opening all the windows. What shall I do next?

Maˈdo (o) miˉnna akete simaimaˈsita ḡa, aˈto ˉnaˈni (o) siˈmasyoˈo ka.

8. I finished locking all the doors. What shall I do next?

Toˈno kaḡiˈ (o) miˉnna kaˈkete siˈmaimaˈsita ḡa, aˈto ˉnaˈni (o) siˈmasyoˈo ka.

B. Substitution Drill

1. I'm putting away the little things.

Koˈmakaˈi moˈnoˈ o siˈmatte imaˈsu.

2. I finished putting away the little things.

Koˈmakaˈi moˈnoˈ (o) siˈmatte simaimaˈsita.

3. I put away the little things for the time being.

Koˈmakaˈi moˈnoˈ (o) siˈmatte okimaˈsita.

4. I had the little things put away.

Koˈmakaˈi moˈnoˈ (o) siˈmatte moraimaˈsita.

5. Shall I put away the little things for you?

Koˈmakaˈi moˈnoˈ (o) siˈmatte aḡemasyoˈo ka.

6. [He] put away the little things for me.

Koˈmakaˈi moˈnoˈ (o) siˈmatte kuremaˈsita.

7. Please put away the little things.

Koˈmakaˈi moˈnoˈ (o) siˈmatte kudasaˈi.

8. Please have the little things put away.

Koˈmakaˈi moˈnoˈ (o) siˈmatte moratte kudasaˈi.

9. I'd like to have the little things put away. . . .

Koˈmakaˈi moˈnoˈ (o) siˈmatte moraitaˈi ñ desu ḡa_

10. The little things have been put away.

Koˈmakaˈi moˈnoˈ (ḡa) siˈmatte arimaˈsu.

C. Substitution Drill

1. [He] cut it fine.

Koˈmakaˈku kiˈrimaˈsita.

2. It isn't fine (i.e. in small pieces).

Koˈmakaˈku aˈrimaseˈñ.

3. It isn't strong.

Tuˈyoku aˈrimaseˈñ.

4. [He] has become strong.

Tuˈyoku naˈrimaˈsita.

5. It has become painful.

Iˈtaˈku naˈrimaˈsita.

6. It isn't painful.

Iˈtaˈku aˈrimaseˈñ.

7. It isn't fast.

Haˈyaku aˈrimaseˈñ.

8. [He] talked fast.

Haˈyaku haˈnasimaˈsita.

9. [He] talked well.

Yoˈku haˈnasimaˈsita.

10. [He] listened carefully.

Yoˈku kiˈkimaˈsita.

D. Substitution Drill [1]

1. Where did you put (i.e. place) it?   Do˹ko ni o˺kima˺sita ka˩

2. Where did you put it (away)?   Do˹ko ni si˺maima˺sita ka˩

3. Where (i.e. into what) did you put it?   Do˹ko ni i˺rema˺sita ka˩

4. Where did you set it out?   Do˹ko ni da˺sima˺sita ka˩

5. Where did you take it?   Do˹ko ni mo˺tte ikima˺sita ka˩

6. What place (for example, what school) have you entered?   Do˹ko ni ha˺irima˺sita ka˩

7. What place did you call (on the telephone)?   Do˹ko ni de˺ñwa o kakema˺sita ka˩

8. Where did you go?   Do˹ko ni i˺kima˺sita ka˩

E. Grammar Drill (based on Grammatical Note 3)

Tutor: Si˹ma˺sita. 'I did it.'
Student: Si˹te okima˺sita. 'I did it in advance, or for future reference, or for the time being, etc.'

1. Kore (wa) a˹no hako ni iremasyo˺o ka.   Kore (wa) a˹no hako ni irete okimasyo˺o ka.

2. Osakana ya yasai (o) su˹˺ko˹si ka˹ima˺sita.   Osakana ya yasai (o) su˹ko˺si ka˺tte okima˺sita.

3. Syo˹kudoo no teeburu no ue˺ ni o˺kima˺sita.   Syo˹kudoo no teeburu no ue˺ ni o˺ite okima˺sita.

4. Ka˹mi˺ ya eñpitu (o) ta˺ku-sañ dasima˺sita.   Ka˹mi˺ ya eñpitu (o) ta˺kusañ da˺site o˺kima˺sita.

5. Ni˹kai no tañsu no na˺ka ni si˺maima˺sita.   Ni˹kai no tañsu no na˺ka ni si˺matte okima˺sita.

6. Su˹ko˺si ya˹sumimasyo˺o.   Su˹ko˺si ya˹su˺ñde o˺kimasyo˺o.

7. Ko˹otuuko˺osya de ki˺ki-ma˺sita.   Ko˹otuuko˺osya de ki˺ite okima˺sita.

8. A˹tarasi˺i meesi (o) tyu˹u-moñ-simasyo˺o ka.   A˹tarasi˺i meesi (o) tyu˹umoñ-site okimasyo˺o ka.

F. Grammar Drill (based on Grammatical Note 1)

Tutor: Si˹te kudasa˺i. 'Please do it.'
Student: Si˹te moratte kudasa˺i. 'Please have it done.' or 'Please have someone do it.'

---

[1] In contrast with the variety of the English equivalents, the Japanese pattern here is identical throughout: a place word + particle _ni_ of goal indicating the place toward or into which motion occurred.

1. O⌐sara (o) aratte kudasa⌐i.   O⌐sara (o) aratte moratte kudasa⌐i.
2. Mi⌐ti (o) osiete kudasa⌐i.   Mi⌐ti (o) osiete moratte kudasa⌐i.
3. Ha⌐yaku na⌐o⌐site kudasai.   Ha⌐yaku na⌐o⌐site mo⌐ratte kudasa⌐i.
4. Se⌐ñse⌐e (o) yo⌐ñde kuda-   Se⌐ñse⌐e (o) yo⌐ñde moratte kuda-
   sa⌐i.   sa⌐i.
5. Ku⌐ruma no kaḡi⌐ (o)   Ku⌐ruma no kaḡi⌐ (o) ⌐ka⌐kete mo-
   ⌐ka⌐kete kudasai.   ⌐ratte kudasa⌐i.
6. Yo⌐kohama e⌐ no miti (o)   Yo⌐kohama e⌐ no miti (o) ki⌐ite mo-
   ki⌐ite kudasa⌐i.   ratte kudasa⌐i.
7. Ni⌐hoñḡo de itte kudasa⌐i.   Ni⌐hoñḡo de itte moratte kudasa⌐i.
8. Ki⌐ree ni ⌐ka⌐ite kudasai.   Ki⌐ree ni ⌐ka⌐ite mo⌐ratte kudasa⌐i.

G. Grammar Drill (based on Grammatical Note 1)

   Tutor: Ta⌐naka-sañ ḡa site kurema⌐sita. 'Mr. Tanaka did it for me.'
   Student: Ta⌐naka-sañ ni site moraima⌐sita. 'I had it done for me by
            Mr. Tanaka.' or 'I had Mr. Tanaka do it for me.'

1. To⌐modati ḡa ma⌐tte ku⌐re-   To⌐modati ni ma⌐tte mo⌐raima⌐sita.
   ma⌐sita.
2. A⌐ni ḡa si⌐ñbuñ (o) katte ku-   A⌐ni ni si⌐ñbuñ (o) katte moraima⌐si-
   rema⌐sita.   ta.
3. Hu⌐miko-sañ ḡa ha⌐ti⌐-zi   Hu⌐miko-sañ ni ha⌐ti⌐-zi made i⌐te
   made i⌐te kurema⌐sita.   moraima⌐sita.
4. Musuko ḡa si⌐ñbuñ (o) motte⌐   Musuko ni si⌐ñbuñ (o) motte⌐ kite mo-
   kite ku⌐rema⌐sita.   ⌐raima⌐sita.
5. Se⌐ñse⌐e ḡa ko⌐re (o) yo⌐ñde   Se⌐ñse⌐e ni ko⌐re (o) yo⌐ñde i⌐tada-
   ku⌐dasaima⌐sita.   kima⌐sita.
6. Ko⌐oka⌐ñsyu ḡa ba⌐ñḡo⌐o (o)   Ko⌐oka⌐ñsyu ni ba⌐ñḡo⌐o (o) i⌐tte mo-
   i⌐tte kurema⌐sita.   raima⌐sita.
7. Mu⌐sume⌐ ḡa syo⌐kuzi no   Mu⌐sume⌐ ni syo⌐kuzi no sitaku (o)
   sitaku (o) site kurema⌐sita.   site moraima⌐sita.
8. Go⌐syu⌐ziñ ḡa mi⌐ti (o) osi-   Go⌐syu⌐ziñ ni mi⌐ti (o) osiete itada-
   ete kudasaima⌐sita.   kima⌐sita.

H. Response Drill (based on Grammatical Note 1)

   Tutor: Si⌐ma⌐sita ka⌐ /tomodati/ 'Did you do it? /friend/
   Student: To⌐modati ni site moraima⌐sita. 'I had it done by a friend.'
            or 'I had a friend do it.'

1. Re⌐ezo⌐oko (o) na⌐osima⌐si-   To⌐modati ni nao⌐site mo⌐raima⌐si-
   ta ka⌐ /tomodati/   ta.
2. Zyu⌐ñsa ni kikima⌐sita ka⌐   Ni⌐hoñzi⌐ñ ni ki⌐ite moraima⌐sita.
   /ni⌐hoñzi⌐ñ/
3. A⌐tarasi⌐i ⌐ka⌐ḡu (o) mi-   Ka⌐nai ni ⌐mi⌐te mo⌐raima⌐sita.
   ⌐ma⌐sita ka⌐ /ka⌐nai/
4. Su⌐misu-sañ ni a⌐ima⌐sita   Ta⌐naka-sañ ni a⌐tte mo⌐raima⌐sita.
   ka⌐ /Tanaka-sañ/
5. Kusuri (o) ka⌐ima⌐sita ka⌐   Mu⌐suko ni katte moraima⌐sita.
   /musuko/

6. To (o) si⌐mema⌐sita ka⌐   Hu⌐miko-tyañ ni ⌐si⌐mete mo⌐rai-
   /Hu⌐miko-tyañ/   ma⌐sita.

7. Ho⌐ndana ni za̅ssi (o)   A⌐no⌐ hito ni si⌐matte moraima⌐si-
   si⌐maima⌐sita ka⌐   ta.
   /a⌐no⌐ hito/

8. Ne⌐ko (o) ⌐so⌐to e da-   Ko⌐domo ni da⌐site mo⌐raima⌐sita.
   ⌐sima⌐sita ka⌐
   /kodomo/

I. Response Drill

     Tutor: To ḡa a⌐ite ima⌐su yo⌐   'You know, the door's open.'
     Student: Da⌐re ḡa a⌐kema⌐sita ka⌐   'Who opened it?'

1. Na⌐ni ka ko⌐bo⌐rete (i)masu   Da⌐re ḡa ko⌐bosima⌐sita ka⌐
   yo⌐

2. I⌐nu⌐ (ḡa) ⌐de⌐te (i)masu yo⌐   Da⌐re ḡa da⌐sima⌐sita ka⌐

3. Ano hako ni ⌐ki⌐ree na   Da⌐re ḡa i⌐rema⌐sita ka⌐
   hu⌐ki⌐ñ ya zo⌐okiñ (ḡa)
   ha⌐itte (i)masu yo⌐

4. Da⌐idokoro no de⌐ñki (ḡa)   Da⌐re ḡa tu⌐kema⌐sita ka⌐
   ⌐tu⌐ite (i)masu yo⌐

5. Ka⌐ḡi⌐ (ḡa) ka⌐ka⌐tte (i)ma-   Da⌐re ḡa ka⌐kema⌐sita ka⌐
   su yo⌐

6. Syo⌐sai no ma⌐do (ḡa) si-   Da⌐re ḡa si⌐mema⌐sita ka⌐
   ⌐ma⌐tte (i)masu yo⌐

J. Level Drill[1]

1. Kyo⌐o no siñbuñ (o) su⌐te-   Kyo⌐o no siñbuñ (o) o⌐sute ni narima⌐
   ma⌐sita ka⌐   ma⌐sita ka⌐

2. A⌐tarasi⌐i ⌐ho⌐ñ (o) si⌐ma-   A⌐tarasi⌐i ⌐ho⌐ñ (o) o⌐simai ni na-
   ima⌐sita ka⌐   rima⌐sita ka⌐

3. Tu⌐kue no ue⌐ ni o⌐kima⌐-   Tu⌐kue no ue⌐ ni o⌐oki ni narima⌐-
   sita ka⌐   sita ka⌐

4. Hi⌐kidasi no na⌐ka ni i⌐re-   Hi⌐kidasi no na⌐ka ni o⌐ire ni nari-
   ma⌐sita ka⌐   ma⌐sita ka⌐

5. I⌐tu-ḡoro hairima⌐sita ka⌐   I⌐tu-ḡoro ohairi ni narima⌐sita ka⌐

6. Do⌐nata kara mo⌐raima⌐sita   Do⌐nata kara o⌐morai ni narima⌐si-
   ka⌐   ta ka⌐

7. Ta⌐naka-sañ ni aima⌐sita   Ta⌐naka-sañ ni oai ni narima⌐sita
   ka⌐   ka⌐

8. Se⌐ñse⌐e (o) yo⌐bima⌐sita   Se⌐ñse⌐e (o) o⌐yobi ni narima⌐sita
   ka⌐   ka⌐

---

[1] Each sentence on the right is the honorific (†) equivalent of the corresponding sentence on the left.

K. Expansion Drill

1. Is [it] in?
   What is in [it]?
   What is inside [it]?

   What is inside that big
   box?

   Ha⌐itte (i)masu ka⌐
   Na⌐ni (g̃a) ⌐ha⌐itte (i)masu ka⌐
   Na⌐ka ni ⌐na⌐ni (g̃a) ⌐ha⌐itte (i)ma-
   su ka⌐
   Ano o⌐oki⌐i hako no ⌐na⌐ka ni ⌐na⌐ni
   (g̃a) ⌐ha⌐itte (i)masu ka⌐

2. I received help.
   I had Mr. Tanaka help me.

   I was very busy so I had
   Mr. Tanaka help me.
   Yesterday morning I was
   very busy so I had Mr.
   Tanaka help me.

   Te⌐tuda⌐tte mo⌐raima⌐sita.
   Tanaka-sañ ni te⌐tuda⌐tte mo⌐raima⌐sita.
   To⌐temo isog̃a⌐sikatta kara, Tanaka-
   sañ ni te⌐tuda⌐tte mo⌐raima⌐sita.
   Ki⌐noo no a⌐sa to⌐temo isog̃a⌐sikatta
   kara, Tanaka-sañ ni te⌐tuda⌐tte
   mo⌐raima⌐sita.

3. Have [it] fixed.
   Have this fixed.
   Have this fixed by someone
   else (lit. another person).
   [I] can't do it so have this
   fixed by someone else.
   I (comparatively speaking)
   can't do it so have this
   fixed by someone else.

   Na⌐o⌐site moratte.
   Ko⌐re (o) nao⌐site moratte.
   Ho⌐ka no hito⌐ ni ko⌐re (o) nao⌐site
   moratte.
   De⌐ki⌐nai kara, ho⌐ka no hito⌐ ni
   ko⌐re (o) nao⌐site moratte.
   Bo⌐ku wa deki⌐nai kara, ho⌐ka no hi-
   to⌐ ni ko⌐re (o) nao⌐site moratte.

4. Have [them] thrown out.
   Have [them] thrown out tomorrow.
   [They] get in the way so
   have [them] thrown out
   tomorrow.
   [They] always get in the
   way so have [them] thrown
   out tomorrow.
   These old papers and magazines and things always
   get in the way so have
   them thrown out tomor-
   row.

   Sutete moratte.
   Asita su̅tete moratte.
   Zya⌐ma ni na⌐ru kara, asita su̅tete
   moratte.
   I⌐tu mo zya⌐ma ni na⌐ru kara, asita
   su̅tete moratte.
   Kono hu⌐ru⌐i siñbuñ ya zassi (wa)
   i⌐tu mo zya⌐ma ni na⌐ru kara,
   asita su̅tete moratte.

5. Is it all right?
   I'd like to rest. Is it all
   right?
   I'd like to rest [this] afternoon. Is it all right?
   I'm tired so I'd like to rest
   [this] afternoon. Is it all
   right?

   Ka⌐maimase⌐ñ ka⌐
   Ya⌐sumita⌐i ñ desu g̃a, ka⌐maimase⌐ñ
   ka⌐
   Go⌐g̃o ya⌐sumita⌐i ñ desu g̃a, ka⌐mai-
   mase⌐ñ ka⌐
   Tu⌐ka⌐rete (i)ru kara, go⌐g̃o ya⌐sumi-
   ta⌐i ñ desu g̃a; ka⌐maimase⌐ñ ka⌐

I'm awfully tired so I'd
like to rest [this] afternoon. Is it all right?

Zu⌐ibuñ tu┏ka┛rete (i)ru kara, go┛-
ḡo ya┏sumita┛i ñ desu ḡa; ka┏mai-
mase┛ñ ka⌐

6. It's all right.

Da⌐izyo┛obu desu yo.

[She] wiped [it] up for me
so it's all right.

Hu⌐ite kureta┛ kara, da⌐izyo┛obu
desu yo.

[She] wiped it up for me
right away so it's all
right.

Su┏ḡu hu┗ite kureta┛ kara, da⌐izyo┛-
obu desu yo.

Fumiko wiped it up for
me right away so it's
all right.

Hu┛miko-sañ (ḡa) ┏su┛ḡu hu┗ite kure-
ta┛ kara, da⌐izyo┛obu desu yo.

I spilled [it] but Fumiko
wiped it up for me right
away so it's all right.

Ko┏bosima┛sita ḡa; Hu┛miko-sañ ḡa
┏su┛ḡu hu┗ite kureta┛ kara, da⌐i-
zyo┛obu desu yo.

I spilled sake but Fumiko
wiped it up for me right
away so it's all right.

Sa┏ke (o) kobosima┛sita ḡa; Hu┛mi-
ko-sañ ḡa ┏su┛ḡu hu┗ite kureta┛
kara, da⌐izyo┛obu desu yo.

I spilled sake on top of the
new table but Fumiko
wiped it up for me right
away so it's all right.

A┛tarasi┛i te┏eburu no ue┛ ni sa┏ke
(o) kobosima┛sita ḡa; Hu┛miko-sañ
ḡa ┏su┛ḡu hu┗ite kureta┛ kara, da⌐i-
zyo┛obu desu yo.

SUPPLEMENTARY SELECTIONS

(with questions)

1. A┛tarasi┛i ┏ho┛ñ o ta┏kusañ katta┛ kara, a┛tarasi┛i ┏ho┛ñdana mo ka┗ima┛-
   sita. Ke┛sa u┏ti e motte┛ kite mo┏raima┛sita ḡa; to┏ttemo isoḡa┛sikatta
   kara, ho┛ñ mo ┏ho┛ñdana mo syo┏sai no su┛mi ni o┗ito┛ite de┏kakema┛si-
   ta ḡa; boku no rusu ni ┏ka┛nai ḡa hi┗to┛ri de so┏no ho┛ñ o mi┏ñna ho┛ñdana
   ni si┗matte kurema┛sita.

   a. Do┛o site a┛tarasi┛i ┏ho┛ñdana o ka┏ima┛sita ka⌐
   b. I┛tu u┏ti e motte┛ kite mo┏raima┛sita ka⌐
   c. Sono ┏ho┛ñ to ┏ho┛ñdana wa ┏do┛ko ni o┏ite okima┛sita ka⌐   Do┛o
      site?
   d. Da┛re ḡa ┏ho┛ñ o si┗matte kurema┛sita ka⌐
   e. Da┛re ni ┏ho┛ñ o si┗matte moraima┛sita ka⌐   *okusan ni hono...*
   f. Da┛re ḡa te┏tudaima┛sita ka⌐   *okusan*

2. Kyo┛o wa ┏a┛sa kara to┏ttemo isoḡa┛sikatta kara, tu┏ka┛rete si┗maima┛sita.
   U┏ti no Ta┛roo ḡa e┏eḡo no ho┛ñ o wa┏sureta┛ kara, ḡa┏kkoo ma┛de mo┗tte
   itte yarima┛sita. Sore kara, u┏ti e ka┛ette; Hu┛miko to issyo ni u┏ti o ka-
   tazukema┛sita. Zyu┏uni┛-zi ni ma̅ta dekakete, Gi┏ñza no depa┛ato e i┏ki-
   ma┛sita. Soko no syokudoo de to┏modati ni a┛tte, issyo ni syo┏kuzi o si-
   ma┛sita. Sore kara, u┏ti no syosai no suto┛obu ḡa ┏mo┛o se┏ñsyuu kara
   dame┛ desu kara; a┛tarasi┛i no o ka┗ima┛sita. Tyo┛tto ┏o┛okikatta kara, de-
   ┏pa┛ato no hi┏┛to┛ ni ┏ta┛kusii made mo┗tte┛ kite moratte; ta┏kusii de ka┏eri-
   ma┛sita. To┏ttemo tuka┛rete i┏ta┛ kara, Hu┛miko ni hi┏to┛ri de ba┏ñḡo┛hañ

no sitaku o site moratte; i⌐ti-zikañ-g͡u⌐rai ya⌐sumima⌐sita.

a. Na⌐ni o ga⌐kkoo ma⌐de mo⌐tte ikima⌐sita ka↵
b. Da⌐re ni mo⌐tte itte yarima⌐sita ka↵ *Taro san*
c. Do⌐o site mo⌐tte itte yarima⌐sita ka↵ *Why, took it for him ?*
d. A⌐sa u⌐ti e ka⌐ette kara, na⌐ni o si⌐ma⌐sita ka↵
e. Hi⌐to⌐ri de si⌐ma⌐sita ka↵
f. Da⌐re ni te⌐tuda⌐tte mo⌐raima⌐sita ka↵ *Fumiko san ni* ____
g. Da⌐re g͡a te⌐tuda⌐tte ku⌐rema⌐sita ka↵
h. Na⌐ñ-zi ni ma⌐ta dekakema⌐sita ka↵
i. Do⌐ko e i⌐kima⌐sita ka↵
j. Do⌐ko de syo⌐kuzi o sima⌐sita ka↵
k. Hi⌐to⌐ri de ta⌐bema⌐sita ka↵
l. Ta⌐bete kara ⌐na⌐ni o ka⌐ima⌐sita ka↵ Do⌐o site?
m. Da⌐re g͡a sore o ⌐ta⌐kusii made mo⌐tte⌐ kite ku⌐rema⌐sita ka↵
n. Ka⌐ette kara ⌐na⌐ni o si⌐ma⌐sita ka↵ Do⌐o site?
o. Hu⌐miko-sañ ni ⌐na⌐ni o si⌐te moraima⌐sita ka↵

SHORT SUPPLEMENTARY DIALOGUES

(In each case, decide whether the speaker is best identified as M, or W, or MW. Change M utterances to W, and W utterances to M.)

1. A: Tu⌐ka⌐retyatta wa↵   W
   B: Bo⌐ku mo.   M

2. A: Eeg͡o o⌐wakari ni na⌐ru?
   B: Wa⌐suretyatta⌐ yo.   *iasuretyatta wa yo (W)*

3. A: Kore ⌐do⌐ko ni o⌐kimasyo⌐o ka.   *Neutral*
   B: A⌐suko ni oito⌐ite kudasai.   *formal* N

4. A: Are ⌐to⌐tte ne?   *inform*
   B: Do⌐o site?
   A: Zya⌐ma ni na⌐ru kara.

5. A: Kono zibiki a͞re to tig͡au?
   B: N̄. A⌐re yo⌐ri a⌐tarasi⌐i yo↵

6. A: Kinoo ko⌐no zassi katta⌐ wa↵   W
   B: A⌐a, bo⌐ku mo o⌐nazi zassi katta⌐ yo.   M

EXERCISES

1. Draw a plan of your home, and describe in Japanese what each room is and the location of the doors, windows, and furniture.

2. Draw a simple house plan, including doors and windows. Using model furniture—or labeled blocks of wood or cardboard—practice giving and

following instructions on where to put each piece of furniture. (This exercise may also be done at the blackboard.   After hearing what is requested, draw the appropriate object in the appropriate location.)

3.) Speaking informally, tell someone to:

    a. put these books away.
    b. put these pens and pencils and such in the top desk drawer.
    c. throw away all these old magazines.
    d. put the beer in the refrigerator.
    e. put this on Mr. Tanaka's desk.
    f. give you a hand.
    g. put all these little things in that box.
    h. get out more paper.
    i. give this to the dog.
    j. give this to the teacher.
    k. wash this with soap.
    l. pass you the salt.   *shio ₤ watasu*
    m. put this under the kitchen table for the time being.
    n. be careful.
    o. have Fumiko buy more of this kind of medicine.

4. Practice the Basic Dialogues with appropriate variations.

Lesson 18. Visiting

BASIC DIALOGUES: FOR MEMORIZATION

(a)

Maid

mem

guest or customer
    kyaku or
    okyaku⁺

put in an appearance or
show up or come
    mi⌐e⌐ru /-ru/   **kimasu**

1. Mr. Tanaka. (Lit. Master.)
Your American guest has
come.
    ~okusama (F)
    Dannasama⌐ A⌐merika⌐ziñ no o-
⌐kyakusa⌐ma ḡa o⌐mie ni narima⌐-
sita.

Host (going to entry hall)

go up or come up or
enter
    aḡaru /-u/

2. Mr. Smith! It was good of
you to come. Please come
in.
    Su⌐misu-sañ. Yo⌐ku i⌐rassyaima⌐-
sita. Do⌐ozo o⌐aḡari-kudasa⌐i.

Smith

3. (Lit. I commit the rudeness
[of entering your home].)
    Si⌐tu⌐ree-simasu.

Host (showing Smith into the living room)

4. This way, please.
    Do⌐ozo kotira e.

Smith

the other day (formal)
    señzitu

5. (Lit. I committed a rudeness
the other day.)
    Señzitu wa si⌐tu⌐ree-simasita.

Host

6. (I was the one [who was
rude].)
    Ko⌐tira ko⌐so.

Smith

rain
fall (of rain, snow, etc.)
weather or good weather
    a⌐me
    hu⌐ru /-u/
    te⌐ñki or
    o⌐te⌐ñki⁺

7. It rained terribly [hard]
yesterday but isn't it a beautiful day today!
    Kinoo ⌐zu⌐ibuñ ⌐a⌐me ḡa hu⌐rima⌐-
sita ḡa, kyo⌐o wa ⌐i⌐i o⌐te⌐ñki desu ⌐ne⌐e.

315

Host

8. [It] certainly [is].   Hoñtoo ni.

    a walk   sañpo
    for a walk   sañpo ni
    is cool   su⌐zusi⌐i /-ku/

9. I went for a walk this   Ke⌐sa sa⌐ñpo ni ikima⌐sita ḡa,* su-
   morning. Hasn't it grown   ⌐zu⌐siku na⌐rima⌐sita ⌐ne⌐e.
   cool!

Smith

    fall or autumn   a⌐ki

10. Yes. Fall has come already, .   E⌐e. Mo⌐o ⌐a⌐ki ni na⌐rima⌐sita
   hasn't it. (Lit. It has be-   ⌐ne⌐e.
   come fall already, hasn't
   it.)

(Maid brings tea)

Host

11. Please [have] some tea.   O⌐tya o do⌐ozo.

Isogashii kara, doozo okamai naku

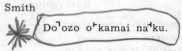

12. Please don't bother. or   Do⌐ozo o⌐kamai na⌐ku.
   Please don't go to any
   trouble.

Host (serving tea)

13. It will get cold, so please   Tu⌐metaku narima⌐su kara, do⌐ozo.
   [go ahead].

Smith

14. (I'll drink it.)   I⌐tadakima⌐su.

Hostess (leading guests to dining room)

15. Please go in.   Do⌐ozo o⌐hairi-kudasaima⌐se.

Smith

16. [Excuse me for going] ahead.   Osaki ni.

    rice-straw floor mat   tatami
    room with floor mats   ta⌐tami no heya⌐
    feeling or mood   kimoti
    is pleasant or agreeable   ki⌐moti ḡa i⌐i

17. Aren't tatami rooms pleas-   Ta⌐tami no heya⌐ (wa) ki⌐moti ḡa i⌐i
   ant!   desu ⌐ne⌐e.

Hostess

    nothing   nani mo /+ negative/   or
                                      nañni mo

18. There's nothing [worth men-   Na⌐ni mo gozaimase⌐n̄ ḡa, do⌐ozo.
    tioning] but please [eat].

                                                            Smith

19. (I'll have some.)   I⌐tadakima⌐su.

                                                            Hostess

        second helping or   kawari or
        additional serving   o⌐ka⌐wari +
20. How about some more?   O⌐ka⌐wari wa?

                                                            Smith

21. No, thank you.   Mo⌐o ⌐ke⌐kkoo desu.

                                                            Hostess

        reserve or restraint   eñryo or
                                             goeñryo
22. Please don't hold back. or   Do⌐ozo go⌐eñryo na⌐ku
    Please don't stand on cere-
    mony.

                                                            Smith

23. Thank you but I've already   A⌐ri⌐ḡatoo gozaimasu ḡa, mo⌐o ta-
    had a lot (so . . .)   ⌐kusañ itadakima⌐sita kara

        mountain   ya⌐ma⌐
        sea or ocean   u⌐mi
        be visible or can see   mi⌐e⌐ru /-ru/
        place   to⌐ko(ro)⌐
24. How beautiful it is here, with Ya⌐ma⌐ mo ⌐u⌐mi mo ⌐mi⌐ete, to⌐t-
    a view of the mountains and   temo ki⌐ree na to⌐koro⌐ desu ⌐ne⌐e.
    the sea! (Lit. Both the
    mountains and the sea being
    visible, it's a very pretty
    place, isn't it!)

                                                            Hostess

25. Thank you.   O⌐so⌐re i⌐rima⌐su.

                                                            Host

        skilled or skillful   zyo⌐ozu⌐ /na/   or
                                             ozyoozu + /na/
26. Isn't your Japanese good,   Su⌐misu-sañ (wa) * nīhoñḡo (ḡa) o-
    Mr. Smith!   ⌐zyoozu de⌐su ⌐ne⌐e.

        still or yet   ma⌐da / + affirmative/
        learn or take lessons   na⌐ra⌐u /-u/
27. Are you still taking les-   Ma⌐da na⌐ra⌐tte (i)masu ka
    sons?

Smith

no more   mo⌐o⌐ / + negative/

28. No, (I'm) not (taking les-   Iie, mo⌐o⌐ na⌐ra⌐tte (i)⌐mase⌐n.
    sons) any more.

not skilled or poor at   he⌐ta⌐ /na/
these days   kono ḡoro
have time   zi⌐kañ ḡa a⌐ru

29. I'm still poor at it, but I   Ma⌐da he⌐ta⌐ desu ḡa, kono ḡoro
    don't have any time these   zi⌐kañ ḡa arimase⌐n kara⌐
    days (so. . .)

(c)

Smith

by means of Japanese   nihoñḡo de
    or in Japanese
say or be named or   iu /-u/ or
   be called   mo⌐osu⌐ /-u/ or
                 o⌐ssya⌐ru⌐ /-aru/

say quote what? or   na⌐ñ to iu or
be named quote what? or   nañ te iu
be called quote what?

30. What is this kind of door   Koñna to (wa) nihoñḡo de ⌐na⌐ñ te
    called in Japanese?   i⌐ima⌐su ka⌐

Tanaka

sliding door (trans-   syoozi
  lucent)
say quote shoji or   syoozi to iu or
  be called quote shoji   syoozi tte iu

31. It's called a " shoji."   Syo⌐ozi tte iima⌐su.

Smith

32. How about that kind (of   A⌐ñna⌐ no wa?
    one)?

Tanaka

sliding door (opaque)   hu⌐suma⌐ [1]
say quote fusuma or   hu⌐suma⌐ to iu or
  be called quote fusuma   hu⌐suma⌐ tte iu

33. That one is called a "fusu- Are wa hu⌐suma⌐ tte iimasu.
    ma."

---

[1] Has commonly occurring unaccented alternant.

Basic Dialogues   319

                                    Smith

34. The outside ones, too?   So⁷to no mo?

                                    Tanaka

    sliding storm door   a⁽ma⁾do
    say quote amado or   a⁽ma⁾do to iu or
    be called quote amado   a⁽ma⁾do tte iu
35. No, no. Those are called   Iie iie. Are wa a⁽ma⁾do tte iimasu.
    " amado. "

                                       (d)

                                    Tanaka

    fine or handsome or   rippa /na/
    magnificent or im-
    posing
    Japanese-style alcove   tokonoma
36. What a handsome tokonoma!   Ri⁽ppa na tokonoma de⁷su ⁽ne⁴e.

    flower or flower ar-   ha⁽na⁷ or
    rangement   ohana⁺
    flower called quote what?   na⁷ñ to iu hana or
                                      na⁷ñ te iu hana
37. What kind of flowers are   Kore (wa) ⁽na⁷ñ te iu ha⁽na⁴ desyoo
    these? (Lit. These are   ka.
    flowers called quote what?)

                                    Smith

    not know how one says [it]   do⁷o iu ka si̅ranai
    or not know how [it] is
    called
38. I don't know what they are   Ni⁽hoñgo de do⁷o iu ka si⁽rimase⁴ñ
    called in Japanese, but there   ga, niwa ni ta⁽kusañ arima⁷su yo◡
    are a lot of them in the gar-
    den.

                                       (e)

                                    Maid

    during someone's absence   rusu-tyuu ni or
    from home   orusu-tyuu ! ni   Kinoshita
39. Someone (lit. a guest) came   Orusu-tyuu ni o⁽kyakusa⁷ñ (ga) o⁴mie
    while you were out. . . .   ni narima⁴sita ga◡   Cane

                                    Tanaka

40. Oh? Who?   So⁷o? Da⁷re?

                                    Maid

    be named quote Ueda or   Ueda to iu or
    be called quote Ueda or   Ueda tte iu
    say quote Ueda
41. His name was Ueda. . . .   U⁽eda to ossyaima⁷sita ga◡

                                      formal — said

Tanaka

say quote what? *or*
 be called quote what?
 or be named quote
 what?
42. What did he say?

na'ñ to iu *or*
 na'ñ te iu

[Na'ñ te itta?

Maid

polite → to say honorific

say quote he'll come,
 go, *or* be
43. He said he'd come again.

i'rassya'ru to o'ssya'ru *or*
 i'rassya'ru tte o'ssya'ru
[Ma'ta irassya'ru tte o'ssyaima'sita.

Tanaka

(ask *[quote]*)will [some-
 one] come
44. Did you ask when he's coming?

(ku'ru ka)*[to]* kiku
[I'tu 'ku'ru ka kiita?

to ask a quest

Maid

clearly *or* distinctly
 or precisely
say quote he doesn't
 understand *or* can't
 tell

ha'kki'ri

o'wakari ni nara'nai to
 o'ssya'ru *or*
 o'wakari ni nara'nai tte o's-
 sya'ru *I asked*

45. Yes. I inquired but he
said he couldn't tell ex-
actly.

normal

(Ha'a. U'kagaima'sita ga, ha'kki'ri
 o'wakari ni nara'nai tte o'ssyaima'-
 sita.

*Hai, kimashita ga hakkiri
 wakaranai ...*

NOTES ON THE BASIC DIALOGUES

1. Remember that -sama is a more polite variant of -sañ.

2. Agaru 'enter' is usually used in reference to entering a Japanese-style
 building—a home, inn, restaurant, etc.—which one enters by stepping up.
 Note also kaidañ o agaru 'go up the stairs.'

3. Si'tu'ree-simasu, lit. 'I commit a rudeness,' covers a multitude of situations in Japanese: it is an apology for entering someone's home or office
 —and for leaving, for taking a seat, even for relaxing!

5. Señzitu wa si'tu'ree-simasita frequently occurs as the formal beginning of
 a conversation between people who have had some recent contact with each
 other. Under similar circumstances, an English speaker might say, 'It
 was nice seeing you the other day.'

6. Ko'so is a particle of strong emphasis. Ko'tira ko'so means 'this side,
 not your side, [committed the rudeness].' Compare:

A: Go'ku'roosama desita. 'It's been a great deal of trouble for you.'
B: A'na'ta koso. 'YOU're the one who has been troubled.'

This exchange might occur for example when two people have been working on a project together.

7. The gerund of huˈru occurs with alternate accents: ˈhuˈtte and huˈtteˈ.

   Teˈñki may be described by words meaning 'good' or 'bad,' but unmodified it means 'good weather.'

8. Hoñtoo ni 'truly': ni is the particle of manner (cf. Lesson 15, Grammatical Note 5).

9. Ni here is the ni of goal or purpose. Note also sañpo-suru 'take a walk.'

   Suˈzusiˈi means 'is cool'—i.e. 'is nice and cool.' Besides referring to typical days of autumn, it is used to describe pleasantly cool days of summer.

10. Note also: huˈyuˈ 'winter'; haˈru 'spring,' naˈtuˈ 'summer.'

11. Otya o is a fragment. A possible major sentence substitute would be: Oˈtya o mesiaĝatte kudasaˈi.

12. Okamai is a derivative of the verbal √kaˈmaˈu /-u/ 'mind,' 'care,' 'bother about,' from which kaˈmawaˈnai (formal, kaˈmaimaseˈñ) 'I don't care,' 'it doesn't matter' is also derived.

14, 19. Remember that iˈtadakimaˈsu is regularly said by a guest as he begins to eat or drink.

16. Osaki ni, depending on context, is either an apology for doing something ahead of someone else, or an invitation to someone else to go ahead. Thus: Osaki ni siˈtuˈree-simasu. 'Excuse me for taking my leave ahead of you.' but Doˈozo osaki ni. 'Please go ahead.'

17. Kiˈmoti ĝa iˈi 'is pleasant or agreeable' and its opposite kiˈmoti ĝa waruˈi 'is unpleasant or disagreeable' are often used in reference to people, as equivalents of English 'feel well' and 'not feel well.' The person or thing to which these sequences refer is followed by particle wa or ĝa, depending upon emphasis.

22. Note also: eñryo-suru 'hold back,' 'be reserved,' 'show restraint,' 'hesitate.'

23. ' so—I don't care for any more.'

24. Toko is an informal alternant of toˈkoroˈ.

25. Oˈsoˈre iˈrimaˈsu, lit. 'I'm overwhelmed [with gratitude or shame],' is an extremely polite way of saying 'Thank you' or 'I'm sorry.' It is used more frequently by women. A commonly occurring alternate form of it is oˈsoˈreirimasu.

27. Naˈraˈu is used in reference to any sort of learning or instruction; beñkyoo-suru is usually used only for scholastic studies.

29. ' so—I've given up taking lessons.'

30. Moˈosu and oˈssyaˈru are polite equivalents of iu. Moˈosu, a humble verbal, is used in reference to the speaker and persons closely connected with him. Oˈssyaˈru, an honorific, refers only to persons other than the speaker, in polite speech.

39. 'but— did you know he was coming?'

Rusu-tyuu: compare sigoto-tyuu 'in the middle of work' and hanasi-tyuu
'in the middle of talking.'

41. 'but— do you know him?'

GRAMMATICAL NOTES

1. Quotatives *[t]* te ~ to

[T] te[1] and its more formal equivalent to are QUOTATIVES. They follow a
quotation (or the gist of a quotation) consisting of any sequence whatsoever— a
word, a part of a word, a sentence, a speech, an utterance in a foreign language, etc.— or nañ 'what?' substituting for a quotation.

Compare:

Ha⌐yaku i⌐ima⌐sita. 'He said [it] quickly.'
Ha⌐yaku to (or tte) i⌐ima⌐sita. 'He said, "Quickly."'

[T] te usually follows quotations of utterances, whereas to also follows
thoughts, written words, etc. Following utterances, *[t]* te is more common
than to in rapid conversational Japanese, particularly in informal and plain
speech. Occurrences of to are usually heard in formal and honorific speech,
and/or in precise speech.

Some quotations repeat the exact words of the original speaker. Usually,
however, a Japanese quotation gives— in the informal style— the gist of what
was said, from the point of view of the person reporting the quotation. The
quotation does retain the tense of the original.

Thus:

Original statement: A⌐gema⌐su. 'I'll give it to you.'
Quoted: Ku⌐reru tte iima⌐sita.[2] 'He said he'd give it to me.'

Original statement: Ki⌐noo itasima⌐sita. 'I did it yesterday.' (Humble)
Quoted: Ki⌐noo nasa⌐tta to o⌐ssyaima⌐sita. 'He said he did it yesterday.'

The person who says or asks something, if expressed, is followed by particle wa or ga, and the person told or asked, by particle ni. Thus:

Tanaka-sañ wa Yámamoto-sañ ni ta⌐bako o yameta tte iima⌐sita.
'Mr. Tanaka said to Mr. Yamamoto that he had quit smoking.'

---

[1] Te follows ñ; tte follows vowels.

[2] Alternate accent: Ku⌐reru⌐ tte i⌐ima⌐sita., with the accent before *[t]* te ~
to the same as that before kara.

The order of the phrases is not fixed: the quotation + quotative is not always followed immediately by the inflected expression it modifies. Thus:

> Tabako o yameta tte, Ya⌐mamoto-sañ ni iima˥sita.
> '[He] said to Mr. Yamamoto that he had quit smoking.'

Sometimes only context and/or intonation distinguish parts of the quotation from modifiers of the following inflected expression. Compare:

> Tanaka-sañ wa ⌐ku˥ru tte i˦ima˦sita.
> 'Mr. Tanaka said that [he][1] would come.'
> (Quotation = ku⌐ru)

and:

> Ta⌐naka-sañ wa ku˥ru tte i˦ima˦sita.
> '[He][1] said that Mr. Tanaka would come.'
> (Quotation = Ta⌐naka-sañ wa ku˥ru)

Compare also:

> Tanaka-sañ ni ⌐a˥tta tte i˦ima˦sita.
> '[He][1] said to Mr. Tanaka that [he][1] had met him.'
> (Quotation = a˥tta)

and:

> Ta⌐naka-sañ ni a˥tta tte i˦ima˦sita.
> '[He][1] said that [he][1] had met Mr. Tanaka.'
> (Quotation = Ta⌐naka-sañ ni a˥tta)

The quotative is often omitted after a quoted question ending with ka; and before ka, the informal non-past copula da is regularly omitted. Accentuation before ka is like that before kara.

Additional examples:

> Ueda-sañ wa i⌐ku tte (i)tte[2] (i)ma˥sita ḡa_
> 'Mr. Ueda was saying that he would go but . . .'   (Lit. 'Mr. Ueda was saying quote he'll go but . . .')
> Mo˥o ⌐mi˦ta tte i˦ima˦sita.   'I said that I had seen it already.'
> (Lit. 'I said quote I have seen it already.')
> I˥i to o⌐ssyaima˦sita ka_   'Did you say that it's all right?'
> Ko⌐no deñwa kosyoo da˥ tte i˦ima˦sita.
> 'He said that this phone is out of order.'
> A⌐sita ka˥eru to ka┌kima˦sita.
> 'He wrote that he is coming home tomorrow.'

---

[1] Or anyone else — made clear by the context.

[2] Following quotative /t/ te, forms of √iu beginning it- (for example, itte, itta, etc.) lose their initial i- in rapid, contracted speech.

I⌐tu de mo i⌐i to, se⌐nse⌐e ni de⌐ñwa-sima⌐sita.
  'He telephoned the teacher that any time will be all right.'
O⌐namae o ka⌐ite kudasai to i⌐ima⌐sita.
  'He said, "Please write your name."'
I⌐tu i⌐ku⌐ ka ki⌐kima⌐sita.
  'I asked when he was going.'
I⌐ssyo ni ikana⌐i ka tte Ta⌐naka-sañ ni kikimasyo⌐o.
  'Let's ask Mr. Tanaka if he won't go with us.'
So⌐no ka⌐ta ⌐do⌐nata ka ki⌐ite kudasaimase⌐ñ ka⌐ [1]
  'Would you be kind enough to ask who that is?'
So⌐re wa na⌐ñ desu ka to ki⌐kima⌐sita.
  'I asked, "What is that?"'
So⌐no ho⌐ñ wa ⌐na⌐ñ te i⌐ima⌐su ka⌐
  'What's the name of that book?' (Lit. 'That book is called quote
  what?')
Ma⌐tuda to moosima⌐su.
  'My name is Matsuda.' (Lit. 'I am called quote Matsuda.')

    A quotation + quotative may be followed by particle wa—particularly in negative sentences. Thus:

        Ma⌐zu⌐i tte wa i⌐imase⌐ñ desita ḡa⌐
        'He didn't say it tasted bad but . . .'   (Lit. 'As for quote it tastes
        bad, he didn't say but . . .')

    The combination X to (or /t/ te) iu Y, in which X is a name or designation (belonging to any word class) and Y is a nominal, is the Japanese equivalent of 'a Y named X' or 'a Y called X.' Na⌐ñ to (or te) iu Y 'a Y named quote what?' is a question equivalent.

    /T/ te (but not to) frequently occurs in statements and questions in sentence-final position, or pre-final before ne⌐e, or ne, following the quotation of someone other than the speaker. Thus:

        De⌐ñki ḡa ki⌐eta⌐ tte. 'He said the light went out.'
        A⌐rimase⌐ñ te? 'Did you say there isn't any?'
        I⌐i tte. 'He said it's all right.'
        So⌐o desu tte ⌐ne⌐e. 'That's what they say, isn't it.'

This use of /t/ te is informal.

---

[1] Note the omission of da before ka.

2. Indirect Questions Containing Interrogative Words

Questions containing interrogative words (na⌐ñ, da⌐re, do⌐ko, i⌐tu, etc.) and ending with particle k a occur as indirect questions before expressions of knowing, understanding, forgetting, informing, etc. They are usually in the informal style. As mentioned in the preceding note, informal non-past da is regularly lost before ka. Accentuation before ka is like accentuation before kara.

Examples:

Direct question:	Do⌐ko e i⌐kima⌐su ka⌐ 'Where are you going?'
Indirect question:	Do⌐ko e i⌐ku⌐ ka si⌐rimase⌐ñ. 'I don't know where you are going.'
Direct question:	Do⌐re ḡa i⌐tibañ taka⌐i desu ka⌐ 'Which one is most expensive?'
Indirect question:	Do⌐re ḡa i⌐tibañ taka⌐i ka wa⌐karimase⌐ñ. 'I can't tell which one is most expensive.'
Direct question:	Da⌐re desu ka⌐ 'Who is he?'
Indirect question:	Da⌐re ka wa⌐surema⌐sita. 'I forgot who he is.'

3. More Imperatives

A nominal consisting of the polite prefix o- + a verbal stem (i.e. the -ma⌐su form minus -ma⌐su)[1] compounded with ku⌐dasa⌐i or (formal) ku⌐dasaima⌐se[2] is a polite imperative. Examples:

o⌐mati-kudasa⌐i 'please wait'
o⌐yobi-kudasa⌐i 'please call'
o⌐kaki-kudasa⌐i 'please write'

If the -kudasa⌐i is dropped, the result is a more informal equivalent.

The following are all used to ask someone to wait, but they differ in their degree of formality and politeness:

	(a)	(b)	(c)
(1)	Ma⌐tte.	Ma⌐tte kudasai.	Ma⌐tte ku⌐dasaima⌐se.
(2)	Omati.	O⌐mati-kudasa⌐i.	O⌐mati-kudasaima⌐se.
(3)	O⌐mati ni na⌐tte.	O⌐mati ni na⌐tte kudasai.	O⌐mati ni na⌐tte ku⌐dasaima⌐se.

Forms in Row (2) are more polite than those in Row (1), and those in Row (3) are most polite. Forms in Column (a) are less formal than those in

---

[1] The combination o- + stem is unaccented.

[2] Forms ending in -ma⌐se are more typical of women's speech.

Column (b). Those in Column (c) are formal women's forms. (3)(a) is also typical of women's speech.

A gerund + ku⌐dasaimase⌐ñ ka (for example, ma⌐tte ku⌐dasaimase⌐ñ ka 'would you be kind enough to wait?'), though not an imperative, is a formal polite form of request. It is softer and less direct than an imperative.

WARNING: Not all verbals have imperatives of the o⌐mati-kudasa⌐i pattern. Use only those which you have heard or checked with a native speaker.

4. ma⌐da + Affirmative; mo⌐o + Negative

Reread Lesson 14, Grammatical Note 5, carefully.

Ma⌐da + an affirmative (except for the special combination ma⌐da desu 'not yet') means 'still' or 'yet.'

Mo⌐o + a negative means '(not) any more.'

As explained in the note referred to above, mo⌐o occurs in the direct iie answer to a ma⌐da question, and ma⌐da occurs in the direct iie answer to a mo⌐o question. Thus:

> Ma⌐da e⌐eḡo o beñkyoo-site ima⌐su ka⌐ 'Are you still studying English?'
> E⌐e, ma⌐da be⌐ñkyoo-site ima⌐su. 'Yes, I'm still studying.'
> Iie, mo⌐o be⌐ñkyoo-site imase⌐ñ. 'No, I'm not studying any more.'
>
> Mo⌐o e⌐eḡo o beñkyoo-site imase⌐ñ ka⌐ 'Aren't you studying English any more?'
> E⌐e, mo⌐o be⌐ñkyoo-site imase⌐ñ. 'No (i.e. that's right), I'm not studying any more.'
> Iie, ma⌐da be⌐ñkyoo-site ima⌐su. 'Yes (i.e. that's wrong), I'm still studying.'
>
> Ma⌐da o⌐oki⌐i desu ka⌐ 'Is it still [too] big?'
> E⌐e, ma⌐da o⌐oki⌐i desu. 'Yes, it's still [too] big.'
> Iie, mo⌐o ⌐o⌐okiku a⌐rimase⌐ñ. 'No, it's not big any more.'

5. na⌐ku in Sentence-Final Position

> O⌐kamai na⌐ku.
> Go⌐eñryo na⌐ku.

Na⌐ku is the -ku form of na⌐i (informal equivalent of a⌐rimase⌐ñ) 'there isn't [any].' The -ku form in final position in these sentences signifies a request. Thus: o⌐kamai na⌐ku 'let there be no bother'; go⌐eñryo na⌐ku 'let there be no reserve.'

Compare also: do⌐ozo yo⌐rosiku (from yorosii 'is good' or 'is favorable') 'let all be well' or 'I request your favor.'

A combination ending with na⌐ku is not limited to sentence-final position:

for example, like other -ku forms, it may occur within a sentence as the modifier of an inflected expression. Compare:

> Ha˥yaku o˩ssya˩tte kudasai. 'Please speak quickly.'

and:

> Go˥eñryo na˥ku o˩ssya˩tte kudasai. 'Please speak freely (lit. without reserve).'

WARNING: Don't make up any —— + na˥ku combinations. Use only those you have heard from a native speaker.

6. mi˥e˥ru

Mi˥e˥ru, an intransitive verbal, occurs in this lesson with two different meanings:

(a) mi˥e˥ru 'put in an appearance,' 'appear,' 'come'

The person who puts in an appearance, if expressed, is followed by wa or ḡa, depending upon emphasis. The polite o˥mie ni na˥ru ᵗ is used to show respect to him. This is never used in reference to the speaker.

Examples:

> O˥mie ni narima˥su ka↲ 'Are you going to put in an appearance?'
> Ta˥naka-sañ ḡa omie ni narima˥sita. 'Mr. Tanaka has appeared.'
> A˥tarasi˥i ko˩oka˩ñsyu ḡa mi˩ema˩sita. 'The new telephone operator has come.'

(b) mi˥e˥ru 'be visible,' 'can see'

The person who can see and the object which is visible, if expressed, are followed by wa or ḡa, depending upon emphasis. The polite o˥mie ni na˥ru ᵗ is used to show respect to the person who can see.

Examples:

> U˥mi ḡa mi˩ema˩sita. 'I could see the ocean.'
>   (i.e. telling what I could see)
> Wa˥takusi ḡa omie ni narima˥su ka↲ 'Can you see me?'
>   (i.e. am I visible as far as you are concerned?)
> Da˥re ḡa mi˩emase˩ñ ka↲ . . . Ta˥naka-sañ ḡa miemase˥ñ.
>   'Who can't see? . . . Mr. Tanaka can't see.' or (depending upon context) 'Whom can't you see? . . . I can't see Mr. Tanaka.'
> Ta˥isi˥kañ to ryo˥ozi˥kañ ḡa mi˥ema˥su ka↲ . . . Ta˥isi˥kañ wa mi˩ema˩su ga, ryo˥ozi˥kañ wa mi˥emase˥ñ.
>   'Can you see the embassy and the consulate? . . . The embassy I can see, but the consulate I can't see.'

Zyo˥ozu˥ da 'be proficient,' su˥ki˥ da 'be pleasing,' wa˥ka˥ru 'be comprehensible,' and de˥ki˥ru 'be possible' are among the many other intransitive inflected words and phrases which are preceded by wa phrases and ḡa phrases but not o phrases.

DRILLS

A. Substitution Drill

1. I haven't anything. or There isn't anything.	Na⌐ni mo na¬i.
2. I can't see anything.	Na⌐ni mo mie¬nai.
3. I can't hear anything.	Nani mo kikoenai.
4. I don't understand any- thing.	Na⌐ni mo wakara¬nai.
5. I don't know anything.	Nani mo siranai.
6. I didn't give [him] any- thing.	Na⌐ni mo yarana¬katta.
7. He didn't give me any- thing.	Na⌐ni mo kurena¬katta.
8. I couldn't do anything.	Na⌐ni mo deki¬nakatta.
9. I didn't do anything.	Na⌐ni mo sina¬katta.
10. I didn't say anything.	Na⌐ni mo iwana¬katta.

B. Substitution Drill

1. Isn't that good Japanese!	* Zyo⌐ozu¬ na ni⌐hoñgo de¬su ⌐ne¬e.
2. Isn't that poor Japanese!	* He⌐ta¬ na ni⌐hoñgo de¬su ⌐ne¬e.
3. Isn't that beautiful Japa- nese!	* Ki⌐ree na ni⌐hoñgo de¬su ⌐ne¬e.
4. Isn't that a beautiful cake!	* Ki⌐ree na o⌐ka¬si desu ⌐ne¬e.
5. Isn't that a wonderful cake!	* Ke⌐kkoo na o⌐ka¬si desu ⌐ne¬e.
6. Isn't that a strange cake!	* He⌐ñ na o⌐ka¬si desu ⌐ne¬e.
7. Isn't he a strange per- son!	* He⌐ñ na hi⌐to¬ desu ⌐ne¬e.
8. Isn't he a fine person!	* Rippa na hi⌐to¬ desu ⌐ne¬e.
9. Isn't he a rude person!	* Si⌐tu¬ree na hi⌐to¬ desu ⌐ne¬e.

C. Substitution Drill

1. Fall has come (lit. it has
    become fall) already, has-
    n't it!
	Mo¬o ⌐a¬ki ni na⌐rima¬sita ⌐ne¬e.

2. Winter has come already, hasn't it!	Mo¬o hu⌐yu¬ ni na⌐rima¬sita ⌐ne¬e.
3. Summer has come already, hasn't it!	Mo¬o na⌐tu¬ ni na⌐rima¬sita ⌐ne¬e.
4. Spring has come already, hasn't it!	Mo¬o ⌐ha¬ru ni na⌐rima¬sita ⌐ne¬e.

5. It has cleared up (lit. be-
    come good weather) al-
    ready, hasn't it!
	Mo¬o o⌐te¬ñki ni na⌐rima¬sita ⌐ne¬e.

6. You've become good at it already, haven't you!	Mo¬o o⌐zyoozu¬ ni narima¬sita ⌐ne¬e.

7. They've become the same already, haven't they!

Mo⌐o o⌐nazi ni narima⌐sita ʰneˤe.

8. You've recovered already, haven't you!

Mo⌐o o⌐geˉňki ni naʳrima⌐sita ⌐neˤe.

D. Substitution Drill

1. What kind of flower is it? (Lit. It's a flower called what?)

Na⌐ñ te iu haʰnaˤ desu ka⌐

2. Is it a man named Tanaka?

Ta⌐naka tte iu hito⌐ desu ka⌐

3. Are they cigarettes called " Peace"?

Pi⌐isu tte iu taʳbako deˤsu ka⌐

4. Is it a department store called " Mitsukoshi"?

Mi⌐tuko⌐si tte iu deʰpaˤato desu ka⌐

5. Is it an American named Smith?

Su⌐misu tte iu Aʰmerikaˤziñ desu ka⌐

6. Is it the magazine "King"?

Ki⌐ňgu tte iu zaʳssi deˤsu ka⌐

7. Is it the newspaper " Mainichi"?

Ma⌐initi tte iu siñbuň deˤsu ka⌐

8. Is it an inn called "Imaiso"?

I⌐mai⌐soo tte iu ryoʰkañ deˤsu ka⌐

E. Substitution Drill

1. This kind of door is called a " shoji" in Japanese.

Koňna to (wa) nĭhoñgo de syo⌐ozi tte iima⌐su.

2. This kind of color is called "aka (red)" in Japanese.

Ko⌐ňna iro⌐ (wa) nĭhoñgo de ⌐a⌐ka tte iimasu.

3. This kind of store is called a " yaoya (vegetable store)" in Japanese.

Ko⌐ňna mise⌐ (wa) nĭhoñgo de ya⌐oya tte iima⌐su.

4. This kind of place is called a " koen (park)" in Japanese.

Ko⌐ňna tokoro⌐ (wa) nĭhoñgo de ko-⌐oeň tte iima⌐su.

5. This kind of building is called a " byoin (hospital)" in Japanese.

Ko⌐ňna tate⌐mono (wa) nĭhoñgo de byo⌐oiň tte iima⌐su.

6. This kind of school is called a " daigaku (university)" in Japanese.

Ko⌐ňna gakkoo (wa) nĭhoñgo de da⌐i-ḡaku tte iima⌐su.

7. This kind of drink is called " kotya (black tea)" in Japanese.

Ko⌐ňna nomi⌐mono (wa) nĭhoñgo de ko⌐otya tte iima⌐su.

8. This kind of place is called a " daidokoro (kitchen)" in Japanese.

Ko⌐ňna tokoro⌐ (wa) nĭhoñgo de da-⌐idokoro tte iima⌐su.

9. This kind of shelf is called a " hondana (book-shelf)" in Japanese.

Konna tana (wa) nihoñgo de ho⌐ñ-dana tte iimasu.

10. This kind of animal is called an " uma (horse)" in Japanese.

Konna doobutu (wa) nihoñgo de u⌐ma⌐ tte iimasu.

F. Substitution Drill

1. Who can't see?[1]
2. Which one can't you see?
3. Which one can't you do?
4. Who can't do it?
5. Who is good at it?
6. Who doesn't understand?
7. Which one don't you understand?
8. Which one do you need?
9. Who needs it?
10. Who doesn't like it?

Da⌐re ga mi⌐emase⌐ñ ka⌐
Do⌐re ga mi⌐emase⌐ñ ka⌐
Do⌐re ga de⌐kimase⌐ñ ka⌐
Da⌐re ga de⌐kimase⌐ñ ka⌐
Da⌐re ga zyo⌐ozu⌐ desu ka⌐
Da⌐re ga wa⌐karimase⌐ñ ka⌐
Do⌐re ga wa⌐karimase⌐ñ ka⌐
Do⌐re ga i⌐rima⌐su ka⌐
Da⌐re ga i⌐rima⌐su ka⌐
Da⌐re ga su⌐ki⌐ zya a⌐rimase⌐ñ ka⌐

G. Substitution Drill

1. I don't know how they say it in Japanese.
2. I can't tell how they say it in Japanese.
3. I forgot how they say it in Japanese.
4. Please tell me how they say it in Japanese.
5. He told me how they say it in Japanese.
6. Let's ask how they say it in Japanese.
7. I had [him] ask how they say it in Japanese.
8. I inquired how they say it in Japanese.

Ni⌐hoñgo de do⌐o iu ka si⌐rimase⌐ñ.
Ni⌐hoñgo de do⌐o iu ka wa⌐karimase⌐ñ.
Ni⌐hoñgo de do⌐o iu ka wa⌐surema⌐-sita.
Ni⌐hoñgo de do⌐o iu ka o⌐siete kuda-sa⌐i.
Ni⌐hoñgo de do⌐o iu ka o⌐siete kure-ma⌐sita.
Ni⌐hoñgo de do⌐o iu ka ki⌐kimasyo⌐o.
Ni⌐hoñgo de do⌐o iu ka ki⌐ite morai-ma⌐sita.
Ni⌐hoñgo de do⌐o iu ka u⌐kagaima⌐-sita.

---

[1] Or, depending on the context, 'Whom can't you see?' or 'Who isn't going to come?' etc.

H. Substitution Drill

1. I don't know how they say it in Japanese.

   Ni⌐hoñgo de do⌐o iu ka si⌐rimase⌐ñ.

2. I don't know who said that.

   <u>Da⌐re ḡa so⌐o itta⌐</u> ka si⌐rimase⌐ñ.

3. I don't know what [he] got.

   <u>Na⌐ni (o) mo⌐ratta⌐</u> ka si⌐rimase⌐ñ.

4. I don't know when [he] entered Tokyo University.

   <u>I⌐tu To⌐odai ni ha⌐itta ka</u> si⌐rimase⌐ñ.

5. I don't know what is wrong with him (lit. what place is bad). [1]

   <u>Do⌐ko ḡa wa⌐ru⌐i ka</u> si⌐rimase⌐ñ.

6. I don't know which one is stronger.

   <u>Do⌐tira no ⌐ho⌐o ḡa tu⌐yo⌐i ka</u> si⌐rimase⌐ñ.

7. I don't know which one was most difficult.

   <u>Do⌐re ḡa i⌐tibañ muzukasi⌐katta ka</u> si⌐rimase⌐ñ.

8. I don't know what floor it is.

   <u>Nañ-ḡai ka</u> si⌐rimase⌐ñ.

9. I don't know which car is his.

   <u>Do⌐no kuruma ḡa a⌐no⌐ hito no ka</u> si⌐rimase⌐ñ.

10. I don't know what day it was.

    <u>Na⌐ñyo⌐obi datta ka</u> si⌐rimase⌐ñ.

I. Level Drill (based on Grammatical Note 3)

[handwritten: stem forms]

Tutor: So⌐ko de ma⌐tte kudasai. ⎫
Student: So⌐ko de omati-kudasa⌐i. ⎭ 'Please wait there.'

1. Do⌐ozo a⌐ḡatte kudasa⌐i.

   Do⌐ozo o⌐aḡari-kudasa⌐i.

2. Ko⌐tira ni ha⌐itte kudasai.

   Ko⌐tira ni ohairi-kudasa⌐i.

3. Do⌐ozo ōsaki ni ⌐ka⌐ette kudasai.

   Do⌐ozo ōsaki ni o⌐kaeri-kudasa⌐i.

4. Koko ni o⌐namae (o) ka⌐ite kudasai.

   Koko ni o⌐namae (o) <u>okaki-kudasa⌐i</u>.

5. Si⌐o⌐ to ko⌐syo⌐o (o) ⌐to⌐tte kudasai.

   Si⌐o⌐ to ko⌐syo⌐o (o) o⌐tori-kudasa⌐i.

6. Kore (o) ⌐ze⌐ñbu tu⌐taete kudasa⌐i.

   Kore (o) ⌐ze⌐ñbu o⌐tutae-kudasa⌐i.

[handwritten: Tsutaemasu - to convey or give message]

---

[1] Refers to someone who is ill.

J.   Grammatical Drill   (based on Grammatical Note 1)

Tutor: Aˈsita kimaˈsu. 'I'll come tomorrow.'
Student: Aˈnoˈ hito wa aˈsita kuˈru tte (iˈimaˈsita). [1] 'He said he'd
          come tomorrow.'

1. Raineñ Toˈodai ni hai-
   rimaˈsu.

2. Naˈñ-zi de mo kamaima-
   seˈñ.

3. Toˈttemo heˈñ desita.

4. Seˈñseˈe desu.

5. Teˈtudaˈtte aḡemasu. [2]

6. Tomodati ni teˈtudaˈtte
   moˈraimaˈsita.

7. Aˈtamaˈ ḡa iˈtaˈi desu.

8. Aˈsitaˈ made iˈmaˈsu.

9. Aˈme ḡa huˈtteˈ (i)ma-
   su.

10. Kinoo deˈkakemaseˈñ de-
    sita.

Aˈnoˈ hito wa raineñ Toˈodai ni haˈ-
iru tte (iˈimaˈsita).

Aˈnoˈ hito wa naˈñ-zi de mo kama-
waˈnai tte (iˈimaˈsita).

Aˈnoˈ hito wa toˈttemo heˈñ datta
tte (iˈimaˈsita).

Aˈnoˈ hito wa seˈñseˈe da tte (iˈimaˈsita).

Aˈnoˈ hito wa teˈtudaˈtte kuˈreruˈ tte
(iˈimaˈsita).

Aˈnoˈ hito wa tomodati ni teˈtudaˈtte
moˈrattaˈ tte (iˈimaˈsita).

Aˈnoˈ hito wa aˈtamaˈ ḡa iˈtaˈi tte
(iˈimaˈsita).

Aˈnoˈ hito wa aˈsitaˈ made iˈruˈ tte
(iˈimaˈsita).

Aˈnoˈ hito wa ˈaˈme ḡa huˈtteˈ (i)ru
tte (iˈimaˈsita).

Aˈnoˈ hito wa kinoo deˈkakenaˈkatta
tte (iˈimaˈsita).

K.   Grammar Drill   (based on Grammatical Note 1)

Tutor: Aˈnoˈ hito (wa) kiˈmaˈsu kaˍ 'Is he coming?'
Student: Aˈnoˈ hito ni ˈkuˈru ka [tte] kiˈkimasyoˈo. [3] 'Let's ask him
          if he is coming.'

1. Aˈnoˈ hito (wa) ˈnaˈni ḡa
   iˈrimaˈsu kaˍ

2. Aˈnoˈ hito (wa) ˈiˈtu made
   iˈsoḡasiˈi desu kaˍ

3. Aˈnoˈ hito (wa) ˈnaˈñ-zi
   ni tuˈkimaˈsita kaˍ

Aˈnoˈ hito ni ˈnaˈni ḡa iˈruˈ ka [tte]
kiˈkimasyoˈo.

Aˈnoˈ hito ni ˈiˈtu made iˈsoḡasiˈi
ka [tte] kiˈkimasyoˈo.

Aˈnoˈ hito ni ˈnaˈñ-zi ni ˈtuˈita ka
[tte] kiˈkimasyoˈo.

---

[1] Practice both the formal (with iˈimaˈsita) and informal (without iˈimaˈsita)
alternants.

[2] Meaning 'I'll help YOU.'

[3] Practice both with and without tte.

4. Aˬnoˈ hito (wa) byoˈoki
   deˈsita kaˌ

   Aˬnoˈ hito ni byoˈoki daˈtta ka /tte/
   kiˈkimasyoˈo.

5. Aˬnoˈ hito (wa) teˈtudaˈtte kuˈremaseˈn kaˌ

   Aˬnoˈ hito ni teˈtudaˈtte kuˈrenaˈi
   ka /tte/ kiˈkimasyoˈo.

6. Aˬnoˈ hito (wa) niˈhoñgo
   (ḡa) dekimaˈsu kaˌ

   Aˬnoˈ hito ni niˈhoñgo (ḡa) dekiˈru
   ka /tte/ kiˈkimasyoˈo.

7. Aˬnoˈ hito (wa) hiˈma
   deˈsu kaˌ

   Aˬnoˈ hito ni hima ka /tte/ kiˈkimasyoˈo.

8. Aˬnoˈ hito (wa) kiˈmoti
   ḡa waruˈi desu kaˌ

   Aˬnoˈ hito ni kiˈmoti ḡa waruˈi ka
   /tte/ kiˈkimasyoˈo.

9. Aˬnoˈ hito (wa) ˬdoˈo site
   kiˈmaseˈn desita kaˌ

   Aˬnoˈ hito ni ˬdoˈo site ˈkoˈnakatta
   ka /tte/ kiˈkimasyoˈo.

10. Aˬnoˈ hito (wa) ˬdoˈo site
    yaˈsumitaˈku aˈrimaseˈn
    kaˌ

    Aˬnoˈ hito ni ˬdoˈo site yaˈsumitaˈku
    ˈnaˈi ka /tte/ kiˈkimasyoˈo.

L. Response Drill (based on Grammatical Note 4)

1. Maˈda ˈaˈme ḡa huˈtteˈ
   (i)masu kaˌ /iie/

   Iie, moˈo huˈtteˈ (i)ˈmaseˈn.

2. Moˈo aˈno uti (o) karite
   (i)maseˈn kaˌ /eˈe/

   Eˈe, moˈo kaˈrite (i)maseˈn.   *to rent*

3. Maˈda saˈmuˈi desu kaˌ
   /iie/

   Iie, moˈo ˈsaˈmuku aˈrimaseˈn.

4. Maˈda eˈeḡo (o) naraˈtte
   (i)masu kaˌ /eˈe/

   Eˈe, maˈda naˈraˈtte (i)masu.

5. Maˈda ˈheˈñ desu kaˌ
   /iie/

   Iie, moˈo ˈheˈñ zya aˈrimaseˈn.

6. Maˈda tuˈkaˈrete (i)masu
   kaˌ /iie/

   Iie, moˈo tuˈkaˈrete (i)ˈmaseˈn.   *tired*

7. Moˈo kōno heñ ni deˈñwa
   (wa) arimaseˈn kaˌ
   /eˈeˈe/

   Eˈe, moˈo aˈrimaseˈn.

8. Moˈo ziˈkañ (wa) arimaseˈñ kaˌ /iie/

   Iie, maˈda aˈɾimaˈsu.

M. Response Drill

(Give iie answers.)

moo — no longer — already
mada — not yet — still

1. Moˈo oˈtomodati ḡa mie-
   maˈsita kaˌ

   Iie, maˈda miˈemaseˈn.

2. Maˈda oˈnazi kaisya ni
   imaˈsu kaˌ

   Iie, moˈo iˈmaseˈn.

3. Moˈo oˈnazi zya arima-
   seˈñ kaˌ

   Iie, maˈda oˈnazi deˈsu.

4. Maˈda Niˈhoˈñ ni tuˈki-
   maseˈñ kaˌ

   Iie, moˈo tuˈkimaˈsita.   *to arrive*

5. Moˈo aˈtuˈi desu kaˌ

   Iie, maˈda ˈaˈtuku aˈrimaseˈn.

6. Maˈda kiˈtanaˈi desu kaˌ

   Iie, moˈo kiˈtanaˈku aˈrimaseˈn.

7. Moˈo oˈyasumi deˈsu
   kaˌ

   Iie, maˈda yaˈsumiˈ zya aˈrimaseˈñ.

8. Ma᷄da i῾ssyo de᷄su ka⌐   Iie, mo᷄o i῾ssyo zya arimase᷄n.
9. Mo᷄o kŏno ka᷄mi᷄ ya eñ-   Iie, ma᷄da i῾rima᷄su.
   pitu wa i῾rimase᷄ñ ka⌐
10. Ma᷄da a῾no ho᷄ñ o ῾yo᷄ñde   Iie, mo᷄o ῾yo᷄ñde (i)᷄mase᷄ñ.
    (i)masu ka⌐

N. Level Drill

        Tutor: Ma῾irima᷄sita. 'I went (or came).' (humble)
        Student: Se῾ñse᷄e mo i῾rassyaima᷄sita. 'The teacher went (or came)
                 too.' (honorific)

be called   *regular*
1. Ta῾naka to moosima᷄su. *iimasu*   Se῾ñse᷄e mo Ta῾naka to ossyaima᷄su.
2. Mo᷄o o῾tya (o) itadaki-   Se῾ñse᷄e mo ῾mo᷄o o῾tya (o) mesia-
   ma᷄sita. *nomimashita*   ḡarima᷄sita.
3. Ha῾zi᷄mete Ta῾naka-sañ   Se῾ñse᷄e mo ha῾zi᷄mete Ta῾naka-sañ
   not no o῾kusañ ni ῾o᷄me ni   no o῾kusañ ni o῾ai ni narima᷄sita.
   kakarima᷄sita.) *aimashita*
to give a 4. Mo᷄o o῾tutae-sima᷄sita.   Se῾ñse᷄e mo ῾mo᷄o o῾tutae ni nari-
message   *tsutaemashita*   ma᷄sita.
5. Zyu᷄u-neñ ῾ma᷄e ni   Se῾ñse᷄e mo ῾zyu᷄u-neñ ῾ma᷄e ni
   To῾odai de beñkyoo-itasi-   To῾odai de beñkyoo-nasaima᷄sita.
   ma᷄sita. *shimashita*
6. Ki῾ree na hu῾rosiki (o)   Se῾ñse᷄e mo ῾ki᷄ree na hu῾rosiki
   itadakima᷄sita. *maraimashita*   (o) omorai ni narima᷄sita.
7. A῾merika-taisi᷄kañ ni   Se῾ñse᷄e mo A῾merika-taisi᷄kañ ni
   tu῾to᷄mete orimasu. *imasu*   tu῾to᷄mete (i)rassyaimasu.
8. Señsyuu ha῾zi᷄mete ko῾ti-   Se῾ñse᷄e mo se῾ñsyuu hazi᷄mete
   ra e mairima᷄sita. *kimashita*   ko῾tira e irassyaima᷄sita.

O. Expansion Drill

   1. Can you see?   Mi῾ema᷄su ka⌐
      Can you see mountains too?   Ya῾ma᷄ mo mi῾ema᷄su ka⌐
      Can you see ocean AND   U᷄mi mo ya῾ma᷄ mo mi῾ema᷄su
      mountains?   ka⌐
      Can you see ocean AND   Otaku kara ῾u᷄mi mo ya῾ma᷄ mo
      mountains from your   mi῾ema᷄su ka⌐
      house?

   2. He ended up forgetting.   Wa῾surete simaima᷄sita.
      He ended up forgetting   Ma῾ta wasurete simaima᷄sita.
      again.
      He said it but he ended up   I῾ima᷄sita ḡa, ma῾ta wasurete si-
      forgetting again.   maima᷄sita.
      He said he wouldn't forget   Wa῾surena᷄i tte i῾ima᷄sita ḡa, ma-
      but he ended up forgetting   ῾ta wasurete simaima᷄sita.
      again.
      He said he wouldn't forget   Mo᷄o wa῾surena᷄i tte i῾ima᷄sita ḡa,
      any more but he ended up   ma῾ta wasurete simaima᷄sita.
      forgetting again.

3. I'm studying.
   I'm still studying.
   Japanese I'm still studying.
   I gave up Spanish, but
   Japanese I'm still
   studying.
   I gave up Spanish be-
   cause I have no time
   but Japanese I'm still
   studying.

   Be⌐ŋkyoo-site (i)ma⌐su.
   Ma⌐da be⌐ŋkyoo-site (i)ma⌐su.
   Ni⌐hoŋgo wa ma⌐da be⌐ŋkyoo-site
   (i)ma⌐su.
   Su⌐peiŋgo o yamema⌐sita ḡa, ni-
   ⌐hoŋgo wa ma⌐da be⌐ŋkyoo-site
   (i)ma⌐su.
   Zi⌐kaŋ ḡa na⌐i kara, Su⌐peiŋgo o
   yamema⌐sita ḡa; ni⌐hoŋgo wa ma⌐-
   da be⌐ŋkyoo-site (i)ma⌐su.

4. It's Mr. Ito.
   The one who's good at it
   is Mr. Ito.
   The one who is best at it
   is Mr. Ito.
   Mr. Yamamoto is good
   too, but the one who is
   best at it is Mr. Ito.
   Both Mr. Tanaka and Mr.
   Yamamoto are good but
   the one who is best at
   it is Mr. Ito.
   Both Mr. Tanaka and Mr.
   Yamamoto are good at
   English, but the one
   who is best at it is Mr.
   Ito.

   I⌐too-saŋ de⌐su.
   Zyo⌐ozu⌐ na no wa I⌐too-saŋ de⌐su.
   I⌐tibaŋ zyoozu⌐ na no wa I⌐too-saŋ
   de⌐su.
   Ya⌐mamoto-saŋ mo zyoozu⌐ desu ḡa,
   i⌐tibaŋ zyoozu⌐ na no wa I⌐too-saŋ
   de⌐su.
   Ta⌐naka-saŋ mo Yamamoto-saŋ mo
   ˙zyoozu⌐ desu ḡa, i⌐tibaŋ zyoozu⌐
   na no wa I⌐too-saŋ de⌐su.
   Eeḡo wa Ta⌐naka-saŋ mo Yamamoto-
   saŋ mo zyoozu⌐ desu ḡa, i⌐tibaŋ
   zyoozu⌐ na no wa I⌐too-saŋ de⌐su.

5. [He] didn't let me know.
   [He] couldn't tell so he
   didn't let me know.
   [He] couldn't tell for sure
   so he didn't let me know.
   He couldn't tell for sure
   so he didn't let me know

   I asked but he couldn't
   tell for sure so he did-
   n't let me know.
   I asked if he would return home but he could-
   n't tell for sure so he
   didn't let me know.
   I asked by what time he
   would return home but
   he couldn't tell for
   sure so he didn't let
   me know.

   O⌐siete kuremase⌐ŋ desita.
   Wa⌐kara⌐nakatta kara, o⌐siete ku-
   remase⌐ŋ desita.
   Ha⌐kki⌐ri wa⌐kara⌐nakatta kara,
   o⌐siete kuremase⌐ŋ desita.
   A⌐no⌐ hito (wa) ha⌐kki⌐ri wa⌐kara⌐-
   nakatta kara, o⌐siete kuremase⌐ŋ
   desita.
   Ki⌐kima⌐sita ḡa; a⌐no⌐ hito (wa) ha-
   ⌐kki⌐ri wa⌐kara⌐nakatta kara, o⌐si-
   ete kuremase⌐ŋ desita.
   Ka⌐eru ka [tte] ki⌐kima⌐sita ḡa; a⌐no⌐
   hito (wa) ha⌐kki⌐ri wa⌐kara⌐nakat-
   ta kara, o⌐siete kuremase⌐ŋ desita.

   Na⌐ŋ-zi made ni ⌐ka⌐eru ka [tte]
   ki⌐kima⌐sita ḡa; a⌐no⌐ hito (wa)
   ha⌐kki⌐ri wa⌐kara⌐nakatta kara,
   o⌐siete kuremase⌐ŋ desita.

I asked Mr. Tanaka by what time he would return home but he couldn't tell for sure so he didn't let me know.

Tanaka-sañ ni ˹na˺n̄-zi made ni ˻ka˩eru ka ⌠tte⌡ ki˹kima˺sita g̃a; a˹no˺ hito (wa) ha˹kki˺ri wa˻kara˩nakatta kara, o˹siete kuremase˺n̄ desita.

6. What shall I do?
    [She] said it. What shall I do?
    Fumiko said [it]. What shall I do?
    Fumiko said [he]'s waiting. What shall I do?

    Fumiko said [he]'s still waiting. What shall I do?

    Fumiko said [he]'s still waiting in the study. What shall I do?

    Fumiko said [he] came and is still waiting in the study. What shall I do?

    Fumiko said that a man named Hamada came and is still waiting in the study. What shall I do?

    Fumiko said that a man named Hamada came while you were out and is still waiting in the study. What shall I do?

Do˺o simasyoo ka.
I˹ima˺sita g̃a, do˺o simasyoo ka.
Hu˹miko-sañ g̃a i˻ima˩sita g̃a, do˺o simasyoo ka.
Ma˺tte (i)ru tte, ˹Hu˺miko-sañ g̃a i˻ima˩sita g̃a; do˺o simasyoo ka.
Ma˺da ˹ma˺tte (i)ru tte, ˹Hu˺miko-sañ g̃a i˻ima˩sita g̃a; do˺o simasyoo ka.
Syosai de ˹ma˺da ˹ma˺tte (i)ru tte, ˹Hu˺miko-sañ g̃a i˻ima˩sita g̃a; do˺o simasyoo ka.
Mi˺ete, syosai de ˹ma˺da ˹ma˺tte (i)ru tte, ˹Hu˺miko-sañ g̃a i˻ima˩sita g̃a; do˺o simasyoo ka.
˹Ha˺mada tte iu hi˻to˩ g̃a ˻mi˩ete, syosai de ˹ma˺da ˹ma˺tte (i)ru tte, ˹Hu˺miko-sañ g̃a i˻ima˩sita g̃a; do˺o simasyoo ka.
Orusu-tyuu ni ˹Ha˺mada tte iu hi˻to˩ g̃a ˻mi˩ete, syosai de ˹ma˺da ˹ma˺tte (i)ru tte, ˹Hu˺miko-sañ g̃a i˻ima˩sita g̃a; do˺o simasyoo ka.

GREETINGS, FAREWELLS, AND ASSORTED SMALL TALK

1. Hostess: Yo˺ku i˻rassyaima˩sita. Do˺ozo o˹ag̃ari-kudasaima˺se.
    Mrs. Tanaka: A˹ri˺g̃atoo gozaimasu. Si˹tu˺ree-itasimasu.

2. Host: Do˺ozo o˹ag̃ari-kudasa˺i.
    Caller: A˹ri˺g̃atoo gozaimasu g̃a, kyo˺o wa ˹tyo˺tto i˻sog̃ima˩su kara_

3. Tanaka: Ma˺tuda-señse˺e, o˹hayoo gozaima˺su.
    Matsuda: O˹hayoo gozaima˺su.
    Tanaka: Señzitu wa si˹tu˺ree-simasita.
    Matsuda: Ko˹tira ko˺so.

4. Host: Tanaka-sañ, ˹yo˺ku i˻rassyaima˩sita. Do˺ozo kotira e.
    Mr. Tanaka: A˹ri˺g̃atoo gozaimasu.
    Host: Osyokuzi wa?

Mr. Tanaka: Mo˥o si˥ma˥sita.
Host: Zya˥a, o˥tya wa ika˥ga desu ka.
Mr. Tanaka: Do˥ozo o˥kamai na˥ku. *cat, drink, smoke*

5. Host: Do˥ozo go˥eñryo na˥ku me˥siagatte kudasa˥i. Do˥ozo ˥do˥ozo.
   Mr. Tanaka: E˥e, i˥tadaite ma˥su. E˥ñryo wa simase˥ñ kara_

6. A: Tyo˥tto o˥negai-sita˥i ñ desu ga_
   B: Na˥ñ desyoo ka. Do˥ozo go˥eñryo na˥ku i˥tte kudasa˥i.

7. Guest: Tyo˥tto de˥ñwa o kaketa˥i ñ desu ga_
   Hostess: Do˥ozo go˥eñryo na˥ku. A˥tira ni gozaima˥su kara, do˥ozo.

8. Smith: Watakusi wa ˹ma˥da Ni˹ho˥ñ wa na˥ñni mo sirimase˥ñ kara, o˥u- *to ask*
   ka˥gai-sita˥i ñ desu ga_
   Tanaka: Do˥ozo go˥eñryo na˥ku.

9. A: Osaki ni.   *go ahead ; please - excuse me*
   B: Do˥ozo.

10. A: Osaki ni. Sayonara.   *going home*
    B: Sayonara.

11. A: Osaki ni si˹tu˥ree-simasu. Sayoonara.
    B: Sayoonara. Mata asita.

12. A: O˹saki ni itadakima˥su.   *I'll eat*
    B: Do˥ozo ˥do˥ozo.

13. Hostess: Tu˹metaku narima˥su kara, do˥ozo ˹su˥gu me˥siagatte kudasai-
    ma˥se.
    Guest: Zya˥a, o˹saki ni itadakima˥su.

14. Tanaka: Tyo˥tto ki˥moti ga waru˥i kara, i˥ma ka˥erita˥i ñ desu ga_
    Smith: Do˥o simasita ka_ Da˹izyo˥obu desu ka_
    Tanaka: O˹naka ga tyo˥tto_
    Smith: Wa˹ru˥i mo˥no˥ o ta˥bemase˥ñ desita ka_
    Tanaka: Sa˥a.
    Smith: Odaizi ni.
    Tanaka: Do˥o mo.

15. Host: Ko˹no isu no ho˥o ga ki˥moti ga i˥i kara, ko˥tira e do˥ozo.
    Mrs. Tanaka: O˹so˥re i˥rima˥su.   *Arigatoo gozaimasu*

16. Hostess: Na˹ni mo gozaimase˥ñ ga, do˥ozo.
    Guest: I˹tadakima˥su.

17. Host: Na˹ni mo arimase˥ñ ga, i˥ssyo ni ta˥bete kudasai.
    Mrs. Tanaka: Do˥o mo o˹so˥re i˥rima˥su.

18. Mrs. Tanaka: Go⌐tisoosama de gozaima⌐sita.
    Hostess: Na⌐ni mo go⌐zaimase⌐ñ de‿

19. Mrs. Tanaka: O⌐so⌐re i⌐rima⌐su ḡa, asita mo⌐o iti-do ira⌐site ku⌐dasai-
    mase⌐ñ ka‿
    Mrs. Yamamoto: Ha⌐a, ka⌐sikomarima⌐sita.

20. Hostess: Yo⌐ku i⌐rassyaima⌐sita. Do⌐ozo o⌐aḡari ni na⌐tte ku⌐dasaima⌐-
    se.
    Mrs. Tanaka: Ha⌐a. O⌐so⌐reirimasu. Si⌐tu⌐ree-itasimasu.

21. Mrs. Tanaka: Nihonḡo ḡa o⌐zyoozu de irassyaima⌐su ⌐ne⌐e.
    Mrs. Smith: O⌐so⌐reirimasu.

22. Mrs. Tanaka: O⌐taku no ozyo⌐osañ wa o⌐tya¹ o nasaima⌐su ka‿   *tea ceremony*   *do, make*
    Mrs. Yamamoto: Ha⌐a, to⌐kidoki itasima⌐su. I⌐ma na⌐ra⌐tte orimasu
    kara‿

23. Smith: Ko⌐ñna heya⌐ wa nihonḡo de syo⌐kudoo tte iima⌐su ka‿
    Tanaka: Iie, so⌐o iimase⌐ñ. Tya⌐noma tte iima⌐su. Ta⌐tami no heya⌐
    desu kara. ²

24. Mrs. Tanaka: A⌐no amerika⌐ziñ wa ⌐i⌐tu mo watakusi ni ăno ne! ăno ne!
    tte i⌐ima⌐su ḡa‿
    Mrs. Yamamoto: Si⌐tu⌐ree desu ⌐ne⌐e.

25. A: Na⌐ñ-zi ni i⌐kimasyo⌐o ka.
    B: Matuda-sañ wa ⌐na⌐ñ-zi de mo ka⌐mawa⌐nai to i⌐tta⌐ kara, ha⌐yaku
    i⌐kimasyo⌐o.

26. Mrs. Tanaka: Yosida-sañ wa ⌐ku⌐-zi made ni i⌐rassya⌐ru to o⌐ssyaima⌐-
    sita ka‿   *come*
    Mrs. Yamamoto: Ha⌐a. Syo⌐kuzi o site⌐ kara ⌐su⌐ḡu i⌐rassya⌐ru to o⌐s-
    syaima⌐sita.   *say, be named*
                         inconvenient
27. A: Ko⌐ma⌐ru tte?
    B: Iie, ka⌐mawa⌐nai tte.

28. A: Su⌐misu-sañ sa⌐simi tabe⌐ru tte?
    B: E⌐e. Da⌐isuki da tte.

---

¹ Otya here refers to the tea ceremony.

² Syokudoo is usually a Western-style room.

29. A: Tanaka-sañ wa ˹ke˺sa deꞪsya de kima˺sita g̃a, kuruma wa ko˹syoo de˺su ka⌟

    B: Ko˹syoo da˺ to wa iˈimaseⁿ desita g̃a, ko˹syoo˞ desyo˹o ˈneˈe.

30. A: Kono zibiki ˹Ziˊroo-sañ no desu ka⌟

    B: So˹o desyoo? Tanaka ˹Ziˊroo to ˈkaˈite ˈaˈru kara⸳

    <u>is written</u>

31. Maid: Go-˹zi-g̃o˺ro Ueda-sañ kara o˹deˈꞪwa g̃a goˈzaimaˈsita.

    Employer: A˺a ˹so˺o. Na˺ñ te?

    Maid: O˹hima na toki˺ ni o˹deˈꞪwa o kuˈdasaˈi to o˞ssyaimaˈsita.

    Employer: Sore dake?

    Maid: Ha˺a, so˹re dake˺ de gozaimasita.

32. Smith: Maˈtuda-sañ no oto˹osañ wa ˹naˈñ to o˞ssyaimaˈsu ka⌟

    Matsuda: Matuda ˹Ziˊroo to moosimasu.

33. Mrs. Tanaka: O˹taku no ozyo˹osañ wa ˹Haˊruko-sañ to o˞ssyaimaˈsu ka⌟

    Mrs. Yamamoto: Iie, Ha˹rue to moosima˺su.

English Equivalents

1. Hostess: I'm so glad you came. Please come in.
   Mrs. Tanaka: Thank you. (Excuse me [for coming into your home].)

2. Host: Please come in.
   Caller: Thank you but today I'm in a bit of a hurry so [I'm afraid I can't].

3. Tanaka: Good morning, Dr. Matsuda.
   Matsuda: Good morning.
   Tanaka: It was nice seeing you the other day. (Lit. I was rude the other day.)
   Matsuda: (I was the one [who was rude].)

4. Host: I'm glad you came, Mr. Tanaka. This way, please.
   Mr. Tanaka: Thank you.
   Host: What about lunch?
   Mr. Tanaka: I've had it already.
   Host: Then how about some tea?
   Mr. Tanaka: Please don't bother.

5. Host: Do please help yourself (lit. eat without reserve).
   Mr. Tanaka: Yes, I'm doing very well (lit. I'm eating). I won't hold back so [don't give it another thought].

6. A: I'd like to ask you a favor. . . .
   B: What is it? Please speak freely.

7. Guest: I'd like to use the telephone. . . .
    Hostess: Please go right ahead. It's over there so please help yourself.

8. Smith: I don't know anything about Japan yet so I'd like to ask you. . . .
    Tanaka: Please, go right ahead.

9. A: [Excuse me for going] ahead.
    B: Go right ahead.

10. A: [Excuse me for leaving] ahead [of you].   Goodbye.
     B: Goodbye.

11. A: Excuse me for leaving ahead of you.   Goodbye.
     B: Goodbye. [See you] again tomorrow.

12. A: Excuse me for eating before you.
     B: Please go ahead.

13. Hostess: Things will get cold so please eat right away.
     Guest: Well then, I'll start (lit. eat) before you.

14. Tanaka: I don't feel well so I'd like to go home now. . . .
     Smith: What happened? Are you all right?
     Tanaka: My stomach is a bit . . .
     Smith: You didn't eat something bad?
     Tanaka: I wonder.
     Smith: Take care of yourself.
     Tanaka: Thanks.

15. Host: This chair is more pleasant so please [sit] here.
     Mrs. Tanaka: Thank you.

16. Hostess: There's nothing here [to speak of] but please [have some].
     Guest: Thank you. (Lit. I'll have some.)

17. Host: We don't have anything [special] but do eat with us.
     Mrs. Tanaka: Thank you very much.

18. Mrs. Tanaka: It was delicious.
     Hostess: There was (lit. being) nothing [to speak of]. . .

19. Mrs. Tanaka: I'm sorry but would you be kind enough to come once more
          tomorrow?
     Mrs. Yamamoto: Yes, certainly.

20. Hostess: I'm so glad you came. Please come in.
     Mrs. Tanaka: Thank you. (Excuse me for entering your home.)

21. Mrs. Tanaka: You are very good in Japanese, aren't you.
     Mrs. Smith: Thank you.

22. Mrs. Tanaka: Does your daughter do the tea ceremony?
    Mrs. Yamamoto: Yes, she does sometimes.   She's taking lessons now
       so. . . .

23. Smith: Is this kind of room called a " shokudo" (dining room) in Japa-
       nese?
    Tanaka: No, we don't call it that.   It's called a " chanoma" (Japanese-
       style family room where meals are eaten)— since it's a tatami room
       [and a " shokudo" is usually a Western-style dining room].

24. Mrs. Tanaka: That American always says, " Hey, hey !" to me   but
       [what can I do?]
    Mrs. Yamamoto: Isn't it rude!

25. A: What time shall we go?
    B: Mr. Matsuda said that any time at all would be all right so let's go
       early.

26. Mrs. Tanaka: Did Mr. Yoshida say that he would come by 9 o'clock?
    Mrs. Yamamoto: Yes. He said that he would come right after he ate.

27. A: Did he say it's inconvenient?
    B: No, he said it doesn't matter.

28. A: Did Mr. Smith say he eats sashimi?
    B: Yes. He said he likes it very much.

29. A: Mr. Tanaka came by (electric) train this morning. Is his car out of
       order?
    B: He didn't say that it was out of order but it probably is (out of order),
       isn't it.

30. A: Is this dictionary Jiro's?
    B: It probably is, don't you think so? — since " Jiro Tanaka" is written
       [on it].

31. Maid: There was a call from Mr. Ueda at about 5 o'clock.
    Employer: Oh? What did he say?
    Maid: He said that you should call (lit. please call) when you are free.
    Employer: [Was] that all?
    Maid: Yes, that was all.

32. Smith: What is your father's name, Mr. Matsuda?
    Matsuda: His name is Jiro Matsuda.

33. Mrs. Tanaka: Is your daughter's name Haruko?
    Mrs. Yamamoto: No, her name is Harue.

EXERCISES

1. Using pictures, models, or actual objects, review vocabulary by taking turns asking and answering the question " What is this called in Japanese? "

2. As a host (or hostess):

      a.   welcome Mr. Yamamoto to your home.
      b.   invite him to come in.
      c.   tell him to come this way.
      d.   offer to let him precede you.
      e.   comment on the weather.
      f.   ask him if he smokes.
      g.   offer him some tea.
      h.   compliment him on his English.
      i.   offer him a second helping.

3. As a guest:

      a.   excuse yourself for going ahead.
      b.   excuse yourself for your rudeness the other day. [1]
      c.   refuse a cigarette.
      d.   tell your host not to go to any trouble.
      e.   refuse a second helping.
      f.   remark on how pretty the garden is.
      g.   remark on how handsome the alcove is.
      h.   remark on how well you can see the mountains.
      i.   remark on how pleasant this kind of room is.

oral

written on Mon.

---

[1] See Basic Sentence 5 and note.

Lesson 19. Transportation

BASIC DIALOGUES: FOR MEMORIZATION

(a) *memorize*

(At the station information booth)

Smith

first class	it-too
second class	ni-too
ticket	kippu

1. Where do you buy second-class tickets?　Do⌈ko de ni-⌐too no kippu (o) kai-ma⌐su ka⌟

Clerk

ticket window	ma⌈do⌉ḡuti
ticket window number seven	na⌈na⌉-bañ no ma⌐do⌐ḡuti

2. It's window number seven.　Na⌈na⌉-bañ no ma⌐do⌐ḡuti desu yo⌟

(At the ticket window)

Smith

(city near Yokohama)	Yokosuka

3. Two second-class tickets for Yokosuka.　Yokosuka, ni-too ⌈ni⌉-mai.

Ticket seller

round trip	oohuku

4. Round trip?　O⌈ohuku de⌉su ka⌟

oohuku ka kikimoshita

Smith

one way	katamiti

5. No, one way, please.　Iie, ka⌐tamiti (o) oneḡai-sima⌐su.

(At the information booth again)

Smith

Yokosuka-bound	Yokosuka-iki or Yokosuka-yuki
track number what?	nañ-bañ-señ

6. On what tracks are the Yokosuka trains? (Lit. The Yokosuka-bound are track number what?)　Yokosuka-iki (wa) na⌈ñ-bañ-señ de⌉-su ka⌟

Clerk

track number seven	nana-bañ-señ
track number eight	hati-bañ-señ

343

7. (They are) track number
    seven and track number
    eight.

    Nana-bañ-señ to haˈti-bañ-señ deˈ-
    su.

Smith

pass through or go
    through or pass in
    front of

toˈoru /-u/

8. Do they go through Yoko-
    hama?

    Yoˈkohama (o) toorimaˈsu ka⌐

    tooru kikinashita

Clerk

come to a halt

tomaru /-u/

9. Yes, they stop at Yoko-
    hama Station.

    Eˈe, Yoˈkohamaˈ-eki ni toˈmarimaˈ-
    su yo⌐

(On the platform)

Smith

second-class car
the second-class car
    stops
the place where the
    second-class car
    stops
what part? or what
    section?

niˈtoˈosya
niˈtoˈosya ḡa tomaru

niˈtoˈosya ḡa tómaru tokoro
    or
niˈtoˈosya no tómaru tokoro
dono heñ

10. Which part [of the platform]
    is the place where the sec-
    ond-class cars stop?

    Niˈtoˈosya no toˈmaru tokoroˈ (wa)
    doˈno heñ deˈsu ka⌐

Stranger

frontmost or furthest
    forward

iˈtibañ maˈe

11. The second-class cars are
    furthest forward so it's
    that part [of the platform].

    Niˈtoˈosya wa iˈtibañ maˈe desu
    kara, aˈno heñ deˈsu yo⌐

(b)

(At the Japan Travel Bureau)

Smith

get on (a vehicle) or
    take (a vehicle) or
    ride
I want to get on or ride
the one I want to get on
    or ride

night
depart or leave for a
    trip

noru /-u/

watakusi ḡa noritai
waˈtakusi ḡa noritaˈi no
    or
waˈtakusi no noritaˈi no
bañ
taˈtu /-u/

depart late at night	bañ o⌐soku ta⌐tu
express	kyuukoo
express that departs late at night	bañ o⌐soku ta⌐tu kyuukoo

12. I'd like to go to Kyoto. The train (lit. one) I want to take is an express that leaves late at night (but. . .)

Kyo⌐oto e i⌐kita⌐i ñ desu ḡa, wa-⌐takusi ḡa norita⌐i no (wa) bañ o-⌐soku ta⌐tu kyu⌐ukoo de⌐su ḡa_

Clerk

leave at 11 o'clock	zyu⌐u-iti⌐-zi ni ⌐de⌐ru
special express	to⌐kubetukyu⌐ukoo or tokkyuu
special express that leaves at 11 o'clock	zyu⌐uiti⌐-zi ni ⌐de⌐ru to⌐kkyuu

13. There's a special express that leaves at 11 o'clock (but. . .)

Zyu⌐uiti⌐-zi ni ⌐de⌐ru to⌐kkyuu (ḡa) arima⌐su ḡa_

Smith

transfer (from one vehicle to another)	norikae

14. That's just fine! Of course there's no changing trains, is there?

Tyo⌐odo i⌐i desu ⌐ne⌐e. Mo⌐ti⌐roñ no⌐rikae wa na⌐i desyoo?

Clerk

15. No (lit. that's right), there isn't.

E⌐e a⌐rimase⌐ñ.

(c)

(At the station)

Smith

leaving at 11 o'clock	zyu⌐uiti⌐-zi hatu _leaving_
Kyoto-bound	Kyooto-iki or Kyooto-yuki

16. What track [is the train] (bound) for Kyoto leaving at 11 o'clock?

Zyu⌐uiti⌐-zi hatu Kyōoto-iki (wa) nāñ-bañ-señ?

Porter

(name of a train)	Ha⌐to

17. Do you mean the Hato? It's track number two.

Ha⌐to desu ka_ Ni-⌐bañ-señ de⌐-su.

what car number?	nañ-ḡo⌐o-sya

18. What is your car number and seat number? (Lit. Your seat is what number in what number car?)

Oseki (wa) nāñ-ḡo⌐o-sya no ⌐na⌐ñ-bañ desu ka_

Smith

car number three
19. Number 17 in car number
3.

sa⌐ñ-g̃o⌐o-sya
Sa⌐ñ-g̃o⌐o-sya no zyu⌐unana⌐-bañ.

(d)

Smith

(name of a train)   Tubame
(section of Tokyo)   Si⌐ñbasi
20. Does the Tsubame stop   Tubame (wa) ⌐Si⌐ñbasi ni to⌐marima⌐su ka↲
at Shimbashi?

Tanaka

down-train (i.e. going   kudari
away from Tokyo)
up-train (i.e. going   nobori
toward Tokyo)
21. The down-train does (stop)   Ku⌐dari wa tomarima⌐su g̃a, nobori wa tõmaranai desyoo?
but the up-train doesn't
(stop), isn't that right?

Yamamoto

opposite   hañtai
22. Isn't it the opposite?   Ha⌐ñtai zya arimase⌐ñ ka↲

Tanaka

get on the train   ki⌐sya⌐ ni nõru   _long distance train_
at the time [someone]   ki⌐sya⌐ ni no⌐ru to⌐ki /ni/
gets on the train
conductor   syasyoo
try asking or ask and   ki⌐ite mi⌐ru
see
23. Oh? Well then, when we   So⌐o? Zya⌐a, ki⌐sya⌐ ni no⌐ru to⌐ki
get on the train let's ask   /ni/ sya⌐syoo ni kiite mimasyo⌐o.
the conductor and find
out.

(e)

(Smith and Tanaka are meeting a train)

Smith

on time   zi⌐kañ-do⌐ori
24. Do you suppose it will   Zi⌐kañ-do⌐ori /ni/ ⌐tu⌐ku desyoo
arrive on time?   ka.

Tanaka

information booth   a⌐ñnaizyo⌐[1]
25. I wonder. Let's ask at   Sa⌐a. Añnaizyo⌐ de ki⌐ite mimasyo⌐o.
the information booth and
find out.

_____
[1] Has unaccented alternant.

(At the information booth)

Tanaka

leaving Kobe or coming from Kobe	Ko⌐obe hatu
arriving at one o'clock	i⌐ti⌐-zi tyaku
26. Will [the train] from Kobe due at one o'clock arrive on time?	Ko⌐obe hatu i⌐ti⌐-zi tyaku (wa) zi-⌐kañ-do⌐ori /ni/ tu⌐kima⌐su ka⌐

Clerk

fall behind or become late	okureru /-ru/
be late	okurete (i)ru
27. No, today it's about ten minutes late.	Iie, kyo⌐o wa zi⌐ppuñ-ḡu⌐rai o⌐kurete (i)ma⌐su.

ADDITIONAL VOCABULARY

1. Is there a first-class car on this train?

Ko⌐no kisya⌐ ni i⌐tto⌐osya (ḡa) a⌐rima⌐su ka⌐

third-class car[1]	sa⌐ñto⌐osya
sleeping car	si⌐ñda⌐isya
dining car	syo⌐kudo⌐osya

2. You need a berth ticket too, you know!

Si⌐ñdaikeñ mo irima⌐su yo⌐

express ticket	kyuukookeñ
special express ticket	tokkyuukeñ
passenger ticket	zyoosyakeñ

NOTES OF THE BASIC DIALOGUES

1. The former three-class system on Japanese trains has been replaced by a two-class system. First-class cars are referred to as gu⌐ri⌐iñsya or gu⌐riiñka⌐a because of their green color. The new high-speed lines are called si⌐ñka⌐ñseñ.

3. Note the use of counter -mai to count tickets.

6. -iki is derived from the verbal iku 'go,' and -yuki from yuku, an alternate form of iku which has the same meaning. Yuku is a slightly more formal form. The place which precedes -iki (or -yuki) is the final destination—the last stop.

8. The area through which (or—in some combinations—in front of which) one passes is followed by particle o. Note the following: ko⌐oeñ o to⌐oru 'pass through the park'; ko⌐oeñ no so⌐ba o ⌐to⌐oru 'pass near the park'; gi⌐ñkoo no ma⌐e o ⌐to⌐oru 'pass in front of the bank,' 'pass the bank.' The last has the shorter alternant gi⌐ñkoo o to⌐oru.

---

[1] Obsolete.

9. Tomaru 'stop'—i. e. 'come to a halt'—is the intransitive partner of the
    transitive tomeru 'stop'—i. e. 'bring to a halt.'   Compare: Ku⌐ruma ḡa
    tomarima⌐sita. 'The c a r s t o p p e d.' and: Ku⌐ruma o tomema⌐sita. 'I
    stopped the car.' Tomaru also occurs as the equivalent of English 'stop
    at a place'—i.e. stay overnight or lodge.

12. 'but—is there such a train?'

    Noru is the intransitive partner of transitive noseru /-ru/ 'give [someone]
    a ride' or 'carry' or 'take on board.'

    Bañ 'night': compare ko⌐ñbañ 'tonight,' ma⌐ibañ 'every night,' ba⌐ñgo⌐hañ
    'dinner'—i.e. evening meal.

    Note the following particles occurring before ta⌐tu: To⌐okyoo o ta⌐tu 'leave
    Tokyo'; To⌐okyoo kara ta⌐tu 'leave from Tokyo'; To⌐okyoo e (or ni) ta⌐tu
    'leave for Tokyo.' The same particles occur with de⌐ru. De⌐ru is a word
    of more general use than ta⌐tu: if Mr. Tanaka leaves Tokyo for a trip to
    America, either de⌐ru or ta⌐tu may be used; if he leaves the office to go
    to lunch, de⌐ru is used.

13. 'but—would that be all right?'

    Tokubetu occurs as an independent nominal meaning 'special.' It may be
    followed by particle ni of manner, meaning 'specially,' 'especially,' 'ex-
    traordinarily.'

14. Norikae is a nominal derived from the verbal no⌐rikae⌐ru /-ru/ 'change
    vehicles' or 'transfer.'

16. Hatu and tyaku (Basic Sentence 26) are nominals which follow time and/or
    place words directly without intervening particles. Note (Basic Sentence
    26) that phrases ending with hatu and tyaku may also follow each other di-
    rectly. Hatu and tyaku expressions are commonly used in reference to
    trains, ships, airplanes, etc.

22. Hañtai is a nominal: hañtai da 'it's the opposite'; ha⌐ñtai zya na⌐i 'it's
    not the opposite.' Note also: hañtai-suru 'oppose.'

24, 26. Ni here is the ni of manner.

27. Note: X ni okureru 'be(come) late for X.'

GRAMMATICAL NOTES

1. Sentence Modifiers

    It has already been explained (a) that a non-past adjectival[1] is an independ-
ent sentence in the informal style (example: Ta⌐ka⌐i. 'It's expensive.') and

---

[1] With sentence intonation, of course.

(b) that non-past adjectivals directly describe following nominals (example: ta⌐ka⌐i ⌐ho⌐ñ 'an expensive book').

Examples in this lesson show that a sentence modifying a nominal does not necessarily consist of a non-past adjectival. Actually, any kind of informal Japanese sentence, consisting of or ending with a non-past or past form, may directly describe a following nominal— subject to the two special points noted below.

Examples:

Nominal:	modified by the sentence:	equals:
hi⌐to⌐ 'man'	Ta⌐bete iru. 'He's eating.'	ta⌐bete iru hito 'the "man who's eating'
hi⌐to⌐ 'man'	Tanaka to iu. 'He is named Tanaka.'	Ta⌐naka to iu hito⌐ 'a man who is named Tanaka'
zi⌐biki⌐ 'dictionary'	Kinoo katta. 'I bought [it] yesterday.'	ki⌐noo katta zibiki⌐ 'the dictionary I bought yesterday'
he⌐ya⌐ 'room'	Na⌐kanaka i⌐i. 'It's quite nice.'	na⌐kanaka i⌐i heya 'a room that's quite nice'
ho⌐ñ 'book'	Ma⌐e ni wa mu⌐zukasi⌐katta. 'It was difficult before.'	ma⌐e ni wa mu⌐zuka-si⌐katta ⌐ho⌐ñ 'a book that was difficult before'
to⌐koro⌐ 'place'	Asita ikitai. 'I want to go tomorrow.'	a⌐sita ikitai tokoro⌐ 'the place where I want to go tomorrow'
zassi 'magazine'	Da⌐re mo yo⌐nde inai. 'No one is reading [it].'	da⌐re mo yo⌐nde inai zassi 'a magazine no one is reading'
bi⌐ru 'building'	Ta⌐isi⌐kañ datta. 'It was the embassy.'	ta⌐isi⌐kañ datta ⌐bi⌐ru 'the building that was the embassy'

considerably

Note that there is no connecting particle between a modifying sentence and the modified nominal.

There are only two differences between an independent sentence and a sentence occurring as the modifier of a nominal, aside from the fact that the latter is almost invariably in the informal style:

(a) The informal non-past da at the end of an independent sentence has the form no or na when the same sentence modifies a nominal. The na alternant regularly occurs (1) if the following nominal is no 'one' or 'ones,' or (2) if the immediately preceding nominal belongs to the special group we designate as na words (cf. Lesson 12, Grammatical

Note (4). Otherwise, the <u>no</u> alternant regularly occurs.

In other words, <u>no</u> and <u>na</u> are special alternants of <u>da</u> which occur only at the end of a sentence which describes a nominal.

Examples:

Nominal:	modifed by the sentence:	equals:
he⌐ya⌐ 'room'	Rippa[1] da. 'It is magnificent.'	ri⌐ppa na heya⌐ 'a room which is magnificent,' 'a magnificent room'
tomodati 'friend'	Su⌐ki⌐[1] da. 'I like [him].'	su⌐ki⌐ na tomodati 'a friend I like'
kodomo 'child'	Ge⌐ŋki[1] da. 'He is healthy.'	ge⌐ŋki na kodomo 'a child who is healthy,' 'a healthy child'
kodomo 'child'	Byooki da. 'He is sick.'	byooki no kodomo 'a child who is sick,' 'a sick child'
no 'one'	Byooki da. 'He is sick.'	byo⌐oki na⌐ no 'one who is sick'
musuko 'son'	Syasyoo da. 'He's a conductor.'	syasyoo no musuko 'my son who is a conductor'[2]
Ta⌐roo 'Taro'	Musuko da. 'He's my son.'	mu⌐suko no Ta⌐roo 'Taro who is my son,' 'my son Taro'
Siñtomi 'Shintomi'	Su⌐si⌐ya da. 'It's a sushi shop.'	su⌐si⌐ya no Siñtomi 'Shintomi which is a sushi shop,' 'the sushi shop "Shintomi"'

(b) The subject of a sentence occurring as a modifier of a nominal is followed by <u>ga</u> or <u>no</u>. No never follows the subject of an independent sentence.

---

[1] A na-nominal.

[2] This can also mean 'the conductor's son,' depending on context.

Examples:

Nominal:	modified by the sentence:	equals:
ziꜜdoꜜosya 'car'	Tomodati ḡa katta. 'A friend bought [it].'	toꜛmodati ḡa katta zidoꜜo-sya <u>or</u> toꜛmodati no katta zidoꜜo-sya 'the car a friend bought'
kaisya 'company'	Boꜜku ḡa tuꜛtoꜜmete iru. 'I am employed.'	boꜜku ḡa tuꜛtoꜜmete iru kaisya <u>or</u> boꜜku no tuꜛtoꜜmete iru kaisya 'the company where I am employed'
kiꜛssaꜜteñ 'tearoom'	Koꜛohiꜜi ḡa oisii. 'The coffee is good.'	koꜛohiꜜi ḡa oꜜisii kissaꜜ-teñ <u>or</u> koꜛohiꜜi no oꜜisii kissaꜜ-teñ 'a tearoom where the coffee is good,' 'a tearoom with good coffee'
hiꜛtoꜜ 'man'	Miꜛmiꜜ ḡa iꜛtaꜜi. '[His] ear hurts.'	miꜛmiꜜ ḡa iꜛtaꜜi hito <u>or</u> miꜛmiꜜ no iꜛtaꜜi hito 'the man whose ear hurts,' 'the man with an earache'

NOTE: Four different <u>no</u>'s have now been introduced:

(a) the nominal meaning 'one,' 'ones'

Example: <u>aꜛkaꜜi no</u> 'red one(s)'

(b) the copula—i.e. a special alternant of <u>da</u>

Example: <u>syasyoo no musuko</u> 'my son who is a conductor'

(c) the particle meaning 'of,' 'pertaining to,' 'belonging to'

Example: <u>boꜜku no zassi</u> 'my magazine'

(d) the particle which follows the subject of a sentence modifier

Example: <u>boꜜku no katta zassi</u> 'the magazine I bought'

A nominal may be described by more than one modifier, any or all of which are sentence modifiers. (Modifiers of nominals which are not sentence modifiers are demonstratives— <u>kono</u>, <u>sono</u>, etc.— or phrases ending in particle <u>no</u> 'of,' 'pertaining to.') For example, in the following sequences, each modifier (underlined by an unbroken line) modifies the nominal at the end. In such sequences, the beginning of a new modifier is also the beginning of a new accent phrase.

tuᒥkue no ueꓶ ni ᒥaꓶru kuᒥroꓶi ᒥhoꓶñ 'the black book which is on top of the desk'

watakusi ḡa karita Taᒥnaka-sañ no zibikiꓶ 'Mr. Tanaka's dictionary which I borrowed'

kinoo katta soᒥno hoꓶñ 'that book which I bought yesterday'

keꓶsa ᒥmiꓶta Siᒥbuya ni aꓶru oᒥokiꓶi uti 'the large house which is in Shibuya, which I saw this morning'

Or, a nominal may be described by a modifier containing or consisting of a word which is itself modified. For example, in the following sequences, the first modifier modifies all or part of the second modifier, which, in turn, modifies the nominal at the end of the sequence:

taᒥisiꓶkañ ni tuᒥtoꓶmete iru tomodati no ᒥhoꓶñ

'a book belonging to a friend who works for the embassy'

keꓶsa itta giñkoo ni tuᒥtoꓶmete iru tomodati

'a friend who works for the bank where I went this morning'

kiᒥnoo kiꓶta tomodati no uti

'the home of the friend who came yesterday'

siᒥñbuñ o yoꓶñde iru hiᒥtoꓶ ḡa ᒥnoꓶñde iru tabako

'the cigarette which the man who is reading the newspaper is smoking'

Note that while there are Japanese equivalents for English sequences like 'the man who ——,' 'the thing which ——,' 'the place where ——,' 'the time when——,' etc., there are no Japanese equivalents for the words 'who,' 'which,' 'where,' 'when' in these sequences.

2. toᒥkiꓶ

Toᒥkiꓶ [1] 'time,' 'occasion,' 'when' is a nominal and the patterns in which it occurs are typical nominal patterns.

---

[1] Also occurs with a first-syllable accent and with no accent.

Sentence modifier + Nominal	Literally:	Normal equivalent:

Compare:

kinoo suteta zassi   'threw-away-yesterday   'the magazine I threw
                              magazine'   away yesterday'

with:

ki⌐noo suteta to⌐ki   'threw-away-yesterday   'when I threw [it]
                              time'   away yesterday'

Also:

Kyo⌐oto e iku tomodati   'go-to-Kyoto friend'   'a friend who's going
                                                          to Kyoto'

with:

Kyo⌐oto e i⌐ku to⌐ki   'go-to-Kyoto time'   'when I go to Kyoto'

To⌐ki⌐ is one of the time words which occur both with and without following particle ni, indicating the time when something happens: cf. Lesson 8, Grammatical Note 4(b). Followed by particles ni + wa, it refers to repeated action— 'at times when——.' Thus:

> Ko⌐obe e i⌐tta toki⌐ [ni] to⌐modati no uti ni tomarima⌐sita.
> 'When I went to Kobe, I stopped at a friend's house.'
> Ko⌐obe e i⌐ku toki⌐ ni wa to⌐modati no uti ni tomarima⌐su.
> 'At times when I go to Kobe, I stop at a friend's house.'

Examples with other particles:

> Bo⌐ku ḡa i⌐tta toki⌐ wa ku̇ruma de go-⌐zikaṅ-ha⌐ṅ ka⌐karima⌐sita
>   ḡa_
> 'When I went (comparatively speaking), it took five and a half hours by car but [I don't know how long it takes now.]'
> Yamada Yu̇kio-saṅ wa wa⌐takusi ḡa gakkoo e itte ita toki⌐ no to⌐modati de⌐su yo_
> 'You know, Yukio Yamada was a friend when (lit. is a friend of the time when) I was going to school.'
> Ko⌐domo no toki⌐ kara ⌐mi⌐ruku ḡa su⌐ki⌐ desu.
> 'I've liked milk since I was a child (lit. from child time).'
> Ga⌐kkoo o de⌐ta toki kara o⌐nazi kaisya ni tuto⌐mete imasu.
> 'I've been working for the same company from the time I left school.'

3. Verbal Gerund + √mi⌐ru

A verbal gerund followed directly in the same accent phrase by √mi⌐ru means 'do so-and-so and see,' 'do so-and-so and find out,' 'try doing so-and-so.'

Examples:

> Yuube sa⌐simi⌐ o ⌐ta⌐bete mi⌐ma⌐sita.
> 'I tried eating sashimi last night.'
> Na⌐ni ḡa ⌐ha⌐itte iru ka wa⌐kara⌐nai kara, a⌐kete mimasyo⌐o.
> 'I can't tell what's in it so let's open it and find out.'
> Si⌐rana⌐i kara, ki⌐ite mima⌐su.
> 'I don't know so I'll ask and see.'

4. C o u n t e r s : -too, -ḡoo-sya, -bañ-señ

-Too occurs with numerals of Series I to name classes as applied to train and boat travel, theater seats, etc.

-Ḡoo-sya combines with the same series of numerals to name the passenger cars of a train.

-Bañ-señ combines with the same series of numerals to name the tracks in a station.

Study the following lists:

it-too	'1st class'	iti-bañ-señ	'track # 1'	i⌐ti-ḡo⌐o-sya	'car # 1'
ni-too	'2d class'	ni-bañ-señ	'track # 2'	ni-⌐ḡo⌐o-sya	'car # 2'
sañ-too	'3d class'	sañ-bañ-señ	'track # 3'	sa⌐ñ-ḡo⌐o-sya	'car # 3'
[higher numbers		yoñ-bañ-señ	'track # 4'	yo⌐ñ-ḡo⌐o-sya	'car # 4'
rare with this		go-bañ-señ	'track # 5'	go-⌐ḡo⌐o-sya	'car # 5'
meaning]		roku-bañ-señ	'track # 6'	ro⌐ku-ḡo⌐o-sya	'car # 6'
				si⌐ti-ḡo⌐o-sya	
		nana-bañ-señ	'track # 7'	or	
		hati-bañ-señ	'track # 8'	na⌐na-ḡo⌐o-sya	'car # 7'
				ha⌐ti-ḡo⌐o-sya	'car # 8'
		kyuu-bañ-señ	'track # 9'	kyu⌐u-ḡo⌐o-sya	'car # 9'
		zyuu-bañ-señ	'track # 10'	zyu⌐u-ḡo⌐o-sya	'car # 10'
nañ-too		nañ-bañ-señ		na⌐ñ-ḡo⌐o-sya	
'what class?'		'what track number?'		'car number what?'	

Musashi Sakai wa
nan ban sen desu ka.

DRILLS

A. Substitution Drill

1. What track is [the train] for Kyoto?

   Kyooto-iki (wa) na⌐ñ-bañ-señ de⌐su ka⌐

2. What track is [the train] arriving at 4 o'clock?

   Yo⌐-zi tyaku (wa) na⌐ñ-bañ-señ de⌐su ka⌐

3. What track is [the train] leaving at 4 o'clock?

   Yo⌐-zi hatu (wa) na⌐ñ-bañ-señ de⌐su ka⌐

4. What track is [the train] from Kobe?

   Ko⌐obe hatu (wa) na⌐ñ-bañ-señ de⌐su ka⌐

5. What track is [the train]   Koobe-yuki (wa) naⁿ-bañ-señ deˈsu
   for Kobe?   ka↵

6. What track is the 7 o'-   Siˈtiˈ-zi no nobori (wa) naⁿ-bañ-señ
   clock up-train?   deˈsu ka↵

7. What track is the 7   Siˈtiˈ-zi no kudari (wa) naⁿ-bañ-señ
   o'clock down-train?   deˈsu ka↵

B. Substitution Drill

1. The special express Hato[1]   Toˈkkyuu no Haˈto (wa) ˈkoˈñbañ
   will arrive late tonight.   oˈsoku tukimaˈsu.

2. My son Taro will arrive   Muˈsuko no Taˈroo (wa) ˈkoˈñbañ
   late tonight.   oˈsoku tukimaˈsu.

3. My (older) brother Yukio   Aˈni no Yukio (wa) ˈkoˈñbañ oˈsoku
   will arrive late tonight.   tukimaˈsu.

4. My (younger) sister Ha-   Iˈmooto no Haˈruko (wa) ˈkoˈñbañ
   ruko will arrive late to-   oˈsoku tukimaˈsu.
   night.

5. My daughter Akiko will   Muˈsume no Aˈkiko (wa) ˈkoˈñbañ
   arrive late tonight.   oˈsoku tukimaˈsu.

6. My friend Mr. Tanaka   Tomodati no Tanaka-sañ (wa)
   will arrive late tonight.   ˈkoˈñbañ oˈsoku tukimaˈsu.

7. My Japanese friend will   Niˈhoñziˈñ no tomodati (wa) ˈkoˈñ-
   arrive late tonight.   bañ oˈsoku tukimaˈsu.

8. My American teacher   Aˈmerikaˈziñ no seˈñseˈe (wa)
   will arrive late tonight.   ˈkoˈñbañ oˈsoku tukimaˈsu.

C. Substitution Drill

1. Is the train that leaves   Zyuˈuitiˈ-zi ni ˈdeˈru kiˈsyaˈ (wa)
   at 11 o'clock an ex-   kyuˈukoo deˈsu ka↵
   press?

2. Is the train that leaves   Koˈñbañ oˈsoku taˈtu kiˈsyaˈ (wa)
   late tonight an express?   kyuˈukoo deˈsu ka↵

3. Is the train that stops   Siˈñbasi ni toˈmaru kisyaˈ (wa)
   at Shimbashi an ex-   kyuˈukoo deˈsu ka↵
   press?

4. Is the train that you   Aˈnaˈta g̃a[2] noˈru kisyaˈ (wa) kyu-
   are going to take an   ˈukoo deˈsu ka↵
   express?

5. Is the train that you   Aˈnaˈta g̃a[2] ˈmaˈtte (i)ru kiˈsyaˈ
   are waiting for an ex-   (wa) kyuˈukoo deˈsu ka↵
   press?

---

[1] I.e. 'the Hato which is a special express.'

[2] Or no.

12-3
21-2
43-1
61-1

6. Is the train that left at
   9 o'clock an express?

Kuˈ-zi ni ˈdeˈta kiˈsyaˈ (wa) kyuˈuˈ
koo deˈsu kaˌ

7. Is the train that is (arrived) on track #2 an
   express?

Ni-ˈbañ-señ ni tuˈite (i)ru kiˈsyaˈ
(wa) kyuˈukoo deˈsu kaˌ

8. Is the train that your
   friend is (riding) on an
   express?

Oˈtomodati g̃a^1 notte (i)ru kisyaˈ
(wa) kyuˈukoo deˈsu kaˌ

9. Is the train that is
   (stopped) on track #4
   an express?

Yoˈñ-bañ-señ ni tomatte (i)ru kisyaˈ (wa) kyuˈukoo deˈsu kaˌ

10. Is the train that your
    (older) brother just got
    on an express?

Niˈisañ g̃a^1 ˈiˈma noˈtta kisyaˈ
(wa) kyuˈukoo deˈsu kaˌ

D. Substitution Drill

1. Is that (man) the man
   who wants to see Mr. Tanaka?

Taˈnaka-sañ ni aitaˈi hito (wa) aˈnoˈ
hito desyoo ka.

2. Is that (man) the man
   whom Mr. Tanaka wants
   to see?

Taˈnaka-sañ g̃a^1 aitaˈi hito (wa) a-
ˈnoˈ hito desyoo ka.

3. Is that (man) the man
   whom the doctor wants
   to look at?

Seˈñseˈe g̃a^1 miˈtaˈi hito (wa) aˈnoˈ
hito desyoo ka.

4. Is that (man) the man
   who wants to have the
   doctor look at him?

Seˈñseˈe ni ˈmiˈte moraitai hito (wa)
aˈnoˈ hito desyoo ka.

5. Is that (man) the man
   who wanted to go by
   taxi?

Taˈkusii de iˈkitaˈkatta hito (wa)
aˈnoˈ hito desyoo ka.

6. Is that (man) the man
   who doesn't want beer?

Biˈiru g̃a^1 iˈranai hitoˈ (wa) aˈnoˈ
hito desyoo ka.

7. Is that (man) the man
   who didn't say any-
   thing?

Naˈni mo iwanaˈkatta hito (wa) aˈnoˈ
hito desyoo ka.

8. Is that (man) the man
   with the toothache?

Haˈ g̃a^1 iˈtaˈi hito (wa) aˈnoˈ hito
desyoo ka.

9. Is that (man) the man
   who isn't very good in
   Japanese?

Niˈhoñg̃o g̃a^1 añmari zyoozuˈ zya
ˈnaˈi hito (wa) aˈnoˈ hito desyoo
ka.

10. Is that (man) the man
    who doesn't have a car?

Kuˈruma g̃a^1 naˈi hito (wa) aˈnoˈ
hito desyoo ka.

---

^{1} Or no.

E. Substitution Drill

1. When I went to the bank this morning, I saw[1] Mr. Hamada.

Keˈsa giˈnkoo e itta toˈki, Haˈmada-sañ ni aˈimaˈsita.

2. When I opened the door, I saw Mr. Hamada.

To ˈ(o) aketa toˈki, Haˈmada-sañ ni aˈimaˈsita.

3. When I bought a newspaper at the station, I saw Mr. Hamada.

Eˈki de siˈnbun (o) katta toˈki, Haˈmada-sañ ni aˈimaˈsita.

4. When I left the house, I saw Mr. Hamada.

Uˈti (o) deˈta toki, Haˈmada-sañ ni aˈimaˈsita.

5. When I arrived at the station, I saw Mr. Hamada.

Eˈki ni ˈtuˈita toki, Haˈmada-sañ ni aˈimaˈsita.

6. When I went into the tearoom, I saw Mr. Hamada.

Kiˈssaˈteñ ni ˈhaˈitta toki, Haˈmada-sañ ni aˈimaˈsita.

7. When I set out early this morning, I saw Mr. Hamada.

Keˈsa ˈhaˈyaku deˈkaketa toˈki, Haˈmada-sañ ni aˈimaˈsita.

8. When I transferred at Shimbashi, I saw Mr. Hamada.

Siˈñbasi de noˈrikaˈeta toki, Haˈmada-sañ ni aˈimaˈsita.

F. Grammar Drill (based on Grammatical Note 1)

Tutor: Kiˈree na huˈrosiki (o) kaimaˈsita. 'I bought a pretty furoshiki.'
Student: Kiˈree na no (o) kaˈimaˈsita. 'I bought a pretty one.'

1. Watakusi no iˈtibañ sukiˈ na oˈsakana (wa) eˈbi deˈsu.

Watakusi no iˈtibañ sukiˈ na no (wa) eˈbi deˈsu.

2. Byooki no kodomo (wa) ˈTaˈroo desu.

Byoˈoki naˈ no (wa) ˈTaˈroo desu.

3. Taˈnaka-sañ no uti daˈtta taˈteˈmono (wa) ˈiˈma ryoˈkañ ni narimaˈsita.

Taˈnaka-sañ no uti daˈtta no (wa) ˈiˈma ryoˈkañ ni narimaˈsita.

4. Itibañ rippa na niwa (wa) ˈKyoˈoto ni ˈaˈru desyoo?

Iˈtibañ rippa naˈ *one* no (wa) ˈKyoˈoto ni ˈaˈru desyoo?

5. Nihoñˈgo ga iˈtibañ zyoozuˈ na hiˈtoˈ (wa) ˈSuˈmisu-sañ desyoo?

Nihoñˈgo ga iˈtibañ zyoozuˈ na no (wa) ˈSuˈmisu-sañ desyoo?

---

[1] I.e. 'met up with.'

G. Grammar Drill (based on Grammatical Note 1)

Tutor: Ke⌐sa ki⌐mase⌐n̄ desita. '[He] didn't come this morning.'
Student: Ke⌐sa ⌐ko⌐nakatta hito (wa) ⌐da⌐re desu ka⌐ 'Who is the person who didn't come this morning?'

1. A⌐na⌐ta ḡa si⌐tte (i)ma⌐su.

A⌐na⌐ta no[1] si⌐tte (i)ru hito⌐ (wa) ⌐da⌐re desu ka⌐

2. A⌐na⌐ta o si⌐tte (i)ma⌐su.

A⌐na⌐ta o si⌐tte (i)ru hito⌐ (wa) ⌐da⌐re desu ka⌐

3. A⌐na⌐ta ni ki⌐ppu o aḡema⌐sita.

A⌐na⌐ta ni ki⌐ppu o aḡeta hito⌐ (wa) ⌐da⌐re desu ka⌐

4. A⌐na⌐ta ni ki⌐ppu o moraima⌐sita.

A⌐na⌐ta ni ki⌐ppu o moratta hito⌐ (wa) ⌐da⌐re desu ka⌐

5. A⌐na⌐ta ḡa ⌐ma⌐tte (i)masu.

A⌐na⌐ta no[1] ⌐ma⌐tte (i)ru hi⌐to⌐ (wa) ⌐da⌐re desu ka⌐

6. A⌐na⌐ta ḡa a⌐ita⌐i desu.

A⌐na⌐ta no[1] a⌐ita⌐i hi⌐to⌐ (wa) ⌐da⌐re desu ka⌐

7. A⌐tama⌐ ḡa i⌐ta⌐i desu.

A⌐tama no[1] ita⌐i hi⌐to⌐ (wa) ⌐da⌐re desu ka⌐

8. Ko⌐domo ḡa arimase⌐n̄.

Ko⌐domo no[1] na⌐i hi⌐to⌐ (wa) ⌐da⌐re desu ka⌐

9. Byo⌐oki de⌐su.

Byo⌐oki no hito⌐ (wa) ⌐da⌐re desu ka⌐

10. O⌐sake ḡa kirai de⌐su.

O⌐sake no[1] kirai na hito⌐ (wa) ⌐da⌐re desu ka⌐

H. Grammar Drill (based on Grammatical Note 1)

Tutor: A⌐no señse⌐e (wa) ni⌐hoñḡo o osiema⌐su. 'That teacher teaches Japanese.'
Student: Ni⌐hoñḡo o osieru señse⌐e desu. 'He's a teacher who teaches Japanese.'

1. A⌐no kisya⌐ (wa) Yo⌐kohama o toorima⌐su.

Yo⌐kohama o to⌐oru ki⌐sya⌐ desu.

2. A⌐no ba⌐su (wa) Yo⌐kohama ni tomarima⌐su.

Yo⌐kohama ni tomaru ba⌐su desu.

3. A⌐no yama⌐ (wa) ko⌐ko kara miema⌐su.

Ko⌐ko kara mie⌐ru ya⌐ma⌐ desu.

4. A⌐no señse⌐e (wa) I⌐too to ossyaima⌐su.

I⌐too to ossya⌐ru se⌐ñse⌐e desu.

5. Ano kodomo (wa) ⌐mi⌐ruku o ko⌐bosima⌐sita.

Mi⌐ruku o ko⌐bo⌐sita ko⌐domo de⌐su.

6. Ano tomodati (wa) e⌐eḡo ḡa wakarimase⌐n̄.

E⌐eḡo no[1] wakara⌐nai to⌐modati de⌐su.

---

[1] Or ḡa.

7. A⌐no musume⌐ (wa) byo-
   ⌐oki de⌐su.

   Byo⌐oki no musume⌐ desu.

8. Ano Tanaka-sañ (wa)
   o⌐hana ḡa zyoozu⌐ desu.

   O⌐hana no^1 zyoozu⌐ na Ta⌐naka-sañ
   de⌐su.

9. Ano kodomo (wa) mi⌐mi⌐
   ḡa i⌐ta⌐i desu.

   Mi⌐mi no^1 ita⌐i ko⌐domo de⌐su.

10. A⌐no⌐ hito (wa) a⌐tarasi⌐i
    kuruma ḡa ka⌐ita⌐i desu.

    A⌐tarasi⌐i kuruma no^1 ka⌐itai hito⌐
    desu.

I. Grammar Drill (based on Grammatical Note 3)

Tutor: Ki⌐kimasyo⌐o. 'Let's ask.'
Student: Ki⌐ite mimasyo⌐o. 'Let's try asking.' or 'Let's ask and
see.' or 'Let's ask and find out.'

1. Ni⌐hoñḡo de iima⌐sita.

   Ni⌐hoñḡo de itte mima⌐sita.

2. A⌐sita no a⌐sa si⌐masyo⌐o.

   A⌐sita no a⌐sa si⌐te mimasyo⌐o.

3. Ha⌐zi⌐mete o⌐sasimi (o) ta-
   bema⌐sita.

   Ha⌐zi⌐mete o⌐sasimi (o) ⌐ta⌐bete mi-
   ⌐ma⌐sita.

4. Do⌐ñna ⌐ho⌐ñ ka wa⌐kari-   *what*
   mase⌐ñ ḡa, yo⌐mita⌐i
   desu.

   Do⌐ñna ⌐ho⌐ñ ka wa⌐karimase⌐ñ ḡa,
   yo⌐ñde mi⌐ta⌐i desu.

5. Da⌐me⌐ desu kara, mi⌐ma-
   syo⌐o.

   since
   Da⌐me⌐ desu kara, mi⌐te mi⌐ma-
   syo⌐o.

6. Asita a⌐no a⌐tarasi⌐i ha-
   ⌐na⌐ya e i⌐kimasyo⌐o.

   Asita a⌐no a⌐tarasi⌐i ha⌐na⌐ya e i⌐tte
   mimasyo⌐o.

7. Amerika no tabako (o)
   i⌐ti-do nomita⌐i ñ desu
   ḡa_

   in
   Amerika no tabako (o) i⌐ti-do no⌐ñ-
   de mi⌐ta⌐i ñ desu ḡa_

8. Na⌐ni ḡa ⌐ha⌐itte iru ka
   wa⌐kara⌐nai kara, a⌐ke-
   masyo⌐o.

   Na⌐ni ḡa ⌐ha⌐itte iru ka wa⌐kara⌐-
   nai kara, a⌐kete mimasyo⌐o.

J. Expansion Drill

1. Does it pass through?
   Does it pass in front?
   Does it pass in front of
   the embassy?
   Which bus passes in front
   of the embassy?

   To⌐orima⌐su ka↩
   Ma⌐e o to⌐orima⌐su ka↩
   Ta⌐isi⌐kañ no ⌐ma⌐e o to⌐orima⌐su
   ka↩
   Do⌐no ⌐ba⌐su ḡa ta⌐isi⌐kañ no ⌐ma⌐e
   o to⌐orima⌐su ka↩

2. It's a number.
   It's the seat number.

   Ba⌐ñḡo⌐o desu.
   Se⌐ki no ba⌐ñḡo⌐o desu.

The thing (lit. one) which
is written is the seat
number.

Ka⌐ite ⌐a⌐ru no wa ⌐se⌐ki no ba⌐ñ-
ḡo⌐o desu.

The thing which is writ-
ten here is the seat
number.

Ko⌐ko ni ka⌐ite ⌐a⌐ru no wa ⌐se⌐ki
no ba⌐ñḡo⌐o desu.

3. How was it?

Do⌐o desita ka⌐

How was the inn?

Ryokañ wa ⌐do⌐o desita ka⌐

How was the inn in Kyo-
to?

Kyo⌐oto no ryokañ wa ⌐do⌐o desita
ka⌐

How was the inn in Kyo-
to where you stopped?

A⌐na⌐ta ḡa tomatta ⌐Kyo⌐oto no ryokañ wa ⌐do⌐o desita ka⌐

4. He's a friend.

To⌐modati de⌐su.

He's a friend who is em-
ployed.

Tu⌐to⌐mete (i)ru to⌐modati de⌐su.

He's a friend who is
working for a bank.

Gi⌐ñkoo ni tuto⌐mete (i)ru to⌐moda-
ti de⌐su.

He's a friend who is
working for the bank
[I] went to this morn-
ing.

Ke⌐sa itta giñkoo ni tu⌐to⌐mete (i)-
ru to⌐modati de⌐su.

He's a friend who is
working for the bank
I went to this morn-
ing.

Watakusi ḡa ⌐ke⌐sa itta giñkoo ni
tu⌐to⌐mete (i)ru to⌐modati de⌐su.

5. It's new, isn't it?

A⌐tarasi⌐i desyoo?

It's newer than the one
[you]'re reading, isn't
it?

Yo⌐ñde (i)⌐ru⌐ no yori a⌐tarasi⌐i
desyoo?

It's newer than the one
you're reading, isn't
it?

A⌐na⌐ta ḡa ⌐yo⌐ñde (i)⌐ru⌐ no yori
a⌐tarasi⌐i desyoo?

The magazine on the ta-
ble is newer than the
one you're reading,
isn't it?

Te⌐eburu ni a⌐ru zassi wa a⌐na⌐ta
ḡa ⌐yo⌐ñde (i)⌐ru⌐ no yori a⌐tara-
si⌐i desyoo?

The magazine on the din-
ing room table is newer
than the one you're
reading, isn't it?

Syo⌐kudoo no teeburu ni a⌐ru zassi wa a⌐na⌐ta ḡa ⌐yo⌐ñde (i)⌐ru⌐
no yori a⌐tarasi⌐i desyoo?

6. I arrived.

Tu⌐kima⌐sita.

I arrived on time.

Zi⌐kañ-do⌐ori /ni/ tu⌐kima⌐sita.

[He] gave me a ride so I
arrived on time.

No⌐sete kurema⌐sita kara, zi⌐kañ-
do⌐ori /ni/ tu⌐kima⌐sita.

[He] gave me a ride in
his car so I arrived on
time.

Zi⌐do⌐osya ni no⌐sete kurema⌐sita
kara, zi⌐kañ-do⌐ori /ni/ tu⌐kima⌐-
sita.

A friend gave me a ride in his car so I arrived on time.	Tomodati ḡa zi⌐do⌐osya ni no┌sete kurema┐sita kara, zi⌐kañ-do⌐ori [ni] tu┌kima┐sita.
I was late for the bus, but a friend gave me a ride in his car so I arrived on time.	Ba┐su ni o⌐kurema┐sita ḡa; tomodati ḡa zi⌐do⌐osya ni no┌sete kurema┐sita kara, zi⌐kañ-do⌐ori [ni] tu┌kima┐sita.
I was late for the 8 o'clock bus but a friend gave me a ride in his car so I arrived on time.	Ha┌ti┐-zi no ┌ba┐su ni o⌐kurema┐-sita ḡa; tomodati ḡa zi⌐do⌐osya ni no┌sete kurema┐sita kara, zi-⌐kañ-do⌐ori [ni] tu┌kima┐sita.

7. It's Haruo.   Ha⌐ruo-sañ de┐su.
   It's Haruo Yamamoto.   Yamamoto Ha⌐ruo-sañ de┐su.

It's Haruo.	Ha⌐ruo-sañ de┐su.
It's Haruo Yamamoto.	Yamamoto Ha⌐ruo-sañ de┐su.
[My] friend is Haruo Yamamoto.	Tomodati wa Yámamoto Ha⌐ruo-sañ de┐su.
My friend is Haruo Yamamoto.	Boku no tomodati wa Yámamoto Ha⌐ruo-sañ de┐su.
There are two people, but my friend is Haruo Yamamoto.	Hu┌tari ima┐su ḡa, boku no tomo-dati wa Yámamoto Ha⌐ruo-sañ de┐su.
There are two people named Yamamoto, but my friend is Haruo Yamamoto.	Ya⌐mamoto to iu hito┐ ḡa hu┌tari ima┐su ḡa, boku no tomodati wa Yámamoto Ha⌐ruo-sañ de┐su.
In this company there are two people named Yamamoto, but my friend is Haruo Yamamoto.	Ko⌐no kaisya ni┐ wa Ya⌐mamoto to iu hito┐ ḡa hu┌tari ima┐su ḡa, bo-ku no tomodati wa Yámamoto Ha⌐ruo-sañ de┐su.

8.

I've forgotten.	Wa⌐surema┐sita.
The name I've forgotten.	Na⌐mae wa wasurema┐sita.
I stopped [there] but I've forgotten the name.	To⌐marima┐sita ḡa, na⌐mae wa wa-surema┐sita.
I stopped at an inn but I've forgotten the name.	Ryo⌐kañ ni tomarima┐sita ḡa, na-⌐mae wa wasurema┐sita.
I stopped at a pleasant inn but I've forgotten the name.	Ki⌐moti no i┐i ryo┌kañ ni tomari-ma┐sita ḡa, na⌐mae wa wasure-ma┐sita.
I stopped at a pretty, pleasant inn, but I've forgotten the name.	Ki┐ree na ki⌐moti no i┐i ryo┌kañ ni tomarima┐sita ḡa, na⌐mae wa wa-surema┐sita.
When I went [there], I stopped at a pretty, pleasant inn, but I've forgotten the name.	I┌tta to┐ki [ni], ki┐ree na ki⌐moti no i┐i ryo┌kañ ni tomarima┐sita ḡa; na⌐mae wa wasurema┐sita.
When I went to Kyoto, I stopped at a pretty, pleasant inn, but I've forgotten the name.	Kyo┐oto e i┌tta to┐ki [ni], ki┐ree na ki⌐moti no i┐i ryo┌kañ ni tomari-ma┐sita ḡa; na⌐mae wa wasurema┐-sita.

QUESTION SUPPLEMENT

1. A⌐sa ta⌐be⌐ru ⌐go⌐hañ wa ⌐na⌐ñ to i⌐ima⌐su ka⌐
2. Kyuukoo no kippu wa ⌐na⌐ñ to i⌐ima⌐su ka⌐
3. Ho⌐ñ o oku tana wa ⌐na⌐ñ to i⌐ima⌐su ka⌐
4. To⌐okyoo no ho⌐o e i⌐ku kisya⌐ wa miñna ⌐na⌐ñ to i⌐ima⌐su ka⌐
5. To⌐kubetu ni haya⌐i kyuukoo wa ⌐na⌐ñ to i⌐ima⌐su ka⌐
6. Nobori no hañtai wa ⌐na⌐ñ desu ka⌐
7. Byo⌐oki no hito⌐ ḡa ta⌐kusañ ha⌐itte iru ta⌐te⌐mono wa ⌐na⌐ñ to i⌐ima⌐su ka⌐
8. Ta⌐tami no na⌐i ta⌐be⌐ru he⌐ya⌐ wa ⌐na⌐ñ to i⌐ima⌐su ka⌐
9. Te⌐ ḡa ki⌐tana⌐ku ⌐na⌐tta to⌐ki⌐ ni wa ⌐na⌐ñ de a⌐raima⌐su ka⌐
10. Zi⌐do⌐osya ḡa ko⌐syoo-sita toki⌐ ni wa ⌐do⌐o simasu ka⌐
11. De⌐ñwaba⌐ñḡoo o si⌐ranai toki⌐ ni wa ⌐na⌐ni o mi⌐ma⌐su ka⌐
12. Zi⌐kañ ḡa wakara⌐nai to⌐ki⌐ ni wa ⌐na⌐ni o mi⌐ma⌐su ka⌐
13. I⌐tibañ taka⌐i kippu wa na⌐ñ-too no⌐ desu ka⌐
14. Ue no hañtai wa ⌐na⌐ñ desu ka⌐
15. Ho⌐ñ ḡa ka⌐itai toki⌐ ni wa ⌐do⌐ñna mi⌐se⌐ e i⌐kima⌐su ka⌐

ya-soya   vey.store

EXERCISES

1. Making any changes necessary, use each of the following sentences within
   a longer sentence, as a modifier of a nominal, and translate the completed
   sentence into English.

   (Example: A⌐soko ni arima⌐sù. 'It's over there.'
   Answer: A⌐soko ni a⌐ru zi⌐biki⌐ wa wa⌐takusi no⌐ desu.
            'The dictionary that's over there is mine.')

   a. Mi⌐ruku o ko⌐bosima⌐sita.
   b. Ni⌐hoñḡo ḡa zyoozu⌐ desu.
   c. Gi⌐ñkoo ni tuto⌐mete (i)rassyaimasu.
   d. Ha⌐ ḡa i⌐ta⌐i desu.
   e. To⌐modati de⌐su.
   f. Wa⌐karimase⌐ñ desita.
   g. Wa⌐takusi ḡa kakima⌐sita.
   h. Ryo⌐ozi⌐kañ desita.
   i. Si⌐rimase⌐ñ.
   j. Si⌐ñbuñ o yo⌐ñde (i)masu.
   k. A⌐soko ni simatte arima⌐su.
   l. Zu⌐ibuñ ta⌐ka⌐i desu.
   m. E⌐ki no ⌐ma⌐e o to⌐orima⌐su.
   n. Ko⌐ohi⌐i ḡa no⌐mita⌐i desu.
   o. Si⌐ta no musume⌐ desu.
   p. Kyo⌐oto e i⌐kima⌐sita.
   q. I⌐ro⌐ ḡa ⌐ki⌐ree desu.

2. Express the following in Japanese.

  a. Buy the following tickets:

    (1) One second-class for Kyoto.
    (2) Two first-class for Yokohama, round trip.
    (3) One first-class for Osaka.
    (4) One second-class round trip for Nikko.

  b. Ask at the information booth:

    (1) when the next train for Yokohama leaves.
    (2) if you need an express ticket.
    (3) if the 8 o'clock train for Nagoya has already left.
    (4) if the 5 o'clock train from Nikko has arrived yet.
    (5) what track the Yokohama trains leave from.
    (6) if the Hato will be on time.

  c. Ask the conductor:

    (1) if the train stops at Shimbashi.
    (2) whether the train has a diner.
    (3) what time you arrive at Tokyo Station.
    (4) where the sleeping cars are.
    (5) where car #3 is.
    (6) where seat #4 is.

  d. Tell Mr. Tanaka that:

    (1) you went from Tokyo to Osaka by train and returned by plane.
    (2) you went from Tokyo to Numazu by electric train and from there to Mito by boat.
    (3) you came from New York to San Francisco by train and from San Francisco to Japan by plane.
    (4) you came from Yokohama to Shimbashi by electric car and from there to the office by taxi.

3. Using a local timetable, take turns asking and answering the following kinds of questions in Japanese:

  a. What time does the train that leaves (place) at (time) arrive at (place)?
  b. What time does the train that arrives at (place) at (time) leave (place)?
  c. Does the train for (place) that leaves (place) at (time) stop at (place)?
  d. How long does it take from (place) to (place) on the train that leaves (place) at (time)?

4. Practice the Basic Dialogues with appropriate variations.

Lesson 20. Transportation (cont.)

BASIC DIALOGUES: FOR MEMORIZATION

(a)

(At the station)

Smith

baggage or things to carry	ni˥motu or o˥ni˥motu˥
is heavy	omoi /-ku/

1. This baggage is terribly heavy, isn't it! — Ko˥no ni˥motu (wa) ˥zu˥ibuñ o˥mo˥i desu ˥ne˥e.

Tanaka

porter or redcap	akaboo
engage	ta˥no˥mu /-u/
come having engaged or go and engage	ta˥no˥ñde ˥ku˥ru *go + ask to come*

2. Shall I go and get a porter? — A˥kaboo (o) tano˥ñde ki˥masyo˥o ka.

Smith

3. Yes, please (go and engage). — E˥e ta˥no˥ñde ki˥te˥ kudasai.

(b)

(At the information booth)

Smith

put into someone else's keeping temporarily or check	a˥zuke˥ru /-ru/
place where one checks	a˥zuke˥ru toko(ro)

4. I'd like to check my baggage. Where is the checking place? — Ni˥motu (o) a˥zuketa˥i ñ desu ga, a˥zuke˥ru to˥ko(ro)˥ (wa) ˥do˥ko desu ka⌐

Clerk

waiting room	ma˥tia˥isitu

5. It's to the right of the waiting room. — Ma˥tia˥isitu no mi˥gi no ho˥o desu.

(c)

(Smith and Tanaka are on the platform after getting off a train)

Smith

subway	tikatetu

6. Shall we take the subway? — Ti˥katetu ni norimasyo˥o ka.

364

Tanaka

even though it is fast (or early) or it is fast (or early) but	ha⌐ya⌐i keredo
become crowded	ko⌐mu /-u/
be crowded	ko⌐ñde (i)ru

7. The subway is fast but it's always crowded so let's go by taxi.

Ti⌐katetu wa haya⌐i keredo; i⌐tu mo ⌐ko⌐ñde (i)ru kara, ta⌐kusii de i⌐ki-masyo⌐o.

Smith

is near	ti⌐ka⌐i /-ku/
place for boarding ve-hicles	noriba

8. [Where is] the nearest stand?
    (Lit. As for the nearest boarding place?)

I⌐tibañ tika⌐i noriba wa?

Tanaka

exit	de⌐ḡuti
one unit of wheeled vehicles	i⌐ti⌐-dai
two or three units of vehicles	ni-sañ-dai
[something] lines up	narabu /-u/
even though they are lined up or they are lined up but	na⌐rañde (i)ma⌐su keredo

intr.

9. <u>Usually</u> two or three [taxis] are lined up at the exit (but. . .)

Taitee ⌐de⌐ḡuti ni ni-⌐sañ-dai na-rañde (i)ma⌐su keredo_

Smith

10. Well, let's go and see.

Zya⌐a, i⌐tte mimasyo⌐o.

(At home)

Husband

intention or plan	tumori
intention of going or a plan to go	iku tumori

11. How do you plan to go? (Lit. A plan of going by what?)

Na⌐ñ de iku tumori?

Wife

(section of Tokyo)	Sibuya
go by riding or ride	notte (i)ku
to a place	
go by transferring	no⌐rika⌐ete (i)ku

even though it is the plan
to go by transferring
<u>or</u>   it is the plan to go
by transferring but

no⌐rika¬ete (i)┌ku tumori da¬
kedo

12. I plan to ride as far as Shibuya on the bus and transfer
(lit. go by transferring) to
the subway there (but. . . .)

Si⌐buya ma¬de ⌐ba¬su ni notte (i)t-
te, [1] asuko de ti⌐katetu ni norika¬-
ete (i)┌ku tumori da¬ kedo⌐

Husband

go down <u>or</u> descend
<u>or</u> get off (a vehicle)

o⌐ri¬ru /-ru/

13. Where will you get off? (Lit.
As for the place where you
get off?)

O⌐ri¬ru toko wa?

Wife

(section of Tokyo)

Toranomoñ

14. Toranomon.

Toranomoñ yo⌐

Husband

15. And from there?

So⌐ko kara¬ wa?

Wife

walk
go by walking <u>or</u>
walk to a place

a⌐ru¬ku /-u/
a⌐ru¬ite (i)ku

16. I'll walk—since it's
close.

A⌐ru¬ite (i)ku wa⌐ —ti┌ka¬i kara.

Husband

come having gone <u>or</u>
go and come

i⌐tte ku¬ru <u>or</u>
i⌐tte ma¬iru┤ <u>or</u>
i⌐tte (i)rassya¬ru┤

17. Well, goodbye (lit. go and
come)!

Zya¬a, i⌐tte (i)rassya¬i.

Wife

18. Goodbye. (Lit. I'll go and
come.)

I⌐tte mairima¬su. *hunble*

. . .   *kimasu — regular*

Wife (returning)

19. Hello! <u>or</u> I'm back!

Tadaima.

---

[1] Accent of contracted alternant: <u>no┌tte¬ tte</u>.

Husband

20. Hello!   O‸kaeri(-nasaˈi).

(e)

Smith

gasoline	gasoriñ
one liter	iˈti-riˈttoru
one or two liters	iˈti-ni-riˈttoru
be(come) left (over) or be(come) left behind	no‸koˈru /-u/
even though they're left (over) or they're left (over) but	no‸koˈtte (i)ru keredo
airport	hikoozyoo
it will be better to have put in (for future use) or [I]'d better put in (for future use)	iˈret(e) oˈita hoo g̃a ˈi‸i

21. Even though there are still one or two liters of gasoline left, since we're going as far as the airport, it would probably be better to put [some] in now (for future use), wouldn't it.

Gasoriñ (g̃a) ˈmaˈda iˈti-ni-riˈttoru no‸koˈtte (i)ru keredo; hi‸koozyoo maˈde iˈkuˈ kara, iˈma iˈret(e) oˈita hoo g̃a ˈiˈi desyoo ˈneˈe.

Tanaka

bridge	ha‸siˈ
go over or go across	wataru /-u/
intersection	yotukado
gasoline station	ga‸soriñsutaˈñdo

22. Yes. You go over that bridge, and there's a big gas station at the next intersection.

Eˈe. Aˈno hasiˈ (o) watatte, tuˈg̃iˈ no yōtukado ni oˈokiˈi ga‸soriñ-sutaˈñdo (g̃a) aˈrimaˈsu yo⌡

• • •

(At the gas station)

Attendant

how many liters?	na‸ñ-riˈttoru
23. How many (liters)?	Na‸ñ-riˈttoru desu ka⌡

Smith

full	~~ippai~~
fill [something] (lit. make full)	ippai ni suru
24. Fill it up.	Iˈppai ni site kudasaˈi.
oil	oˈiru
tire	taiya

air
be sufficient
enough

ku˺uki
tariru /-ru/
zyu˺ubu˺ñ /na/   adv. or adj.

25. Look at the oil, too, and
then there's too little air
in the front tires so put in
the right amount (lit. air
of the front tires is insuf-
ficient so put it in suffi-
ciently).

O˺iru mo ˺mi˺te; sore kara, ma˺e
no taiya no ˺ku˺uki (ḡa) ta˺rina˺i
kara, zyu˺ubu˺ñ /ni/ irete.

Tanaka

26. I'm sorry you were kept
waiting.

O˺matidoosama de˺sita.

become punctured
become completely flat

pañku-suru
pañku-site simau or
pañku-sityau

27. I'm late because I had a
flat.

Ta˺iya (ḡa) pañku-sityatta˺ kara,
o˺soku narima˺sita.

Smith

awful or dreadful or
terrible or a nuisance

taiheñ /-na/

28. Don't mention it. What a nuisance it must have been!
(Lit. It was a nuisance, was-
n't it?)

Do˺o itasimasite. Ta˺iheñ da˺tta
desyoo?

oneself

zibuñ or
gozibuñ˺

by oneself
exchange

zibuñ de
torikaeru /-ru/

29. Did you change [it] yourself?

Go˺zibuñ de torikaema˺sita ka↲

Tanaka

garage

ga˺re˺ezi

30. No, I had [it] changed at a
garage right nearby.

Iie, su˺ḡu ˺so˺ba no ga˺re˺ezi de
to˺rikaete moraima˺sita yo.

(g)

Smith

even though there
isn't or there
isn't but
brakes
condition
is funny

na˺i keredo

bu˺re˺eki
guai
o˺kasi˺i /-ku/

look into or check
or investigate

si⌐rabe⌐ru /-ru/

it will be better to have
had [them] checked
or [I] should have
[them] checked

si⌐ra⌐bete mo⌐ratta ho⌐o ḡa ⌐i⌐i

you had better have someone check (for you)

31. Even though we don't have
very much time, there's
something funny about the
brakes (lit. the condition
of the brakes has become
funny) so I guess I should
have them checked right
away, shouldn't I.

Zi⌐kañ (ḡa) añmari na⌐i keredo;
bu⌐re⌐eki no guai (ḡa) o⌐ka⌐siku
⌐na⌐tta kara, ha⌐yaku si⌐ra⌐bete
mo⌐ratta ho⌐o ḡa ⌐i⌐i desyoo ⌐ne⌐e.

Tanaka

important

taisetu /na/

32. Yes. You'd better do it
quickly (lit. the fast alternative is good)—be-
cause brakes are impor-
tant.

E⌐e, ha⌐ya⌐i hoo ḡa ⌐i⌐i desu yo↲
—bu⌐re⌐eki wa ta⌐isetu da⌐ kara.

• • •

(At the garage)

Attendant

go around

mawaru /-u/

33. Brakes? I'm sorry but
please go around toward
the back. [That's] be-
cause this (place) is just
[for] gas and oil and
things like that.

Bu⌐re⌐eki desu ka↲ Su⌐mimase⌐ñ
ḡa, u⌐siro no ho⌐o e ma⌐watte ku-
dasa⌐i. Kotira wa ga⌐soriñ ya o⌐i-
ru da⌐ke⌐ desu kara.

NOTES ON THE BASIC DIALOGUES

1. The opposite of omoi is karui /-ku/ 'is light (i.e. not heavy).'

2. Note: hi⌐to⌐ o ta⌐no⌐mu 'engage a person,' 'retain a person'; mo⌐no⌐ o ta-⌐no⌐mu 'order or request a thing'; hi⌐to⌐ ni ta⌐no⌐mu 'order or request from a person.'

4. Note also: a⌐zuka⌐ru 'receive in custody,' 'take charge of,' 'keep.'

9. 'but—I don't know whether or not there are any there now.'

The opposite of de⌐ḡuti is iriḡuti 'entrance.'

Narabu is the intransitive partner of transitive naraberu /-ru/ 'line [things or people] up'

12. 'but—do you think that's all right?'

13. Note: X o o⌐ri⌐ru (or, less commonly, X kara o⌐ri⌐ru) 'go down from X'
    or 'get off X.' (For particle o, see Lesson 7, Grammatical Note 3.) O⌐ri⌐-
    ru is the intransitive partner of transitive o⌐ro⌐su /-u/ 'lower' or 'let
    down' or 'discharge (a passenger).'

17. I⌐tte irassya⌐i is the farewell regularly said by the person remaining be-
    hind, to someone leaving his own home (or, in some circumstances, his
    office, his town, city, or country, etc.).   Sayonara is not used in this
    situation.   I⌐rassya⌐i (formal women's form, i⌐rassyaima⌐se) is the im-
    perative of i⌐rassya⌐ru.

18. I⌐tte mairima⌐su, or a less polite equivalent, is the farewell regularly
    said by someone leaving his home, to the person remaining behind. It is
    the reply to Sentence 17, preceding. Men regularly use i⌐tte kima⌐su or
    i⌐tte ku⌐ru.

19. Tadaima, lit. 'just now'—i.e. '[I've] just now [returned],' is the greeting
    regularly said by someone returning home.

20. O⌐kaeri(-nasa⌐i), an imperative of ka⌐eru 'return home,' is the greeting
    regularly said to someone who has just returned home. It is the reply to
    Sentence 19, preceding. The formal women's form is o⌐kaeri-nasaima⌐se.

21. No⌐ko⌐ru is the intransitive partner of transitive no⌐ko⌐su /-u/ 'leave be-
    hind,' 'leave over (for another time).'

22. For particle o, see Lesson 7, Grammatical Note 3.

    Wataru is the intransitive partner of watasu /-u/ 'hand over.'

    Yotukado is an intersection of two streets forming four corners.

24. Ippai is a nominal: ippai da '[it] is full'; i⌐ppai zya na⌐i '[it] is not full';
    i⌐ppai ni na⌐ru 'become full'; ippai ni suru 'fill' (lit. 'make full'). It oc-
    curs without a following particle as an expression of manner: ippai ireru
    'fill up' (lit. 'insert fully'). The opposite of ippai is ka⌐ra⌐ 'empty,' also
    a nominal.

25. In expressions of manner, zyu⌐ubu⌐n occurs both with and without particle
    ni.

26. O⌐matidoosama (de⌐sita) is used in the same kinds of situations as
    o⌐matase-itasima⌐sita, but the latter is more polite.

28. Some other English equivalents of taihen da are: 'Good heavens!' 'Good
    night!' 'What a mess!' 'What a fix to be in!' Taihen also occurs without
    a following particle as an expression of manner, meaning 'awfully,'
    'very,' 'terribly.'

29. Compare: zibun de 'by oneself—i.e. by one's own power or ability' and
    hi⌐to⌐-ri de 'by oneself—i.e. unaccompanied.' Zibun also occurs followed
    by particle no, meaning 'one's own.'

    Note: X o Y to torikaeru 'exchange X for (lit. with) Y.'

30. Ga⌐re⌐ezi usually refers to a garage where cars are repaired. Garages
    attached to homes for private cars are rare in Japan.

31. Many of the Japanese words for parts of a car are, like bu⌐re⌐eki and

taiya, loan-words from English. Thus: e⌐nziñ 'engine,' ho⌐oñ 'horn,'
ba⌐tterii 'battery,' kya⌐burettaa 'carburetor,' etc.

Note: gu⌐ai ḡa i⌐i 'be in good condition' or 'be fine' or 'be in good health';
gu⌐ai ḡa waru⌐i 'be in bad condition' or 'be out of order' or 'feel unwell'
or 'be sick.'

O⌐kasi⌐i, like 'funny' in English, means either 'strange' or 'amusing.'

33. Mawaru is the intransitive partner of transitive mawasu /-u/ 'send
around.'

GRAMMATICAL NOTES

1. Gerunds of Condition and Manner; Errands

(Reread Lesson 15, Grammatical Note 5.)

A verbal gerund, by itself or at the end of a sequence, may occur as the
modifier of another verbal, an adjectival, or a phrase ending in √da. In one
such pattern, the gerund (or sequence ending in the gerund) asks or answers
the question 'how?' or 'in what condition?' For example, in ti⌐katetu ni notte
kima⌐sita 'I rode here on the subway' (lit. 'I came by riding on the subway'),
tikatetu ni notte describes ki⌐ma⌐sita and tells how I came.

In this pattern, the action or state represented by the gerund may precede
or be simultaneous with that represented by the inflected expression it modifies.

The gerund does not always immediately precede the word or phrase it
modifies.

Examples:

> A⌐ru⌐ite i⌐kima⌐sita. 'I walked (to a specific place)'— lit. 'I went by
> walking.'
> O⌐kurete tukima⌐sita. 'I arrived late.'
> Ki⌐otuke⌐te o⌐sara o aratte kudasa⌐i. 'Please wash the dishes care-
> fully.'
> I⌐so⌐ide ikitai. 'I want to go in a hurry.' (informal style)
> I⌐so⌐ide u⌐ti e kaerita⌐i ñ desu ḡa— 'I'd like to go home in a hur-
> ry. . . .'
> Na⌐ñ ni notte Yo⌐kosuka e ikima⌐sita ka— 'How (lit. riding on what)
> did you go to Yokosuka?'

This pattern also covers errand situations in Japanese— situations involving going somewhere, doing something, and coming back. In such cases, √ku⌐-
ru (or a more polite equivalent) follows the appropriate gerund of doing, and
the first step— the going— is usually not mentioned. (Compare English, which
normally omits mentioning the last step— the coming back.) Thus, the Japanese equivalent of 'go and buy' is ka⌐tte ku⌐ru 'buy and come,' 'come having
bought.'

Examples:

> Si⌐ñbuñ o katte kima⌐su. 'I'll go and buy a paper.' (Lit. 'I'll come

having bought a paper.')

Ki⌐ite kimasyo⌐o ka. 'Shall I go and ask?' (Lit. 'Shall I come having asked?')

De͡nwatyoo o sira⌐bete mairimasu. 'I'll go and check the phone book.' (Lit. 'I'll come having checked the phone book.')

Actually, most uses of the gerund introduced thus far are covered by the statement at the beginning of this note. For example:

(a) a⌐ru⌐ku + ku⌐dasa⌐i > a⌐ru⌐ite kudasai 'please walk'
(b) a⌐ru⌐ku + iru > a⌐ru⌐ite iru '[I] am walking'
(c) a⌐ru⌐ku + ka⌐eru > a⌐ru⌐ite ⌐ka⌐eru '[I] will walk home'
(d) sañpo-suru + ka⌐eru > sañpo-site, ka⌐eru '[I] will take a walk, and then go home'

In patterns (a) and (b) only, the gerund is always immediately followed in the same accent phrase by the inflected word it modifies.

Patterns (c) and (d) are distinguished by intonation: in pattern (d), [1] the gerund usually ends with comma intonation and the word following the gerund starts a new accent phrase.

2. keredo 'even though'

Keredo 'even though' or 'although' is a particle which follows verbals, adjectivals, and √da, non-past, past, and tentative. When it occurs in the middle of a sentence, it regularly ends with comma intonation. If the final inflected form in the sentence is informal, only the informal occurs before medial keredo; otherwise it may be preceded by formal or informal forms. Before keredo, an unaccented verbal or copula expression regularly acquires an accent on its final syllable and an unaccented adjectival on its pre-final syllable.

Examples:

Mo⌐o wa⌐ka⌐tta (or wa⌐karima⌐sita) keredo, mo⌐o iti-do itte kudasaimase⌐ñ ka⌐ 'Even though I've already understood, would you please say it again?'
A⌐tu⌐i (desu) keredo, ma⌐do wa a⌐ketaku arimase⌐ñ. 'Even though it's hot, I don't want to open the window.'
Ki⌐ree da keredo, a͡nmari oisiku na⌐i. 'Even though it's pretty, it's not very tasty.'
Da⌐izyo⌐obu da⌐tta desyo⌐o keredo, ta⌐bemase⌐ñ desita. 'Even though it was probably safe, I didn't eat it.'

---

[1] Described in Lesson 7, Grammatical Note 5.

Like ḡa, keredo within a sentence implies contrast or is simply a clause connective (cf. Lesson 4, Note 1); but as an indication of contrast, medial keredo is a slightly stronger 'but.' Thus:

Yo⌐mima⌐sita ḡa, mo⌐o wa⌐surema⌐sita. 'I read it but I've forgotten it already.'

Yo⌐ñda keredo, mo⌐o wa⌐surema⌐sita. 'Even though I read it, I've forgotten it already.'

Kedo is a less formal, contracted equivalent of keredo; there is also a more formal equivalent, keredomo.

The use of keredo and kedo in sentence-final position closely resembles that of sentence-final ḡa. Thus:

Ikitai ñ desu ḡa_ ⎫
Ikitai ñ desu keredo_ ⎬ 'I'd like to go but. . . .'
Ikitai ñ desu kedo_ ⎭

Note that whereas an informal inflected form before ḡa occurs only in men's informal speech, informal forms before keredo occur in formal and informal speech of men and women.

3. **tumori** 'intention'

Tumori (honorific, otumori [1]) 'intention' is a nominal which is always preceded by a modifier—usually a sentence modifier consisting of a non-past affirmative verbal or negative adjectival— and is followed by some form of √da (including no before another nominal). Tumori in statements usually refers to the speaker's own intentions, and in questions to those of the person addressed. Thus:

I⌐ku tumori de⌐su. 'I intend to go,' 'I expect to go,' 'I plan to go,' etc.
I⌐ku tumori de⌐su ka_ 'Do you intend to go?' 'Do you expect to go?' 'Do you plan to go?' etc.

A negative may precede or follow tumori. Compare:

I⌐kanai tumori de⌐su. 'I intend not to go,' 'It is my intention not to go.'

and:

I⌐ku tumori zya arimase⌐ñ. 'I don't intend to go,' 'It is not my intention to go.'

Additional examples:

Ko⌐ñbañ ⌐na⌐ni o su⌐ru otumori de⌐su ka_ 'What do you intend to do this evening?'
Ki⌐no⌐o wa de⌐kakenai tumori da⌐tta keredo, de⌐kakete simaima⌐sita. 'Yesterday I planned not to go out, but I ended up by going out.'
Ka⌐u tumori zya na⌐katta keredo; a⌐ñmari ya⌐sukatta kara, ka⌐tte simaima⌐sita. 'Even though I didn't intend to buy it, it was so cheap that (lit. because it was so cheap) I ended up by buying it.'

Zyu⌈uni⌉-zi ni ta⊦be⊣ru tumori no mo⊦no⊣ o zyu⌈uiti⌉-zi ni ⊦ta⊣bete si⊦maima⊣sita. 'At 11 I ate up the things I planned to eat at 12.'
Do⌉n̄na tumori de i⊦tta⊣ ka wa⌈karimase⌉n̄ ḡa... 'What sort of thing he had in mind when he said it I can't tell but . . .' (Lit. 'Being what kind of intention he said [it] I can't tell but . . .')

The immediately preceding sentence is an example of the pattern — tumori de suru 'do with a — intention,' 'do with — in mind'; de is the gerund of da, and suru stands for any verbal.

4. Further Notes on Comparisons

Reread Lesson 15, Grammatical Note 2.

When comparing two courses of action, the nominal ho⌉o 'alternative' is preceded by a sentence modifier consisting of— or ending with— an affirmative verbal or a negative adjectival. A non-past before ho⌉o is more often used in general statements, whereas the past often refers to action on a specific occasion (lit. 'the alternative of having done will be —').

Thus:

Ko⌈n̄na ho⌉n̄ no ⊦ho⊣o ḡa o⊦mosiro⊣i. 'This kind of book is more interesting.'

but:

Ko⌈n̄na ho⌉n̄ o ⊦yo⊣mu hoo ḡa o⊦mosiro⊣i. 'Reading this kind of book is more interesting.'

and:

Ko⌈n̄na ho⌉n̄ o ⊦yo⊣n̄da hoo ḡa o⊦mosiro⊣i. 'It will be more interesting to read (lit. to have read) this kind of book.'

The combination si⌈ta ho⌉o ḡa ⊦i⊣i '[lit.] the alternative of having done [it] will be good' is often equivalent to English '[someone] had better do [it].' Sita may be replaced by other past verbals in this pattern.

Additional examples:

Hi⌈ko⌉oki de i⊦ku ho⊣o ḡa ha⊦ya⊣i. 'It's faster to go by plane.' (Lit. 'The alternative of going by plane is fast.')
Ni⌈hon̄go o yo⌉mu hoo ḡa mu⊦zukasi⊣i desyoo? 'It's more difficult to read Japanese, isn't it?'
Ha⌉yaku na⊦o⊣sita hoo ḡa ⌈i⌉i desu yo. 'You'd better fix it quickly.' (Lit. 'The alternative of having fixed it quickly will be good.')
Ko⌉n̄ban̄ i⊦tta ho⊣o ḡa ⌈i⌉i desyoo ⊦ne⊣e. 'I guess I'd better go tonight!' (Lit. 'The alternative of having gone tonight will probably be good, won't it.')
Na⌈ni mo iwanai ho⌉o ḡa ⊦i⊣i desyoo? 'It's better to say nothing, isn't it?'

A sequence consisting of— or ending with— an informal non-past affirmative verbal or negative adjectival + yori 'more than' indicates the course of action with which another is being compared. Before yori, a normally unaccented inflected word regularly acquires an accent—a verbal on its final syllable, and an adjectival on its pre-final syllable.

Examples:

Ki⌐sya⌐ de i⌐ku⌐ yori hi⌐ko⌐oki de i⌐ku ho⌐o ḡa ha⌐ya⌐i. 'It's faster to go by plane than to go by train.' (Lit. 'More than going by train, the alternative of going by plane is fast.')

Ha⌐na⌐su yori nihoñḡo o ⌐yo⌐mu hoo ḡa mu⌐zukasi⌐i desyoo? 'It's more difficult to read Japanese than to speak, isn't it?'

Ra⌐isyuu ma⌐de ⌐ma⌐tu yori ⌐ha⌐yaku na⌐o⌐sita hoo ḡa ⌐i⌐i desu yo⌐ 'You'd better fix it quickly rather than wait until next week.'

A⌐sita iku⌐ yori ⌐ko⌐ñbañ i⌐tta ho⌐o ḡa ⌐i⌐i desyoo ⌐ne⌐e. 'I guess I'd better go tonight rather than go tomorrow.'

5. Approximate Numbers

The combination of two consecutive numerals of Series I, from 1 to 9, plus a single counter, indicates approximation equivalent to English patterns like '1 or 2 hours,' '2 or 3 days,' '3 or 4 months,' etc.

The same pattern occurs in approximations of higher rank, like these:

ni-sañ-zeñ	'2 or 3 thousand'
si-ḡo-hyaku	'4 or 5 hundred'
ro⌐ku-siti-zyu⌐u	'60 or 70' (lit. '6 or 7 tens')

In this pattern, the consecutive numerals occurring in pairs are from 1 through 9 only. Kyu⌐uzyuu means '90'—not '9 or 10.'

Some combinations are irregular and must be memorized separately, but in general si⌐ '4' and si⌐ti⌐ '7' are the more common alternants of those numerals; and before ku⌐/kyu⌐u '9,' ha⌐ti⌐ occurs in its hak- alternant.

Examples:

iti-ni-mai	'1 or 2 thin, flat objects'
ni-⌐sañ-zi⌐kañ	'2 or 3 hours'
sañ-si-hoñ	'3 or 4 long, cylindrical objects'
si-⌐ḡo⌐-niti	'4 or 5 days'
go-⌐ro⌐p-puñ	'5 or 6 minutes'
ro⌐ku-siti-syu⌐ukañ	'6 or 7 weeks'
si⌐ti-hak-ka⌐ḡetu	'7 or 8 months'
hak-ku-neñ	'8 or 9 years'

6. Counters: -dai, -rittoru

The counter -dai combines with numerals of Series I to count units of wheeled vehicles—cars, busses, carts, carriages, etc. The numbers from one to ten are:

i⌐ti⌐-dai	'1 wheeled vehicle'
ni⌐-dai	'2 wheeled vehicles'
sa⌐ñ-dai	'3 wheeled vehicles'
yo⌐ñ-dai or yo-dai	'4 wheeled vehicles'
go-dai	'5 wheeled vehicles'
ro⌐ku⌐-dai	'6 wheeled vehicles'
na⌐na⌐-dai or si⌐ti⌐-dai	'7 wheeled vehicles'
ha⌐ti⌐-dai	'8 wheeled vehicles'
kyu⌐u-dai	'9 wheeled vehicles'
zyu⌐u-dai	'10 wheeled vehicles'
na⌐ñ-dai	'how many wheeled vehicles?'

The counter -rittoru combines with numerals of Series I to count liters. [1]

The numbers from one to ten are:

i⌐ti-ri⌐ttoru	'1 liter'
ni-⌐ri⌐ttoru	'2 liters'
sa⌐ñ-ri⌐ttoru	'3 liters'
yo⌐ñ-ri⌐ttoru	'4 liters'
go-⌐ri⌐ttoru	'5 liters'
ro⌐ku-ri⌐ttoru	'6 liters'
na⌐na-ri⌐ttoru or si⌐ti-ri⌐ttoru	'7 liters'
ha⌐ti-ri⌐ttoru	'8 liters'
kyu⌐u-ri⌐ttoru	'9 liters'
zyu⌐u-ri⌐ttoru	'10 liters'
na⌐ñ-ri⌐ttoru	'how many liters?'

-Rittoru is one of a large number of counters borrowed from English metric system terms. Others are -meetoru 'meter,' -kiro(meetoru) 'kilometer,' -guramu 'gram,' -kiro(guramu) 'kilogram,' etc.

In the late 1950's Japan adopted the metric system as its official measurement system. Before that time, three systems were in use simultaneously: along with the metric system, there was a native Japanese system with its own terms, and the American system with another set of borrowed terms (-yaado 'yard,' -iñti 'inch,' -garoñ 'gallon,' -poñdo 'pound,' etc.). The various measures of the last two systems are being—or have already been—abandoned since the official adoption of the metric system.

*

---

[1] One liter = 1.06 quarts.

DRILLS

A. Substitution Drill

1. Please get off now.   I¹ma ⸢o⸣rite kudasai.   vi oriru
2. Please let me off now.   I¹ma o⸢ro⸣site kudasai.   vt.
3. Please get on now.   I¹ma no⸢tte kudasa¹i.   vi   noru
4. Please let me on now.   I¹ma no⸢sete kudasa¹i.   vt.   noseru
5. Please line up now.   I¹ma na⸢rande kudasa¹i. i   ne n
6. Please line [them] up now.   I¹ma na⸢rabete kudasa¹i. t.   narabu
7. Please go across now.   I¹ma wa⸢tatte kudasa¹i. i.
8. Please hand [it] over now.   I¹ma wa⸢tasite kudasa¹i. t.
9. Please go around now.   I¹ma ma⸢watte kudasa¹i. i.
10. Please send [it] around now. I¹ma ma⸢wasite kudasa¹i. t.

B. Substitution Drill

1. There are 1 or 2 taxis left. . . .
    Ta¹kusii (ḡa) i⸢ti-ni-dai noko¹tte (i)masu ḡa_

2. There are 2 or 3 portions of sashimi left. . . .
    Osasimi (ḡa) ni-⸢sañ-niñ-mae noko¹tte (i)masu ḡa_

3. There are 3 or 4 pencils left. . . .
    Eñpitu (ḡa) sa⸢ñ-si-hoñ noko¹tte (i)masu ḡa_

4. There are 4 or 5 glasses of beer left. . . .
    Bi¹iru (ḡa) si-⸢go-hai noko¹tte (i)masu ḡa_

5. There are 5 or 6 children left. . . .
    Kodomo (ḡa) go-⸢roku-niñ noko¹tte (i)masu ḡa_

6. There are 6 or 7 liters of gasoline left. . . .
    Gasoriñ (ḡa) ro⸢ku-siti-ri¹ttoru no-⸢ko⸣tte (i)masu ḡa_

7. There are 7 or 8 books left. . . .
    Ho¹ñ (ḡa) si⸢ti-has-satu noko¹tte (i)masu ḡa_

8. There are 8 or 9 sheets of paper left. . . .
    Ka⸢mi¹ (ḡa) ha⸢k-ku-mai noko¹tte (i)masu ḡa_

C. Substitution Drill

1. I went to the airport in a taxi.
    Hikoozyoo e ⸢ta¹kusii ni no⸐tte iki-ma⸣sita.

2. I walked to the airport.
    Hikoozyoo e a⸢ru¹ite i⸐kima⸐sita.

3. I went to the airport happily.
    Hikoozyoo e yo⸢roko¹ñde i⸐kima⸐sita.

4. I went to the airport in a hurry.
    Hikoozyoo e i⸢so¹ide i⸐kima⸐sita.

5. I went to the airport late.
    Hikoozyoo e o⸢kurete ikima¹sita.

6. I went back to the airport.
    Hikoozyoo e mo⸢do¹tte i⸐kima⸐sita.

7. I went to the airport, [after] transferring to a bus.
    Hikoozyoo e ⸢ba¹su ni no⸐rika⸐ete i⸐kima⸐sita.

8. I went to the airport by way of (lit. passing through) the park.
    Hikoozyoo e ko⸢oeñ (o) to¹otte i⸐kima⸐sita.

D. Substitution Drill

1. Shall I go and hire a por-   A⌐kaboo (o) tano⌐nde ki⌐masyo⌐o ka.
    ter?
2. Shall I go and check the   Ni⌐motu (o) a⌐zu⌐kete ki⌐masyo⌐o
    baggage?   ka.
3. Shall I go and get (lit. put   Ga⌐soriñ (o) irete kimasyo⌐o ka.
    in) some gas?
4. Shall I go and look up the   De⌐ñwaba⌐ñḡoo (o) si⌐ra⌐bete ki⌐ma-
    phone number?   syo⌐o ka.
5. Shall I go and buy a pa-   Si⌐ñbuñ (o) katte kimasyo⌐o ka.
    per?
6. Shall I go and ask at the   A⌐ñnaizyo de kiite kimasyo⌐o ka.
    information booth?
7. Shall I go and call the   Se⌐ñse⌐e (o) yo⌐ñde kimasyo⌐o ka.
    doctor?
8. Shall I go and pick up the   Ni⌐motu (o) to⌐tte kimasyo⌐o ka.
    baggage?

E. Substitution Drill

1. Even though I didn't have   Zi⌐kañ ḡa añmari na⌐katta keredo,
    much time, I went.   i⌐kima⌐sita.
2. Even though I didn't feel   Gu⌐ai ḡa wa⌐rukatta keredo, i⌐kima⌐-
    well, I went.   sita.
3. Even though I was very   To⌐ttemo tuka⌐rete (i)⌐ta⌐ keredo,
    tired, I went.   i⌐kima⌐sita.
4. Even though I wanted to   Ya⌐sumita⌐katta keredo, i⌐kima⌐sita.
    rest, I went.
5. Even though it was raining,   A⌐me ḡa hu⌐tte⌐ (i)ta keredo, i⌐kima⌐-
    I went.   sita.
6. Even though I didn't want to   I⌐kitaku na⌐katta keredo, i⌐kima⌐sita.
    go, I went.
7. Even though it was winter,   Hu⌐yu⌐ datta keredo, i⌐kima⌐sita.
    I went.
8. Even though it was awfully   Zu⌐ibuñ to⌐o⌐katta keredo, i⌐kima⌐-
    far, I went.   sita.
9. Even though it wasn't very   A⌐ñmari tika⌐ku ⌐na⌐katta keredo,
    near, I went.   i⌐kima⌐sita.
10. Even though I was very   Ta⌐iheñ isoḡa⌐sikatta keredo, i⌐kima⌐-
    busy, I went.   sita.

F. Substitution Drill

1. I plan to go (riding) on the   Ba⌐su ni no⌐tte iku tumori da⌐
    bus (but . . .)[1]   kedo_

---

[1] 'but—I'm not sure I will' or 'but—it isn't definite,' etc.

2. I plan to get off in front of the park (but. . .)
Koꜜoeñ no maꜜe de oꜛriꜛru tuꜛmori daꜜ kedo‿

3. I plan to deposit ¥ 5000 in the bank (but. . .)
Giñkoo ni goꜜseñ-eñ azukeꜜru tuꜛmori daꜜ kedo‿

4. I plan to have the car checked (but. . .)
Kuꜜruma (o) siraꜜbete moꜛrau tumori daꜜ kedo‿

5. I plan to leave early in the morning (but. . .)
Aꜜsa ꜛhaꜜyaku ꜛtaꜛtu tuꜛmori daꜜ kedo‿

6. I plan to stop at an inn in Kyoto (but. . .)
Kyoꜜoto no ryoꜛkañ ni tomaru tuꜛmori daꜜ kedo‿

7. I plan to check the baggage at the station (but. . .)
Eꜜki de ꜛniꜜmotu (o) aꜛzukeꜜru tuꜛmori daꜜ kedo‿

8. I plan to return to America next week (but. . .)
Raisyuu Aꜛmerika e kaꜜeru tuꜛmori daꜜ kedo‿

9. I plan to study English next year (but. . .)
Raineñ eꜛeꜛgo (o) beñkyoo-suru tuꜛmori daꜜ kedo‿

10. I plan to transfer to the bus at Yokohama (but. . .)
Yokohama de ꜛbaꜜsu ni noꜛrikaꜜeru tuꜛmori daꜜ kedo‿

G. Grammar Drill (based on Grammatical Note 3)

Tutor: Iꜛkimaseꜜñ. 'I'm not going to go.'
Student: Iꜛkanai tumori deꜜsu. 'I plan not to go.'

1. Koꜜñbañ deꜛkakemaseꜜñ.
Koꜜñbañ deꜛkakenai tumori deꜜsu.

2. Asita kiꜛmaseꜜñ.
Asita ꜛkoꜜnai tumori desu.

3. Koñna siꜛgoto wa ꜛmoꜛo siꜛmaseꜜñ.
Koñna siꜛgoto wa ꜛmoꜛo siꜛnai tumori deꜜsu.

4. Raꜛineñ maꜜde wa kaꜛerimaseꜜñ.
Raꜛineñ maꜜde wa kaꜛeraꜜnai tumori desu.

5. Zeꜜñbu wa siꜛmaseꜜñ.
Zeꜜñbu wa siꜛnai tumori deꜜsu.

6. Soꜛñna hitoꜜ ni wa naꜜni mo yarimaseꜜñ.
Soꜛñna hitoꜜ ni wa naꜛni mo yaranai tumori deꜜsu.

what kind person / anything — nothing (handwritten)

H. Response Drill

Tutor: Huꜛruꜜi desu ka‿ 'Is it old?'
Student: Huꜛruku aꜛrimaseꜜñ. Aꜛtarasiꜜi desu yo‿ 'It isn't old. It's new.'

1. Oꜛmoꜜi desu ka‿
Oꜛmoku arimaseꜜñ. Kaꜛruꜜi desu yo‿

2. Tiꜛkaꜜi desu ka‿
Tiꜛkaꜜku aꜛrimaseꜜñ. Toꜛoi desu yo‿

3. Zyoꜛozuꜜ desu ka‿
Zyoꜛozuꜜ zya aꜛrimaseꜜñ. Heꜛtaꜜ desu yo‿

4. Tuꜛmetaꜜi desu ka‿
Tuꜛmetaku arimaseꜜñ. Aꜛtuꜜi desu yo‿

5. Oꜛisiꜜi desu ka‿
Oꜛisiku arimaseꜜñ. Maꜛzuꜜi desu yo‿

6. Oꜛmosiroꜜi desu ka‿
Oꜛmosiꜜroku aꜛrimaseꜜñ. Tuꜛmaraꜜnai desu yo‿

7. A'kema'su ka⌐   A'kemase'ñ. Si'mema'su yo⌐
8. Ko'i desu ka⌐   Ko'ku a'rimase'ñ. U'su'i desu yo⌐
9. Ka'ra' desu ka⌐   Ka'ra' zya a'rimase'ñ. I'ppai de'-
                            su yo⌐
10. Su'ppa'i desu ka⌐   Su'ppa'ku a'rimase'ñ. A'ma'i desu
                            yo⌐

I. Response Drill (based on Grammatical Note 4)

      Tutor: I'kimasyo'o ka. 'Shall I go?'
      Student: E'e, i'tta ho'o ga 'i'i desyoo? 'Yes, you'd better go, don't
              you think so?'

1. Ha'yaku si'ra'bete mo-   E'e, si'ra'bete mo'ratta ho'o ga
   'raimasyo'o ka.   'i'i desyoo?
2. Gasoriñ (o) i'rete okima-   E'e, i'ret(e) o'ita hoo ga 'i'i desyo'o ka.   syoo?
3. Akaboo (o) ta'nomimasyo'o   E'e, ta'no'ñda hoo ga 'i'i desyoo?
   ka.
4. Ha'si' (o) wa'tarimasyo'o   E'e, wa'tatta ho'o ga 'i'i desyoo?
   ka.
5. Kono taiya (o) to'rikaema-   E'e, to'rikaeta ho'o ga 'i'i desyo'o ka.   syoo?
6. Oohuku no kippu (o) ka'i-   E'e, ka'tta ho'o ga 'i'i desyoo?
   masyo'o ka.
7. Ka'gi' (o) ka'kemasyo'o   E'e, ka'keta hoo ga 'i'i desyoo?
   ka.
8. A'ma'do (o) si'memasyo'o   E'e, si'meta hoo ga 'i'i desyoo?
   ka.
9. To'kkyuu ni norimasyo'o ka.   E'e, no'tta ho'o ga 'i'i desyoo?
10. Sya'syoo ni kiite mimasyo'o   E'e, ki'ite mi'ta hoo ga 'i'i de-
   ka.   syoo?

J. Level Drill

     (Change all formal inflected forms except the final one to the infor-
     mal.)

1. Zi'p-puñ 'ma'e ni ta'nomi-   Zi'p-puñ 'ma'e ni ta'no'ñda kere-
   ma'sita keredo, ma'da mo-   do, ma'da mo'tte kimase'ñ.
   'tte kimase'ñ.
2. I'ti-do aima'sita keredo,   I'ti-do a'tta keredo, mo'o wa'su-
   mo'o wa'surete simaima'-   rete simaima'sita.
   sita.
3. I'ti-zikañ-gu'rai 'ma'e ni   I'ti-zikañ-gu'rai 'ma'e ni su'to'-
   su'to'obu (o) tu'kema'sita   obu (o) tu'ke'ta keredo, ma'da
   keredo, ma'da sa'mu'i   sa'mu'i desyoo?
   desyoo?
4. To'oi' desu kara, zu'ibuñ   To'oi' kara, zu'ibuñ zi'kañ ga ka-
   zi'kañ ga kakarima'su ke-   ka'ru keredo; i'kima'su yo⌐
   redo; i'kima'su yo⌐

5. A⌐no⌐ hito wa wa⌐karimase⌐ñ keredo, i⌐tu mo wa⌐ka⌐ru tte i⌐tte (i)ma⌐su ⌐ne⌐e.

A⌐no⌐ hito wa wa⌐kara⌐nai keredo, i⌐tu mo wa⌐ka⌐ru tte i⌐tte (i)ma⌐su ⌐ne⌐e.

6. Mo⌐o ni-⌐sañ-do mima⌐sita keredo; a⌐ñmari omosiro⌐i desu kara, ma⌐ta mita⌐i desu yo.

Mo⌐o ni-⌐sañ-do mi⌐ta keredo; a⌐ñmari omosiro⌐i kara, ma⌐ta mita⌐i desu yo.

7. Se⌐ñse⌐e ga so⌐o ossyaima⌐sita keredo, ho⌐ñtoo zya arimase⌐ñ yo⌐

Se⌐ñse⌐e ga so⌐o ossya⌐tta keredo, ho⌐ñtoo zya arimase⌐ñ yo⌐

8. Ki⌐koemase⌐ñ desita keredo, yo⌐ku mi⌐ema⌐sita.

Ki⌐koena⌐katta keredo, yo⌐ku mi⌐ema⌐sita.

9. I⌐ku tumori de⌐su keredo, ma⌐da si⌐taku wa simase⌐ñ.

I⌐ku tumori da⌐ keredo, ma⌐da si-⌐taku wa simase⌐ñ. *prepared*

10. De⌐kakenai tumori de⌐sita keredo, de⌐kakete simaima⌐sita.

De⌐kakenai tumori da⌐tta keredo, de⌐kakete simaima⌐sita.

K. Expansion Drill

1. [He] didn't see me.
   [He] was waiting at the exit so he didn't see [me].
   My friend was waiting at the exit so he didn't see me.

   A⌐imase⌐ñ desita.
   De⌐guti de ⌐ma⌐tte (i)⌐ta⌐ kara, a⌐imase⌐ñ desita.
   To⌐modati wa de⌐guti de ⌐ma⌐tte (i)⌐ta⌐. kara, a⌐imase⌐ñ desita.

   I was waiting in the waiting room but my friend was waiting at the exit so he didn't see me.

   Ma⌐tia⌐isitu de ⌐ma⌐tte (i)⌐ta⌐ keredo; to⌐modati wa de⌐guti de ⌐ma⌐tte (i)⌐ta⌐ kara, a⌐imase⌐ñ desita.

   I was waiting in the waiting room for about a half hour but my friend was waiting at the exit so he didn't see me.

   Sa⌐ñ-zip-puñ-gu⌐rai ma⌐tia⌐isitu de ⌐ma⌐tte (i)⌐ta⌐ keredo; to⌐modati wa de⌐guti de ⌐ma⌐tte (i)⌐ta⌐ kara, a⌐imase⌐ñ desita.

2. I ended up by going.
   I ended up by going (riding) in the car.

   I⌐tte simaima⌐sita.
   Ku⌐ruma ni notte itte simaima⌐sita.

   There wasn't enough time so I ended up by going (riding) in the car.

   Zi⌐kañ ga tarina⌐katta kara, ku⌐ruma ni notte itte simaima⌐sita.

   Even though I planned to walk (lit. go walking), there wasn't enough time so I ended up by going (riding) in the car.

   A⌐ru⌐ite i⌐ku tumori da⌐tta keredo; zi⌐kañ ga tarina⌐katta kara, ku⌐ruma ni notte itte simaima⌐sita.

   Even though I planned to walk to the station, there wasn't enough time so I

   E⌐ki e a⌐ru⌐ite i⌐ku tumori da⌐tta keredo; zi⌐kañ ga tarina⌐katta kara, ku⌐ruma ni notte itte

ended up by going (riding)
in the car.

Even though I planned to
walk to the station this
morning, there wasn't
enough time so I ended up
by going (riding) in the
car.

simaima˺sita.

Ke˺sa ˹e˺ki e a˹ru˺ite i˹ku tumori
da˹tta keredo; zi˹kañ ḡa tarina˺-
katta kara, ku˹ruma ni notte itte
simaima˺sita.

3. I ended up by going. (M)[1]

I ended up by going (riding)
on the bus.

I arrived late so I ended
up by going (riding) on the
bus.

I arrived at the station late,
so I ended up by going
(riding) on the bus.

I intended to take the train
but I arrived at the sta-
tion late, so I ended up
by going (riding) on the
bus.

I intended to take a train
that stops at Numazu but
I arrived late, so I ended
up by going (riding) on the
bus.

I˹ttyatta˺ yo.

Ba˹su ni no˹tte (i)ttyatta˺[2] yo.

O˹kurete tu˹ita kara, ba˹su ni
no˹tte (i)ttyatta˺ yo.

E˹ki ni o˹kurete tu˹ita kara, ba˹su
ni no˹tte (i)ttyatta˺ yo.

Ki˹sya˺ ni no˹ru tumori da˺tta kedo; e˹ki ni o˹kurete tu˹ita kara,
ba˹su ni no˹tte (i)ttyatta˺ yo.

Nu˹mazu ni tomaru ki˹sya˺ ni no-
˹ru tumori da˺tta kedo, e˹ki ni
o˹kurete tu˹ita kara, ba˹su ni
no˹tte (i)ttyatta˺ yo.

4. [He] didn't say.

[He] didn't say anything.

Nobody said anything.

I ended up by going in but
nobody said anything.

I ended up by going in
through (lit. from) the
exit but nobody said any-
thing.

I couldn't tell so I ended up
by going in through the exit, but nobody said any-
thing.

I˹imase˺ñ desita yo⌐

Na˹ni mo iimase˺ñ desita yo⌐

Da˹re mo nani mo iimase˺n desita
yo⌐

Ha˹itte si˹matta˺ kedo, da˹re mo
nani mo iimase˺ñ desita yo⌐

De˹ḡuti kara ˹ha˹itte si˹matta˺ kedo, da˹re mo nani mo iimase˺ñ
desita yo⌐

Wa˹kara˹nakatta kara, de˹ḡuti kara
˹ha˹itte si˹matta˺ kedo; da˹re mo
nani mo iimase˺ñ desita yo⌐

---

[1] M = more typical of men's speech.

[2] Notte itte is regularly contracted to notte tte in informal speech.

I couldn't tell which was the
entrance so I ended up by
going in through the exit, but
nobody said anything.

Do˥tira ga ˥iriguti ka wa˥kara˥naka-
tta kara, de˥guti kara ˥ha˥itte si-
˥matta˧ kedo; da˥re mo nani mo
iimase˥ñ desita yo˩

5. There isn't enough. (Lit.
It has become insuffi-
cient.)

Ta˥rinaku narima˥sita.

Again there isn't enough.

Ma˥ta tarinaku narima˥sita.

Even though I had [some]
put in, again there isn't
enough.

I˥rete moratta˧ keredo, ma˥ta tarinaku narima˥sita.

Even though I had enough
put in, again there is-
n't enough.

Zyu˥ubu˥ñ i˥rete moratta˧ kedo, ma-
˥ta tarinaku narima˥sita.

There wasn't enough (lit.
it had become insuffi-
cient) so I had the right
amount put in, but again
there isn't enough.

Ta˥rinaku na˥tte (i)˥ta˧ kara, zyu˥u-
bu˥ñ i˥rete moratta˧ kedo; ma˥ta
tarinaku narima˥sita.

There wasn't enough air
so I had the right amount
put in, but again there is-
n't enough.

Ku˥uki ga ta˥rinaku na˥tte (i)˥ta˧
kara, zyu˥ubu˥ñ i˥rete moratta˧
kedo; ma˥ta tarinaku narima˥si-
ta.

There wasn't enough air in
the tires so I had the right
amount put in, but again
there isn't enough.

Ta˥iya no ku˥uki ga ta˥rinaku na˥tte
(i)˥ta˧ kara, zyu˥ubu˥ñ i˥rete mo-
ratta˧ keredo; ma˥ta tarinaku na-
rima˥sita.

There wasn't enough air in
the tires this morning so
I had the right amount
put in, but again there is-
n't enough.

Ke˥sa ta˥iya no ku˥uki ga ta˥rinaku
na˥tte (i)˥ta˧ kara, zyu˥ubu˥ñ i˥re-
te moratta˧ keredo; ma˥ta tarinaku
narima˥sita.

6. Let's go (and come).

I˥tte kimasyo˥o.

Let's go to the J. T. B.

Ko˥otuuko˥osya e i˥tte kimasyo˧o.

Let's go to the J. T. B. right
nearby.

Su˥gu ˥so˥ba no ko˥otuuko˥osya e
i˥tte kimasyo˧o.

[They] are waiting so let's
go to the J. T. B. right
nearby.

Ma˥tte (i)ru kara, su˥gu ˥so˥ba no
ko˥otuuko˥osya e i˥tte kimasyo˧o.

[They] are waiting in line
so let's go to the J. T. B.
right nearby.

Na˥rañde ma˥tte (i)ru kara, su˥gu
˥so˥ba no ko˥otuuko˥osya e i˥tte
kimasyo˧o.

Lots of people are waiting
in line so let's go to the
J. T. B. right nearby.

Hi˥to˥ ga ta˥kusañ narañde ma˥tte
(i)ru kara, su˥gu ˥so˥ba no ko˥o-
tuuko˥osya e i˥tte kimasyo˧o.

Lots of people are always
waiting in line so let's go
to the J. T. B. right nearby.

I˥tu mo hi˥to˥ ga ta˥kusañ narañde
ma˥tte (i)ru kara, su˥gu ˥so˥ba
no ko˥otuuko˥osya e i˥tte kima-
syo˧o.

Lots of people are always waiting in line at the ticket windows so let's go to the J. T. B. right nearby.

Maˊdoˈgˍuti ni wa ⌐iˈtu mo hiˊtoˈ gˍa taˈkusañ narañde maˈtte (i)ru kara, suˈgˍu ˈsoˈba no koˈotuukoˈ-osya e iˈtte kimasyoˈo.

Lots of people are always waiting in line at the ticket windows in this station so let's go to the J. T. B. right nearby.

Koˈno eˈki no maˊdoˈgˍuti ni wa ⌐iˈ-tu mo hiˈtoˈ gˍa taˈkusañ narañde maˈtte (i)ru kara, suˈgˍu ˈsoˈba no koˈotuukoˈosya e iˈtte kima-syoˈo.

QUESTION SUPPLEMENT

(The following questions are based on the Basic Dialogues of this lesson.)

(a)   1. Suˈmisu-sañ to Tānaka-sañ wa ⌐doˈko de haˈnaˈsite imasu ka⌐

      2. Tanaka-sañ wa ⌐doˈo site aˈkaboo o tanoˈñde kiˈmaˈsu ka⌐

(b)   3. Suˈmisu-sañ wa ⌐naˈni o aˈzuketaˈi ñ desu ka⌐

      4. Aˈzukeˈru toˈkoroˈ wa ⌐doˈko desu ka⌐

      5. Suˈmisu-sañ wa ⌐doˈko de oˈsiete moraimaˈsita ka⌐

      6. Eˈki no hiˈto o maˈtu heˈyaˈ wa ⌐naˈñ to iˈimaˈsu ka⌐

(c)   7. Tanaka-sañ wa ⌐doˈo site tiˈkatetu ni noritaku arimaseˈñ ka⌐

      8. Tanaka-sañ wa ⌐naˈñ ni noˈritaˈi ñ desu ka⌐

      9. Taˈkusii no iˈtibañ tikaˈi noriba wa ⌐doˈko desu ka⌐

    10. Taitee ⌐eˈki no ˈdeˈgˍuti ni ⌐naˈni gˍa naˈrañde imaˈsu ka⌐

(d) 11. Oˈkusañ wa ⌐naˈñ to ⌐naˈñ ni noˈtte iku tumori deˈsu ka⌐

    12. Oˈkusañ wa ⌐doˈko made ⌐baˈsu ni noˈtte iku tumori deˈsu ka⌐

    13. Oˈkusañ wa Sîbuya de ⌐naˈni o suˈru tumori deˈsu ka⌐

    14. Oˈkusañ wa ⌐doˈko de tiˈkatetu o oriˈru desyoo ka.

    15. Oˈkusañ wa Toˈranomoñ de oˈrite kara ⌐doˈo simasu ka⌐

    16. Goˈsyuˈziñ mo iˈkimaˈsu ka⌐

    17. Niˈhoñziˈñ wa ziˈbuñ no uti o deˈru toˈkiˈ ni wa ⌐naˈñ to iˈimaˈsu ka⌐

    18. Niˈhoñziˈñ wa ziˈbuñ no uti ni kaˈetta toˈkiˈ ni wa ⌐naˈñ to iˈimaˈ-su ka⌐

    19. Uˈti ni iru hitoˈ wa deˈkakeru hitoˈ ni ⌐naˈñ to iˈimaˈsu ka⌐

    20. Uˈti ni iru hitoˈ wa uˈti ni kaˈette ˈkiˈta hiˈtoˈ ni ⌐naˈñ to iˈimaˈsu ka⌐

(e) 21. Suˈmisu-sañ no ziˈdoˈosya ni gāsoriñ gˍa naˈñ-rittoru-gˍuˈrai noˈ-koˈtte imasu ka⌐

    22. Doˈo site ˈiˈma gāsoriñ o ˈmoˈtto iˈrete oˈita hoo gˍa ⌐iˈi desyoo ka.

    23. Taˈnaka-sañ no sitte iru gasoriñsutaˈñdo wa ⌐doˈko desyoo ka.

    24. Suˈmisu-sañ wa gaˈreˈezi de ⌐naˈni o siˈte moraimaˈsu ka⌐

(f) 25. Tanaka-sañ wa ⌐do⌐o site o⌐soku narima⌐sita ka⌐
    26. Tanaka-sañ wa zi⌐buñ de pañku-sita taiya o torikaema⌐sita ka⌐
(g) 27. Su⌐misu-sañ wa ⌐do⌐o site ga⌐re⌐ezi e i⌐kima⌐sita ka⌐
    28. Su⌐misu-sañ wa zi⌐buñ de bure⌐eki o si⌐rabema⌐sita ka, ga⌐re⌐ezi
        no hi⌐to⌐ ni si⌐ra⌐bete mo⌐rau tumori de⌐su ka⌐

SUPPLEMENTARY CONVERSATION

Smith: Ga⌐soriñ o ireta⌐i ñ desu ḡa, kono heñ ni ga⌐soriñsuta⌐ñdo wa ⌐na⌐i desyoo ⌐ne⌐e.

Tanaka: Sa⌐a.   . . . A, asuko ni zyu⌐ñsa ḡa iru⌐ kara, ki⌐ite mimasyo⌐o.
(To policeman) Tyo⌐tto u⌐kaḡaima⌐su ḡa, kono heñ ni ga⌐soriñsuta⌐ñdo wa a⌐rimase⌐ñ ka⌐

Policeman: Ga⌐soriñsuta⌐ñdo desu ka⌐ Kono miti o mo⌐o suko⌐si itte, hasi no temae o mi̅ḡi e maḡatte; sore kara, ni-⌐sañ-byaku-meetoru-ḡu⌐rai saki ni o⌐oki⌐i ga⌐re⌐ezi mo ga⌐soriñsuta⌐ñdo mo arimasu.

Tanaka: Wa⌐karima⌐sita. Do⌐o mo a⌐ri⌐ḡatoo gozaimasita.

        . . .

Smith: A, mi⌐ema⌐su yo⌐ — ha⌐si⌐ ḡa.
Tanaka: Mi̅ḡi no ho⌐o desu ne?
Smith: E⌐e.

(At the gas station)

Smith: O⌐neḡai-sima⌐su.
Attendant: O⌐matase-sima⌐sita.
Smith: Ga⌐soriñ oneḡai-sima⌐su.
Attendant: I⌐ppai ni simasyo⌐o ka.
Smith: E⌐e.   . . .   O⌐iru mo mi̅zu mo ⌐mi⌐te ne?
Attendant: Ha⌐a, ka⌐sikomarima⌐sita.
Tanaka: Ta⌐iya wa daizyo⌐obu desu ka⌐
Smith: E⌐e, da⌐izyo⌐obu desyoo. Señsyuu si⌐ra⌐bete mo⌐ratta⌐ kara.
Tanaka: Mi⌐ti ḡa waru⌐i kara, taiya ḡa ⌐su⌐ḡu ⌐wa⌐ruku narimasu ⌐ne⌐e.
Smith: Ho̅ñtoo de⌐su ⌐ne⌐e. Ki⌐no⌐o mo ⌐ma⌐e no ta⌐iya ḡa pañku-sima⌐sita yo.
Tanaka: Kono kuruma ⌐na⌐ñ-neñ no desu ka⌐
Smith: Yo-⌐neñ ma⌐e no desu ḡa, e⌐ñziñ no guai ḡa ⌐ma⌐da to⌐temo i⌐i desu kara⌐
Tanaka: So⌐re wa i⌐i desu ⌐ne⌐e.
Attendant: Omatidoosama. Gasoriñ wa sa⌐ñzyuu-ri⌐ttoru i⌐rema⌐sita. O⌐iru mo mi̅zu mo ⌐ma⌐da da⌐izyo⌐obu desu kara⌐
Smith: A⌐a ⌐so⌐o. Do⌐o mo go⌐ku⌐roosama.
Attendant: Maido a⌐ri⌐ḡatoo gozaimasu.

English Equivalent

Smith: I'd like to get (lit. put in) some gas, but there probably isn't a gas station around here, is there.

Tanaka: I wonder. . . .   Oh, there's a policeman over there so let's ask him and find out.
               (To policeman) Excuse me but is(n't) there a gas station around here?
Policeman: A gas station? You go a little further along this street, turn right this side of the bridge, and then about two or three hundred meters ahead there's a big garage and gas station.
Tanaka: I understand. Thank you very much.

                                  . . .

Smith: Oh, I see it—the bridge.
Tanaka: It's to the right, isn't it?
Smith: Yes.

               (At the gas station)

Smith: Will you wait on me?
Attendant: I'm sorry to have kept you waiting.
Smith: Let me have some gas.
Attendant: Shall I fill it up?
Smith: Yes. . . .   look at (both) the oil and water, will you?
Attendant: Yes, certainly.
Tanaka: Are the tires all right?
Smith: Yes, I think they're all right. (Because) I had them checked last week.
Tanaka: The roads are bad so the tires go bad right away, don't they.
Smith: They certainly do.   Why, I had a flat in the front tire yesterday again (lit. too).
Tanaka: What year is this car? (Lit. This car is one of what year?)
Smith: It's four years old but the engine is still in very good condition so. . . (Lit. It's one of four years ago but the condition of the engine is still very good so. . . .)
Tanaka: Isn't that fine!
Attendant: I'm sorry to have kept you waiting. I put in 30 liters of gas. (Both) the oil and water are still all right (so. . .)
Smith: Oh. Thanks very much for your trouble.
Attendant: Thank you (again and again).

EXERCISES

1. Make up questions based on the immediately preceding conversation, and then practice the questions and answers.

2. Tell the porter:

         a. that you want to check your luggage.
         b. to take your luggage to the waiting room.
         c. to take only the heavy luggage.
         d. that you will take the light things.

3. Ask a stranger:

         a. where the waiting room is.

    b. which way the airport is.

    c. where you get the subway. *no noriba wa*   *or Doko de*

    d. if the next station is Shibuya.

    e. if there's a gas station around here. *ガソリンスタンド*

4. Tell the garage attendant:

    a. that you want 20 liters of gasoline. *ニ十 rittoru o kudasai*

    b. to fill the tank. *ippai ni shite kudasai*

    c. that there isn't enough air in the tires. *taiyaa no kuuki ga tarimasen*

    d. that there's something wrong with the engine. *engine no guai ga okashii desu.*

    e. that you have a flat. *taiyaa ga pankushityatta*

    f. that your brakes are out of order. *bureeki ga kooshoo desu.*

    g. to check the oil and water.

5. Tell Mr. Tanaka:

    a. that you walked here. *Koko e aruite ikimashita*

    b. that you came here on the subway. *notte kimashita*

    c. that you got on at Shimbashi. *norimashita*

    d. that you got off at Shibuya. *sh. de orimashita*

    e. that you came here by transferring at Shibuya. *norikaete kimashita*

    f. that you are going to go and buy a newspaper. *o katte kimasu*

    g. that he'd better check his luggage. *azuketa hoo ga iidesu*

    h. that he'd better get (lit. engage) a porter. *tanonde kita hoo ...*

    i. that it will be faster to go by taxi. *de iku hoo ga hayai desu.*

    j. that you plan to try walking to the office tomorrow.

    k. that you plan to walk to Mr. Tanaka's house and ride back.

    l. that you plan to have the engine of your car checked tomorrow.

j. *Ashita*, *jimusho e* あるいて (itte) 見るつもりです。

k. 田中さんのうち へ あるいて 徒 それから のって 帰えるつもりです。

l. あした 車の エンジン を しらべて もらう 方が つもりです。

Japanese–English Glossary

Except for proper names, the following list contains all the vocabulary introduced in this text—words occurring in the Notes and as additional vocabulary as well as those appearing in the Basic Dialogues. Numbers following the entries refer to lessons: a number alone means that the entry first occurs in the Basic Dialogues of that lesson; a number followed by '-A' refers to the Additional Vocabulary of that lesson; a number followed by '-N' indicates that the item first occurs in the Notes of that lesson. CI and Int. refer to Classroom Instructions [1] and Introductory Lesson respectively. An asterisk (*) means that the item is included in the Index to the Grammatical Notes, with a reference to the location of the appropriate note(s).

Except in special cases, verbals and adjectivals are listed in their citation form only. Every verbal is identified as transitive /tr/ or intransitive /intr/ [2] and is assigned to the appropriate subclass; [3] its gerund is also given. For example, akeru /tr:-ru:akete/ identifies akeru as a transitive verbal belonging to the -ru subclass (i.e. the subclass to which ta⌐be⌐ru 'eat' and mi⌐ru 'see' belong), with gerund akete.

Every adjectival is identified by '/-ku/.' [4] after the citation form. Thus, the adjectival meaning 'is big' appears as: o⌐oki⌐i /-ku/.

All forms of the copula which occur in the text are listed and identified.

Nominals occur with no special designation, except that the members of the subclass of na-nominals [5] are identified by a following '/na/.'

Particles and quotatives are so identified. All are marked with asterisks, since all are included in the index.

Pre-nominals are identified by the designation '/+ nom/.'

Counters are so identified and are listed with a preceding hyphen.

'/M/' and '/W/' follow entries typical of men's or women's speech respectively.

---

[1] Words designated as CI are those which occur only in the Classroom Instructions.

[2] For a description of transitive and intransitive verbals, see Lesson 16, Grammatical Note 1.

[3] For a description of verbal subclasses, see Lesson 11, Grammatical Note 1.

[4] See Lesson 2, Grammatical Note 1.

[5] See Lesson 12, Grammatical Note 4.

Except in a few special cases, words having a polite alternant that differs from the plain alternant only in the addition of the polite prefix o- or go- are listed only in the plain alternant.

For purposes of alphabetizing, hyphens and the macron of ḡ are ignored. Syllabic ñ is assigned to the position immediately following nonsyllabic n.

In most cases, combinations occurring as indented sublistings match the first occurrence in the lessons; but a simpler, more generally occurring example of the pattern is cited in cases where the combination which occurs first in the lessons seems less desirable as the model for a pattern of wide general use.

A

a oh! 4
a⌐a oh! Int.
(a⌐a /M/ yes 16)
abunai /-ku/ is dangerous 7
aḡaru /intr:-u:aḡatte/ go up, come up,
    enter 18
aḡeru /tr:-ru:aḡete/ give (to someone
    other than the speaker) 17
  site aḡeru do for someone 17
aida interval, space between 7
  Tookyoo to Yokohama no aida be-
    tween Tokyo and Yokohama 7
akaboo porter, redcap 20
akai /-ku/ is red 4
akeru /tr:-ru:akete/ open [it] 16
a⌐ki autumn, fall 18
aku /intr:-u:aite/ [it] opens 16
a⌐ma⌐do sliding storm door 18
amai /-ku/ is sweet or sugary or
    insufficiently salted 14-A
a⌐me rain 18
  a⌐me ḡa ⌐hu⌐ru it rains 18
a⌐merika⌐ziñ an American 10
a⌐na⌐ta you Int.
ane older sister 11-A
a⌐ni older brother 11-A
ano* /+ nom/ that —— over there 3
Ano ne! Say! Hey there! 13
añmari /+ negative/ not very much,
    not so much, not too much 3
    /+ affirmative/ so much, too much
    14
aña* that kind, that kind of 5
añnaizyo, a⌐ñnaizyo⌐ information booth 19
a⌐o blue, green 16
a⌐o⌐i /-ku/ is blue or green 4; is
    pale 14
a⌐pa⌐ato apartment house 16
arau /tr:-u:aratte/ wash 17
are* that thing over there 2

bañ night 19
-bañ /counter for naming numbers in
    a series/ 12
ba⌐ñgo⌐hañ evening meal, dinner 15-N
ba⌐ñḡo⌐o number 12
-bañ-señ /counter for naming track
    numbers/ 19
ba⌐su bus 8
ba⌐ta butter 14-A
ba⌐tterii battery 20-N
be⌐ekoku⌐ziñ an American 10-A

A⌐ri⌐ḡatoo (gozaimasita).+ Thank you
    (for what you did). Int.
A⌐ri⌐ḡatoo (gozaimasu).+ Thank you.
    Int.
a⌐ru* /intr:-u:a⌐tte; neg:na⌐i/ be lo-
    cated (of inanimate objects), have 2
  si⌐mete ⌐a⌐ru have been closed 16
a⌐ru⌐ku /intr:-u:a⌐ru⌐ite/ walk 20
a⌐sa morning 9
a⌐sago⌐hañ breakfast 15-N
a⌐si⌐ leg, foot 17-A
a⌐sita⌐ tomorrow 1
asoko that place over there, over there
    6
asuko /see asoko/ 6
a⌐tama⌐ head 17
  a⌐tama⌐ ḡa i⌐ta⌐i have a headache
    17
a⌐tarasi⌐i /-ku/ is new or fresh 2
a⌐t(a)taka⌐i /-ku/ is warm 16
atira that one (of two); that way, there-
    abouts, over there 6
a⌐to later, afterward 4
  a⌐to de later, at a later time 4
  A⌐to ⌐na⌐ni o simasyoo ka. What
    shall I do next? 17
a⌐tti⌐ /see atira/ 6
a⌐tu⌐i /-ku/ is hot 14
a⌐u /intr:-u:a⌐tte/ meet, see (and talk
    to) a person 11
  Ya⌐mada-sañ ni a⌐u meet or see Mr.
    Yamada 11
a⌐zuka⌐ru /tr:-u:a⌐zuka⌐tte/ receive
    in custody, take charge of, keep
    20-N
a⌐zuke⌐ru /tr:-ru:a⌐zu⌐kete/ put into
    someone else's keeping tempo-
    rarily, check, deposit 20

B

beñkyoo-suru /tr:irreg:beñkyoo-site/
    study 11
be⌐ñzyo⌐ /M/ toilet 6-A
be⌐tto bed 17-A
betu ni /+ negative/ not especially
    13
bi⌐iru beer 14
bi⌐ru building (Western style) 6
bo⌐ku, boku /M/ I, me 5
bo⌐ttyañ† son 11-A
bu⌐re⌐eki brakes 20

buta   pig   17-A
byooiñ   hospital   7

byooki   sickness, sick   11

D

da* /copula: informal non-past/
-dai /counter for vehicles/ 20
daidokoro   kitchen   17
daiḡaku   university   13
da'isuki /na/   very pleasing   15
da'izi /na/   important, valuable   11-N
    Odaizi ni.   Take care of yourself!
       11
da'izyo'obu /na/   safe, all right   7
da'ke* just, only   4
    so're dake' just that, that's all   4
    mi-'ttu' dake   just three (units)   5
da'me /na/   no good, bad, broken   2
da'nnasa'ma ' master   12
da're who?   10
    dare mo /+ negative/   nobody   13
da'su /tr:-u:da'site/   put out, send out,
    take out   17
da'tta* /copula: informal past/
de* /copula: gerund/
de* /particle/   by means of   7;
    at, in   7
de'ḡuti   exit   20
dekakeru /intr:-ru:dekakete/   set out,
    go out   13
de'ki'ru /intr:-ru:de'kite/   be possible,
    can do   9; come into being, be-
    (come) completed   15
    ni'hoñḡo ḡa deki'ru   can [speak] Japa-
    nese   9
de'ñki   electricity, electric light   16
de'ñsya, deñsya   electric train, street
    car   8
deñwa   telephone   6
    de'ñwa o kake'ru   telephone (verb)
    12
de'ñwaba'ñḡoo   telephone number   12
deñwa-suru /intr:irreg:deñwa-site/
    make a telephone call   12
deñwatyoo   telephone book   12
de'pa'ato   department store   6
de'ru /intr:-ru:de'te/   go out, leave   9

de'sita* /copula: formal past/
de'su* /copula: formal non-past/
de'syo'o* /copula: formal non-past
    tentative/
-do /counter for number of times/   1
do'a   door (Western style)   16
doituḡo   German language   11-A
do'itu'ziñ   a German   10-A
do'ko   what place? where?   6
do'nata ' who?   10
do'no* /+ nom/   which— ?   3
dono-ḡurai   about how long? about how
    much?   8
do'ñna* what kind? what kind of?   5
do'o   how? what way?   2
    Do'o itasimasite. ' Don't mention it.
    You're welcome.   Int.
    do'o mo   in every way   Int.
    Do'o mo.   [Thanks] very much.   Int.
    do'o sita   what happened?   14
    do'o site   why? how?   11
    do'o suru   do what? act how?   13
doobutu   animal   17-A
-doori /see to'ori'/   avenue, street
    7-N
-doori   in accordance with   19
    zi'kañ-do'ori   on time   19
do'ozo   please   Int.
do're* which thing (of three or more)?
    2
    do're de' mo   whichever (of three or
    more) it is, any one at all   15
do'tira   which one (of two)?; which
    way? whereabouts? where?
    6
    do'tira de' mo   either one   15
    do'tira no 'ho'o   which alternative?
    15
    dotira mo   both   10
do'tirasama ' who?   12
do'tti /see do'tira/   6
do'yo'o(bi), doyoo   Saturday   8

E

e* /particle/   to, into, onto   7
ebi   shrimp, prawn   14
e'e   yes; that's right   Int.

e'eḡa'kañ   movie theater   7
eeḡo   English language   11-A
e'ekoku'ziñ   Englishman   10-A

e⌐ki station 6
-eñ /counter for yen/ 3
eñpitu pencil 2
eñryo reserve, restraint 18

eñryo (cont.)
Go⌐eñryo na⌐ku. Don't hold back.
Don't stand on ceremony. 18
e⌐ñziñ engine 20-N

G

ḡa* /particle/ 4
Ha⌐iza⌐ra ḡa arimasu. There's an
ashtray. 4
Ki⌐ree desu ḡa— It's pretty but . . .
4
gaikoku foreign country 11-N
gaikokuḡo foreign language 11
ga⌐ikoku⌐ziñ foreigner 11-N
ga⌐imu⌐syoo Foreign Office 11
-ḡaisya /see kaisya/ company
12-N
gaiziñ foreigner, Westerner, American 11-N
gakkoo school 6-A
ga⌐ñneñ the year 1, first year of an
emperor's reign 8-N
ga⌐re⌐ezi garage (commercial) 20
gasoriñ gasoline 20
ga⌐soriñsuta⌐ñdo gas station 20
ga⌐suḡa⌐isya gas company 12-N
-ḡatu /counter for naming the months
of the year/ 8
gekizyoo theater 6-A
ge⌐ñkañ entry hall 16
ge⌐ñki /na/ health, pep, good spirits
Int.
(O)⌐ge⌐ñki desu ka— Are you well?
How are you? Int.
ge⌐tuyo⌐o(bi), getuyoo Monday 8
giñkoo bank 6
go⌐ five 3
go⌐ḡo afternoon, p.m. 9

go⌐hañ cooked rice, food 14-A; meal
15
Go⌐ku⌐roosama (desita). Thanks for your
trouble. 1
Go⌐meñ-kudasa⌐i(ma⌐se). Excuse me
(for breaking away or interrupting). 12
-ḡoo-sya /counter for naming train
car numbers/ 19
-ḡo⌐ro* approximate point of time,
about 8
ha⌐ti-ḡatu-ḡo⌐ro about August 8
gotisoo a feast, delicious food and/or
drink 14-N
Go⌐tisoosama (de⌐sita). It was a
feast. Thank you for the delicious
refreshments. 14
go⌐za⌐ru+* /intr:-aru/ be located (of
inanimate objects), have Int.
go⌐zeñ a.m. 9-N
go⌐zo⌐ñzi da † know 13
guai condition 20
gu⌐ai ḡa i⌐i be in good condition, be
fine, be in good health 20-N
gu⌐ai ḡa waru⌐i be in bad condition,
be out of order, feel unwell, feel
sick 20
gu⌐riiñka⌐a 'green car' (i.e. first-
class car) 19-N
gu⌐ri⌐insya 'green car' (i.e. first-
class car) 19-N
-ḡu⌐rai* approximate extent, about 8
dono-ḡurai about how much? 8
ni-⌐syuukañ-ḡu⌐rai about two weeks
8
gyuunyuu cow's milk 14-A

H

ha⌐ tooth 17-A
ha⌐a+ yes; that's right 4
ha⌐ha mother 11-A
ha⌐i yes; that's right Int.; here you
are 3
-hai /counter for glassfuls and cup-
fuls/ 14
haiiro gray 16
ha⌐iru /intr:-u:ha⌐itte/ enter, go in
17
ha⌐itte (i)ru be inside 17

ha⌐iza⌐ra ashtray 3
ha⌐kki⌐ri clearly, distinctly, precisely
18
hako box 17
hana nose 17-A
ha⌐na⌐ flower 6-A; flower arrangement 18
ha⌐nasi⌐ talking, a talk, a story 13
hanasi-tyuu in the middle of talking;
the line is busy 13
ha⌐na⌐su /tr:-u:ha⌐na⌐site/ speak, talk 13

ha⌐na'ya flower shop, florist 6-A
-ha'n half 8
  sa'n-zikan-ha'n three hours and a half 8
  go-'zi-ha'n 5:30 9
ha⌐nbu'n half, half part 14
hantai opposite 19
hantai-suru /intr:irreg:hantai-site/ oppose 19-N
ha'ru spring (season) 18-N
ha'si chopsticks 14-A
ha⌐si' bridge 20
ha'tati 20 years of age 10-N
ha⌐ti' eight 3
hatu leaving 19
  zyu⌐uiti'-zi hatu leaving at 11 o'-clock 19
  Ko'obe hatu leaving Kobe, coming from Kobe 19
hatu-ka 20 days; twentieth day of the month 8
ha⌐ya'i /-ku/ is fast or early 9
Ha⌐zimema'site. How do you do? 11
ha⌐zi'mete the first time 11
  Ha⌐zi'mete ome ni kakarimasu.
    How do you do? 11
he'bi snake 17-A
hen area, section, part 6
  kono hen this area, around here 6
  do'no hen what part? what section? 19
he'n /na/ strange 13
he⌐ta' /na/ unskilled, poor at 18
he⌐ya' room 13
hi day 15
hidari left 6
  hi⌐dari no ho'o left side; toward the left 6
hikidasi drawer 17
hi⌐ko'oki airplane 8
hikoozyoo airport 20
hima /na/ free time, leisure 12
  hi'ma na toki' time when [someone] is free 12
hi'ru' noon, daytime 15-N
hi⌐rugo'han noon meal, lunch 15
hito, hi⌐to' person 10
  o'nna' no hito woman 10
  o⌐toko' no hito man 10
hi⌐to'-ri one person; single (person) 10
  hi⌐to'-ri de alone, by oneself 17

hi⌐to'-tu one unit 5
hodo* approximate extent 15
  tenpura hodo su⌐ki' zya 'na'i [I] don't like [it] as much as tempura 15
hoka other, another, other than 4
  hoka ni in addition 4
  Tanaka-san no hoka ni in addition to Mr. Tanaka, other than Mr. Tanaka 15-N
  hoka no hi another day 15
ho'n book 2
-hon /counter for long, cylindrical units/ 5
ho'ndana bookshelf 17
hontoo truth, true 3
ho'nya bookstore, book dealer 6-A
ho'o side; direction; alternative 6
  hi⌐dari no ho'o left side, toward the left 6
  ko⌐tira no ho'o this side, this direction 6
  mi⌐gi no ho'o right side, toward the right 6
  si⌐ta ho'o ga ⌐i'i it will be better to have done [it], [you]'d better do [it] 20
ho'oku fork 14-A
ho'on horn 20-N
ho'teru hotel 6
hu⌐ki'n dishrag, dish cloth, cloth 17
huku /tr:-u:huite/ wipe 17
hu'ne ship, boat 8
-hun /counter for naming and counting minutes/ 8
huransugo French language 11-A
hu⌐ransu'zin Frenchman 10-A
hu⌐roba' bathroom (not toilet) 17-A
hurosiki furoshiki (cloth square for wrapping) 4
hu'ru /intr:-u:hu'tte, hu'tte'/ fall (of rain, snow, etc.) 18
  a'me ga ⌐hu'ru it rains 18
hu⌐ru'i /-ku/ is old (i.e. not new) or stale 2-A
hu⌐suma', husuma sliding door (opaque) 18
hu⌐ta-tu two units 5
hu'yu' winter 18-N
hya⌐ku' one hundred 3
-hyaku /counter for hundreds/ 3

I

i⌐girisu⌐ziñ Englishman 10-A

i⌐i /yo⌐ku/ is good or fine or all
   right; never mind 2

iie no; that's not right Int.

i⌐ka⌐ga how? 4
   I⌐ka⌐ga desu ka⌐ How are you?
   How are things? How about it
   (offering something)? 4

I⌐kemase⌐ñ ⌐ne⌐e. That's too bad.
   11

ikenai /-ku/ it won't do, that's too bad
   11

-iki -bound 19
   Kyooto-iki bound for Kyoto 19

iku* /intr:-u:itte/ go 1

i⌐kura how much? 3

i⌐kutu how many units? 5; how old (of
   people)? 10

i⌐ma now 7

i⌐ma⌐ living room 17-A

i⌐mo⌐oto younger sister 11-A

i⌐nu⌐ dog 17

i⌐ñdo⌐ziñ an Indian (from India) 10-A

ippai full 20
   i⌐ppai ni na⌐ru become full 20-N
   ippai ni suru fill [something] 20

i⌐rassya⌐ru ⌐ * /intr:-aru:i⌐rassya⌐tte ~
   i⌐ra⌐site/ be 6; go 7; come
   8
   I⌐rassya⌐i(ma⌐se). Welcome! 4
   Do⌐nata de (i)rassyaimasu ka⌐ ⌐
   Who is it? Who are you? 10

ireru /tr:-ru:irete/ put in, insert
   17

iriguti entrance 20-N

i⌐ro⌐ color 5
   do⌐ñna iro what (kind of) color? 5

iru* /intr:-ru:ite/ be located (of animate beings) 6
   beñkyoo-site (i)ru be studying 11

iru (cont.)
   hu⌐tte (i)ru be raining 18
   kekkoñ-site (i)ru be married 10

iru /intr:-u:itte/ be necessary, need,
   want 4

i⌐sogasi⌐i /-ku/ is busy 13

i⌐so⌐gu /intr:-u:i⌐so⌐ide/ be in a hurry 7

issyo together 15
   Sa⌐itoo-sañ to issyo together with
   Mr. Saito 15

isu chair 17-A

itadaku ⌐ /tr:-u:itadaite/ eat, drink
   14; receive, accept 17

i⌐ta⌐i /-ku/ is painful 17

i⌐ta⌐mu /intr:-u:i⌐ta⌐ñde/ be(come)
   hurt or spoiled 14
   i⌐ta⌐ñda ebi spoiled shrimp 14

itasu ⌐ /tr:-u:itasite/ make, do 13
   Do⌐o itasimasite. ⌐ Don't mention it.
   You're welcome. Int.

i⌐ti⌐ one (numeral) 3

itibañ, i⌐ti⌐bañ* to the highest degree
   15
   i⌐tibañ taka⌐i is most expensive 15

i⌐to⌐ko cousin 11-A

I⌐tte irassya⌐i. Goodbye. (Lit. Go and
   come.) 20

I⌐tte kima⌐su. Goodbye. (Lit. I'll go
   and come.) 20-N

I⌐tte mairima⌐su. ⌐ Goodbye. (Lit. I'll
   go and come.) 20

i⌐tto⌐osya first-class car 19-A

i⌐tu when? 8
   i⌐tu mo always 9

i⌐tu⌐-tu five units 5

iu /tr:-u:itte/ say, be named, be
   called 1

i⌐ya /M/ no; that's not right 16

K

ka* /sentence particle/ (question) Int.
   O⌐ge⌐ñki desu ka⌐ ⌐ Are you well?
   Int.

-ka ~ -niti /counter for naming and
   counting days/ 8

ka⌐do street corner 7

ka⌐eru /intr:-u:ka⌐ette/ return (home)
   9

-kagetu /counter for number of months/
   8

ka⌐gi⌐ key 16
   ka⌐gi⌐ ga ka⌐ka⌐ru [something] locks 16

kaˈgiˈ (cont.)
   kaˈgiˈ o kaˈkeˈru   lock [something]
      16
kaˈgu   furniture   17-A
-kai   /counter for naming and counting
      floors/   16
kaidañ   stairway   17-A
kaikee   bill, accounting, check   15
kaisya   business company, company
      office   12
kaˈkaˈru   /intr:-u:kaˈkaˈtte/   be re-
      quired, take   8; be suspended
      11
   kaˈgiˈ ga kaˈkaˈru   [something]
      locks   16
   oˈme ni kakaˈru   see (a person),
      meet   11
   Haˈziˈmete ome ni kakarimasu.
      How do you do.   11
   ziˈkañ ga kakaˈru   take time
      8
kaˈkeˈru   /tr:-ru:kaˈkete/   hang [some-
      thing]   12
   deˈñwa o kakeˈru   telephone (verb)
      12
   kaˈgiˈ o kaˈkeˈru   lock [something]
      16
kaˈku   /tr:-u:kaˈite/   write, draw   7
kaˈmaˈu   /intr:-u:kaˈmaˈtte/   mind, care
      about   18-N
   kaˈmawaˈnai   doesn't matter, makes
      no difference, is all right   9
kaˈmiˈ   paper   5
kaˈnai   wife (one's own)   11
kaˈñkokuˈziñ   a South Korean   10-A
kao   face; expression   14
   aˈoˈi kao o suru   be pale   14
kara*   /particle/   from   8; because
      11; after   16
   sore kara   from that point, after
      that, and then, and   4
karada   body   17-A
kaˈraˈi   /-ku/   is spicy or salty   14
kariru   /tr:-ru:karite/   borrow, rent
      [from someone]   13
karui   /-ku/   is light (i.e. not heavy)
      20-N
Kaˈsikomarimaˈsita.   Certainly. I'll
      do as you have asked.   4
kaˈtaˈ   person   10
   oˈñna no kataˈ   woman   10
   oˈtoko no kataˈ   man   10
katamiti   one-way   19
kaˈtazukeˈru   /tr:-ru:kaˈtazuˈkete/
      straighten up   16

kau   /tr:-u:katte/   buy   4
kaˈwaˈku   /intr:-u:kaˈwaˈite/   become
      dry   15
kawari   a change; a second helping   18
kaˈyoˈo(bi), kayoo   Tuesday   8
kaˈzoku   family   11-A
kedo   /see keredo/   20
kekkoñ-suru   /intr:irreg:kekkoñ-site/
      marry   10
   kekkoñ-site (i)ru   be married   10
keˈkkoo   /na/   fine, all right   9
   Moˈo ˈkeˈkkoo desu.   I'm fine as I
      am. I've had enough already.   14
ke(re)do*   /particle/   although   20
keˈsa   this morning   9
kesu   /tr:-u:kesite/   turn off, extin-
      guish, erase   16
kieru   /intr:-ru:kiete/   become extin-
      guished, go out   16-N
kiiroi   /-ku/   is yellow   4
kikoeru   /intr:-ru:kikoete/   be audi-
      ble, can hear   13
kiku   /tr:-u:kiite/   ask a question, lis-
      ten, hear   12
kimoti   feeling, mood   18
   kiˈmoti ga iˈiˈ   is pleasant or agree-
      able   18
kiˈnoˈo, kinoo   yesterday   1
kiˈñyoˈo(bi), kiñyoo   Friday   8
kiˈotukeˈru   /intr:-ru:kiˈotukeˈte/   be
      careful   17
kippu   ticket   19
kirai   /na/   displeasing   15
kiˈree   /na/   pretty, clean   3
kiˈru   /tr:-u:kiˈtte, kiˈtteˈ/   cut, cut
      off, hang up (the telephone)   13
kiˈssaˈteñ, kissateñ   tearoom   14-A
kiˈsyaˈ   (steam) train   8
kiˈtanaˈi   /-ku/   is dirty   16
ko   child   10
   oˈñnaˈ no ko   little girl   10
   oˈtokoˈ no ko   little boy   10
koˈboreˈru   /intr:-ru:koˈboˈrete/   [some-
      thing] spills   17
   koˈboˈrete (i)ru   be spilled   17
koˈboˈsu   /tr:-u:koˈboˈsite/   spill
      [something]   17-N
kodomo   child   10
koˈe   voice   13
   oˈokiˈi ˈkoˈe de   or   oˈoki na ˈkoˈe
      de   with a loud voice   13
koˈi   /-ku/   is strong or thick (of li-
      quids); is dark (of colors)   14-A
koko   this place, here   6
koˈkoˈno-tu   nine units   5

ko꜀maka˥i /-ku/ is small or fine or
    detailed 17
ko꜀ma˥ru /intr:-u:ko꜀ma˥tte/ be(come)
    distressing or troublesome or
    annoying or inconvenient or per-
    plexing 9
ko꜀me˥ uncooked rice 14-A
ko꜀mu /intr:-u:ko꜀ñde/ be(come) crowded 20
    ko˥ñde (i)ru be crowded 20
kono* /+ nom/ this — 3
kono-goro these days, nowadays 18
ko˥ñbañ this evening, tonight 13
    Koñbañ wa. Good evening. Int.
koñgetu this month 10
koñna* this kind, this kind of 5
    Koñniti wa. Good afternoon. Int.
koobañ police box 7
kooeñ park 6-A
ko꜀ohi˥i coffee 14
ko꜀ohiizya˥wañ cup (with handles) 14-A
ko꜀oka˥ñsyu telephone operator 12
koori ice 14-A
ko꜀otuuko˥osya Japan Travel Bureau
    12
kootya black tea 14-A
koppu glass for drinking 14-A
kore* this thing 2
ko꜀si˥ lower part of the back 17-A
ko꜀syo˥o pepper 14-A
kosyoo out of order 13
kosyoo-suru /intr:irreg:kosyoo-site/
    break down 13-N
ko꜀tae˥ru, ko꜀ta˥eru /intr:-ru:ko꜀ta˥ete/
    answer CI
kotira this one (of two); this way,
        hereabouts, here 6; this per-
        son 11; the person speaking 12
    ko꜀tira no ho˥o this side, this di-
        rection 6
kotori bird 17-A
kotosi this year 8
kotozuke message; the giving of a mes-
    sage 13

ko꜀tti˥ /see kotira/ 6
ku˥ nine 3
kubi neck 17-A
ku꜀da˥mono fruit 14-A
kudari down-train (i.e. going away
    from Tokyo) 19
ku꜀dasa˥i* /imperative of ku꜀dasa˥ru/
    give me 1
    Ko꜀re o kudasa˥i. Please give me
    this one. 4
    Ma˥tte kudasai. Please wait. 1
    I꜀soga˥nai de kudasai. Please don't
    hurry. 7
ku꜀dasa˥ru ˺ * /tr:-aru:ku꜀dasa˥tte ~
    ku꜀dasu˥tte/ give me 4
    ka˥ite ku꜀dasaimase˥ñ ka_ ˺
    would (lit. won't) you be kind
    enough to write (or draw) for me?
    7
-kuñ /M/ /suffix attached to men's
    and boys' names; familiar/ 13
kureru /tr:-ru:kurete/ give me 17
    ta꜀no˥ñde kureru request (or order)
    for me 17
ku꜀ro˥i /-ku/ is black 4
ku˥ru * /intr:irreg:ki꜀te˥/ come 5
    ta꜀no˥ñde kuru come having engaged,
    go and engage 20
kuruma car, cart 7
kusuri medicine 6-N
kusuriya drugstore, druggist 6-A
kuti mouth 17-A
ku˥uki air 20
kya˥burettaa carburetor 20-N
kyaku guest, customer 18
kyo˥neñ last year 10-A
kyo˥o today 1
kyo˥odai brothers and/or sisters
    11-A
kyu˥u nine 3
kyuukoo express 19
kyu꜀uko˥okeñ express ticket 19-A

M

ma˥a oh well; I guess 4
ma˥da* /+ affirmative/ still, yet
    18; /+ negative/ not yet 14
    ma˥da da it is yet to happen; not
    yet 14
made* /particle/ as far as; up to and
    including 7

made (cont.)
    To꜀okyo˥o-eki made as far as Tokyo
    Station 7
    na˥ñ-zi made until what time? 9
    zyu꜀u-gatu˥ made ni by October 9
ma˥do window 16
ma꜀do˥guti ticket window 19

ma⌐e front 6; before 8
    e⌐ki no ⌐ma⌐e   front of the station
      6
    zi⌐p-pu⌐ñ mae   ten minutes before
      the hour 8
    zi⌐p-puñ ma⌐e, zi⌐p-puñ ⌐ma⌐e   ten
      minutes ago 8
maḡaru /intr:-u: maḡatte/   make a turn
      7
    ka⌐do o maḡaru   turn at the corner,
      turn the corner 7
ma⌐ḡo⌐ grandchild 11-A
-mai /counter for thin, flat units/   5
ma⌐iasa every morning 9-N
ma⌐ibañ every night 19-N
maido every time 4
    Ma⌐ido ari⌐ḡatoo gozaimasu.⁺
      Thank you again and again. 4
maiḡetu every month 9-N
maineñ every year 9-N
ma⌐initi every day 9
ma⌐iru⌐* /intr:-u: ma⌐itte/   go 7;
      come 8
maisyuu every week 9-N
maitosi every year 9-N
maituki every month 9-N
ma⌐kita⌐bako cigarette 3-N
ma⌐ma⌐ condition 16
    so⌐no mama⌐ de   being that condition
      as it is 16
-mañ /counter for ten thousands/ 3
ma⌐ssu⌐ḡu straight 7
mata again 4
    Ma⌐ta do⌐ozo. Please [come] again. 4
ma⌐tia⌐isitu waiting room 20
ma⌐tti match 3
ma⌐tu /tr:-u: ma⌐tte/   wait, await, wait
      for 1
mawaru /intr:-u: mawatte/   go around
      20
mawasu /tr:-u: mawasite/   send around
      20
ma⌐zu⌐i /-ku/ is bad-tasting 14
me⌐ eye 17-A
me⌐e niece 11-A
me⌐eḡosañ⁺ niece 11-A
meesi name card, calling card 13
me⌐ezi Meiji Era (1868-1912) 8
mesiaḡaru⁺ /tr:-u: mesiaḡatte/   eat;
      drink; smoke 14
mi⌐dori green 16-N
mi⌐e⌐ru* /intr:-ru: mi⌐ete/   be visible,
      can see; put in an appearance,
      show up, come 18

miḡi right (i.e. not left) 6
    mi⌐ḡi no ho⌐o   right side, toward the
      right 6
mi⌐mi⌐ ear 17-A
mi⌐na⌐sañ⁺ everyone 11
mi⌐ñna⌐ everyone; everything 11
mi⌐ru* /tr:-ru: mi⌐te/   look at, see
      12
    si⌐te mi⌐ru   try doing, do and see
      19
mi⌐ruku milk 14
mi⌐se⌐ store, shop 6-A
mi⌐se⌐ru /tr:-ru: mi⌐sete   show, let
      [someone] see 4
miti street, road, way 7
mi-⌐ttu⌐ three units 5
mizu cold water 14
mo* /particle/ also, too 4
    a⌐o⌐i no mo   blue one(s) too 4
    de⌐pa⌐ato ni mo   in the department
      store too 6
    o⌐oki⌐i no mo ti⌐isa⌐i no mo   both
      big ones and small ones 5
    do⌐o mo   in every way Int.
    i⌐tu mo   always 9
    dotira mo   both 10
    dare mo /+ negative/ nobody
      13
mo⌐do⌐ru /intr:-u: mo⌐do⌐tte/   go back,
      back up 7
mo⌐kuyo⌐o(bi), mokuyoo Thursday 8
momoiro pink 16-N
mo⌐no⌐ thing (tangible) 14
moo* /+ quantity expression/   more,
      additional 1
    moo iti-do   one time more 1
    mo⌐o suko⌐si   a little more, a few
      more 4
mo⌐o* /+ affirmative/ already, yet,
      now already, soon now 14
    /+ negative/ no more 18
    mo⌐o su⌐ḡu   soon now, any minute
      now 15
mo⌐osu⌐⁺ /tr:-u: mo⌐osite/   say, be
      named, be called 18
morau /tr:-u: moratte/   receive, get
      17
    site morau   have [someone] do [it],
      have [something] done 17
mo⌐simosi   hello (on the telephone);
      say there! 12
mo⌐ti⌐roñ   of course 15
motte iku   take [something somewhere]
      14-N

mo⌐tte ku⌐ru   bring [something]   14
mo⌐tto*   more   5
mukoo   beyond, over there; the far
   side   6
   bi⌐ru no mukoo   beyond the building   6
   mu⌐koo no bi⌐ru   the building over
      there   6

N

na*   /pre-nominal alternant of da/
   12
   hi⌐ma na toki⌐   time when [someone]
      is free   12
naḡaisu   couch, sofa   17-A
na⌐ḡasi⌐   sink   17-A
na⌐ihu   knife   14-A
naiseñ   telephone extension   12
na⌐ka   inside   17
   hi⌐kidasi no na⌐ka   inside the draw-
      er   17
nakanaka   considerably; more than ex-
      pected   11
namae   name   10
na⌐na   seven   3
na⌐na⌐-tu   seven units   5
na⌐ni   what?   2
   na⌐ni ka   something, anything   4
   nani mo   /+ negative/ nothing
      18
naniiro   what color?   5-N
nanizin̄   what nationality?   10-A
na⌐n̄   what?   2
   na⌐n̄ de⌐ mo   no matter what it is,
      anything at all   15
nañni mo   /see nani mo/   18
na⌐o⌐ru   /intr:-u:na⌐o⌐tte/   get well,
      recover   14
na⌐o⌐su   /tr:-u:na⌐o⌐site/   fix, repair
      13
na⌐pukiñ   napkin   14-A
naraberu   /tr:-ru:narabete/   line
      [something or someone] up
      20-N
narabu   /intr:-u:narañde/   [something
      or someone] lines up   20
na⌐ra⌐u   /tr:-u:na⌐ra⌐tte/   learn, take
      lessons   18
na⌐ru*   /intr:-u:na⌐tte/   become, get
      to be   10
   o⌐okiku ⌐na⌐ru   get big   10
   ya-⌐ttu⌐ ni ⌐na⌐ru   get to be eight
      years old   10

mu⌐ne⌐   chest (part of the body)   17-A
mu⌐ra⌐saki   purple   16-N
musuko   son   11-A
mu⌐sume⌐   daughter   11-A
mu-⌐ttu⌐   six units   5
muzukasii   /-ku/   is difficult   11

na⌐ru   (cont.)
   o⌐kaeri ni na⌐ru ↑   /honorific equiv-
      alent of ka⌐eru/   9
na⌐sa⌐ru ↑   /tr:-aru:na⌐sa⌐tte ~ na⌐su⌐-
      tte/   do, make   13
na⌐tu⌐   summer   18-N
na⌐ze   why?   11
ne?*   /sentence particle/   isn't it
      true?   do you agree?   13
ne⌐e*   /sentence particle/   isn't it true!
      don't you agree!   1
   Do⌐ko desyoo ka ⌐ne⌐e.   Where
      WOULD it be!   I wonder where it
      is!   11
ne⌐esañ ↑   older sister   11-A
ne⌐ḡa⌐u ↑   /tr:-u:ne⌐ḡa⌐tte/   request
      Int.
   O⌐negai-sima⌐su. ↑   I'd like it.
      Please let me have it.   Please do
      so.   I have a request to make of
      you.   Int.
ne⌐ko   cat   17-A
-neñ   /counter for naming and counting
      years/   8
ni⌐   two   3
ni*   /particle/   in, on, at   6;   into,
      onto, to   7;   by   17
   hoka ni   in addition   4
   To⌐okyoo ni a⌐ru   be in Tokyo   6
   sa⌐n̄-zi ni iku   go at 3 o'clock   8
   koko ni oku   put here   17
   tomodati ni iu   say to a friend   18
   to⌐modati ni tuku⌐tte morau   have a
      friend make [it]   17
ni⌐ḡa⌐i   /-ku/   is bitter   14-A
nihoñḡo   Japanese language   11
ni⌐hoñzi⌐ñ   a Japanese   10
ni⌐isañ ↑   older brother   11-A
ni⌐ku⌐   meat   6-N
ni⌐ku⌐ya   meat market, butcher   6-A
ni⌐motu   baggage, things to carry   20
-niñ   /counter for people/   10
-niñmae   /counter for portions/   15

nippoño̱go Japanese language 11
niˈppoñziˈñ a Japanese 10-A
-niti /counter for naming and counting
   days/ 10
niˈtiyoˈo(bi), nitiyoo Sunday 8
niˈtoˈosya second-class car 19
niwa garden 17-A
no* one, ones 4
  aˈkaˈi no red one(s) 4
  kyoˈo no wa as for today's (one) 5
no* /particle/
  Toˈokyoo no tiˈzu map of Tokyo 5
  kyoˈo no siñbuñ today's newspaper
    5
  watakusi no siñbuñ my newspaper 5
  niˈtoˈosya no tomaru tokoro the place
    where the second-class cars stop 19
no* /pre-nominal alternant of da/
   19-N
  byooki no kodomo sick child 19-N
nobori up-train (i.e. going toward Tokyo) 19

o* /particle/
  Huˈrosiki o miˈsete kudasai. Please
   show me a furoshiki. 4
  Kono miti o maˈssuˈg̱u iˈtte kudasaˈi. Please go straight along
   this street. 7
oba aunt 11-A
oˈbaˈasañ grandmother; old lady
   11-A
obasañ aunt; woman 11-A
oboñ tray 14-A
Odaizi ni. Take care [of yourself]!
   11
Oˈhayoo (gozaimaˈsu). Good morning.
   Int.
oi nephew 11-A
oˈide ni naˈru be, come, go 9-N
oig̱osañ nephew 11-A
oimotosañ younger sister 11-A
oˈiru oil (for automobiles) 20
oisii /-ku/ is delicious 14
oˈkaˈasañ mother 11-A
Oˈkaeri-nasaˈi. Welcome home.
   Hello. 20
okag̱esama de thanks to you; thanks
   for asking Int.
Oˈkamai naˈku. Don't bother. Don't
   go to any trouble. 18
oˈkaˈsi cake, sweets 14-A

noˈdo throat 15
  noˈdo g̱a kaˈwaˈku become thirsty
   15
noˈkoˈru /intr:-u:noˈkoˈtte/ be(come)
   left over or left behind 20
noˈkoˈsu /tr:-u:noˈkoˈsite/ leave behind, leave over (for another
   time) 20-N
noˈmiˈmono a drink, beverage 15
noˈmu /tr:-u:noˈñde/ drink 14
noriba place for boarding vehicles 20
norikae a transfer (from one vehicle
   to another) 19
noˈrikaeˈru, noˈrikaˈeru /intr:-ru:no-
   ˈrikaˈete/ change vehicles, transfer 19-N
noru /intr:-u:notte/ get on (a vehicle),
   take (a vehicle), ride 19
noseru /tr:-ru:nosete/ give [someone]
   a ride, carry, take on board 19-N
notihodo later 12
ñ /M/ yeah 16
ñˈmaˈ horse 17-A

O

oˈkasiˈi /-ku/ is funny (strange or
   amusing) 20
okosañ child 10
oku* /tr:-u:oite/ put, place 17
  site oku do in advance, do now for
   later reference 17
okureru /intr:-ru:okurete/ fall behind, become late 19
  okurete (i)ru be late 19
oˈkusañ wife; madam; mistress 11
Oˈmatase-(ita)simaˈsita. I'm sorry
   to have kept you waiting. 4
Oˈmatidoosama deˈsita. I'm sorry you
   were kept waiting. 20
oˈme ni kakaˈru see (a person), meet
   11
  Haˈziˈmete ome ni kakarimasu.
   How do you do? 11
omoi /-ku/ is heavy 20
oˈmosiroˈi /-ku/ is interesting, is unusual, is fun 2
onaka stomach 15
  onaka g̱a suku become hungry 15
onazi same 2
  onazi kusuri same medicine 17
  kore to onazi same as this 17
Oˈneg̱ai-simaˈsu. Please (speaker
   requesting something; lit. I make
   a request). Int.

o⌐nna⌐ female 10
  o⌐nna⌐ no hito woman 10
  o⌐nna no kata⌐ ⁺ woman 10
  o⌐nna⌐ no ko little girl 10
oohuku round trip 19
o⌐oki * /na/ big 13
  o⌐oki na ˩ko˩e loud voice 13
o⌐oki⌐i /-ku/ is big 2
o⌐ri⌐ru /intr:-ru:o⌐rite/ go down, descend, get off (a vehicle) 20
o⌐ro⌐su /tr:-u:o⌐ro⌐site/ lower, let
  down, discharge (from a vehicle)
  20-N
o⌐ru ⁺ * /intr:-u:o⌐tte/ be located (of
  animate beings) 6
  ke⌐kkoñ-site o⌐ru ⁺ be married
    10
  be⌐ñkyoo-site o⌐ru ⁺ be studying
    11
  hu⌐tte ˩o⌐ru ⁺ be raining 18
Osaki ni. ⁺ [Excuse me for going]
  ahead. 18
  Do⌐ozo, osaki ni. ⁺ Please [go]
    ahead. 18-N
osieru /tr:-ru:osiete/ teach, inform
  7
osiire closet (for clothing, quilts,
  etc.) 17-A

pa⌐ñ bread 14-A
pañku-suru /intr:irreg:pañku-
  site/ become punctured
  20

ra⌐iĝetu next month 16-N
raineñ next year 16-N
raisyuu next week 16
ra⌐itaa lighter 4
ra⌐zio radio 16
re⌐e zero 12
re⌐ezo⌐oko refrigerator 17-A
re⌐ñzi stove (for cooking) 17-A
re⌐sutorañ restaurant 14-A
-ri ~ -niñ /counter for people/
  10
rippa /na/ fine, handsome, magnifi-
  cent, imposing 18

osoi /-ku/ is late or slow 11
O⌐so⌐reirimasu. Thank you. I'm sorry. 18
o⌐ssya⌐ru ⁺ /tr:-aru:o⌐ssya⌐tte/ say,
  be named, be called 13
otaku ⁺ home, household 9
  otaku no pertaining or belonging
    to your household
    10
o⌐toko⌐ male 10
  o⌐toko⌐ no hito man 10
  o⌐toko no kata⌐ ⁺ man 10
  o⌐toko⌐ no ko little boy 10
o⌐to⌐osañ ⁺ father 11
o⌐tooto⌐ younger brother 11-A
o⌐toto⌐i, ototoi day before yesterday
  8
otya ⁺ tea 14
oya parent 11-A
oyaĝosañ ⁺ parent 11-A
O⌐yasumi-nasa⌐i. Good night.
  Int.
oyu ⁺ hot water 14-A
ozi uncle 11-A
o⌐zi⌐isañ ⁺ grandfather; old man 11-A
ozisañ ⁺ uncle; man 11-A
o⌐zyo⌐osañ ⁺ daughter; young girl; little girl 11-A

P

pañku-suru (cont.)
  taiya ĝa pañku-suru have a flat
    tire 20
pe⌐ñ pen 2

R

-rittoru /counter for liters/ 20
ro⌐ku⌐ six 3
rooka hall, corridor 17-A
rosiaĝo Russian language 11-A
ro⌐sia⌐ziñ a Russian 10-A
ru⌐su away from home 12
  rusu-tyuu ni during [someone's] ab-
    sence from home 18
ryokañ inn (Japanese style) 6-A
ryo⌐ori⌐ya restaurant (Japanese style) 14-A
ryoᵈosiñ both parents 11-A
ryo⌐ozi⌐kañ consulate 6

S

sa⌐a hmm. . . 6

sakana fish 6-N

sakanaya fish market, fish man 6-A

sake rice wine 14

saki ahead 6

   kono saki up ahead from here 7

-sama † (more polite alternant of -sañ)
   12

sa⌐mu⌐i /-ku/ is cold (of weather or
   atmosphere) 14

sañ three 3

-sañ † Mr., Mrs., Miss Int.

sañpo a walk 18

sañpo-suru /intr:irreg:sañpo-site/
   take a walk 18-N

sa⌐ñto⌐osya third-class car 19-A

sara plate, dish 14-A

sa⌐simi⌐ sashimi (raw fish) 14-A

sa⌐to⌐o sugar 14-A

-satu /counter for books, magazines,
   etc./ 5

Sayonara. Goodbye. Int.

sayoo that way, thus, so 12

Sayoonara. Goodbye. Int.

seereki Western calendar, Christian
   Era 8-N

se⌐ki, seki seat, assigned place 12

sekkeñ soap 17

senaka back (part of the body) 17-A

se⌐ñ thousand 3

-señ /counter for thousands/ 3

se⌐ñgetu last month 14

se⌐ñme⌐ñki wash basin 17-A

señmeñzyo washroom, lavatory 17-A

se⌐ñse⌐e teacher, doctor 16

señzitu the other day 18

si⌐ four 3

si⌐ba⌐raku a while (short or long) 11

   Si⌐ba⌐raku desita. It's been a long
      time [since I last saw you]. 11

si⌐goto work 10

   si⌐goto-tyuu in the middle of work
      12

si⌐ka⌐si however, but 15

si⌐ma⌐ru /intr:-u:si⌐ma⌐tte/ [some-
   thing] closes or shuts 16

simau * /tr:-u:simatte/ put away, store
   17

simau (cont.)

   irete simau finish putting in, put in
      for good, end up by putting in 17

si⌐me⌐ru /tr:-ru:si⌐mete/ close or
   shut [something] 16

siñbuñ newspaper 2

siñdai bed 17-A

si⌐ñda⌐ikeñ berth ticket 19-A

si⌐ñda⌐isya sleeping car 19-A

si⌐ñka⌐ñseñ new trunk-line 19-N

siñsitu bedroom 17-A

si⌐o⌐ salt 14-A

si⌐rabe⌐ru /tr:-ru:si⌐ra⌐bete/ look into, check, investigate 20

si⌐ro⌐i /-ku/ is white 4

siru /tr:-u:sitte/ come to know 10

   sitte (i)ru know 10

sita under, below, bottom, youngest
   10

   si⌐ta no ho⌐ñ bottom book 10-N

   ho⌐ñ no sita under the book 10-N

sitaku preparation 16

   sitaku o suru prepare 16

si⌐ti⌐ seven 3

si⌐tu⌐ree /na/ rudeness, rude 10

   Si⌐tu⌐ree desu ğa_ Excuse me
      but. . . 10

   Si⌐tu⌐ree(-simasu). Excuse me (on
      leaving). Int.

   Si⌐tu⌐ree(-simasita). Excuse me
      (for what I did). Int.

so⌐ba vicinity 6

   e⌐ki no ⌐so⌐ba near the station 6

   so⌐ba no ⌐e⌐ki a nearby station 6

   su⌐ğu ⌐so⌐ba immediate vicinity 6

so⌐ba noodles 14-A

so⌐ba⌐ya noodle shop 14-A

so⌐bo grandmother 11-A

so⌐hu grandfather 11-A

soko that place, there 6

sono * /ᐩnom/ that— 3

soñna * that kind, that kind of 5

so⌐o that way, thus, so 2

   So⌐o desu. That's right. 2

   So⌐o desu ka. Is that right? Oh?
      2

   So⌐o desu ⌐ne⌐e. That's right, isn't
      it. 2; Let me see. . . Hmm. . .
      4

soozi-suru /tr: irreg: soozi-site/ clean 16

sore* that thing 2
  sore kara after that, and then, and 4

sotira that one (of two); that way, thereabouts, there 6; that person 11; the person addressed 12

so⌉to outside 17

so⌐tti⌉ /see sotira/ 6

su⌐ḡi⌉ past, after 8
  ni-⌐hu⌉n suḡi two minutes after 8

su⌉ḡu soon, any minute, right away 5
  su⌉ḡu ⌐so⌉ba immediate vicinity 6

su⌐iyo⌉o(bi), suiyoo Wednesday 8

su⌐ki⌉ /na/ pleasing; like [something] 15

sukiyaki sukiyaki (stew of vegetables with meat or chicken or fish) 14-A

su⌐ko⌉si a little, a few 4
  mo⌐o suko⌉si a little more, a few more 4

suku /intr: -u: suite/ become empty 15
  onaka ḡa suku become hungry 15

su⌉mai residence 16

su⌉mi corner (of a room) 17

Su⌐(m)imase⌉n. I'm sorry. Thank you for your trouble. Int.

Su⌐(m)imase⌉n desita. I'm sorry (for what I did). Thank you (for the trouble you took). Int.

supeiñḡo Spanish language 11-A

su⌐ppa⌉i /-ku/ is acid or sour 14-A

su⌐pu⌉uñ spoon 14-A

suru* /tr: irreg: site/ do, perform, make 1

su⌐si⌉ sushi (rice with fish, seaweed, egg, etc.) 14-A

su⌐si⌉ya sushi shop 14-A

sutañdo lamp 17-A

suteru /tr: -ru: sutete/ throw away 17

su⌉to⌉obu heater 16

suu /tr: -u: sutte/ smoke (cigarettes, cigars, etc.) 14

su⌐zusi⌉i /-ku/ is cool 18

syasyoo train conductor 19

syokudoo dining room 14-A

syo⌐kudo⌉oosya dining car 19-A

syokuzi dining, a meal 15
  syokuzi o suru dine, eat a meal 15

syo⌉osyoo a little 4

syoowa Showa Era (1926-   )   8

syooyu soy sauce 14-A

syoozi sliding door (translucent) 18

syosai study (i.e. a room) 17

-syuukañ /counter for number of weeks/ 8

syu⌉ziñ husband 11-A

T

tabako cigarette, tobacco 3

tabakoya cigar store 6-A

ta⌐bemo⌉no, ta⌐bemono⌉ food, edibles 15-N

ta⌐be⌉ru /tr: -ru: ta⌉bete/ eat 14

Tadaima. Hello, I'm back. 20

taiheñ /na/ awful, dreadful, terrible, a nuisance; very 20

taisetu /na/ important 20

ta⌐isi⌉kañ embassy 6

taisyoo Taisho Era (1912-1926) 8

taitee usual, usually 9
  ta⌐itee no Amerika⌉ziñ most Americans 15

taiya tire 20

ta⌐ka⌉i /-ku/ is expensive 3

ta⌐kusa⌉n, takusañ much, many 5

ta⌉kusii taxi 7

ta⌐ma⌉ḡo egg 14-A

tana shelf 17-A

ta⌐no⌉mu /tr: -u: ta⌐no⌉nde/ make a request, place an order 14; engage, hire 20

tañsu chest of drawers 17-A

tariru /intr: -ru: tarite/ be sufficient 20

tatami rice-straw floor mat 18
  ta⌉tami no heya⌉ room with tatami 18

ta⌐temo⌉no, ta⌐te⌉mono building 6

ta⌉tu /intr: -u: ta⌉tte/ depart, leave for a trip 19

te⌉ hand 17-A

te⌐a⌉rai toilet 6-A

teeburu   table   17
temae   this side   6
   byooiñ no temae   this side of the
   hospital   6
te⌐ñki   weather; good weather   18
teñpura   tempura (batter-fried fish or
   vegetables)   14
teñpuraya   tempura shop   14-A
te⌐rebi   television   16
te⌐tuda⌐u   /tr:-u:te⌐tuda⌐tte/   help,
   lend a hand   17
tiḡau   /intr:-u:tiḡatte/   be wrong; be
   different   2
   sore to tiḡau   be different from that
   17
   Ti⌐ḡaima⌐su.   Wrong number (on the
   telephone).   13
ti⌐isa /na/   small   13-N
   ti⌐isa na ⌐ko⌐e   a low voice   13-N
ti⌐isa⌐i /-ku/   is small   2
ti⌐ka⌐i /-ku/   is near   20
tikatetu   subway   20
ti⌐ti⌐   father   11
ti⌐zu   map   5
to* /particle/   and   4; with   15
   ho⌐ñ to zassi   book and magazine
   4
   Sa⌐itoo-sañ to issyo   together with
   Mr. Saito   15
to* /quotative/   18
   na⌐ñ to iu   say what?   be named or
   called what?   18
to   door   16
todana   cupboard (with shelves)   17
to⌐ire(tto)   toilet   6-A
tokee   clock, watch   8
to⌐ki⌐*   time, occasion   12
   no⌐ru toki⌐ /ni/   when [someone]
   rides   19
to⌐kidoki⌐   sometimes   9
tokkyuu   special express   19
to⌐kkyu⌐ukeñ   special-express ticket   19-A
tokonoma   Japanese-style alcove   18
to⌐ko(ro)⌐   place   18
tokubetu   special   19-N
to⌐kubetukyu⌐ukoo   special express   19
tomaru   /intr:-u:tomatte/   come to a
   halt; stop at, lodge   19
tomeru   /tr:-ru:tomete/   bring to a
   halt   7

tomodati   friend   10
tonari   next door, adjoining   6
   e⌐ki no tonari   next door to the station   6
To⌐ñde mo na⌐i.   Heavens no!   8
to⌐o   ten units   5
-too /counter for naming classes/   19
Toodai   Tokyo University   13
tooi /-ku/   is far   13
   deñwa ḡa tooi   have trouble hearing (on the telephone)   13
to⌐ori⌐   avenue, wide street   7
to⌐oru   /intr:-u:to⌐otte/   pass through,
   go through, pass in front of   19
to⌐osuto   toast   14-A
tori   bird   17-A; chicken, fowl   14-A
torikaeru /tr:-ru:torikaete/   exchange
   20
to⌐ru /tr:-u:to⌐tte/   take up, take away,
   remove, take off, pass [to someone]
   17
totemo   exceedingly, very   8
tottemo   exceedingly, very   8
to⌐zi⌐ru /tr:-ru:to⌐zite/   close [some-
   thing]   CI
/t/te* /quotative/   18
   na⌐ñ te iu   say what?   be named
   or called what?   18
-/t/tu /counter for number of units/
   5; /counter for years of people's
   age/   10
tu⌐ḡi⌐   next   7
   tu⌐ḡi⌐ no ⌐ka⌐do   next corner   7
tu⌐itati⌐   first day of the month   8
tu⌐kare⌐ru /intr:-ru:tu⌐ka⌐rete/   become tired   17
tu⌐ke⌐ru /tr:-ru:tu⌐ke⌐te/   attach,
   turn [something] on   16
tukiatari   end of a street or corridor
   7
tu⌐ku /intr:-u:tu⌐ite/   arrive   9;
   [something] becomes attached or
   turned on   16
tukue   desk   17
tu⌐mara⌐nai /-ku/   is dull or boring;
   is trifling   2
tumetai /-ku/   is cold   14
tumori*   intention, plan   20
   iku tumori da   [I] intend to go, [I]
   plan to go   20
tutaeru /tr:-ru:tutaete/   report,
   communicate, convey a message
   13

tu⌐tome⌐ru /intr:-ru:to⌐to⌐mete/ become employed 10
tu⌐to⌐mete (i)ru be employed 10
tu⌐yo⌐i /-ku/ is strong 17
tyairo brown 16
tyaku arriving 19
  i⌐ti⌐-zi tyaku arriving at 1 o'-
    clock 19
tyanoma family room (Japanese
  style) 17-A
-tyañ ⌐ /suffix added to children's
  given names/ 10
tyawañ cup or small bowl (Japanese
  style) 14-A
tyoodo exactly 8
-tyoome /counter for naming
  chomes/ 7

tyooseñḡo Korean language
  11-A
tyo⌐oseñzi⌐ñ a Korean 10-A
tyo⌐tto a bit, a little 1; just
  5
  Tyo⌐tto. Say there! 4
  tyo⌐tto_ I'm afraid it won't
    do... 4
-tyuu in the middle of —, now busy
  with — 12
  siḡoto-tyuu in the middle of work
    12
tyuuḡokuḡo Chinese language 11-A
tyu⌐uḡoku⌐ziñ a Chinese 10-A
tyuumoñ-suru /tr:irreg:tyuumoñ-site/
  place an order 14

U

u⌐de⌐ arm 17-A
u⌐e⌐, ue over, above, top, topmost,
  oldest 10
  u⌐e no ho⌐ñ top book 10-N
  ho⌐ñ no ue top of the book
    10-N
ukaḡau ⌐ /tr:-u:ukaḡatte/ inquire 6
  tyo⌐tto u⌐kaḡaima⌐su ḡa excuse
    me but ; I'm just going to ask
    [you something] but 6
ukaḡau ⌐ /intr:-u:ukaḡatte/ visit 16
u⌐ma⌐ horse 17-A
u⌐mi sea, ocean 18
usaḡi rabbit 17-A
usi bull, cow 17-A

usiro back, rear 7
  ta⌐isi⌐kañ no usiro back of the em-
    bassy 7
usui /-ku/ is weak or thin (of
  liquids); is light (of colors)
  14
u⌐ti⌐, uti home, house, household
  9
  uti no our household's, our
    10
uti among 15
  A to B to C no uti /de/ /being/
    among A and B and C
    15

W

wa* /sentence particle/ /W/ 16
wa* /particle/ as for, comparative-
  ly speaking Int.
  A⌐na⌐ta wa? How about you? Int.
  Sore wa ⌐na⌐ñ desu ka_ What is
    that? (Lit. As for that, what is
    it?) 2
  Si⌐ñbuñ wa kaimase⌐ñ desita. A
    newspaper I didn't buy. 4
  Ko⌐ko ni⌐ wa a⌐rimase⌐ñ. Here
    there isn't one. 6

wa⌐ka⌐ru /intr:-u:wa⌐ka⌐tte/ be comprehensible, understand, can tell 1
wañ bowl 14-A
wa⌐ru⌐i /-ku/ is bad 2-A
wasureru /tr:-ru:wasurete/ forget 4
watakusi I, me 5
  watakusi no my, mine 5
wataru /intr:-u:watatte/ go over, go
  across 20
watasu /tr:-u:watasite/ hand over
  20-N

Y

ya* /particle/ and 17
  ho˺n̄ ya zassi   books and maga-
    zines and the like   17
ya˺ḡi   goat   17-A
ya⌐ma˺   mountain   18
yameru /tr:-ru:yamete/ quit, give up 14
yaoya   vegetable store   6-A
yaru /tr:-u:yatte/   give (to someone
  other than the speaker)   17
yasai   vegetable   14-A
yasasii /-ku/   is easy   11
ya⌐su˺i /-ku/   is cheap   3
ya⌐sumi˺   vacation, holiday, time off   8
ya⌐su˺mu /tr:-u:ya⌐su˺n̄de/   rest, re-
    lax, take time off   17
ya-⌐ttu˺   eight units   5
yo* /sentence particle/   2
  Pe⌐n̄ desu yo.   It's a pen (I tell
    you).   2
yobu /tr:-u:yon̄de/   call, summon
    13
yo˺i /-ku/   is good   2-N
yoko   side   6
  de⌐pa˺ato no yoko   the side of the
    department store   6
yo˺ku /adverbial of i˺i∼ yo˺i/   well,
  a good deal, often   1

yo˺mu /tr:-u:yon̄de/   read   13
yo˺n̄   four   3
yori* /particle/   more than   15
  ko⌐re yo˺ri ˺i˺i   is better than
    this   15
yo⌐roko˺bu /intr:-u:yo⌐roko˺n̄de/   take
  pleasure in   16
yo⌐roko˺n̄de /gerund of yo⌐roko˺bu/
  gladly, with pleasure   16
yorosii /-ku/   is good or fine or
  all right; never mind   5
  Do˺ozo yorosiku.   (Lit. Please
  [treat me] favorably.)
  11
  Mi⌐na˺san̄ ni yorosiku.   Give my regards to everyone.   11
yo˺ru   night, night-time   16
yo-⌐ttu˺   four units   5
yotukado   intersection   20
yu⌐bi˺   finger   17-A
-yuki   -bound   19
  Yokosuka-yuki   Yokosuka-bound
    19
yu⌐kku˺ri   slowly   13
yuku /alternant of iku/   19-N
yu⌐ube˺   last night   11
yu⌐ubi˺n̄kyoku   post office   6

Z

zassi   magazine   2
ze⌐n̄bu   all, the whole thing   1
ze˺ro   zero   12
-zi /counter for naming o'clocks/
    8
zi⌐biki˺   dictionary   2
zibun̄   oneself   20
  zibun̄ de   by oneself   20
  zibun̄ no   one's own   20
zi⌐do˺osya   automobile   7
zikan̄   time   18
  zi⌐kan̄ ḡa a˺ru   have time
    18
  zi⌐kan̄-do˺ori   on time   19
-zikan̄ /counter for hours/   8
zi⌐mu˺syo   office   9
zi˺syo   dictionary   2
zo⌐n̄zi˺nai ˺ /-ku/   don't know   13
zo⌐n̄zite ˺o˺ru ˺   know   13

zookin̄   cleaning rag   17
zu˺ibun̄   extremely,   to a considerable
  degree   3
zutto   by far   15
  zu⌐tto ma˺e kara   since a long time
    ago   15
zya /contraction of de˺ wa/   2
  e⌐n̄pitu zya na˺i   it isn't a pencil
    2
zya˺/a/   then, well then, in that case
    2
zyama /na/   hindrance, bother   17
  zya⌐ma ni na˺ru   become a bother,
    get in the way   17
zyo⌐osya˺ken̄   passenger ticket   19-A
zyo⌐ozu˺ /na/   skilled, skillful   18
zyu⌐n̄sa, zyun̄sa   policeman   7
zyu˺u   ten   3
zyu⌐ubu˺n̄ /na/   enough   20

Index to the Grammatical Notes

References are to Lesson and Grammatical Note; for example, 6.4 refers to Lesson 6. Grammatical Note 4.

407